CRIMINAL LAW

SEVENTH EDITION

Other Books in the *Essentials of Canadian Law* Series

ESSENTIALS OF CANADIAN LAW

CRIMINAL LAW

SEVENTH EDITION

KENT ROACH

Faculty of Law
University of Toronto

Published in 2018 by

Irwin Law Inc.
14 Duncan Street
Suite 206
Toronto, ON
M5H 3G8

www.irwinlaw.com

ISBN: 978-1-55221-490-9
e-book ISBN: 978-1-55221-491-6

Library and Archives Canada Cataloguing in Publication

Roach, Kent, 1961–, author
        Criminal law / Kent Roach, Faculty of Law, University of Toronto. — Seventh edition.

(Essentials of Canadian law)
Includes bibliographical references and index.
Issued in print and electronic formats.
ISBN 978-1-55221-490-9 (softcover).—ISBN 978-1-55221-491-6 (PDF)

        1. Criminal law—Canada. I. Title. II. Series: Essentials of Canadian law.

KE8809.R62 2018   345.71   C2018-903917-5
KF9220.ZA2R59 2018   C2018-903918-3

Printed and bound in Canada.

2 3 4 5   22 21 20 19

SUMMARY
TABLE OF CONTENTS

DETAILED
TABLE OF CONTENTS

CHAPTER 3:

THE PROHIBITED ACT, OR *ACTUS REUS*　92

CHAPTER 4:

UNFULFILLED CRIMES AND PARTICIPATION IN CRIMES 143

CHAPTER 5:

THE FAULT ELEMENT, OR *MENS REA* 184

FOREWORD

It is a great pleasure to write this foreword to the seventh edition of my colleague Kent Roach's book, *Criminal Law*. There is no Canadian book like it and all those studying criminal law will be indebted to Professor Roach for his very readable and careful analysis of Canadian criminal law. This book will be an excellent companion for students in criminal law courses both in the law schools and criminology and criminal justice departments. As is demonstrated by its citation by the Supreme Court and other courts, even judges and seasoned criminal lawyers will benefit from reading the thoughtful views on the basic principles of criminal law articulated in this book. In addition, it deals with many new developments in criminal law, such as new developments relating to sexual assault offences and the provocation defence, as well as infanticide. The fact that Professor Roach has acted as counsel in a number of important *Charter* and sentencing cases discussed in the book provides an added dimension to this work. This thoroughly revised seventh edition, like the earlier editions, is destined to be widely used and praised. I look forward to many future editions of this valuable book.

Martin L Friedland, CC, QC
Professor of Law and University Professor Emeritus
University of Toronto

PREFACE
TO THE SEVENTH EDITION

This book is designed to provide a concise and current discussion of the basic principles of Canadian criminal law. To this end, the heart of this book examines the principles of the general part of the criminal law: the elements of offences and the relevant defences. It follows the traditional conceptualization of the general part, but it examines unfulfilled crimes and participation in crimes earlier than other works because of their great practical importance and their effective expansion of the prohibited act. Regulatory offences and corporate criminal liability are examined together because of their functional and contextual similarities.

A few chapters attempt to place the general principles of the criminal law in context. Chapter 1 provides an overview of all the topics examined in the book and some basic and current criminal justice statistics. Chapter 2 examines the constitutional principles that affect the investigation of crime, the criminal trial process, and the substantive criminal law as they relate to fault requirements and defences. This chapter includes new developments in the interpretation of the legal rights in the *Charter* with the reasonable limits provision in section 1 of the *Charter* in *R v KRJ*.[1] It also includes discussion of new developments in bail in *R v Antic*[2] and of the right to a trial in a reasonable time, as well as new developments concerning the important principle under section 7 of the *Charter* that criminal offences should not be overbroad.

---

1   [2016] 1 SCR 906.
2   [2017] 1 SCR 509.

Chapter 3, dealing with both the prohibited act and ignorance of the law, has been rewritten and reorganized in order to make it clearer. The examination of voluntariness has been expanded to include a discussion of the defence of accident as it relates to the prohibited act. Chapter 5 has also been revised to include a discussion of the defence of accident as it relates to fault. The policy elements of the prohibited act are discussed at the end of Chapter 3, including discussion of the prohibited act of bestiality in *R v DLW*,[3] as well as an expanded discussion of the prohibited act of possession.

Chapter 5 has expanded discussion of objective fault and examines continued confusion in applying wilful blindness as a form of subjective fault. Chapter 6 has expanded discussion of the due diligence defence and its relation to statutory standards; and Chapter 7 discusses the implications of the Court's interpretation of the critical distinction between general and specific intent in *R v Tatton*.[4]

Chapter 9 has been updated to examine disagreements between the Ontario Court of Appeal and the Manitoba Court of Appeal about whether the exclusion of murder from the offence of duress can be justified.[5] This chapter also includes how various courts of appeal are interpreting the self-defence and defence of property provisions added to the *Criminal Code* in 2012, while we await a case when the Supreme Court provides its interpretation.

The discussion of provocation in Chapter 10 has been thoroughly updated to take account both of the Supreme Court's and Parliament's recent restrictions on the controversial defence and to simplify the discussion as much as possible. Similarly, the discussion of infanticide has been expanded to take into account the Supreme Court's decision in *R v Borowiec*.[6] The discussion of sexual assault has been revised to take account of important decisions from the Alberta and Nova Scotia Court of Appeals and Bill C-51, which will make several changes to sexual assault offences.

Chapter 10 on selected aspects of the special part, as well as subsequent chapters on sentencing (Chapter 11) and themes in the criminal law (Chapter 12), are not intended to be comprehensive. Each deserves a book in its own right, but it is hoped they will provide readers with a fuller sense of the criminal law than would be provided if the book were restricted to the general part of the criminal law. For example, Chapter 11 examines the Supreme Court's restrictive approach for when a judge

---

3   2016 SCC 22.
4   2015 SCC 33.
5   *R v Willis*, 2016 MBCA 113; *R v Aravena*, 2015 ONCA 250.
6   2016 SCC 11.

can depart from joint sentencing submissions from the accused and the prosecution.[7] In doing so, it helps explain the reality of a criminal justice system in which most accused pled guilty and are often rewarded for doing so.

I have included more caselaw from the courts of appeal in this edition in part because the Supreme Court, especially in appeals as of right, has been more inclined to endorse the reasoning of the courts of appeal. I have generally avoided the temptation to engage in extended criticisms of decided cases in order to focus on how each case fits into the overall structure of the criminal law. Unfortunately, the fit is not always natural and my impression after almost thirty years of teaching is that Canadian criminal law is complex, challenging, and at times incoherent, even for the brightest of students.

Fortunately, Parliament has addressed and considerably simplified the law of both self-defence and defence of property, and Chapter 9 contains an extensive examination of these provisions. Not all of Parliament's interventions or the Court's decisions create simplicity. Chapter 8 on mental disorder examines some 2014 amendments that will unsettle previous determinations that the provisions for the detention of those found not criminally responsible on account of mental disorder satisfy the *Charter*, and Chapter 10 discusses the blunt, categorical, and arguably arbitrary and overbroad restrictions that Parliament placed on the defence of provocation in 2015. The Supreme Court has also attempted to unify the statutory and common law defences of duress in *R v Ryan*.[8] The overall effect is to make common law and statutory duress defences more consistent but, alas, more complex.

I am grateful to many colleagues and students who have read the book and made encouraging comments or helpful suggestions for improvement. Don Stuart deserves particular credit for his generous yet challenging and helpful review of the first edition. I have benefitted greatly from discussions with Sanjeev Anand, Benjamin Berger, Alan Brudner, Emma Cunliffe, Michael Code, Markus Dubber, Craig Forcese, Marty Friedland, Anil Kapoor, Martha Shaffer, Simon Stern, Hamish Stewart, James Stribopoulos, and Gary Trotter about many of the issues discussed in this book.

KR
May 2018

---

7   *R v Anthony-Cook*, 2016 SCC 43.
8   2013 SCC 3.

OVERVIEW

Criminal law is enacted and applied in Canada in an increasingly complex constitutional framework that is examined in Chapter 2. The basic elements of criminal and regulatory offences are the prohibited act and the required fault element, which are examined in Chapters 3 and 5, respectively. Chapter 4 examines how criminal offences are expanded by various provisions prohibiting attempted and unfulfilled crimes and participation as an accomplice in crimes. Special provisions governing regulatory offences and corporate crime are examined in Chapter 6. Various defences to crimes are examined in subsequent chapters, including intoxication (Chapter 7), mental disorder and automatism (Chapter 8), and self-defence, necessity, and duress (Chapter 9). Chapter 10 examines the application of general principles of criminal liability in the context of some selected specific offences, including the various forms of homicide, sexual, property, and terrorism offences. It also examines the provocation defence, which only applies to reduce murder to manslaughter. Punishment depends on the exercise of sentencing discretion, which is examined in Chapter 11. A final chapter examines models of the criminal justice system and trends in the criminal law.

A. CRIME IN CANADA

A 2014 victimization study suggests that about 20 percent of all Canadians are victims of crime in a year, down from 25 percent in 2004. In 2014, this amounted to 6.4 million criminal incidents, including various forms of theft (50 percent), assault (22 percent), sexual assault (10 percent), and robbery (3 percent). The perpetrator of most violent crime is often someone known to the victim, and the site of most violence is the home.

In only 31 percent of cases in the 2014 survey did victims report the crime to the police. The reasons for not reporting vary, but often relate to a perception that the incident was too minor to justify reporting or it was a personal matter. Other reasons included concerns that the offender would not be adequately punished or the police would not be effective or that the victim did not want to be involved with the courts.

In 2016, there were just over 1.9 million crimes reported to the police. This represented a 28 percent decrease in crime reported per capita since 2006. There were 611 homicides and 777 attempted murders. There were also about 220,000 assaults and 21,000 sexual assaults reported to the police. Although they receive the most attention in the press and in appeal court cases, homicides make up only 0.2 percent of violent crimes reported to the police. The majority (80 percent) of crimes reported to the police are non-violent. They include 70,500 incidents related to impaired driving, of which 96 percent involved alcohol and 4 percent other drugs.

The majority of crimes reported to the police do not result in charges. The majority of cases in which charges are laid are resolved without a trial and end in a finding of guilt. In a process commonly known as plea bargaining, the prosecutor may withdraw some charges or take certain positions on sentence if the accused agrees to plead guilty. The accused may receive a more lenient sentence because he or she has pled guilty, with judges only departing from joint submissions by prosecutors and the defence about an appropriate sentence if the recommended sentence will bring the administration of justice into disrepute.

In 2014/15, there were 328,028 cases completed in adult court. These cases disposed of 992,635 charges, which reflects the fact that most accused face three or more charges from the many criminal offences that Parliament has enacted and continues to enact. There was a plea or finding of guilt in 63 percent of cases, withdrawal or a stay generally by the prosecutor in 32 percent of cases, acquittals in 4 percent of cases, and alternative findings, such as not criminally responsible by reason of mental disorder, in 1 percent of cases.

The most frequently occurring offences were theft (10 percent), impaired driving (10 percent), and common assault (9 percent). Men are the accused in 80 percent of cases and 98 percent of cases involving sexual assault. There was a sentence of custody in 37 percent of the cases where the accused was found guilty with a median sentence of 30 days.

Over 99 percent of these cases were resolved in provincial court with only 0.4 percent being resolved in superior court where the judges are appointed by the federal government and the lawyers wear gowns.

Only a very small minority of either convictions or acquittals are ever appealed. Nevertheless, appeal cases are crucial to the development of the criminal law. Appeal courts, most notably the Supreme Court of Canada, interpret the *Criminal Code*. They also develop judge-made common law, so long as this law is not inconsistent with the *Code* and does not create new offences. Appeal courts also apply the *Canadian Charter of Rights and Freedoms* (the *Charter*) to the activities of police and prosecutors, as well as to laws enacted by legislatures.

Canada imprisons people at a rate of 139 per 100,000 population, a rate much lower than the United States. In 2015/16, there were on average 41,049 adults and youth imprisoned in Canada, with close to 87,000 more people on probation in the community. Men represent the majority of prisoners, but women account for 8 percent of admissions to federal custody for those serving two years' imprisonment or more and 11 percent of offenders admitted to custody in provincial facilities for those serving less than two years. The majority of those imprisoned in provincial jails (14,899) are people who have not been convicted but are facing charges and have been denied bail because of concerns that they will not show up for trial or will commit offences if released or that their release will undermine public confidence in the administration of justice.

Prisoners have significantly less education and employment history than other Canadians. Indigenous people, including First Nations, Inuit, and Metis people, represent 28 percent of admissions to federal custody and 26 percent of admissions to provincial custody but are only 4 percent of the population. Indigenous people are also more likely than non-Indigenous people to experience a violent victimization with almost one in three reporting victimization in the 2014 survey compared to less than one in five for non-Indigenous persons. The chart that follows illustrates how the criminal law affects only a small percentage of crimes committed.

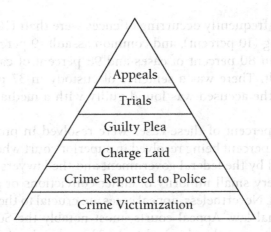

Appeals

Trials

Guilty Plea

Charge Laid

Crime Reported to Police

Crime Victimization

B. THE CRIMINAL PROCESS

The criminal law assumes concrete meaning when it is administered through the criminal justice system or the criminal process. The process starts with a decision of a legislature to make certain conduct illegal. The criminal law is then enforced by the police who respond to the decisions of crime victims to report crime and sometimes, especially in drug and prostitution cases, proactively investigate the crime themselves. As examined in Chapter 2, the investigative activities of the police are restricted by various rights under the *Charter*, such as the right to counsel and the right against unreasonable search and seizure.

If the accused is charged, then the trial process begins. The accused may be released by the police or detained for a bail hearing before a judge. A prosecutor (sometimes called the Crown) will decide what if any charges are warranted and can make a decision to divert the charges out of court to alternative-measure programs. If charges proceed, the accused will have to make a decision whether to hire a lawyer or, if a lawyer cannot be afforded, to apply for legal aid to have a lawyer paid by the state.

The trial process may include pre-trial detention by the denial of bail and in the most serious cases may include the holding of a preliminary inquiry and trial by jury. The vast majority of cases in Canada are decided by a judge without a jury. As noted above, most cases do not result in full trials, and the judge only has to engage in sentencing after the accused has pled guilty to some offence. The trial process is affected by various *Charter* rights, such as the right not to be denied reasonable bail without just cause and the right to be tried in a reasonable time. If the accused is convicted, the judge must then sentence the accused and the accused may appeal. Jails and penitentiaries are the end of the criminal process, and parole boards have powers to determine if a prisoner will be released from custody before the expiry of his or her sentence.

Each year, governments spend about $10 billion on the criminal process with 60 percent of this money going to the police, 25 percent to corrections, 9 percent to courts, and 6 percent to legal aid for those who cannot afford a defence lawyer. The chart that follows outlines the major steps in the criminal process.

The Major Steps in the Criminal Process

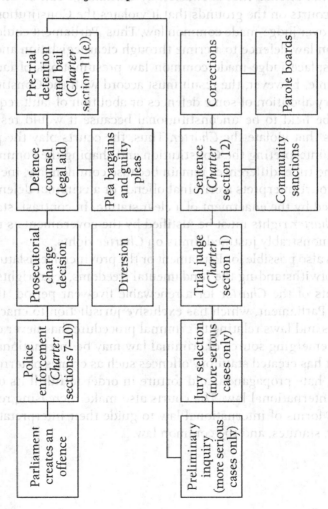

C. SOURCES OF CRIMINAL LAW

There are three main sources of criminal law in Canada: (1) the Constitution, including both the division of powers and the *Canadian Charter of Rights and Freedoms*; (2) statutes enacted by legislatures, including the *Criminal Code* and other statutes creating offences; and (3) judge-made common law in the form of defences that have not been codified in the *Criminal Code* and common law presumptions of fault.

Not all sources of the criminal law are equal. The Constitution is the supreme law and prevails over both statutes and common law. Thus, a criminal offence that is enacted by Parliament can be struck down by the courts on the grounds that it violates the Constitution. Statutes prevail over judge-made common law. Thus, Parliament could abolish a common law defence to a crime through clear legislation and they can also displace judge-made common law presumptions of fault. At the same time, however, the result must accord with the Constitution and statutory abolition of some defences or abolition of fault requirements might be held to be unconstitutional because it would result in convictions that violate the *Charter*. Thus, the courts play the prime role both in interpreting the Constitution and shaping the common law. At the same time, differences remain because common law, including the way a court interprets a criminal offence or a criminal defence, can be displaced by the enactment of a clear statute. In contrast, statutes that limit *Charter* rights must be justified by the government as reasonable and demonstrably justified limits on *Charter* rights.

It is also possible for Parliament or the provincial legislature to enact laws notwithstanding the fundamental freedoms, legal rights, or equality rights of the *Charter* for a renewable five-year period, though the federal Parliament, which has exclusive jurisdiction to enact criminal offences and laws relating to criminal procedure, has never done this.

An emerging source of criminal law may be international law. Parliament has created statutory offences such as crimes of terrorism, war crimes, hate propaganda, and torture in order to fulfill its obligations under international law. The courts also make increasing reference to various forms of international law to guide their interpretation of the *Charter*, statutes, and the common law.

D. CRIMINAL OFFENCES

Criminal law in Canada is enacted only by the federal Parliament. The *Criminal Code* contains many offences, ranging from traditional crimes such as murder, assault, robbery, and theft to newer crimes such as driving with a blood alcohol level over 80. Some offences such as assault or sexual assault protect bodily integrity, while others such as theft protect property. Crimes such as firearms and drunk-driving offences attempt to prevent conduct that presents a significant risk of harm to others. Crimes against the possession and sale of illegal drugs or obscene material may prevent harm, but they also proclaim standards of socially acceptable behaviour. Criminal laws are primarily designed to denounce and to punish inherently wrongful behaviour and to deter people from committing crimes or engaging in behaviour that presents a serious risk of harm. Courts consider these purposes when sentencing offenders, but they are also concerned with the incapacitation and rehabilitation of the particular offender and with providing reparation to the victim and the community for the crime committed.

E. THE CRIMINAL LAW AND THE CONSTITUTION

Criminal offences must be consistent with the supreme law of the Constitution. In Canada, this means that only the federal Parliament can enact criminal laws. The provinces (and their delegates, the municipalities) can, however, enact regulatory offences and such offences can even be punished by imprisonment. In addition, a criminal law may be unconstitutional if it infringes a right or a freedom protected under the *Charter*, and if it cannot be justified under section 1 as a reasonable and demonstrably justified limit on a right.

Sections 7 and 11(d) of the *Charter* are particularly important to the criminal law. Section 7 provides that people cannot be deprived of life, liberty, and security of the person except in accordance with the principles of fundamental justice. Imprisonment most definitely affects the liberty or security of the person. Thus, it is necessary that the criminal law be in accord with the principles of fundamental justice. These principles have been defined as the fundamental tenets of the legal system. They address the substantive fairness of criminal laws to ensure that the morally innocent are not convicted and that people who could not have reasonably been expected to obey the law are not punished for conduct committed in a morally involuntary fashion. As well, the principles of fundamental justice support the procedural fairness of the criminal law to ensure that the accused is treated fairly. Section 11(d) protects the accused's right to be presumed innocent and to receive a fair and public hearing by an independent and impartial court.

F. SUBSTANTIVE FAIRNESS

A criminal law or a regulatory offence can be declared invalid by the courts if it results in an unjustified violation of a *Charter* right, such as freedom of expression. Expression has been interpreted broadly to include non-violent attempts to convey meaning. Thus, offences prohibiting hate literature, communication for the purposes of prostitution, defamatory libel, or pornography must be justified by the government under section 1 of the *Charter* as a reasonable limit on the *Charter* right.

The principles of fundamental justice in section 7 of the *Charter* have been interpreted as prohibiting the use of vague, arbitrary, overbroad, or grossly disproportionate laws. Section 7 of the *Charter* also prohibits the punishment of the morally innocent who are not at fault, as well as those who act in a morally involuntary manner in dire circumstances where there was no other realistic choice but to commit the crime. The question of what constitutes moral innocence or morally involuntary conduct depends very much on the particular context. What is required under section 7 of the *Charter* to sustain a conviction for murder or war crimes is quite different from what is required to sustain a manslaughter conviction. It is also quite different from what is required for a conviction of a regulatory offence. Fault requirements should generally increase with the seriousness of the offence and intentional crimes should be punished more severely than those committed negligently.

A denial or a restriction on a defence, such as the defences of intoxication, mental disorder, or duress, may also violate section 7 of the *Charter* if it results in a deprivation of liberty in a manner that is not in accordance with the principles of fundamental justice. For example, it would be fundamentally unjust to convict a person for involuntary conduct or for committing a crime where threats or dire circumstances meant that there was no other realistic choice but to commit the crime. Section 7 jurisprudence, as it affects criminal and regulatory offences, will be examined at various junctures of this book.

G. PROCEDURAL FAIRNESS

Both the police and the prosecutor must comply with the accused's *Charter* rights, or risk having the trial process diverted from the issue of guilt or innocence by the accused seeking a *Charter* remedy for the violation of his or her legal rights. Sections 8 and 9 of the *Charter* provide individuals with the rights to be free from unreasonable searches and seizures and from arbitrary detentions during the investigative process. Section 10 ensures that people will know why they have been arrested or detained and that they can obtain legal advice from a lawyer. Sections 7 and 11 of the *Charter* protect an accused's right to a fair trial. These rights include the right to a trial in a reasonable time, and the right to a trial by jury when the accused faces five years' imprisonment or more. The prosecutor, often known as the Crown, has special obligations of fairness and must disclose relevant evidence in its possession to the accused.

An important procedural protection is the presumption of innocence protected under section 11(d) of the *Charter*. The Crown must bear the burden of proving that the accused is guilty beyond a reasonable doubt. A reasonable doubt is not imaginary or frivolous, but is based on reason and common sense derived from the evidence or absence of evidence. The Crown must go well beyond demonstrating that it is probable or likely that the accused is guilty, but does not have to establish guilt as an absolute certainty. The accused is entitled to the benefit of any reasonable doubt about any matter essential to conviction. The matters essential to conviction include the elements of the offence, as well as the existence of any defence that would excuse or justify the commission of the offence. The presumption of innocence is offended if an accused is required to prove that he or she did not have one of the elements of the offence or even if he or she did not have a defence to the crime. The presumption of innocence is designed to ensure that the accused always receives the benefit of any reasonable doubt as to guilt and that the judge or jury are never forced by the law to convict the accused even though they may have a reasonable doubt. At the same time, violations of the presumption of innocence may be justified under section 1 of the *Charter* on the basis that they are necessary to protect social interests.

H. THE ELEMENTS OF CRIMINAL OFFENCES

The basic elements of a criminal offence are the act or omission that is prohibited by the legislation, or the *actus reus*, and the fault element, or *mens rea*, with which the accused must commit the prohibited act or omission. The Crown must prove beyond a reasonable doubt that the accused committed the prohibited act and did so with the required fault element. There is also a general requirement that the accused have the necessary fault or *mens rea* at the same time as the prohibited act or *actus reus* occurred. For murder, the Crown would have to prove that the accused committed the prohibited act of causing another person's death, and at the same time had the fault element of knowing that the victim's death was likely to occur. It is possible that the accused could commit a criminal act without the required fault, and in such a case, the accused would not be convicted.

The Crown must, subject to exceptions justified under section 1 of the *Charter*, also prove beyond a reasonable doubt that the accused did not have a relevant defence. An accused will, for example, be acquitted of murder if there is a reasonable doubt that he or she acted in self-defence as defined by the *Criminal Code*, or if there is a reasonable doubt that intoxication prevented him or her from knowing that the victim was likely to die. A few defences, most notably mental disorder and automatism, must be established by the accused on a balance of probabilities even though this violates the presumption of innocence by allowing a conviction even if there is a reasonable doubt about the existence of a defence. If the Crown proves the prohibited act and fault element beyond a reasonable doubt, and there is no defence, then the accused will be convicted.

I. THE PROHIBITED ACT, OR *ACTUS REUS*

Every criminal or regulatory offence will have a prohibited act or omission, or *actus reus*. The prohibited act depends on how the legislature has worded the offence. For example, the prohibited act of theft is defined by Parliament in section 322(1) of the *Criminal Code* as the taking and conversion of anything. The prohibited act also depends on how the courts interpret the words of an offence. Sometimes the courts interpret these words restrictively to benefit the accused, but they may not do so if a restrictive interpretation defeats the clear purpose of the offence. The Supreme Court has interpreted the word *anything* in the offence of theft not to include the taking of confidential information from a computer screen, even though taking a piece of paper with confidential information on it would be theft. Parliament could always amend the criminal law to state clearly that confidential information constitutes a thing that can be stolen, or it could create a new offence of stealing confidential information from a computer. The definition of the prohibited act is perhaps the most important policy component of the criminal law. The trend is towards expansive legislative definitions of the prohibited act, with the most obvious example being the replacement of the offence of rape with sexual assault.

The *actus reus* is usually defined as an overt act, such as the taking of another person's property. The legislature can, however, define the prohibited conduct as an omission or a failure to take action. For example, a parent can be guilty of the criminal offence of failing to provide the necessities of life to his or her child. Regulatory offences may often prohibit the failure to take action, such as keeping proper business records or taking health and safety precautions. The definition of the criminal act must not be so vague or broad that it fails to give fair notice to the accused or to limit law enforcement discretion. Although each offence must have an *actus reus* that is not excessively vague or overbroad, it is generally no excuse that the accused did not know that his or her conduct was illegal.

Whether the accused has committed the prohibited act is usually a distinct issue from whether the accused had the required fault element. For example, a person commits the prohibited act of theft if he or she mistakenly takes another person's jacket at a party. If the person honestly believes that it is his or her jacket, however, then the person may not have committed the crime with the fault element required for theft. The person would have taken another's property, but not with the required moral fault, or *mens rea*. There is some blurring of the concepts of *actus reus* and *mens rea* when a person acts in an involuntary manner because, for example, he or she is sleepwalking or having a seizure. In such cases, it may not be fair to say even that the accused has committed the criminal act.

J. ATTEMPTS AND OTHER UNFULFILLED CRIMES

The criminal law intervenes even before the accused has committed the criminal act required for a complete crime. Thus, a person who attempts to steal an object but fails can be charged with attempted theft. Section 24 of the *Criminal Code* states that anyone, having an intent to commit an offence, who does or omits to do anything beyond mere preparation to commit a criminal offence is guilty of attempting to commit the offence regardless of whether or not it was possible to commit an offence. A person who had just entered a backyard to steal a barbecue, but had not started to remove it, could be guilty of attempted theft. The Crown would have to prove beyond a reasonable doubt that the accused had gone beyond mere preparation to commit the offence and had the intent to steal the barbecue. A person punished for an attempted crime is punished more for his or her intent to commit the crime than for the harm caused.

Sometimes activity that is preparatory to completing a crime is defined by Parliament as a completed crime. Section 322(2) of the *Criminal Code* provides that a person commits theft when, with the intent to steal, he or she moves an item or even begins to cause it to become movable. A person who has cut a chain on a backyard barbecue to make it movable with the intent to steal could be guilty of theft as opposed to attempted theft. Similarly, terrorism offences relating to the financing or facilitation of terrorism generally apply to conduct done in preparation to commit an actual act of terrorism.

In addition to attempts, a person could be guilty of conspiracy to commit a theft if he or she had agreed with others to commit the theft. This offence would apply even though they had done nothing more than agree to commit a crime. A person could also be guilty of counselling a crime if he or she had procured, solicited, or incited another person to commit an offence, even though that second person never committed the offence. For example, Jane could be guilty of counselling theft if she attempted to persuade Sam to steal a barbecue, even though Sam never stole the item and never intended to do so. If Sam did go on to steal the barbecue, Jane could be guilty of theft as a party or accomplice to the offence. Finally, a person who knowingly assists another person to escape after a crime can be guilty of the separate crime of being an accessory after the fact.

As can be seen, the criminal law prohibits and punishes not only complete crimes such as theft or murder, but also attempts to commit crimes, conspiracies to commit crimes, counselling other people to commit crimes, and assisting known criminals to escape. All of these offences, with the exception of conspiracies, are not subject to as severe punishment as the commission of the complete crime, but they are crimes nevertheless.

K. PARTICIPATION IN CRIMES

Often a crime is committed by more than one person. A person who assists in the commission of an offence can be convicted of the same offence as the person who commits the offence. Section 21 of the *Criminal Code* provides that people are parties to an offence and guilty of that offence not only if they commit the offence, but also if they aid or abet the commission of the offence. A person would aid a theft if he or she acted as a lookout or caused a distraction for the purpose of allowing another person time to take the property without being caught. A person would abet a crime if he or she encouraged or procured the commission of a crime. A store clerk might, for example, encourage and knowingly allow a customer to shoplift. The clerk could also be guilty of the crime under section 22 of the *Criminal Code* if she counselled or incited someone to commit a crime even though she did not actually commit the offence herself.

Section 21(2) provides that once two or more people have formed a common intent to carry out an unlawful purpose, they are guilty of every offence that each of them commits, provided they knew or ought to have known that the commission of the crime would be a probable consequence of carrying out the unlawful purpose. If Jane and Sam agreed to assault a person and, in carrying out that assault, Jane also steals the victim's wristwatch, then Sam would be guilty of theft if he knew or ought to have known that it was probable that Jane would also steal when assaulting the victim. If Jane murdered the victim during the assault, Sam would not be guilty of murder, because of the special stigma and penalty that accompany a murder conviction, unless he subjectively knew that it was probable that Jane would also murder the victim they had planned to assault.

The parties' provisions in section 21 mean that people who had different levels of involvement in a crime may be found guilty of the same offence. Because section 21 makes those who actually commit an offence, as well as those who aid or abet the offence, a party to the offence, a jury can convict a person of the crime without necessarily agreeing on whether the person committed the crime or aided or abetted the crime. Both the person who performs the actual theft and a person who assists in the theft can be convicted of theft. The extent of an offender's participation in a crime will be considered by the judge when determining the appropriate sentence.

Expansive definitions of the criminal act are found in the above criminal prohibitions that apply to those who have attempted or planned to commit a crime, and to those who have assisted others in committing a crime. In order to convict a person of an attempted crime or for being a party to an offence, however, the Crown must also prove that the person had the fault or mental element of intending to commit the full offence or intending to assist the other person in the commission of the crime. In other words, the commission of a broadly worded prohibited act, or *actus reus*, is not enough; the accused must also have acted with the required fault element, or *mens rea*.

L. THE FAULT ELEMENT, OR *MENS REA*

A great variety of fault elements are used in criminal and regulatory offences. Sometimes the fault element is specified in the wording of an offence by words such as *intentionally, knowingly, recklessly,* or *negligently.* Frequently, however, the courts will have to infer what type of fault element is required. Often a distinction between subjective and objective fault elements is drawn. A subjective fault or mental element depends on what was in the particular accused's mind at the time that the criminal act was committed. In determining this condition, the judge or jury must consider all the evidence presented, even if it reveals factors, such as the accused's diminished intelligence, that are peculiar to the accused. On the other hand, an objective fault element does not depend on the accused's own state of mind, but on what a reasonable person in the circumstances would have known or done.

The criminal law increasingly accepts objective negligence as a legitimate form of criminal fault. That said, negligence for the purpose of imposing criminal liability and punishment is different than ordinary negligence used in private law to require one party to compensate the other or negligence or lack of due diligence that will be the required fault for most regulatory offences. Under the criminal law, the prosecutor must establish beyond a reasonable doubt that the accused engaged in a marked departure from what a reasonable person would have done in order to distinguish criminal from civil negligence. Personal characteristics of the accused such as age are generally not relevant in applying objective fault standards of negligence, but they may be relevant if they render the accused incapable of appreciating the relevant risk. The courts have also stressed that negligence liability cannot be determined in the abstract or deduced from the commission of the prohibited act. The judge or jury must consider all the circumstances and all the evidence, including any explanation offered by the accused and the accused's state of mind. That said, the purpose of this process is not, as it is with respect to subjective fault, to determine what was in the accused's state of mind, but only to determine whether the accused engaged in a marked departure from reasonable standards.

Courts will often presume that a criminal offence requires proof of a subjective fault element unless the offence clearly or by implication only requires proof of objective fault. There are significant gradations among subjective mental elements. To be convicted of theft, for example, an accused must act with a fraudulent purpose or intent. A person who mistakenly takes another's coat at a party does not act with the fraudulent purpose of taking and keeping that person's coat. Other forms of subjective *mens rea* require less elaborate thought processes. As will be seen, it is enough in a murder case to prove that the accused knew that death was likely to occur, even though he or she may not have had the purpose or intent to kill. In many other cases, some subjective awareness of the prohibited conduct or consequence will be enough. In Canada, this is called recklessness. It is distinct from negligence because it requires some awareness of the prohibited risk by the accused, and it is not sufficient to conclude that a reasonable person would have been aware of the risk. Sam would recklessly commit theft if the thought crossed his mind that the coat he took might not belong to him. He would negligently commit theft if his conduct was a marked departure from what a reasonable person in his situation would have done to determine the proper ownership of the coat. The actual offence of theft, however, requires more than negligence or even recklessness.

The Supreme Court has found that sometimes the principles of fundamental justice under section 7 of the *Charter* require that the Crown prove that the accused subjectively knew that the prohibited act was likely to occur. This principle has only been applied with respect to a few serious crimes — murder, attempted murder, and war crimes — that because of their stigma and penalty have a constitutionally required form of subjective *mens rea*. Thus, in order to obtain a conviction for murder, the Crown must prove that the particular accused knew that the victim was likely to die, not simply that a reasonable person in the accused's position would have recognized the likelihood of death. Note, however, that knowledge is not the highest form of subjective *mens rea* and it is not necessary under section 7 of the *Charter* to prove that an accused's intent or purpose was to kill the victim. The *Charter* only provides minimum standards and Parliament could require such higher forms of *mens rea*. The courts have constitutionalized subjective *mens rea* only for a few serious crimes.

Another important consideration is the relation between the fault element and the prohibited act. As discussed earlier in this chapter, the fault element must generally occur at the same time as the commission of the prohibited act, though the latter may be defined in a broad manner, for example, to include the whole process of causing death. In addition, there is a general principle that the fault element relate to all parts of the prohibited act. In the case of murder, the fault element of knowledge must relate to the prohibited act of causing death. In other cases, however, such a matching or symmetry between the *actus reus* and the *mens rea* is not required. Thus, the fault element for unlawful act manslaughter relates to negligence with respect to the risk of causing non-trivial bodily harm, whereas the prohibited act requires that the accused have caused the victim's death. A number of other crimes, such as dangerous or impaired driving causing death or bodily harm, recognize the consequences of the accused's actions, but do not require proof of fault with respect to these consequences. Other crimes such as attempts may require a fault element that extends beyond the *actus reus* and contemplates the commission of a complete crime. In other words, the *mens rea* or fault element does not always relate to the *actus reus* or prohibited act.

M. REGULATORY OFFENCES AND CORPORATE CRIME

The *Criminal Code* contains many crimes, but they constitute only a small number of all the offences in Canada. Most offences are regulatory offences that can be defined in legislation enacted by the federal Parliament, provinces, or municipalities. Regulatory offences include traffic offences such as speeding, environmental offences, offences for engaging in a regulated activity without a licence or proper records, and offences relating to harmful commercial practices, such as misleading advertising or not complying with health and safety regulations. The primary purpose of regulatory offences is to deter risky behaviour and prevent harm before it happens, rather than to punish intrinsically wrongful and harmful behaviour. The standards used to govern the investigation of regulatory offences and to impose convictions for such offences are more favourable to the state than the standards used for criminal offences.

Traditionally, courts were in a dilemma of interpreting a regulatory offence to require either absolute liability, for which a conviction follows from the commission of the prohibited act, or subjective fault, as is presumed for criminal offences. As will be seen, both of these options were problematic.

An absolute liability offence could punish a person who was morally innocent or without fault. The Supreme Court invalidated an absolute liability offence under section 7 of the *Charter* on the basis that it could send a person to jail for driving with a suspended licence when that person did not have subjective fault (that is, she did not know or was not aware of the risk that her licence was suspended) and did not have objective fault (that is, a reasonable person in her circumstances would not have known that the licence was suspended). Although absolute liability offences offend the principles of fundamental justice by punishing the morally innocent, they will not violate section 7 of the *Charter* unless they threaten the accused's right to life, liberty, and security of the person. The courts have upheld absolute liability offences that could not result in imprisonment.

Requiring proof of subjective fault for a regulatory offence would mean that the Crown would have to prove some form of subjective fault beyond a reasonable doubt even if the conduct was risky and harmful and could have been avoided by reasonable precautions. The legislature requires such forms of fault for some regulatory offences. Nevertheless, the courts do not assume that a regulatory offence requires proof of subjective fault, as they do for criminal offences.

Rather, Canadian courts assume that regulatory offences are "strict liability" offences that in Canadian criminal law is a compromise between absolute liability and subjective fault. Strict liability offences give the accused an opportunity to establish on a balance of probabilities that they were not negligent in the form of establishing a defence of due diligence or reasonable and mistaken belief in facts that would render their conduct innocent. For example, an accused would not be convicted of a strict liability if they did all that could reasonably be expected to expect some prohibited act to happen. Courts will look at many factors including the severity of harm and industry standards in determining whether those accused of a regulatory offences have a due diligence defence.

Requiring the accused to prove a defence or lack of fault to escape a conviction violates the presumption of innocence, which requires the state to prove all aspects of guilt beyond a reasonable doubt. It would, however, generally be justified as a reasonable and proportionate limit under section 1 of the *Charter* because of the difficulty that the Crown might have in establishing beyond a reasonable doubt that a person or corporation accused of a regulatory offence was negligent. Placing the onus on the accused to establish the due diligence defence to a strict liability regulatory offence also creates incentives on those individuals and corporations who enter a regulated field to take reasonable precautions to prevent harms.

Corporations and other organizations may be charged not only with regulatory offences, but also with more serious criminal offences that require some form of *mens rea*. Until 2003, only a "directing mind" of a corporation, namely, a senior official with responsibility for creating corporate policy, could have his or her fault or *mens rea* attributed to the corporation for the purpose of determining the corporation's liability for criminal offences. In 2003, Parliament amended the *Criminal Code* to make it somewhat easier to convict corporations and other organizations of criminal offences. The fault of "senior officers" is now attributed to the corporation, and senior officers are defined in the *Criminal Code* to include not only those who play an important role in the establishment of the organization's policies, but also those who are responsible for managing an important aspect of the organization's activities.

A corporation can be held liable for a subjective fault crime if the responsible senior officer commits the offence or intentionally directs the work of any representative of the corporation (including contractors and agents of the corporation) so that they commit the offence. In addition, the corporation may be liable if the senior officer knows that any representative is committing or is about to commit an offence but fails to take all reasonable measures to stop the representative from committing the offence. A corporation can be liable for a negligence-based crime if the responsible senior officer(s) depart markedly from the standard of care that, in the circumstances, could reasonably be expected to prevent representatives from committing the offence.

N. DEFENCES

Even if the Crown proves that the accused committed the prohibited act and had the required fault element, the accused may still avoid conviction by raising a relevant defence. Some common defences, such as mistake of fact and intoxication, are not really defences, but conditions that prevent the Crown from proving the required mental or fault element beyond a reasonable doubt. A person accused of murder could be so intoxicated that he or she did not know that the victim was likely to die. Likewise, a hunter accused of murder could commit the prohibited act of causing another hunter's death but have had the mistaken impression that he or she was shooting a deer. In such instances, the Crown can prove the commission of the prohibited act, but will be unable to prove that the accused had the mental element required for murder. The defences of intoxication and mistake of fact are derived from the fault element of the particular crime. For example, an offence requiring objective negligence will allow a defence of mistake of fact only if the mistake was a reasonable one. It will also generally not allow any intoxication defence because the reasonable person is sober.

Other defences may excuse or justify conduct, even though the accused committed the offence with the required fault element. Those who defend themselves may have a defence of self-defence, even if they intentionally kill or harm the attacker. Those who commit a crime in reasonable response to serious threats of harm by third parties may have a defence of duress, even if they commit the crime with the required fault element. An example would be the person who goes along with a robbery with a gun at his or her head. Similarly, a person who commits a crime in response to circumstances of dire peril may have a defence of necessity. This would apply to a lost hiker who intentionally breaks into a cabin because he or she desperately needs food and water. Those who have valid defences of duress and necessity act in a morally involuntary manner because in the dire circumstances it was impossible for them to comply with the law, there was no safe and lawful avenue of escape, and there was proportionality between the harm avoided and the harm inflicted. The defences of necessity and duress are usually thought to excuse but not justify conduct, but like self-defence they also lead to a full acquittal.

Defences are related to the appropriate disposition of the accused. Provocation is a special defence that reduces murder to manslaughter, thus avoiding murder's mandatory sentence of life imprisonment. The defence of intoxication has traditionally been available only as a defence to some offences, known as specific intent offences, but not to others, known as general intent offences. A specific intent offence, such as robbery, requires more complicated mental processes that often require some thought beyond the immediate commission of the act, while a general intent offence, such as assault, requires less complicated thought processes. Traditionally, an accused so intoxicated as to be unable to have the subjective foresight of death would be acquitted of murder, a specific intent offence, but almost always convicted of manslaughter, a general intent offence. Manslaughter is a less serious offence than murder, and it generally allows for the exercise of sentencing discretion.

Defences related to mental disorders are also influenced by concerns about the appropriate disposition of the accused. The insanity or mental disorder defence applies to those who, because of a mental disorder, cannot appreciate the physical consequences of the prohibited act they commit or know that it is legally or morally wrong. Such a person, although not convicted, would be detained and examined to determine if further detention was required to protect the public from a significant threat of danger. Automatism refers to involuntary behaviour that may prevent the Crown from proving the fault element or even the prohibited act of a crime. An accused found to be in such a state will not be convicted. If the automatism is caused by a mental disorder, however, the accused can be subject to detention as a person held not criminally responsible by reason of mental disorder. If the automatism is caused by a factor that is not a mental disorder, such as a blow on the head, the accused is simply acquitted. The accused now has the burden of establishing both the mental disorder and non-insane automatism defences on a balance of probabilities. Courts increasingly assume that automatism is caused by mental disorder because people found not criminally responsible by reason of mental disorder can be subject to detention for public safety reasons.

Many defences require that the accused act in a reasonable fashion. To be able to claim self-defence, the accused must not only subjectively believe that force or threat of force is being used against them or others, but there must also be a reasonable basis for such beliefs. In addition, the new section 34(1)(c) of the *Code* requires that acts of self-defence be reasonable in the circumstances.

The criminal law generally excuses crimes committed in response to threats and dire circumstances only if a reasonable person in the accused's circumstances would have committed the crime. The use of objective standards in defences raises the question of who is the reasonable person. Unlike in the case of objective fault elements, the trend in Canada is to consider the particular accused's own experiences and characteristics when applying objective standards relating to defences such as provocation, self-defence, duress, and necessity. In the self-defence context, the Supreme Court has indicated that what is reasonable to expect of a man in a barroom brawl may not be reasonable to expect of a woman who has been previously battered by the person she kills. In judging whether an ordinary person would have lost self-control when provoked, the courts consider the accused's characteristics and experiences, as they affect the gravity or meaning of the provoking act. This provides a more generous defence that is sensitive to the particular experiences and frailties of the accused, but it also risks blurring the conceptual distinction between objective and subjective standards. The courts attempt to contextualize the reasonable person while maintaining common standards of reasonable behaviour that apply to all.

Restrictions on a defence may violate the principles of fundamental justice protected under section 7 of the *Charter*. The Supreme Court has held that the complete denial of an intoxication defence when a person is charged with a general intent offence, such as an assault or sexual assault, violates the principles of fundamental justice. It could result in the conviction of a person who acted in an involuntary manner because of extreme intoxication. Statutory restrictions on the defence of duress also offend the principles of fundamental justice because they allow a person to be convicted even though he or she acted in a morally involuntary manner in response to threats. A person acts in a morally involuntary manner if any reasonable person in the same circumstances with the same characteristics would have committed the offence. A conviction of a person who acts in a morally involuntary manner because of external pressures offends section 7 of the *Charter* because it would deprive a person of liberty in a manner that is not in accordance with the principles of fundamental justice. Although the mental disorder defence is at times unpopular, its repeal would also probably violate section 7 of the *Charter* because it would allow people to be punished for morally involuntary conduct.

O. THE SPECIAL PART: SOME SELECTED OFFENCES

The focus of this book is on general principles that define criminal liability and provide excuses or justifications for the commission of all crimes. Nevertheless, it is useful to have a sense of some of the most serious or important offences and how they are informed by contextual considerations that are specific to the particular crime.

Although homicide offences are statistically rare, they are the place where much criminal law is developed. There are three homicide offences: murder, manslaughter, and infanticide. In addition, the most serious murders are classified as first-degree murder, which requires the proof of additional fault such as planning and deliberation or the commission of another serious crime during the killing. Provocation is a controversial defence available only to accused charged with murder. It applies when an accused kills in a rage produced by a sudden and wrongful act or insult (since 2015 this wrongful act has to also be an indictable offence punishable by five years' imprisonment or more, such as assault or sexual assault) that would have caused an ordinary person to lose self-control. This defence does not lead to a complete acquittal, but reduces murder to manslaughter. This avoids the mandatory penalty of life imprisonment that follows a murder conviction.

Sexual assault has been a particularly controversial offence and the subject of much law reform. In 1982, the offence of rape was replaced with offences of sexual assault that were designed to stress the violence in sexual crimes and to expand the prohibited act. There are three forms of sexual assault that mimic the offences of assault: assault with a weapon or causing bodily harm, and aggravated assault. In 1992, new provisions were enacted that addressed both the prohibited act and fault element for sexual assault offences. These reforms were designed to reflect the particular circumstances of sexual violence. They were called the "no means no" reforms and provided concrete examples of circumstances where consent to sexual activity would not be valid. They also modified the controversial defence that the accused had a mistaken belief that the victim consented, in part, by providing that the defence would not apply if the accused did not take reasonable steps in the circumstances known to him to ascertain whether the complainant was consenting. In this way, Parliament combined subjective and objective fault elements in a creative and innovative manner. Bill C-51, passed by the House of Commons but not by the Senate before the 2018 summer recess, would amend both section 273.1, defining consent, and section 273.2, defining the fault element of sexual assault. This amendment would codify a judicial interpretation that an unconscious complainant could not consent while making clear that this was not the only ground to find that the complainant was incapable of consenting. It would also make clear that a belief in consent on grounds prohibited by law would be a mistake of law, which under section 19 of the *Code* is not an excuse for a crime.

P. SENTENCING

Most accused plead guilty to some charge and proceed directly to sentencing without a criminal trial. A majority of those who do go to trial are convicted of some offence and are subject to sentencing. In Canada, judges have traditionally had significant sentencing discretion guided only by general principles in the *Criminal Code* and high maximum penalties. Robbery, for example, is subject only to a maximum punishment of life imprisonment, with no minimum sentence. Committing a robbery with a firearm, however, does have a mandatory minimum sentence of five years' imprisonment. Mandatory penalties can be challenged as violating the right against cruel and unusual punishment, but judges cannot craft exemptions under the *Charter* from mandatory sentences. Another constraint on a sentencing judge can be a joint submission by both the accused and the prosecutor about the appropriate sentence.

The fundamental principle of sentencing is that a sentence must be proportionate to the gravity of the offence and the degree of responsibility of the offender. This is an important principle, given the various types of conduct that can be caught under broad legislative definitions of the prohibited act, and the provisions that make parties to an offence guilty of the same offence as those who actually pull the trigger. This principle also suggests that the punishment should fit the crime and that an offender should not be treated more harshly than the crime warrants, in order to deter others or to incapacitate or even rehabilitate the offender. A sentence that is grossly disproportionate will constitute cruel and unusual punishment under section 12 of the *Charter*.

Despite the fundamental principle that a sentence must fit the crime, there are other legitimate purposes of sentencing, including deterring others from committing crimes; deterring the particular offender from reoffending; incapacitating the particular offender from committing more crimes; rehabilitating the particular offender; and providing reparation for harm done to victims or the community. In fulfilling these multiple purposes, judges can impose punishments other than actual imprisonment, including community service orders and discharges with conditions in the form of probation orders, fines, and restitution orders. Conditional sentences allow offenders to serve sentences of imprisonment in the community so long as they satisfy prescribed conditions. They cannot be used if the accused is subject to any mandatory term of imprisonment and Parliament has in recent years imposed other restrictions on their use. If a person is imprisoned, he or she can usually apply to a parole board before the end of the sentence for various forms of supervised release into the community. There are also provisions that allow repeat offenders to be declared dangerous and subject to indeterminate detention.

CONCLUSION

The criminal law is the result of a complex process that starts with the decision of a legislature to define something as a prohibited act. The next steps are usually the investigation by the police and the prosecution by the Crown. These phases of the criminal process must be procedurally fair, or the accused will be able to seek a remedy for the violation of his or her rights under the *Charter*.

The offence and the available defences must ensure that the morally innocent are not punished and that people are also not punished if they act in a morally involuntary manner. The Crown must also prove beyond a reasonable doubt to the judge or jury that the accused committed the prohibited act with the required fault element. The accused has available various defences, most of which will apply if there is a reasonable doubt as to their existence. Some defences such as self-defence lead to a complete acquittal, whereas others such as intoxication and provocation may result in the accused being acquitted of a serious offence such as murder but still convicted of a less serious offence such as manslaughter. The mental disorder defence leads to a special disposition in which the accused, although not convicted, may be subject to further detention or treatment if he or she presents a significant threat to public safety. The judge can, subject to statutory restrictions, exercise sentencing discretion to tailor punishment to the offender's degree of responsibility, but also to consider what punishment will best deter, rehabilitate, or incapacitate the particular offender, deter others from committing the same crime, and provide reparation to the victims and the community for the crime.

FURTHER READINGS

KEIGHLEY, K. "Police-Reported Crime Statistics in Canada, 2016" (2017) 37(1) *Juristat*, online: www.statcan.gc.ca/pub/85-002-x/2017001/article/54842-eng.pdf.

MATHEWS, A. "Adult Criminal Court Statistics, 2014/2015" (2017) 37(1) *Juristat*, online: www.statcan.gc.ca/pub/85-002-x/2017001/article/14699-eng.pdf.

PERREAULT, S. "Criminal Victimization in Canada, 2014" (2015) 35(1) *Juristat*, online: www.statcan.gc.ca/access_acces/alternative_alternatif.action?l=eng&loc=/pub/85-002-x/2015001/article/14241-eng.pdf.

REITTANO, J. "Adult Correctional Services in Canada 2015/2016" (2017) *Juristat*, online: www.statcan.gc.ca/pub/85-002-x/2017001/article/14700-eng.pdf.

CHAPTER 2

THE CRIMINAL LAW AND THE CONSTITUTION

In order to understand criminal law in Canada, it is increasingly necessary to understand constitutional law. The Constitution, which is the supreme law of the land, has always played a role in the criminal law. The constitutional division of powers between the federal and provincial governments, created in 1867, allows only the federal Parliament to enact laws concerning criminal law and procedure. The provinces can, however, enact regulatory offences to help them govern matters within their jurisdiction, such as liquor licensing. The federal government can also enact regulatory offences to help it govern matters such as navigation and shipping that are within federal jurisdiction. In deciding whether an offence is within federal or provincial jurisdiction, the courts are concerned with the law's primary purpose.

In 1982 the *Canadian Charter of Rights and Freedoms* was added to the Constitution, and it places new restraints on the state's ability to enact and apply criminal laws. It does so by recognizing various rights, such as the right to be free of unreasonable searches and seizures, the right to counsel, and the right to a fair trial. In most cases, people will have the incentive to invoke their *Charter* rights only when they are charged with an offence. Hence, most *Charter* litigation arises in criminal cases. Many of the rights in the *Charter* require procedural fairness or due process in the investigation and prosecution of crime. Other rights are concerned that the substance of the law is fair and does not punish a person who is morally innocent, responds to threats in a morally involuntary manner that a reasonable person could not resist, or is only exercising constitutional rights, such as freedom of expression. A law or practice can infringe a *Charter* right because it has the effect of violating an individual's right, even if it was enacted for a valid and legitimate purpose.

If a criminal or regulatory offence or procedural provision violates a right protected under the *Charter*, the government will have an opportunity to justify the law under section 1 of the *Charter* as a reasonable limit that is demonstrably justifiable in a free and democratic society. The government must demonstrate not only that the law has been enacted for an important purpose, but also that there is no other reasonable manner to fulfill that purpose except by violating the accused's rights and the good that the law achieves in advancing its objective outweighs the harm to the *Charter* right. If the accused's rights have been violated and the violation is not justified under section 1, the courts can order a range of constitutional remedies. For example, they can strike down an unconstitutional offence, terminate a prosecution through a stay of proceedings, or exclude relevant evidence because it was obtained through a *Charter* violation such as an unconstitutional search or interrogation.

The new emphasis on the accused's rights in Canadian criminal law has diverted some trials away from their traditional focus on whether the accused was factually guilty. The *Charter* protects the rights of the accused to due process or fair treatment, but section 1 allows the government to justify some restrictions on the accused's rights as necessary for crime control or some other important objective. Other people affected by a criminal law, including victims, witnesses, or the media, may also have *Charter* rights, such as the rights to privacy and the equal protection and benefit of the law. The *Charter* does not eliminate the need to balance competing interests in criminal laws and prosecutions, but it provides a new framework for reconciling these interests.

A. CRIMINAL JUSTICE AND THE DIVISION OF POWERS

1) Federal Jurisdiction over Criminal Law

Under section 91(27) of the *Constitution Act, 1867*, only the federal Parliament can enact laws concerning criminal law and procedure. Most criminal law is contained in the *Criminal Code*[1] although the *Controlled*

---

1   RSC 1985, c C-46 [*Code*].

Drugs and Substances Act[2] and the *Youth Criminal Justice Act*[3] are often considered criminal law. Not all laws enacted by the federal government fall under its power to enact criminal law and procedure. For example, a federal law prohibiting the sale of margarine or establishing the alcohol content of light beer would not be a valid criminal law.[4] Courts have, however, been quite generous in allowing the federal government to enact laws that facilitate the administration of the criminal law. For example, federal laws regulating the detention of the criminally insane or those found unfit to stand trial because of a mental disorder[5] and enabling judges to order the accused to make restitution to the victims of crime[6] have been upheld as valid criminal law. Parliament's criminal law power has also been interpreted broadly to allow laws restricting the advertising of tobacco,[7] prohibiting pollution,[8] prohibiting the possession of marijuana,[9] requiring all guns to be registered,[10] and regulating assisted suicide.[11] When the federal government relies on its criminal law power, it must emphasize the use of prohibitions and punishments, as opposed to other forms of regulation such as licensing and inspections. At the same time, something that is not necessarily immoral can still be prohibited by the criminal law.

Unlike in the United States and Australia, the provinces (or states) cannot make laws that are classified by the courts as having the dominant purpose of prohibiting acts by the criminal sanction. Provincial and municipal attempts to prohibit the propagation of ideas,[12] the use of streets for prostitution,[13] or abortions,[14] have all been struck down as infringing the federal government's exclusive jurisdiction over criminal law. A provincial offence or a municipal bylaw will be unconstitutional if its prime purpose is to punish behaviour as criminal. Before

---

2   SC 1996, c 19.

3   SC 2002, c 1.

4   *Canadian Federation of Agriculture v Quebec (AG)*, [1951] AC 179 (PC); *Labatt Breweries of Canada Ltd v Canada (AG)*, [1980] 1 SCR 914.

5   *R v Swain* (1991) 63 CCC (3d) 481 (SCC); *R v Demers* [2004] 2 SCR 489.

6   *R v Zelensky* (1978), 41 CCC (2d) 97 (SCC).

7   *RJR-MacDonald Inc v Canada (AG)* (1995), 100 CCC (3d) 449 (SCC). The advertising restrictions were, however, struck down under the *Charter* as an unjustified restriction on freedom of expression.

8   *R v Hydro–Quebec* (1997), 118 CCC (3d) 97 (SCC).

9   *R v Malmo-Levine* (2003), 179 CCC (3d) 417 (SCC) [*Malmo-Levine*].

10   *Reference re Firearms Act (Can)*, [2000] 1 SCR 783 [*Firearms Reference*].

11   *Carter v Canada (Attorney General)*, 2015 SCC 5 [*Carter*].

12   *Switzman v Elbling* (1957), 117 CCC 129 (SCC).

13   *R v Westendorp* (1983), 2 CCC (3d) 330 (SCC).

14   *R v Morgentaler* (1993), 85 CCC (3d) 118 (SCC)

the enactment of the *Charter*, these restrictions acted as an indirect but important protection of civil liberties.

Provincial or municipal laws have also been upheld if found to have the primary purpose of responding to the conditions that cause crime as part of provincial jurisdiction over local matters.[15] The courts have recently upheld various provincial laws designed to prevent and respond to crimes by various preventive and remedial measures even though there were already provisions in the federal criminal law addressing the same mischief.[16]

2) Provincial Jurisdiction to Enact Regulatory Offences

Under section 92(15) of the *Constitution Act, 1867*, the provinces (and their delegates, the municipalities) can create offences punishable by fine, penalty, or imprisonment for matters within their jurisdiction. The provinces have been allowed to enact highway traffic offences,[17] and to make provisions for the classification and censorship of films,[18] and even the compulsory treatment of heroin addicts.[19] Provincial offences will be constitutional provided that their dominant purpose is to regulate some matter within areas of provincial jurisdiction, such as property and civil rights and matters of a local and private nature. The fact that a provincial scheme for roadside breath testing and licence suspensions is designed to deter or prevent the crime of impaired driving is not fatal to holding that the scheme is within provincial powers.[20]

Provincial offences are often classified as regulatory or public welfare offences. They can be tried in the same courts as criminal offences and can even result in imprisonment. The standards for investigation

---

15   *Bedard v Dawson*, [1923] SCR 681; *Canada (Attorney General) v Dupond*, [1978] 2 SCR 770.

16   See *Chatterjee v Ontario* [2009] 1 SCR 624, upholding provincial laws for forfeiture of proceeds and instruments of crime; *R v Banks* (2007), 216 CCC (3d) 19 (Ont CA), upholding provincial law against soliciting from people in a parked vehicle; *R v Dyck*, 2008 ONCA 309, upholding a provincial requirement that all sexual offenders register with the police; and *Baril v Obnecki* (2007), 279 DLR (4th) 304 (Man CA), upholding provincial protection orders targeting domestic violence. In all four cases, the laws were also held to be consistent with the *Charter*.

17   *O'Grady v Sparling* (1960), 128 CCC 1 (SCC).

18   *McNeil v Nova Scotia (Board of Censors)* (1978), 44 CCC (2d) 128 (SCC).

19   *R v Schneider* (1982), 68 CCC (2d) 449 (SCC).

20   *Goodwin v British Columbia (Superintendent of Motor Vehicles)*, 2015 SCC 46 [*Goodwin*]. The Court did, however, find that the provincial scheme violated the right against unreasonable searches and seizures under s 8 of the *Charter* because of the absence of a meaningful review of the accuracy of a failure on a roadside breath test.

and conviction of regulatory offences are generally less protective of the accused than those for criminal offences.[21] The federal government can also enact regulatory offences under other areas of its jurisdiction, such as its power over fisheries. In terms of offences and prosecutions, regulatory offences far outnumber criminal offences. Individuals are more likely to be charged with speeding or performing an act without a licence than with crimes such as murder, theft, or break and enter.

3) Prosecutors, Police, and Prisons

The Attorney General of a province will generally prosecute offences under the *Criminal Code*,[22] but the federal Attorney General may prosecute drug offences and also prosecute offences in the territories and various crimes with international implications.[23] The fact that the person ultimately responsible for prosecutions is an elected representative who sits in Cabinet is constitutional, but it would violate the principles of fundamental justice if that person acted for partisan or other improper motives.[24]

The provinces can establish police forces to enforce the *Criminal Code* (this power in turn often being delegated to a municipality or a region) but the federal Royal Canadian Mounted Police (RCMP) investigate other offences under federal law, including those relating to threats to national security. Many provinces, however, purchase policing services from the RCMP. Peace officers (including the public police, customs officials, and jail guards, but not usually private police or security guards) have special powers, duties, and protections under the *Criminal Code*.[25] A fundamental feature of the rule of law is that peace officers are bound by the law including the *Criminal Code* and the *Charter*. Ordinary individuals have legal powers to arrest a person fleeing from the commission of a serious offence[26] and to go before a judicial

---

21 See Chapter 6.
22 *Code*, above note 1, s 2. The Attorney General of Canada through the Public Prosecution Service of Canada is the prosecutor for the Northwest and Yukon Territories and Nunavut. The Attorney General of Canada can also prosecute certain *Criminal Code* crimes with extraterritorial effect and crimes involving terrorism or otherwise affecting the security of Canada, United Nations personnel, or capital market frauds.
23 *Code*, above note 1, s 2 definition of Attorney General; *R v Hauser* (1979), 46 CCC (2d) 481 (SCC).
24 *R v Cawthorne*, 2016 SCC 32.
25 *Code*, above note 1, ss 25, 129, 270, 495, and 503. Peace officers are defined in s 2.
26 *Ibid*, s 494(1).

official to establish reasonable and probable grounds that a criminal offence has been committed.[27]

The provinces have jurisdiction over those sentenced to less than two years' imprisonment, while the federal government administers penitentiaries for those sentenced to longer periods.[28] The provinces generally administer probation orders, while provincial and federal parole boards administer gradual release or parole from imprisonment before an offender's sentence has expired.

4) Trials and Trial Courts

The vast majority (over 99 percent) of criminal cases are resolved in provincial courts formerly known as magistrates' courts. Provincial court judges are appointed by the provinces and cannot sit with a jury. They can, however, hear most serious indictable offences,[29] provided that the accused decides or elects to be tried in provincial court without a jury or a preliminary inquiry to determine whether there is enough evidence to put the accused on trial. The least serious indictable offences can be tried only in provincial court,[30] and provincial courts or justices of the peace also hear the least serious criminal offences, known as summary conviction offences, as well as provincial regulatory offences enacted under section 92(15) of the *Constitution Act, 1867*. Both summary conviction and provincial offences can generally be punished only by up to six months' imprisonment and $5,000 in fines.[31] A growing number of offences, such as sexual assault, if prosecuted by way of summary conviction, can be punished by up to eighteen months' imprisonment and there is a proposal to create two-year maximum sentences for summary conviction offences. The only constitutional restraints on the creation of summary offences is that under section 11(f) of the *Charter* anyone who faces five years' or more imprisonment has a right to trial by jury and only superior courts sit with juries.

In "hybrid" offences, the Crown has the discretion to prosecute the offence by indictment or as a less serious summary conviction offence. If the prosecutor elects to prosecute the offence as a summary conviction offence, the accused is not entitled to a preliminary inquiry or a trial by jury but the maximum punishment is limited. The prosecutor's

---

27   *Ibid*, ss 504 and 507.

28   *Constitution Act, 1867* (UK), 30 & 31 Vict, c 3, ss 91(28) and 92(6) [*CA 1867*]; *Code*, above note 1, s 743.1.

29   But not those, such as murder, listed in the *Code, ibid*, s 469.

30   Including theft and other offences listed in the *Code, ibid*, s 553.

31   *Ibid*, s 787.

election to prosecute by summary conviction or indictment may also determine what maximum and minimum penalty will apply if the accused is convicted.

Those under eighteen years of age are generally tried in youth court, which in most provinces is the provincial court. Youth sentences are lower than those available upon conviction of the same offence in adult court. In some cases, however, adult sentences can be imposed on young offenders; but the Supreme Court has held that a presumption that a young person would receive an adult sentence for specified offences violates a principle of fundamental justice, which presumes that young people are less blameworthy for crimes because of their age, vulnerability, and reduced capacity for moral judgment.[32]

Only federally appointed superior court judges can sit with a jury in what is known in different provinces as the Superior Court, Supreme Court, or Queen's Bench.[33] Murder charges must be tried by a superior court judge, usually with a jury.[34] Superior court judges may also try most other indictable offences, provided the accused elects to be tried in this higher level of trial court. The accused can elect to be tried in the superior court with a preliminary inquiry (heard by a provincial court judge or justice of the peace) and with or without a jury. The appearance of a superior court trial can be impressive (for example, the lawyers are gowned), but it should be remembered that the vast majority of criminal cases are resolved in the less formal and more hectic atmosphere of the provincial courts.

Trial judges have to provide reasons for their decisions and these reasons should set out all the elements of an offence for a conviction. Such reasons, however, can be briefer in cases of an acquittal based on the fact that the Crown has not proven one of the elements of the offence.[35] This also reflects a fundamental asymmetry in the criminal law in which the state has to establish guilt beyond a reasonable doubt and the accused is given the benefit of reasonable doubt about guilt.

5) Appeals and Appellate Courts

Canada has a generous appellate structure that allows both the accused and the Crown wide rights of appeal. Appeals in summary conviction offences can be made by either the accused or the prosecutor and are heard by a superior court judge with further appeals on questions of

---

32   R v DB, 2008 SCC 25 [DB].
33   CA 1867, above note 28, s 96.
34   Code, above note 1, s 469.
35   R v Sheppard, [2002] 1 SCR 869; R v Walker, 2008 SCC 34.

law to the court of appeal.[36] Appeals for indictable offences go directly
to the provincial court of appeal, which has federally appointed judges
and hears appeals in panels of three and sometimes five judges. The accused has broad rights of appeal and can appeal matters of fact or law,
as well as the fitness of his or her sentence.[37] The accused's appeal can
be allowed on three grounds: (1) that the conviction is unreasonable or
cannot be supported by the evidence; (2) that the conviction entails a
miscarriage of justice; or (3) that the trial judge made an error of law.
In the last case, the appeal can be denied if the appeal court concludes
that notwithstanding the legal error, "no substantial wrong or miscarriage of justice has occurred."[38] If the accused's appeal is successful, a
new trial will usually be ordered, but in some cases an acquittal may
be entered. In addition, the minister of justice can order a new trial or
direct an appeal to a provincial court of appeal when he or she is "satisfied that there is a reasonable basis to conclude that a miscarriage of
justice likely occurred" after having inquired into an application by a
person convicted of an offence whose appeal rights have been exhaust-
ed.[39] A similar power was used to order new appeals in cases involving
miscarriages of justice, such as the wrongful convictions of Donald
Marshall, Jr., David Milgaard, and William Mullins-Johnson.

The prosecutor may appeal questions of law and the fitness of sentence to the court of appeal.[40] If the appeal is allowed and the prosecutor
can show that the outcome would not have been the same without the
legal error, a new trial will be ordered. In rare cases, the appeal court
might enter a conviction instead of ordering a new trial, but this cannot
be done if the accused was acquitted at trial by a jury. The right of the
prosecutor to appeal acquittals and to have new trials ordered is broader
in Canada than in either the United States or the United Kingdom.

Either the accused or the prosecutor can appeal to the highest
court, the Supreme Court of Canada, with nine federally appointed
judges. Appeals to that Court are of right on any question of law from
which a judge in the provincial court of appeal dissents, and by leave
on any matter of law of national importance.[41]

36   *Code*, above note 1, ss 813, 830, and 839.
37   *Ibid*, s 675.
38   *Ibid*, s 686(1)(b)(iii).
39   *Ibid*, s 696.3(3). Pardons may also be granted under s 748 of the *Code* and pursu-
      ant to the royal prerogative of mercy.
40   *Ibid*, s 676.
41   *Ibid*, ss 691 and 693; *Supreme Court Act*, RSC 1985, c S-26, s 40.

B. CRIMINAL LAW AND THE *CHARTER OF RIGHTS*

In 1982 the *Canadian Charter of Rights and Freedoms* was added to the Canadian Constitution. The *Charter*'s greatest impact has been on the criminal justice system, and it provides constitutional standards that affect the criminal process from the investigation of crime to the punishment of offenders. A violation of the *Charter* may occur if police, prosecutorial, or correctional practices or some law has the effect of violating the accused's rights. Under section 24 of the *Charter*, courts can provide a range of remedies if police, prosecutors, or prison officials violate the *Charter* rights of the accused. These remedies can include the termination of a prosecution through a stay of proceedings, the release of a person, and the exclusion of unconstitutionally obtained evidence. Criminal laws passed by Parliament can also be struck down by the courts under section 52 of the *Constitution Act, 1982*, if they are found to violate one of the rights in the *Charter* and the government cannot justify the violation under section 1 of the *Charter* as a proportionate and reasonable means to fulfill an important purpose. Parliament and the provincial legislatures retain the final, but very rarely exercised, option to declare that a law will operate notwithstanding the fundamental freedoms, legal rights, or equality rights otherwise guaranteed under the *Charter*.[42]

1) Division of Powers and the *Charter* Compared

The division of powers in the *Constitution Act, 1867* and the *Charter* provides a complex constitutional framework that governs the enactment of criminal and regulatory offences in Canada. The history of legislation requiring Sunday observance provides a good illustration. At the turn of the twentieth century, provincial legislation requiring Sunday observance was struck down on the grounds that it was a criminal law that only Parliament could enact.[43] The federal *Lord's Day Act*[44] was subsequently upheld as valid criminal law because it was designed with the religious purpose of requiring the observance of the Christian

---

42 *Canadian Charter of Rights and Freedoms*, Part I of the *Constitution Act, 1982*, being Schedule B to the *Canada Act 1982* (UK) 1982, c 11, s 33 [*Charter*].

43 *Ontario (AG) v Hamilton Street Railway Co*, [1903] AC 524 (PC). Subsequent provincial attempts to compel observance of religious holidays were struck down as invasions of federal jurisdiction over criminal law. *Henry Birks & Sons v (Montreal) Ltd (City)* (1955), 113 CCC 135 (SCC).

44 RSC 1970, c L-13.

Sabbath.[45] By that time, however, the *Charter* had been enacted, and the Supreme Court decided that a law enacted with the religious purpose of compelling observance of a common Sabbath was a direct violation of freedom of conscience and religion as protected under section 2(a) of the *Charter*.[46] Since the law was based on a purpose contrary to *Charter* values, it could not be justified by the government under section 1 and was declared to be invalid.

A year later, the Supreme Court had to decide the constitutionality of a provincial law requiring Sunday closing. The Court found that the law had been enacted for the secular purpose of establishing a common rest day, a matter of civil and property rights within provincial jurisdiction. At the same time, however, the Court found that the law violated the right to freedom of religion and conscience because it had the effect (but not the purpose) of placing burdens on those who, because of their religious beliefs, could not open their stores on either Sunday or their own religious Sabbath.[47] That conclusion did not end the constitutional analysis, however, because the Court held that the government had justified the law under section 1 of the *Charter* as a reasonable limit that was necessary to ensure a common rest day. There is no equivalent to section 1 under the division of powers in allowing the government to justify limits on rights as reasonable and proportionate. Courts have interpreted section 1 to require the government to demonstrate that a law that limits *Charter* rights is rationally connected to a legislative objective that is important enough to limit a *Charter* right. In addition, the limit must also limit the *Charter* right as little as is necessary to achieve its objectives and the beneficial effects of the law in achieving its objectives must be greater that its harmful effects. The Court has recently affirmed the importance of this last overall benefit aspect of its proportionality test.[48]

The federal Parliament's ability to require all gun owners to register firearms was upheld under the division of powers on the basis that the law's purpose or "pith and substance" was to protect public safety by controlling access to firearms through prohibitions and penalties. At the same time, the Court stressed that this holding would not preclude other constitutional challenges to the law based on the *Charter* or Indigenous rights and that it was not concerned with the wisdom or

---

45   *R v Big M Drug Mart Ltd* (1985), 18 CCC (3d) 385 (SCC).
46   *Ibid.*
47   *R v Edwards Books & Art Ltd* (1986), 30 CCC (3d) 385 (SCC).
48   *R v Oakes* (1986), 24 CCC (3d) 321 (SCC) [*Oakes*]. For a recent affirmation of
        the important role of the final balancing test, see *R v KRJ*, 2016 SCC 31 [*KRJ*].

efficacy of the law.[49] The law was subsequently repealed by a different federal government. The Court held that it was a policy choice within federal power over criminal law to destroy the data from the long-gun registry even though some provinces had indicated their intent to create their own gun registry under provincial jurisdiction. A minority dissented on the basis that the destruction of the data related to provincial jurisdiction and violated principles of cooperative federalism.[50]

2) The *Charter* and the Investigation of Crime

Before the enactment of the *Charter*, courts conducting a criminal trial were generally not concerned with the manner in which the police investigated crime. The failure of the police to warn suspects that their statements might be used against them did not affect the admissibility of their statements[51] and evidence could not be excluded because it was unfairly obtained.[52] The only real restraint was that confessions had to be proven to be voluntary in the sense that they were not obtained through fear or hope of advantage. This was done to ensure the reliability of confessions more than their fairness.

The *Charter* has changed this exclusive emphasis on crime control by recognizing rights to be secure against unreasonable search and seizures (section 8); rights not to be arbitrarily detained or imprisoned (section 9); and rights to be informed of the reason for arrest or detention and to retain and instruct counsel without delay (sections 10(a) & (b)). A violation of any of these rights can result in the exclusion of relevant evidence from the criminal trial if its admission will bring the administration of justice into disrepute (section 24(2)).

a) Search and Seizure
Section 8 of the *Charter* provides that everyone has a right to be secure against unreasonable search and seizure.

i) *Reasonable Expectations of Privacy*
This provision protects all reasonable expectations of privacy, and such expectations are not sacrificed simply because an accused was committing a criminal offence or risked that the state would discover his

---

49   *Firearms Reference*, above note 10.
50   *Quebec (AG) v Canada (AG)*, 2015 SCC 14.
51   *R v Boudreau* (1949), 94 CCC 1 (SCC).
52   *R v Wray*, [1970] 4 CCC 1 (SCC).

or her illegal activities.[53] The Court has held that the right to privacy includes the right of anonymity with respect to internet usage[54] and text messages.[55] This does not mean that the protection of privacy is absolute, but that reasonable measures, such as obtaining a judicial warrant on a showing of reasonable grounds to believe that a crime has been committed and that the search will obtain evidence of a crime, should be taken. Such protections are not, however, required if there is no reasonable expectation of privacy as determined on the basis of the totality of the circumstances including whether the accused had a subjective expectation of privacy and whether that expectation was reasonable. For example, the Court has held that the use of technology to detect heat arising from homes for drug enforcement purposes does not invade a reasonable expectation of privacy because the technology does not permit inferences about the precise activity causing the heat.[56] Searches of garbage put out for collection also do not invade reasonable expectations of privacy.[57] People who are trespassing or squatting on premises do not have a reasonable expectation in those premises.[58]

Individuals and businesses operating in a regulated field have diminished expectation of privacy over their business records.[59] Regulatory inspections, like regulatory offences, are thought to carry with them less stigma and for this reason the state is given greater scope in its activities. Similarly, a demand by government investigators for the production of documents is seen as less intrusive than an actual search.[60] The Supreme Court has made clear, however, that reasonable expectations of privacy and warrant requirements apply when regulators "cross the Rubicon" from regulation to prosecution. This occurs when the predominant purpose of their inquiries is the determination of penal liability.[61] Complex issues are raised when regulatory search and seizure powers are intertwined with searches for evidence of crime.[62] In some contexts, such as the use of sniffer dogs, all the

---

53   *R v Duarte* (1990), 53 CCC (3d) 1 (SCC) [*Duarte*]; *R v Wong* (1990), 60 CCC (3d) 460 (SCC) [*Wong*].

54   *R v Spencer*, 2014 SCC 43.

55   *R v Jones*, 2017 SCC 60 at para 37; *R v Marakah*, 2017 SCC 59.

56   *R v Tessling*, [2004] 3 SCR 432.

57   *R v Patrick*, [2009] 1 SCR 579.

58   *R v Simpson*, 2015 SCC 40 at para 51.

59   *R v Potash* (1994), 91 CCC (3d) 315 (SCC).

60   *Thomson Newspapers Ltd v Canada (Director of Investigation & Research)* (1990), 54 CCC (3d) 417 (SCC); *R v McKinlay Transport Ltd* (1990), 55 CCC (3d) 530 (SCC).

61   *R v Jarvis* (2002), 169 CCC (3d) 1 (SCC).

62   *R v Nolet*, [2010] 1 SCR 851.

Court requires is a reasonable suspicion to justify a search despite the recognition that searches on suspicion mean only that there is a reasonable possibility that evidence of wrongdoing will be obtained and even though such a standard will result in more innocent people being searched.[63] The standards that will apply in the regulatory context depend on the context. The Court has found a section 8 violation when drivers could be subject to a ninety-day licence suspension under provincial law but have no meaningful means to challenge the accuracy of the failure of a roadside breath-testing device.[64]

It is not only those who operate in a regulatory context who have diminished or no expectations of privacy. An individual who occasionally stays at an intimate friend's home may have no reasonable expectation of privacy when that friend's home is searched,[65] and passengers may not have a reasonable expectation of privacy when the car they are driving in is searched.[66] Students in schools also have diminished expectations of privacy from searches,[67] as do prisoners,[68] drivers asked to produce their licences,[69] individuals who pass customs,[70] and those whose power consumption can be determined by access to commercial records.[71]

ii) Warrant Requirements

If there is a reasonable expectation of privacy, the state must generally obtain prior judicial authorization to authorize a search and seizure, except if there are exigent and urgent circumstances that make it impossible to obtain a warrant.[72] The police need not wait to obtain a warrant if there is imminent danger that evidence of a crime will be destroyed or that someone will be harmed. At the same time, section 8 requires some form of accountability for searches even in such exigent circumstances. The Court has struck down a scheme of warrantless electronic surveillance in exigent circumstances on the basis that the scheme did not even require notification after the fact of those who had their conversations electronically recorded.[73]

---

63 *R v Chehil*, [2013] 3 SCR 220.
64 *Goodwin*, above note 20.
65 *R v Edwards* (1996), 104 CCC (3d) 136 (SCC).
66 *R v Belnavis* (1997), 118 CCC (3d) 405 (SCC); *R v Paterson*, 2017 SCC 15.
67 *R v M(MR)* (1998), 129 CCC (3d) 361 (SCC).
68 *Weatherall v Canada (AG)* (1993), 83 CCC (3d) 1 (SCC).
69 *R v Hufsky* (1988), 40 CCC (3d) 398 (SCC) [*Hufsky*].
70 *R v Simmons* (1988), 45 CCC (3d) 296 (SCC); *R v Jacques* (1996), 110 CCC (3d) 1 (SCC).
71 *R v Plant* (1993), 84 CCC (3d) 203 (SCC); *R v Gomboc*, [2010] 3 SCR 211.
72 *R v Grant* (1993), 84 CCC (3d) 173 (SCC).
73 *R v Tse*, 2012 SCC 16 [*Tse*].

When prior judicial authorization for a search and seizure is sought, it should generally be granted only if there are reasonable and probable grounds established on oath to believe that an offence has been committed and that the search will reveal evidence of it.[74] Searches must also be authorized by law, and the law must be reasonable.[75] In response to numerous decisions holding warrantless and illegal searches to be unreasonable, Parliament has enacted new laws to grant warrants and authorizing warrantless searches in exigent circumstances. For example, the Court's decision that wearing a wire without a warrant violated section 8 of the *Charter* was followed by the enactment of new provisions allowing judges to issue such warrants and also authorizing the use of wires without warrants in urgent circumstances and to prevent bodily harm.[76] The Court's decision declaring the warrantless use of videotaping to be a violation of section 8 of the *Charter* led to the enactment of a new general warrant provision that allows a judge to grant a warrant authorizing any investigative technique that, if not authorized, would constitute an unreasonable search and seizure.[77] When the Supreme Court declared the common law rule that allowed a warrantless search of a dwelling house in order to make an arrest violated section 8 of the *Charter*, Parliament enacted new provisions that allowed such warrants to be granted and also authorized warrantless entries into dwelling houses to make arrests in exigent circumstances.[78] Search warrants should in most instances specifically authorize the search of a computer because of the vast and private information that may be stored on computers.[79]

---

74 *Canada (Director of Investigation & Research, Combines Investigation Branch) v Southam Inc* (1984), 14 CCC (3d) 97 (SCC).

75 *R v Collins* (1987), 33 CCC (3d) 1 (SCC); *Wakeling v United States of America*, [2014] 3 SCR 549.

76 *Duarte*, above note 53. See *Code*, above note 1, ss 184.1–184.4. See now *Tse*, above note 73.

77 *Wong*, above note 53. See now *Code*, above note 1, ss 184.1–184.4 and 487.01. This general warrant provision does not authorize interference with bodily integrity. Parliament, however, has enacted other provisions that allow warrants to be obtained to seize DNA samples and take body impressions. See *Code*, *ibid*, ss 487.04–487.09 and 487.091.

78 *R v Feeney* (1997), 115 CCC (3d) 129 (SCC). See *Code*, above note 1, ss 487.04–487.09, 487.091, and 529. Exigent circumstances are defined to include the need to prevent imminent bodily harm or death and the imminent loss or destruction of evidence. *Code*, *ibid*, s 529.3.

79 *R v Vu*, [2013] 3 SCR 657.

iii) Consent Searches and Searches Incident to Arrest
The police do not need to obtain a warrant if the person consents to
a search or if they are conducting a reasonable search incident to arrest.[80] Searches incident to arrest must not be conducted in an abusive
fashion and do not include the power to seize bodily samples from the
accused for DNA testing[81] or to take body impressions.[82] The Court
distinguished these to hold that a penile swab could be taken from an
arrested person without a warrant. It reasoned that there was urgency
because the swab was to obtain the complainant's DNA which could
degrade over time as opposed to the arrestee's own DNA.[83]

The power to conduct a strip search does not follow automatically from
the power to conduct a less intrusive search incident to arrest. There must
be reasonable and probable grounds for concluding that a strip search is
necessary in the particular circumstances of the arrest in order to discover weapons or evidence.[84] The power of search incident to arrest does
include the power to search a suspect's cellphone provided that the
search is done truly incidental to arrest and is fully documented.[85]

iv) Remedies for Breach
Evidence obtained in violation of section 8 of the *Charter* will not automatically be excluded under section 24(2) of the *Charter*. Judges will
apply a three-part test that examines the seriousness of the *Charter*
violation, the impact of the *Charter* violation on the accused's *Charter*-
protected interests, and society's interests in an adjudication on the
merits.[86] The courts will balance the seriousness of the *Charter* violation and the impact of the *Charter* violation on the accused's *Charter*-
protected interests against the harm to the repute of the administration
of justice caused by the exclusion of evidence.

---

80 *Cloutier v Langlois* (1990), 53 CCC (3d) 257 (SCC); *R v Caslake* (1998), 121 CCC
    (3d) 97 (SCC).
81 *R v Stillman* (1997), 113 CCC (3d) 321 (SCC) [*Stillman*]. Warrants can be issued
    for obtaining DNA samples. See *Code*, above note 1, ss 487.04–487.091. These
    warrant provisions have been upheld under the *Charter: R v SAB*, [2003] 2 SCR
    678.
82 *Stillman*, above note 81. But see *Code*, above note 1, s 487.092, for warrants to obtain
    body impressions.
83 *R v Saeed*, 2016 SCC 24.
84 *R v Golden*, [2001] 3 SCR 679 at 733.
85 *R v Fearon*, 2014 SCC 77. Three judges in dissent would have required prior
    judicial authorization or exigent circumstances to justify the search.
86 *R v Grant*, [2009] 2 SCR 353 [*Grant*].

b) Arbitrary Detention and Imprisonment

Section 9 of the *Charter* provides that everyone has the right not to be arbitrarily detained or imprisoned. Detention has been defined broadly under both sections 9 and 10 of the *Charter* to include detention with respect to a demand or direction that may have legal consequences, such as a demand for a breath sample, physical restraint, and psychological compulsion that leaves individuals with the reasonable belief that they have no choice but to comply with the police.[87] People are detained when pulled over to the side of the road by the police, and laws authorizing random vehicle stops violate section 9 because they provide no objective criteria to govern who is detained. Nevertheless, these laws have been upheld under section 1 as reasonable limits necessary to prevent drunk driving and to ensure traffic safety[88] despite a strong dissent that argued that the Court was allowing "any individual officer to stop any vehicle, at any time, at any place. The decision may be based on any whim. Individual officers will have different reasons."[89] Random stops are permissible when undertaken for reasons of traffic safety.

The Supreme Court has held that a person will not be detained under section 9 if questioned by the police in a non-adversarial manner, for example, with respect to emergency calls or accidents. Other relevant factors include the nature of the police conduct and the characteristics of the individual, including age and minority status. In *Grant*, the accused was not detained when a police officer asked him his name and address but was detained when the police officer told him to keep his hands in front of him.[90]

Section 9 provides protection against only arbitrary detention, not all detention. A detention will be arbitrary if it is not authorized by law or if the law that authorizes the detention is itself arbitrary.[91] A detention may also be arbitrary if the officer "was biased towards a person of a different race, nationality or colour" or had "a personal enmity"[92] towards a particular detainee.

The Supreme Court has recognized and effectively created powers of investigative detention that allow a person to be briefly detained if there are reasonable grounds to suspect that he or she is connected to a particular crime and the detention is reasonably necessary. In such cases, a person is detained, but the detention is not arbitrary. Rea-

---

87   *Ibid* at para 31.
88   *Hufsky*, above note 69; *R v Ladouceur* (1990), 56 CCC (3d) 22 (SCC).
89   *Ladouceur*, *ibid* at 29.
90   *Grant*, above note 86 at paras 36–37, 44, and 48–52.
91   *Ibid* at para 54.
92   *R v Storrey*, [1990] 1 SCR 241 at 251–52.

sonable suspicion will generally require individualized suspicion.[93] If a stop goes beyond a brief detention, however, it may be characterized as an arbitrary detention.[94] There is some evidence in Canada that unpopular minorities are disproportionately targeted for investigative stops by the police.[95]

If the accused has been arbitrarily detained, there is a limit to what the criminal court can do. If evidence was obtained, it can be excluded under section 24(2). In *Grant*,[96] however, the Court was unwilling to exclude drugs and a gun discovered as a result of an arbitrary detention of a young African-Canadian man. A criminal court cannot award damages, but courts can reduce the accused's sentence if convicted in response to *Charter* violations and other abuses of power.[97] Halting the prosecution by a stay of proceedings may be an option if the violation is very serious.

c) Right to Counsel

i) Trigger upon Arrest or Detention

Section 10(b) of the *Charter* provides those who are subject to arrest or detention with both a right to retain and instruct counsel without delay and a right to be informed of that right. Detention has been interpreted broadly to include not only deprivation of liberty by physical constraint, but also the assumption of control over a person by a demand with significant legal consequences that would otherwise impede access to counsel and psychological compulsion in the form of a reasonable perception of a lack of freedom of choice. Even a brief five-minute detention in the back of a police car may require a right to counsel warning, if the police ask questions.[98] A person is detained when required to provide a breath sample, either at the roadside or at a police station. However, the denial of the right to counsel for a person who must give a breath sample into a roadside screening device has been held to be justified under section 1 of the *Charter* as a reasonable limit required

---

93   *R v Mann*, [2004] 3 SCR 59.
94   *R v Clayton*, 2007 SCC 32 at para 19.
95   *Report of the Manitoba Aboriginal Justice Inquiry* (Winnipeg: Queen's Printer, 1991); *Report of the Commission on Systemic Racism in the Ontario Criminal Justice System* (Toronto: Queen's Printer, 1995); Ontario Human Rights Commission, *Paying the Price: The Human Cost of Racial Profiling* (Toronto: Ontario Human Rights Commission, 2004).
96   *Grant*, above note 86.
97   *R v Nasogaluak*, [2010] 1 SCR 206.
98   *R v Elshaw* (1991), 67 CCC (3d) 97 (SCC).

to combat drunk driving.[99] This section 1 limit has also been extended to requests by the police that the driver answer questions about his or her drinking and perform roadside sobriety tests even though these actions were not specifically authorized by legislation.[100] Nevertheless, a person facing a demand for a breath sample at the police station must be informed of his or her right to retain and instruct counsel without delay[101] and the limitations under section 1 that apply to *Charter* rights at the roadside only apply for a limited time.[102]

ii) Informational Requirements
Upon arrest or detention, the police must inform detainees not only that they can consult a lawyer, but also about the availability of publicly funded legal aid for those who cannot afford a lawyer and duty counsel who can provide temporary legal advice regardless of the suspect's financial status.[103] Most provinces have established toll-free telephone numbers that allow detainees to contact duty counsel on a twenty-four-hour basis. The police must generally inform detainees of available services, including the toll-free telephone number, but the Supreme Court has refused to require governments to establish such services despite evidence that they are efficient and practical.[104]

Section 10(a) of the *Charter* also requires a person to be informed promptly of the reason for detention or arrest. This does not require an explicit warning if the matter being investigated was obvious.[105] The right was violated, however, when an accused was not aware that he was also held for a second, more serious sexual assault[106] or when he believed he was being held for drug offences, not murder.[107] If an attempted murder becomes a murder after the victim dies, the accused should be so informed and have another opportunity to consult counsel.[108]

iii) Implementation Requirements
The police must hold off eliciting evidence until the suspect has had a reasonable opportunity to contact counsel. The Court has indicated

99 R v Thomsen (1988), 40 CCC (3d) 411 (SCC).
100 R v Orbanski, [2005] 2 SCR 3.
101 R v Therens (1985), 18 CCC (3d) 481 (SCC).
102 R v Woods, [2005] 2 SCR 205.
103 R v Brydges (1990), 53 CCC (3d) 330 (SCC) [Brydges].
104 R v Prosper (1994), 92 CCC (3d) 353 (SCC).
105 R v Evans (1991), 63 CCC (3d) 289 (SCC) [Evans].
106 R v Borden (1994), 92 CCC (3d) 404 (SCC).
107 Evans, above note 105.
108 R v Black (1989), 50 CCC (3d) 1 (SCC).

that a standard caution that asked the accused "do you wish to say anything" immediately after he was informed of the right to counsel violated the holding off requirement.[109] Once a detainee asks to speak to a lawyer, the police must facilitate access to counsel by offering the use of a telephone.[110] The police officer does not have a duty to give a suspect his or her own cellphone, but they must facilitate access to a telephone even if the accused is in a hospital.[111] The detainee should be allowed, within reason, to consult a lawyer of his or her own choice and to consult with that lawyer in privacy. The detainee must, however, exercise the right to contact counsel with reasonable diligence and the police do not have to hold off in cases where detainees wish to speak to a particular lawyer who is likely to be unavailable.[112]

iv) Continued Interrogation

Once an accused has been given a reasonable opportunity to consult counsel, questioning may resume without again informing the accused of the right to counsel or providing another reasonable opportunity to consult counsel.[113] There is no right to have a lawyer present during police questioning as there is in the United States, but the police may have to give the detainee another opportunity to speak to counsel before asking the detainee to engage in non-routine procedures, such as participating in a lineup or a polygraph. The ability of the police to continue to interrogate applies even in cases where the accused and/or counsel have indicated a desire not to talk and the interrogation is lengthy and involves confronting the accused with actual or fake evidence.[114] The right to counsel may, however, be violated by prolonged questioning without counsel being present, police denigration of counsel, or the offer of a plea bargain without counsel being present.[115] The courts have also not required the police to videotape or audiotape interrogations,[116] though this may help ensure proper interrogation.

---

109 R v GTD, 2018 SCC 7.

110 R v Manninen (1987), 34 CCC (3d) 385 (SCC) [Manninen].

111 R v Taylor, [2014] 2 SCR 495.

112 R v Smith (1989), 50 CCC (3d) 308 (SCC); R v Willier, [2010] 2 SCR 429; R v McCrimmon, [2010] 2 SCR 402.

113 R v Hebert (1990), 57 CCC (3d) 1 (SCC).

114 R v Sinclair, [2010] 2 SCR 310.

115 R v Burlingham (1995), 97 CCC (3d) 385 (SCC) [Burlingham].

116 R v Barrett (1995), 96 CCC (3d) 319 (SCC).

v)   Waiver of Right to Counsel

The accused's right to counsel can be subject to informed and voluntary waiver. A murder suspect who was too drunk to be aware of the consequences cannot waive her rights to counsel.[117] Accused persons who answered baiting questions or participated in a lineup before being given a reasonable opportunity to consult counsel have not waived their right to counsel.[118] An accused who asked about legal aid, but was not informed about its availability, did not waive the right to counsel when he subsequently answered questions.[119] An accused who confessed after the police had insulted his counsel of choice also did not waive the right to counsel.[120]

vi)   Remedy for Breach

Statements taken in violation of the right to counsel will presumptively be excluded because of the importance of the police respecting the right to counsel, the adverse effect of such statements on *Charter*-protected interests such as the right to silence, and concerns about the reliability of statements taken in violation of the *Charter*. Nevertheless, exclusion of evidence taken in violation of section 10(b) is not automatic especially in cases of minor violations.[121]

d)   Entrapment

Before the advent of the *Charter*, Canadian courts were reluctant to recognize a defence of entrapment. In the 1982 case of *R v Amato*,[122] the Supreme Court affirmed a conviction for trafficking in narcotics even though an undercover police officer had persistently solicited the accused to sell him cocaine and made implied threats of violence. In a strong dissent, Estey J concluded that entrapment should be recognized as a common law defence designed to ensure that the administration of justice is not brought into disrepute. He would have stayed proceedings because of the police conduct in the case. Six years later in *R v Mack*,[123] the Supreme Court recognized the defence of entrapment. The Court stressed that the defence could be available even though the accused committed the *actus reus* with the requisite degree of fault. A finding of entrapment results in a permanent stay of proceedings rather than

---

117 *R v Clarkson* (1986), 25 CCC (3d) 207 (SCC).
118 *Manninen*, above note 110; *R v Ross* (1989), 46 CCC (3d) 129 (SCC).
119 *Brydges*, above note 103.
120 *Burlingham*, above note 115.
121 *Grant*, above note 86 at paras 89–98.
122 (1982), 69 CCC (2d) 31 (SCC).
123 (1988), 44 CCC (3d) 513 (SCC) [*Mack*].

an acquittal. Because it is a matter independent of guilt or innocence, entrapment must be established by the accused on a balance of probabilities, and the determination of entrapment can be left until after the accused's guilt has been established. The judge, rather than the jury, decides whether entrapment has been made out because the judge is the best person to determine whether the state's activities would bring the administration of justice into disrepute.

Entrapment occurs if the state offers a person an opportunity to commit a crime without reasonable suspicion that the person was engaged in criminal activity *or* while not engaged in a *bona fide* inquiry into crime in a high-crime area. The state must provide an opportunity to commit a crime and a simple drug buy may not even constitute offering an opportunity.[24] Even if there is a reasonable suspicion or a *bona fide* inquiry, entrapment will also occur if the state goes beyond providing the accused with an opportunity to commit a crime and actually induces its commission.

A reasonable suspicion is less than reasonable and probable grounds to believe a person has committed a specific crime. In *Mack*, the Court determined that the police acted with reasonable suspicion in conducting a six-month drug sting because the accused was a former drug user with several drug convictions, and even though the accused told the police informer he was only interested in real estate. On the other hand, the police officer in *R v Barnes* who had a (correct) hunch that a scruffily dressed male who looked around a lot was selling marijuana did not have a reasonable suspicion because her impressions of the suspect were too general and subjective.[25]

Even though the police did not have a reasonable suspicion and engaged in random virtue testing in *Barnes*, the Supreme Court held there was no entrapment because the police were acting pursuant to a *bona fide* inquiry into criminal activity by offering a person an opportunity to commit the crime because he was present in a place (the Granville Street Mall in Vancouver) associated with the particular criminal activity. Justice McLachlin dissented on the basis that the high-crime area was described very broadly and that insufficient attention had been paid to the likelihood of the crime at the location targeted, its seriousness, the number of innocent people affected, and the availability of less intrusive investigative techniques. In any event, the majority's approach would allow random virtue testing of those found in areas associated with drugs or prostitution. In other words, the police can offer someone

---

124 *R v Imoro*, 2010 ONCA 122, aff'd [2010] 3 SCR 62 [*Imoro*].
125 (1991), 63 CCC (3d) 1 (SCC).

an opportunity to sell drugs or solicit prostitution simply because that person is in an area associated with that crime and even if they do not have a reasonable suspicion that the person is engaged in the particular crime. Other courts following the majority have held that random virtue testing did not amount to entrapment so long as it was done as part of a *bona fide* investigation into a variety of crimes ranging from child prostitution, to drugs, to selling tobacco to children.[126]

Even if they have reasonable suspicion or are acting on a *bona fide* inquiry, the police should never go beyond providing the suspect an opportunity to commit a crime and actually induce the commission of a crime. The police will go over this line if their conduct is so objectionable that it brings the administration of justice into disrepute and would have induced an average person to have committed the crime. In the context of extensive "Mr Big" operations, where undercover police pose as criminals and attempt to have a suspect confess to a crime as a pre-condition of joining a criminal organization, the Supreme Court has indicated that an abuse of process would occur where the police overcome the will of the accused and coerce a confession by, for example, violence or threats of violence or exploiting vulnerabilities such as mental health and addiction issues.[127] A few phone calls to an old friend to set up a drug buy do not go over the line, but persistent solicitation accompanied by veiled threats does.[128] A brief conversation between an undercover officer and a person selling drugs will also not constitute entrapment.[129]

The nature of the entrapment defence is influenced by the fact that, if established by the accused on a balance of probabilities, it will result in a permanent stay of criminal proceedings against the accused. The courts will also examine the proportionality between the conduct of the state and the accused and whether the state had instigated the crime and exploited the accused. In almost all cases, the courts will also balance the competing interests in stopping and conducting a prosecution before entering a stay of proceedings as a remedy for entrapment as a form of abuse of process.[130] The fact that the police may have acted illegally in selling the accused narcotics does not automatically merit a stay unless the activity would shock the conscience of the community and be so detrimental to the proper administration of justice that it

---

126 *R v Chiang*, 2012 BCCA 85; *R v Clothier*, 2011 ONCA 27; *R v Bayat*, 2011 ONCA 778; *R v Faqi*, 2011 ABCA 284.

127 *R v Hart*, 2014 SCC 52 at paras 115–18.

128 *Mack*, above note 123; *R v Showman* (1988), 45 CCC (3d) 289 (SCC).

129 *Imoro*, above note 124.

130 *R v Babos*, 2014 SCC 16.

warrants judicial intervention.[131] When determining whether the state has gone beyond providing an opportunity, the focus is on the propriety of the conduct of police and their agents. There may still be entrapment even though the accused was predisposed to commit the crime and had the intent to commit the crime.[132] At the same time, the fact that the police or a state informant violated the law does not automatically result in entrapment and a stay of proceedings.[133] There will not be an entrapment defence when the accused is entrapped into committing a crime by private individuals not acting for the state. Depending on the threats used, such an accused may nevertheless have a defence of duress. That defence is examined in Chapter 9.

3) The *Charter* and the Criminal Trial Process

The *Charter* also plays an important role in the criminal trial process by ensuring that the trial is conducted in a fair manner. Section 7 of the *Charter* provides the basic guarantee that everyone has the right to life, liberty, and security of the person and that these rights can be taken away only "in accordance with the principles of fundamental justice." This broad guarantee affects all aspects of the criminal process, with section 11 of the *Charter* articulating specific rights possessed by any person charged with a criminal offence or one that gives rise to penal consequences such as imprisonment or a punitive fine.[134] Section 11 includes the right to be tried within a reasonable time (11(b)); not to be compelled to be a witness in proceedings against that person in respect of the offence (11(c)); to be presumed innocent until proven guilty according to law in a fair and public hearing by an independent and impartial tribunal (11(d)); to reasonable bail with just cause (11(e)); to trial by jury where the maximum punishment for the

---

131 *R v Campbell* (1999), 133 CCC (3d) 257 (SCC) [*Campbell*]. See *R v Nuttall*, 2016 BCSC 1404, a case where terrorism charges were stayed on findings that the police did not have a reasonable suspicion when they offered two suspects the opportunity to commit terrorist crimes; that the police had induced the commission of the offence and that an abuse of process meriting a stay of proceedings was also required, in part because the police committed several terrorism offences in the course of an extensive "Mr Big"-type sting operation.

132 *R v S(J)* (2001), 152 CCC (3d) 317 (Ont CA).

133 *Campbell*, above note 131. See now s 25.1 of the *Code*, above note 1 authorizing the police to do acts that would otherwise constitute an offence.

134 Section 11 does not apply to those who are subject to provincial licence suspensions or subject to administrative penalties under the *Income Tax Act*. *Goodwin*, above note 20.

offence is imprisonment for five years or more (11(f)); and protection from double jeopardy (11(h)).

a) Disclosure

One of the most important rights in the criminal trial process is the Crown's obligation to disclose to the accused all relevant evidence in its possession. Disclosure is considered necessary to protect the accused's right to make full answer and defence under section 7 of the *Charter*. The Crown has a special obligation within an adversarial system of criminal justice to treat the accused fairly. The Supreme Court has explained:

> [T]he fruits of the investigation which are in the possession of coun-sel for the Crown are not the property of the Crown for use in secur-ing a conviction but the property of the public to be used to ensure that justice is done. In contrast, the defence has no obligation to as-sist the prosecution and is entitled to assume a purely adversarial role toward the prosecution.[135]

In general, all relevant evidence in the Crown's possession should be disclosed to the accused and there is no distinction between inculpatory and exculpatory evidence. The investigating police force also has a duty to participate in this disclosure, including disclosing misconduct relating to the investigation or that could reasonably impact the case against the accused.[136] Evidence disclosed to the defence will usually include state-ments that witnesses made to the police and physical evidence seized at the crime scene. The Crown can decide what evidence is relevant and can delay disclosure for legitimate reasons, such as protecting informers.

In controversial decisions, the Supreme Court has ruled that the Crown must disclose to the accused all medical and therapeutic rec-ords in its possession without regard to the privacy and equality inter-ests of complainants in sexual assault trials[137] and stayed proceedings because a rape crisis centre had shredded its records of an interview with a complainant.[138] Parliament responded to these decisions with new legislation restricting the accused's access to the personal rec-ords of complainants in sexual assault cases including material in the Crown's possession. The legislation has been upheld as a reasonable balance of the accused's and complainant's rights.[139] Criminal courts

---

135 *R v Stinchcombe* (1991), 68 CCC (3d) 1 at 7 (SCC).
136 *R v McNeil*, [2009] 1 SCR 66.
137 *R v O'Connor* (1995), 103 CCC (3d) 1 (SCC).
138 *R v Carosella* (1997), 112 CCC (3d) 289 (SCC).
139 *Code*, above note 1, ss 278.1–278.89. Upheld in *R v Mills*, [1999] 3 SCR 668.

may also award costs and order new trials as remedies for disclosure violations.[140]

b) Right to Full Answer and Defence

Section 7 of the *Charter* also has been interpreted to provide the accused with a right to make a full answer and defence in response to criminal charges. In general, the prejudice of evidence must substantially outweigh its probative value before the accused is prevented from calling evidence. In *R v Seaboyer*,[141] the Supreme Court held that section 277 of the *Code*, which bans evidence about sexual reputation to challenge or support the credibility of the complainant in a sexual assault trial, did not violate section 7 because there was no logical link between one's sexual reputation and one's truthfulness. The Court did, however, find that a "rape shield" provision that restricted the admissibility of the complainant's prior sexual conduct with people other than the accused did violate the accused's right to make full answer and defence in part because such conduct might be relevant to the controversial defence that the accused honestly but perhaps not reasonably had a mistaken belief that the complainant consented. Parliament responded to this ruling by modifying the mistaken belief in consent defence and by establishing a new procedure that requires judges to balance the accused's right to make full answer and defence against other factors, including society's interest in encouraging the reporting of sexual assaults, the need to remove discriminatory bias from fact-finding and potential prejudice to the complainant's rights of privacy, personal security, and the full protection and benefit of the law.[142] This new provision has been held to be consistent with the accused's rights.[143] The right to full answer and defence also requires that the accused be able to conduct a thorough cross-examination of the Crown's witnesses,[144] as well as call his or her own witnesses.

c) Right to Reasonable Bail

A detainee has a right under section 11(e) of the *Charter* not to be denied reasonable bail without just cause. A person can be detained for valid reasons such as ensuring his or her appearance in court or preventing the commission of a crime. Despite recognizing the difficulty

---

140 *R v 974649 Ontario Inc* (2001), 159 CCC (3d) 321 (SCC); *R v Taillefer*, [2003] 3 SCR 307.

141 (1991), 66 CCC (3d) 321 (SCC).

142 *Code*, above note 1, s 276.

143 *R v Darrach* (2000), 148 CCC (3d) 97 (SCC).

144 *R v Lyttle*, [2004] 1 SCR 193.

of predicting future danger, the Supreme Court has upheld denial of bail to prevent the substantial likelihood of future crime or interference with the administration of justice on the basis that "the bail system . . . does not function properly if individuals commit crimes while on bail."[145] The Court also upheld a reverse onus that required those charged with drug trafficking to establish why they should not be detained.[146] The Court did strike down pre-trial detention in the public interest as excessively vague on the basis that "a standardless sweep does not become acceptable simply because it results from the whims of judges and justices of the peace rather than the whims of law enforcement officials. Cloaking whims in judicial robes is not sufficient to satisfy the principles of fundamental justice."[147] In 1997, Parliament responded by authorizing the denial of bail for

> any other just cause . . . and, without limiting the generality of the foregoing, where detention is necessary in order to maintain confidence in the administration of justice, having regard to all the circumstances, including the apparent strength of the prosecution's case, the gravity of the nature of the offence, the circumstances surrounding its commission and the potential for a lengthy term of imprisonment.[148]

The Supreme Court held that this provision, with the exception of the vague phrase "any other just cause," did not violate section 11(e) of the *Charter* because the maintenance of confidence in the administration of justice was a legitimate object of the bail system. Four judges dissented and argued that the new section was not fundamentally different from the prior and vague public interest ground and that it could allow an accused's liberty to be deprived on the basis of subjective and irrational fears by the public.[149]

The Supreme Court subsequently ruled that it was an error (and an improper preference for the dissenting judgment in the above case) for judges to reserve the denial of bail on public confidence grounds to rare or exceptional cases or even to use it only as a residual ground in cases where denial of bail was not necessary to ensure the accused's attendance at trial or to prevent the commission of a crime. Public confidence should be judged on the basis of the reasonable and well-informed person as opposed to a "legal expert familiar with all the basic principles

---

145 *R v Morales*, [1992] 3 SCR 711 at 738 [*Morales*].
146 *R v Pearson* (1992), 77 CCC (3d) 124 (SCC).
147 *Morales*, above note 145 at 729.
148 *Code*, above note 1, s 515(10) as am by SC 1997, c 18, s 59.
149 *R v Hall* (2002), 167 CCC (3d) 449 (SCC) [*Hall*].

of the criminal justice system, the elements of criminal offences or the subtleties of criminal intent and of the defences that are available to accused persons."[150] The Court stressed the importance of the judge examining all the circumstances but also concluded: "if the crime is serious or very violent, if there is overwhelming evidence against the accused and if the victim or victims were vulnerable, pre-trial detention will usually be ordered."[151] The Court has also held that public confidence as judged by the standard of the well-informed and reasonable person, as well as public safety, should be considered in determining whether it is in the public interest to grant bail to an accused who has been convicted pending an appeal.[152]

The Court has subsequently not decided a section 11(e) *Charter* challenge to a provision allowing cash bail or surety supervision for accused who live out of province or more than 200 km away from where they are detained in custody. Instead, the Court held that the bail review judge had ignored the "ladder principle" in section 515(3) of the *Code* by requiring a cash deposit of $100,000 as opposed to simply a monetary pledge. The Court stressed that section 11(e) requires not only that bail only be denied with "just cause," but that bail be set at reasonable terms. It stressed that the Crown must demonstrate why more restrictive terms of bail are required and "it is an error of law for a justice or judge to order a more restrictive form of release without justifying the decision to reject the less onerous forms."[153]

d) Trial in a Reasonable Time

An important right in the pre-trial process is the Crown's obligation under section 11(b) of the *Charter* to provide a trial in a reasonable time. If the accused's section 11(b) right is violated, the accused is entitled to a stay of proceedings.[154] This right does not usually apply to delay before a charge is laid,[155] and there is no statute of limitations that prevents the prosecution of indictable offences committed long ago.[156] Courts have allowed charges to proceed even though the allegations

---

150 *R v St-Cloud*, 2015 SCC 27 at para 80.

151 *Ibid* at para 88.

152 *R v Oland*, 2017 SCC 17 [*Oland*].

153 *R v Antic*, [2017] 1 SCR 509 at para 67.

154 *R v Askov* (1990), 59 CCC (3d) 449 (SCC).

155 The Court has recognized that pre-charge delay could in some circumstances violate s 7 of the *Charter* but has been reluctant to so find. *R v L(WK)*, [1991] 1 SCR 1091 [*L(WK)*]; *R v Hunt*, 2017 SCC 25.

156 There is a six-month statute of limitations on less serious summary conviction offences but this can be waived with the agreement of the prosecutor and the accused. The accused might agree to waive the limitation in cases in which the

relate to matters that occurred decades ago.[157] A stay of proceedings might be entered if the passage of time has made it impossible for the accused to exercise the right to full answer and defence because of the unavailability of crucial evidence.[158]

Whether the accused's right to a trial in a reasonable time has been violated depends on the length of the delay (delays of more than eight to ten months can be suspect) and the explanation for the delay (some delays may be attributable to the accused, but systemic delay caused by a backlog of cases and unavailability of judges is charged to the Crown). It also depends on whether the accused has waived his or her rights by consenting to the delay, and whether the accused has suffered prejudice. This latter factor has been stressed more in cases after the 1990 *Askov* decision, indicating that delays beyond six to eight months were unreasonable, led to the stay of more than 50,000 charges.[159] Even under this more deferential approach there are limits to how much delay will be tolerated. A thirty-month delay in a case where the defence did not contribute to the delay led to the stay of proceedings of a sexual assault case.[160]

In *R v Jordan*,[161] the Court returned to the type of presumptive limits used in *Askov* because of its concerns about the uncertainty of its more case-specific approach. The presumptive limits of eighteen months for cases resolved in provincial court and thirty months for more serious cases in superior court were considerably higher than in *Askov*. They are also subject to exceptional circumstances exceptions outside of the Crown's control relating both to discrete events and the complexity of cases. Time waived by the accused or delay caused by the accused will also not count towards the new *Jordan* limits. Despite the escape hatches from these new limits as well as their much greater length than the previous *Askov* limits, there are many concerns that criminal cases will be stayed because of delay. So far, however, there has not been the same magnitude of stays imposed because of section 11(b) violations than after *Askov*. The Court in *Jordan* also signalled its willingness to

---

prosecutor has the discretion to lay the charge as a more serious indictable offence. *Code*, above note 1, s 786(2).

157 L(WK), above note 155.

158 *R v MacDonnell* (1997), 114 CCC (3d) 145 (SCC).

159 *R v Morin* (1992), 71 CCC (3d) 1 (SCC).

160 *R v Godin*, [2009] 2 SCR 3.

161 2016 SCC 27. The Court also allowed transitional periods for cases before its decisions but held in companion cases that a sexual assault charge should be stayed because of a 33.5-month delay before trial and a possession of cocaine for the purpose of trafficking charge stayed because of a 36-month delay before trial. *R v Williamson*, 2016 SCC 28; *R v Vassell*, 2016 SCC 26. See also *R v Cody*, 2017 SCC 31.

reconsider whether the drastic remedy of a stay of proceedings was the minimum remedy for a section 11(b) violation.

e) Pre-trial Publicity

The *Criminal Code* provides for mandatory publication bans at the accused's request on evidence heard at bail hearings or at preliminary inquiries.[162] The Supreme Court has upheld the former as a reasonable limit on freedom of expression in large part because of the importance of ensuring a fair trial and an expeditious bail process.[163] Trial proceedings when the jury is not present, such as a *voir dire* to determine the admissibility of evidence, also cannot be published until the jury retires to consider its verdict.[164]

A discretionary publication ban must be justified on the basis that it is necessary to prevent a real and substantial risk to the fairness of the trial because alternative measures will not prevent the risks. Courts should attempt to harmonize the public's right to freedom of expression with the accused's right to a fair trial by devising, where possible, alternatives short of publication bans.[165] Alternatives include adjournments of trials; changing the location or venue of the trial to where there has been less publicity; allowing the accused to question prospective jurors more closely; sequestering juries and instructing them to disregard matters that they heard outside the courtroom. Even if a publication ban is the only way to protect the accused's right to a fair trial, it must be as limited in scope and time as possible, and the Court must determine that the good achieved by the ban in protecting a fair trial or other important interests outweighs the harm the ban causes to freedom of expression.

f) Right to a Jury Trial

An accused who faces five years of imprisonment or more has a right to trial by jury under section 11(f) of the *Charter*. The fact that a person subject to a maximum punishment of five years less a day can also be subject to a high fine does not entitle that person to a jury trial.[166] If the accused fails to appear for trial, however, he or she can subsequently be denied trial by jury.[167] If the accused is charged with an indictable

---

162 *Code*, above note 1, ss 517 and 539.
163 *Toronto Star Newspapers Ltd v Canada*, [2010] 1 SCR 721.
164 *Code*, above note 1, s 648.
165 *Dagenais v Canadian Broadcasting Corp* (1994), 94 CCC (3d) 289 (SCC); *R v Mentuck*, [2001] 3 SCR 442.
166 *R v Aitkens*, 2017 SCC 14.
167 *R v Lee* (1989), 52 CCC (3d) 289 (SCC).

offence that is not listed in section 553 of the *Criminal Code*, he or she may elect or select a trial by jury.

A jury is composed of twelve citizens who should represent a fair cross-sample of the public in the place where the case is tried. There is no right for people from groups to be represented in proportion to their population in either the pool of prospective jurors or the twelve people selected to serve on the jury. The Court has held that dramatic under-representation of Indigenous people living on reserves on the panel of prospective jurors is consistent with the *Charter* so long as reasonable efforts were made to select an impartial and representative jury. It also held that the honour of the Crown and *Gladue* principles rooted in substantive equality were not relevant to jury selection and that an Indigenous accused did not have standing to raise the equality rights of Indigenous people who were or could be prospective jurors.[168] Two judges dissented in part on the basis that Indigenous people living on reserves were only 4 percent of the jury pool but between 22 and 32 percent of the population of the northern district. They stressed that the jury should be a random sample of the relevant community and that the state should make efforts to increase Indigenous representation on juries.[169]

In selecting the jury, the Crown and the accused can challenge prospective jurors for cause, with the most important ground being that the person is not indifferent between the Crown and the accused. They can ask prospective jurors questions provided a judge has decided that the questions respond to a realistic potential for partiality.[170] These questions may be aimed at the possibility of racial bias against the accused but need not include the interracial nature of an alleged crime or possible partiality with respect to the complainant[171] or bias based on the nature of the charge faced by the accused.[172] The accused and the Crown each have the same limited number of peremptory challenges they can use to remove prospective jurors without giving any reasons,[173] though there are proposals before Parliament to abolish per-

---

168 *R v Kokopenace*, 2015 SCC 28 at paras 98 and 128.

169 Justice Cromwell concluded in dissent: "an Aboriginal man on trial for murder was forced to select from a jury roll which excluded a significant part of the community on the basis of race — his race. This in my view is an affront to the administration of justice and undermines public confidence in the fairness of the criminal process." *Ibid* at para 195.

170 *R v Williams* (1998), 124 CCC (3d) 481 (SCC).

171 *R v Spence*, [2005] 3 SCR 458.

172 *R v Find*, [2001] 1 SCR 863.

173 *Code*, above note 1, s 634. The accused's right to a fair trial was violated by previous provisions that effectively gave the Crown over four times as many peremp-

emptory challenges to prevent their discriminatory use. The jury delib-
erates in secret and they must agree unanimously to a verdict of guilt or
innocence. If they cannot agree, they are a "hung jury" and a new trial
may be held. An instruction from the judge that the jury must convict
violates the right to a trial by jury under section 11(f).[174] Except in very
limited circumstances, it is a criminal offence for a juror to disclose
information about the jury's deliberations.[175]

Section 11(d) protects the right to a fair and public hearing by an
independent and impartial tribunal. Judges must have security of tenure
and can only be removed for cause related to their capacity to perform judicial functions. They must also have financial security and independ-
ence over their administration as it bears directly upon the exercise
of their judicial function. Provincial court judges and even part-time
judges have been held to be sufficiently independent, but military officers acting as court martial judges have not.

The accused's right to a fair trial will in more complex cases include
a right to have a lawyer if the accused cannot afford one. In such cases,
courts can stay proceedings until a lawyer is appointed or order that
counsel be provided. The accused also has a right to effective assistance
of counsel. To violate that right, however, it is necessary that the accused
establish both that the performance by the lawyer was unreasonable and
that it caused prejudice in the form of a miscarriage of justice.[176]

g) Right to Be Presumed Innocent

Section 11(d) also provides that the accused has the right "to be presumed innocent until proven guilty according to law in a fair and public hearing by an independent and impartial tribunal." The first part
of the right embraces the presumption of innocence, which has been
referred to as the "one golden thread" running "throughout the web of
the English common law."[177] The presumption of innocence refers to
the burden placed on the Crown to prove the accused's guilt. It also
includes the requirement that the Crown prove guilt by a high degree
or quantum of proof. Chief Justice Dickson has stated that "[t]he presumption of innocence confirms our faith in humankind; it reflects our
belief that individuals are decent and law-abiding members of the community until proven otherwise."[178]

---

tory challenges as the accused. *R v Bain* (1992), 69 CCC (3d) 481 (SCC).

174 *R v Krieger*, [2006] 2 SCR 501.

175 *Code*, above note 1, s 649.

176 *R v B(GD)* (2000), 143 CCC (3d) 289 (SCC).

177 *Woolmington v DPP*, [1935] AC 462 at 481 (HL).

178 *Oakes*, above note 48 at 333–34.

i)   Quantum of Proof

Proof beyond a reasonable doubt is not easily defined, but it requires the Crown to go beyond the burden used in private law cases of proving that something is more probable than not. If proof on a balance of probabilities as required in civil cases (and when an accused in a criminal trial bears a reverse onus) represents something like a "51 percent rule," then proof beyond a reasonable doubt requires the Crown to establish a significantly higher likelihood that the crime was committed. This mathematical analogy is quite rough and ready and should not be used by judges in their directions to juries.

In *R v Lifchus*,[179] the Supreme Court held that the meaning of reasonable doubt must be explained to a jury and undertook that difficult task. The Court indicated that the jury should be told that the reasonable doubt standard is related to the presumption of innocence. It requires more than proof that the accused is probably guilty, but does not require proof to an absolute certainty. A reasonable doubt is not a frivolous or imaginary doubt, but rather a doubt based on reason and common sense that must logically be derived from evidence or absence of evidence. The Supreme Court approved of the following suggested charge to the jury, which explains the meaning of a reasonable doubt and relates it to the presumption of innocence.

> The accused enters these proceedings presumed to be innocent. That presumption of innocence remains throughout the case until such time as the Crown has on the evidence put before you satisfied you beyond a reasonable doubt that the accused is guilty.
>
> What does the expression "beyond a reasonable doubt" mean?
>
> The term "beyond a reasonable doubt" has been used for a very long time and is a part of our history and traditions of justice. It is so engrained in our criminal law that some think it needs no explanation, yet something must be said regarding its meaning.
>
> A reasonable doubt is not an imaginary or frivolous doubt. It must not be based upon sympathy or prejudice. Rather, it is based on reason and common sense. It is logically derived from the evidence or absence of evidence.
>
> Even if you believe the accused is probably guilty or likely guilty, that is not sufficient. In those circumstances you must give the benefit of the doubt to the accused and acquit because the Crown has failed to satisfy you of the guilt of the accused beyond a reasonable doubt.

---

179   (1997), 118 CCC (3d) 1 (SCC).

On the other hand you must remember that it is virtually impossible to prove anything to an absolute certainty and the Crown is not required to do so. Such a standard of proof is impossibly high.

In short if, based upon the evidence before the Court, you are sure that the accused committed the offence you should convict since this demonstrates that you are satisfied of his guilt beyond a reasonable doubt.[180]

In *R v Starr*,[181] a majority of the Supreme Court held that trial judges would err if they did not make clear to the jury that the reasonable doubt standard was much closer to absolute certainty than the balance of probabilities standard used in civil trials and everyday life. In a series of complex cases, the Court has warned trial judges that they must not simply decide criminal cases on the basis of whether they find the Crown's witnesses and cases to be more credible than the accused's. Triers of fact, whether the trial judge or the jury, must still be convinced of guilt beyond a reasonable doubt. In other words, the Crown still has a burden to prove every element of the offence beyond a reasonable doubt and the accused should always be given the benefit of a reasonable doubt.[182]

ii) Persuasive Burdens

The presumption of innocence is infringed whenever the accused is liable to be convicted despite the existence of a reasonable doubt about a factor essential for conviction. In *Oakes*, section 11(d) was violated by a statutory provision that required, once the Crown had proven beyond a reasonable doubt the possession of narcotics, that the accused establish on a balance of probabilities that he or she did not have the intent to traffic in order to escape a conviction for the offence of possession of narcotics with the intent to traffic. Chief Justice Dickson explained how the provision could allow a conviction despite a reasonable doubt:

If an accused bears the burden of disproving on a balance of probabilities an essential element of an offence, it would be possible for a conviction to occur despite the existence of a reasonable doubt. This would arise if the accused adduced sufficient evidence to raise a

---

180 *Ibid* at 14.
181 (2000), 147 CCC (3d) 449 (SCC).
182 *R v W(D)*, [1991] 1 SCR 742; *R v JHS*, [2008] 2 SCR 152 at para 13 ("it must be made crystal clear to the jury that the burden *never* shifts from the Crown to prove *every* element of the offence beyond a reasonable doubt . . . ." [emphasis in original]).

reasonable doubt as to his or her innocence but did not convince the jury on a balance of probabilities that the presumed fact was untrue.[183]

Another approach is to examine the relationship between the element that the Crown proves (in this case, possession of narcotics) and the element that is presumed (in this case, the intent to traffic in the narcotics) unless the accused satisfies the burden placed upon him or her. The substitution of one element for an essential element of an offence violates section 11(d) unless "if upon proof beyond reasonable doubt of the substituted element it would be unreasonable for the trier of fact not to be satisfied beyond a reasonable doubt of the essential element."[184] In *Oakes*, there was not this extremely close or inexorable link between what was proved (possession of narcotics) and what was presumed (intent to traffic), and the provision violated section 11(d). In many cases, the jury may have been satisfied beyond a reasonable doubt that the accused had the intent to traffic upon proof of possession of a large quantity of narcotics. The problem was that the provision stated that the jury must draw such a conclusion in all cases. This would include those where the accused failed to provide enough evidence to prove on a balance of probabilities that there was no intent to traffic, but the jury still had a reasonable doubt about the intent to traffic. An important purpose of the presumption of innocence is to ensure that the jury always has the ability to find a reasonable doubt on the basis of any evidence in the case.

iii) Presumption Applies to Elements of Offences, Collateral Factors, and Defences

The presumption of innocence applies not only to essential elements of an offence but also to defences and collateral factors. This makes sense once it is recognized that whether something is an element of an offence, a defence, or a collateral matter is a simple matter of legislative drafting. For example, murder could be redrafted to include all killings, with the accused then having the ability to establish on a balance of probabilities a defence of a lack of intent to kill. Similarly, Parliament could provide that the intent to kill be presumed unless the accused established a collateral factor, such as the victim's death was unavoidable. If the presumption of innocence was not applied to these defences and factors, the accused could still be convicted despite a reasonable doubt as to his or her guilt. As Dickson CJ has explained:

---

183 *Oakes*, above note 48 at 343.
184 *R v Vaillancourt* (1987), 39 CCC (3d) 118 at 136 (SCC) [*Vaillancourt*].

The exact characterization of a factor as an essential element, a collateral factor, an excuse, or a defence should not affect the analysis of the presumption of innocence. It is the final effect of a provision on the verdict that is decisive. If an accused is required to prove some fact on the balance of probabilities to avoid conviction, the provision violates the presumption of innocence because it permits a conviction in spite of a reasonable doubt in the mind of the trier of fact as to the guilt of the accused.[185]

In R v Whyte, the Court examined a provision that required an accused found in the driver's seat while intoxicated to prove an absence of intent to put the vehicle in motion in order to escape a presumption that the accused was in care and control of the vehicle. This provision violated section 11(d) because it required the accused to be convicted even if he or she was able to raise a reasonable doubt about the intent to put the vehicle in motion but was unable to prove on a balance of probabilities that there was no such intent. This, in turn, triggered a mandatory presumption that the accused was in care and control of the vehicle, which was an essential element of the offence of care and control of a vehicle while impaired. Looked at another way, proof of the substituted fact (being in the driver's seat), plus the accused's inability to prove on a balance of probabilities that there was no intent to drive the car, did not lead inexorably to the conclusion that the presumed fact (care and control) exists. The accused could be convicted even though there was a reasonable doubt about whether he was guilty.

Subsequent to Whyte, the Court has held that requiring an accused to prove a defence on a balance of probabilities violates section 11(d) because it allows a conviction despite a reasonable doubt about a factor essential for a conviction. For example, section 319(3) of the Criminal Code violates section 11(d) because it requires the accused to prove on a balance of probabilities the defence of truth when charged with a hate propaganda offence. The accused could be convicted even though there was a reasonable doubt that his or her statements were true.[186] Requirements that an accused prove a defence of due diligence when charged with a regulatory offence violate section 11(d), because the accused could be convicted even though there was a reasonable doubt that he or she was negligent.[187] Similarly, a requirement that the accused establish the mental disorder defence on a balance of probabilities also

---

185 R v Whyte (1988), 42 CCC (3d) 97 at 109 (SCC).
186 R v Keegstra (1990), 61 CCC (3d) 1 (SCC) [Keegstra].
187 R v Wholesale Travel Group Inc (1991), 67 CCC (3d) 193 (SCC) [Wholesale Travel Group].

violates section 11(d), because the accused could be convicted despite a reasonable doubt about his or her sanity.[188] In all these cases, however, the Court found that the legislation was justified under section 1 of the *Charter* as a reasonable limit on section 11(d), because of the difficulties of requiring the Crown to prove beyond a reasonable doubt that the accused did not have the respective defences.

To justify an infringement of section 11(d) or any *Charter* right under section 1 of the *Charter*, the Crown must demonstrate that the objective of the limit is a compelling objective. Moreover, the Crown must then show that there is a rational connection between the violation and the objective. In *R v Laba*,[189] the Supreme Court held that it is not necessary for there to be a rational connection between the proven and the presumed factors for a reverse onus to be justified under section 1 of the *Charter*. The Court did note, however, that the lack of a rational connection between the proven and presumed factors would increase the danger of convicting the innocent.[190]

Even if the section 11(d) violation is rationally connected with a compelling objective, it must also be the least restrictive means of advancing the objective, and there must be proportionality between the objective and the rights violation. In *Laba*, the Court held that a reverse onus requiring a seller of precious metals to prove legal ownership was not a proportionate limitation on the presumption of innocence because the objective of deterring the theft of such metals could be as effectively advanced by the less restrictive alternative of requiring the accused to meet an evidential burden as to the presence of legal authorization. Once the accused pointed to some evidence of legal authorization, the Crown would still have to prove beyond a reasonable doubt that the accused did not have such authorization. An evidential burden is a less restrictive alternative to a persuasive burden, even though, as will be seen, it also violates section 11(d) if accompanied by a mandatory presumption.

The courts have on their own initiative imposed persuasive burdens on the accused. In the pre-*Charter* case of *R v Sault Ste Marie (City)*,[191]

---

188 *R v Chaulk* (1990), 62 CCC (3d) 193 (SCC).

189 *R v Laba* (1994), 94 CCC (3d) 385 at 417 (SCC) [*Laba*].

190 A rational connection between the proven and the presumed fact would not be sufficient under s 11(d) of the *Charter*, above note 42, because it means only that upon proof of the proven fact, it is probable that the presumed fact was present. Section 11(d) contemplates that the Crown must prove its case beyond a reasonable doubt, not on a simple balance of probabilities. In other words, s 11(d) requires an inexorable connection between the proven element and the presumed element, a condition that would make it unreasonable for the jury to have even a reasonable doubt about the presumed factor.

191 (1978), 40 CCC (3d) 353 (SCC).

the Supreme Court imposed a persuasive burden on the accused to establish a new defence of due diligence to strict liability offences. If the accused did not establish this defence, it would be presumed to have been negligent in allowing the *actus reus* to have occurred. The Court also reasoned that the accused was in a good position to prove due diligence. The Court has upheld such reverse onuses under the *Charter* as a reasonable limit on the presumption of innocence.[192]

Even after the *Charter* entrenched the presumption of innocence, courts have imposed burdens on the accused. In *R v Daviault*,[193] the Supreme Court imposed a persuasive burden on the accused to prove a defence of extreme intoxication to a general intent offence such as manslaughter or assault, even though the traditional defence of intoxication applies whenever there was a reasonable doubt that the accused had the intent for a specific intent offence such as murder or robbery. In *R v Stone*,[194] the Court again on its own initiative held that the accused must establish the defence of non-mental disorder automatism on a balance of probabilities. Thus, an accused no longer will have the benefit of a reasonable doubt that he or she acted in an involuntary manner because of a condition such as sleepwalking or a severe physical or emotional blow. The Court was concerned about consistency in the law and noted that the accused already had to establish the mental disorder and extreme intoxication defences on a balance of probabilities.

In some cases, the presumption of innocence seems to be honoured more in its breach. This makes it easier for the Crown to obtain a conviction, but it also opens the possibility for a conviction even though there may be a reasonable doubt that the accused was not guilty.

iv) Evidential Burdens and Mandatory Presumptions

The Supreme Court has held that section 11(d) is violated not only by persuasive burdens that require an accused to prove some factor on a balance of probabilities, but also by evidential burdens that only require the accused to point to evidence to raise a reasonable doubt about a mandatory presumption. In *R v Downey*,[195] the Court held that a provision violated section 11(d) when it required the trier of fact to conclude "in the absence of evidence to the contrary" that an accused was guilty of the offence of living off the avails of prostitution once the prosecution had proven that the accused was habitually in the company of prostitutes. Justice Cory stressed: "the fact that someone lives with a

192 *Wholesale Travel Group*, above note 187; *R v Ellis-Don Ltd*, [1992] 1 SCR 840.
193 *R v Daviault* (1994), 93 CCC (3d) 21 (SCC) [*Daviault*].
194 *R v Stone* (1999), 134 CCC (3d) 353 (SCC) [*Stone*].
195 (1992), 72 CCC (3d) 1 (SCC).

prostitute does not lead inexorably to the conclusion that the person is living off the avails."[196] This mandatory presumption violated section 11(d), even though it could be displaced by an accused pointing to some evidence in either the Crown's or the accused's case to raise a reasonable doubt as to the presumed fact and did not require the accused to establish on a balance of probabilities that he did not live off the avails of prostitution. The Court, however, held that the mandatory presumption that could be displaced by satisfying an evidential burden was justified under section 1 of the *Charter* because of the difficulties of requiring prostitutes to testify against their pimps and the ease that a person in a lawful relationship with a prostitute would have in pointing to some evidence that could raise a reasonable doubt about the presumption.[197]

v)   Threshold "Air of Reality" Tests

The above combination of an evidential burden with a mandatory presumption should be distinguished from the requirement that there be an air of reality to justify the judge in instructing the jury about a particular issue or defence. These sorts of burdens of establishing an air of reality are quite common. They do not require the accused to prove anything and they make no mandatory presumptions about the commission of the crime. They have generally been seen as a matter of efficient and orderly trial administration and not as raising any presumption of innocence problems.

At the same time, air of reality tests can be quite important and determine the practical meaning of a particular defence. For example, the administration of the defence of mistaken belief in the complainant's consent in sexual assault cases often depends on whether there is an air of reality to justify instructing the jury about the controversial defence.[198]

The air of reality test may also be influenced by whether the accused bears a persuasive burden on the issue. In both *Daviault*[199] and *Stone*,[200] the Court indicated that in order to establish an air of reality about the extreme intoxication and automatism defences, respectively, the accused must point to evidence upon which a properly instructed

---

196   *Ibid* at 14.

197   Three judges dissented on the basis that there was not only no inexorable but also no rational connection between the proven fact (living with a prostitute) and the presumed fact (living off the avails). The requirement of such a connection under s 1 has now been rejected in *Laba*, above note 189.

198   See Chapter 5, Section D(4) and Chapter 10, Section B(3)(b).

199   *Daviault*, above note 193.

200   *Stone*, above note 194 at 430.

jury will find that the defence has been established on a balance of probabilities. The holding in *Stone* has been qualified in the subsequent case of *Fontaine*[201] in which the Court stressed that the judge should not determine whether evidence is credible or will support proof by the accused on a balance of probabilities of a defence such as extreme intoxication or automatism. Justice Fish stated that the threshold air of reality test is not "intended to assess whether the defence is likely, unlikely, somewhat unlikely or very likely to succeed at the end of the day. The question for the trial judge is whether the evidence discloses a real issue to be decided by the jury and not how the jury should ultimately decide the issue. The 'air of reality' test . . . should not be used to . . . introduce a persuasive requirement."[202] The Court also noted that "the cost of risking a wrongful conviction and possibly violating the accused's constitutionally protected rights by inadvisably withdrawing a defence from the jury is a high one."[203]

In *R v Cinous*,[204] a majority of the Supreme Court indicated that a consistent air of reality test should be applied throughout the criminal law. The test justifies not instructing the jury about a particular defence if there was no evidence that a properly instructed jury acting reasonably could use to acquit on the basis of the evidence. There must be an air of reality on every requirement of a defence to justify instructing the jury about the defence, but the judge should not determine the credibility of the evidence when assessing whether it has an air of reality. In *Fontaine*,[205] a unanimous Court similarly stated: "In determining whether the evidential burden has been discharged on any defence, trial judges, as a matter of judicial policy, should therefore always ask the very same question: Is there in the record any evidence upon which a reasonable trier of fact, properly instructed and acting judicially, could conclude that the defence succeeds?" Although the Court in both cases stressed that the accused did not have a persuasive burden to overcome the air of reality test and that the credibility of evidence should be left to the jury, decisions about whether there is an air of reality about a particular defence can be very important in a criminal trial. The air of reality test for each defence depends on the necessary elements of the particular defence and will be discussed in subsequent chapters in relation to various defences.

---

201 *R v Fontaine*, 2004 SCC 27 [*Fontaine*].

202 *Ibid* at paras 68 and 70.

203 *Ibid* at para 61, quoting Arbour J in dissent in *R v Cinous* (2002), 162 CCC (3d) 129 at para 200 (SCC).

204 (2002), 162 CCC (3d) 129 (SCC).

205 Above note 201 at para 57.

vi) Summary

Section 11(d) of the *Charter* has been interpreted broadly, so that it is violated any time a statutory provision allows an accused to be convicted in the face of a reasonable doubt as to any factor essential to conviction, including any applicable defences. It also has been interpreted to apply to evidential burdens that only require the accused to point to some evidence to raise a reasonable doubt about a mandatory presumption. At the same time, however, the courts frequently uphold violations of section 11(d) under section 1 of the *Charter* and have on their own initiative imposed a persuasive burden on the accused to establish the defences of extreme intoxication and automatism. Statutory requirements that the accused prove the defence of due diligence in regulatory offences or the defences of mental disorder have also been upheld on the basis that it would be too difficult for the Crown to prove beyond a reasonable doubt that the defence did not apply. There need not be a rational connection between the proven and presumed factors for a presumption to be upheld under section 1 of the *Charter*. Even though an evidential burden with a mandatory presumption itself violates section 11(d), it can be a less drastic alternative to a persuasive burden.

h) Other Legal Rights

Accused have the right in section 14 of the *Charter* to continuous, competent, and contemporaneous interpretation at trial if they are deaf or do not understand or speak the language in which the proceedings are conducted.[206] Under section 11(c), accused cannot be compelled to testify in their own trials. This protection does not extend to corporations and an officer of a corporation can be compelled to testify against his or her corporation.[207]

Other *Charter* rights are designed to protect the principle of legality by requiring that a person charged with an offence has the right "to be informed without unreasonable delay of the specific offence" (section 11(a)). Section 11(i) protects the accused against the burden of retroactive punishment[208] and section 11(g) protects against retro-

---

206 *R v Tran* (1994), 92 CCC (3d) 218 (SCC).

207 *R v Amway Corp*, [1989] 1 SCR 21.

208 This also includes retroactive restrictions on liberty through prohibitions: *KRJ*, above note 48. The retroactive imposition of restrictions on using the internet against those convicted of sexual offences against children violated s 11(i), but was justified under s 1 because the benefits in protecting children from sexual offenders outweighed the harms to offenders. In contrast, the Court found that the harms to the accused of a retroactive imposition of a ban on contact with anyone under sixteen years of age were greater than the benefits achieved by

active criminal laws. The latter right, however, has an exception to allow retroactive laws if the conduct was contrary to international law, or was criminal according to the general principles of law recognized by the community of nations. The latter phrase was included to allow for the prosecution of war crimes committed in other nations, and such legislation has been upheld under the *Charter*.[209] At the same time, the Court indicated that because of the special stigma of such crimes, the Crown must prove the accused knew or was wilfully blind to facts and circumstances that would bring his acts within the definition of war crimes or crimes against humanity.[210]

4) The *Charter* and Substantive Criminal Offences and Defences

Although they have been primarily concerned with the procedural fairness of investigations and prosecutions, courts under the *Charter* have also evaluated the substance of offences and defences. An accused cannot be convicted if the criminal offence itself results in an unjustified violation of one of the rights guaranteed by the *Charter*. Criminal offences have generally been challenged on the grounds that they violated fundamental freedoms, such as freedom of expression, or the principles of fundamental justice.

a) Fundamental Freedoms
Section 2(b) of the *Charter* has been interpreted broadly to include protection for all forms of expression short of violence or threats of violence. At the same time, however, the courts have recognized that criminal prohibitions on some types of expression can be justified as a reasonable limit under section 1 of the *Charter*.

A criminal offence prohibiting solicitation in a public place for the purpose of prostitution has been held to violate freedom of expression, but to be justified as a reasonable response to "the social nuisance of street solicitation."[211] The restriction in section 163 of the *Criminal Code* on the making and distribution of obscene materials also has been found to violate freedom of expression. This restriction, however, is a reasonable limit on freedom of expression provided it is interpreted

---

such a retrospective form of punishment and could not be justified under s 1 of the *Charter*.

209 *R v Finta* (1994), 88 CCC (3d) 417 (SCC) [*Finta*].

210 *Ibid* at 503.

211 *Reference re ss 193 & 195.1(1)(c) of the Criminal Code (Canada)* (1990), 56 CCC (3d) 65 at 77 (SCC).

not to "proscribe sexually explicit erotica without violence that is not degrading or dehumanizing."[212] The Supreme Court has indicated that the criminal law cannot be used to enforce morality *per se*, but that it can act to respond to Parliament's "reasoned apprehension of harm" even if the causal links between the expression and the harm of violence against women and children are not conclusive. The Court also approved of the use of the criminal law "to enhance respect for all members of society, and non-violence and equality in their relations with each other," especially as this relates to the enforcement of "*Charter* values" such as equality.[213]

The crime of possession of child pornography that depicts a person under eighteen years of age in explicit sexual activity or that encourages unlawful sexual activity with those under eighteen years of age has also been held to be a reasonable limit on freedom of expression. The Supreme Court, however, indicated that defences of artistic merit, educational, scientific, or medical purpose or the public good should be liberally interpreted to protect freedom of expression. In addition, exceptions for expressive material created and held privately and for consensual visual recordings of lawful sexual activity that are held privately and not distributed publicly were read into the offence by the Court in order to protect freedom of expression and privacy.[214]

A provision prohibiting the wilful promotion of hatred against an identifiable group has been held to be a reasonable limit on freedom of expression. Chief Justice Dickson stressed that the requirements that the accused have the intent of wilfully promoting hatred and that the Attorney General approve any prosecution restrict the reach of the provision. He also argued that Parliament can act to prevent the serious harms caused by racial and religious hatred and to respond to "the severe psychological trauma suffered by members of those identifiable groups targeted by hate propaganda."[215]

Two years later, the Supreme Court struck down a provision prohibiting wilfully spreading false news that is likely to injure the public interest. Justice McLachlin argued that although the provision could be used to prohibit statements, such as the accused's denial of the Holocaust, which denigrate vulnerable groups,

> [i]ts danger, however, lies in the fact that by its broad reach it criminalizes a vast penumbra of other statements merely because they might

---

212 *R v Butler* (1992), 70 CCC (3d) 129 at 165 (SCC).
213 *Ibid* at 168.
214 *R v Sharpe*, [2001] 1 SCR 45.
215 *Keegstra*, above note 186 at 58.

be thought to constitute a mischief to some public interest, however successive prosecutors and courts may wish to define these terms. The danger is magnified because the prohibition affects not only those caught and prosecuted, but those who may refrain from saying what they would like to because of the fear that they will be caught.[216]

This provision was struck down because it was broader and less narrowly tailored than the hate propaganda provision examined above. The crime of defamatory libel was also upheld as a justified restriction on freedom of expression, given the need to protect reputations and to establish that the accused intended to make defamatory statements.[217]

In summary, an offence that prohibits any form of expression short of violence will likely violate freedom of expression. Depending on the objective and reach of the offence, however, the courts may find it to be a reasonable limit on expression that can be justified under section 1 of the *Charter.*

b) Principles of Fundamental Justice

i) Everyone

Section 7 of the *Charter* provides that "everyone has the right to life, liberty, and security of the person and the right not to be deprived thereof except in accordance with the principles of fundamental justice." Corporations are not entities that enjoy rights to life, liberty, and security of the person.[218] Nevertheless, courts have allowed corporations to challenge offences that they are charged with on the basis that the offence can also apply to natural persons who enjoy rights under section 7 of the *Charter.*[219] A corporation should be precluded from bringing a section 7 challenge to provisions that only apply to corporations,[220] because section 7 of the *Charter* does not protect the principles of fundamental justice in the abstract, but only in cases where a human being is deprived of the right to life, liberty, and security of the person.

ii) Right to Life, Liberty, and Security of the Person

As a threshold matter, a law must affect either the right to life, liberty, or security of the person. A deprivation of those rights alone is not sufficient. In other words, "[s]ection 7 does not promise that the state will never

---

216 R v Zundel (1992), 75 CCC (3d) 449 at 521 (SCC).
217 R v Lucas (1998), 123 CCC (3d) 97 (SCC).
218 Irwin Toy Ltd v Quebec (AG), [1989] 1 SCR 927.
219 Wholesale Travel Group, above note 187.
220 See, for example, Code, above note 1, ss 22.1–22.2 on organizational liability, which is discussed in Chapter 6.

interfere with a person's life, liberty or security of the person — laws do this all the time — but rather that the state will not do so in a way that violates the principles of fundamental justice."[221]

In *Carter v Canada (Attorney General)*,[222] the Court held that the assisted suicide offence deprived persons of life by requiring those with debilitating illnesses to take their lives before they might otherwise desire so as to ensure that those who assisted them when they were physically unable to do so would not face criminal liability.

The right to liberty is affected if a person is liable to be imprisoned. It is also affected by other restrictions on their fundamental autonomy, dignity, and bodily integrity including probation orders that restrain the person's liberty in the community.[223] The only sure way to guarantee that liberty is not infringed when a person is subject to a fine is to provide that imprisonment cannot be used if the offender fails to pay the fine.[224] Prohibitions on smoking marijuana have not been found to violate a person's right to liberty.[225]

A person's security of the person is infringed by state-imposed interference with personal choices and bodily integrity. An offence that criminalized abortion except where certain conditions were satisfied violated women's security of the person.[226] Laws that exposed sex workers to increased danger by prohibiting them from working in brothels, from hiring bodyguards, or from screening customers in public were all held to violate security of the person even though the ultimate harm that they would be exposed to would be inflicted by third parties.[227] At the same time, high fines without the possibility of imprisonment have been held not to infringe security of the person.[228]

iii) *Principles of Fundamental Justice*
The test for whether a rule or principle constitutes a principle of fundamental justice is that (1) the proposition must be a legal principle; (2) there must be a consensus that the rule or principle is fundamental to the way the legal system ought fairly to operate; and (3) the rule or principle must be identified with sufficient precision to constitute a

---

221 *Carter*, above note 11 at para 71.
222 *Ibid* at paras 57–58.
223 *Re BC Motor Vehicle Reference*, [1985] 2 SCR 486 at 512 [*Re BC Motor Vehicle Reference*].
224 *R v Pontes* (1995), 100 CCC (3d) 353 (SCC).
225 *R v Clay*, [2003] 3 SCR 735 at paras 31–32.
226 *R v Morgentaler*, [1988] 1 SCR 30 [*Morgentaler (No 2)*].
227 *Canada (Attorney General) v Bedford*, [2013] 3 SCR 1101 at paras 58–92 [*Bedford*].
228 *R v William Cameron Trucking* (2003), 180 CCC (3d) 254 (Ont CA).

manageable standard to measure deprivations of life, liberty, or security of the person.[229] There is no free-standing right to respect for the principle of fundamental justice. Rather, it must be respected when the state infringes the right to life, liberty, or security of the person.[230]

The test for what constitutes a principle of fundamental justice can be quite restrictive, and long-standing principles such as the idea that the criminal law should be used only to prevent harms to others or that the law should respect the best interests of children have been held not to be principles of fundamental justice.

In *R v Malmo-Levine*,[231] the Supreme Court considered whether section 7 of the *Charter* restricted Parliament to criminalizing conduct that harmed others. The accused challenged the criminal offence that prohibited the possession of marijuana. The majority of the Court rejected the idea that the harm principle was a principle of fundamental justice or that Parliament could only criminalize conduct that harmed others. It held that there was no consensus that the criminal law should be used only to respond to harms to others and that there was little agreement about what constituted harm. The Court's subsequent finding that there was a reasonable apprehension of harm for criminalizing marijuana suggests that even the constitutionalization of the harm principle would not have been a robust tool for demanding parliamentary restraint in the use of the criminal sanction. The courts below, which, unlike the Supreme Court, had applied the harm principle as a principle of fundamental justice, also found that there was sufficient harm to justify criminalizing the possession of marijuana.[232]

The Court has also found that the principle that the law should pursue the best interests of children was not a principle of fundamental justice because there was no consensus that it was vital or fundamental to justice and it fails to produce manageable standards.[233]

On the other hand, the Court has stressed that principles of fundamental justice are not a closed category and they will continue to evolve. The Court held that the presumption that young people are less blameworthy for offences is a principle of fundamental justice with a majority holding that the principle was violated by a presumption that young offenders convicted of certain serious offences should receive an adult

---

229 *Malmo-Levine*, above note 9 at para 113; *DB*, above note 32 at paras 46 and 125.
230 *Re BC Motor Vehicle Reference*, above note 223 at 512.
231 Above note 9.
232 See also *R v Murdock* (2003), 11 CR (6th) 43 (Ont CA).
233 *Canadian Foundation for Children, Youth and the Law v Canada (AG)*, [2004] 1 SCR 76 at paras 11–12 [*Canadian Foundation for Children*].

sentence.[234] More recently, the Court has indicated that arbitrariness, overbreadth, and gross disproportionality are all distinct principles of fundamental justice that if violated can require a law that infringes life, liberty, or security of the person to be struck down. The Court has recently used these concepts, especially overbreadth and gross disproportionality, to strike down a number of criminal offences, including laws prohibiting brothels, living off the avails of prostitution, public solicitation of prostitution, and assisted suicide.

iv) Relation of Section 7 and Section 1
The Supreme Court has never held that a violation of section 7 was justified and reasonable under section 1. Some cases suggest that the court would only make such a finding in a state of emergency, but more recent cases have not stressed this limitation to the same extent. The Court's caution in accepting even well-established legal principles such as the harm and best interests of the child standard as principles of fundamental justice may in part be related by its position that "violations of s. 7 are seldom salvageable by s. 1."[235] At the same time, some principles of fundamental justice come close to replicating some of the proportionality analysis that is conducted under section 1. For example, the principle that excessively vague laws would violate section 7 mimics some of the role of the requirement under section 1, that limits on rights be "prescribed by law." Similarly, the principle of fundamental justice against laws that are arbitrary and bear no relation to their objective is similar to the section 1 requirement that a law limiting a right be rationally connected to the legislative objective. The section 7 principle against overbroad laws is similar to the section 1 requirement that a law should limit rights as little as is reasonably possible to achieve its objective. Finally, the principle of fundamental justice against gross disproportionality has some relation to the overall balance stage of section 1 analysis. These analogies should be used with caution because the Court in *Bedford*[236] stressed that the section 7 inquiry is focused on the comparative harms that a law seeks to prevent and that it imposes and not, as under section 1, on the social benefits and costs of the law. The analysis under section 7 is more abstract and qualitative

234 *DB*, above note 32.
235 *Ibid* at para 89, quoting Lamer J in *Re BC Motor Vehicle Reference*, above note 223, stating: "[s]ection 1 may, for reasons of administrative expediency, successfully come to the rescue of an otherwise violation of s. 7, but only in cases arising out of exceptional conditions, such as natural disasters, the outbreak of war, epidemics, and the like."
236 Above note 227 at para 121. See also *Malmo-Levine*, above note 9 at para 181.

and focused on the individual than under section 1. In other words, a law can be arbitrary, overbroad, or grossly disproportionate under section 1 because of its effect on simply one person, and overall social costs and benefits are considered under section 1. Another important difference is that an applicant bears the burden of establishing that section 7 rights have been violated, whereas the government bears the burden of justification under section 1 of the *Charter*.[237]

c) Vagueness, Arbitrariness, Overbreadth, and Gross Disproportionality

i) Vagueness

The principles of fundamental justice in section 7 of the *Charter* are offended by offences that are so vague that they fail to give fair notice to citizens and provide no limit for law enforcement discretion. The Court has stressed that an excessively vague law "mock[s] the rule of law"[238] and that "condemning people for conduct that they could not have reasonably known was criminal is Kafkaesque and anathema to our notions of justice."[239] At the same time, "a court can conclude that a law is unconstitutionally vague only after exhausting its interpretive function."[240]

Courts are very reluctant to hold that criminal laws are unconstitutionally vague with commentators reasonably concluding that vagueness challenges "are virtually doomed to fail."[241] They make allowances for the ability of courts to add an interpretative gloss on vague words. For example, the Supreme Court has upheld criminal offences and defences from vagueness challenges even when they use open-ended language such as "unduly"[242] and "reasonable."[243] In other words, judicial interpretations of laws, even creative interpretations, can save them from being held to violate section 7 of the *Charter* because of vagueness.[244] The Supreme Court stressed the need to give the accused fair notice and to avoid excessively vague laws when it interpreted the

---

237 *Bedford*, above note 227 at paras 123–28.
238 *R v Levkovic*, [2013] 2 SCR 204 at para 1 [*Levkovic*].
239 *R v Mabior*, [2012] 2 SCR 584 at para 14.
240 *Levkovic*, above note 238 at para 47.
241 Morris Manning QC & Peter Sankoff, *Criminal Law*, 5th ed (Markham, ON: LexisNexis Canada, 2015) at 2.92.
242 *R v Nova Scotia Pharmaceutical Society*, [1992] 2 SCR 606.
243 *Canadian Foundation for Children*, above note 233.
244 See *Canadian Foundation for Children*, *ibid*, where the reference to the use of reasonable corrective force against children was saved by the majority of the Court by adopting a restrictive and quasi-legislative interpretation of what force is reasonable.

offence of failure to obtain assistance in childbirth to require that the child would likely have lived.[245]

A law's vagueness may also be a consideration in determining whether the law violates another *Charter* right. As discussed above, the Court has struck down under section 11(e) of the *Charter*: the vague terms "public interest" and "just cause" for the denial of bail.[246] The vagueness of a law that violates a *Charter* right may also be relevant to whether it can be justified under section 1 of the *Charter*. A limitation on a *Charter* right under section 1 must be "prescribed by law" and provide an intelligible standard to determine the manner in which the legislature has limited a *Charter* right.

ii) Arbitrariness

A law is arbitrary if its infringement of life, liberty, or security of the person is not rationally connected to the objective of the law. The Supreme Court explained in *Bedford*: "There must be a rational connection between the object of the measure that causes the s. 7 deprivation, and the limits it imposes on life, liberty, or security of the person . . . . A law that imposes limits on these interests in a way that bears *no connection* to its objective arbitrarily impinges on those interests."[247]

Arbitrariness is a difficult standard to establish, but not an impossible one. For example, the requirement that abortions be performed only in a hospital was arbitrary to the objective of the law because there was no connection between the restriction on a woman's security and liberty and the government's objective of protecting a woman's health.[248]

The Court also found that the denial of a statutory exemption from drug trafficking laws to an on-site safe injection site was arbitrary because, on the evidence, there was no connection between the denial and the government's objectives of protecting health and preventing crime.[249] In *R v Smith*[250] the Court found that a medical marijuana exemption that allowed the smoking of marijuana for medical purposes but not other uses of marijuana was arbitrary to the legislative

---

245 *Levkovic*, above note 238.

246 *Morales*, above note 145; *Hall*, above note 149. But the Court has accepted that bail after a conviction and pending appeal can be denied on the basis of the "public interest" as interpreted by the Court as including public safety and public confidence. *Oland*, above note 152.

247 *Bedford*, above note 227 at paras 111 and 113.

248 *Morgentaler (No 2)*, above note 226.

249 *Canada (AG) v PHS Community Services Society*, 2011 SCC 44.

250 2015 SCC 34 at paras 25–26. The same lack of connection between the prohibition and its objection meant that the law could not be justified under s 1 as rationally connected to the legislative objectives of health and safety.

objectives of promoting health and safety, given findings that smoking can present health risks and use of cannabis derivatives could be more effective in relieving health problems. The law was arbitrary because there was a "total disconnect between the limit on liberty and security of the person imposed by the prohibition and its object" and the same disconnect meant that extending the prohibition to cannabis derivatives could not be justified under section 1 because of a lack of a rational connection with the objectives of health and safety.[251]

It should be noted, however, that none of the prostitution laws challenged in *Bedford* were found to be arbitrary. They were all related to legitimate objectives and their mischief was going beyond what was required for the objective or gross disproportionality between the objectives and the role of the offences in exposing sex workers to danger. Similarly, the assisted suicide offence was not arbitrary because in some cases it would prevent people from being coerced into taking their own lives, even though it was overbroad in its application to those who made a free choice to end their lives, but because of physical disability required assistance in doing so.[252] Rational laws should not be found to be arbitrary.

iii) Overbreadth

A law is overbroad when it goes beyond what is necessary to achieve its legislative objectives and is not rationally connected to those objectives. An early example was the Court's decision in *R v Heywood*[253] to strike down a law that prevented all convicted sexual offenders from loitering in a broad range of public places. The law restricted liberty more than was necessary to achieve its objective of preventing sexual abuse of children because it applied to all sex offenders and in places where children would not reasonably be present. The majority of the Court was influenced by the fact that Parliament had enacted a more modern and carefully tailored law that better targeted the danger of sexual abuse of children. It should be noted, however, that four judges in dissent would have interpreted the overbroad law restrictively so it would apply only to those who had an intent to sexually abuse children. In many cases, restrictive interpretations can save a law from being found to be overbroad in violation of section 7 of the *Charter*.[254]

---

251 *Ibid* at para 27.
252 *Carter*, above note 11.
253 [1994] 3 SCR 761.
254 See *R v Khawaja*, [2012] 3 SCR 555, where the Court rejected an overbreadth challenge to a broad terrorism law by interpreting it not to apply to innocent

Overbreadth differs from arbitrariness because, while an arbitrary law is irrational in the sense that it bears no relation to its purpose, an overbroad law bears some relation to its purpose but goes further than is necessary. The Supreme Court has explained:

> Overbreadth deals with a law that is so broad in scope that it includes *some* conduct that bears no relation to its purpose. In this sense, the law is arbitrary *in part*. At its core, overbreadth addresses the situation where there is no rational connection between the purposes of the law and *some*, but not all, of its impacts . . . . Overbreadth allows courts to recognize that the law is rational in some cases, but that it overreaches in its effect in others.[255]

In other words, the vagrancy offence in *Heywood* was not arbitrary because it would in some cases apply to potential child abusers; it was overbroad because it applied in cases where there was no danger of child sexual abuse.

Overbreadth has emerged as one of the most powerful principles of fundamental justice to curb broadly drawn offences. The offence of living off the avails or earnings of prostitution was found to be overbroad in *Bedford* because it would apply to relationships other than exploitative "pimping" relations. At the same time, the offence was not arbitrary because it would apply to some such relations. Similarly, the Supreme Court found the assisted suicide offence to be overbroad in *Carter* because, while it would apply to some people who were coerced into taking their lives against their will, it would apply to many who made voluntary choices to take their lives.[256]

A critical feature in overbreadth analysis is how courts define the relevant legislative objective. If the objectives are defined too broadly, then laws will hardly ever be found to be overbroad but if the legislative objective is defined too narrowly, laws will often be overbroad. A provision that denied those with prior convictions credit for time spent in jail awaiting trial was overbroad (and also not rationally connected) to the legislative objective of public safety.[257] In contrast, a provision that allows members of the military to be prosecuted in the military justice system for certain off-duty conduct was not overbroad because of its rational connection with the legislative objective of maintaining disci-

---

activities, including the professional assistance of doctors or lawyers who may assist terrorist groups.

255 *Bedford*, above note 227 at para 112 [emphasis in original].

256 *Carter*, above note 11.

257 *R v Safarzadeh-Markhali*, 2016 SCC 14.

pline, morale, and efficiency in the military.[258] Prosecutorial discretion cannot be relied upon to save an overbroad law because nothing would prevent the conviction of such persons should they be prosecuted.[259]

Although overbroad laws cannot be saved by prosecutorial discretion, in most cases, Parliament should be able to respond to a ruling by crafting a more carefully tailored offence. Parliament can often respond to a finding that an offence must be struck down on overbreadth grounds by enacting a narrower offence with a closer fit between the legislative objective and the scope of the offence. After *Bedford*, Parliament enacted a new offence, making it a crime to receive financial benefits from prostitution but with exemptions for "a legitimate living arrangement," the purchase of good and services on the same terms as provided to the general public or in a manner that does not encourage the purchaser to provide sexual services for money.[260] Parliament also responded by narrowing the assisted suicide offence so it would not apply to medical or nurse practitioners who provided medical assistance in death to adults under certain conditions.[261]

iv) Gross Disproportionality

A law will be grossly disproportionate "in extreme cases where the seriousness of the deprivation is totally out of sync with the objective of the measure. This idea is captured by the hypothetical of a law with the purpose of keeping the streets clean that imposes a sentence of life imprisonment for spitting on the sidewalk. The connection between the draconian impact of the law and its object must be entirely outside the norms accepted in our free and democratic society."[262] Less hypothetically, the Court in *Bedford* held that the offence against keeping bawdy houses or brothels for sex workers and of public solicitation for prostitution were both grossly disproportionate because the objective of controlling neighbourhood nuisances was not nearly as important as the harms to the life and safety of sex workers required to work in more dangerous conditions because of the offences. Citing the example of a bawdy house (Grandma's House) that when closed exposed sex workers to a serial killer, the Court concluded: "Parliament has the power to regulate against nuisances, but not at the cost of the health, safety and lives of prostitutes. A law that prevents street prostitutes from resorting

---

258 *R v Moriarity*, 2015 SCC 55, [2015] 3 SCR 485.
259 *R v Appulonappa*, [2015] 3 SCR 754 at para 74.
260 *Code*, above note 1, s 286.2.
261 *Ibid*, ss 241–241.4.
262 *Bedford*, above note 227 at para 136.

to a safe haven such as Grandma's House while a suspected serial killer prowls the streets, is a law that has lost sight of its purpose."[263]

The holding of the prostitution-related laws as grossly dispropor-tionate in *Bedford* may be exceptional. It depended on clear evidence that Parliament was only targeting neighbourhood nuisances and that the criminal offences had the effect of endangering the lives of sex workers. In other cases, courts have not held laws to be grossly dispro-portionate. For example, offences against possession of marijuana are not grossly disproportionate because Parliament acted with a reasoned expectation that in some extreme cases, marijuana could be harmful. The Court also assumed that judges would use their sentencing discre-tion not to imprison those who possess marijuana for personal use.[264] The Court struck down the assisted suicide offence only on the basis of overbreadth[265] and did not compare the relative harms that the of-fence attempted to avoid and that the law imposed. If it had, it might have found the harms to be relatively similar or at least not grossly disproportionate. A lower court has held the offence of polygamy not to be grossly disproportionate or arbitrary given Parliament's reasoned apprehension of harms caused by plural marriages.[266]

Parliament responded to *Bedford* not by reaffirming the relatively low value of legislating to respond to social nuisances but rather with a more ambitious attempt as outlined in a legislative preamble to re-spond to and denounce exploitation, violence, and the "commodifica-tion" of sex and the "objectification of the human body." The focus is on those who purchase sex and there are some exceptions for those who sell sex.[267] The Court's approach to gross disproportionality suggests that the focus in inevitable *Charter* challenges to this new law, at least with respect to gross disproportionality, may be on the importance of the non-nuisance-related harms Parliament addresses such as violence and exploitation (and not Parliament's effectiveness in addressing these harms) compared to the harms the new law may impose on sex workers

---

263 *Ibid.*

264 *Malmo-Levine*, above note 9.

265 *Carter*, above note 11.

266 *Reference re Section 293*, 2011 BCSC 1588 at paras 1202–205 and 1226. The Court, however, did hold that the offence was overbroad as it could be applied to minors between twelve and seventeen years of age who could be married, because of the harms that would be caused to them by prosecution.

267 SC 2014, c 25, adding to the *Criminal Code* s 213(1.1) limiting communication offences of offering sexual services to places near schools and playgrounds and ss 286.1–286.5 providing various offences for purchasing sexual services, re-ceiving material benefits from their sale, procuring sexual services, or advertis-ing sexual services.

who may again have to work in the shadows in order to protect their customers from possible criminal charges.

d) Fault Requirements

Fault requirements will be discussed in greater detail in Chapters 5 and 6. Nevertheless, at this juncture it will be helpful to provide a somewhat less detailed overview of how section 7 of the *Charter* requires certain minimal fault requirements.

i) Moral Innocence and Absolute Liability

In the *BC Motor Vehicle Reference*,[268] the Supreme Court indicated that a "law enacting an absolute liability offence will violate section 7 of the *Charter* only if and to the extent that it has the potential of depriving of life, liberty, and security of the person." In that case, there was no doubt that the regulatory offence would deprive an accused of liberty because it set a minimum penalty of seven days' imprisonment. The law specifically stated that the offence was one of absolute liability so that an accused would be convicted of driving with a suspended licence regardless of whether the accused knew that his or her licence was suspended or was negligent in respect to whether it was suspended. The Supreme Court concluded that the offence could allow the morally innocent to be punished and suggested that a better alternative would have been to allow the accused a defence of due diligence or lack of negligence once the Crown proved the prohibited act of driving with a suspended licence. A strict liability offence, as opposed to one of absolute liability, would do "nothing more than let those few who did nothing wrong remain free."[269]

In *R v Pontes*,[270] the Supreme Court subsequently upheld an absolute liability offence but only on the basis that an accused could not be imprisoned for violating it. The rationale would seem to be that while absolute liability offends the principles of fundamental justice by allowing the morally innocent to be punished, it does not violate section 7 of the *Charter* because a sentence other than imprisonment does not affect the accused's rights to life, liberty, or security of the person. At the same time, the Court has not yet decided whether a fine that may result in imprisonment if the accused defaults on payment also affects the accused's right to liberty and security of the person. The Court has also invalidated as absolute liability offences part of a misleading

---

268 *Re BC Motor Vehicle Reference*, above note 223 at 515. See Chapter 6, Section A for further discussion.

269 *Ibid* at 521.

270 Above note 224.

advertising offence punishable by imprisonment that required the accused to make forthwith corrections regardless of whether the accused knew or ought to have known that the advertisement was misleading. The Court stressed that such mandatory retraction requirements were considerably more onerous than the due diligence defence that is generally available to those charged with regulatory offences and could apply in situations where the accused could not reasonably know that there was any misleading advertising requiring correction.[271]

The Supreme Court has held that absolute liability criminal offences also violate section 7 of the *Charter*. In *R v Hess*,[272] the Court held that a "statutory rape" offence that made sex with a girl under fourteen years of age a crime regardless of whether the accused had an honest belief that she was older constituted an absolute liability offence. The Court held that "a person who is mentally innocent of the offence — who has no *mens rea* with respect to an essential element of the offence — may be convicted and sent to prison."[273] The majority also held that the violation of the accused's section 7 rights could not be justified under section 1 of the *Charter* because a person who honestly believed a girl was over fourteen could not be deterred from committing the crime and, in any event, it would be unjust to punish a morally innocent person in order to deter others. The Court also noted that Parliament had already replaced the unconstitutional offence with one that allowed the accused a defence that he had taken "all reasonable steps to ascertain the age of the complainant."[274] This new provision violated the accused's rights less because it allowed an honest and reasonable mistake that the child was older than fourteen years of age to be a defence. In other words, the new offence imposed fault on the basis of negligence and not simply on the basis that the accused committed the criminal act.

ii) Negligence as a Sufficient Fault Element Under the Charter for Most Offences

The above cases indicate that absolute liability offences, where a conviction follows from proof of the prohibited act, will violate section 7 of the *Charter* whenever the offence has the potential to deprive the accused of

---

271 *Wholesale Travel Group*, above note 187.

272 (1990), 59 CCC (3d) 161 (SCC).

273 *Ibid* at 168.

274 *Code*, above note 1, s 150.1(4).

life, liberty, or security of the person.[275] In these circumstances, section 7 of the *Charter* requires a fault element of at least negligence.[276]

The courts have been more cautious about striking down offences because they do not have fault elements higher than negligence. Criminal offences prohibiting unlawfully causing bodily harm,[277] dangerous driving,[273] careless use of a firearm,[279] and failing to provide the necessities of life[280] have all been upheld on the basis that they require proof of a marked departure from the standard of care that a reasonable person would take in the circumstances. In addition, subjective fault or subjective knowledge of the prohibited consequences is not required to convict an accused of "unlawful act manslaughter"[281] or of misleading advertising.[282] In other words, "an objective fault requirement is constitutionally sufficient for a broad range of offences other than those falling within the relatively small group of offences"[283] so far including only murder, attempted murder, and war crimes.

Objective fault is sufficient even for serious crime such as manslaughter that may be punished by up to life imprisonment. An objective fault element of reasonable foresight of non-trivial bodily harm was held in *Creighton* not to violate section 7 of the *Charter* because

> by the very act of calling the killing *manslaughter* the law indicates that the killing is less blameworthy than murder. It may arise from negligence, or it may arise as the unintended result of a lesser unlawful act. The conduct is blameworthy and must be punished, but its stigma does not approach that of murder.[284]

Section 7 of the *Charter* will not be violated so long as (1) the *mens rea* and the available penalties reflect the particular nature of the crime and its stigma; (2) the punishment is proportionate to the moral blame-

---

275 Corporations do not enjoy life, liberty, or security of the person. Section 7 of the *Charter*, above note 42, would not apply if the offence was drafted to apply only to corporations, but corporations are allowed to argue that an offence is unconstitutional because of its effects on natural persons. *Wholesale Travel Group*, above note 187.

276 Negligence can be defined in various ways. See Chapter 5, Section C.

277 *R v DeSousa* (1992), 76 CCC (3d) 124 (SCC).

278 *R v Hundal* (1993), 79 CCC (3d) 97 (SCC) [*Hundal*].

279 *R v Gosset* (1993), 83 CCC (3d) 494 (SCC); *R v Finlay* (1993), 83 CCC (3d) 513 (SCC) [*Finlay*].

280 *R v Naglik* (1993), 83 CCC (3d) 526 (SCC).

281 *R v Creighton* (1993), 83 CCC (3d) 346 (SCC) [*Creighton*].

282 *Wholesale Travel Group*, above note 187.

283 *Creighton*, above note 281 at 354–55, Lamer CJ in dissent, but not on this issue.

284 *Ibid* at 374 [emphasis added].

worthiness of the offender; and (3) those who cause harm intentionally are punished more severely than those who cause harm unintentionally. As will be seen, the courts have held that murder, attempted murder, and war crimes have a special stigma that requires subjective fault in relation to the prohibited act. Although the third standard could affect that ability of Parliament to combine objective and subjective forms of liability, the preceding three principles listed above have so far made a minimal impact on the substantive criminal law.

iii) Negligence Standards: Marked Departure from the Standards of a Non-individuated Reasonable Person

Section 7 of the *Charter* has been interpreted to require more than simple or civil negligence, but rather "a marked departure from the standards of a reasonable person,"[285] in order to convict a person of a criminal offence based on objective fault. This applies even if the offence seems to contemplate a lower standard of negligence, such as carelessness, because "the law does not lightly brand a person as a criminal."[286] In *R v Beatty*,[287] the Court explained:

> if every departure from the civil norm is to be criminalized, regardless of the degree, we risk casting the net too widely and branding as criminals persons who are in reality not morally blameworthy. Such an approach risks violating the principle of fundamental justice that the morally innocent not be deprived of liberty.

Negligence as a criminal form of fault that can result in the deprivation of liberty requires the prosecutor to prove that the accused's conduct was a marked departure from the standard of care that would be used in the circumstances by the reasonable person.

The question remains, however, who is the reasonable person who is used for the purpose of determining negligence as a form of criminal fault? A majority of the Court in *Creighton* held that when applying an objective standard, personal characteristics of the accused are only relevant if they establish incapacity to appreciate the nature and quality of one's conduct or incapacity to appreciate the risk involved in one's conduct.[288] Four judges dissented and argued that the accused's personal characteristics should be factored into the objective standard to

---

285 *Ibid* at 371–72, quoting *Hundal*, above note 278. See Chapter 5, Section C for further discussion.

286 *Finlay*, above note 279 at 521.

287 2008 SCC 5 at para 34 [*Beatty*].

288 Above note 281 at 384–85, McLachlin J. For further discussion, see Chapter 5, Section C(2).

the extent that they indicate either enhanced or reduced foresight from that of a reasonable person.[289] Section 7 is thus not offended by applying objective standards without consideration of the accused's own characteristics, at least when those characteristics do not render the accused incapable of appreciating the relevant risk.

In *Beatty*,[290] the Court affirmed that a modified objective approach that takes into account the personal characteristics of the accused is not required when applying standards of criminal negligence. At the same time, the Court affirmed that all negligence used for criminal liability must be a marked departure in order to distinguish criminal from civil negligence. It also suggested that judges examine the accused's state of mind, but only to determine if there is a reasonable doubt about whether a reasonable person in the accused's position would have been aware of the risk created by this conduct.[291] It is not clear whether this latter requirement is based on section 7 of the *Charter* as is the requirement for a marked departure of standards of reasonable care. It could simply be a reminder for judges and juries to consider all the circumstances of the case in determining whether the accused was criminally negligent.

iv) No Requirement of Correspondence or Symmetry Between Prohibited Act and Fault Element

A majority of the Court in *Creighton* held that section 7 of the *Charter* does not require that objective fault relate to all the prohibited consequences in the offence, so that proof of objective foresight of bodily harm (as opposed to death) is sufficient to convict a person of manslaughter.[292] Four judges dissented and argued that the fault element of objective foresight should be related to the prohibited consequences of the offence. Section 7 is thus not offended by offences that punish a person for causing certain harm even though the accused may not have subjectively or objectively been at fault for causing the harm that forms part of the *actus reus*.

---

289 *Ibid*, Lamer CJ.

290 Above note 287 at paras 37–40.

291 *Ibid* at para 49.

292 Chief Justice McLachlin stated: "It is important to distinguish between criminal law theory, which seeks the ideal of absolute symmetry between *actus reus* [the prohibited act] and *mens rea* [the required fault requirement], and the constitutional requirements of the *Charter*. Provided an element of mental fault or moral culpability is present, and provided that it is proportionate to the seriousness and consequences of the offence charged, the principles of fundamental justice are satisfied." *Creighton*, above note 281 at 378–79. For further discussion, see Chapter 5, Section A(1).

v) Subjective Fault Required in Relation to the Prohibited Act for a Few Offences with Special Stigma

The Supreme Court has held that section 7 of the *Charter* requires proof of subjective fault for only a limited number of offences. *R v Vaillancourt*[293] and *R v Martineau*[294] established that because of its stigma and mandatory life imprisonment, the offence of murder requires proof that the accused either intended to cause death or knew that death was likely to occur. In those cases, the Court struck down "felony" or constructive murder provisions that allowed an accused committing some other serious offence such as robbery or sexual assault to be convicted of murder "whether or not the person means to cause death to any human being and whether or not he knows that death is likely to be caused."[295] In *Vaillancourt*, the section provided that a person committing a serious offence such as robbery was guilty of murder if death resulted from the use or possession of a weapon. In *Martineau*, the section provided that a person was guilty of murder if he or she meant to cause bodily harm for the purpose of facilitating a serious offence. The Court also suggested that it was unconstitutional to convict a person of murder under section 229(c) of the *Criminal Code* on the basis that while pursuing an unlawful object, he or she ought to have known that death was likely to result. Under section 7 of the *Charter*, the Crown must at least prove that an accused has subjective knowledge that death is likely to result before that person can be convicted of murder.[296]

The Supreme Court has also stated that section 7 is violated by provisions that allowed an accused to be convicted as a party to attempted murder on the basis that he or she ought to have known death was likely to result.[297] Even though the penalty was not mandatory life imprisonment, the Court stressed that a person convicted of attempted murder would suffer the same stigma as a murderer. Hence, the Crown must establish as a constitutional minimum that the accused subjectively knew that death was likely to occur. The *Charter*, however, only establishes minimum standards and, as will be seen, the courts have gone above

---

293 *Vaillancourt*, above note 184.
294 *R v Martineau* (1990), 58 CCC (3d) 353 (SCC) [*Martineau*].
295 *Code*, above note 1, s 230.
296 At the same time, the Court has defined manslaughter quite broadly to apply to an accused who causes death when a reasonable person would have foreseen the likelihood of bodily harm, provided that the accused had the capacity to see such a risk. *Creighton*, above note 281.
297 *R v Logan* (1990), 58 CCC (3d) 391 (SCC).

the minimum constitutional standards by requiring proof of an intent to commit murder as the fault requirement for attempted murder.[298]

In Finta,[299] the Court indicated that the "stigma and opprobrium" that would accompany conviction of crimes against humanity or war crimes required the Crown to prove that the accused knew, was aware of, or was wilfully blind to the aggravating facts and circumstances that would make crimes such as robbery or manslaughter a war crime or a crime against humanity. In the subsequent Mugesera v Canada (Minister of Citizenship and Immigration) case,[300] the Court recognized that in international criminal law "it is now well settled that in addition to the mens rea for the underlying act, the accused must have knowledge of the attack and must know that his or her acts comprise part of it or take the risk that his or her acts will compromise part of it."[301] The Court has reformulated the Finta holding as requiring that "the accused must have knowledge of the attack and must know that his or her acts are part of the attack [constituting a crime against humanity], or at least take the risk that they are part of the attack."[302] The Court did not advert to the requirements of section 7 of the Charter, but this reformulated fault requirement would allow recklessness with respect to the conditions that make a crime a war crime or a crime against humanity. Although recklessness is a subjective form of fault that requires proof that the accused adverted to the prohibited risk, it is a lower and lesser form of fault than knowledge or even wilful blindness, which was previously the lowest constitutionally required fault element for war crimes. Knowledge remains the minimal fault requirement under section 7 of the Charter with respect to murder and attempted murder.

Beyond the limited context of murder, attempted murder, and war crimes, the Supreme Court has refused to require subjective fault under section 7 of the Charter. The Court has held that the stigma attached to offences such as unlawfully causing bodily harm, dangerous driving, misleading advertising, careless use of a firearm, failure to provide the necessities of life, and unlawful act manslaughter is not sufficient to require proof of subjective as opposed to objective fault. The stigma concept has often been criticized as circular and tautological, but there is no consensus that the Court should constitutionalize subjective fault beyond the offence of murder and attempted murder.

---

298 R v Ancio, [1984] 1 SCR 225, discussed in Chapter 4.
299 Finta, above note 209 at 499–503.
300 [2005] 2 SCR 100.
301 Ibid at para 173 [emphasis in original].
302 Ibid at para 176.

Even if subjective fault is required as an essential element of an offence under section 7 of the *Charter*, it is theoretically possible that another fault element could be substituted for that essential element. Following the section 11(d) jurisprudence outlined above, Parliament can substitute proof of another element for an essential element if proof of the substituted element leads inexorably to proof of the essential element, so that the trier of fact could not have a reasonable doubt about the essential element. In *Martineau*, the majority held that proof of the *mens rea* for the underlying offence and the intent to cause bodily harm did not lead inexorably to the conclusion that the accused had the essential element of subjective foresight of death.[303] Proving under section 230(c) of the *Criminal Code* that the accused "wilfully stops, by any means, the breath of a human being" also does not lead inexorably to proof that the accused had subjective foresight of death.[304] In cases of suffocation, it is now necessary to charge the accused with murder under section 229 of the *Criminal Code* and prove that he or she had subjective foresight that death was likely to result. The jury could infer from the attempt at suffocation that the accused knew that death was likely, but it cannot be required by the wording of the offence to draw this inference. Following the presumption of innocence, the jury would be obliged to acquit the accused of murder if it had a reasonable doubt about his or her subjective foresight of death for any reason, including intoxication or diminished intelligence.

In both *Vaillancourt* and *Martineau*, the Supreme Court considered whether the violation of sections 7 and 11(d) of the *Charter* could be justified under section 1 of the *Charter*. The Court stated that the goals of the "felony murder" provisions — namely, deterring the carrying of weapons and the use of force when committing serious crimes such as robbery — were important enough to justify overriding a constitutional right. The Court also conceded that there was a rational connection between the objective of deterrence and convicting those who caused death but did not have subjective knowledge that death would result. However, in both cases the Court concluded that the restrictions on sections 7 and 11(d) were not reasonable because there were

---

303 In dissent, L'Heureux-Dubé J argued that proof of the substituted element would lead to the "inexorable conclusion" that there was objective foreseeability of death which, in her view, should be the constitutionally required minimal mental element for murder. *Martineau*, above note 294 at 375.

304 *R v Sit* (1991), 66 CCC (3d) 449 at 453 (SCC). Similar reasoning would apply to *Code*, above note 1, s 230(b), providing that a person who "administers a stupefying or overpowering thing" in order to facilitate an offence was guilty of murder if death ensues.

other ways Parliament could achieve its objectives. Parliament could punish for the possession of a weapon while committing an offence as a separate offence.[305] In cases where death results from the possession of a weapon or the infliction of harm, "very stiff" sentences for manslaughter would be available. The Court concluded that

> [t]o label and punish a person as a murderer who did not intend or foresee death unnecessarily stigmatizes and punishes those whose moral blameworthiness is not that of a murderer, and thereby unnecessarily impairs the rights guaranteed by ss. 7 and 11(d) of the *Charter*.[306]

In other words, departures from constitutional requirements of subjective fault could not be justified under section 1 of the *Charter* because of the availability of other means more respectful of *Charter* rights to pursue the state's legitimate objective of deterring the use of weapons and violence in the commission of crimes.

e) Criminal Defences

As will be examined in greater depth in Chapters 7 through 9, statutory or common law restrictions on defences may also violate the *Charter*. One exception is if a defence would be inconsistent with the very purpose of an offence. For example, intoxication is not recognized as a defence for impaired driving.[307] At the same time, however, the courts have been most active with respect to the defence of intoxication and have held that various common law restrictions on that defence violate section 7 of the *Charter*. They have expressed concern that not considering evidence of extreme intoxication when an accused is charged with a general intent offence such as assault or sexual assault could result in the conviction of the morally innocent, at least in cases where the accused is so extremely intoxicated that he or she is in a state akin to automatism and acts in an involuntary manner.[308] The Court has also changed traditional common law rules that focus on whether evidence of intoxication raises a reasonable doubt about the accused's capacity to commit a specific intent crime such as murder because they

---

305 The use of a firearm while committing an offence is punishable as a separate offence with a mandatory minimum sentence of one year's imprisonment. *Code, ibid*, s 85. The commission of certain offences with a firearm such as robbery now has a mandatory minimum sentence of five years. *Code, ibid*, s 344.

306 *Martineau*, above note 294 at 362.

307 *R v Penno* (1990), 59 CCC (3d) 344 (SCC).

308 *Daviault*, above note 193. But see now *Code*, above note 1, s 33.1, both discussed in Chapter 7, Section E(2).

could allow the conviction of an accused who may have been capable of having the required intent, but did not actually have the intent.[309]

The Supreme Court has held that section 43 of the *Criminal Code*, which authorizes parents and teachers to use reasonable force to correct a child or pupil, does not violate sections 7, 12, or 15 of the *Charter*. The Court acknowledged that the defence affected the security of the person of children, but held that it was not so vague or overbroad as to violate section 7 of the *Charter*. As suggested above, this case demonstrates how judicial interpretation of a law can save it from being held to violate section 7 because of vagueness or overbreadth.

The Court also indicated that the "best interests of the child" was not a principle of fundamental justice; that the application of reasonable force was not cruel and unusual; and that the offence did not demean the equal dignity of children. The later holding was related to the adverse effects that striking down section 43 would have on families and ultimately on children because it would criminalize all applications of force without the child's consent. The Court also indicated that restrictions or denials of defences could violate the *Charter* with the exception of cases in which the defence would be inconsistent with the nature of the offence. For example, the purpose of the offence of intoxicated driving would be defeated if the *Charter* was interpreted to allow an accused to raise the defence of intoxication.[310]

f) Physical and Moral Involuntariness
The principles of fundamental justice may be violated if the accused was convicted for involuntary conduct. The courts have recognized two forms of involuntariness: physical and moral involuntariness.

The courts have long held that it is unfair to convict a person in the absence of a "willing mind at liberty to make a definite choice or decision."[311] A person who lost control of a vehicle because of involuntary actions after a heart attack, a seizure, or a sudden injury could not be said to be acting voluntarily. The Supreme Court has recognized that voluntariness in this basic physical sense is a long-recognized principle of fundamental justice and concluded that "punishing a person whose actions are involuntary in the physical sense is unjust because it conflicts with the assumption in criminal law that individuals are autonomous and freely choosing agents."[312] It has similarly indicated that "according to a traditional fundamental principle of the common

---

309 *R v Robinson* (1996), 105 CCC (3d) 97 (SCC).
310 *Canadian Foundation for Children*, above note 233.
311 *R v King* (1962), 133 CCC 1 at 3 (SCC).
312 *R v Ruzic*, 2001 SCC 24 at paras 46 & 47 [*Ruzic*].

law, criminal responsibility can result only from the commission of a voluntary act. This important principle is based on a recognition that it would be unfair in a democratic society to impose the consequences and stigma of criminal responsibility on an accused who did not voluntarily commit an act that constitutes a criminal offence."[313]

The Court has also recognized the related but different notion that the principles of fundamental justice will be violated by punishing a person who commits a crime in a "morally involuntary" manner. A person acts in a morally involuntary manner if he or she did not have "any realistic choice" in the circumstances but to commit the crime. "In the case of morally involuntary conduct, criminal attribution points not to the accused but to exigent circumstances facing him, or to threats of someone else . . . . Depriving a person of liberty and branding her with the stigma of criminal liability would infringe the principles of fundamental justice if the accused did not have any realistic choice."[314] A person who commits a crime in such exigent circumstances acts in a morally involuntary manner even though he or she committed the crime with a physically voluntary act and with the required fault element and even if he or she cannot be said to be morally innocent.

Applying the principle of fundamental justice that a person should not be punished for morally involuntary actions, the Supreme Court has held that severe statutory restrictions under section 17 of the *Criminal Code* on the defence of duress violate section 7 of the *Charter* because they would allow the conviction of a person who had no realistic choice but to commit the crime in response to threats. The Court struck down the requirement under section 17 of the *Criminal Code* that threats must be of immediate death or bodily harm from a person who is present when the offence is committed.[315] In that case and subsequently in *R v Ryan*,[315] the Supreme Court left open the question of whether the categorical restrictions in section 17 on the commission of a long list of offences in response to threats would also violate section 7 of the *Charter*.[317] The decision in *Ruzic* points in the direction of striking down such offence-based exclusion on the defence of duress if the accused committed such offences when he or she had no realistic choice but to do so. If the accused acted in a morally involuntary manner then a conviction should violate section 7 of the *Charter*. The Court

---

313   *R v Bouchard-Lebrun*, [2011] 3 SCR 575 at para 45 [*Bouchard-Lebrun*].
314   *Ruzic*, above note 312 at para 46.
315   *Ibid.*
316   [2013] 1 SCR 14.
317   Courts of appeal have reached different conclusions on the exclusion of the murder offence from the defence of duress. See Chapter 9, Section D(2).

in *Ruzic* indicated that violations of section 7 of the *Charter* can be justified only in "exceptional circumstances, such as the outbreak of war or a national emergency"[318] and the Court has never held that a section 7 violation was justified under section 1. Even if it was willing to do so, categorical restrictions on the section 17 defence will be difficult for the government to justify because the common law duress defence has been applied to serious crimes, including murder.

A person who qualifies for a mental disorder defence under section 16 of the *Charter* also acts in a morally involuntary manner because he or she has no "moral control"[319] over his or her actions. A person who qualifies for the mental disorder defence "is incapable of morally voluntary conduct. The person's actions are not actually the product of his or her free will . . . . Convicting a person who acted involuntarily would undermine the foundations of the criminal law and the integrity of the judicial system."[320] One consequence of holding that those with a section 16 mental disorder defence act in a morally involuntary manner is that an attempt to repeal or restrict the sometimes unpopular defence would violate the principle of fundamental justice that a person not be punished for morally involuntary conduct. As seen above, the courts have not yet accepted section 1 justifications for violations of section 7 of the *Charter*, though section 7, like other legal rights, can be subject to a temporary and renewable override under section 33 of the *Charter*, again a feature that has not yet been used with respect to the criminal law.

5) The *Charter* and Punishment

The *Charter* places restrictions on the state's ability to punish people for criminal offences. Section 12 provides that everyone has the right not to be subjected to cruel and unusual treatment or punishment and the Court's jurisprudence on this issue will be examined in Chapter 11. In general, however, section 12 of the *Charter* prohibits grossly disproportionate punishments.[321] A judge who concludes that a mandatory sentence imposes cruel and unusual punishment must strike down the sentence and is not allowed to craft a constitutional exception or exemption from the mandatory sentence.[322]

In a landmark case, the Supreme Court has interpreted section 7 of the *Charter* generally to preclude the extradition of a fugitive to face trial

---

318 *Ruzic*, above note 312 at para 92.
319 *Bouchard-Lebrun*, above note 313 at para 47.
320 *Ibid* at para 51.
321 *R v Smith* (1987), 34 CCC (3d) 97 (SCC); *R v Nur*, 2015 SCC 15.
322 *R v Ferguson*, 2008 SCC 6.

in another country unless assurances are received that the death penalty will not be applied. The Court stressed both an emerging international consensus on this issue and the risk of wrongful convictions.[323] This decision reviews a number of wrongful convictions that have occurred in Canada, the United Kingdom, and the United States and stands as an important reminder of the inherent fallibility of the criminal process.

Section 11(h) provides protection against double jeopardy, which is being tried or punished twice for the same offence. This does not preclude criminal trials after a person has been tried on disciplinary charges at work or in prison.[324] In Canada, protection against double jeopardy applies only if a person has been "finally acquitted of the offence." This right accommodates the generous rights of appeal that the prosecutor enjoys in Canada, which allow an appeal even after a jury has acquitted the accused.[325] The section is violated, however, if the accused is retried for the same offence after an acquittal, as opposed to having the Crown take a more limited appeal on specific grounds that the trial court had made errors of law.[326] The principle of double jeopardy also prohibits conviction for multiple offences if there are no additional or distinguishing elements among the offences.[327] Thus, an accused could not be convicted of using a firearm while committing an indictable offence and of pointing a firearm, because there is no distinguishing element between these two offences.[328] It can also be violated in cases where the parole ineligibility of convicted offenders is increased dramatically and retroactively.[329]

CONCLUSION

Constitutional law has a pervasive and foundational influence on criminal law and it is relevant at all stages of the criminal process. The division of powers limits the enactment of criminal law to Parliament but allows provinces and municipalities to enact regulatory offences.

---

323 *United States of America v Burns and Rafay* (2001), 151 CCC (3d) 97 (SCC), effectively reversing *Kindler v Canada (Minister of Justice)* (1991), 67 CCC (3d) 1 (SCC).

324 *R v Wigglesworth* (1987), 37 CCC (3d) 385 (SCC); *R v Shubley* (1990), 52 CCC (3d) 481 (SCC).

325 *Morgentaler (No 2)*, above note 226.

326 *Corp professionelles des médecins (Québec) v Thibault* (1988), 42 CCC (3d) 1 (SCC).

327 See also *Code*, above note 1, s 12.

328 *R v Krug* (1985), 21 CCC (3d) 193 (SCC). See also *R v Kienapple* (1974), 15 CCC (2d) 524 (SCC).

329 *Canada (AG) v Whaling*, [2014] 1 SCR 392.

Sections 7 to 10 of the *Charter* restrain the investigative activities of the police. These rights are enforced primarily by the decisions of courts under section 24(2) of the *Charter* to exclude unconstitutionally obtained evidence if its admission would bring the administration of justice into disrepute. In the *Charter* era, Canadian courts are also prepared to stay proceedings if the accused has been entrapped into committing a crime. At the same time, the entrapment defence allows police to offer people an opportunity to commit a crime so long as they have a reasonable suspicion that the suspect is engaged in criminal activity or the suspect is present in a high-crime area. Even if they have a reasonable suspicion or are acting on a *bona fide* inquiry into crime, the police cannot actually induce the commission of a crime by shocking activity that would bring the administration of justice into disrepute.

The *Charter* affects the trial process by giving the accused various rights including the right to make full answer and defence and the right to be presumed innocent. The presumption of innocence is violated whenever the accused has to establish an element of an offence or a defence on a balance of probabilities because this allows a conviction to occur despite a reasonable doubt. Even mandatory presumptions that can be displaced by satisfying an evidential burden violate the presumption of innocence. At the same time, the courts have frequently accepted limitations on the presumption of innocence as reasonable limits and have, on their own initiative, required the accused to establish the defences of extreme intoxication and automatism on a balance of probabilities.

The *Charter* also affects substantive criminal offences that infringe freedom of expression, are excessively vague, overbroad, arbitrary, grossly disproportionate, or allow the punishment of the morally innocent. These matters will be discussed in greater depth in subsequent chapters, but it should be noted that section 7 of the *Charter* is offended by imprisonment of the morally innocent who have committed a prohibited act but through no fault of their own. The courts have found that because of their penalty and stigma, a few crimes —murder, attempted murder, and war crimes— require proof of subjective fault in relation to their *actus reus*. The Court has not, however, extended such requirements to the vast majority of crimes. For crimes such as manslaughter, objective fault is constitutionally sufficient and does not have to extend to all aspects of the *actus reus* or require that the reasonable person be endowed with the same characteristics as the accused. Section 7 of the *Charter* also prevents people from being convicted for conduct that is either physically or morally involuntary.

Section 7 of the *Charter* may also be violated by restrictions on defences. As examined in greater depth in Chapters 7 and 9, restrictions on the intoxication and duress defences have been struck down under section 7 of the *Charter*. The Court has recognized a general principle under section 7 of the *Charter* that people should not be punished for crimes that are committed in a morally involuntary manner in the sense that they have no realistic choice but to commit the crime. This principle protects a variety of defences, including duress and mental disorder, from legislative repeal. Although many of these matters will be revisited in subsequent chapters, it is important to have a sense of how the *Charter* affects the entire criminal process and how constitutional law has become fundamental to the criminal law in Canada.

FURTHER READINGS

BERGER, B, & J STRIBOPOULOS, EDS. *Unsettled Legacy: Thirty Years of Criminal Justice under the* Charter (Toronto: LexisNexis, 2012).

CAMERON, J, & J STRIBOPOULOS, EDS. *The* Charter *and Criminal Justice: Twenty-Five Years Later* (Markham, ON: LexisNexis, 2008).

COUGHLAN, S. *Criminal Procedure*, 3d ed (Toronto: Irwin Law, 2016).

HOGG, PW. *Constitutional Law of Canada*, 5th ed (Toronto: Carswell, 2007) ch 18–19, 33–41, and 44–52.

PENNEY, S, V RONDINELLI, & J STRIBOPOULOS. *Criminal Procedure in Canada*, 2d ed (Markham, ON: LexisNexis, 2016).

QUIGLEY, T. *Procedure in Canadian Criminal Law*, 2d ed (Toronto: Carswell, 2005).

ROACH, K. *Constitutional Remedies in Canada*, 2d ed (Aurora, ON: Canada Law Book, as updated) ch 9 & 10.

————. *Due Process and Victims' Rights: The New Law and Politics of Criminal Justice* (Toronto: University of Toronto Press, 1999) ch 2–5.

SHARPE, RJ, & K ROACH. *The Charter of Rights and Freedoms*, 6th ed (Toronto: Irwin Law, 2017).

STEWART, H. *Fundamental Justice: Section 7 of the* Charter (Toronto: Irwin Law, 2012).

STUART, D. Charter *Justice in Canadian Criminal Law*, 7th ed (Toronto: Carswell, 2018).

CHAPTER 3

THE PROHIBITED ACT, OR *ACTUS REUS*

The *actus reus*, or prohibited act, is defined by the legislation creating the specific criminal or regulatory offence. In order to ensure that there is fixed predetermined law, the courts cannot create crimes on their own. For similar reasons, the *Charter*[1] provides important protections against vague or retroactive criminal laws. For example, laws may be struck down under section 7 of the *Charter* if they are so vague that they do not provide fair notice of what is prohibited, or any limitation on law enforcement discretion. Retroactive criminal laws would also violate section 11(g) of the *Charter* because they would fail to give people fair notice of the act or omission that is prohibited and section 11(i) similarly protects against retroactive punishments.

Although legislatures define the prohibited act, courts play an important role in interpreting the words used to define crimes. The determination of the precise scope of the prohibited act is largely a matter of statutory interpretation. Courts will interpret all statutes in a manner designed to achieve their purposes, but in cases of reasonable ambiguity, they will resort to a doctrine of strict construction of the criminal law that will favour the liberty of the accused as well as the need for clarity and fair notice in defining what is prohibited. This is also consistent with the ideal of a fixed predetermined law that clearly alerts people to what is prohibited.

---

1   *Canadian Charter of Rights and Freedoms*, Part I of the *Constitution Act, 1982,* being Schedule B to the *Canada Act 1982* (UK), 1982, c 11 [*Charter*].

The ideal of a fixed, predetermined law should in theory allow citizens to determine beforehand whether conduct is illegal. This is important because the criminal law has traditionally not allowed ignorance or mistakes about the law to be an excuse for a crime. Section 19 of the *Criminal Code* provides that ignorance of the law is not an excuse. This generally means that a mistaken belief by accused that their actions are legal will not be a defence to a crime whereas mistakes about the existence of essential facts can be an excuse that will prevent the prosecution from establishing *mens rea*. There are limited exceptions to this rule with respect to officially induced error and particular forms of *mens rea* for theft and fraud that allow accused to argue that they were acting with a "colour of right" in that they thought they were legally entitled to take property. This chapter will examine not only the prohibited act, but the related principle that legal ignorance or mistakes are not excuses.

In order to obtain a conviction for a criminal or a regulatory offence, the Crown must always prove beyond a reasonable doubt that the accused committed the prohibited act (*actus reus*).[2] The *actus reus* is only one element of a criminal offence. In theory, the prohibited act must coincide with the fault element, or *mens rea*, for a crime to be committed. It will be seen in this chapter that the courts have sometimes finessed this requirement, often by defining the criminal act in a broad fashion so that it overlaps with a time in which the accused had the required fault element.

Although the criminal law generally keeps the physical and mental elements of crimes distinct, an emerging line of authority suggests that an accused who acts involuntarily may not have committed an *actus reus*. This interpretation effectively builds a minimal mental element into the *actus reus*. As a practical matter, it could prevent the court from convicting an accused who acted in an involuntary and unconscious manner even though the offence may have no fault element or one based on negligence. The accused can raise a defence of accident as a means to raise a reasonable doubt about the voluntariness of the criminal act.

Sometimes when determining whether the accused has committed the *actus reus*, it is necessary to determine if he or she caused some prohibited result. Causation is defined broadly in homicide cases so that an accused may be held to have caused another's death even though

---

2   The Supreme Court has held that it is an error of law for the trial judge to instruct the jury that they must find an unlawful act. *R v Gunning*, 2005 SCC 27 at paras 30–31 [*Gunning*].

other factors, such as lack of medical treatment or the victim's "thin skull," contributed to the death. This approach fits into the trend towards expansive definitions of the criminal act.

The criminal law has traditionally been reluctant to punish an omission or a failure to act, but some criminal and regulatory offences punish people for failing to act or to fulfill specific legal duties. The *Criminal Code* tends to impose duties on specific groups of persons such as parents and guardians and not the public at large. For example, it is an offence for parents and guardians to omit or fail to provide children with the necessities of life,[3] but it is not a crime for a person not to take reasonable steps to help a stranger in peril.

Finally, this chapter will examine how the *actus reus* or prohibited act as initially enacted by the legislature and then interpreted by the courts has important policy components. For example, in 1983 the offence of rape, which was defined as non-consensual sexual intercourse by a man with a woman who was not his wife, was replaced with the broader, gender-neutral offence of sexual assault that applied to all persons. In 1992 the law of sexual assault was again changed, with Parliament defining consent and stating specific instances in which consent did not exist. The Supreme Court subsequently decided that for purposes of determining the *actus reus*, consent should be based on the subjective views of the complainant. In 2018, Parliament returned to the definition of the *actus reus* of sexual assault. Bill C-51 provides that no consent is obtained if the complainant is unconscious or otherwise incapable of consenting and that consent must be present at the time of the sexual activity. It also stated that a number of situations where consent is claimed are questions of law,[4] thus making clear that section 19 of the *Code* prohibiting ignorance or mistakes of law applied.

Courts also contribute to the policies that inform different definitions of the *actus reus*. Examples include the Supreme Court's decision that consent for the purpose of assault will be nullified or vitiated for reasons of public policy when serious bodily harm is intended and caused.[5] This ruling had the effect of turning some consensual fist fights into assaults. Finally, the broad nature of many of the prohibited acts

---

3   *Criminal Code*, RSC 1985, c C-46, s 215 [*Code*].
4   Bill C-51, *An Act to Amend the Criminal Code and the Department of Justice Act and to Make Consequential Amendments to Another Act*, 1st Sess, 42nd Parl, 2017, proposed s 273.1 (in committee, Senate).
5   *R v Jobidon*, [1991] 2 SCR 714 [*Jobidon*]; *R v Paice*, [2005] 1 SCR 339 [*Paice*].

in the *Criminal Code*[6] requires the judge to distinguish at sentencing among the relative culpability of various levels of participation in crimes.

A. THE LEGISLATIVE CREATION AND JUDICIAL INTERPRETATION OF THE CRIMINAL ACT

1) Codification

Since 1953, section 9 of the *Criminal Code* has provided that no person shall be convicted of an offence at common law (judge-made law) except contempt of court. To be convicted of a criminal or regulatory offence in Canada, a person must do something that is prohibited by a valid statute or regulation enacted by the legislature. This requirement accords with the ideal that one should not be punished except in accordance with fixed, predetermined law.

Even before the enactment of section 9 of the *Criminal Code,* Canadian courts were reluctant to create common law or judge-made crimes on the basis that they

> would introduce great uncertainty into the administration of the criminal law, leaving it to the judicial officer trying any particular charge to decide that the acts proved constituted a crime or otherwise, not by reference to any defined standard to be found in the *Code* or in reported decisions, but according to his individual view as to whether such acts were a disturbance of the tranquillity of people tending to provoke physical reprisal.[7]

The Court thus held that a common law charge of acting in a manner likely to cause a breach of the peace by being a "peeping Tom" was not sustainable.[8] In contrast, courts in England continue to exercise "a residual power, where no statute has yet intervened to supersede the common law, to superintend those offenses which are prejudicial to the

---

6   Including the provisions governing liability as a party or accomplice to an offence and prohibiting attempts to commit crimes. See Chapter 4.

7   *Frey v Fedoruk* (1950), 97 CCC 1 at 14 (SCC). The Supreme Court interpreted a previous offence against conspiring to effect an unlawful purpose to require a purpose contrary to federal and provincial legislation as opposed to the common law. *R v Gralewicz* (1980), 54 CCC (3d) 289 (SCC).

8   Parliament subsequently enacted a new crime of loitering and prowling at night on the property of another person near a dwelling house. See *Code,* above note 3, s 177.

public welfare."[9] Crimes such as conspiracy to corrupt public morals or to outrage public decency have been created under this common law power. In Canada, a person can only be convicted for conspiring to commit an offence created by a legislature and defined in law.

The only remaining judge-made crime in Canada, contempt of court, has been upheld under the *Charter* on the basis that codification is not required as a principle of fundamental justice and that uncodified crimes can still be consistent with the principle of fixed, predetermined law. The Court stressed that an accused could predict in advance if conduct constituted contempt of court and that a prohibited act and fault must be proven beyond a reasonable doubt to result in a conviction for contempt of court.[10] Thus, there is no constitutional requirement under section 7 of the *Charter* that all crimes be codified by legislation. This does not, however, mean that the *Charter* cannot be applied to the exercise of the contempt power. Some attempts by judges to punish people for contempt of court have been found to violate *Charter* rights, such as the right to an impartial tribunal and to freedom of expression.[11] At the same time, the very concept of a judge-made or common law offence does not offend the principles of fundamental justice.

2) Territorial and Age-Based Restrictions in the Application of the *Criminal Code*

The basic rule in section 6(2) of the *Criminal Code* is that no person can be convicted for offences committed outside Canada.[12] This rule is subject to various exceptions including for war crimes, crimes committed on aircrafts, crimes in relation to dangerous nuclear materials, sexual offences committed against children by Canadians while abroad, and crimes of terrorism.[13] The conspiracy provisions in section 465 are also

---

9   *Shaw v DPP*, [1962] AC 220 at 268 (HL).

10   *UNA v Alberta (AG)* (1992), 71 CCC (3d) 225 at 253–54 (SCC).

11   *R v Martin* (1985), 19 CCC (3d) 248 (Ont CA); *R v Kopyto* (1987), 39 CCC (3d) 1 (Ont CA). Before determining whether a person is guilty of contempt of court, judges should give the person notice and an opportunity to be represented by counsel and to make representations. The judge should avoid making determinations that will taint the fairness of the trial. *R v K(B)* (1995), 102 CCC (3d) 18 (SCC); *R v Arradi*, [2003] 1 SCR 280.

12   A person in Canada who has committed a crime elsewhere can, subject to *Charter* standards, be sent back or be extradited to that country. *Extradition Act*, RSC 1985, c E-23.

13   *Code*, above note 3, s 7. See also s 46(3) (treason); s 57 (forging a passport); s 58 (fraudulent use of citizenship certificate); s 74 (piracy); s 290 (bigamy); s 462.3 (enterprise crime).

worded broadly to apply to those who conspire outside Canada to commit a crime within Canada, and to those who conspire inside Canada to commit a crime outside Canada. Other crimes including treason and torture are defined so that they can apply to conduct outside Canada.

Section 13 of the *Criminal Code* provides that no person shall be convicted of an offence committed while that person was under twelve years of age.[14] Before 1983, only those under seven were deemed incapable of committing a crime, and those between seven and fourteen years of age could be convicted only if they "were competent to know the nature and consequence of their conduct and to appreciate that it was wrong."[15]

3) The *Charter* and the Criminal Act

The value of certainty and having a predefined criminal law is supported by some *Charter* rights. As discussed in Chapter 2, section 11(a) gives an accused the right to be informed without unreasonable delay of the specific offence charged; section 11(g) provides that the act or omission must, at the time it was committed, have been illegal under Canadian or international law and section 11(i) protects against retroactive punishment by giving the accused the benefit of any lesser punishment.

As discussed in Chapter 2, a law that is excessively vague because it does not give fair notice to citizens of what is prohibited, or place any limits on law enforcement discretion, violates section 7 of the *Charter*. This is sometimes known as the "void for vagueness doctrine." Although the words used in statutes to define criminal acts cannot provide certainty, they should provide some boundaries of permissible and non-permissible conduct. When determining whether an offence is excessively vague, the courts examine not only the words used by Parliament, but also the cases in which courts have interpreted those words. In other words, "a court can conclude that a law is unconstitutionally vague only after exhausting its interpretive function."[16] In many cases, these interpretations add more certainty about what is prohibited, and limit the extent of the criminal prohibition. For example, the Supreme Court has held that statutory prohibitions against "bawdy houses," or commercial behaviour that "lessens, unduly, competition,"

---

14 Those who are twelve years of age but under eighteen may be convicted of *Criminal Code* offences, but they are tried and punished under the provisions of the *Youth Criminal Justice Act*, SC 2002, c 1.

15 *Criminal Code*, RSC 1970, c C-34, s 13.

16 *R v Levkovic*, [2013] 2 SCR 204 at para 47 [*Levkovic*].

are not vague, in large part because courts have been able to give these statutory phrases ascertainable meanings.[17] As McLachlin J has stated:

> Laws must of necessity cover a variety of situations. Given the infinite variability of conduct, it is impossible to draft laws that precisely foresee each case that might arise. It is the task of judges, aided by precedent and considerations like the text and purpose of a statute, to interpret laws of general application and decide whether they apply to the facts before the court in a particular case. This process is not in breach of the principles of fundamental justice; rather, it is in the best tradition of our system of justice.[18]

Most challenges to criminal laws as excessively vague have failed. The Supreme Court has upheld a regulatory offence against impairing the quality of the natural environment for any use that can be made of it, on the basis that the legislature should be able to use broadly worded offences to protect the environment.[19] Statutes that allow people to be detained in order to protect public safety have also been found not to be excessively vague.[20] A challenge that the offence of failing to obtain assistance in childbirth was unconstitutionally vague failed, but only after the Court interpreted the offence to require proof that the child would have been likely to have lived. The fact that expert testimony might be required to determine this standard did not render the offence unconstitutionally vague.[21]

Section 43 of the *Criminal Code* was held by a majority of the Court not to be unduly vague or overbroad in authorizing the use of force to correct children that is "reasonable under the circumstances." Chief Justice McLachlin noted that "the criminal law often uses the concept of reasonableness to accommodate evolving mores and avoid successive 'fine-tuning' amendments. It is implicit in this technique that current social consensus on what is reasonable may be considered." The fact that the defence had been subject to varying interpretations in the past was not fatal because it could still be given "a core meaning in tune with contemporary standards" and because it "sets real boundaries and a risk

---

17   *Reference re ss 193 & 195(1)(c) of the Criminal Code (Canada)* (1990), 56 CCC (3d) 65 (SCC); *R v Nova Scotia Pharmaceutical Society* (1992), 74 CCC (3d) 289 (SCC).

18   *Winko v British Columbia (Forensic Psychiatric Institute)* (1999), 135 CCC (3d) 129 at 166–67 (SCC) [*Winko*].

19   *R v Canadian Pacific Ltd* (1995), 99 CCC (3d) 97 (SCC).

20   *R v Morales* (1992), 77 CCC (3d) 91 (SCC); *Winko*, above note 18.

21   *Levkovic*, above note 16.

zone for criminal sanction."[22] In this case, the Court placed several new restrictions on the ambit of the defence that clarified its availability. For example, the Court indicated that it would not be reasonable to use force on children under two or over twelve years of age or to use objects or blows to the head. This case affirms that the key question in "void for vagueness" challenges is not the vagueness of the language used by Parliament or even the variety of interpretations placed on the law in the past, but rather the Court's ability to interpret the law in an intelligible manner that establishes a "risk zone" for the use of the criminal law. One consequence of the Court's approach is that the public and law enforcement officials can be misled by simply reading the terms Parliament has employed in the *Criminal Code* and that they will have to consult the Court's jurisprudence to understand the precise extent of the criminal law.

4) Strict and Purposive Construction of the Criminal Law

Another means that pre-dates the *Charter* of ensuring that the criminal law is fixed and predetermined is for courts to apply the doctrine that it should be interpreted or construed strictly to the benefit of the accused. This doctrine has been defined by the Supreme Court as follows:

> It is unnecessary to emphasize the importance of clarity and certainty when freedom is at stake . . . . [I]f real ambiguities are found, or doubts of substance arise, in the construction and application of a statute affecting the liberty of a subject, then that statute should be applied in such a manner as to favour the person against whom it is sought to be enforced. If one is to be incarcerated, one should at least know that some Act of Parliament requires it in express terms, and not, at most, by implication.[23]

This doctrine was used most extensively three hundred years ago when even comparatively minor criminal offences, such as theft, were subject to capital punishment. The Supreme Court has stated that "while the original justification for the doctrine has been substantially eroded, the seriousness of imposing criminal penalties of any sort demands that reasonable doubts be resolved in favour of the accused."[24] For example, the word "conceals" in the criminal offence of removing, concealing, or disposing of property with the intent to defraud creditors has been

---

22 *Canadian Foundation for Children, Youth and the Law v Canada (AG)*, 2004 SCC 4 at paras 36, 39, and 42 [*Canadian Foundation for Children*].

23 *Marcotte v Canada (Deputy AG)* (1976), 19 CCC (2d) 257 at 262 (SCC).

24 *R v Paré* (1987), 38 CCC (3d) 97 at 106 (SCC) [*Paré*].

interpreted as requiring "a positive act done for the purpose of secreting the debtor's property."[25] The accused would have concealed property if he had hidden it in a remote warehouse, but he did not conceal it simply because he failed to tell bankruptcy officials about its existence. Similarly, people would be guilty of causing a public disturbance only if their shouting, swearing, or singing caused a foreseeable interference with the use of a public place, not mere mental annoyance.[26] Similarly, the offence of failure to seek assistance in childbirth applies only if the child was likely to have lived.[27]

Strict construction in favour of the liberty of the accused suggests that offences, but not defences, should be given a restrictive reading. In *R v McIntosh*,[28] the Court invoked strict construction as a rationale for giving the statutory defence of self-defence a reading that favoured the liberty of the accused, as opposed to one that expanded the scope of criminal liability. This rule is not, however, absolute. The Court saved the defence in section 43 of the *Code* of using "reasonable" corrective force against children from a challenge that it was vague and overbroad under section 7 of the *Charter* by reading several categorical restrictions into the defence that was available to the accused.[29] The Court has also recently added common law requirements, such as a reasonable belief in threats, no safe avenue of escape, and proportionality between harm threatened and caused, that have the effect of restricting the duress defence as defined by Parliament in section 17 of the *Code*.[30] In both the sections 43 and 17 cases, the Court's interpretation restricted defences that were available to the accused, indicating that strict construction of the criminal law in favour of the accused and liberty interest is not an invariable rule.

Strict construction of offences in the criminal law is in some tension with modern purposive approaches to statutory interpretation. Purposive approaches acknowledge the limits of grammatical or dictionary-based interpretation of words and instruct courts to look at the broader purposes of a particular statute. For example, section 12 of the *Inter-*

---

25   *R v Goulis* (1981), 60 CCC (2d) 347 (Ont CA). The accused was acquitted of the criminal offence, but at the same time convicted of regulatory offences under the *Bankruptcy Act*, RSC 1985, c B-3, which required him to divulge such information.

26   *R v Lohnes* (1992), 69 CCC (3d) 289 (SCC).

27   *Levkovic*, above note 16.

28   (1995), 95 CCC (3d) 481 at 493 (SCC).

29   *Canadian Foundation for Children*, above note 22.

30   *R v Ryan*, 2013 SCC 3 [*Ryan*], discussed in Chapter 9.

pretation Act,[31] which applies to all federal law including the *Criminal Code*,[32] states:

> Every enactment is deemed remedial, and shall be given such fair, large and liberal construction and interpretation as best ensures the attainment of its objects.

The purposive approach to statutory interpretation has been reconciled with the doctrine of strict construction by holding that the preference for the interpretation that most favours the accused applies only if, after consulting the purposes of a statute, reasonable ambiguities remain in its meaning. Thus, a criminal law should first be given a purposive reading and the doctrine of strict construction applied only if there are still reasonable ambiguities after such a broad interpretation.

There are several examples of courts interpreting criminal laws in a purposive manner, even though more restrictive interpretations were grammatically possible. For example, in *Paré*,[33] the Supreme Court recognized that while "it is clearly grammatically possible to construe the words 'while committing' . . . as requiring murder to be classified as first degree only if it is exactly coincidental" with the offences listed in section 231(5) of the *Criminal Code*, it was not reasonable to attribute such a restrictive meaning to the provision. The Court held that the purpose of section 231(5) is to punish, as more severe, murders that were committed while the victim was being unlawfully dominated by the commission of an underlying offence. In the result, the Court held that a murder committed two minutes after the accused had indecently assaulted the victim was indeed committed while the indecent assault took place. The murder was part of the same transaction and the same continuous sequence of events involving the illegal domination of the young victim. There was no resort to the doctrine of strict construction because, considering the purpose of the provision, there was no reasonable ambiguity in the provision. Similar purposive reasoning has been applied to hold that an accused murders a person "while committing" a sexual assault, even if the sexual assault takes place after the victim has died;[34] that a police officer is murdered "acting in the course

---

31   RSC 1985, c I-21.

32   *R v Robinson* (1951), 100 CCC 1 (SCC); *R v Hasselwander* (1993), 81 CCC (3d) 471 (SCC) [*Hasselwander*]; *R v Gladue* (1999), 133 CCC (3d) 385 (SCC). The *Charter*, above note 1, is also accorded a broad and purposive interpretation by courts. See *Canada (Director of Investigation & Research Combines Investigation Branch) v Southam Inc* (1984), 14 CCC (3d) 97 (SCC).

33   Above note 24.

34   *R v Richer* (1993), 82 CCC (3d) 385 (Alta CA).

of his duties" when on duty, but not actually enforcing the law;[35] and that a firearm is a prohibited weapon "capable of firing bullets in rapid succession" if it can readily be converted to do so.[36]

In *R v Russell*,[37] the Supreme Court went beyond *Paré* to hold that first-degree murder can be committed even if the underlying offence was committed against a third party and not the person murdered. The Court stressed that strict construction was not relevant because the ordinary words of section 231(5) of the *Criminal Code* did not require that the underlying offence be committed against the victim. It dismissed the idea in *Paré* that first-degree murders were united by the unlawful domination of the murder victim as too narrow and restrictive given the wording of the statute. All that was necessary under section 231(5) was that the killing was "closely connected, temporally and causally, with an enumerated offence. As long as the connection exists, however, it is immaterial that the victim of the killing and the victim of the enumerated offence are not the same."[38] This case underlines that courts will not lightly resort to the doctrine of strict construction and will often give even the most serious criminal offences a generous reading if supported by the language of the enactment.

Resort is made to the doctrine of strict construction only if there are reasonable ambiguities in a law after it has been interpreted in a purposive manner consistent with its intent.[39] As the *Criminal Code* is federal legislation enacted in both French and English, both officially authoritative versions of the *Code* should be consulted to see if one of them resolves an ambiguity that may be present in the other version.[40] If, however, the English and French versions of the *Criminal Code* are not consistent, the Court should select the provision more restrictive to the state and favourable to the accused.[41] Such an approach is consistent

---

35   *R v Prevost* (1988), 42 CCC (3d) 314 (Ont CA).

36   *Hasselwander*, above note 32.

37   [2001] 2 SCR 804.

38   *Ibid* at para 43.

39   *CanadianOxy Chemicals v Canada*, [1999] 1 SCR 743 at para 14; *Bell Express Vu v Canada* (2002), 212 DLR (4th) 1 at para 21 (SCC).

40   *R v Mac* (2002), 163 CCC (3d) 1 (SCC) (ambiguity in English version resolved by French version); *R v Lamy* (2002), 162 CCC (3d) 353 (SCC) (ambiguity in French version resolved by English version).

41   "It would not be fair to propose an interpretation whereby in one language the elements of the *actus reus* would be met, but not in the other. If we adopted the English version, which is broader than the French one, this Court would be making an undue judicial amendment of the statute. For these reasons, the Court must favour the French version." *R v Daoust* (2004), 180 CCC (3d) 449 at para 37 (SCC). The Court has also applied this approach to the interpretation of

with the doctrine of the strict construction of the criminal law and its concerns that there be fair notice about criminal liability and that reasonable doubts be resolved in favour of the accused. After consulting the French version of the *Code*, the Ontario Court of Appeal acquitted an accused of forcible entry after he entered a friend's house while fleeing from the police. Although such an act could have constituted the prohibited act, the fact that the accused had visited the house before suggested that his entry was not likely to cause a breach of the peace or even a reasonable apprehension of a breach of a peace as required under section 72(1) of the *Code*.[42]

Although the Court has not made reference to the doctrine of strict construction, it has interpreted some indecency offences quite narrowly so as to maximize privacy and autonomy interests. In *R v Labaye*,[43] the Court overturned a conviction of keeping a common bawdy house with respect to a private and locked floor of a club that was used as a place for members and their guests to engage in group sex. A common bawdy house is defined as a place resorted to for the purpose of prostitution or acts of indecency. The Court interpreted acts of indecency to require conduct that by its nature

> causes harm or presents a significant risk of harm to individuals or society in a way that undermines or threatens to undermine a value reflected in and thus formally endorsed through the Constitution or similar fundamental laws by, for example: (a) confronting members of the public with conduct that significantly interferes with their autonomy and liberty; or (b) predisposing others to anti-social behaviour; or (c) physically or psychologically harming persons involved in the conduct, and that the harm or risk of harm is of a *degree* that is incompatible with the proper functioning of society.[44]

On the facts of the case, there was no evidence of harm or anti-social conduct in this case that involved consenting adults behind closed doors. Two judges dissented on the basis that the Court was substituting a new harm-based test for the traditional test of community tolerance that had been used to measure indecency. They concluded that

---

the *Charter* reading the reference to the requirement in s 24(2) that unconstitutionally obtained evidence shall be excluded if its admission "would" bring the administration of justice into disrepute as "could" on the basis of the reference in "less onerous" to the accused French use of "est susceptible." *R v Collins*, [1987] 1 SCR 265 at para 43.

42   *R v D(J)* (2002), 171 CCC (3d) 188 at paras 23–24 (Ont CA).

43   [2005] 3 SCR 728.

44   *Ibid* at para 62 [emphasis in original].

the actions, even if consensual, breached community standards of tolerance.[45] In another case, the Court acquitted a man, who was observed
masturbating in his house, of committing an indecent act in a public
place on the basis that his home was not a public place; a public place
was interpreted as a place to which the public has physical as opposed
to visual access.[46] The Court did not rely on strict construction to reach
this conclusion but rather contextual interpretation based on the fact
that, in other parts of the *Criminal Code*, Parliament had extended offences to apply not only to public places but also to places on private
property that were exposed to public view.[47] In both cases, however,
the Court opted for the interpretation of an offence that was most consistent with the liberty of the accused.

5) Requirements for Marked Departure

Another form of strict construction is whether courts should add interpretative glosses to criminal offences to limit their reach. The Canadian courts are not always consistent in their approach. In some cases,
they have interpreted the prohibited act to require that the conduct be
a marked departure from expected conduct even when Parliament has
not so provided, but in other cases, they have not.

In *R v Gunning*,[48] the Supreme Court suggested that the offence of
careless use of a firearm required that "the conduct in question" constitute a "marked departure" from the standard of care expected of a reasonable person. As will be seen in Chapter 5 on fault, the Court clearly
requires that there be a "marked departure" from reasonable standards
when negligence is used as a form of objective fault, but in this case,
the Court also seemed to require that the act of careless use of a firearm also be a marked departure. In *R v Boulanger*,[49] the Supreme Court
similarly interpreted the *actus reus* of the offence of breach of trust by a
public officer to require a marked departure from the standards of conduct required by public officials so as to ensure that the prohibited act
of the criminal offence would be distinguished from ethical breaches
that could be dealt with by internal discipline within the public service. The accused, the director of public security, had asked a police
officer to fill out a supplementary report about an accident involving

---

45   *Ibid* at paras 73–76.
46   *R v Clark*, [2005] 1 SCR 6.
47   See, for example, s 174(1)(b) defining the offence of nudity on private property
     while "exposed to public view."
48   Above note 2 at para 21.
49   [2006] 2 SCR 49 [*Boulanger*].

his daughter, but he did not ask that the report be falsified. Although it would have been better to have the insurance company communicate directly with the officer, the accused's conduct was characterized as "an error in judgment" and not a marked departure from the standards that would be expected from a person in a position of public authority.[50]

In *R v Beatty*,[51] a majority of the Court did not read in a requirement of marked departure into the *actus reus* of dangerous driving. The majority focused on interpreting the words used by Parliament to define the *actus reus* while at the same time reading in the marked departure requirement into the fault element of negligence that applied to that offence. Although this approach is at odds with that taken in *Boulanger*, it recognizes the traditionally dominant role accorded to the legislature in defining the criminal act. There is a danger that reading in a requirement of a marked departure into every criminal act will alter the clear intent of the legislature in defining the criminal act. Interpreting the *actus reus* should be a matter of statutory interpretation and reading marked departure standards into prohibited acts may strain legislative intent.

6) The *De Minimis* Defence

Another way to ensure restraint in the use of the criminal law would be the application of an old common law concept of "*de minimis non curat lex.*" This concept recognizes that the law should not punish a "mere trifle."[52] It would allow for an acquittal of those who were technically guilty of the *actus reus* because they possessed a minute amount of drugs, stole something of limited value, or engaged in a trivial assault.

Given the breadth of many prohibited acts as they are defined by Parliament and the rejection of the idea that it is a principle of fundamental justice that the criminal law must always respond to proven harms,[53] the doctrine of *de minimis non curat lex* should be recognized as a common law defence designed to ensure that the criminal law does

---

50 *Ibid* at para 67.

51 *R v Beatty*, 2008 SCC 5 at para 45 [*Beatty*]. McLachlin CJC (Binnie and LeBel JJ concurring) dissented on this point and held that the marked departure should be read into the act of dangerous driving as well as its fault requirement and that this approach was supported by concerns about both restraint in the use of criminal law and the need for symmetry between the fault and act requirements. *Ibid* at paras 57–67.

52 "The Reward" (1818), 165 ER 1482 at 1484.

53 *R v Malmo-Levine*, [2003] 3 SCR 571, discussed in Chapter 2.

not lightly brand someone with a stigma of a criminal offence.[54] Such a defence would not distort Parliament's intent for the offence and could be shaped and limited by the courts.

The *de minimus* doctrine has not yet been adopted by a majority of the Supreme Court even in the context of acceptance of a benefit by a public servant.[55] The Court has strongly rejected the *de minimis* defence in the context of sexual assault as it might be applied to kissing or cuddling a sleeping partner who is not capable of providing contemporaneous consent to the sexual activity. Chief Justice McLachlin rejected the *de minimus* defence on the basis that "even mild non-consensual touching of a sexual nature can have profound implications for the complainant."[56] Justice Fish in dissent similarly stated: "I do not view sexual assault of any kind as a trifling matter."[57] The *de minimus* defence has also been rejected by courts of appeal in relation to assaults[58] and the possession of small or trace amounts of drugs.[59] At the same time, the possession of a minute and old trace of a drug may lead to a conclusion that the accused did not actually have the *actus reus* of present possession.[60]

Although not yet definitely recognized, a *de minimus* defence could provide more narrowly tailored relief from potentially overbroad criminal offences than either reading in a marked departure requirement to the definition of all criminal acts or holding that the vagueness or overbreadth of the law violates section 7 of the *Charter*. A *de minimus* defence could also recognize that courts now make less frequent resort to strict construction of the criminal law and that Parliament often errs on the side of defining criminal acts too broadly rather than too narrowly. The *de minimus* defence could be developed in the context of the facts of exceptional cases and it would avoid having to reach a strained interpretation of a prohibited act that could distort Parliament's intent and would shape all subsequent applications of the offence. Section 8(3) of the *Criminal Code* contemplates that courts can

---

54   For an argument that the doctrine exists under s 8(3) of the *Criminal Code*, see *Canadian Foundation for Children*, above note 22 at paras 200–7, Arbour J in dissent but not on this point.

55   *R v Hinchey*, [1996] 3 SCR 1128 at para 69. But see *Ontario v Canadian Pacific Ltd*, [1995] 2 SCR 1031 at para 65, approving of the *de minimus* defence when interpreting a regulatory offence of impairing the environment.

56   *R v JA*, [2011] 2 SCR 440 at para 63.

57   *Ibid* at para 121.

58   *R v Kubassek* (2004), 188 CCC (3d) 307 (Ont CA); *R v RHL*, 2008 NSCA 100; *R v Gosselin* 2012 QCCA 1874.

59   *R v Quigley* (1954), 111 CCC 81 (Alta CA); *R v Lima*, 2017 SKCA 108.

60   *R v McBurney* (1975), 24 CCC (2d) 44 (BCCA).

as a matter of judge-made law develop new common law defences. Although a *de minimus* doctrine could be abused, courts would have to justify its use and they could be corrected on appeal.

B. IGNORANCE OF THE LAW

Codification, and the doctrines of strict construction of the criminal law and void for vagueness discussed above, help promote the principle that people should be punished only by fixed, predetermined laws. These doctrines are especially important because the criminal law has historically not allowed ignorance of the law to be an excuse to a criminal offence. Early cases held that people were guilty even if they committed an act they could not have known had recently been made illegal or was not illegal in their home country.[61]

Since the *Criminal Code* was enacted in 1892, it has provided that "ignorance of the law by a person who commits an offence is not an excuse for committing that offence."[62] This provision is uncontroversial when applied to offences that a person should know are crimes. It can, however, have harsh results when applied to matters that one may reasonably believe to be legal. That said, the Canadian courts have not recognized a defence of reasonable ignorance or mistake of law, though they have developed a range of devices to limit some of the harshest effects of the section 19 principles.

In *R v Molis*,[63] the Supreme Court held that the principle that ignorance of the law is no excuse precluded an accused from arguing that he had a defence of reasonable mistake in believing that drugs he manufactured were not prohibited under the *Food and Drug Act*. The accused had tried to determine if the drugs were legal, and the drugs in question had only recently been added to the prohibited list. Given his efforts, the accused would have most likely had a valid defence of due diligence if he had made a factual mistake about the nature of the drugs,[64] as opposed to a legal mistake as to whether the drugs had been prohibited under the relevant law. Courts have also rejected as an excuse the accused's reliance on a lower court judgment, which wrongly

---

61 *R v Bailey* (1800), 168 ER 651 (CCR); *R v Esop* (1836), 173 ER 203.

62 *Code*, above note 3, s 19.

63 (1980), 55 CCC (2d) 558 (SCC).

64 In *R v Beaver*, [1957] SCR 531 [*Beaver*], the Supreme Court held that those in possession of a prohibited drug had a defence because they believed it was a harmless substance. See Chapter 5 for discussion of the mistake of fact defence.

held that the activity in question was legal.[65] People rely on their own knowledge of the law, or even a lawyer's advice, at their peril. The ignorance of the law is no excuse principle can have harsh effects on a person who has made genuine and reasonable attempts to ascertain what the law is and to comply with it.

Nevertheless, the Supreme Court has affirmed that ignorance of the law is no excuse in the post-*Charter* era by stating that "it is a principle of our criminal law that an honest but mistaken belief in respect of the legal consequences of one's deliberate actions does not furnish a defence to a criminal charge, even when the mistake cannot be attributed to the negligence of the accused."[66] An accused who makes reasonable mistakes about the law will generally not have a defence, even though reasonable mistakes about the facts will provide a defence to most criminal and regulatory offences.[67] Even a reasonable mistake about the obligations of complex regulatory offences will not be recognized as a defence.[68]

An accused's argument that he mistakenly thought he was legally authorized to possess a firearm in Nova Scotia when he was only authorized to possess it in Alberta was dismissed by the Supreme Court as a defence on the basis of the section 19 ignorance of the law is no excuse principle.[69] The Court did, however, express some concern that the trial judge could not treat the accused's mistake of law as a mitigating factor in sentencing because of a mandatory minimum sentence of three years' imprisonment.[70] The Court subsequently held that "an honest but mistaken belief in the legality of his or her actions" could be a mitigating factor at sentencing by reducing the moral blameworthiness of the accused's actions.[71] This falls into a pattern of courts both upholding the traditional principle that ignorance or mistake of the law is not an excuse but attempting to mitigate some of its harsher effects.

---

65 *R v Campbell* (1972), 10 CCC (2d) 26 (Alta Dist Ct); *R v MacIntyre* (1983), 24 MVR 67 (Ont CA).

66 *R v Forster* (1992), 70 CCC (3d) 59 at 64 (SCC).

67 A person accused of a strict liability offence would have a defence if he or she "reasonably believed in a mistaken set of facts which, if true, would render the act or omission innocent." *R v Sault Ste Marie (City)* (1978), 40 CCC (2d) 353 at 374 (SCC). See Chapter 6.

68 *La Souveraine, Compagnie d'assurance générale v Autorité des marchés financiers*, [2013] 3 SCR 756 [*La Souveraine*].

69 *R v Macdonald*, [2014] 1 SCR 37 at paras 56–61 [*Macdonald*].

70 *Ibid* at para 61.

71 *R v Suter*, 2018 SCC 34 at para 64.

1) Distinguishing Mistakes of Law and Fact

The refusal to recognize a mistake of law as a defence means that an accused could be convicted of selling obscene material even though the accused relied reasonably on a newspaper report, a case, or a lawyer's advice that the material was not obscene. On the other hand, if the accused made a mistake about the facts, as opposed to the law, then he or she would have a defence.[72] This would apply, for example, to a vendor who believed that a magazine contained pictures of consenting adults, not children, engaged in sexual activity. Thus, the Supreme Court has acquitted a vendor on the basis that he had no knowledge of the features of videotapes that made them obscene while at the same time indicating that the vendor's belief that the videotapes were not legally obscene was not relevant. Even the fact that the videos had been approved by a provincial film board was not a defence because it only supported the accused's claim to have made a mistake about the law of obscenity.[73]

The Court has rejected arguments that the accused's belief that he was legally authorized to possess a firearm is a matter going to *mens rea* on the basis that such an interpretation would allow mistake of law to be a defence and require the Crown to prove that the accused was aware of the law.[74] In *R v Jones*,[75] the Court similarly held that the accused did not have a defence because they believed they were not legally required to have a provincial licence to operate a bingo on an Indigenous reserve. The Court stressed that the mistake was not a defence because it related not "to those facts here . . . [but] in believing that the law does not apply because it is inoperative on the reserves."[76] The accused might have had a defence if they, for example, had mistakenly believed that the Band had obtained a provincial licence for the bingo. The ignorance of the

---

72 *R v Metro News Ltd* (1986), 29 CCC (3d) 35 (Ont CA).

73 *R v Jorgensen* (1995), 102 CCC (3d) 97 (SCC) [*Jorgensen*]. But the decision of Lamer CJ, who would have held that the board's approval of the films provided a defence of officially induced error, was subsequently approved by the Supreme Court in *Lévis (City) v Tétreault*, [2006] 1 SCR 420 [*Lévis*] so that now the accused might be entitled to a stay of proceedings if they reasonably relied on erroneous legal advice from an official responsible for the administration of the law. Reliance by their accused on their own legal research or his own lawyer's advice would still not be a defence under the ignorance of the law is not an excuse principle.

74 *Macdonald*, above note 69 at paras 55–56.

75 (1991), 66 CCC (3d) 512 (SCC) [*Jones*].

76 *Ibid* at 517. The Court did note that the accused had not formally challenged the validity of the law as inconsistent with Indigenous or treaty rights protected under s 35 of the *Constitution Act, 1982*, being Schedule B to the *Canada Act 1982* (UK), 1982, c 11.

law is no excuse principle punishes those who have formed a mistaken belief about the legality of their actions more than a person who has made a mistake about the facts. This may seem unjust, but, as will be examined in Chapter 5, it is consistent with the general tendency of focusing on the accused's immediate intent in relation to the prohibited act as opposed to the accused's underlying motive or rationale for intentionally committing an act that in law constitutes an offence. The ignorance of the law principle as articulated in *Jones* means that Indigenous people who conclude that they are exercising an Indigenous or treaty right are often put in the difficult position of having to violate a regulatory law and then defend the violation on the basis of their rights. If the court accepts the validity of their claim of right, they will not be convicted. If, however, the court rejects their claim of right, their honest and perhaps reasonable mistake of law will not be an excuse to criminal or regulatory liability.

The distinction between a mistake of law, which is no excuse, and a mistake of fact, which may be an excuse, can be slippery and difficult. In 1979, a majority of the Supreme Court stated that a driver's knowledge of whether his licence was suspended was a matter of fact. As such, a driver who believed his licence was not suspended could have a defence of a lack of *mens rea* to a *Criminal Code* offence of driving while disqualified.[77] Three years later, the Court distinguished this finding and stated that while knowledge of a licence suspension was still a matter of fact when the accused was charged with a *Criminal Code* offence, it was a matter of law when the accused was charged with a provincial offence.[78] These rulings had the effect of protecting an accused who was mistaken about the law from a more serious *Criminal Code* conviction, but not the less serious regulatory conviction under provincial law.

The Supreme Court subsequently recognized in *R v Pontes*[79] that such arbitrary distinctions should not be maintained, with Cory J stating that it "cannot be that a mistake as to the law under the *Criminal Code* constitutes a mistake of fact, whereas a mistake as to the provisions of the provincial statute constitutes a mistake of law." Unfortunately, the Court was not clear on what precedent should be maintained. As will be seen, the Court held in that case that the offence of driving with a suspended licence should be classified as an absolute liability offence

---

77   *R v Prue* (1979), 46 CCC (2d) 257 (SCC).

78   *R v MacDougall* (1982), 1 CCC (3d) 65 (SCC).

79   *R v Pontes* (1995), 100 CCC (3d) 353 at para 40 (SCC) [*Pontes*].

because section 19 deprived the accused of any possible defence based on the automatic suspension of a driver's licence.

2) Preclusion of Mistake of Law as the Only Defence Making an Offence One of Absolute Liability

In *Pontes*, Cory J suggested for the majority that where section 19 operates to deny the accused his only possible defence, then the offence should be classified as one of absolute liability for which imprisonment cannot be imposed.[80] In the case, he held that the accused's lack of knowledge that his licence was suspended was the only possible defence to the offence of driving without a valid licence. Because the licence was automatically and without notice suspended upon the accumulation of a certain amount of demerit points, the defence that the accused did not know that his licence was suspended must amount to a mistake of law and as such be prohibited. An example given by the Court was those who as a result of a *Criminal Code* conviction received a licence suspension and who honestly and reasonably believed that they could drive after the *Criminal Code* suspension because they did not recognize that their licence was automatically suspended for a longer period under provincial law. This preclusion of the only available defence by the mistake of law is not an excuse principle led the majority of the Court to characterize the offence as one of absolute liability. This meant that the accused could not be imprisoned under section 7 of the *Charter* for violation of an absolute liability. This again fits into a pattern observed above of the courts in the *Charter* era mitigating some of the harshest edges of the ignorance of the law is not an excuse principle while still accepting and applying the basic principle. Four judges in dissent in *Pontes* argued that while the conviction of the accused because of ignorance and mistake of the law might be harsh, it has long been accepted in the criminal law. The majority's decision in *Pontes* preserves the ignorance of the law is no excuse principle, but somewhat mitigates its harshness by, in this one limited context, taking imprisonment away as a sentencing option.

3) Non-publication

There are some exceptions to the principle that ignorance of the law is not an excuse. A person may not be convicted of violating a law or

---

80   *Ibid* at 368.

regulation that has not been officially promulgated or published.[81] The rationale would be that it would be impossible for a person to ascertain and comply with a law that was not available to the public. Fortunately, Canadian laws are available electronically today.

4) *Mens Rea*, Colour of Right, and Mistake of Law

Sometimes the *mens rea*, or fault element, of specific offences will be defined in a manner that can make the accused's mistake of law a matter that will negate proof of *mens rea*. In other words, a person may not be convicted if the fault element required for a particular offence includes some knowledge of the relevant law. Thus, an accused has been acquitted of wilfully breaching his probation order because he wrongly believed that he had not committed the offence of care and control of a vehicle while impaired because the car was not moving.[82] If the accused thought he was doing something perfectly legal, it could not be said that he was wilfully breaching his parole. This was tied to the complex or high fault element implicit in the offence of wilfully breaching parole.[83] Similarly, a mistake about the extent of one's legal obligations to pay taxes can prevent proof of the high *mens rea* that one has wilfully evaded income tax. That said, the court held that there was no defence when a person did not pay taxes because he did not believe that the federal government had the constitutional power to impose taxes.[84]

A legal error about who owns property may afford a defence to theft and other property offences because the fault element of the crime itself contemplates that an accused act "without colour of right."[85] Theft

---

81   *R v Ross* (1944), 84 CCC 107 (BC Co Ct); *Lim Chin Aik v R*, [1963] AC 160 (PC); *R v Catholique* (1980), 49 CCC (2d) 65 (NWTSC). See also *Statutory Instruments Act*, RSC 1985, c S-22, s 11(2).

82   *R v Docherty* (1989), 51 CCC (3d) 1 (SCC) [*Docherty*].

83   Parliament subsequently amended the offence to provide that an accused was guilty when a probation order was breached "without reasonable excuse." *Code*, above note 3, s 733.1. It is possible that a court might find that the accused's genuine belief that he was not acting illegally and in breach of a probation order constituted a reasonable excuse, but the Supreme Court's decision in *Docherty*, *ibid*, was based on the high level of *mens rea* employed in the previous offence.

84   *R v Klundert* (2004), 187 CCC (3d) 417 (Ont CA).

85   The fault element of theft requires that the accused act "fraudulently and without colour of right." *Code*, above note 3, s 322(1). A person "who is honestly asserting what he believes to be an honest claim cannot be said to act 'without colour of right,' even though it may be unfounded in law or in fact." *R v DeMarco* (1973), 13 CCC (2d) 369 at 372 (Ont CA). See also *R v Shymkowich* (1954), 110 CCC 97 (SCC); *R v Howson*, [1966] 3 CCC 348 (Ont CA); *R v Spot Supermarket Inc* (1979), 50 CCC (2d) 239 (Que CA); *R v Lilly*, [1983] 1 SCR 794 [*Lilly*]. Section 429

has a particularly complex and high fault element and this makes some mistakes of law relevant to proof of *mens rea*.

A colour of right based on a mistaken belief by the accused about his or her legal entitlement to property can prevent the Crown from establishing the particular fault element of theft beyond a reasonable doubt.[86] The issue is the accused's belief about the law and not the actual legal entitlement.[87] The accused's belief in a moral as opposed to a legal entitlement is not sufficient.[88] There must be an air of reality to the accused's claim of colour of right, but if there is an air of reality, the prosecutor must prove beyond a reasonable doubt that the colour of right does not exist.[89]

The colour of right exceptions to the ignorance of the law principle depend on the particular fault element of the particular offence and the presence of a specific defence of colour of right.[90] They are limited exceptions that would not exonerate an accused who simply argued that he or she did not think that theft or care and control of a vehicle while impaired was illegal. The colour of right defence has been denied to Indigenous and environmental protesters on the basis that they believed they had a moral and not a legal right to occupy land or on the basis that they did not think that the *Criminal Code* applied to their activities.[91] Colour of right defences are a limited incursion on the principle that ignorance of the law is not an excuse. They generally relate to mistaken beliefs by the accused that they have a personal right or entitlement to property as opposed to more global beliefs that the criminal law is invalid or beyond constitutional limits.

5) Officially Induced Error

The Supreme Court has recognized a defence of officially induced error for all criminal and regulatory offences. The Court affirmed its commit-

---

provides that no person shall be convicted of property offences under ss 439–46 including mischief, arson, and cruelty to animals if she acted with colour of right. This phrase has been interpreted as requiring an honest belief in facts and law that would support the accused's property or possessory rights. It does not include the accused's belief that she was outside the jurisdiction of Canadian criminal law. *R v Watson* (1999), 137 CCC (3d) 422 (Nfld CA) [*Watson*].

86   *R v Dorosh* (2003), 183 CCC (3d) 224 (Sask CA).

87   *Lilly*, above note 85 at 798–99.

88   *Watson*, above note 85.

89   *R v Simpson*, 2015 SCC 40, [2015] 2 SCR 827 at para 32.

90   Colour of right does not apply to offences such as the illegal operation of a bingo: *Jones*, above note 75.

91   *R v Billy* (2004), 191 CCC (3d) 410 (BCSC); *Watson*, above note 85.

ment to the principle that ignorance of the law is not an excuse, but recognized that an inflexible approach to this rule could cause injustice "where the error in law of the accused arises out of an error of an authorized representative of the state" while at the same time the state prosecutes the accused. The accused must establish the defence of officially induced error on a balance of probabilities and it results in a stay of proceedings.

The defence applies to (1) errors of law or mixed law and fact where (2) the accused "considered the legal consequences of his or her actions" and (3) obtained erroneous legal advice "from an appropriate official," (4) the advice was reasonable (5) but erroneous and (6) the accused "relied on the advice in committing the act." The Court stressed the need for both the legal advice and the reliance placed on the advice to be reasonable. Hence, it "is not sufficient in such cases to conduct a purely subjective analysis of the reasonableness of the information."[92] The defence did not apply in the case because the accused relied on an "administrative practice" that they would receive a renewal notice when their licences expired and they did not obtain a specific legal opinion from responsible officials about the consequences of their actions or rely on that opinion.[93] This novel defence responds to the injustice of the state with one hand approving of conduct that it on the other hand prosecutes. It has been accepted in a case in which custom officials appeared to accept documentation offered at the border by protesting farmers as they left Canada to sell their wheat in the United States on the basis that they relied on legal advice from appropriate customs officials.[94]

The Court has refused an invitation to recognize a more general defence of reasonable mistake of law or to extend the limited defence of officially induced error. The case involved a corporation that wrote to a regulator setting out its understanding of its legal obligations, but heard no reply for six months until the regulator charged it with many regulatory offences. The Court was aware that the regulator's conduct was problematic and that reasonable mistakes could be made about complex regulatory laws, but it still confirmed the convictions.[95] This decision affirms that the courts will not recognize reasonable mistakes about the law as a defence even when an accused has sought legal advice and attempted without success to clarify the law with appropriate

---

92   *Lévis*, above note 73 at paras 26–27 following the approach taken by Lamer CJ in *Jorgensen*, above note 73 at paras 28–35.

93   *Jorgensen, ibid* at para 34.

94   *R v Charles* (2005), 197 CCC (3d) 42 (Sask CA).

95   *La Souveraine*, above note 68. Justice Abella in dissent would have extended the defence of officially induced error to the regulator's passivity.

governmental officials. At the same time, the Court stressed that it was dealing with a claim by an insurance company that had entered a highly regulated field requiring special knowledge.

Officially induced error is a fairly limited defence that leaves intact the general principle that ignorance of the law is no excuse. It did not apply in a case where wildlife officials relied on advice from a police officer about their arrest powers because the advice was not obtained from an appropriate official and was not reasonable. The Court expressed doubts that officials could even rely on the defence, stating that its rationale was "to protect a diligent person who first questions a government authority about the interpretation of legislation so as to be sure to comply with it and then is prosecuted by the same government for acting in accordance with the interpretation the authority gave him or her."[96] The advice has to come from an appropriate governmental official responsible for administering the law and it cannot be based on tacit non-enforcement of the law in the past.[97] Even in cases where there has been advice from an appropriate governmental official, reliance on the advice must be objectively reasonable. The defence has been recognized, but restrictively circumscribed. It also must be established by the accused on a balance of probabilities. If successful, the officially induced error defence results in a stay of proceeding rather than an acquittal, again indicating that it is only a limited exception to the basis principle that neither ignorance nor mistake of law are defences.

C. VOLUNTARINESS OF THE ACT

The criminal law has traditionally kept distinct the issue of whether the accused has committed the *actus reus* from whether he or she had the required fault element. In many cases, this does not create a practical problem because a person who commits a prohibited act while asleep or having an involuntary seizure will also not have the required fault element. Problems emerge in those cases in which the Crown is not required to prove some fault element or perhaps fault based on objective negligence. For example, a person brought into the country under custody has been convicted of the regulatory offence of being an illegal

---

96 *R v Bédard*, 2017 SCC 4 at para 1.
97 *Canada v Shiner*, 2007 NLCA 18; *Canada (Public Prosecutions, Director) v Marsland*, 2011 SKQB 207.

alien even though the jury believed she was guilty through circumstances beyond her control.[98]

The Supreme Court of Canada has been a pioneer in building a voluntariness requirement into the *actus reus*.[99] In the 1962 case of *King*, the Supreme Court refused to convict a person of impaired driving when the impairment was caused by involuntarily consuming a drug at the dentist's office. One judge argued that "there can be no *actus reus* unless it is the result of a willing mind at liberty to make a definite choice or decision."[100] This approach builds a minimal mental or fault element into the *actus reus* and suggests that an accused who acts involuntarily may not have committed the *actus reus* of an offence.

In *R v Théroux*,[101] McLachlin J stated that the *mens rea* of an offence "does not encompass all of the mental elements of a crime" because "the *actus reus* has its own mental element" — namely, that "the act must be the voluntary act of the accused for the *actus reus* to exist." Justice McLachlin and Lamer CJ have also stated that the involuntary conduct that would accompany a heart attack, an epileptic seizure, a detached retina, or a bee sting would prevent the Crown from proving the *actus reus* of dangerous driving.[102] Justice La Forest has indicated that the unconscious and involuntary behaviour that results in a defence of automatism "is conceptually a subset of the voluntariness requirement which in turn is part of the *actus reus* component of criminal liability."[103] In *R v Daviault*,[104] Lamer CJ stated that extreme intoxication that produced involuntary or unconscious behaviour should be seen as negating the *actus reus* of the offence. The majority of the Court held that extreme intoxication would negate the mental element of the assault but seemed to concede that such a condition could also prevent the voluntary formation of the *actus reus*. In *R v Stone*,[105] the Court also acknowledged that, subject to the mental disorder defence, an accused

---

98 *R v Larsonneur* (1933), 24 Cr App Rep 74 (CCA).

99 See also the statement of New Zealand judges that the commission of the *actus reus* cannot be involuntary or unconscious. *Kilbride v Lake*, [1962] NZLR 590 (SC).

100 *R v King* (1962), 133 CCC 1 at 3 (SCC). In England, however, an accused was convicted despite the involuntary consumption of drugs. *R v Kingston*, [1994] 3 WLR 519 (HL).

101 *R v Théroux* (1993), 79 CCC (3d) 449 at 458 (SCC).

102 *R v Hundal* (1993), 79 CCC (3d) 97 (SCC). But see *Beatty*, above note 51 at para 43 where it is suggested that such a sudden occurrence may also be relevant to determining even objective *mens rea* or fault requirements.

103 *R v Parks* (1992), 75 CCC (3d) 287 at 302 (SCC). See Chapter 8.

104 *R v Daviault* (1994), 93 CCC (3d) 21 at 25 (SCC) [*Daviault*]

105 *R v Stone* (1999), 134 CCC (3d) 353 (SCC).

should be acquitted if he or she acted in an involuntary manner. In *R v Ruzic*,[106] the Court again referred to the requirement of voluntariness as a fundamental principle of criminal law and a fundamental principle of justice under section 7 of the *Charter*. It related the principle of voluntariness to the requirement that people be punished only if they acted as "autonomous and freely choosing agents."

Courts seem increasingly willing to consider a lack of voluntary or conscious conduct as something that prevents the commission of the criminal act, or *actus reus*. This means a lack of voluntariness may be a defence to all criminal and regulatory offences, regardless of the fault element required. In practice, this will be most important in cases with no fault element or one based on negligence because involuntary conduct should usually be inconsistent with subjective forms of fault. One example would be that a person who learned about the presence of a loaded weapon while in a moving car could not instantly be guilty of possession of such a weapon until he had an opportunity to safely exit the vehicle.[107]

1) Accident and Voluntariness

A number of Courts of Appeal have recognized that the so-called defence of accident can in some cases raise a reasonable doubt about the voluntariness of the *actus reus*.[108] Justice Healy has stated for the Quebec Court of Appeal: "For an act to be attributed to the responsibility of a person in the criminal law it must be voluntary. Accidents are, by definition, not voluntary. A voluntary act is the expression of a conscious choice and conscious control by the person who commits it. To this extent the *actus reus* of an offence includes a mental element."[109] Similarly Trotter JA for the Ontario Court of Appeal has distinguished "between an accident, in the sense of being an involuntary act (i.e., accidentally discharging the firearm), as opposed to a voluntary act leading to unintended consequences (i.e., discharging the gun but unintentionally shooting" a person).[110]

Reference to voluntariness as opposed to unintentional acts better captures the idea that voluntariness is required for an *actus reus* and

---

106 (2001), 153 CCC (3d) 1 (SCC) at paras 42 and 46.

107 *R v Swaby* (2001), 54 OR (3d) 577 (CA).

108 *R v Barton*, 2017 ABCA 216 at para 286; *Primeau c R*, 2017 QCCA 1394 [*Primeau*]; *R v Parris*, 2013 ONCA 515 at paras 106–8.

109 *Primeau*, above note 108 at para 25. See also *Fils c R*, 2007 QCCA 56 at para 38 stressing the importance of distinguishing questions of intent from voluntariness.

110 *R v Spence*, 2017 ONCA 619 at para 32.

that in some cases an accidental action such as stumbling can produce involuntary conduct. In the sense of involuntary conduct, accident could be a defence for all offences.

Even if the accused acted in a voluntary manner and committed the *actus reus*, the defence of accident may also be relevant to whether the Crown has established a particular form of *mens rea*. In some cases, to be discussed in Chapter 5, a claim of accident in the form of unintended consequences may raise a reasonable doubt about subjective fault but not necessarily objective fault that punishes criminal negligence.[111] It would be helpful for courts, litigants, and students to be clear about whether any specific claim of accident is directed towards the voluntariness of the *actus reus* and/or the particular fault element of the offence charged.

D. THE COINCIDENCE OF THE *ACTUS REUS* AND *MENS REA*

A traditional principle of criminal law has been that the accused must commit the criminal act at the same time that he or she has the fault element required for the particular crime.[112] This requirement, sometimes called the simultaneous principle, establishes the principle that accused are judged on their conduct at the time when they committed the prohibited act and not on the basis of past bad acts. It is also generally used when applying defences. The focus is on whether the accused has a valid defence at the time the prohibited act was committed and not on past behaviour.

Although the simultaneous principle is a traditional principle of the criminal law, it has not yet been recognized as a principle of fundamental justice under section 7 of the *Charter* and it has at times been finessed by the courts. For example, in *Fagan v Metropolitan Police Commissioner*,[113] the accused accidentally drove his car on a police officer's foot. After being informed of this fact, the accused switched off the ignition and swore at the officer, before eventually moving the car. The accused was convicted of assaulting a police officer and the conviction upheld on appeal. In his dissent, Bridge J noted the theoretical dilem-

---

111 See Chapter 5, Section A(2).

112 The Latin phrase is *actus non facit reum, nisi mens sit rea*, or "the intent and the act must both concur to constitute the crime." *Fowler v Padget* (1798), 101 ER 1103 at 1106 (KB).

113 (1968), [1969] 1 QB 439.

ma that when the accused committed the initial act of assault, he did not know what he was doing, while when the accused did know that he was assaulting the officer, he did not act. The majority, however, took a more practical approach and held that the *actus reus* was not complete when the accused first drove onto the officer's foot, but continued while the force of the car was applied and the accused became aware of his actions. Thus, the mental element of knowledge coincided with this expanded definition of the act of assault. An alternative to the continuous act approach would be to hold that the accused, having created a danger by driving onto the officer's foot, was under a duty to take reasonable steps to rectify the situation.[114] This would make the failure to act a sufficient criminal act even though it might not technically fit the definition of the crime of assaulting a police officer.

In murder cases, courts have also been prepared to hold the accused guilty if the mental element was present at any point of time during the transaction that culminated in death. In R v Meli,[115] the accused struck the victim with the intent to kill, and then threw him over a cliff. The victim survived those events, but died some time later of exposure. The Privy Council upheld the murder conviction, stating that the accused had formed the intent to kill and it was impossible to divide the transaction that resulted in the victim's death. In R v Cooper,[116] the Supreme Court of Canada adopted *Meli* and upheld a murder conviction, on the basis that at some point during two minutes of strangulation the accused formed the intent to kill. The accused need not have had the intent throughout the entire transaction and the possibility that he may have "blacked out" because of intoxication did not excuse so long as the accused had the fault at some time during the strangulation. Justice Cory concluded: "It was sufficient that the intent and the act of strangulation coincided at some point. It was not necessary that the requisite intent continue throughout the entire two minutes required to cause the death of the victim."[117]

Another departure from the requirement that the fault element and the prohibited act occur at the same time has been the traditional rule with respect to intoxication for general intent offences such as assault or sexual assault. If the accused was so intoxicated at the time the assault was committed that he did not have the minimal mental element required, then the fault in becoming so intoxicated would be sufficient

114   *R v Miller*, [1983] 2 AC 161 (HL) [*Miller*].
115   [1954] 1 WLR 228 (PC) [*Meli*].
116   (1993), 78 CCC (3d) 289 (SCC).
117   *Ibid* at 298.

to convict the person of the general intent offence.[118] The fault in becoming extremely intoxicated would be formed long before the prohibited act was committed, but would be sufficient. This departure from the simultaneous principle has been held by the Supreme Court to violate sections 7 and 11(d) of the *Charter* by substituting the fault of becoming extremely intoxicated for the mental element of a general intent offence, when the former does not lead inexorably to the latter.[119] Parliament has, however, responded by deeming the fault of becoming extremely intoxicated to be sufficient for a conviction of violent offences,[120] thus affirming the common law approach of judging the accused's conduct through a wider lens than simply focusing on whether the accused had the required fault element at the time when the prohibited act was committed.

Criminal and regulatory offences based on negligence may also constitute a departure from the principle that fault occurs at the same time as the prohibited act. An accused can be found to be negligent for failing to take precautionary measures long before the prohibited act was committed. For example, an oil tanker may spill its contents and the shipping company be negligent because the tanker was not inspected and repaired the last time it was in harbour. The purpose of regulatory and negligence-based offences, of course, is to prevent harm before it occurs, and some departure from the simultaneous principle may be necessary to achieve this end. Conversely, however, the Supreme Court has recognized that a momentary lapse of attention at the time of the prohibited act may not justify a conviction for a negligence-based offence such as dangerous driving causing death.[121] The rationale would seem to be that the accused's entire course of driving did not demonstrate the necessary negligence.

E. PROHIBITED ACTS BASED ON CAUSING PROHIBITED CONSEQUENCES AND CAUSATION

When the criminal act prohibits a consequence or a result, it is necessary to determine if the accused's actions have actually caused the prohibited

---

118 *R v Majewski* (1976), 62 Cr App Rep 262 (HL); *R v Leary* (1977), 33 CCC (2d) 473 (SCC). See Chapter 7.

119 *Daviault*, above note 104.

120 *Code*, above note 3, s 33.1. See Chapter 7, Section E.

121 *Beatty*, above note 51; *R v Roy*, 2012 SCC 26.

consequence or result. Canadian criminal law does not take an overly strict approach to causation and allows a person to be held liable for causing consequences even if the consequences are caused, in part, by the victim's peculiar and perhaps unforeseeable vulnerabilities. This is often called the "thin skull" rule, or the principle that accused take their victims as they find them. In addition, it is not necessary that the accused's acts be the sole operative cause of the prohibited consequences. This fits into the general trend towards expansive definitions of the criminal act, but may have some harsh results in particular cases. The unanticipated harm caused by actions may be a mitigating factor in sentencing, particularly in manslaughter, which has no minimum penalty.

1) Statutory Provisions Concerning Causation

Parliament remains free to impose its own statutory rules to define the test for when a person will be held responsible for causing a prohibited consequence or result as part of its ability to define the prohibited act. As will be examined in greater detail in Chapter 10, Parliament has generally defined causation broadly for the purpose of homicide offences. For example, section 222(1) provides that a person commits homicide when, directly or indirectly, by any means, he or she causes the death of a human being. This is a broad definition that has been satisfied in a case where an accused abducted a child who subsequently died of hypothermia when left in a car.[122]

Parliament has enacted specific causation rules in sections 224 to 226 of the *Criminal Code* to deal with certain issues of remoteness between the accused's actions and the victim's actual death and some intervening causes such as treatment. The Supreme Court has noted that "ss. 224 and 225 of the *Criminal Code* provide that the chain of causation is not broken if death could otherwise have been prevented by resorting to proper means (s. 224), or if the immediate cause of death is proper or improper treatment that is applied in good faith (s. 225)."[123] Finally, there are also specific and more restrictive causation rules under the first-degree murder provisions in section 231(5) that require that the death be caused while the accused is committing or attempting to commit a list of enumerated offences, including sexual assault, kidnapping, and hostage-taking.[124]

---

122 *R v Younger* (2004), 186 CCC (3d) 454 (Man CA).
123 *R v Maybin*, 2012 SCC 24 at para 52 [*Maybin*].
124 *R v Harbottle*, [1993] 3 SCR 306, discussed in Chapter 10, Section A(1)(c).

2) General Principles of Causation

The *Criminal Code* does not comprehensively codify all causation issues. As the Supreme Court has stated, "[w]here the factual situation does not fall within one of the statutory rules of causation in the *Code*, the common law general principles of criminal law apply to resolve any causation issues that may arise."[125] In *R v Smithers*,[126] the Supreme Court upheld a manslaughter conviction on the basis that the accused's action of kicking the deceased in the stomach "was at least a contributing cause of death, outside the *de minimis* range," even though the death was in part caused by the victim's malfunctioning epiglottis, which caused him to choke to death on his own vomit. Justice Dickson upheld the applicability of the thin skull principle in the criminal law of homicide by stating:

> Death may have been unexpected, and the physical reactions of the victim unforeseen, but that does not relieve the [accused] . . . .
>
>   It is a well-recognized principle that one who assaults another must take his victim as he finds him.[127]

One court of appeal has stated that the contributing cause and thin skull principles set out in *Smithers* establish "a test of sweeping accountability" for causing death that might be vulnerable to challenge under section 7 of the *Charter* as infringing the principles of fundamental justice.[128]

   Nevertheless, the *Smithers* approach to causation in homicide cases survived under the *Charter*. In *R v Cribbin*,[129] the Ontario Court of Appeal concluded that the *de minimis* causation test and thin skull principles approved in *Smithers* and *Creighton* are consistent with the principles of fundamental justice that forbid the punishment of the morally innocent. Justice of Appeal Arbour stated that the requirement for proof of fault in addition to the criminal act removed any risk that the broad causation test would punish the morally innocent.[130] A manslaughter conviction was upheld in *Cribbin* because the accused's assault had contributed to the victim's death, even though the victim had been subject to more serious assaults by another person and had died because he drowned in his own blood.

---

125 *Ibid.*
126 (1977), 34 CCC (2d) 427 (SCC).
127 *Ibid* at 437.
128 *R v F(DL)* (1989), 52 CCC (3d) 357 at 365 (Alta CA).
129 (1994), 89 CCC (3d) 67 (Ont CA) [*Cribbin*].
130 *Ibid* at 88.

In *R v Nette*,[131] the Supreme Court revisited *Smithers*. Although the Court did not overrule *Smithers*, it reformulated and arguably elevated the test for causation in homicide cases. Justice Arbour for a majority of the Court concluded that "the causation standard expressed in *Smithers* is still valid and applicable to all forms of homicide" (that is, murder, manslaughter, and infanticide). Nevertheless, she added:

> In order to explain the standard as clearly as possible to the jury, it may be preferable to phrase the standard of causation in positive terms using a phrase such as "significant contributing cause" rather than using expressions phrased in the negative such as "not a trivial cause" or "not insignificant." Latin terms such as *de minimis* are rarely helpful.[132]

Justice L'Heureux-Dubé with three other judges dissented and would have maintained the negative formulation contemplated under *Smithers*. She argued that "[t]here is a meaningful difference between expressing the standard as 'a contributing cause that is not trivial or insignificant' and expressing it as a 'significant contributing cause.'"[133]

All the judges were agreed, however, that the accused had caused the death of a ninety-five-year-old widow he had left hog-tied and alone after robbing her home. The victim died of asphyxiation some twenty-four to forty-eight hours later. Medical evidence showed that a number of factors contributed to the death, including the hog-tied position, a moderately tight ligature that the accused had left around the victim's neck, as well as the victim's age, asthma, and congestive heart failure. Justice Arbour concluded that "the fact that the appellant's actions might not have caused death in a different person, or that death might have taken longer to occur in the case of a younger victim, does not transform this case into one involving multiple causes."[134]

Courts now describe causation in the positive terms of whether the accused's actions were a significant contributing cause as opposed to the older formulation of a cause that is not trivial or insignificant.[135] They have indicated that "evidence that an act was possibly a cause of death cannot provide the evidentiary basis for a finding beyond a reasonable doubt that the act significantly contributed to the death."[136] The

---

131 [2001] 3 SCR 488 [*Nette*].

132 *Ibid* at para 71.

133 *Ibid* at para 6.

134 *Ibid* at para 81. See also *R v Knight*, [2003] 1 SCR 156.

135 *R v Pangowish* (2003), 171 CCC (3d) 506 (BCCA), leave to appeal to SCC refused (2003), 176 CCC (3d) vi (SCC).

136 *R v Talbot* (2007), 217 CCC (3d) 415 at para 82 (Ont CA).

causation requirement, like other elements of the prohibited act, must be established beyond a reasonable doubt.

3) Concurrent Causes and New Acts That Sever the Chain of Causation

Courts have concluded that an accused caused death when he or she set off a chain of events that ended in a person's death, even though the immediate cause of death had not been at the accused's hands. In *R v Maybin*,[137] the Supreme Court stressed that the ultimate issue was whether the accused's actions still constituted a significant cause of death. It indicated that the test of whether the intervening act was reasonably foreseeable from the accused's actions and whether the intervening act was independent of the accused's actions were only analytical aids and not new legal tests of causation in determining whether a particular intervening act was sufficient to break the chain of causation so that the accused's actions were no longer a significant cause of the victim's death. In holding that brothers who assaulted another patron in a bar were still responsible for the patron's death even though a bouncer also punched the victim (who died of bleeding in the brain) in the back of the head, the Court stressed that it was reasonably foreseeable that either bouncers or other patrons would join in the fight.[138] The Court also held that the bouncer's assault on the victim was not so independent an act that it rendered the accused's initial assault so remote to suggest that the accused "were morally innocent of the death."[139] The approach to causation taken in this case is broad, but it is also based on statutory interpretation of the relevant prohibited act, in this case, the test that requires that the accused's actions be a significant but not necessarily the only cause of a death.

Although an accused may still be held responsible for causing death when there are concurrent causes of the death, it will be necessary in some cases for the jury to be instructed about whether an intervening event has "severed the chain of causation" in such a manner that the accused's actions are no longer a significant contributing cause of the victim's death. For example, the Supreme Court in a 4:3 decision reversed a murder conviction and ordered a new trial in a case where the victim, who was shot in the stomach and barely survived, died as a result of a blood clot a few days after being released from hospital.

---

137 2012 SCC 24.
138 *Ibid* at para 41.
139 *Ibid* at para 59.

A new trial would include the possible verdict of attempted murder because the pathologist would not rule out the possibility that while the blood clot was probably related to the shooting, it could have been caused by cocaine ingested by the victim shortly before his death.[140]

In a case where the accused rendered the deceased unconscious by a headlock but the victim died when his friends' attempts at resuscitation had the unfortunate effect of causing the victim to choke to death on his own vomit, the Nova Scotia Court of Appeal concluded that the jury should be asked whether it was "satisfied beyond a reasonable doubt that the actions [of the accused] are so connected to the death . . . that they can be said to have had a significant causal effect which continued up to the time of his death, without having been interrupted" by the intervening act of the botched resuscitation. The Court of Appeal added that the jury must not be convinced that the accused's actions were "the sole cause" of the death but rather, consistent with *Nette*, that they were "a significant contributing cause."[141] This approach remains valid after *Maybin*, with the questions of whether the risk of the botched resuscitation was reasonably foreseeable or independent from the accused's action described as analytical guides to determining the ultimate issue of whether the accused's action was a significant contributing cause.

The accused's actions do not have to be the sole cause of death, but there may be situations where the chain of causation will be broken so that the accused's actions are no longer the significant cause of death. For example, the accused would not be responsible for causing a person's death if he or she assaulted a victim, leaving the victim unconscious, but the victim was then killed by a subsequent and independent fire or building collapse. A reasonable doubt about whether the accused caused the prohibited consequences may leave the accused vulnerable to charges that he nevertheless attempted to commit the crime because he had the required intent for the crime and did an act that even if it did not cause the prohibited result.

4) Causation in Non-homicide Cases

Causation issues sometimes arise in non-homicide cases. In *R v Winning*,[142] a conviction of obtaining credit by false pretences was overturned because even though the accused made false statements in her application

---

140 *R v Sarrazin*, 2011 SCC 54 at paras 6, 20, and 42.

141 *R v Reid and Stratton* (2003), 180 CCC (3d) 151 at para 89 (NSCA).

142 (1973), 12 CCC (3d) 449 (Ont CA).

for a credit card, the company did not rely on these statements when issuing the credit card. If the accused had the necessary intent, however, it might be possible to convict him or her of attempting to obtain credit by false pretences because the *actus reus* for attempts only requires some step beyond mere preparation to commit the offence. When a person is charged with impaired driving causing bodily harm or death, the Crown must show that the accused's impairment was a contributing cause outside the *de minimis* range to the bodily harm or death. It cannot simply rely on the fact that the driver was impaired with alcohol.[143]

A distinction is sometimes drawn between legal and factual causation with factual causation referring to whether the accused is the "but for" cause of prohibited consequences and legal causation referring to whether the accused should be held criminally responsible for the prohibited consequences. In *R v Williams*[144] a man was charged with aggravated assault on the basis that he had sex with a woman, knowing he was HIV-positive. The man learned he was HIV-positive in November and failed to inform the victim, but the sexual relationship had begun in June. The woman became HIV-positive, but there was no certainty about exactly when she became so infected. The Supreme Court held that the man should be acquitted of aggravated assault because it was possible that the woman was already infected at the point in time at which the accused had sex with her knowing he was HIV-positive. This case suggests that the accused will have the benefit of any reasonable doubt about factual causation. It also illustrates the continued need for a coincidence between the *actus reus* and *mens rea*. When the accused had the required fault of knowingly risking HIV transmission, he could not commit the *actus reus* because the woman was already infected. When the accused may have committed the act of infecting the victim, he did not have the guilty knowledge.

---

143   *R v Ewart* (1989), 53 CCC (3d) 153 (Alta CA); *R v Powell* (1989), 52 CCC (3d) 403 (Sask CA); *R v Stephens* (1991), 27 MVR (2d) 24 (Ont CA); *R v Fisher* (1992), 13 CR (4th) 222 (BCCA); *R v Laprise* (1996), 113 CCC (3d) 87 (Que CA).
144   2003 SCC 41.

5) Attempts and Accomplice Liability as Alternative Forms of Liability in Cases of Reasonable Doubt About Factual Causation

Although Williams was acquitted of aggravated assault on the basis of a reasonable doubt that he was the factual cause of the victim's HIV infection at the time he knew he was HIV-positive, the Court held that he was guilty of attempted aggravated assault. Liability for attempts as well as accomplice or party liability will be examined in Chapter 4, but it should be noted that both can provide alternative forms of legal liability in cases where doubts about whether the accused caused the prohibited consequences may prevent the accused from being held responsible as the principal offender who caused the prohibited consequences.

The accused in *R v Williams* was convicted of attempted aggravated sexual assault because at the time he had the necessary fault of knowing he was HIV-positive and not telling the woman, he committed an act that was sufficient to constitute the very broadly defined *actus reus* of attempt. A person can be guilty of an attempted crime even though the commission of the completed offence may be impossible.[145] Similarly, accomplice or party liability as an aider or abettor may also be an alternative form of legal liability in cases where there may be doubts as to whether a particular accused was the factual cause of a prohibited consequence.[146] This would apply in a case where there was a reasonable doubt about whom of multiple accused actually killed the victim, but it is clear that all the accused assisted in the killing through aiding or abetting the killing.[147]

---

145 As examined in Chapter 4, Section A(2), accused under s 24 of the *Code* may be guilty of an attempted crime if they do or omit to do "anything" beyond mere preparation to commit the crime with the intent to commit the crime. It is no defence that the commission of the complete crime was impossible.

146 As explained by Lebel J, in dissent in *R v Pickton*, [2010] 2 SCR 198 at paras 60–61, where he states, "party liability as codified in s. 21 of the *Criminal Code* often bridges the gap which might otherwise exist between factual and legal causation" and may apply in a case where there is reasonable doubt whether an accused factually caused a prohibited consequence such as causing death.

147 As examined in Chapter 4, Section E(2), accused under s 21(1) of the *Code* may be guilty of committing an offence if they purposefully aided or abetted the offence as well as if they actually committed it.

F. OMISSIONS: THE FAILURE TO ACT AS A PROHIBITED ACT

One possible exception to the trend to wide definitions of the criminal act is the traditional reluctance to use a failure to act as an *actus reus*. Traditionally, the criminal law has prohibited harmful conduct; it has not required socially desirable conduct. An omission or failure to act will generally form the *actus reus* of a criminal offence only when an individual has a specific legal duty to act.

Legal duties to act can be found throughout the *Criminal Code* and other statutes. Section 215 of the *Criminal Code* provides that a parent, spouse, or guardian has a legal duty to provide the necessaries of life for his or her child under sixteen years of age, spouse or common law partner, or dependent charge,[148] and makes it an offence to fail to do so without lawful excuse. If a person commits this offence,[149] or is criminally negligent in omitting to perform another duty imposed by law,[150] he or she can be convicted of manslaughter by means of an unlawful act, or criminal negligence.[151]

Those who undertake to do an act have a legal duty to perform the act, if an omission to do the act is or may be dangerous to life.[152] This duty could apply to a person who agreed to be a lifeguard, but who did not make reasonable efforts to save a drowning person. On the other hand, a person who had not agreed to be a lifeguard would be under no such duty. He or she legally could walk away from a drowning person. The Ontario Court of Appeal has stressed that only binding and intentional commitments will suffice to expose an accused to criminal liability for failing to act. A mere expression of words will not normally be enough to create a duty under section 217.[153]

---

148 This can include a dependent who is an adult. The Ontario Court of Appeal has stated: "The duty arises when one person is under the other's charge, is unable to withdraw from that charge, and is unable to provide himself or herself with necessaries of life." The phrase "necessaries of life" includes not only food, shelter, care, and medical attention necessary to sustain life, but also appears to include protection of the person from harm. Thus, s 215(1)(c) obligations are driven by the facts and the context of each case. *R v Peterson* (2005), 201 CCC (3d) 220 at para 34 (Ont CA), leave to appeal to SCC refused, [2005] SCCA No 539.

149 *R v Naglik* (1993), 83 CCC (3d) 526 (SCC).

150 *Code*, above note 3, s 219.

151 *Ibid*, ss 222(5)(a)–(b).

152 *Ibid*, s 217.

153 *R v Browne* (1997), 116 CCC (3d) 183 (Ont CA), leave to appeal to SCC refused, [1997] SCCA No 398.

There is a duty to use reasonable care when providing medical treatment or other lawful acts that may endanger the life of others.[154] This duty was breached by a person who donated blood that he knew was infected with HIV.[155] It is also an offence not to use reasonable care in handling explosives;[156] to disobey a court order;[157] to fail to assist a peace officer when requested;[158] to abandon a child;[159] not to obtain assistance in childbirth;[160] to fail to stop when your vehicle is involved in an accident;[161] to neglect animals;[162] and to fail to take steps to protect holes in ice or open excavations.[163] A new duty provides that those who direct others to perform tasks or how to work have "a legal duty to take reasonable steps to prevent bodily harm to that person, or any other person, arising from that work or task."[164] Regulatory offences even more frequently penalize the failure to act, by, for example, mandating safety measures or keeping proper records. As criminal and regulatory offences are used to regulate conduct, there seems to be a trend away from the traditional reluctance to penalize omissions.

Duties may also be implicit in particular crimes. In *R v Colucci*,[165] the accused was convicted of publishing a false statement with intent to deceive shareholders when he failed to inform them about an engineer's report, which stated that there were no prospects for development of a particular mine. A refusal to identify yourself to a police officer who saw you commit a crime has been held to be an obstruction of a police officer under section 129 of the *Criminal Code*.[166] In that case, however, Dickson J wrote a strong dissent warning that "the criminal law is no place within which to introduce implied duties, unknown to statute and common law, breach of which subjects a person to arrest and punishment."[167]

---

154 *Code*, above note 3, s 216.

155 *R v Thornton* (1993), 82 CCC (3d) 530 (SCC).

156 *Code*, above note 3, ss 79–80.

157 *Ibid*, s 127.

158 *Ibid*, s 129(b).

159 *Ibid*, s 218. Note that in *Levkovic*, above note 16, this duty was interpreted to apply only in cases where the baby was likely to have lived, and this form of interpretation narrowed the ambit of the duty.

160 *Code*, above note 3, s 242.

161 *Ibid*, s 252.

162 *Ibid*, s 446.

163 *Ibid*, s 263.

164 *Ibid*, s 217.1.

165 [1965] 4 CCC 56 (Ont CA).

166 *R v Moore* (1978), 43 CCC (2d) 83 (SCC).

167 *Ibid* at 96.

There is also the possibility of courts creating common law duties on their own. In *Miller*,[168] the House of Lords held that a person who accidentally set a house on fire had a duty to take reasonable steps to extinguish the fire or to call the fire department. In the Canadian context, however, such common law duties come precariously close to creating common law crimes contrary to section 9 of the *Criminal Code*. Common law duties challenge the principle of legality because they are created and applied retroactively by courts. In Canada, the preferred approach to *Miller* is found in the Court of Appeal's decision, which did not create a free-standing common law duty but instead found that the accused had adopted the act of setting the fire when he awoke and did not take steps to put out the fire.[169] The controlling principle is not that society is not justified in imposing duties on people to take reasonable steps to respond to dangers, but that this should be done by the democratic enactment of general, accessible, and prospective duties in the *Criminal Code* and not by judges imposing retroactive common law duties on a case-by-case basis.

G. POLICY ELEMENTS IN THE DEFINITION OF THE *ACTUS REUS*

The definition of the prohibited act is an important policy component of the criminal law. The legislative definition of the *actus reus* indicates what conduct will be prohibited and criminalized in our society. Both Parliament in enacting offences and the courts in interpreting those offences add to the policy component in shaping what is prohibited and not prohibited in the criminal law. The general trend is towards more expansive definitions of prohibited act. It should also be recalled that the accused's failure to know about the expanded nature of a crime and even a reasonable mistake about what is prohibited will generally not be a defence to a crime.

1) Consent and Sexual Offences

Rape used to be defined in the *Criminal Code* as sexual intercourse with a female person who is not the accused's wife.[170] In 1983, the offence of rape was replaced with offences of sexual assault, sexual assault with

---

168 Above note 114.
169 *Ibid.*
170 *Code*, above note 3, s 135.

a weapon or threats, and aggravated sexual assault. In an attempt to emphasize the violence in sexual offences, Parliament broadened the prohibited act to include all intentional applications of force without consent in circumstances that were objectively sexual.[171] The marital rape exception was also repealed as a means to ensure that people, usually women, were protected from sexual violence from their spouses.

In a further attempt to protect the sexual integrity of women and spell out that "no means no," Parliament in 1992 further defined consent for the purpose of sexual assault as "the voluntary agreement of the complainant to engage in the sexual activity in question." Moreover, it provided that no consent is obtained where

(a) the agreement is expressed by the words or conduct of a person other than the complainant;

(b) the complainant is incapable of consenting to the activity;

(c) the accused induces the complainant to engage in the activity by abusing a position of trust, power or authority;

(d) the complainant expresses, by words or conduct, a lack of agreement to engage in the activity; or

(e) the complainant, having consented to engage in sexual activity, expresses, by words or conduct, a lack of agreement to engage in the activity.[172]

This provision defines certain examples where the accused will be precluded from arguing that the prohibited act of sexual assault did not occur because the complainant consented. It establishes as an objective statement of law that consent is a voluntary agreement to engage in the particular sexual activity and that there cannot be consent if (a) agreement is given by a third party; (b) the complainant is incapable of consenting;[173] (c) the complainant is induced to participate by abuse of a position of trust, power, and authority; or (d, e) the complainant expresses a lack of agreement, by either words or comments, to engage or continue to engage in sexual activity. Bill C-51 would add that consent must be present at the time of the sexual activity in question and no consent exists if the complainant is unconscious or for any other reason incapable of consenting to the activity.[174] The above examples of

---

171　*R v Chase* (1987), 37 CCC (3d) 97 (SCC).

172　*Code*, above note 3, s 273.1, introduced in *An Act to Amend the Criminal Code (Sexual Assault)*, SC 1992, c 38, s 1.

173　For cases rejecting the idea that an unconscious complainant could have given prior consent, see *R v Humphrey* (2001), 143 OAC 151 (CA); *R v Ashlee* (2006), 212 CCC (3d) 477 (Alta CA).

174　Bill C-51, above note 4, s 19, proposed amendment of s 273.1 (2.1).

deemed non-consent are not exhaustive and the Ontario Court of Appeal has held that there was no consent or voluntary agreement when a man threatened to distribute nude photographs of his ex-girlfriend if she did not have sex with him.[175]

The Supreme Court has rejected the defence of either advance[176] or implied[177] consent to sexual assault. As a matter of determining the *actus reus* of consent "[t]he absence of consent . . . is subjective and determined by reference to the complainant's subjective internal state of mind toward the touching, at the time it occurred."[178] This requires that the complainant be conscious at the time of the sexual activity in question and prevents the use of advance consent in a case where the complainant was unconscious at the time of the commission of the prohibited act.[179] This finding would be codified in the Bill C-51 amendments to the sexual assault offence.[180]

In rejecting the concept of implied consent, the Supreme Court has stated that the trier of fact "may only come to one of two conclusions: the complainant either consented or not. There is no third option. If the trier of fact accepts the complainant's testimony that she did not consent, no matter how strongly her conduct may contradict that claim, the absence of consent is established."[181] The existence of consent for the purpose of defining the *actus reus* of sexual assault thus depends on the subjective perceptions of the victims as opposed to external and objective standards of law. Similarly, consent will be negated by the complainant's fear of the application of force regardless of the reasonableness of the fear or whether it was communicated to the accused. A statement by the victim that she did not consent or did so because of fear will be determinative unless it is found not to be a credible statement of her state of mind at the time the offence occurred. The Court is understandably concerned about maximizing the physical and sexual integrity of women and rejecting the rape myths that women implicitly consent to sexual activity unless they protest or resist or clearly express fear. The Court's vehicle for rejecting these myths is to make the issue of consent for the purpose of defining *actus reus* dependent on the subjective perceptions of the complainant even if they are uncommunicated and unreasonable.

---

175 *R v DS* (2004), 72 OR (3d) 223 (CA), aff'd [2005] 1 SCR 914.
176 *R v JA*, [2011] 2 SCR 440 [*JA*].
177 *R v Ewanchuk* (1999), 131 CCC (3d) 481 (SCC) [*Ewanchuk*].
178 *Ibid* at 494.
179 *JA*, above note 176.
180 Bill C-51, above note 4, proposed amendment of s 273.1 (2.1).
181 *Ewanchuk*, above note 177 at 495.

2) Consent and HIV Disclosure

The Court took a different, more objective approach with respect to the issue of whether a person's non-disclosure of his positive HIV status constitutes fraud that vitiates consent to unprotected sexual intercourse. In *R v Cuerrier*,[182] Cory J stated that in determining whether consent was obtained fraudulently, "[t]he actions of the accused must be assessed objectively to determine whether a reasonable person would find them to be dishonest."[183] A person only had a duty to disclose if the failure to disclose presented a significant risk of serious bodily harm. The rest of the Court rejected L'Heureux-Dubé J's view that any fraud designed to induce the complainant to consent would nullify the consent. There was a concern that her view would trivialize the criminal process by allowing consent to be nullified because, for example, the accused lied about his age or his job. This approach was confirmed in *R v Mabior*,[184] where the Court held that consent would be vitiated where failure to disclose would cause a significant risk of harm and where the complainant would not have consented had he or she been informed. The Court interpreted the significant risk of harm standard as applying to a realistic possibility of harm. It defended such a standard as objective and appropriate for the criminal law.

In *R v Hutchinson*,[185] a majority of the Court extended the fraud exception to convict a man of aggravated sexual assault who deceptively poked holes in a condom with the knowledge that the complainant would not have unprotected sex. It held that pregnancy satisfied the requirement of a significant risk of harm. Three other judges also would have convicted, but on the different basis that the complainant had agreed to have sex only with a condom. These cases remain controversial with some criticizing them for extending the criminal sanction too far and others criticizing them for not extending the criminal sanction far enough. Nevertheless, they illustrate the continued policy controversies over how consent should be defined. They also suggest

---

182 (1998), 127 CCC (3d) 1 (SCC) [*Cuerrier*]. In *R v Esau* (1997), 116 CCC (3d) 289 at 312 (SCC), McLachlin J also stated that "[a]t issue, as elsewhere in dealing with consent, is the social act of communicating consent, not the internal state of mind of the complainant. The accused is not expected to look into the complainant's mind and make judgments about her uncommunicated thoughts. But neither is he entitled to presume consent in the absence of communicative ability." It is possible, however, that both the above statements might be characterized as relating to the *mens rea* as opposed to the *actus reus* of the offence.

183 *Cuerrier*, above note 182 at 49.

184 [2012] 2 SCR 584.

185 [2014] 1 SCR 346.

that greater clarity might be achieved if Parliament more specifically addressed these issues in its definition of the prohibited act.

Parliament has defined what is meant by consent for policy reasons in other sections of the *Criminal Code*. For example, section 14 provides that people cannot consent to their death, and section 286 provides that consent is no defence to the abduction of a child. Section 150.1(1) provides that the complainant's consent is no defence to various sexual offences involving those under the age of sixteen.[186] This provision defines consent for the purpose of determining the *actus reus*. Section 150.1(4) addresses the accused's fault or mental element by providing that a subjective belief that the complainant was sixteen or older is not a defence "unless the accused took all reasonable steps to ascertain the age of the complainant."[187]

3) Restrictions on Consent to Assault for Policy Reasons

Assault is defined broadly in section 265 to include not only the non-consensual and intentional application of direct or indirect force on another person, but also attempts or threats "by an act or a gesture, to apply force to another person" if the accused causes the complainant to believe on reasonable grounds that he or she has the present ability to effect his purpose. It also includes begging or accosts on another person while openly carrying a weapon or imitation thereof. Section 265(3) also provides that there is no consent to assault if a complainant "submits or does not resist" because of threats or fear of the application of force, application of force to a third party, fraud, or the exercise of authority.

Despite the breadth of the assault offence and the clear exemption of consensual applications of force from its ambit, the Supreme Court has expanded the *actus reus* of assault by interpretation. In *R v Jobidon*,[188] the Supreme Court held that a person could not consent to an assault that intentionally causes "serious hurt or non-trivial bodily harm . . . in the course of a fist fight or brawl," and that a minor could not consent to an adult's intentional application of force in a fight. Justice Gonthier recognized that "some may see limiting the freedom of an adult to consent to applications of force in a fist fight as unduly paternalistic and a violation of self-rule," but he argued:

---

186 Some exceptions are made if the accused is under sixteen years of age, less than two years older than the complainant, and not in a position of trust, authority, or dependency with the complainant. *Code*, above note 3, s 151.1(2).

187 See Chapter 10, Section B(3).

188 *Jobidon*, above note 5.

All criminal law is "paternalistic" to some degree — top-down guidance is inherent in any prohibitive rule. That the common law has
developed a strong resistance to recognizing the validity of consent
to intentional applications of force in fist fights and brawls is merely
one instance of the criminal law's concern that Canadian citizens
treat each other humanely and with respect.[189]

The Court did indicate that consent would not be negated if the bodily
harm was trivial or an accepted part of socially valued activity such as
sports. Subsequent cases have made clear that "*Jobidon* requires serious
harm both intended and caused for consent to be vitiated."[190]

In dissent in *Jobidon*, Sopinka J argued that the above rule interfered
with Parliament's decision to make lack of consent a requirement for
an assault and allowed judges to use the common law to expand the
breadth of the offence of assault. On the facts of the case, however, even
Sopinka J found no consent, because what had started as a consensual
fist fight had become a severe beating resulting in death. Subsequent
cases have found that minors cannot consent to fights where serious
harm is intended and caused, but they can consent to schoolyard scuf-
fles where serious harm is not intended or caused.[191] Whether by statutory words or judicial interpretation, the definition of the prohibited act
is an important policy element of the criminal law.

4) Bestiality

In *Jobidon*, the Court effectively expanded the crime of assault by
holding that consent would not be valid if serious harm was intended
and caused in an otherwise consensual fist fight. More recently and
with respect to bestiality, the Court took a different approach that left
the task of expanding criminal offences to Parliament. It determined
that the crime of bestiality under section 160 of the *Criminal Code* incorporated the traditional common law definition of the term and as
such required proof of human penetration of an animal. The Court
stressed that "[t]o to accept the Crown's invitation to expand the scope
of bestiality would be to turn back the clock and re-enter the period . . .
when the courts rather than the Parliament could change the elements

---

189 *Ibid.*
190 *Paice*, above note 5 at para 18.
191 *R v W(G)* (1994), 90 CCC (3d) 139 (Ont CA); *R v M(S)* (1995), 97 CCC (3d) 281
     (Ont CA). Consent will not be vitiated so long as non-trivial bodily harm is
     not intended even though it may be caused. *R v B(TB)* (1994), 93 CCC (3d) 191
     (PEICA); *R v McIlwaine* (1996), 111 CCC (3d) 426 (Que CA).

of criminal offences"[192] even though this was arguably what the Court had done in *Jobidon*. The Court appealed to both the interests in stability of the law and strict construction of the criminal law. It also noted that Parliament retained the ancient word "bestiality" even as it broadened the *actus reus* of other sexual offences better to protect interests in sexual integrity. Justice Abella dissented on the basis that Parliament had moved away from requiring proof of penetration for other sexual offences. She also argued that Parliament had acted on a "common sense assumption that since penetration is physically impossible with most animals and for half the population, requiring it as an element of the offence eliminates from censure most sexually exploitive conduct with animals."[193] This decision will likely result in legislative expansion of the crime, which will be clearer and provide more notice to accused, than expansions of crime through common law interpretation of the type seen in *Jobidon*.

5) Possession

Section 4(3) defines possession broadly to include not only personal possession, but also knowingly having something in the actual possession or custody of another person or in another place whether or not the place belongs or is occupied by the accused. Joint possession is also deemed under section 4(3)(b) where "one of two or more persons, with the knowledge and consent of the rest, has anything in his custody or possession." This definition is also used under the *Controlled Drugs and Substances Act*[194] where most issues of possession arise. This definition fits into a pattern seen throughout Canadian criminal law of defining the prohibited act broadly while relying on *mens rea* to mitigate the potentially harsh effects of such broad definitions. For example, the Supreme Court, in one of its most celebrated *mens rea* decisions, has held that those who possess drugs thinking they were an innocent substance would not have the necessary *mens rea* for possession even though they physically possessed them.[195]

Not all questions of possession can, however, be resolved by relying on *mens rea* requirement. The Supreme Court upheld the quashing of a conviction of the offence of possession of stolen goods when an accused might have known that a car he was riding in was stolen but

---

192 *R v DLW*, 2016 SCC 22 at para 3.
193 *Ibid* at para 149.
194 SC 1996, c 19, s 2.
195 *Beaver*, above note 64.

did not have control over the car.[196] Joint possession has been interpreted as requiring knowledge, consent, and a measure of control, and constructive knowledge requires knowledge and control.[197] A person with knowledge and control can have constructive knowledge even if he or she requires the third party actually to possess the prohibited substance.[198] Courts have also been understandably reluctant to hold that people possess illicit material when they retain them for a brief time for the purpose of handing them over to authorities.[199]

The Supreme Court has also indicated that possession of child pornography requires downloading files and not merely looking at them, but in reaching this conclusion gave weight to Parliament's creation of a separate offence of viewing child pornography. Justice Fish also observed that "[i]nterpreting possession to apply only to the underlying data file is also more faithful to a traditional understanding of what it means to 'possess' something. The traditional objects of criminal possession — for example, contraband, drugs, and illegal weapons — are all things that could, potentially at least, be transferred to another person."[200] He would not extend constructive possession to viewing material on a distant server that the accused had no control over but left open the possibility whether it might include storage in the cloud without downloading to a personal computer.

6) Theft

Section 322 defines theft as the taking or conversion of anything. Despite this apparently broad definition of the *actus reus* of theft, the Supreme Court has excluded the taking of confidential information from the offence of theft on the basis that information alone does not constitute property as protected under the criminal law, and its theft does not deprive the possessor of the use or possession of the confidential

---

196 *R v Terrence* (1983), 4 CCC (3d) 193 (SCC).

197 *R v Pham* (2005), 203 CCC (3d) 326 (Ont CA), aff'd 2006 SCC 26.

198 *R v Bremner*, 2007 NSCA 114.

199 The British Columbia Court of Appeal acquitted a warehouse owner who, fearing that goods had been deposited by others in his warehouse, moved them off his property, and the court stated, "Personal possession is established where an accused person exercises physical control over a prohibited object with full knowledge of its character, however brief the physical contact may be, and where there is some evidence to show the accused person took custody of the object willingly with intent to deal with it in some prohibited manner." *R v York*, 2005 BCCA 74 at para 20.

200 *R v Morelli*, 2010 SCC 8 at para 28.

information.[201] The Court's interpretation of the *actus reus* of theft means that taking confidential information alone is not presently theft, but taking a piece of paper that contains confidential information may be theft. This definition seems anachronistic in the computer age. Parliament can, of course, always amend the crime of theft to make clear that taking confidential information does indeed constitute theft, or it can enact a new offence.[202]

CONCLUSION

Codification, *Charter* rules against excessively vague or retroactive laws and the doctrine of strict construction all serve the purposes of a fixed, pre-determined criminal law that provides fair notice to the accused and limits law enforcement discretion. In reality, however, courts have been very reluctant to strike down laws under section 7 of the *Charter* on the basis that they are excessively vague.[203] They have also not recognized the doctrine of *de minimus non curat lex* to ensure that the criminal law is used with restraint and does not apply to trifles.

Courts have added interpretative glosses on offences and defences so that they diverge in significant ways from the words of the statute, sometimes restricting offences by reading in requirements that acts be marked departures from reasonable conduct[204] but in other cases not doing so.[205] They have also effectively expanded the ambit of assault offences by reading in policy-based restrictions against consent to serious harm[206] and have restricted defences through their interpretations.[207] Courts only apply the doctrine of strict construction if there are reasonable ambiguities after the criminal law has been given a purposive interpretation designed to achieve its objects. In general, the interpretation of the criminal act should be a matter of statutory interpretation and courts should avoid strained interpretation of what the legislature has prohibited.

---

201 *R v Stewart* (1988), 41 CCC (3d) 481 at 494–95 (SCC).
202 For example, see *Code*, above note 3, ss 326 and 342.1, prohibiting the taking of electricity, gas, or telecommunication services and unauthorized use of a computer.
203 *R v Heywood* (1994), 94 CCC (3d) 481 (SCC).
204 *Gunning*, above note 2.
205 *Beatty*, above note 51.
206 *Jobidon*, above note 5.
207 *Canadian Foundation for Children*, above note 22; *Ryan* above note 30.

Courts should consider going beyond the limited exceptions they have made to the traditional and often harsh rule that ignorance of the law is not an excuse. This means that an accused who makes even reasonable mistakes about what is prohibited will be convicted unless the theft or other property-based offences specifically allows for a colour of right defence. The *mens rea* of most crimes do not make beliefs by the accused that they are acting legally relevant and the section 19 ignorance or mistake of the law principle still applies.

The Supreme Court has now recognized that reasonable reliance on mistaken legal advice from an official who administers the law will provide a defence of officially induced error. This defence must be established by the accused on a balance of probabilities and it will result in a stay of proceedings. The recognition of the new defence of officially induced error is a positive development that should prevent the state from encouraging and prosecuting conduct at the same time.[208] Nevertheless, the defence is a limited qualification of the ignorance of the law is not an excuse principle. For example, it would not be available to accused who reasonably relied on their own legal research or even that of their lawyer. The Court has not extended it to cases where there is passive reliance on a refusal by state officials to make even complex laws clear to those who are regulated by the laws.

The Supreme Court has also suggested that the operation of section 19 can in some cases turn what might otherwise be a strict liability offence that allows a defence of due diligence into an absolute liability offence.[209] This somewhat mitigates the harshness of the ignorance of the law is no excuse principle because, as will be discussed in Chapter 6, an accused cannot be imprisoned for an absolute liability offence. At the same time, it does not fundamentally challenge the ignorance of the law is no excuse principle. In general, only prosecutorial or sentencing discretion can mitigate the harshness of convicting a person who acted under a reasonable mistake of law.

There is an emerging principle that involuntary actions may not constitute the prohibited act and this constitutes an important restraint on criminal law, particularly in those cases where there is no fault element. The issue of voluntariness has largely been left to judicial development and it would be helpful if voluntariness requirements were also articulated in the *Criminal Code*. More attention is being paid to the defence of accident, which can in some cases raise a reasonable doubt about the

---

208 *Lévis*, above note 73.
209 *Pontes*, above note 79.

voluntariness of the prohibited act, but in other cases can be relevant to criminal fault.

Although the criminal act and the fault requirement are supposed to coincide, the courts can often finesse this requirement. One factor is that many criminal acts are defined broadly so that it is only necessary for the fault element to coincide with one part of a broadly defined act. Conversely, the fault element of negligence has encouraged courts to judge the accused's conduct through a broader lens than simply focusing on the moment in which the *actus reus* has been committed.

The criminal law is not particularly forgiving when it comes to holding people responsible for prohibited consequences and this is consistent with the general trend to broad legislative and judicial definitions of the criminal act. The Supreme Court has indicated that the general test in homicide cases is one of a significant contributing cause and that any other tests are simply analytical aids in answering this question.[210] It is clear that the accused can be held responsible for causing death even if there are other concurrent causes of death, including in some cases improper medical treatment, the contributing actions of others, or of the victim's own "thin skull." The accused's actions need not be the sole cause of the prohibited consequences, but the possibility that intervening events will break the chain of causation so that the accused's actions are no longer a significant contributing cause should be considered. Causation, like other elements of the prohibited act, should be proven beyond a reasonable doubt.

Parliament has under the *Criminal Code* been relatively restrained in criminalizing omissions or failures to act, though such requirements are more prevalent in regulatory offences. Failure to act is generally only criminal under the *Criminal Code* in limited circumstances, the most important being the requirement that parents, guardians, and others provide children with the necessaries of life. Although legislatures can and have punished failures to act, this underlines the need for clarity in the criminal law especially when the ignorance of the law principle is considered.

Finally, the definition and interpretation of the criminal act is perhaps the most important policy component of the criminal law. The present trend is towards broad legislative definitions of the prohibited act. The Supreme Court is also not immune from this policy trend and it has made decisions that have expanded crimes like assault and sexual assault for policy reasons related to the discouragement of consensual fighting, concerns about the failure of a person to disclose they

---

210 *Nette*, above note 131; *Maybin*, above note 123.

have HIV, and better protection of the sexual integrity of complainants. There will always be a need for judicial interpretation, but controversial policy issues, such as whether a person can consent to non-trivial bodily harm[211] and whether consent should be based on the subjective views of the complainant in a sexual assault case,[212] should probably be specifically addressed by Parliament.

FURTHER READINGS

ASHWORTH, A. *Positive Obligations in Criminal Law* (Oxford: Hart Publishing, 2013).

BOYLE, C, & S DE GROOT. "The Responsible Citizen in the *City of Levis*: Due Diligence and Officially Induced Error" (2006) 36 CR (6th) 249.

BUTT, J. "Removing Fault from the Law of Causation" (2017) 65 *Criminal Law Quarterly* 72.

COLVIN, E, & S ANAND. *Principles of Criminal Law*, 3d ed (Toronto: Thomson Carswell, 2007) ch 3 & 4.

COMISKEY, M, & M SULLIVAN. "Avoidance, Deception and Mistake of Law: The *Mens Rea* of Tax Evasion" (2006) 51 *Criminal Law Quarterly* 303.

FEHR, C. "Reconceptualizing De Minimis Non Curat Lex" (2017) 64 *Criminal Law Quarterly* 200.

FERGUSON, G, "Causation and the *Mens Rea* for Manslaughter: A Lethal Combination" (2013) 99 *Criminal Reports* (6th) 351.

GALLOWAY, D. "Causation in Criminal Law: Interventions, Thin Skulls and Lost Chances" (1989) 14 *Queen's Law Journal* 71.

GRANT, I, D CHUNN, & C BOYLE. *The Law of Homicide* (Toronto: Carswell, 1994) ch 3.

HART, HLA, & T HONORE. *Causation in the Law*, 2d ed (Oxford: Oxford University Press, 1985) ch 12–14.

MANNING, M, & P SANKOFF. *Criminal Law*, 5th ed (Markham: LexisNexis, 2015) ch 4.

---

211 *Jobidon*, above note 5.
212 *Ewanchuk*, above note 177.

SHAFFER, M. "Sex, Lies and HIV" (2013) 63 *University of Toronto Law Journal* 467.

STEWART, H. "Mistake of Law under the *Charter*" (1998) 40 *Criminal Law Quarterly* 279.

STUART, D. *Canadian Criminal Law: A Treatise*, 7th ed (Toronto: Carswell, 2014) ch 2, 4, & 5.

VANDERVORT, L. "HIV, Fraud, Non-Disclosure, Consent and a Stark Choice: *Mabior* or Sexual Autonomy" (2013) 60 *Criminal Law Quarterly* 301.

WILLIAMS, G. "Criminal Omissions: The Conventional View" (1991) 107 *Law Quarterly Review* 86.

CHAPTER 4

UNFULFILLED CRIMES AND PARTICIPATION IN CRIMES

The trend towards broad definitions of the criminal act examined in the last chapter is a means of expanding the breadth of the criminal sanction. The provisions examined in this chapter also cast the net of criminal liability broadly to include those who attempt but fail to complete a crime; those who encourage or plan the commission of a crime; and those who assist others to commit a crime.

A person who goes beyond mere preparation to rob a bank, with the intent to commit the robbery, can be convicted of attempted robbery, even though no robbery took place and it may have been impossible for the complete crime to ever occur. An attempted robbery is, however, subject to less punishment than a robbery. On the other hand, a person who assists in the robbery by driving the getaway car can be convicted of being a party to the robbery by aiding the robbery, even though he or she never took the property with force. Similarly, a bank teller who helped the robber plan the heist might also be guilty of the robbery as a person who abets the crime. The provisions governing attempts and parties to a crime will be considered separately, but they are united in imposing the criminal sanction on those who do not actually commit the complete crime. The relatively high level of *mens rea* required for attempts and parties, however, generally limits these provisions to those who act with guilty intent or knowledge. Sentencing discretion also plays an important role in distinguishing the various degrees of culpability caught by the broad definitions of criminal attempts and parties to a crime.

In section 24 of the *Criminal Code*, Parliament has prohibited attempts to commit criminal offences. Any act beyond mere preparation may be a sufficient *actus reus* for an attempted crime, even if the act does not amount to a moral wrong or a social mischief. The counterbalance to this broad definition of the *actus reus* is that the Crown must prove beyond a reasonable doubt that the accused acted with the intent to commit the complete offence.

In addition to attempts, a person who counsels or solicits the commission of a crime or is part of an agreement to commit a crime may also be guilty of the separate crimes of counselling or conspiracy, even though the complete crime was never committed. These unfulfilled crimes are designed to discourage the commission of the complete offence and to recognize that the accused had the intent to commit the complete crime. They are, however, separate offences and, with the exception of conspiracy, subject to less punishment than the complete crime.

The law concerning parties to a crime is in some respects even broader and harsher than the law relating to inchoate crimes such as attempts, counselling, and conspiracy. Parliament has provided in section 21(1)(b) and (c) of the *Criminal Code* that those who assist the person committing the actual criminal offence through aiding or abetting are guilty as parties of the same criminal offence as the person who commits the crime. The person who acts as lookout or drives the getaway car can be convicted of robbery just as the person who takes the money by force. The *actus reus* is defined to include acts of assistance and acts of encouragement but not mere presence. At the same time, however, the Crown must prove the *mens rea* that the accused intentionally and knowingly aided or abetted the offence. A person who unwittingly delivers a package containing a bomb assists in the bombing, but would not have the intent required to be guilty as an aider or abettor to the bombing.

Section 21(2) makes an accused who has formed an unlawful purpose with an accomplice responsible for crimes that the accused knew or ought to have known would be a probable consequence of carrying out their common purpose. This section requires the formation of an unlawful purpose and either subjective or objective foresight of the additional crimes. The fault element of objective foresight has been found to be unconstitutional when applied to parties charged with murder and attempted murder. Thus, an accused who agreed with an accomplice to assault a person could not be convicted of murder unless he knew that it was likely that the accomplice would actually kill the victim. A requirement for a high level of *mens rea* may counterbalance the broad definition of the prohibited act. At the same time, the courts have indicated that the accused who forms an unlawful purpose does not necessarily have to desire that unlawful purpose. In addition, objective foresight of the further crime is all that is required under section 21(2) for crimes other than murder and attempted murder.

The provisions for attempted crimes and participation in crimes examined in this chapter apply to all criminal offences in the *Code* and constitute important extensions of criminal liability. For example, the September 11 terrorists could have been charged with attempted murder or conspiracy to commit murder if they were apprehended before they boarded the planes. Similarly, those who knowingly and intentionally assisted them in carrying out their plots could be charged as parties to their offences. At the same time, however, Parliament may create new crimes that may apply to conduct that might or might not constitute an attempt to commit a crime or a form of participation in the commission of the crime.

New crimes can serve as a functional substitute for attempted crimes. For example, charges of attempted sexual assault or attempted sexual interference may not be necessary if a person is guilty of the crime of inviting a person under sixteen years of age to engage in sexual touching or new offences relating to luring children over the internet.[1] New crimes such as financing, facilitating, or instructing a person to carry out activities for the benefit of a terrorist group may be broader alternatives to establishing that a person is guilty of attempting or conspiracy to commit the crime intended to be committed by the terrorists.[2] Crimes based on participation in the activities of a terrorist group[3] or a criminal organization[4] can be used instead of charging a person as a party to a crime committed by the group or with an attempt to commit the crime or with a conspiracy to commit the crime.

The Supreme Court has called a new computer luring offence under section 172.1 of the *Code* an "incipient or 'inchoate' offence, that is, a preparatory crime that captures otherwise legal conduct meant to culminate in the commission of a completed crime."[5] It has stressed that it was appropriate to require subjective fault in relation to all the elements of the offence including the age of the child and the purpose of facilitating a sexual offence given the remoteness of the offence to actual harm.[6] Nevertheless, the Court also indicated that a person may be

---

1   *Criminal Code*, RSC 1985, c C-46, ss 152 and 172.1 [*Code*].
2   *Ibid*, ss 83.02, 83.03, 83.04, 83.19, 83.21, & 83.22.
3   *Ibid*, s 83.18.
4   *Ibid*, s 467.11.
5   *R v Legare*, 2009 SCC 56 at para 25.
6   *Ibid* at para 33.

guilty under such offences even if the secondary crime was not likely to have been committed in a case involving a man luring a thirteen-year-old girl in a different province over the computer.[7] The Court has held that an accused can be guilty of influence peddling even if they do not succeed or even attempt to influence the conduct of government as a result of receiving a benefit in relation to government business.[8] It will be important that such statutory inchoate crimes have a high level of fault given their expansion of criminal liability. It is also possible that such broadly defined completed crimes may go beyond the traditional inchoate crimes. The courts, for example, have refused to combine in-choate forms of liability and have refused to create a crime of attempted conspiracy on the basis that the criminal law should not expand so far as to criminalize a "risk that a risk"[9] of a completed crime will occur. Statutory offences such as computer luring or terrorist financing may, however, criminalize conduct that presents a risk that a particularly dangerous risk may occur.

A. ATTEMPTS

Section 24 of the *Criminal Code* provides:

(1) Every one who, having an intent to commit an offence, does or omits to do anything for the purpose of carrying out his intention is guilty of an attempt to commit the offence whether or not it was possible under the circumstances to commit the offence.

(2) The question whether an act or omission by a person who has an intent to commit an offence is or is not mere preparation to commit the offence, and too remote to constitute an attempt to commit the offence, is a question of law.

Section 463 sets out the punishment for attempted crimes. A person guilty of an attempted crime is generally subject to one-half of the longest term to which a person guilty of the completed offence is liable.[10] A few substantive offences, including bribery and obstructing justice, include attempts as part of the completed offence and, as such, punish them in

---

7   *Ibid* at para 44.

8   *R v Carson*, 2018 SCC 12.

9   *R v Déry*, [2006] 2 SCR 669 at para 50 [*Déry*].

10 An attempt to commit an offence punishable on summary conviction is itself punishable on summary conviction: *Code*, above note 1, s 463(c). Attempted murder is subject to life imprisonment: *Code*, *ibid*, s 239.

the same fashion as the completed offence.[11] A broadly defined offence may also be a substitute for charging a person with an attempted crime. For example, many acts that may have been attempted rapes before 1983 could now constitute sexual assaults. Similarly, some unsuccessful thefts could still qualify as thefts if the accused, with the intent to steal, begins to move the object to be stolen.[12] The crime of assault is also defined broadly by Parliament to include not only the striking of another person, but also attempts or threats, by act or gesture, to apply force. Thus, there would be no need to charge a person with attempted assault if he or she threatened a person in a manner that made that person reasonably believe that he or she could be assaulted.[13]

1) Mens Rea for Attempts

The mens rea, or fault element, is the most important element of attempted crimes because the actus reus will, by definition, not include the completed crime. As the Ontario Court of Appeal has observed, "whereas in most crimes it is the actus reus which the law endeavours to prevent, and the mens rea is only a necessary element of the offence, in a criminal attempt, the mens rea is of primary importance and the actus reus is the necessary element."[14] Similarly, the Supreme Court has recognized that "the criminal element of the offence of attempt may lie solely in the intent."[15]

After having initially interpreted "the intent to commit an offence" in section 24(1) to include any intent provided in the Criminal Code to commit the completed offence,[16] the Supreme Court now interprets the intent to commit an offence as the specific intent to commit the completed offence. In the context of murder, McIntyre J reasoned as follows:

> The completed offence of murder involves a killing. The intention to commit the complete offence must therefore include an intention to kill . . . . I am then of the view that the mens rea for an attempted murder cannot be less than the specific intent to kill . . . .
>
> Section 24 defines an attempt as "having an intent to commit an offence." Because s. 24 is a general section it is necessary to "read in" the offence in question. The offence of attempted murder then is defined as "having an intent to commit murder." . . .

11   Code, ibid, ss 119(1)(a)(iii), 123(2), and 139(1).
12   Ibid, s 322(2).
13   Ibid, s 265(b)(ii).
14   R v Cline (1956), 115 CCC 18 at 27 (Ont CA).
15   R v Ancio (1984), 10 CCC (3d) 385 at 402 (SCC) [Ancio].
16   R v Lajoie (1973), 10 CCC (2d) 313 (SCC).

The fact that certain mental elements, other than an intent to kill, may lead to a conviction for murder where there has been a killing does not mean that anything less than an intent to kill will suffice for an attempt at murder.[17]

The intent that is "read in" for attempted murder is the intent to kill in section 229(a)(i), even though it is constitutionally permissible to convict a person of the completed offence of murder on the basis of a lesser intent.[18] It should be noted that *Ancio* was a decision made without any reference to the *Charter* and articulates principles that should apply to all attempts.[19]

a)   Constitutional Fault Element for Attempted Murder

In *R v Logan*,[20] the Supreme Court considered the fault element required under section 7 of the *Charter* for a conviction of attempted murder. Chief Justice Lamer held that the minimal fault element for attempted murder should be the same as for the commission of murder, on the grounds that the stigma of being convicted of the two offences was the same. He reasoned:

> The stigma associated with a conviction for attempted murder is the same as it is for murder. Such a conviction reveals that, although no death ensued from the actions of the accused, the intent to kill was still present in his or her mind. The attempted murderer is no less a killer than a murderer: he may be lucky — the ambulance arrived early, or some other fortuitous circumstance — but he still has the same killer instinct.[21]

In determining whether subjective foresight of death was constitutionally required, "the crucial consideration is whether there is a continuing serious social stigma which will be imposed on the accused upon conviction"[22] and not the existence of sentencing discretion that is

---

17   *Ancio*, above note 15 at 402–3.
18   Namely, subjective foresight of death as required in *R v Martineau* (1990), 58 CCC (3d) 353 (SCC) [*Martineau*], discussed in Chapter 2, Section B(4)(d)(v).
19   As Doherty JA has stated: "I do not agree that there is a meaningful difference in how the *Criminal Code* treats attempted murder and other attempts. Like all attempts, the requisite elements of the offence of attempted murder are found in s 24 of the *Code*. Attempted murder, like other attempts, requires proof of 'an intent to commit an offence' (s 24(1)) and an act that goes beyond 'mere preparation' (s.24(2))." *R v Sarrazin*, 2010 ONCA 577 at para 54.
20   (1990), 58 CCC (3d) 391 (SCC) [*Logan*].
21   *Ibid* at 399.
22   *Ibid* at 400.

available for attempted murder but not murder.[23] *Logan* suggests that the minimum fault requirement for attempted murder is the knowledge that death will result and that Parliament could lower the *mens rea* of attempted murder to that point but not below. Nevertheless, it does not overtake the higher standard of an intent to kill that is required by *Ancio.* It is an error to instruct the jury that knowledge that the victim is likely to die is a sufficient *mens rea* for attempted murder: the Crown must rather prove the *Ancio* standard of an intent to kill.[24] The *Charter* provides minimum standards of fairness towards the accused, not maximum standards.

b) *Mens Rea* for Other Attempted Offences

On the basis of *Ancio,* in principle, nothing less than the specific intent to obtain the prohibited result will suffice, even if a conviction for the completed offence could be based on some lesser form of intent. In *R v Colburne,*[25] the Quebec Court of Appeal stated that an attempt requires a specific intent to carry out the crime, even if the completed offence requires a lesser intent. On this basis, it could be argued that an attempted sexual assault must be based on the subjective intent to engage in non-consensual sexual activity, even though a person could now be convicted of the completed offence of sexual assault on the basis of recklessness, wilful blindness, or a failure to "take reasonable steps, in the circumstances known to the accused at the time, to ascertain that the complainant was consenting."[26] A discussion of the requirements of the crime of attempted sexual assault may, in many cases, be academic, given the wide definition of the *actus reus* of the completed crime of sexual assault.[27] That said, Canadian courts should not follow other jurisdictions that allow attempts to be punished on the basis of recklessness or knowledge with respect to the completed offence.[28] The

---

23 Attempted murder is punishable by up to life imprisonment, whereas murder has a mandatory sentence of life imprisonment.

24 *R v Latoski* (2005), 77 OR (3d) 505 at paras 11–12 (CA).

25 (1991), 66 CCC (3d) 235 at 240 and 248–49 (Que CA).

26 *Code,* above note 1, s 273.2.

27 Section 265(b) of the *Code* defines the *actus reus* of assaults to include attempts or threats to apply force, provided the accused causes the complainant to believe on reasonable grounds that he has the present ability to effect his purpose.

28 See E Colvin & S Anand, *Principles of Criminal Law,* 3d ed (Toronto: Thomson Carswell, 2007) at 528–30. The authors examine the Australian and British law and argue in favour of recognizing conditional intent or knowledge, but not recklessness, as a sufficient *mens rea* for attempts, in part because knowledge is a sufficient form of fault for most completed offences including murder. As suggested above, however, the fact that knowledge is sufficient for serious

essence of an attempt crime is the accused's clear intent to commit the completed offence. This is particularly the case when it is considered that the *actus reus* of the attempt may not in itself be a crime or even a social mischief. It is unclear whether courts will accept crimes such as attempted manslaughter or an attempt to commit a strict liability offence as offences because of the difficulties of reconciling such crimes with the idea that attempts require a specific intent to carry out the complete crime.

In *R v Williams*,[29] the Supreme Court recognized the relevance of the high-intent standard contemplated in *Ancio* outside the context of attempted murder. In this case, the Court convicted a man of attempted aggravated assault for having unprotected sex when he knew he was HIV-positive. As discussed in Chapter 3, an attempt conviction was entered because there was at least a reasonable doubt that the accused's partner was already infected with HIV when the accused had sex with her, knowing that he was infected. This *actus reus* of aggravated assault was not proven beyond a reasonable doubt, but there was a sufficient *actus reus* for attempted aggravated assault. On the *mens rea* issue, Binnie J stated for the Court:

> The crime of attempt, as with any offence, requires the Crown to establish that the accused *intended* to commit the crime in question: *R. v. Ancio*, [1984] 1 S.C.R. 225 at pp. 247–48. The requisite intent is established here . . . . The respondent, knowing . . . he was HIV-positive, engaged in unprotected sex with the complainant intending her thereby to be exposed to the lethal consequences of HIV.[30]

Attempted crimes, by their very nature of not resulting in the prohibited consequences of a completed crime, are characterized by the intent of the accused to carry out the completed crime. Attempts are, in the words of the Supreme Court, crimes where "the *mens rea* of the completed offence is present entirely."[31] Attempts to commit crimes will often require proof of a higher form of *mens rea* than the completed crime because of their very nature as inchoate offences. An intent to commit the complete

---

completed offences does not justify its use for attempted crime, which may not have involved even the commission of a harmful act, let alone the completed offence. For similar criticisms but with some suggestion that wilful blindness might suffice for an attempt, see M Manning & P Sankoff, *Criminal Law*, 5th ed (Markham, ON: LexisNexis, 2015) at 7.16.

29 2003 SCC 41 [*Williams*].

30 *Ibid* at para 62 [emphasis in original].

31 *Ibid* at para 65, quoting *United States of America v Dynar*, [1997] 2 SCR 462 at para 74 [*Dynar*].

crime is required for attempt, whereas knowledge or even recklessness will be a sufficient *mens rea* for most complete crimes.

2) The *Actus Reus* of Attempts

Although section 24(2) of the *Criminal Code* states that it is a question of law whether an act or omission "is not mere preparation to commit the offence, and too remote to constitute an attempt to commit the offence," Canadian courts have not been able to provide a universal definition of the prohibited act in criminal attempts. In *R v Cline*,[32] the Ontario Court of Appeal stated that "a precise and satisfactory definition of the *actus reus* is perhaps impossible," while concluding that "each case must be determined on its own facts, having due regard to the nature of the offence and the particular acts in question." The Court of Appeal added that the *actus reus* for an attempt need not "be a crime or a tort or even a moral wrong or social mischief," nor demonstrate by its nature an unequivocal intent.[33] The *actus reus* must not be mere preparation to commit a crime, but it can be the next step done with the intent to commit the crime after preparation is complete. On the facts, the Court of Appeal held that the accused had gone beyond mere preparation when, following his pattern of past indecent assaults, he approached and offered a young boy money to help carry his suitcases. By donning large sunglasses and selecting a secluded alley, the accused had finished preparing to commit the crime, and his approach to the young boy was a sufficient *actus reus*.

In *R v Deutsch*,[34] the Supreme Court took a fact and offence specific approach to determine when preparation has ended and the *actus reus* for a criminal attempt has begun. Justice Le Dain stated:

> [T]he distinction between preparation and attempt is essentially a qualitative one, involving the relationship between the nature and quality of the act in question and the nature of the complete offence, although consideration must necessarily be given, in making that qualitative distinction, to the relative proximity of the act in question to what would have been the completed offence, in terms of time, location, and acts under the control of the accused remaining to be accomplished.[35]

The Supreme Court held that the accused had gone beyond mere preparation for the crime of attempted procurement of prostitution when

32   Above note 14 at 26 and 28.
33   *Ibid* at 28. See also *R v Sorrell* (1978), 41 CCC (2d) 9 (Ont CA) [*Sorrell*].
34   (1986), 27 CCC (3d) 385 (SCC) [*Deutsch*].
35   *Ibid* at 401.

he indicated to job applicants that they could earn up to $100,000 a year and might be required to have sex with clients in order to secure business contracts. By holding out large financial awards in the course of the job interviews, the Court concluded that the accused had gone beyond mere preparation, even though no formal job offer was made and any prostitution would happen "a considerable period of time" in the future.

Determining whether the accused has gone beyond mere preparation and committed an *actus reus* for an attempted crime is difficult to predict. In a subsequent case, the Supreme Court has observed that "the distinction between preparation and attempt is essentially a qualitative one, involving the relationship between the nature and quality of the act in question and the nature of the complete offence." It indicated that "consideration must necessarily be given, in making that qualitative distinction, to the relative proximity of the act in question to what would have been the completed offence, in terms of time, location, and acts under the control of the accused remaining to be accomplished." The Court found that the accused had gone beyond preparation and there was "sufficient proximity" to the completed offence of selling illegally obtained fish when the accused had brought a sample of illegally obtained fish to a store and asked the owner if he was "interested."[36]

In a practical sense, the determination of whether the act has gone beyond mere preparation may depend in part on the strength of the evidence of wrongful intent. Going through the glove compartment of a car has been held to be the *actus reus* for its attempted theft when the accused indicated that he was searching for keys to steal the car.[37] The accused's actions in pointing a loaded gun at and following his ex-wife have been held sufficient for an attempted murder, even if the accused did not fire the gun.[38] On the other hand, making a plasticine impression of a car key has been held to be only preparation to steal the car and thus not sufficient for the prohibited act of an attempt.[39] Approaching a store with balaclavas and a gun could be a sufficient *actus reus* for attempted robbery, but retreat when informed that the store was closed may reveal

---

36   *R v Gladstone* (1996), 109 CCC (3d) 193 at 202 (SCC).

37   *R v James* (1971), 2 CCC (2d) 141 (Ont CA).

38   *R v Boudreau* (2005), 193 CCC (3d) 449 (NSCA). For another case where pointing a gun was a sufficient *actus reus*, see *R v Goldberg*, 2014 BCCA 313. See also *R v Mantley*, 2013 NSCA 16, where entering a hospital with a loaded weapon where the intended victim was present was held to be a sufficient *actus reus* for attempted murder.

39   *R v Lobreau* (1988), 67 CR (3d) 74 (Alta CA).

a reasonable doubt about the intent to commit the robbery.[40] In practice, a more remote *actus reus* will be accepted if the intent is clear. Another factor may well be the magnitude of the planned crime. In a case in which the accused intends to commit murder or even mass murder, the approach in *Deutsch* of holding that the accused has gone beyond mere preparation and committed the *actus reus* of an attempt even though the completed crime may still be months away makes eminent sense.

Some countries recognize abandonment or desistance as a defence to attempt. The Canadian authorities have rejected abandonment as an independent defence that is not contemplated in section 24,[41] while at the same time recognizing that it may create a reasonable doubt about whether the accused had the intent to commit the crime in the first place.[42] Although an act beyond mere preparation is required, the emphasis throughout the law of attempts should be on the accused's intent to commit the completed offence. Abandonment may raise a reasonable doubt about whether the accused had the intent to commit the complete offence in the first place, but in Canada, it is not an independent defence to an attempted crime.

Something that goes beyond mere preparation may still constitute the *actus reus* of attempt in cases where the complete crime does not and even cannot occur. In *R v Detering*,[43] the accused had gone well beyond mere preparation in their attempt to commit fraud, but were convicted of attempted fraud as opposed to fraud because the intended victims were not deceived. In *Williams*,[44] unprotected acts of sexual intercourse by an accused who knew he was HIV-positive constituted the *actus reus* of attempted aggravated assault. The accused "took more than preparatory steps. He did everything he could to achieve the infection of the complainant." The fact that it may have been impossible to infect the complainant because she was already infected with HIV did not prevent the conviction of the accused for attempt.

---

40   *Sorrell*, above note 33.
41   *R v Kosh*, [1965] 1 CCC 230 at 235 (Sask CA), stating that "once the essential element of intent is established, together with overt acts towards the commission of the intended crime, the reason why the offence was not committed becomes immaterial. Once these elements are established, it makes no difference whether non-commission was due to interruption, frustration or a change of mind."
42   *Sorrell*, above note 33.
43   (1982), 70 CCC (2d) 321 (SCC) [*Detering*].
44   *Williams*, above note 29 at para 64.

3) Impossibility and Attempts

The theoretical issue of whether an accused should be held liable for attempts when it was impossible to commit the completed offence has been settled by section 24(1) of the *Criminal Code*, which states that a person can be guilty of attempt "whether or not it was possible under the circumstances to commit the offence." This provision precludes either legal or factual impossibility as a possible defence to an attempted crime. Factual impossibility would include a case in which an accused attempted to pick a pocket that contained no money[45] and the case of a person who tried to infect someone with HIV even though she was already infected.[46] Legal impossibility would include attempting to receive goods believed to be stolen, but which were in law not stolen.[47] The distinction between factual and legal impossibility has been rejected on the basis that under section 24 "[t]here is no legally relevant difference between the pickpocket who reaches into the empty pocket [that is, factual impossibility] and the man who takes his own umbrella from a stand believing it to be some other person's umbrella [legal impossibility]."[48] In both cases, the accused had the *mens rea* of a thief, had taken steps beyond preparation to consummate the crime, and was thwarted by circumstances over which he had no control.

On several occasions, the Supreme Court has indicated that impossibility is not a defence to attempted crimes in Canada.[49] In *Dynar*,[50] the Court again affirmed that impossibility was not a defence to an attempt. Thus, an accused who believed he was engaged in laundering drug money could be convicted of attempted money-laundering even though the money was government money provided by the police in a sting operation and not drug money. Similarly, a person who stabs a corpse with the intent to murder a real person would be guilty of attempted murder.[51] A person who accepts a package believing it to contain a large

---

45   *R v Scott*, [1964] 2 CCC 257 (Alta CA).
46   *Williams*, above note 29.
47   For an acquittal in this scenario, see *Anderton v Ryan*, [1985] AC 560 (HL). This case was overruled a year later in *R v Shivpuri*, [1986] 2 All ER 334 (HL).
48   *Dynar*, above note 31 at para 62.
49   *Detering*, above note 43; *R v Kundeus* (1975), 24 CCC (2d) 276 (SCC).
50   *Dynar*, above note 31 at para 67. In any event, the offence was subsequently amended to criminalize laundering money either knowing or believing that it was the proceeds of crime. *Code*, above note 1, s 462.31(1).
51   In dissent, Major J pointed out that this approach could lead to what he saw as the absurdity of convicting someone of attempted murder who placed a voodoo stick in a doll thinking that this would cause the death of a person. *Dynar*, above note 31 at para 173.

amount of drugs would be guilty of attempting to possess drugs for the purpose of trafficking even if the package did not contain any drugs.[52] A person who comes to a hotel hoping to have sex with an eleven-year-old is still guilty of attempting to procure the sexual services of a child even though no child was involved in the police sting operation.[53]

The only time impossibility could be a defence would be if a person intended to commit an "imaginary crime." Thus, a person who believed that the possession of $100 bills was illegal would be innocent because that person has "no *mens rea* known to law" and "has not displayed any propensity to commit crimes in the future." It is highly unlikely that a person would ever be charged with the commission of an imaginary crime and it is best simply to conclude that factual or legal impossibility is not a defence to an attempted crime. What matters is whether the accused had the intent to commit the crime and went beyond mere preparation to commit the crime.

B. CONSPIRACY

A conspiracy, like an attempt, is something that occurs before a completed offence is committed. The Supreme Court has indicated that "conspiracy is in fact a more 'preliminary' crime than attempt, since the offence is considered to be complete before any acts are taken that go beyond mere preparation to put the common design into effect. The Crown is simply required to prove a meeting of the minds with regard to a common design to do something unlawful, specifically the commission of an indictable offence."[54] Unlike attempts, however, conspiracies are generally punished as severely as the completed offence.

Section 465(1)(c) establishes the general offence of conspiracy by providing that "every one who conspires with any one to commit an indictable offence . . . is guilty of an indictable offence and liable to the same punishment as that to which an accused who is guilty of that offence would, on conviction, be liable."[55] A general provision for conspiracies to effect an unlawful purpose was repealed after the Supreme Court indicated a reluctance to recognize conspiracies to commit common

---

52   *R v Chan* (2003), 178 CCC (3d) 269 at paras 63–64 (Ont CA) (*obiter* ruling) [*Chan*].

53   *R v Kerster* (2003), 175 CCC (3d) 28 (BCCA).

54   *Dynar*, above note 31 at para 87.

55   *Code*, above note 1, s 465(1)(d), now provides that everyone who conspires to commit a summary conviction offence is guilty of an offence punishable on summary conviction and it is not yet clear whether this includes provincial and regulatory offences that can be prosecuted as summary conviction offences.

law as opposed to statutory crimes.[56] There are specific provisions relating to conspiracy to commit murder;[57] conspiracy to prosecute a person known to be innocent;[58] conspiracy with extraterritorial effects;[59] and conspiracy in restraint of trade.[60] The agreement of more than one person to commit a crime is seen as a particular menace to society that deserves punishment even before the conspirators have taken steps beyond preparation and attempted to commit the crime. In practice, conspiracy charges are most often brought in cases involving organized crime and drug trafficking. Other offences such as participation in the activities in a terrorist organization or a criminal organization may be functional substitutes for conspiracy charges.

1) The *Actus Reus* of Conspiracy

The *actus reus* of conspiracy is an agreement to carry out the completed offence. "The essence of criminal conspiracy is proof of agreement. On a charge of conspiracy the agreement is the gist of the offence. The *actus reus* is the fact of agreement."[61] The commission of acts in furtherance of the scheme does not constitute the *actus reus*; there must be an agreement and meeting of minds to commit the offence.[62] Once an agreement to commit an offence is reached, it is not necessary to do anything else. In the context of a conspiracy to commit murder, "the crime is complete when two or more persons agree to kill a third party. No one need be killed; nor is it necessary that any steps be taken to bring about the murder."[63] A criminal plot may be a conspiracy long before it has gone beyond the preparation necessary for a criminal attempt. Thus, "[c]onspiracy is in fact a more 'preliminary' crime than attempt, since the offence is considered to be complete before any acts are taken that go beyond mere preparation to put the common design into effect. The Crown is simply required to prove a meeting of the minds with regard to a common design to do something unlawful, specifically

---

56   *R v Gralewicz* (1980), 54 CCC (2d) 289 (SCC).

57   *Code*, above note 1, s 465(1)(a).

58   *Ibid*, s 465(1)(b).

59   *Ibid*, ss 465(3) & (4).

60   *Ibid*, ss 466 & 467.

61   *R v Cotroni* (1979), 45 CCC (2d) 1 at 17 (SCC) [*Cotroni*]. See also *R v Douglas* (1991), 63 CCC (3d) 29 (SCC).

62   *R v HA* (2005), 206 CCC (3d) 233 at paras 46–48 (Ont CA); *R v JF*, [2013] 1 SCR 565 at para 44 [*JF*] ("an act done in furtherance of the unlawful object is not an element of the offence of conspiracy.")

63   *JF, ibid* at para 21.

the commission of an indictable offence."[64] An agreement to launder money could be a conspiracy even though the money was not yet transferred between the parties and there would not be a sufficient *actus reus* for an attempt.

Although an agreement must be between two or more people, a person can be convicted of conspiracy even if, for some other reason, the co-conspirators are not convicted.[65] As discussed in the next section, however, the conspirators must not only intend to agree, but also intend to carry out their common design. There must be communication for an agreement to be reached, but an implicit or tacit agreement to commit an offence is enough to prove the act of conspiracy:[66] "So long as there is a continuing overall, dominant plan there may be changes in methods of operation, personnel, or victims, without bringing the conspiracy to an end. The important inquiry is not as to the acts done in pursuance of the agreement, but whether there was, in fact, a common agreement."[67] The *actus reus* of conspiracy is thus an agreement, but the agreement itself need not be etched in stone or carried out.

a) Attempted Conspiracies and Other Attempts to Combine Inchoate Forms of Liability

The courts have refused to recognize an offence of attempted conspiracy when an agreement is not reached between the parties. In *R v Déry*,[68] the Supreme Court set aside a conviction of an attempt to conspire on the basis that it would extend the criminal law too far and criminalize "bad thoughts of this sort that were abandoned before an agreement was reached, or an attempt made, to act upon them." The Court distinguished an attempt to conspire, which it characterized as "a risk that a risk will materialize,"[69] from both conspiracies and attempts that pose more direct risks.

At the same time, the Court noted that "unilateral conspiracies," in which there was no agreement, "will in any event normally be caught under our law by the offence of 'counselling an offence not committed'"[70] under section 464 of the *Code*.[71] A person who unsuccessfully attempts to enter a conspiracy may nevertheless be guilty of the independent

---

64 *Dynar*, above note 31 at para 87.
65 *R v Murphy* (1981), 60 CCC (2d) 1 (Alta CA); *Cotroni*, above note 61.
66 *Atlantic Sugar Refineries Co v Canada (AG)* (1980), 54 CCC (2d) 373 at 381 (SCC).
67 *Cotroni*, above note 61 at 17–18.
68 *Déry*, above note 9 at para 51.
69 *Ibid* at para 50.
70 *Ibid* at para 36.
71 See also *R v Dungey* (1979), 51 CCC (2d) 86 (Ont CA); *Chan*, above note 52.

offence of counselling a crime that is not committed. In addition, a person who abets or encourages any of the conspirators to pursue the object of the conspiracy can be guilty of being a party to the conspiracy even though he or she did not actually agree to the conspiracy.[72] A person who pursues a unilateral conspiracy beyond the point of mere preparation would also be guilty of an attempt to commit the crime. Given all these other offences, there is no need for an offence of attempted conspiracy.

The Court in *Déry* left open the question of whether one could attempt to commit an offence such as treason that is defined to include a conspiracy to commit the offence.[73] It could be argued that the dangers of these specified offences justify punishment of attempts to commit them and that the form of the offence allows cases such as *Déry* to be distinguished.[74] Nevertheless, the courts should not be overly influenced by form because cases such as *Déry* are based on sound principles about the need for restraint in the criminal law and the dangers of punishing people simply for bad thoughts and reckless talk.

An alternative to such an extension of conspiracy offences is the creation of a statutory offence that can be completed as a separate crime even though the accused may only be preparing or conspiring to commit some ultimate form. Parliament increasingly enacts such broad offences. One example is the definition of terrorist activities in section 83.01 of the *Criminal Code*, which includes attempts, counselling, threats, and conspiracies to commit terrorist activities. In turn, terrorist activities are included in the definition of offences such as participation in a terrorist group, which can cover situations where people may be planning acts of terrorism. The Supreme Court rejected the idea that this broad offence in section 83.18 ran afoul of the principle of restraint in *Dery* and also concluded that when given a purposive interpretation and the harms of terrorism, the statutory participation offence was not unconstitutionally overbroad.[75] As criminal prohibitions are extended to include and punish as complete crimes conduct that is very remote from the ultimate harms punished, it will be especially important for courts to insist on the need for the proof of high levels of *mens rea* and

---

72   *R v McNamara (No 1)* (1981), 56 CCC (2d) 193 (Ont CA); *R v Vucetic* (1998), 129 CCC (3d) 178 (Ont CA).

73   *Déry*, above note 9 at para 20. The completed offence of treason is defined in s 46(2)(c) of the *Code*, above note 1, to include a conspiracy to use force or violence for the purpose of overthrowing the government. See also s 466, *ibid*, providing a complete offence of conspiracy in restraint of trade.

74   Colvin & Anand, above note 28 at 526.

75   *R v Khawaja*, [2012] 3 SCR 555.

to ensure proportionality between what the accused actually did and the punishment. That said, courts may defer more to Parliament in its definition of statutory crimes than in their own approach under the common law, which has generally rejected the combination of different forms of inchoate liability and the criminalization of remote risks that a completed crime might be committed.

2) The *Mens Rea* for Conspiracy

The *mens rea* for conspiracy includes both the "intention to agree" and the "intention to put the common design into effect." Justice Taschereau explained:

> Although it is not necessary that there should be an overt act in furtherance of the conspiracy to complete the crime, I have no doubt that there must exist an intention to put the common design into effect . . . . The intention cannot be anything else but the will to attain the object of the agreement. I cannot imagine several conspirators agreeing to defraud, to restrain trade, or to commit any indictable offence, without having the intention to reach the common goal.[76]

In that case, no conspiracy was found because only one of the parties to the agreement actually had the intent to carry out the kidnapping. An agreement between one person and an undercover officer could not be a conspiracy because the officer would not intend to carry out the offence.[77] An agreement between two people and an undercover officer could, however, be a conspiracy because in that case two or more people would intend to commit the crime.

In *R v Sokoloski*,[78] the Supreme Court convicted two people of conspiracy to traffic in a controlled drug on the basis that the seller of the large quantity of the drugs must have known that the purchaser would in turn sell the drugs. A minority criticized this decision as an unwarranted extension of conspiracy, because the seller and the buyer had not agreed to carry out the trafficking enterprise in common. To support a conspiracy, there should be something more than mere knowledge that drugs will be sold, but rather an agreement on a common design and an intent to implement that agreement.

---

76   *R v O'Brien* (1954), 110 CCC 1 at 3 (SCC).

77   As examined in the next section, the suspect might be guilty of the separate crime of counselling a crime that was not committed.

78   (1977), 33 CCC (2d) 495 (SCC).

In *R v Nova Scotia Pharmaceutical Society*,[79] the Supreme Court indicated that to be convicted of conspiracy to lessen competition unduly, it was necessary to prove that the accused had a subjective intent to enter into an agreement and knowledge of its terms. An objective fault element, however, was sufficient in relation to the aims of the agreement, so that the accused would be guilty if reasonable business-people in their position would have known that the agreement would unduly lessen competition. An accused who deliberately entered into an agreement could be guilty even if he or she did not intend or know the agreement would unduly lessen competition.

The nature of conspiracy as an agreement between two or more persons to commit a crime also led the Supreme Court in *R v JF*[80] to hold that an accused would be guilty of aiding and abetting a conspiracy only if he or she assisted in the formation of the agreement as opposed to the broader proposition of carrying out the aims of the conspiracy.

3) Impossibility and Conspiracy

Given the rejection of impossibility as a defence to an attempted crime, it is not surprising that impossibility is also not a defence to the related crime of conspiracy. Thus, two accused[81] could conspire to launder drug money even though it was impossible to launder the money because the money was government money provided in a sting operation. The accused still reached an agreement (the *actus reus*) and their intention to agree and launder drug money (the *mens rea*) remained the same "regardless of the absence of the circumstance that would make the realization of that intention possible . . . . The essential element of conspiracy is the existence of the agreement to put the intention of the conspirators into effect."[82] As with attempts, impossibility would prevent a conspiracy conviction only if two or more people agree to commit what they may think is a crime, but what is actually only an imaginary crime. There is no possible social interest in punishing an agreement to do something that is not a crime.

---

79   (1992), 74 CCC (3d) 289 at 326 (SCC).

80   Above note 62.

81   The two accused would have to both intend to agree and intend to carry out the agreement so that an agreement between one person and an undercover officer would not be sufficient.

82   *Dynar*, above note 31 at para 108.

C. COUNSELLING A CRIME THAT IS NOT COMMITTED

As discussed above, a person could not be convicted of conspiracy for agreeing with an undercover police officer to commit a crime because one party to the agreement would not have the intent to put the common design into effect. In that case, or in any case, where a person attempts to solicit another to commit a crime and the second person is unwilling to do so, the appropriate charge will be counselling a crime that is not committed. This is a separate offence under section 464 of the *Criminal Code* and it is subject to the same reduced punishment as an attempt. It is distinct from counselling an offence that is committed, which under section 22 of the *Code* is a method by which a person becomes a party to an offence and is punished as if he or she had committed the complete offence.

1) The *Actus Reus* of Counselling a Crime That Is Not Committed

Section 22(3) provides that for the purposes of the *Criminal Code* "counsel" includes procure, solicit, or incite. It does not matter whether the person counselled acts on the solicitation or has any intention of doing so.[83] This means that a person can be guilty of counselling an undercover officer to commit a crime, even if the person so solicited would never commit the offence. The Supreme Court has indicated that "the *actus reus* for counselling will be established where the materials or statements made or transmitted by the accused *actively induce or advocate* — and do not merely *describe* — the commission of an offence."[84] The Ontario Court of Appeal has stated that a person can be guilty of counselling, even if the person solicited immediately rejects the idea of going through with the offence.[85] Of course, if the person counselled does carry out the crime, then the person who counselled the crime is guilty as a party to the offence that is eventually committed.[86]

---

83   *R v Glubisz (No 2)* (1979), 47 CCC (2d) 232 (BCCA).

84   *R v Hamilton*, [2005] 2 SCR 432 at para 15 [emphasis in original] [*Hamilton*]. See also *Mugesera v Canada (Minister of Citizenship and Immigration)*, [2005] 2 SCR 100 at para 64 [*Mugesera*], stating: "[T]he offence of counselling requires that the statements, viewed objectively, actively promote, advocate or encourage the commission of the offence described in them."

85   *R v Gonzague* (1983), 4 CCC (3d) 505 (Ont CA).

86   *Code*, above note 1, s 22, discussed later in this chapter.

2) The *Mens Rea* for Counselling a Crime That Is Not Committed

The *mens rea* in section 464 is not spelled out, but given the possible breadth of the *actus reus*, it will be important to require subjective knowledge of the crime counselled and an actual intent by the accused (but not necessarily the person counselled) that the crime be performed. In *R v McLeod*,[87] Georgia Strait Publishing Ltd was convicted of counselling the illegal cultivation of marijuana by publishing an article explaining how to grow marijuana. The Court of Appeal concluded that the paper was deliberately counselling readers of the paper to cultivate marijuana, but held that the evidence was insufficient to prove that the editor of the paper had this intent. If this case arose today, the protection of freedom of expression in section 2(b) of the *Charter* would also be a factor.[88]

In *R v Janeteas*,[89] the Ontario Court of Appeal issued a comprehensive judgment that stressed the importance of *mens rea* in a counselling offence. Justice of Appeal Moldaver stated that, as with the other inchoate crimes of attempts and conspiracy, the accused must intend the commission of the offence in order to be guilty of the crime of counselling an offence that is not committed. Recklessness was not a sufficient form of fault because it could result in the conviction of a person who made only casual comments about the possibility of a crime being committed. The Court of Appeal rejected the policy argument that a person should be convicted simply because he may have placed a dangerous thought about the commission of a crime into another's mind. The Alberta Court of Appeal has likewise stressed the requirement of intent as opposed to lesser forms of subjective *mens rea* such as recklessness or wilful blindness for the section 464 offence. It has related this high *mens rea* standard to the fact that the offence relates to counselling a crime that is not committed.[90] The decisions are helpful in their recognition that counselling a crime that is not committed is, like an attempt or a conspiracy, a form of inchoate liability. As such, it should require an intent to commit the complete offence.

Unfortunately, the Supreme Court of Canada in a 6:3 decision held that the *mens rea* of counselling an offence included not only an intent

---

87   (1970), 1 CCC (2d) 5 at 8 (BCCA).
88   *Iorfida v MacIntyre* (1994), 93 CCC (3d) 395 (Ont Ct Gen Div) (law restricting sale or promotion of drug literature an unjustified violation of freedom of expression).
89   (2003), 172 CCC (3d) 97 (Ont CA).
90   *R v Hamilton* (2003), 178 CCC (3d) 434 at paras 5 and 27 (Alta CA).

to commit the substantive crime, but also a lesser form of *mens rea* in the form of knowingly counselling a crime while aware of an unjustified risk that the offence was likely to be committed as a result of the accused's conduct.[91] Although described as a "relatively demanding standard," the majority of the Court has lowered the fault element to something perhaps less than knowledge by its reference of knowledge of an unjustified risk that the offence will likely be committed as a result of the accused's conduct. Justice Charron in a strong dissent contemplated a *mens rea* requirement that was both higher, simpler, and easier to explain to the jury when she stated that "the counsellor must intend that the counselled offence be committed for the offence to be made out."[92]

The majority's judgment in *R v Hamilton* should not be interpreted as encompassing recklessness as a sufficient fault for the offence of counselling a crime not committed. Although the majority does refer to a risk of an offence being committed, it requires that the risk be that the offence is likely to be committed, which is a higher standard than a reckless awareness of the possibility that an offence would be committed.[93]

In *Mugesera*,[94] the Court also considered section 464, albeit in the context of immigration law. The Court indicated that the accused's knowledge that a speech given during the Rwandan genocide would be understood as incitement to commit murder demonstrated that "Mr. Mugesera not only intentionally gave the speech, but also intended that it result in the commission of murders." Thus, this case is consistent with the requirement that an accused intend or at least have knowledge of the complete crime to be guilty of the offence of counselling an offence. A requirement that the Crown only have to prove recklessness as opposed to intent or knowledge could result in a counselling offence that would be a disproportionate restriction on intemperate speech. As Charron J recognized, "[I]f mere recklessness as to the communication's potential power of persuasion were to suffice, some may argue that the publication of Shakespeare's *Henry VI*, with its famous phrase

---

91   *Hamilton*, above note 84 at para 29.
92   *Ibid* at para 82.
93   Professors Colvin and Anand, however, interpret *R v Hamilton* as including recklessness liability, above note 28 at 570, as does Professor Don Stuart in *Canadian Criminal Law*, 7th ed (Scarborough, ON: Thomson Carswell, 2014) at 746. See also Manning & Sankoff, above note 28 at 7.109. Although Fish J's reference to "risk" suggests recklessness, his statement about the need for the accused to know that the offence will "likely" be committed and his reference to the "demanding" nature of the fault requirement suggest that he did not intend to include recklessness as the lowest form of subjective fault as a sufficient fault element for an inchoate crime.
94   Above note 84 at para 79.

'let's kill all the lawyers', should be subject to state scrutiny!"[95] Recklessness would also raise other constitutional issues, at least as applied to the offence of counselling a murder that was not committed.[96] That said, it would have been more principled for the Court in *Hamilton* to have recognized that a common feature of all inchoate offences, at least in the absence of a clear legislative intent to the contrary, is that they require proof of an intent to commit the completed offence. If the accused is being punished primarily for his or her intent, then it makes sense to require proof of a clear intent to commit the completed offence.

3) Impossibility and Counselling

Given the willingness to convict an accused for impossible attempts and conspiracies and for counselling crimes that are immediately rejected by the person solicited, it would be expected that impossibility would not be a defence to the crime of counselling a crime that is not committed. In *R v Richard*,[97] however, the Manitoba Court of Appeal held that an adult accused could not be convicted of counselling the commission of an indecent assault because the child he attempted to procure was incapable of committing the completed offence because she was under twelve years of age.[98] This strange and impractical result helps to explain Parliament's enactment of a separate offence of inviting a child under sixteen to engage in sexual touching.[99] A broadly worded offence may be a substitute for an inchoate crime such as an attempt or counselling a crime that is not committed.

Parliament has now provided in section 23.1 of the *Criminal Code* that a person could be guilty of being a party to an offence even though the person aided or abetted, counselled or assisted, cannot be convicted of the offence. Strangely, this provision may not change the result in *Richard*, because it applies only to offences that are committed, not to the separate offence in section 464 of counselling a crime that is not committed. Nevertheless, an accused in Richard's position could be charged with the separate crime of inviting a child to engage in sexual

---

95   *Hamilton*, above note 84 at para 76 (in dissent).

96   It could be argued that such an offence would have the same stigma as attempted murder and should require knowledge as a constitutional minimum form of *mens rea*. See *Logan*, above note 20.

97   (1986), 30 CCC (3d) 127 (Man CA). It is also surprising that the Crown did not charge the accused with an attempt to commit indecent assault.

98   As examined in Chapter 3, Section A(2), s 13 of the *Code*, above note 1, deems those under twelve years of age incapable of committing any criminal offence.

99   *Code, ibid*, s 152.

touching or attempted sexual interference. For these crimes, as well as for crimes in sections 21 to 23 of the *Code*, it does not matter that the other person involved could not be convicted of an offence. Thus, adults who counsel young children under twelve years to commit drug offences can be convicted even though the child they tried to recruit could not be prosecuted.

D. COUNSELLING A CRIME THAT IS COMMITTED

Section 22(1) provides that a person who counsels a crime that is committed becomes a party to that offence and, as such, is subject to the same punishment as if he or she had actually committed the offence. This provision applies "notwithstanding that the offence was committed in a way different from that which was counselled." An accused who counsels a person to kill another with a bomb would still be guilty of murder if the person counselled used a gun instead. In addition, section 22(2) expands liability further by providing that a counsellor becomes a party "to every offence that the other commits in consequence of the counselling that the person who counselled knew or ought to have known was likely to be committed in consequence of the counselling."

1) The *Actus Reus* of Counselling a Crime That Is Committed

The *actus reus* of counselling remains the act of procuring, soliciting, or inciting a crime. In addition, a crime must then be committed by the person counselled. The crime need not be committed in the same way as was counselled or even be the same crime that was counselled. It must, however, be a crime that was reasonably foreseeable from the counselling. Under section 23.1, an accused could be convicted of counselling even though the person who actually committed the offence could not. For example, an adult who involved children under twelve years of age in the drug trade could be convicted even though the children could not. Similarly, a person who procured a reluctant person to commit an offence could be guilty even though the reluctant person might have a valid defence such as duress.

2) The Mens Rea for Counselling a Crime That Is Committed

The accused must intentionally counsel a criminal offence under section 22(1). It would not be fair to hold that an accused is a party to an offence for comments that were not intended to solicit or incite a crime, but which had that effect. Under section 22(2), an accused who intentionally counsels an offence is also a party "to every offence that the other commits in consequence of the counselling that the person who counselled knew or ought to have known was likely to be committed in consequence of the counselling." This extends liability not only to the offence intentionally counselled but to any other offence that the person knew or ought to have known would be committed as a result of the counselling.

The latter fault element of objective foreseeability would violate section 7 of the *Charter* when applied to murder or attempted murder, which has a minimum fault element of subjective foresight of death.[100] Nevertheless, objective foreseeability would be a constitutionally sufficient fault element for most other crimes. For example, an accused who counselled a severe beating could be convicted of manslaughter because he or she ought to have known that manslaughter could result.[101] The accused would, however, be guilty of murder only if he or she actually knew that death was likely to result.

Section 22(2) incorporates objective forms of fault while section 464 always requires subjective fault even though both offences are based on the counselling of a crime. A rationale for the different approaches is that counselling under section 22 constitutes a form of participation in a completed crime whereas counselling under section 464 is a form of inchoate liability that applies when the crime counselled has not been committed.

E. AIDING AND ABETTING

Section 21(1) of the *Criminal Code* provides that everyone is a party to an offence who "actually commits it; or does or omits to do anything for the purpose of aiding any person to commit it; or abets any person

---

100 *Martineau*, above note 18; *Logan*, above note 20; *R v Chenier* (2006), 205 CCC (3d) 333 at para 62 (Ont CA).

101 Because of the fault element required for manslaughter, this conviction requires only objective foreseeability that bodily harm would result. *R v Jackson* (1993), 86 CCC (3d) 385 at 391 (SCC).

in committing it." The courts have found that a person actually commits an offence even if the completion of the crime depends on a subsequent but causally connected action of an innocent agent.[102]

A person who either aids or abets an offence is a party to that offence and guilty of the same offence as the person who actually commits the offence, often known as the principal. It is not necessary for the Crown to specify whether a person is guilty as the principal offender or as an aider or abettor of the offence. In the famous Colin Thatcher case, the Crown was able to argue that the accused was guilty of murder on the alternative theories that he actually killed his ex-wife or he assisted others to do the killing.[103] In the Robert Pickton serial murder case, the jury was initially instructed according to the Crown's theory of the case that Pickton personally shot his multiple victims. The Supreme Court, however, upheld a subsequent jury instruction that left open the possibility that Pickton would be guilty if he was "otherwise an active participant" in the killings and indicated that it was not necessary that Pickton be the actual shooter to be guilty of murder. Relying on the *Thatcher* case, the Court stressed that section 21(1) was designed to put the aider or abettor on the same footing as the person who committed the crime.[104]

A number of accused could be convicted of murder if they all knowingly assisted in causing the victim's death even though it was unclear which one of the accused actually killed the victim.[105] Imposing the same liability and maximum penalty on a person who has knowingly assisted an offence as on the person who actually committed the offence may seem harsh in some cases. Limited participation in a crime may,

---

102 The Ontario Court of Appeal has observed that "the classic example of innocent agency is employing unwitting drug mule." *R v King*, 2013 ONCA 417 at para 22. See also *R v Berryman* (1990), 57 CCC (3d) 375 (BCCA) [*Berryman*].

103 *R v Thatcher* (1987), 32 CCC (3d) 481 (SCC).

104 *R v Pickton*, [2010] 2 SCR 198 at para 33 Justice Charron for the majority indicated that it would have been preferable had the jury been instructed specifically about aiding and abetting but that the omission of such an instruction could only have benefited the accused; *ibid* at para 12. The dissenters in the case agreed that the alternatives of aiding and abetting could be put to the jury, but stated that "the phrases 'active participation,' 'acting in concert,' or 'joint venture' do not in and of themselves adequately convey the law of party liability to a trier of fact"; *ibid* at para 38.

105 *Chow Bew v The Queen*, [1956] SCR 124; *R v Issac*, [1984] 1 SCR 74 at 80–81; *R v McMaster*, [1996] 1 SCR 740 at para 33; *R v McQuaid*, [1998] 1 SCR 244; *R v Biniaris*, [2000] 1 SCR 381; *R v Suzack* (2000), 141 CCC (3d) 449 (Ont CA); *R v H(LI)* (2003), 17 CR (6th) 338 at para 60 (Man CA); *R v Portillo* (2003), 17 CR (6th) 362 at para 71 (Ont CA) [*Portillo*]; *R v JFD* (2005), 196 CCC (3d) 316 at para 14 (BCCA); *R v Rojos* (2006), 208 CCC (3d) 13 (BCCA).

however, be a mitigating factor in sentencing though the mitigating factor may be limited by the existence of a mandatory minimum penalty.

1) The *Actus Reus* of Aiding and Abetting

It is common to speak of aiding and abetting together, but the two concepts are distinct, and liability can flow from either one. Broadly speaking, "[t]o aid under s. 21(1)(b) means to assist or help the actor . . . . To abet within the meaning of s. 21(1)(c) includes encouraging, instigating, promoting or procuring the crime to be committed."[106] Abetting has been held to include intentional encouragement whether by acts or words.[107] A person who distracts a security guard so that his or her friend can shoplift may aid a theft, whereas a salesclerk who encourages or allows a customer to shoplift would abet the theft. Both people would be guilty of theft, even though they did not themselves steal the merchandise. The terms "aiding" and "abetting" are generally used together, but they remain distinct forms of liability for being a party to an offence.

In *Dunlop v R*,[108] Dickson J stated that a person is not guilty of aiding or abetting a rape

> merely because he is present at the scene of a crime and does nothing
> to prevent it . . . . If there is no evidence of encouragement by him,
> a man's presence at the scene of the crime will not suffice to render
> him liable as aider and abettor. A person who, aware of a rape taking
> place in his presence, looks on and does nothing is not, as a matter
> of law, an accomplice. The classic case is the hardened urbanite who
> stands around in a subway station when an individual is murdered.

In the case, the accused were acquitted of rape on the basis that there was no evidence that they "rendered aid, assistance, or encouragement" to the gang rape of a young woman. Justice Dickson did indicate, however, that presence at the commission of an offence can be evidence of aiding and abetting if accompanied by other factors such as prior knowledge that the crime was going to be committed. Similarly, presence at a crime that prevents the victim's escape or prevents the victim receiving assistance is a sufficient *actus reus*.[109] Some members of the Supreme

---

106 *R v Briscoe*, [2010] 1 SCR 411 at para 14 [*Briscoe*], citing *R v Greyeyes*, [1997] 2
    SCR 825 at para 26 [*Greyeyes*].

107 *R v Wobbes*, 2008 ONCA 567; *R v Hennessey*, 2010 ABCA 274 at para 39.

108 (1979), 47 CCC (2d) 93 at 111 (SCC) [*Dunlop*].

109 *R v Black*, [1970] 4 CCC 251 (BCCA); *R v Stevenson* (1984), 11 CCC (3d) 443
    (NSCA).

Court have disapproved of a case in which an accused was found not to be a party to a rape, despite having witnessed the crime with his pants down.[110] At the same time, the Court has recently affirmed as sound the proposition in *Dunlop* that "an accused's mere presence at the scene of a crime in circumstances consistent with innocence will not support a conviction."[111] In that case it upheld a conviction of a man producing marijuana, on the basis that there was evidence beyond his mere presence to convict him because he was found sleeping in a camouflaged tent with fertilizer at a remote marijuana plantation. Two judges dissented, however, on the basis that there was no evidence of anything beyond the accused's presence at the site. In another case, the Court indicated that gang members who provided protection for a drug trafficking network aided the trafficking by preventing or hindering interference with the criminal act.[112]

The Court has also upheld the acquittal of a mother who found that her son was growing a large quantity of marijuana on her land, because the mother was presented with a crime that was "a fait accompli" and did not intend to assist in its commission.[113] At the same time, a person can be guilty of aiding a kidnapping if he or she knows or is wilfully blind that someone has been kidnapped, then provides assistance and support in the continued confinement.[114]

The position that mere presence and passive acquiescence in a crime is not sufficient to make a person an aider or abettor mirrors the criminal law's traditional reluctance to penalize omissions. As with omissions, however, courts recognize exceptions to this principle in cases where the person who stands by is under a specific legal duty to act. Owners of cars who do nothing while others engage in dangerous driving have been held to have abetted the dangerous driving because they did not exercise their power to control the use of their vehicle.[115] A senior officer in charge of a police lock-up has also been found to have aided and abetted an assault on a prisoner by failing to exercise his statutory duty to protect a prisoner in his charge.[116] The conclusion in these cases that a failure to act can amount to aiding and abetting is strengthened by the fact that section 21(1)(b) provides that one who

---

110 *R v Salajko*, [1970] 1 CCC 352 (Ont CA), disapproved of in *R v Kirkness* (1990), 60 CCC (3d) 97 at 106 (SCC), Wilson J (L' Heureux-Dubé J concurring) [*Kirkness*].
111 *R v Jackson*, 2007 SCC 52 at paras 3 and 9 [*Jackson*].
112 *R v Knapczyk*, 2016 SCC 10.
113 *R v Rochon*, [2012] 2 SCR 673, aff'g 2011 QCCA 2012.
114 *R v Vu*, [2012] 2 SCR 411 at paras 59–60 [*Vu*].
115 *R v Halmo* (1941), 76 CCC 116 (Ont CA); *R v Kulbacki*, [1966] 1 CCC 167 (Man CA).
116 *R v Nixon* (1990), 57 CCC (3d) 97 (BCCA).

omits to do anything for the purpose of aiding any person to commit an offence may be charged as a party to that offence.

2) The *Mens Rea* for Aiding and Abetting

The broad definition of the *actus reus* of aiding and abetting is balanced with a requirement that the act or omission of assistance be committed for the purpose of assisting in the commission of the offence. The Supreme Court has explained: "a person becomes a party to an offence when that person — armed with *knowledge* of the principal's intention to commit the crime and with the intention of assisting the principal in its commission — does (or, in some circumstances, omits to do) something that assists or encourages the principal in the commission of the offence."[117] There are thus two different *mens rea* requirements for aiding and abetting: (1) the intent to assist the principal offender and (2) knowledge of the type but not the exact nature of the crime committed.[118]

Section 21(1)(b) requires that the accused act or omit to do anything for the purpose of aiding any person to commit an offence. A person who unwittingly delivers a bomb or administers a poison would not be guilty as a party to an offence, even though he or she may have committed the *actus reus* of assisting the commission of the offence.[119] Such a person would not have acted for the purpose or with the intent of aiding the offence.

The requirement that the accused act with the purpose of aiding the offence does not mean that the accused must desire that the offence be committed or even share the exact same *mens rea* as the principal offender. A person who assists in a robbery by driving the getaway car will have acted with the purpose of aiding the offence, even though he or she participated only because of death threats. Chief Justice Lamer has concluded that "the expression 'for the purpose of aiding' in section 21(1)(b), properly understood, does not require that the accused actively view the commission of the offence he or she is aiding as desirable in and of itself. As a result, the *mens rea* for aiding under section

---

117   *Vu*, above note 114 at para 58 [emphasis in original], citing *Briscoe* above note 106 at paras 14–18. See also *R v Morgan* (1993), 80 CCC (3d) 16 at 21 (Ont CA); *R v Maciel*, 2007 ONCA 196 at para 88; *R v Chambers*, 2016 ONCA 684 at para 37; *R v Phillips*, 2017 ONCA 752 at para 196; *R v Kelsie*, 2017 NSCA 89 at paras 89–90.

118   *Briscoe*, above note 106 at para 16.

119   *Berryman*, above note 102.

21(1)(b) is not susceptible of being 'negated' by duress."[120] The issue should be whether the accused intended to assist the principal offender. The jury should not be confused by being asked to consider duress both in relation to *mens rea* and in relation to the separate defence of duress. A person who arranges a drug buy may intend to aid or abet in trafficking even though his or her motivation may have only been to assist the purchaser.[121] This follows the traditional position that motive is not normally relevant to subjective fault.[122] Similarly, a person may intentionally assist others to commit a planned and deliberate murder without necessarily planning and deliberating as the principal offenders did.[123]

The Ontario Court of Appeal has concluded with respect to section 21(1)(b) that "purpose is synonymous with intent and does not include recklessness."[124] It has also indicated that the high level of *mens rea* for section 21(1)(b) is justified not only by the specific purpose requirement in the section, but also by the need to ensure that a person who assists in the commission of an offence has a sufficient level of fault to justify convicting that person of the same offence as the person who actually committed the offence. The high subjective *mens rea* of aiding and abetting applies even in cases where the principal offender may be convicted on the basis of an objective fault requirement.[125] Recklessness is not a sufficient form of fault to convict a person as a party to an offence under section 21(1)(b).[126] This is appropriate because an aider and abettor's involvement with the crime will be more peripheral than that of the

---

120 *R v Hibbert* (1995), 99 CCC (3d) 193 at 214 (SCC) [*Hibbert*]. Such a person could be acquitted on the basis of the common law defence of duress if there was no safe avenue of escape from the threats. See Chapter 9, Section D.

121 *Greyeyes*, above note 106 at 349.

122 See Chapter 5, Section B(2).

123 The Court has stated:

> [T]he aider to a murder must 'have known that the perpetrator had the intent required for murder.' . . . The perpetrator's intention to kill the victim must be known to the aider or abettor; it need not be shared. *Kirkness* should not be interpreted as requiring that the aider and abettor of a murder have the same *mens rea* as the actual killer. It is sufficient that he or she, armed with *knowledge* of the perpetrator's intention to commit the crime, acts with the intention of assisting the perpetrator in its commission. It is only in this sense that it can be said that the aider and abettor must intend that the principal offence be committed.

> *Briscoe*, above note 106 at para 18.

124 *R v Roach* (2004), 192 CCC (3d) 557 at para 36 (Ont CA); *R v Helsdon*, 2007 ONCA 54 at paras 32–33 [*Helsdon*].

125 *Helsdon, ibid* at paras 36–38.

126 *Hibbert*, above note 120 at para 26; *R v L* (2003), 172 CCC (3d) 44 at para 48 (BCCA).

principal offender(s) and this lesser form of physical involvement should be counterbalanced by higher fault requirements.

In addition to the intent or purpose to assist the principal offender, an aider or abettor must also know that the principal offender will commit the crime, but not necessarily precisely how the crime will be committed.[127] In other words, it is not necessary that the aider or abettor know all the details of the crime committed; it is sufficient that he or she was "aware of the type of crime to be committed"[128] and knew "the circumstances necessary to constitute the offence he is accused of aiding."[129] In R v Briscoe,[130] the Supreme Court held that in an appropriate case wilful blindness could be substituted for this knowledge requirement and distinguished wilful blindness as a form of "deliberate ignorance" that is distinct from recklessness. This suggests that the mens rea requirements for section 21(1)(b) are quite high and that recklessness will not suffice either for the intent to assist requirement or the knowledge of the crime that is being assisted.

The courts are reluctant to find purchasers of drugs guilty of aiding and abetting trafficking on the basis of the purchase alone.[131] They are concerned that such people do not deserve the stigma of a trafficking conviction and are more appropriately convicted of possession of narcotics or possession with the intent to traffic, either as a principal offender or an aider or abettor. Assisting a person to purchase drugs is another matter. In Greyeyes, the Supreme Court upheld the trafficking conviction of a person who located a seller for a purchaser, negotiated the purchase price, and accepted $10 for his efforts.[132] The Court reasoned that these were not the acts of a mere purchaser, but rather the acts of one who offered crucial assistance to the trafficking. The accused had the dual mens rea of intending to assist the trafficking and knowledge that trafficking was being assisted. The accused, who acted as a go-between between the purchaser and the seller and assisted the trafficking transaction, was convicted and sentenced as a drug trafficker. It is hoped his rather peripheral involvement in the trafficking enterprise would be considered at sentencing.

---

127 Ibid at para 17; R v Nateways, 2017 SCC 5, aff'g 2015 SKCA 120 at para 19 [Nateways].
128 R v Yanover (1985), 20 CCC (3d) 300 at 329 (Ont CA).
129 R v FW Woolworth Co (1974), 18 CCC (2d) 23 at 32 (Ont CA).
130 Briscoe, above note 106 at paras 22–25.
131 R v Poitras (1974), 12 CCC (3d) 337 (SCC); R v Meston (1975), 28 CCC (2d) 497 (Ont CA). As L'Heureux-Dubé J has stated, "despite his or her crucial assistance in helping to complete the sale of narcotics, the purchaser cannot by this action alone be found guilty of the offence of aiding and abetting the offence of trafficking." Greyeyes, above note 106 at 340 [emphasis in original].
132 Greyeyes, ibid.

A person can be guilty of aiding or abetting a conspiracy but only if his or her actions assist in the formation of the agreement or assist a person to join a pre-existing conspiracy. The Court has rejected a broader approach that would hold that all those who aid in furthering the object of the conspiracy are guilty of aiding and abetting the conspiracy on the basis that the conspiracy is based on an agreement to commit a crime and not the carrying out of an unlawful objective.[133]

3) Abandonment

Abandonment will prevent conviction to "ensure that only morally culpable persons are punished" and because "there is a benefit to society in encouraging individuals involved in criminal activities to withdraw from those activities and report them."[134] Nevertheless, a fairly strict test is applied. An accused who supplied her husband with drugs to kill their children in a murder-suicide pact did not abandon her intent to aid and abet their murder when she told her husband they should not go through with the plan. In addition to timely and unequivocal notice and an intention to withdraw from an unlawful purpose, there must also be evidence "that the accused took, in a manner proportional to his or her participation in the commission of the planned offence, reasonable steps in the circumstances either to neutralize or otherwise cancel out the effects of his or her participation or to prevent the commission of the offence."[135] Here the accused could have hidden the drugs or removed her children, but she did not. Justice Fish dissented on the basis that it was "fundamentally unfair"[136] to impose the new requirement of reasonable steps for the accused to cancel her participation retroactively to her case. Through their interpretation of the requirements for abandonment, the courts effectively imposed common law judge-made requirements on accused, albeit only accused who are already guilty of offences.

4) Impossibility

What is the relevance of impossibility to a charge of aiding and abetting? In *R v Chan*,[137] the Ontario Court of Appeal applied the Supreme Court's

---

133 *JF*, above note 62.
134 *R v Gauthier*, [2013] 2 SCR 403 at para 40.
135 *Ibid* at para 50.
136 *Ibid* at para 96.
137 *Chan*, above note 52.

reasoning in *Dynar*[138] to a case where an accused was convicted of possessing drugs when he thought he was participating in the purchase of a large quantity of heroin. The drugs had been previously intercepted by the police and only contained a very small amount of heroin. The Court of Appeal held that what mattered in determining the *mens rea* was the accused's belief that he was dealing with heroin and not the truth of the matter.[139] This suggests that the accused might have had the *mens rea* even if there were no drugs in the package that was received. The question then would be whether the accused had the necessary *actus reus* to be guilty of aiding or abetting the offence. If there were no drugs present, then it would be difficult to conclude that the accused had aided and abetted a drug offence. The accused would not necessarily be acquitted because he or she could be guilty of the separate offence of attempting to possess the heroin. As in the Supreme Court's *Williams*[140] case, the accused would have the *mens rea* both for the complete and attempted offence and would have the *actus reus* for the attempt offence, because he or she would have done an act beyond mere preparation to commit the crime.[141]

F. COMMON INTENTION TO COMMIT AN UNLAWFUL PURPOSE AND SECTION 21(2)

Section 21(2) enlarges the scope of who is a party to an offence beyond those who knowingly aid or abet an offence by providing that those who "form an intention in common to carry out an unlawful purpose and to assist each other therein" are parties to any consequential offence committed by one of them provided that the accused "knew or ought to have known that the commission of the offence would be a probable consequence of carrying out the common purpose." Thus, a person who forms a common unlawful intent (for example, to engage in a robbery) is a party to other offences that he or she knew or ought to know would probably occur (such as forcible confinement or manslaughter). In practice, section 21(2) applies when the principal has committed crimes beyond which the parties have intended to aid and abet.[142]

---

138 Above note 31.
139 *Chan*, above note 52 at para 40.
140 Above note 29.
141 *Chan*, above note 52 at para 64.
142 *R v Simpson* (1988), 38 CCC (3d) 481 (SCC).

1) The *Actus Reus* of Section 21(2)

Under section 21(2) there must be a formation of a common intent to assist each other in carrying out an unlawful purpose, but not necessarily any act of assistance.[143] It could be argued that this requires an agreement akin to conspiracy, although most cases do not dwell on the issue. In addition, it is assumed that the unlawful purpose means a purpose contrary to the *Criminal Code*. The subsequent offence committed has to be one that the accused either knows or ought to have known would be a probable consequence of carrying out the common purpose. In *R v Jackson*,[144] the Supreme Court held that the offence is not confined to that which the principal was convicted, but encompasses any included offence. For example, a party to an unlawful purpose could be convicted of manslaughter, even though the principal was convicted of murder. This would happen when the party did not have the subjective foresight of death required for a murder conviction, but did have objective foresight of bodily harm necessary for a manslaughter conviction. Less clear is whether a party with the *mens rea* for murder can be convicted of murder even though the principal offender was convicted only of manslaughter. There is some authority that the party could only be convicted of the same offence as the principal offender,[145] but general principles as well as section 23.1 suggest that a party with the required *mens rea* could be convicted of a more serious offence than a principal offender. For example, a sober or unprovoked accomplice might have the *mens rea* for murder even though the actual drunken or provoked killer might have only the *mens rea* for manslaughter.[146]

2) The *Mens Rea* for Section 21(2)

There are two distinct mental or fault elements for section 21(2): the first is the formation of the common unlawful purpose and the second is either subjective knowledge or objective foresight that the actual offence would be a probable consequence of carrying out the unlawful purpose.

a) Common Unlawful Purpose
In *R v Paquette*,[147] the Supreme Court held that a person who drove others to a robbery had not formed a common unlawful purpose to

---

143 *R v Moore* (1984), 15 CCC (3d) 541 at 555 (Ont CA).

144 Above note 101.

145 *R v Hébert* (1986), 51 CR (3d) 264 (NBCA).

146 *R v Rémillard* (1921), 62 SCR 21.

147 (1976), 30 CCC (2d) 417 (SCC).

assist them in the robbery because he had been forced at gunpoint to cooperate. Justice Martland stated:

> A person whose actions have been dictated by fear of death or of grievous bodily injury cannot be said to have formed a genuine common intent to carry out an unlawful purpose with the person who has threatened him with those consequences if he fails to co-operate.[148]

In *Hibbert*, the Supreme Court subsequently rejected this interpretation on the basis that section 21(2) requires only a common intent to commit the offence and not "a mutuality of motives and desires between the party and the principal."[149] On this reasoning, Paquette would have had the required mental element because he intended to commit a robbery even though he did not truly desire to commit the robbery. The fact that he wanted to commit a robbery only because his life was threatened would be a matter of motive that is not relevant to the mental element. It would, however, be relevant to whether Paquette had a common law defence of duress that would prevent his conviction.[150] As with section 21(1)(b), the Court has rejected the idea that intent requires proof of desire even though section 21(2) requires the formation of an intention in common to assist in the commission of an offence. It was concerned that cases such as *Paquette* would complicate the task of the jury by considering duress as both a matter relevant to *mens rea* and as a separate defence and that it would not fulfill Parliament's purpose in widening the net of criminal liability to catch those who assist in the commission of crimes.

As with aiding and abetting, it is possible that an accused might abandon the common unlawful purpose through timely notice. The Court's decision in *Hibbert*, however, suggests that reluctance to engage in the common unlawful purpose will not be inconsistent with the *mens rea*. In addition, abandonment including surrender to the authorities or remorse after the commission of the relevant *actus reus* and *mens rea* should not relieve accused of responsibility for having committed the crime. That said, an accused who forms a common unlawful purpose is not automatically responsible for all the crimes that his or her accomplice commits while pursuing that purpose. As will be seen later in this chapter, the accused is only liable for crimes that he or she knows or in

---

148 *Ibid* at 423.

149 *Hibbert*, above note 120 at 216. See *Dunbar v R* (1936), 67 CCC 20 (SCC), also drawing a distinction between intention and motive when an accused was threatened if he did not assist in a robbery.

150 See Chapter 9, Section D(1).

most cases ought to have known would be a probable consequence of carrying out the common unlawful purpose.

b) Knew or Ought to Have Known That the Crime Would Be Committed

In most cases the accused will be liable if he or she either knew or ought to have known that the commission of the offence was a probable consequence of the common unlawful purpose. In *Logan*,[151] however, the Supreme Court declared the phrase "ought to have known" to be an unjustified violation of the *Charter* when the accused is charged with murder or attempted murder. Section 7 of the *Charter* requires subjective as opposed to objective foresight of death for a conviction of murder or attempted murder. As Lamer CJ explained:

> When the principles of fundamental justice require subjective foresight in order to convict a principal of attempted murder, that same minimum degree of *mens rea* is constitutionally required to convict a party to the offence of attempted murder. Any conviction for attempted murder, whether of the principal directly or of a party pursuant to s. 21(2), will carry enough stigma to trigger the constitutional requirement. To the extent that s. 21(2) would allow for the conviction of a party to the offence of attempted murder on the basis of objective foresight, its operation restricts s. 7 of the *Charter*.[152]

In cases of murder and attempted murder, the objective arm of section 21(2) should not be left to the jury and the jury should convict only if a party has actual foresight or knowledge that the principal offender would attempt to kill a person while carrying out their common unlawful purpose.[153]

Logan is a case of limited application. The Court stated that "because of the importance of the legislative purpose, the objective component of section 21(2) can be justified with respect to most offenses."[154] Chief Justice Lamer concluded that it was not a principle of fundamental justice that a person convicted as a party to an offence have as high a *mens rea* as the principal offender. This means that a party could be convicted under the objective arm of section 21(2) even though subjective *mens rea* was required to convict the principal. For example, an accused who formed an unlawful purpose to rob a bank could be convicted of assault

---

151 Above note 20.
152 *Ibid* at 401.
153 *R v Rodney* (1990), 58 CCC (3d) 408 (SCC); *R v Laliberty* (1997), 117 CCC (3d) 97 at 108 (Ont CA); *Portillo*, above note 105 at paras 72–73.
154 Above note 20 at 403.

on the basis that he or she ought to have known an assault would occur, whereas the person who actually assaulted one of the guards or tellers would be convicted on the basis of a subjective intent to apply force. In upholding the objective arm of section 21(2) as constitutional in most cases, the Court emphasized the importance of recognizing different degrees of involvement when exercising sentencing discretion.[155] A fundamental principle of sentencing is that the punishment be proportionate to the degree of the offender's responsibility.

The subjective or objective foresight required by section 21(2) does not need to extend to the precise means or the identity of the victim of a crime that is committed in furtherance of a common unlawful purpose. Thus, the Court has approved of a manslaughter conviction under section 21(2) on the basis that a reasonable person in the circumstances would have foreseen the risk of bodily harm to any other individual as a result of carrying out an unlawful purpose.[156]

G. ACCESSORY AFTER THE FACT

Section 23 provides a separate offence for receiving, comforting, or assisting a person that one knows has been a party to an offence for the purpose of enabling that person to escape. An accessory after the fact is not a party to an offence but is punished under section 463 as if he or she had been guilty of an attempt of the crime that the person assisted committed.

1) The *Actus Reus* of Being an Accessory After the Fact

The *actus reus* for this provision requires a person to receive, comfort, or assist a person who has committed a crime. This requires more than the

---

155 Chief Justice Lamer stated:

> It must be remembered that within many offences there are varying degrees of guilt and it remains the function of the sentencing process to adjust the punishment for each individual offender accordingly. The argument that the principles of fundamental justice prohibit the conviction of a party to an offence on the basis of a lesser degree of *mens rea* than that required to convict the principal could only be supported, if at all, in a situation where the sentence for a particular offence is fixed. However, currently in Canada, the sentencing scheme is flexible enough to accommodate the varying degrees of culpability resulting from the operation of ss 21 and 22.

> *Ibid* at 398.

156 *Natewayes*, above note 127 at paras 20–21 (SKCA).

mere failure to inform authorities about the fugitive's whereabouts.[157] At the same time, advising fugitives that the police had their names and licence numbers is enough.[158] This again mirrors the traditional reluctance in the criminal law to punish an omission or failure to act.

Section 23(2) used to provide that a married person cannot be guilty of assisting his or her spouse after the commission of a crime, but it was repealed in 2000. Section 23.1 allows a person to be convicted of being an accessory after the fact even though the person assisted has not been convicted of an offence. The Supreme Court has upheld the conviction of an accused for being an accessory after the fact by assisting her brother by transporting him from a killing and orchestrating a false alibi even though her brother was eventually acquitted of the murder.[159]

2) The Mens Rea for Being an Accessory After the Fact

Section 23(1) requires two distinct mental elements: (1) subjective knowledge that the person assisted has been a party to an offence, and (2) assisting the fugitive for the purpose of assisting him or her to escape.

With respect to knowledge that the person assisted was a party to the offence, the accused must know or be wilfully blind to the fact that the other accused has committed a specific offence such as murder; knowledge that the accused may have committed some general crime is not sufficient.[160]

With respect to the second fault requirement of acting for the purpose of assisting the fugitive to escape, it is not sufficient that the acts of assistance simply have the effect of helping the person escape[161] or were taken only to help those accused of being an accessory to escape liability themselves.[162] A majority of the Supreme Court held that the acts of a person who told the police that "nothing happened" because he was afraid was not sufficient to make the person an accessory after the fact.[163] Four judges in dissent, however, concluded that the person was an accessory after the fact because he made the "nothing happened" statement with the intent of helping the perpetrator escape liability.[164]

---

157 *R v Dumont* (1921), 37 CCC 166 (Ont CA).

158 *Young v R* (1950), 98 CCC 195 (Que CA).

159 *R v S(FJ)* (1997), 115 CCC (3d) 450 (NSCA), aff'd (1998), 121 CCC (3d) 223 (SCC).

160 *R v Duong* (1998), 124 CCC (3d) 392 (Ont CA).

161 *R v McVay* (1982), 66 CCC (2d) 512 (Ont CA).

162 *R v Morris*, [1979] 1 SCR 1041 at 1069 [*Morris*], citing with approval *Sykes v DPP*, [1962] AC 528 (HL).

163 *Morris*, above note 162 at 1070.

164 *Ibid* at 1053.

The important point is that to be convicted as an accessory after the fact, the Crown must establish not only the accused's knowledge of the perpetrator's crime, but the subjective purpose of assisting the perpetrator to escape. This latter requirement that the accused act with the purpose of assisting a known criminal to escape is a high form of subjective *mens rea* that may be more difficult for the Crown to prove than lower forms of subjective mental elements such as knowledge or recklessness. It should also be noted that some specific crimes such as obstruction of justice or harbouring a terrorist may in some circumstances be functional alternatives to the general crime under section 23 of being an accessory after the fact.[165]

CONCLUSION

The following chart summarizes how various provisions of the *Criminal Code* expand the net of criminal liability to apply to those who did not themselves perform the complete crime. The underlying rationale seems to be that society is justified in intervening and punishing people for their criminal intent or fault and participation in crimes even if they do not commit the complete criminal act.

Counselling a crime that is not committed s 464	Conspiracy s 465	Attempts s 24	Counselling a crime that is committed s 22	Unlawful purpose and commission of further offence s 21(2)	Aiding or abetting s 21(1)(b) & (c)	Accessory after the fact s 23
			Party to the offence	Party to the offence	Party to the offence	

An accused could be convicted of counselling murder under section 464 simply for asking an undercover officer to kill someone. The same person could be convicted under section 465 of conspiracy to commit murder if he or she agreed with another person that they would kill someone and both intended to carry out the agreement. That person could not be convicted of attempted conspiracy because the courts

---

165   *R v Catton*, 2015 ONCA 13 at para 38 (noting obstruction charge, an alternative to an accessory after the fact charge where the accused falsely told the police she was the driver of a car involved in accident).

have refused to recognize such a crime because of concerns about extending criminal liability too far.

If an accused acted alone with respect to a murder, he or she could be convicted of attempted murder under section 24 if he or she did anything beyond mere preparation for the purpose of carrying out the intent to kill. The accused may be held to have gone beyond mere preparation to commit an offence by for example purchasing a weapon even though the murder would not happen until sometime in the future. The fact that it was impossible to kill the intended victim because he was already dead would not be a defence. The accused would be punished more for having the intent to kill than the harm that was caused or could have been caused.

An accused could be guilty of murder under section 22 if he or she counselled another person to commit a murder and that person went on to actually commit the murder. The accused would be guilty of murder under section 21(2) if he or she formed an unlawful purpose with another person and he or she knew that it was likely that his accomplice would kill the victim while carrying out the unlawful purpose. For crimes other than murder and attempted murder,[166] all that would have to be proven under section 21(2) would be the formation of the unlawful purpose and that the accused ought to have known that his accomplice would commit the further crime. If the accused aided or abetted the murder with the fault required for murder[167] (the minimum fault is subjective foresight of death), the accused would also be guilty of murder under section 21(1).

Assisting a person to escape after a crime can be punished as a separate offence under section 23. It requires some act of assistance by an accused who knows or is wilfully blind that the person assisted was a party to the offence and acted for the subjective purpose of assisting that person to escape.

There is also the possibility that some complete offences such as participation in a terrorist or criminal organization could also apply to those who prepare for or have assisted in the commission of murders. Although these offences are not inchoate forms of liability, they do extend criminal liability in a manner similar to both the inchoate and parties provisions examined in this chapter. In all cases, the fact that the accused is liable for actions that may be remote from the actual commission of harm makes it important that high levels of subjective fault be proven to justify criminal liability.

---

166 *Logan*, above note 20; *Jackson*, above note 111.
167 *Kirkness*, above note 110.

Although there is a consensus that participation in crime should be criminal, the law could be made clearer and less complex. Any distinctions among counselling, aiding, and abetting under sections 21(1) and 22 are quite fine and could be eliminated by a generic provision criminalizing the intentional assistance and encouragement of crime. There is less agreement about whether criminal liability should be extended under section 21(2). The existing law is complex because the objective fault element provided under section 21(2) is unconstitutional as applied to murder and attempted murder but continues to apply to other crimes.[168] One reform option would be to eliminate section 21(2) altogether while another would be to require subjective foresight for all crimes that are committed in furtherance of an unlawful objective. A requirement of subjective foresight, however, would blur the practical distinction between section 21(2) and aiding and abetting under section 21(1)(b) and (c). The Supreme Court has simplified the law somewhat by holding that duress cannot negate the *mens rea* requirements under either section 21(1)(b) or 21(2). The requirements in those sections that the accused act with the purpose of aiding and form an intention in common to carry out an unlawful purpose should not be equated with either desire or motive.[169]

The law concerning attempts is relatively settled, but there remains uncertainty in determining exactly when an accused's actions will have gone beyond mere preparation[170] and whether an intent to commit the complete offence is required for all crimes.[171] Given that attempts are driven by concerns about intent and not social harm, the intent to commit the complete offence should be established for all attempted crimes, not just murder. There is a case for keeping the *actus reus* flexible and in practice more remote forms of *actus reus* may be accepted if the *mens rea* is clear or if the magnitude of the attempted crime is great. It should now be crystal clear that impossibility will not be a defence to either an attempt or conspiracy. This also makes sense when it is recognized that society is intervening primarily to punish criminal intent, not the complete crime.

---

168 *Jackson*, above note 111.
169 *Hibbert*, above note 120.
170 *Deutsch*, above note 34.
171 *Ancio*, above note 15; *Williams*, above note 29.

FURTHER READINGS

COLVIN, E, & S ANAND. *Principles of Criminal Law*, 3d ed (Toronto: Thomson Carswell, 2007) ch 9 & 10.

MACKINNON, P. "Making Sense of Attempts" (1982) 7 *Queen's Law Journal* 253.

MANNING, M, & P SANKOFF. *Criminal Law*, 5th ed (Markham, ON: LexisNexis, 2015) ch 6 & 7.

MANSON, A. "Re-Codifying Attempts, Parties, and Abandoned Intentions" (1989) 14 *Queen's Law Journal* 85.

MEEHAN, E, & J CURRIE. *The Law of Criminal Attempt*, 2d ed (Toronto: Carswell, 2000).

RAINVILLE, P. "Le Verbe Fait Crime" (2007) 11 *Canadian Criminal Law Review* 177.

RANKIN, M. "Party Liability for Continuing Offences" (2013) 60 *Criminal Law Quarterly* 174.

ROSE, G. *Parties to an Offence* (Toronto: Carswell, 1982).

STUART, D. *Canadian Criminal Law: A Treatise*, 7th ed (Toronto: Thomson Carswell, 2014) ch 9 & 10.

CHAPTER 5

THE FAULT ELEMENT, OR *MENS REA*

Generic references to *mens rea* are confusing because each different crime has a specific fault element that must be related to the *actus reus* of the specific crime. In 1889 Stephen J indicated that *mens rea* exists only in relation to particular definitions of crime, so that,

> "*Mens rea*" means in the case of murder, malice aforethought; in the case of theft, an intention to steal; in the case of rape, an intention to have forcible connection with a woman without her consent; and in the case of receiving stolen goods, knowledge that the goods were stolen. In some cases it denotes mere inattention. For instance, in the case of manslaughter by negligence it may mean forgetting to notice a signal. It appears confusing to call so many dissimilar states of mind by one name.[1]

In Canada, confusion about *mens rea* continues because Parliament has not clearly and consistently defined fault elements such as "purposely," "knowingly," "recklessly," or "negligently" or specified what particular fault element applies for each offence.[2] As a result, the fault element must often be inferred by the courts from the legislative definition of each separate offence. This means that criminal offences that may appear at first reading to have no fault element may actually be interpreted as requiring fault. In some cases, courts will require the proof of fault in relation to all

---

1   *R v Tolson* (1889), 23 QBD 168 at 185 (CCR) [*Tolson*].
2   But see *Criminal Code*, RSC 1985, c C-46, ss 433 and 436 [*Code*], for clear definitions of separate offences of intentional and negligent arson.

aspects of the prohibited act and in some cases they will not. References in the *Criminal Code* to carelessness, dangerousness, or negligence are misleading because the courts now require proof of a marked departure from standards of reasonable care in order to distinguish criminal from civil negligence. The fault element for crimes is often uncertain and complex in part because Parliament has long resisted reform proposals to define fault elements and provide for residual fault rules.

A. CONCEPTUAL CONSIDERATIONS

In order to explain the fault element of any criminal offence accurately, it is necessary to specify (1) the circumstances and consequences to which the fault element is directed, including its relation to the *actus reus* of the offence; and (2) the precise fault element required. It is not very helpful to say the *mens rea* for murder is subjective. A more precise approach would be to say the *mens rea* for murder requires at least subjective knowledge that the victim would likely die. Similarly, stating that the *mens rea* of manslaughter is objective tells only part of the story. The fault is objective foreseeability of bodily harm. The degree of negligence should also be explained, as should who is the reasonable person used to apply the objective fault or negligence standard.

It is also important to understand the differences between constitutional requirements and common law presumptions of particular forms of *mens rea* and how the so-called defences of intoxication and mistake of fact are really conditions that prevent the prosecutor from establishing the fault element beyond a reasonable doubt.

1) The Relation of the Fault Element to the Prohibited Act

The fault element does not exist in the air or in the abstract but must be related to certain consequences or circumstances. As McLachlin J has stated,

> Typically, *mens rea* is concerned with the consequences of the prohibited *actus reus*. Thus, in the crimes of homicide, we speak of the consequences of the voluntary act — intention to cause death, or reckless and wilfully blind persistence in conduct which one knows is likely to cause death.[3]

---

3   *R v Théroux* (1993), 79 CCC (3d) 449 at 458 (SCC) [*Théroux*]. This is not an absolute rule, as seen in her own majority judgment in *R v Creighton* (1993), 83 CCC (3d) 346 (SCC) [*Creighton*] and discussed below at note 5.

On this principle, a person is not guilty of assaulting a peace officer in the execution of his or her duties unless the accused has the *mens rea* for assault and subjective knowledge that the person is a peace officer. Similarly, the Court classified the old offence of statutory rape as absolute liability because Parliament had excluded fault in relation to a crucial aspect of the *actus reus*, namely, the age of the girl.[4] The fault element should generally extend to all the elements of the prohibited act.

The Supreme Court has recognized that the criminal law "has traditionally aimed at symmetry between the *mens rea* and the prohibited consequence of the offence" as discussed above. Nevertheless, a majority in *R v Creighton* concluded:

> It is important to distinguish between criminal law theory, which seeks the ideal of absolute symmetry between the *actus reus* and *mens rea* and the constitutional requirements of the *Charter* . . . .
>
>   I know of no authority for the proposition that the *mens rea* of an offence must always attach to the precise consequence which is prohibited as a matter of constitutional necessity.[5]

In the result, McLachlin J held that objective foresight of the risk of bodily harm was a sufficient fault element for the crime of unlawful act manslaughter, even though the *actus reus* of the crime was causing death as opposed to causing bodily harm. Offences that do not require a fault element in relation to all aspects of the *actus reus* are sometimes called offences of partial intent, constructive crimes, or crimes based on predicate offences. The Supreme Court has indicated that requiring fault elements for every element of an offence "would bring a large number of offences into question" including impaired causing death and sexual assault causing bodily harm. It has ruled that it is generally acceptable "to distinguish between criminal responsibility for equally

---

4   *R v Hess* (1990), 59 CCC (3d) 161 (SCC), discussed in Chapters 2 and 6.

5   Above note 3 at 378–79. In *R v DeSousa*, [1992] 2 SCR 944 at 966 [*DeSousa*], the Court noted that a number of offences punish a person more severely because of the consequences of his or her actions even though there is no fault requirement with regard to those aggravating consequences. Examples cited included "manslaughter (s. 222(5)), criminal negligence causing bodily harm (s. 221), criminal negligence causing death (s. 220), dangerous operation causing bodily harm (s. 249(3)), dangerous operation causing death (s. 249(4)), impaired driving causing bodily harm (s. 255(2)), impaired driving causing death (s. 255(3)), assault causing bodily harm (s. 267(1)(b)), aggravated assault (s. 268), sexual assault causing bodily harm (s. 272(c)), aggravated sexual assault (s. 273), mischief causing danger to life (s. 430(2)), and arson causing bodily harm (s. 433(b)). As noted by Professor Colvin, "[i]t would, however, be an error to suppose that *actus reus* and *mens rea* always match in this neat way."

reprehensive acts on the basis of the harm actually caused,"[6] but not intended. This means that fault is not necessarily required in relation to all parts of the prohibited act.

Constructive murder violates section 7 of the *Charter* because while it required the fault of a predicate offence (such as robbery) and the fault of causing bodily harm, it did not require fault with respect to the prohibited act of killing and did not satisfy the constitutional requirement that a murderer at least have subjective foresight of death.[7] The Supreme Court pulled back, however, from declaring as a general constitutional principle that people could not be punished for the consequences of their actions in the absence of some fault or responsibility for those consequences. Thus, a person can be punished for causing death in a manslaughter case even though his or her fault only related to the objective risk of causing bodily harm. Similarly, they can be punished for dangerous driving causing bodily harm even though their fault related only to the dangerous driving and not the causing of bodily harm.

Other offences require a *mens rea* that extends beyond the commission of the *actus reus*. Any attempted crime is a good example because it requires a *mens rea* that goes further than the *actus reus* committed by the accused. Discharging a firearm with the intent to wound also requires proof of an intent to wound, even though an actual wounding is not part of the *actus reus*. Such offences are sometimes called ulterior intent offences, because they require an intent beyond the *actus reus* that is committed.

Although the relation between the prohibited act and the *mens rea* should be clarified in discussions of fault, it is important to keep the two elements conceptually distinct and not to assume that just because the prohibited act or *actus reus* occurred that the accused had the necessary fault. A jury should "be instructed to avoid reasoning backwards. That is, they should avoid the logical fallacy of assuming that, because the victim died, [the accused] must have known that death was likely."[8] In short, fault, as distinct from the prohibited act, must be proven by the prosecution beyond a reasonable doubt.

2) Subjective and Objective Fault Elements

A broad distinction is often drawn between subjective and objective fault elements. A subjective fault or mental element requires the Crown

---

6   *DeSousa*, *ibid* at 964.

7   *R v Martineau*, [1990] 2 SCR 633 [*Martineau*].

8   *R v Shand*, 2011 ONCA 5 at para 210.

to establish that the accused subjectively had the required guilty knowledge in relation to the specified circumstances or consequences, whereas an objective fault element requires only that a reasonable person in the accused's position would have had the required guilty knowledge or would have acted differently.

A distinction should be made between the subjective mental elements that the Crown must prove and the means used to establish such guilty knowledge. The judge or jury who must determine what was in an accused's mind must rely on inferences from the evidence presented in the case. In deciding whether to draw these inferences, the trier of fact will almost inevitably consider what a reasonable person in the accused's place would have thought or recognized. As Martin JA has explained,

> Since people are usually able to foresee the consequences of their acts, if a person does an act likely to produce certain consequences it is, in general, reasonable to assume that the accused also foresaw the probable consequences of his act and if he, nevertheless, acted so as to produce those consequences, that he intended them. The greater the likelihood of the relevant consequences ensuing from the accused's act, the easier it is to draw the inference that he intended those consequences. *The purpose of this process, however, is to determine what the particular accused intended, not to fix him with the intention that a reasonable person might be assumed to have in the circumstances, where doubt exists as to the actual intention of the accused.*[9]

In other words, what the reasonable person would have known may provide the basis for the jury to conclude that the accused had a particular subjective mental element, but it never requires the jury to make such a determination.[10] The trier of fact must remain open to all the evidence presented in the case (especially evidence relating to peculiarities about the accused) and acquit the accused if any evidence raises a reasonable doubt as to whether that particular person, with all of his or her frailties and experiences, had the required subjective mental element.

Subjective *mens rea* operates as a doctrine that prevents the conviction of an accused who, for whatever reason, does not have the know-

---

9   *R v Buzzanga* (1979), 49 CCC (2d) 369 at 387 (Ont CA) [emphasis added] [*Buzzanga*]. "Where liability is imposed on a subjective basis, what a reasonable man ought to have anticipated is merely evidence from which a conclusion may be drawn that the accused anticipated the same consequences. On the other hand, where the test is objective, what a reasonable man should have anticipated constitutes the basis of liability." *R v Tennant* (1975), 23 CCC (2d) 80 at 91 (Ont CA).

10   This formulation also accords with the presumption of innocence. See Chapter 2, Section B(3)(g).

ledge and foresight that a reasonable person would have. It operates to protect those who because of impaired reasoning or lack of thought do not recognize or intend what may be obvious to the reasonable observer. The function of subjective *mens rea* is "to prevent the conviction of the morally innocent — those who do not understand or intend the consequences of their acts."[11]

The Supreme Court has kept clear the distinctions between subjective and objective fault elements, but it has been increasingly willing to see the latter as an appropriate form of fault. In *R v Wholesale Travel Group Inc*,[12] Cory J stated:

> It should not be forgotten that *mens rea* and negligence are both fault elements . . . . *Mens rea* focuses on the mental state of the accused and requires proof of a positive state of mind such as intent, recklessness or wilful blindness. Negligence, on the other hand, measures the conduct of the accused on the basis of an objective standard, irrespective of the accused's subjective mental state. Where negligence is the basis of liability, the question is not what the accused intended but rather whether the accused exercised reasonable care.

The preceding statement was made in the context of regulatory offences outside of the *Criminal Code*, but the Court has also accepted that negligence, albeit modified for the purposes of imposing criminal as opposed to civil liability, can be a sufficient fault level for most criminal offences.

There are a number of important differences between subjective and objective forms of fault. One is the reasoning process used by the trier of fact. In determining subjective fault, the trier of fact may reason from what a reasonable person would recognize were the probable consequences or circumstances of an act, but the judge or jury must be attentive to any evidence (including the accused's idiosyncrasies) that raises a reasonable doubt about whether the accused had the required subjective form of fault. The trier of fact must also be attentive to all of the evidence in determining objective fault, but does so for the purpose of determining what the reasonable person in the same circumstances would have done or recognized.

In the context of *Criminal Code* offences based on negligence, the Supreme Court has indicated that there must be "a marked departure from the standard of care that a reasonable person would observe in

---

11   *Théroux*, above note 3 at 458.
12   (1991), 67 CCC (3d) 193 at 252 (SCC).

the accused's situation."[13] In R v Beatty, the Court arguably elevated the marked departure standard to a constitutional requirement when it warned:

> If every departure from the civil norm is to be criminalized, regardless of the degree, we risk casting the net too widely and branding as criminals persons who are in reality not morally blameworthy. Such an approach risks violating the principle of fundamental justice that the morally innocent not be deprived of liberty.[14]

In addition to the requirement of a marked departure from reasonable standards, the Court in Beatty also held that courts should examine the actual mental state of the driver to determine whether it might raise a reasonable doubt about whether the accused was criminally negligent. The Court called this approach a modified objective approach, which is potentially confusing because it does not modify the standards demanded by the reasonable person standard to reflect matters such as the accused's age or gender. Rather, the focus is on administering the objective standard in a contextual manner that is sensitive to the possibility that "a reasonable person in the position of the accused would not have been aware of the risk or, alternatively, would not have been able to avoid creating the danger."[15]

In Beatty, the Court upheld an acquittal for dangerous driving causing death on the basis that the accused had engaged in only a momentary lapse when his vehicle went over the centre line and killed three people. In R v Roy,[16] the Court similarly entered an acquittal for dangerous driving causing death and stressed that the commission of the actus reus of pulling into the path of an overcoming tractor trailer in foggy weather with poor visibility only established "a single and momentary error in judgment with tragic consequences" as opposed to the fault of a marked departure from the standard of care expected of a reasonable person in the same circumstances. These decisions affirm that objective fault will not always follow from the commission of a prohibited

---

13 R v Hundal, [1993] 1 SCR 867 at para 43 [Hundal]; Creighton, above note 3 at 361 (Lamer CJ) and 383 (McLachlin J). In R v Tutton (1989), 48 CCC (3d) 129 at 140 (SCC) [Tutton], McIntyre J (L'Heureux-Dubé J concurring) stated in relation to criminal negligence: "The test is that of reasonableness, and proof of conduct which reveals a marked and significant departure from the standard which could be expected of a reasonably prudent person in the circumstances will justify a conviction of criminal negligence." Other means of adapting negligence as a principle of criminal liability will be discussed later in this chapter.

14 [2008] 1 SCR 49 at para 34 [Beatty].

15 Ibid at para 37.

16 2012 SCC 26 at para 55 [Roy].

act and that in all cases the prosecutor must prove a marked departure from reasonable standards considering all the evidence in the case.

3) Common Law Presumptions of *Mens Rea*

It is important to keep distinct the issues of what is required under section 7 of the *Charter* and what the courts will presume as a matter of judge-made common law in the absence of a clear legislative intent or design to the contrary. The Supreme Court has been reluctant to constitutionalize subjective *mens rea* for all but the most serious crimes, but it has long relied on common law presumptions in favour of subjective *mens rea* in relation to all aspects of the *actus reus*.[17]

Long before the enactment of the *Charter*, the Supreme Court presumed that criminal offences would require subjective *mens rea*.[18] Thus, an offence of possession of narcotics was interpreted in 1957 to require proof that the accused had knowledge of the substance that in law constituted the illegal drugs even though Parliament did not specifically require that the offence be the "knowing" possession of drugs. The Court recognized that "[i]t would, of course, be within the power of Parliament to enact that a person who, without any guilty knowledge, had in his physical possession a package which he honestly believed to contain a harmless substance such as baking soda but which in fact contained heroin, must on proof of such facts be convicted of a crime and sentenced to at least 6 months' imprisonment." Nevertheless, the Court would not adopt an interpretation with the "monstrous consequences" of allowing the conviction of the morally innocent unless "the words of the statute were clear and admitted of no other interpretation."[19] Similarly, when interpreting an offence of knowingly or wilfully contributing to the delinquency of a child, the Court concluded that the fault element should be established with regards to all the elements of the *actus reus*, including whether the accused had subjective knowledge that the girl he had sexual intercourse with was actually under eighteen years of age. It was always open for Parliament to provide that the accused's belief about the age of the child was

---

17   As will be examined in Chapter 6, the Court has also relied on a common law presumption in *R v Sault Ste Marie (City)* (1978), 40 CCC (2d) 353 (SCC) [*Sault Ste Marie*] that regulatory offences will be crimes of strict as opposed to absolute liability.

18   *R v Watts* (1953), 105 CCC 193 (SCC); *R v Rees* (1956), 115 CCC 1 (SCC) [*Rees*]; *R v Beaver* (1957), 118 CCC 129 (SCC) [*Beaver*]; *R v Prue* (1979), 46 CCC (2d) 257 (SCC).

19   *Beaver*, above note 18 at 141.

not relevant, but in this case, Parliament had not made such a clear statement. Hence a requirement of subjective knowledge would be presumed in relation to all aspects of the *actus reus*.

The leading statement of the common law presumption of *mens rea* is contained in *R v Sault Ste Marie*.[20] In that case, Dickson J stated:

> Where the offence is criminal, the Crown must establish a mental element, namely, that the accused who committed the prohibited act did so intentionally or recklessly, with knowledge of the facts constituting the offence, or with wilful blindness toward them. Mere negligence is excluded from the concept of the mental element required for conviction. Within the context of a criminal prosecution a person who fails to make such inquiries as a reasonable and prudent person would make, or who fails to know facts he should have known, is innocent in the eyes of the law.

This means that the courts should presume that criminal offences require some form of subjective *mens rea* — intent, knowledge, recklessness, or wilful blindness — in relation to all aspects of the *actus reus* unless Parliament clearly indicates otherwise. A judicial reluctance to impose criminal liability on the basis of negligence explains why recklessness in Canadian law requires proof that the accused subjectively was aware of the prohibited risk.[21]

Common law presumptions concerning *mens rea* remain valid and the Court has recently demonstrated increased interest in them. For example, it has applied such presumptions to require subjective fault

---

20   *Sault Ste Marie*, above note 17 at 362. Justice Dickson reaffirmed this presumption in *R v Pappajohn*, [1980] 2 SCR 120 at 138–39 [*Pappajohn*], when he stated:

> There rests now, at the foundation of our system of criminal justice, the precept that a man cannot be adjudged guilty and subjected to punishment, unless the commission of the crime was voluntarily directed by a willing mind . . . . Parliament can, of course, by express words, create criminal offences for which a guilty intention is not an essential ingredient. Equally, *mens rea* is not requisite in a wide category of statutory offences which are concerned with public welfare, health and safety. Subject to these exceptions, *mens rea*, consisting of some positive states of mind, such as evil intention, or knowledge of the wrongfulness of the act, or reckless disregard of consequences, must be proved by the prosecution.

Note that both of these articulations of the common law presumption were quoted with approval by the Supreme Court in *R v ADH*, 2013 SCC 28 at paras 23 and 27 [*ADH*].

21   *R v Sansregret*, [1985] 1 SCR 570, 18 CCC (3d) 223 [*Sansregret*]. In some parts of English law, however, recklessness was an objective form of liability that only requires the accused's failure to advert to an obvious risk. *Metropolitan Police Commissioner v Caldwell* (1981), [1982] AC 341 (HL).

for the offence of abandoning a child[22] and for firearms offences.[23] The Court has stated that while the presumption of subjective fault in relation to all the aspects of the *actus reus* "must — and often does — give way to clear expressions of a different legislative intent, it nonetheless incorporates an important value in our criminal law, that the morally innocent should not be punished."[24] The Court has affirmed the importance of the presumption but also carefully examined the text and the context of the offence. The presumption will apply if based on all these factors, Parliament had not displaced it by, for example, requiring the accused to take "reasonable precautions" or by prohibiting "careless" or "dangerousness" conduct[25] or by punishing conduct such as assault causing bodily harm or dangerous driving causing death more severely because of its consequences.

Common law presumptions remain quite important given the frequency with which Parliament enacts criminal offences without specifying any fault element, though the modern trend tends to be for Parliament to specify particular forms of fault when enacting new offences. Common law presumptions will, however, be overcome once Parliament has clearly indicated, through either the words or design of the offence, that it has intended some other result. Common law presumptions require Parliament to clearly state when it does not desire subjective *mens rea* when enacting a criminal offence.[26]

4) Constitutional Requirements of *Mens Rea*

The topic of *mens rea* has become more complex in part because there are a number of different principles of fundamental justice that govern the fault element. Some of these principles require proof of subjective fault, some of them require a proportionality between the moral blameworthiness of an offence and its punishment, including maintaining distinctions between the seriousness of subjective and objective fault offences, and some of them modify objective fault standards to ensure that they can be used to impose criminal liability.

---

22   *ADH*, above note 20 at para 23.

23   *R v Macdonald*, [2014] 1 SCR 37 at para 54.

24   *ADH*, above note 20 at para 27.

25   *ADH*, *ibid* at para 73.

26   As examined in Chapter 6, the common law presumption in *Sault Ste Marie*, above note 17, that regulatory offences will be strict liability, requires legislatures to clearly state if they desire a regulatory offence to be an absolute liability offence.

a) Requirements of Subjective Fault in Relation to Prohibited Act for Special Stigma Crimes: Murder, Attempted Murder, and War Crimes

As seen earlier in this chapter, there are common law presumptions that require proof of subjective *mens rea* — at least recklessness — in relation to all elements of the prohibited act, but these can be displaced by clear legislation. A constitutional requirement of subjective *mens rea* under section 7 of the *Charter* would leave Parliament far fewer options than a common law presumption. Violations of section 7 of the *Charter* are almost never upheld under section 1 of the *Charter*[27] and the substitution of elements for essential elements are also almost never accepted under section 11(d) of the *Charter*. The remaining legislative option would be the rather draconian use of the section 33 override to allow the legislation to operate for at least five years notwithstanding the legal rights in the *Charter*. The finality of constitutional requirements of *mens rea* may help explain the Supreme Court's caution about constitutionalizing subjective *mens rea* in relation to the prohibited act under section 7 of the *Charter*.

In *R v Vaillancourt*,[28] Lamer J expressed preference for a general constitutional principle of subjective *mens rea* in relation to all aspects of the prohibited act, while recognizing that many crimes were based on objective fault. He stated:

> It may well be that, as a general rule, the principles of fundamental justice require proof of a subjective *mens rea* with respect to the prohibited act, in order to avoid punishing the "morally innocent." . . . There are many provisions in the *Code* requiring only objective foreseeability of the result or even only a causal link between the act and the result. As I would prefer not to cast doubt on the validity of such provisions *in this case*, I will assume, but only for the purposes of this appeal, that something less than subjective foresight of the result may, sometimes, suffice for the imposition of criminal liability for causing that result through intentional criminal conduct.[29]

Subsequent cases have made it clear that subjective foresight of the prohibited consequences is not required for all crimes. Indeed, subjective *mens rea* so far has only been required under section 7 of the *Char-*

---

27   *Re BC Motor Vehicle Reference S 94(2)*, [1985] 2 SCR 486 at 518; *R v DB*, 2008 SCC 25 at para 89.
28   (1987), 39 CCC (3d) 118 (SCC) [*Vaillancourt*].
29   *Ibid* at 133–34 [emphasis in original].

ter for murder,[30] attempted murder,[31] and war crimes.[32] The Supreme Court has ruled that it is not required for many other crimes, including unlawfully causing bodily harm,[33] dangerous driving,[34] unlawful act manslaughter,[35] careless use of a firearm,[36] and failing to provide the necessities of life.[37] As will be discussed in Chapter 6, the *Charter* also does not require proof of subjective *mens rea* for regulatory offences found outside of the *Criminal Code* in various provincial and federal statutes.[38]

What then distinguishes murder, attempted murder, and war crimes as crimes that require subjective *mens rea* in relation to the prohibited act? Murder is the easiest to explain because "a conviction for murder carries with it the most severe stigma and punishment of any crime in our society."[39] Attempted murder only has a maximum penalty of life imprisonment and not a mandatory penalty of life imprisonment as does murder. Nevertheless, the Court has stressed that it carries with it the same stigma as murder because one who commits attempted murder has the same intent or "killer instinct" as a murderer but was "lucky — the ambulance arrived early, or some other fortuitous circumstance."[40] With respect to both murder and attempted murder, the constitutionally required *mens rea* is knowledge of the probability that death will be caused.

The Court was more divided on whether war crimes and crimes against humanity also were special stigma crimes that required proof of subjective knowledge in relation to all aspects of the prohibited act. The majority of the Court in *Finta*[41] stressed that a person convicted of war crimes would be subject to "additional stigma and opprobrium" associated with war crimes that would not normally be associated with the underlying crimes charged in that case: unlawful confinement, robbery, kidnapping, and manslaughter of Jews during the Holocaust. The minority relied on the general principle that section 7 of the *Charter*

---

30   *Martineau*, above note 7.
31   *R v Logan*, [1990] 2 SCR 731 [*Logan*].
32   *R v Finta* (1994), 88 CCC (3d) 417 (SCC) [*Finta*].
33   *DeSousa*, above note 5.
34   *Hundal*, above note 13.
35   *Creighton*, above note 3.
36   *R v Finlay* (1993), 83 CCC (3d) 513 (SCC) [*Finlay*]; *R v Gosset* (1993), 83 CCC (3d) 494 (SCC) [*Gosset*].
37   *R v Naglik* (1993), 83 CCC (3d) 526 (SCC) [*Naglik*].
38   *Hundal*, above note 13.
39   *Martineau*, above note 7 at 645.
40   *Logan*, above note 31 at 743.
41   Above note 32.

does not require proof of fault in relation to all aspects of the prohibited result and that any additional stigma attached to a war crimes conviction would be caused by the surrounding circumstances as opposed to the nature of the offence.

The theory behind special stigma offences appears to be that fair labelling is required, albeit only for the most serious of crimes. It is difficult to see what other crimes might be added to this short list of special stigma crimes, although terrorist offences may qualify given the stigma and enhanced penalties associated with them. In *R v Khawaja*,[42] the Supreme Court avoided deciding whether terrorism crimes were stigma offences that required proof of subjective fault in relation to the prohibited act. It did, however, stress that the offence under section 83.18 had a high subjective *mens rea* requirement that the accused have "the *subjective* purpose of enhancing the ability of a terrorist group to facilitate or carry out a terrorist activity." The requirement of subjective purpose goes beyond the constitutionally required minimum of subjective knowledge for the stigma crimes of murder, attempted murder, and war crimes.

b) Principles of Fundamental Justice as Outlined in *Creighton*

Constitutional requirements of subjective knowledge in relation to the prohibited result for crimes of special stigma do not exhaust constitutional requirements of fault. In *Creighton*,[43] McLachlin J indicated that the following considerations were relevant in determining constitutional requirements of *mens rea*:

1. the stigma attached to the offence, and the available penalties requiring a *mens rea* reflecting the particular nature of the crime;
2. whether the punishment is proportionate to the moral blameworthiness of the offender; and
3. the idea that those causing harm intentionally must be punished more severely than those causing harm unintentionally.

This articulates constitutional requirements of *mens rea* at a greater level of generality than often circular conclusions about whether the stigma, penalty, or moral blameworthiness of particular crimes demands a greater degree of *mens rea*.

The first *Creighton* proposition builds on a line of cases culminating in *Martineau* and *Logan* that indicated that murder and attempted murder because of their nature and labelling effects will require a sub-

---

42   [2012] 3 SCR 555 at para 46 [*Khawaja*].
43   *Creighton*, above note 3 at 374.

jective *mens rea* in relation to the *actus reus* of the crime. As discussed earlier, the Supreme Court in its first war crimes case concluded, albeit in a 4:3 decision, that the prosecutor must establish not only the fault of the underlying offence but also subjective fault, including wilful blindness, of the circumstances that elevated the crime from an ordinary crime into a war crime.[44] The first *Creighton* proposition will only be relevant with respect to a small number of crimes with a special stigma.

The second *Creighton* proposition relates to proportionality between the moral blameworthiness of the offender and the punishment. The Court has not elaborated on this particular concept, but subsequent to *Creighton* it has indicated that a law that is grossly disproportionate to a state interest would also violate section 7 of the *Charter*.[45] The Court refused to strike down either the offence of possession of marijuana in *Malmo-Levine* or the offence of manslaughter in *Creighton* under section 7 of the *Charter*, and in both cases relied on the notion that sentencing discretion, including the option of alternatives to imprisonment, would allow judges to tailor punishment to moral blameworthiness. At the time of both decisions, there were no mandatory minimum sentences for either crime. This raises the question of whether the Court's analysis would be different if there were a mandatory sentence of imprisonment as there is now with respect to manslaughter committed with a firearm.[46] The question under section 7 would be whether the existence of a mandatory sentence meant that the punishment was no longer proportionate to the moral blameworthiness of the offence. The existence of safety valves such as sentencing discretion may be quite important to maintaining proportionality between punishment and moral blameworthiness required by section 7 of the *Charter*.

The idea expressed in the third *Creighton* proposition that the intentional causing of harm should be punished more severely than the unintentional causing of harm was easily satisfied because of the important distinction between murder and manslaughter. Nevertheless,

---

44 *Finta*, above note 32.

45 *R v Malmo-Levine* (2003), 179 CCC (3d) 417 (SCC). See also *Canada (Attorney General) v Bedford*, 2013 SCC 72; *Carter v Canada (Attorney General)*, 2015 SCC 5.

46 *Code*, above note 3, s 236 provides for a four-year mandatory minimum penalty for manslaughter when a firearm is used in the commission of an offence. Note that in *R v Morrisey*, [2000] 2 SCR 90, the Court held that a similar four-year sentence was not cruel and unusual punishment contrary to s 12 of the *Charter*. In subsequent cases, however, the Court has indicated that mandatory sentences for broadly defined offences may often violate s 12 unless the offence is defined more narrowly or sentencing judges are allowed to make and justify exceptions from the mandatory penalty. See *R v Lloyd*, 2016 SCC 13 at paras 35–36. For further discussion, see Chapter 11.

this principle creates the possibility that section 7 might be violated by some broadly defined crimes such as sexual assault,[47] the new organizational criminal liability provisions for subjective intent offences,[48] and the new restrictions on the defence of extreme intoxication,[49] which combine objective and subjective fault elements. This approach, however, would require courts to scrutinize the policy reasons that Parliament may have for broadly defining crimes to include a range of culpable conduct. Courts may very well retreat to the notion, firmly established in the cases, that the stigma, penalty, and blameworthiness of only a few crimes demand a *mens rea* that reflects the particular nature of the crime. Thus, courts may well conclude that the stigma and penalty that accompany a sexual assault conviction,[50] or most subjective offences committed by organizations, do not require proof of subjective fault for every element of the offence or the creation of a separate, less serious offence of negligent sexual assault.

In addition, the third *Creighton* proposition may discount that sometimes it may be quite appropriate for Parliament to combine subjective and objective fault elements and that this may not result in disproportionate punishment that punishes those who cause harm unintentionally more than those who cause harm intentionally. Rather, the result may be to punish those who had elements of both subjective and objective fault. As with the second *Creighton* principle of ensuring that punishment is proportionate to the moral blameworthiness of the offender, the existence of sentencing discretion may also play a role in ensuring compliance with section 7 of the *Charter*.

c) Constitutional Requirements with Respect to Criminal Negligence

Section 7 of the *Charter* also plays a role in shaping negligence standards when they are used to determine criminal liability resulting in imprisonment. There are at least three constitutional requirements all designed to ensure that objective standards of criminal liability are applied in a fair manner that avoids punishing the morally innocent and ensures that it is fundamentally fair to impose the criminal sanction.

Starting with *R v Creighton*, the Court has indicated that while the accused's personal characteristics should not be factored into the reasonable person standard, the accused's characteristics would be relevant and prevent criminal liability if they indicated that the particular accused

---

47   *Code*, above note 2, s 273.2(b), discussed in Chapter 10, Section B(3).
48   *Code*, *ibid*, s 22.2(c), discussed in Chapter 6, Section D(2)(e)(iii).
49   *Code*, above note 2, s 33.1, discussed in Chapter 7, Section E(3).
50   See *R v Daviault*, [1994] 3 SCR 63 [*Daviault*], Sopinka J in dissent.

"is not capable of appreciating the risk" or not capable to avoid creating the risk.[51] Because the Court has often dealt with this factor in the context of licensed driving, it is difficult to point to concrete examples in the jurisprudence where the accused is incapable of appreciating or controlling a risk. Possible examples could include situations where the accused's illiteracy made it impossible for him or her to appreciate a risk that was the subject of a written warning or where the accused's mental deficiencies were so extreme that it was not possible for that person to avoid a specific risk that requires some degree of mental foresight or planning. At present, however, it is not possible to point to specific examples of courts applying these incapacity-based exceptions to prevent the application of objective standards of fault.

A second constitutional requirement is that negligent conduct must at a minimum constitute a marked departure from reasonable conduct so as to distinguish criminal from civil negligence. As Charron J explained:

> If every departure from the civil norm is to be criminalized, regardless of the degree, we risk casting the net too widely and branding as criminals persons who are in reality not morally blameworthy. Such an approach risks violating the principle of fundamental justice that the morally innocent not be deprived of liberty.[52]
>
> The constitutional requirement that criminal uses of negligence be distinguished from civil uses of negligence by proof of a marked departure explains why the Court has interpreted crimes such as careless use of a firearm and dangerous driving to require proof of a marked departure from reasonable standards of care despite statutory language that suggests an intent to punish mere carelessness that would ordinarily only be sufficient for imposing civil liability.[53]

This requirement not only distinguishes criminal from civil negligence but requires a higher marked departure standard for criminal negligence as opposed to the fault element of negligence or more specifically lack of due diligence used for regulatory offences to be examined in the next chapter.

A third and somewhat more recent constitutional requirement with respect to the administration of objective and negligence-based fault requirements in the criminal law is the need to consider all the evidence, including the actual mental state of the accused, to determine if it

---

51   *Creighton*, above note 3; *Beatty*, above note 14 at para 40; *Roy*, above note 16 at para 38.
52   *Beatty*, above note 14 at para 34.
53   *Hundal*, above note 13; *Finlay*, above note 36; *Beatty*, above note 14.

raises a reasonable doubt about whether a reasonable person in similar circumstances would have been aware of the risk created by the conduct.[54] This contextual approach would, for example, take into account whether the driver charged suffered an unexpected heart attack, seizure, detached retina, or loss of consciousness. It does not, however, require that the reasonable person have the same characteristics of the accused or that the accused has subjectively adverted to the prohibited risk.

Although the Court has upheld the constitutionality of using objective fault for most offences other than those that have special stigma, it has stressed that section 7 of the *Charter* requires (1) that objective standards not be applied to convict those incapable of appreciating or avoiding a prohibited risk, (2) proof of at a minimum marked departure from a reasonable standard of care, and (3) consideration of all the evidence, including the accused's actual mental state, before determining whether the accused has engaged in such a marked departure from standards of reasonable care.

d) Substituted Elements for Constitutionally Required Elements

As discussed earlier, constitutional requirements concerning fault elements will be less easily overcome than common law presumptions. The Supreme Court has concluded that because of the stigma and penalty of a murder conviction, section 7 of the *Charter* requires proof that the accused knew that the victim was likely to die. Thus, subjective knowledge of the *actus reus* is a constitutional requirement for the offence of murder.

It is theoretically possible to substitute another fault element for the fault element required under section 7 of the *Charter*. As examined in Chapter 2, however, the Court has been quite stringent and held that another element could only be substituted for a required element if proof of the substituted element would lead inexorably, or prove beyond a reasonable doubt, that the required element was present.[55] In *Martineau*,[56] the Supreme Court held that proof that the accused means to cause bodily harm for the purpose of facilitating a serious offence — the *mens rea* required for constructive murder under section 230(a) — could not be substituted for proof of the essential element of murder required for a murder conviction under section 7 of the *Charter* — namely, proof of subjective knowledge that the victim was likely to die. Similarly, proof under section 230(c) that the accused wilfully stops the breath of a hu-

---

54   *Beatty, ibid* at para 49.
55   *R v Whyte* (1988), 42 CCC (3d) 97 (SCC), as discussed in Chapter 2, Section B(3)(g).
56   *Martineau*, above note 7.

man being for the purpose of facilitating a serious offence could not be substituted for the essential element under section 7 of the *Charter* of knowledge of death. Proof of the substituted element in section 230 did not lead inexorably to a conclusion that the state had proven beyond a reasonable doubt the existence of the essential element required under section 7 of the *Charter*.[57]

Another possibility would be to justify the violation of section 7 caused by providing some other fault element as a reasonable limit under section 1 of the *Charter*. The Supreme Court has, however, been extremely reluctant to hold that violations of section 7 of the *Charter* are justified under section 1 of the *Charter*. In both *Vaillancourt* and *Martineau*, the Court held that it was not necessary or proportionate for the Court to use a lesser fault element than knowledge of death in order to advance the important objective of deterring the use of weapons and violence in the commission of serious offences. The Court noted that Parliament could and does punish the use of weapons in the commission of offences and that the accused could always receive a stiff sentence for manslaughter. In other cases, the Court seems even more categorical, even suggesting that a section 7 violation could be justified under section 1 only in exceptional circumstances such as war and other emergencies.[58] A final means to overcome a constitutional requirement of fault would be for Parliament to re-enact an offence, such as the constructive murder offence, notwithstanding section 7 of the *Charter*. This section 33 override would have to be re-enacted by Parliament after a five-year period.

A constitutional requirement of *mens rea* under section 7 of the *Charter* is much more difficult for Parliament to overcome than a common law presumption. All Parliament need do in response to a common law presumption of subjective *mens rea* is to indicate clearly that the common law presumptions are not desired. A constitutional requirement of *mens rea* can be overcome only by satisfying the rigorous and almost impossible standards for substituting elements under section 11(d) of the *Charter* or the equally difficult burden of justifying a violation of section 7 of the *Charter* under section 1. This may help explain why the Supreme Court has been relatively cautious in constitutionalizing subjective *mens rea* under section 7 of the *Charter* while it did not hesitate before the *Charter* to apply robust common law presumptions of subjective *mens rea*. It should be remembered that constitutional

---

57   *R v Sit* (1991), 61 CCC (3d) 449 (SCC).

58   *BC Motor Vehicle Reference*, above note 27 at 518; *R v Heywood*, [1994] 3 SCR 761 at 802; *New Brunswick v G(J)*, [1999] 3 SCR 46 at para 99; *R v Ruzic*, 2001 SCC 24 at para 92.

requirements are a bare minimum. As the content of constitutional requirements become more minimal, the common law presumptions will become more important.

5) Fault Elements in Relation to the Defences of Mistake of Fact, Intoxication, and Accident

Understanding fault elements is sometimes confused by reference to the "defences" of mistake of fact, intoxication, and accident. The availability of these defences often depends on a reasonable doubt about the fault element of the specific offence.

Both mistake of fact and intoxication defences are primarily derived from the fault element of the particular offence. As will be discussed in depth in Chapter 7, evidence that the accused was intoxicated may raise a reasonable doubt whether the accused had the required mental element for a specific intent offence such as murder or robbery. The Supreme Court has made clear that the issue is the accused's actual intent, not his or her capacity for the intent.[59] The relation of the intoxication defence to the fault element is less clear for offences that are classified as general intent offences. General intent offences such as assault are thought to involve less complex mental processes. Only extreme intoxication may negate such mental elements.[60] It might also be thought that intoxication may never be relevant to offences that only require an objective fault element because the reasonable person would not be intoxicated. Nevertheless, extreme intoxication may raise a reasonable doubt as to whether the accused had voluntarily committed the *actus reus*.[61]

The derivative nature of the mistake of fact defence is revealed by comparing the availability of the defence for crimes with various and no-fault elements. Mistake of fact will not be an issue for an absolute liability offence because the only issue is whether the accused has committed the *actus reus*. What the particular accused thought or even what a reasonable person in the accused's position would have perceived is not relevant. If objective negligence is the fault element, a mistake of fact will prevent a conviction only if it is one that a reasonable person would have made. In other words, a mistake of fact would have to be honest and reasonable. If the offence requires a subjective fault element, this opens up the possibility that an honest but not ne-

---

59   *R v Robinson* (1996), 105 CCC (3d) 97 (SCC).
60   *Daviault*, above note 50.
61   See Chapter 3, Section B(4) and Chapter 7, Section E, for more discussion of this proposition.

cessarily reasonable mistake of fact will suffice. The issue is what the actual accused perceived, not what a reasonable person perceived. The more unreasonable the accused's mistake, the less likely the jury will be to accept it as genuine and honest, but the ultimate issue is the perceptions of the particular accused. As will be seen later in this chapter, it is possible to combine subjective and objective fault elements and require that a mistake of fact be based on reasonable behaviour given the accused's actual subjective knowledge of the circumstances.

As discussed in Chapter 3, an accident may raise a reasonable doubt that the accused's conduct was involuntary and as such could negate proof of the *actus reus* or prohibited act.[62] At the same time, the defence of accident may also relate to fault or *mens rea*.[63] In such cases, distinctions between objective and subjective fault may be critical.

A claim of accident may result in a reasonable doubt that the accused acted with subjective intent or knowledge of the prohibited circumstances or consequences. This would be relevant in cases of struggles between the accused and the victim where the victim is accidentally killed or injured. Such a conclusion, however, may not result in a full acquittal, especially if there is a lesser included offence based on objective forms of fault. In a 1942 case, the Supreme Court drew this distinction when it stated that "even if the jury thought the pistol went off by accident (or were not satisfied that it did not go off in that manner)" in a struggle between a robber and a store owner, they could still conclude "that the conduct of the accused was such that he ought to have known it to be likely to induce such a struggle as that which actually occurred, and that somebody's death was likely to be caused thereby . . . ."[64] Today, a person who accidentally kills another while

---

62   See Chapter 3, Section C(1)

63   M Manning & P Sankoff, *Criminal Law*, 5th ed (Markham, ON: LexisNexis, 2015) at 13.171. On the need to relate the defence of accident to the particular *mens rea*, see *R v O'Brien*, 2003 NBCA 28; *R v McKenna*, 2015 NBCA 32. Note that "the defence of accident" applies if there is a reasonable doubt either to *actus reus* or *mens rea*. See *R v Stasiuk*, 1942 CanLII 371 (Man CA); *R v Kolbe*, 1974 ALTASCAD 44 at para 62; *R v Parrington* (1985), 20 CCC (3d) 184 (Ont CA); *R v Sutherland* (1993), 84 CCC (3d) 484 (Sask CA); *R v Samuels*, 2005 CanLII 15700 at para 32 (Ont CA); *R v Shannon*, 2014 BCCA 250 at paras 18–19.

64   *R v Hughes*, [1942] SCR 517 at 522 referring to what at the time was an alternative form of murder liability based on objective foresight of death. It would be an error for a judge to conclude that accident in the form of unintended consequence cannot be relevant to the subjective foresight of death that is today required under s 229(c) of the *Code*. *R v Belcourt*, 2015 BCCA 126 at paras 105–7. For a case where the Supreme Court held that the manslaughter should have been left to the jury where the accused claim that the killing was accidental, see *R v Kuzmack*, [1955] SCR 292.

committing another unlawful act could be not guilty of murder because of a reasonable doubt about subjective knowledge of the likelihood of death, but might nevertheless be guilty of unlawful act manslaughter which only requires a voluntary and unlawful act and objective fault in the form that a reasonable person in the accused's circumstances has objective foresight that non-trivial bodily harm may result from the commission of the unlawful act.[65]

B. THE DEGREES OF SUBJECTIVE *MENS REA*

There are important practical differences among the various forms of subjective *mens rea*. A person who might not be guilty of acting with the purpose or intent to commit a crime might, nevertheless, have acted with subjective knowledge that the prohibited result would occur. Similarly, a person who cannot be said to have acted with subjective knowledge that the prohibited result would occur may, nevertheless, have acted with subjective recklessness in adverting to or being conscious of a risk that the prohibited result could occur or the prohibited circumstances might be present. Such a person could also be wilfully blind by not inquiring into the prohibited risk, when he or she knows there is need for further inquiry. References to "subjective *mens rea*" are unhelpful, and the exact degree of subjective fault must be specified.

1) Intent, Purpose, or Wilfulness

The highest level of subjective *mens rea* is that which requires the accused to act with the intent or purpose to achieve the prohibited result, or to wilfully pursue such a result. An example would be section 229(a)(i), which prohibits murder where the accused "means to cause . . . death." This high level of *mens rea* is used relatively infrequently. Common law presumptions and even constitutional requirements of subjective *mens rea* do not require proof of intent and are satisfied by lower forms of *mens rea* such as knowledge and even recklessness. Where Parliament has specifically used the words "with intent," this will generally exclude lower forms of subjective *mens rea* such as recklessness.[66]

Proof of purpose is required under the various parties provisions in the *Criminal Code*. As examined in the last chapter, these provisions

---

65 *R v Parris*, 2013 ONCA 515 at paras 106–8; *R v Barton*, 2017 ABCA 216 at paras 288–92.

66 *R v Chartrand* (1994), 91 CCC (3d) 396 (SCC) [*Chartrand*].

can make a person guilty of an offence simply for assisting in the commission of a crime and thus it makes sense to require a fairly high level of *mens rea*. Section 21(1)(b) requires a party to do or omit "to do anything for the purpose of aiding any person" to commit an offence, and section 21(2) requires the formation of an "unlawful purpose." Similarly, attempts require "an intent to commit the offence," and an accessory after the fact must act for the purpose of enabling a known criminal to escape. Attempts and conspiracy also require a high level of intent to commit the completed crime.[67] The more peripheral the accused's involvement to the completed crime, the more sense it makes to require a higher form of subjective *mens rea*.

The potential difference between guilty intent and guilty knowledge can be illustrated in cases where the accused knowingly engages in prohibited conduct but does so for another purpose such as avoiding harm. In *R v Steane*, the accused was charged with assisting the enemy with the "intent to assist the enemy" after he made wartime propaganda broadcasts. The Court of Appeal held that, given the intent required for the offence, it was wrong for the trial judge to have left the jury with the impression that "a man must be taken to intend the natural consequences of his acts." It was possible that Steane acted not with the intent to assist the enemy, but rather with "the innocent intent of a desire to save his wife and children from a concentration camp."[68] In *R v Paquette*,[69] the Supreme Court similarly indicated:

> A person whose actions have been dictated by fear of death or of grievous bodily injury cannot be said to have formed a genuine common intent to carry out an unlawful purpose with the person who has threatened him with those consequences if he fails to co-operate.

In that case, the accused was held not to have formed a common intent under section 21(2) to rob a store when he drove the robbers to the store after being threatened at gunpoint. In both cases, the accused certainly acted with the knowledge that his actions would contribute to the prohibited result. The difficult issue is whether the accused acted with the intent or purpose to achieve the prohibited result.

The Supreme Court in *R v Hibbert*[70] has overruled *Paquette* on the basis that it confused intent and purpose with motive and desire. Chief Justice Lamer stated that a person, like Paquette, who participates in

---

67 *R v Ancio* (1984), 10 CCC (3d) 385 at 402 (SCC) and *R v O'Brien* (1954), 110 CCC 1 at 3 (SCC) as discussed in Chapter 4.

68 [1947] KB 997 at 1006 (CA).

69 (1976), 30 CCC (2d) 417 at 423 (SCC) [*Paquette*].

70 *R v Hibbert* (1995), 99 CCC (3d) 193 (SCC) [*Hibbert*].

a robbery because of threats to his life nevertheless forms an "unlawful purpose" under section 21(2) to commit the robbery. His desire or motive of saving his own life does not prevent the formation of the unlawful purpose of intentionally committing the robbery. Similarly, Paquette would act with the purpose of assisting the robbery required under section 21(1)(b) if he intended to drive the getaway car and by doing so assist the robbery. It would not matter to the question of *mens rea* that Paquette's desire or motive was to save his own life. The Supreme Court has rejected the idea that intent or purpose under section 21 should be equated with the accused's desires and motivations. Some caution is in order before applying this ruling to all forms of subjective *mens rea*. The Court made clear it only reached these conclusions for section 21 in large part because an accused who responded to threats could still claim a common law defence of duress.[71] Depending on how the offence was structured, the fact that a person acted as a result of threats could, in some instances, be relevant to the question of whether he or she possessed the *mens rea* necessary to commit the offence. Thus, a person in Steane's position could perhaps still argue that he did not wilfully act with an intent or purpose to assist the enemy even though he surely knew that his actions would have that effect.

Knowledge that something is very certain to occur, however, may be equated with an intent or a purpose to achieve the prohibited result. In *Buzzanga*,[72] Martin JA stated that "as a general rule, a person who foresees that a consequence is certain or substantially certain to result from an act which he does to achieve some other purpose, intends that consequence." Consistent with the presumption of innocence, however, an accused should be allowed to raise a reasonable doubt as to whether he or she intended the consequence, if that is the required mental element.

A requirement that the accused wilfully achieve a prohibited result imposes a high degree of subjective *mens rea*. In *Buzzanga*,[73] the Ontario Court of Appeal interpreted a prohibition against wilfully promoting hatred against an identifiable group as requiring proof that the accused's "conscious purpose in distributing the document was to promote hatred against that group," or knowledge that the promotion of hatred "was certain or morally certain" to result from their actions. This requires knowledge of a much higher degree of probability of the prohibited act than either knowledge that requires that the accused

---

71   See Chapter 9, Section D.

72   *Buzzanga*, above note 9 at 384–85, approved in *Chartrand*, above note 66 at 415.

73   *Buzzanga*, above note 9 at 385. This analysis has been approved with reference to a "with intent" requirement. *Chartrand*, above note 66.

know that the prohibited act is probable or recklessness that requires knowledge that the prohibited act is possible.

In *R v Docherty*,[74] the Supreme Court stated that the word "wilfully" "stresses intention in relation to the achievement of a purpose. It can be contrasted with lesser forms of guilty knowledge, such as 'negligently' or even 'recklessly.' In short, the use of the word 'wilfully' denotes a legislative concern for a relatively high level of *mens rea*." In that case, the accused was held not to have wilfully breached his probation order because he believed that what he was doing, sitting in the driver's seat of a motionless car while drunk, was not a crime that would place him in breach of probation. Parliament subsequently deleted the requirement that the prosecutor prove that the accused "wilfully" breached parole. Instead there is a simple prohibition against breaching parole without a reasonable excuse.[75] Courts have interpreted the *mens rea* of wilfully obstructing justice as requiring a specific intent to pervert justice and not to include "a simple error of judgment."[76]

In *R v ADH*,[77] the Supreme Court interpreted a reference in section 214 of the *Code* to abandoning or exposing a child as including "a wilful omission to take charge of a child by a person who is in a legal duty to do so" as an indication that the offence required subjective fault. Justice Cromwell commented that a wilful omission is the antithesis of a crime involving a mere failure to act in accordance with some minimum level of behaviour. If Parliament had meant to include in the terms "abandon" and "expose" situations in which there is no more than a failure to meet a standard of reasonable conduct, it would not make sense to require that omissions to observe that standard would have to be "wilful."

Nevertheless, Parliament retains the power within the broad confines of *Charter* requirements to define wilful in a different way. This is seen in *R v Carker (No 2)*,[78] where a prisoner was convicted of wilfully damaging public property when he smashed plumbing fixtures in his cell during a prison riot, even though he performed the act only after fellow prisoners had threatened to injure him if he did not. It

---

74 (1989), 51 CCC (3d) 1 at 7 (SCC).

75 *Code*, above note 2, s 733.1. Applying the common law presumption of subjective *mens rea* discussed above, this new offence would only require proof that accused recklessly breached probation by being aware of the risk that their actions would breach probation.

76 *R v Beaudry*, [2007] 1 SCR 190 at para 52. See also *R v Murray*, 2000 CanLII 22378 (Ont SCJ).

77 *ADH*, above note 20 at paras 36 and 49.

78 (1966), [1967] 2 CCC 190 (SCC).

could be argued that Carker did not truly intend to damage public property because he was acting for the purpose of self-preservation. Carker was, however, found to have the necessary *mens rea*, because "wilful" was defined by Parliament for the purpose of the offence as including knowledge or recklessness that the prohibited result would occur.[79] Carker knew he was damaging public property, even though his ultimate purpose or intent may have been to save his life. The Court has subsequently indicated outside this specific statutory context that those who act under duress and with a desire to save themselves from threats may nevertheless have the *mens rea* of acting with an unlawful purpose.[80] In another prison case that did not involve a legislative definition of purpose, a majority of the Court in *R v Kerr*[81] interpreted the offence of possession of a weapon for a purpose dangerous to the public peace in a manner that seemed to equate purpose with knowledge[82] and even with recklessness.[83] It can no longer be maintained with great confidence that a *mens rea* requirement of intent, purpose, or wilfulness will be sharply differentiated from a requirement of knowledge.

2) Intent, Purpose, or Wilfulness Distinguished from Motive

The criminal law does not generally require proof of a motive for a crime, and an argument that the accused had no motive or some innocent motivation will not exonerate one who has otherwise committed the crime with the necessary guilty intent. As Dickson J has stated,

> In ordinary parlance, the words "intent" and "motive" are frequently used interchangeably, but in the criminal law they are distinct. In most criminal trials, the mental element, the *mens rea* with which the Court

---

79   *Code*, above note 2, s 429(1).

80   *Hibbert*, above note 70. In some circumstances, they might have a defence of duress. See Chapter 9.

81   [2004] 2 SCR 371.

82   *Ibid* at para 55, Bastarache J (Major J concurring). Justice Bastarache held that the accused did not have the purpose requirement because he possessed the shank in order to defend himself.

83   *Ibid* at para 77, LeBel J (Arbour J concurring). Justice LeBel elaborated: "Criminal liability under s. 88(1) thus applies not only to an accused who intends to do harm to persons or property, but also an accused who is aware of a risk of harm to persons or property and persists with his or her intention despite that risk. It does not establish an objective standard of dangerousness however." *Ibid* at para 88. He held that the accused did possess the weapon for a purpose dangerous to the public peace but ruled that the offence was excused because of the defence of necessity.

is concerned, relates to "intent," i.e., the exercise of a free will to use particular means to produce a particular result, rather than with "motive," i.e., that which precedes and induces the exercise of the will. The mental element of a crime ordinarily involves no reference to motive.[84]

The Crown does not have to prove motive, but evidence relating to motive can be relevant in a criminal trial and can assist the Crown and sometimes the accused. In *Buzzanga*, the fact that the accused may have intended to counter apathy among francophones when they circulated an anti-French document was relevant in determining whether they were wilfully promoting hatred against that group. On the other hand, Martin JA indicated that if the accused were indeed intentionally promoting hatred against francophones, they would be guilty even if their motive was to produce a reaction that would help establish a French language school. Motive, of course, could be relevant to the exercise of either prosecutorial or sentencing discretion.[85]

One exception to the principle that motive is not an essential element of offences are the terrorism offences created by Parliament at the end of 2001. The prosecutor must not only prove various forms of intent beyond a reasonable doubt, but also that the act was "committed in whole or in part for a political, religious, or ideological purpose, objective, or cause."[86] In other words, a political or religious motive is an essential element of crimes involving the commission of a terrorist activity. The motive requirement was defended as necessary to distinguish terrorism from ordinary crime. This seems unlikely given that the activities also have to be committed with the intent to intimidate the public or compel governments or persons to act. Concerns were raised that the motive requirement would require the police to investigate the political and religious beliefs of terrorist suspects and that these matters would be front and centre in any terrorist trial. In response, Parliament enacted section 83.01(1.1), which provides that "the expression of a political, religious, or ideological thought, belief, or opinion" would not fall under the definition of terrorist activity unless the other intent requirements were satisfied. The Supreme Court has upheld the use of the political and religious motive requirement on the basis that no rule prevents Parliament from including motive in the

---

84 *R v Lewis* (1979), 47 CCC (2d) 24 at 33 (SCC).

85 Manning & Sankoff, above note 63 at 4.64. They also suggest that motive may be relevant to defences such as duress and necessity. See Chapter 9 examining these structured defences, which require a reasonable perception of threats and proportionality between harm avoided and inflicted in addition to the subjective motive to save oneself or others.

86 *Code*, above note 2, s 83.01(1)(b)(I)(A).

definition of a crime. It also indicated that the particular political or religious motive requirement in relation to the definition of terrorist activities did not limit freedom of expression or religion, especially given the exemption for expression of political opinion or religious belief.[87]

Motive can be difficult to distinguish from intent, and cases on this issue have not always been consistent. In a 1936 case, the Supreme Court held that a person who assisted in a robbery had formed a common intent to commit the crime. The fact that his motivation may have been to avoid threats of death from his accomplices was irrelevant to the issue of *mens rea*.[88] In 1976, however, the Court indicated that a person who assisted in a robbery in response to threats of death could not have formed a genuine intent to carry out the unlawful purpose.[89] In 1995, however, the Supreme Court reverted to its former approach when it overruled the 1976 case on the basis that a person could act with the purpose of assisting a crime under section 21(1)(b) or form a common intent to carry out an unlawful purpose to engage in a crime under section 21(2), even though his or her motives and desires were to avoid threats from accomplices.[90] The Court indicated that in most cases, the motive of avoiding harm to self or others would not negate the issue of intent.

The Supreme Court has continued to draw a broad distinction between motive and intent. Justices Cory and Iacobucci have stated that "[i]t does not matter to society, in its efforts to secure social peace and order, what an accused's motive was, but only what the accused intended to do. It is no consolation to one whose car has been stolen that the thief stole the car intending to sell it to purchase food for a food bank."[91] Good motive is no defence to intentional crimes. It may, however, be relevant to the exercise of prosecutorial or sentencing discretion.

a) Motive, Mistake of Law, and Colour of Right

The criminal law's general lack of concern about motive may also help explain the ignorance of the law is not an excuse principle found in section 19 of the *Criminal Code* and discussed previously in Chapter 3. This principle means that accused who have formed honest and even reasonable but mistaken beliefs that their actions are legal may still be found to have the necessary *mens rea* to commit the offence. In most cases, *mens rea* relates only to the accused's intent or knowledge in rela-

---

87   *Khawaja*, above note 42 at paras 82–84.
88   *Dunbar v R* (1936), 67 CCC 20 (SCC).
89   *Paquette*, above note 69.
90   *Hibbert*, above note 70.
91   *United States of America v Dynar* (1997), 115 CCC (3d) 481 at 509 (SCC) [*Dynar*].

tion to the commission of the immediate act and not to more elaborate processes relating either to why the accused acted or whether the accused thought that the act was legal. This may help explain why mistakes about the legality and legal consequences of actions are generally not excuses, but a mistake about the existence of the more immediate factual elements of the offences may, as will be discussed later in this chapter, be a factor that will prevent the prosecutor from establishing *mens rea*.

As in many areas, there are some exceptions. The *mens rea* of some offences, notably theft, are defined in a robust way that allows the accused's mistaken beliefs about legal claims to the property to be relevant to proof of *mens rea*. Section 322(1) of the *Code* provides a particularly high level of *mens rea*, which requires proof that an accused who commits theft "fraudulently and without colour of right" takes or converts property.[92] The courts have held that an accused's mistaken belief about his legal entitlement to the property can prevent proof of *mens rea* for this particular crime.[93] Consistent with the focus on the accused's mental state, the issue is the accused's belief in legal entitlement and not the actual legal entitlement.[94] Mistaken beliefs about legal entitlement can prevent the proof of this particular fault element. The Court has refused to extend this colour of right concept to other offences that do not contain this formulation. Thus, the belief by Indigenous persons that they are exercising their legal rights will not provide a defence in cases where courts reject their claim of rights even though this may speak to the motive for their actions.[95] This is another reminder about the need to be specific about the precise nature of *mens rea* for specific offences. Although neither motive nor beliefs about legality are relevant for most criminal offences, they may be relevant to some offences such as theft and other property offences that allow a colour of right defence.

3) Knowledge

Knowledge is a slightly lower form of subjective *mens rea* than intent or purpose. Section 229(c) of the *Criminal Code* states that a person is guilty of murder if he "knows" that he "is likely to cause death to

---

92   The colour of right concept will not be read into other crimes that do not contain such language. See *R v Jones*, [1991] 3 SCR 110 (not reading in colour of right concept into offence of operating unlicensed bingo).

93   *R v Howson*, [1966] 3 CCC 348 (Ont CA); *R v Dorosh*, 2003 SKCA 134.

94   *R v Lilly*, [1983] 1 SCR 794 at 798–99.

95   *R v Jones*, [1991] 3 SCR 110 (convicting accused who mistakenly believed that *Criminal Code* betting restrictions did not apply on their reserve).

a human being, notwithstanding that he desires to effect his object without causing death or bodily harm to any human being."[96] Similarly, section 229(a)(ii) also emphasizes the requirement of guilty knowledge by providing that a person who intentionally causes bodily harm is guilty of murder if he or she knows that the harm is likely to result in death. This requirement of guilty knowledge of the likelihood of death has been held to be sufficient under section 7 of the *Charter* to sustain a murder conviction.[97] A person may have guilty knowledge that his or her victim will die without necessarily desiring or having the motive of causing death or even intending or meaning to cause death under section 229(a)(i).

Knowledge is a common form of *mens rea* for possession-based offences. In *Beaver*,[98] the Supreme Court held that a person in physical possession of a substance could not be said to possess that substance unless he or she knew the nature of the substance. Justice Cartwright explained that a person with an honest belief that a substance was baking soda would not have the *mens rea* for possession even if the substance turned out to be heroin. "The essence of the crime is the possession of the forbidden substance and in a criminal case there is in law no possession without knowledge of the character of the forbidden substance."[99] As discussed in Chapter 3, however, a person who makes a mistake about whether a particular drug is illegal would not have a defence because ignorance of the law is no excuse.

In *R v Lucas*,[100] the Supreme Court interpreted the requirement that the prosecutor prove that an accused who has been charged with defamatory libel know that the statements were false as requiring proof of the accused's subjective knowledge. The Court then qualified this correct statement by indicating that the accused's

> subjective understanding of the statements . . . should not be determinative if this position was adopted, it would always be open to an accused to argue that the "real" meaning which they believed to be true was quite different from the meaning which would be object-

---

96 The reference in that section to objective foreseeability that occurs when the accused ought to know that his or her actions would cause death is unconstitutional because s 7 of the *Canadian Charter of Rights and Freedoms*, Part I of the *Constitution Act, 1982*, being Schedule B to the *Canada Act 1982* (UK), 1982, c 11 [*Charter*] has been interpreted as requiring a minimal *mens rea* for murder of knowledge that death is likely to occur. *Martineau*, above note 7.

97 *Martineau*, *ibid*, discussed in Chapter 2, Section B(4)(d).

98 *Beaver*, above note 18.

99 *Ibid* at 140.

100 (1998), 123 CCC (3d) 97 at 131 (SCC).

ively attributed to it by any reasonable reader. Rather the question should be whether the appellants knew that the message, as it would be understood by a reasonable person, was false.

This formulation runs the risk of confusing subjective and objective standards of liability and diluting the relatively high level of subjective *mens rea* required by proof of guilty knowledge. Knowledge is a subjective form of *mens rea* and a person who claims to ignore what a reasonable person would know runs the real risk of being found guilty. Nevertheless, the ultimate issue is the particular accused's knowledge, not what a reasonable person would know.

In *Dynar*,[101] the Supreme Court observed that knowledge has "two components — truth and belief" and that only belief is relevant to the determination of a subjective *mens rea*. The truth of the matter is an objective fact that is required to establish the *actus reus* not the *mens rea*. Thus, an accused who stabbed a manikin believing it to be human would have the subjective *mens rea* of murder. Because the manikin was not in truth a human being, however, there would be no *actus reus* for murder. Even though the accused had the *mens rea* required for murder, he or she could only be charged with attempted murder.

4) Wilful Blindness

A more recent and controversial form of subjective *mens rea* is wilful blindness, which is now seen as a substitute for knowledge in cases where an accused subjectively sees the need for further inquiries about the existence of prohibited consequences or circumstances but deliberately fails to make such inquiries because he or she does not want to know the truth.[102] The Supreme Court stated in *Sansregret*:

> Wilful blindness is distinct from recklessness because, while recklessness involves knowledge of a danger or a risk and persistence in a course of conduct which creates a risk that the prohibited result will occur, wilful blindness arises when a person who has become aware of the need for some inquiry declines to make the inquiry because he does not wish to know the truth. He would prefer to remain ignorant. The culpability in recklessness is justified by consciousness of the risk and by proceeding in the face of it, while in wilful blindness it is

---

101 *Dynar*, above note 91 at 506.
102 *R v Briscoe*, [2010] 1 SCR 411 at paras 21 and 24 [*Briscoe*].

justified by the accused's fault in deliberately failing to inquire when
he knows there is reason for inquiry.[103]

On the facts of the case, the trial judge had acquitted the accused of rape
on the basis that while the risk that the complainant had not consented
would have been obvious to anyone "in his right mind," it was not to
the accused, who "saw what he wanted to see, heard what he wanted to
hear, believed what he wanted to believe." The Supreme Court reversed
and entered a conviction on the basis that the accused was wilfully
blind to the lack of consent because he "was aware of the likelihood of
the complainant's reaction to his threats." To proceed in the circumstances was "self-deception to the point of wilful blindness . . . . Where
the accused is deliberately ignorant as a result of blinding himself to
reality the law presumes knowledge, in this case knowledge of the nature of the consent."[104]

Some commentators have argued that if the accused in *Sansregret*
genuinely believed that the complainant consented, there was no reason for him to make the inquiry, and the Court was actually imposing
liability on the basis of negligence. This interpretation seems strained,
given the facts of the case, which included a break-in and violence, as
well as a similar encounter less than a month earlier in which the same
complainant had reported that she had been raped by the accused. The
Supreme Court seems to suggest that given these facts, the accused
knew there was a likelihood that the complainant was not consenting,
but he deliberately blinded himself to that possibility. This reading is
supported by the Court's reliance on Glanville Williams's text in *Sansregret* where he states that "a court can only properly find wilful blindness only where it can almost be said that the defendant actually knew.
He suspected the fact, he realized its probability, but he refrained from
obtaining the final confirmation because he wanted in any event to be
able to deny knowledge."[105]

In subsequent cases, the Supreme Court has defined wilful blindness as "deliberately choosing not to know" when the accused strongly
suspects that such an inquiry would fix them with guilty knowledge.[106]
The Court has made clear that a mere failure to inquire, though it may
be evidence of negligence, will not be enough for a finding of wilful

---

103 *Sansregret*, above note 21 at 235 (cited to CCC).
104 *Ibid.*
105 Glanville Williams, *Criminal Law: The General Part*, 2d ed (London: Stevens,
1961) at 159, cited in *Sansregret*, above note 21 at 586 (cited to SCR), and *Briscoe*,
above note 102 at para 22.
106 *R v Jorgensen* (1995), 102 CCC (3d) 97 at 135 (SCC).

blindness. In *R v Briscoe*, the Court adopted Professor Don Stuart's description of wilful blindness as deliberate ignorance and ruled that the trial judge erred in not instructing the jury that wilful blindness was available as a substitute fault element for knowledge in a case where the accused had a "strong, well-founded suspicion" that the victim would be sexually assaulted and killed but had declared: "[W]hatever you guys wanna do just do it. Don't do it around me. I don't want to see nothing."[107]

The Court has made clear that wilful blindness is a subjective form of fault, distinct and greater than both recklessness and negligence. At the same time, wilful blindness is still a difficult concept to administer especially with respect to the ambiguous statement that an accused will only be wilfully blind if they "suspect" the prohibited consequence or circumstance.[108] It is clear that the accused must subjectively suspect, but it is still not clear whether the subjective suspicion must relate to the mere possibility or probability that the prohibited consequences or circumstances exist.

In order to be equated with knowledge and distinguished from recklessness, wilful blindness should require more than a subjective suspicion about a mere possibility but rather a well-founded suspicion that is closer to knowledge of a probability that the prohibited circumstances or consequences will occur. The fact that the accused should have been suspicious or only recognized the possibility as opposed to the probability of the unlawful act occurring should not be sufficient if wilful blindness is truly to be the equivalent of guilty knowledge.

The Ontario Court of Appeal has reversed convictions on the basis of wilful blindness where the trial judge focused simply on the accused's

---

107 *Briscoe*, above note 102 at para 25.

108 The Quebec Court of Appeal has stressed the subjective nature of wilful blindness by stating that the issue was not whether the accused "'*should*' have known or should '*normally*' have known from the suspicious circumstances that her husband was probably involved in a conspiracy to import cocaine. The question was whether the circumstances were such that she, herself, was, in fact, suspicious that this was the case, but deliberately refrained from making inquiries so that she could remain in ignorance as to the truth." *R v Comtois Barbeau* (1996), 110 CCC (3d) 69 at 95 (Que CA) [emphasis in original]. The Ontario Court of Appeal has similarly stressed that "culpability on the basis of wilful blindness rests on a finding of deliberate ignorance. An accused who suspects that property is stolen but declines to make the inquiries that will confirm that suspicion, preferring instead to remain ignorant is culpable." *R v Lagace* (2003), 181 CCC (3d) 12 at para 28 (Ont CA). The Court of Appeal also referred to "actual suspicion, combined with a conscious decision not to make inquiries which could confirm that suspicion, is equated in the eyes of criminal law with knowledge." *R v Duong* (1998), 124 CCC (3d) 392 at para 23.

suspicions or used the colloquial phrase "turning a blind eye."[109] It also explained that wilful blindness "does not involve a failure to inquire, but an active decision not to inquire so as to avoid being fixed with knowledge."[110] The Saskatchewan Court of Appeal has overturned a finding of wilful blindness based in the accused's "indifference" because such a definition of wilful blindness did not stress the requirement of deliberate ignorance and a conscious decision by the accused not to obtain knowledge as stressed by the Supreme Court in *Briscoe*.[111] These cases suggest that some trial judges still struggle with the concept of wilful blindness despite the guidance provided by *Briscoe* that it is a high form of subjective fault that is the equivalent of knowledge.

5) Recklessness

Recklessness is a lower form of *mens rea* than intent, purpose, wilfulness, knowledge, or wilful blindness, but in Canada it is still a form of subjective *mens rea*. In Canadian criminal law, a person acts recklessly if he or she has adverted to or become aware of the risk of the prohibited conduct. In *Sansregret*,[112] the Supreme Court stressed the importance of distinguishing recklessness from negligence:

> In accordance with well-established principles for the determination of criminal liability, recklessness, to form a part of the criminal *mens rea*, must have an element of the subjective. It is found in the attitude of one who, aware that there is danger that his conduct could bring about the result prohibited by the criminal law, nevertheless persists, despite the risk. It is, in other words, the conduct of one who sees the risk and who takes the chance.

Recklessness requires subjective advertence to the prohibited risk and can be distinguished from negligence, which requires only that a reasonable person in the accused's circumstances would have recognized the risk.[113] A person recklessly commits sexual assault if he recognizes the risk that the woman is not consenting, while a person would negligently commit sexual assault if a reasonable person in his circum-

---

109 *R v Duncan*, 2013 ONCA 774 at para 9; *R v Farmer*, 2014 ONCA 823 at para 26; Trotter JA defined wilful blindness as "a subjective suspicion about a fact, circumstance or situation, but deciding not to make inquiries, preferring to remain ignorant of the true state of affairs." *R v Pilgrim*, 2017 ONCA 309 at para 66.

110 *R v Downey*, 2017 ONCA 789 at para 5.

111 *R v Spencer*, 2017 SKCA 54 at paras 78 and 80.

112 *Sansregret*, above note 21 at 233 (cited to CCC).

113 *O'Grady v Sparling* (1960), 128 CCC 1 at 13 (SCC).

stances would have known there was a risk that the woman does not consent. As will be seen, the actual fault element for sexual assault falls somewhere in between recklessness and negligence.

Recklessness requires that the accused is subjectively aware of the possibility of the prohibited act, whereas knowledge requires that the accused be aware of the probability of the prohibited act.[114] Recklessness is a common form of subjective *mens rea*. Justice Martin has stated that "the general *mens rea* which is required and which suffices for most crimes where no mental element is mentioned in the definition of the crime, is either the intentional or reckless bringing about of the result which the law, in creating the offence, seeks to prevent."[115] Similarly, the common law presumption in *Sault Ste Marie*[116] that a criminal offence have subjective *mens rea* includes recklessness. Recklessness requires only subjective awareness of the risk of the prohibited act, as opposed to knowledge of the likelihood of the prohibited act.

6) Transferred Subjective *Mens Rea*

Section 229(b) codifies the common law doctrine of transferred intent. The *mens rea* of intentionally or knowingly causing death to one person is transferred to the killing of the victim, even though the accused "does not mean to cause death or bodily harm" to the victim and does so "by accident or mistake." This provision was applied in *R v Droste (No 2)*[117] to convict an accused who, in a deliberate attempt to kill his wife, set fire to a car, causing two children buckled in the back seat to die of asphyxiation. The Court concluded that because the attempted murder of the accused's wife was planned and deliberate, the intent of planning and deliberation, as well as the guilty knowledge that death would result, could be transferred to the children's deaths.

The Manitoba Court of Appeal has decided that section 229(b) should not be applied when the accused intends to kill himself but ends up killing another person. The Court of Appeal held that a person who intends to kill himself does not have the same moral blameworthiness

---

114 Some commentators argue that recklessness requires subjective advertence to the probability of the prohibited risk. (Manning & Sankoff, above note 63 at 4.83). My concern with such a reading is that it risks obliterating the distinction between knowledge and recklessness, something that would especially be undesirable given that knowledge is the constitutionally required *mens rea* for stigma offences.

115 *Buzzanga*, above note 9 at 381.

116 Above note 17 at 362.

117 (1984), 10 CCC (3d) 404 (SCC).

as a person who intends to kill another person, but then kills yet another person by accident or mistake.[118]

The courts may transfer intent in other contexts. An accused has been convicted of assault causing bodily harm when, in an attempt to strike another person, he caused bodily harm to a bystander.[119] Statutory and common law doctrines of transferred intent allow *mens rea* directed towards one person to be transferred to an *actus reus* that occurs in relation to another person.

C. THE DEGREES OF OBJECTIVE *MENS REA*

The Supreme Court has indicated that objective, as opposed to subjective, fault is constitutionally sufficient for unlawful act manslaughter and other criminal offences less serious than murder, attempted murder, and war crimes. The Court has recognized that indicia of criminal offences that only require proof of objective fault include the use of words such as "dangerousness," "careless," "negligence," and requirements for "reasonable" conduct or precautions. It also recognized that objective fault is more likely to be used with regards to regulated and licensed activity such as driving, offences that impose specific duties on persons, and offences that are based on a predicate offence such as dangerous driving, but are designed to punish the person for additional and objectively foreseeable consequences such as causing death or bodily harm.[120] This is a fairly long list and the use of objective forms of liability can no longer be seen as exceptional.

Despite increasing acceptance of objective fault as a form of *mens rea*, there has been some uncertainty about how such a standard should be applied in a criminal prosecution. This topic raises some of the same dilemmas encountered when the courts apply objective standards to defences such as self-defence,[121] though the Court's resolution of these dilemmas for objective forms of fault has been much less generous to the accused than for defences that also require the accused to act as the reasonable person would have in the same circumstances. As will be

---

118   *R v Fontaine* (2002), 168 CCC (3d) 263 at paras 40–45 (Man CA), rejecting *R v Brown* (1983), 4 CCC (3d) 571 (Ont HCJ), holding that an intent to commit suicide could be transferred under s 229(b) of the *Code*.

119   *R v Deakin* (1974), 16 CCC (2d) 1 (Man CA).

120   *ADH*, above note 20 at paras 56–74. See also the dissenting opinion of Moldaver J, which also stressed that duty-based crimes should escape common law presumptions of subjective fault.

121   See Chapter 9.

seen, the Court will only consider the accused's own characteristics in applying objective forms of fault if they render the accused unable to appreciate or control the risk. At the same time, the courts have insisted that the Crown prove as a minimum a marked departure from reasonable conduct as a means to distinguish negligence under the criminal law from less onerous standards used in civil law or with respect to regulatory offences. They have also instructed courts to consider all the circumstances, including the accused's own subjective perceptions when applying objective forms of fault. These interpretations have placed a considerable and complex judicial gloss on crimes based on objective fault.

1) Who Is the Reasonable Person?

Some judges have been attracted to the idea of making the reasonable person resemble the accused, but this has not won majority support in the Supreme Court. In *Tutton*,[122] Lamer J would have applied an objective standard to determine criminal negligence, but he would have modified it by making "'a generous allowance' for factors which are particular to the accused, such as youth, mental development, education." He noted that if this was done, "the adoption of a subjective or an objective test will, in practice, nearly if not always produce the same result."[123] In *Creighton*,[124] Lamer CJ elaborated his views and held that the reasonable person used to determine objective liability should be invested with "any human frailties which might have rendered the accused incapable of having foreseen what the reasonable person would have foreseen," as well as any "enhanced foresight" derived from the accused's special knowledge or skill. Human frailties were defined as "personal characteristics habitually affecting an accused's awareness of the circumstances which create risk."[125] They had to be characteristics that the accused could not control or manage in the circumstances. On the one hand, Lamer CJ would have factored in the inexperience, youth, and lack of education of a mother who did not provide the necessities of life to her child,[126] while on the other hand, he would have considered the enhanced foresight of risk that an experienced drug or gun user would have when dealing with those dangerous objects.[127] Making the

---

122 *Tutton*, above note 13 at 140.
123 *Ibid* at 143.
124 *Creighton*, above note 3 at 359–60.
125 *Ibid* at 362–63.
126 *Naglik*, above note 37.
127 *Creighton*, above note 3; *Gosset*, above note 36.

reasonable person more like the accused could make it more difficult to convict an accused who habitually was unaware of prohibited risks, while it could also make it easier to convict an accused who was more sensitive to the prohibited risk than the reasonable person.

The Lamer approach to individualizing the reasonable person has not been accepted by a majority of the Supreme Court.[128] In *Creighton*,[129] McLachlin J for a 5:4 majority rejected the Lamer approach on the basis that it "personalizes the objective test to the point where it devolves into a subjective test, thus eroding the minimum standard of care which Parliament has laid down by the enactment of offenses of manslaughter and penal negligence." Justice McLachlin stressed the need for minimal objective standards to be applied without regard to the accused's age, experience, and education when the accused made voluntary decisions to be involved in activities such as driving that could injure and kill others. The only personal characteristics of the accused that are relevant in the majority's approach would be those that establish incapacity to appreciate the nature and quality of the prohibited conduct and consequences. Justice McLachlin elaborated:

> Mental disabilities short of incapacity generally do not suffice to negative criminal liability for criminal negligence. The explanations for why a person fails to advert to the risk inherent in the activity he or she is undertaking are legion. They range from simple absent-mindedness to attributes related to age, education and culture. To permit such a subjective assessment would be "co-extensive with the judgment of each individual, which would be as variable as the length of the foot of each individual" leaving "so vague a line as to afford no rule at all, the degree of judgment belonging to each individual being infinitely various." . . . Provided the capacity to appreciate the risk is present, lack of education and psychological predispositions serve as no excuse for criminal conduct, although they may be important factors to consider in sentencing.[130]

---

128 In *Hundal*, above note 13 at 104, there was some recognition that "[t]he potential harshness of the objective standard may be lessened by the consideration of certain personal factors." These were, however, held inapplicable to the offence of dangerous driving because licensing requirements ensure "that all who drive have a reasonable standard of physical health and capability, mental health and a knowledge of the reasonable standard required of all licensed drivers." *Ibid* at 108.

129 *Creighton*, above note 3 at 381–82.

130 *Ibid* at 390–91.

In short, the reasonable person will not be invested with the personal characteristics of the accused unless the characteristics are so extreme as to create an incapacity to appreciate or avoid the prohibited risk. The accused's age and level of education, however, would not normally be considered when applying the reasonable person standard.

Chief Justice Lamer subsequently accepted this unmodified objective approach and justified it on the basis that it applied to those who make a voluntary decision to perform conduct that is subject to punishment for negligence.[131] The Court has continued in *Beatty* to apply a strict reasonable person standard with respect to crimes of negligence:

> Short of incapacity to appreciate the risk or incapacity to avoid creating it, personal attributes such as age, experience, and education are not relevant. The standard against which the conduct must be measured is always the same — it is the conduct expected of the reasonably prudent person in the circumstances.[132]

As will be seen in Chapter 9, however, Lamer CJ's modified objective approach of endowing the reasonable person with similar characteristics, frailties, and experiences as the accused has won the day with respect to defences in which the accused is held up to standards of reasonable conduct. The justification for the different approaches would appear to be that an accused who commits a crime with a valid defence such as provocation, self-defence, duress, or necessity does not voluntarily commit the crime and that the accused's characteristics and experiences must be considered in determining whether he or she had no realistic choice but to commit the crime. In contrast, accused make voluntary decisions to engage in conduct such as driving that is judged by objective fault standards.

2) Inability to Appreciate or Avoid the Risk

Although the reasonable person standard for the purposes of objective forms of liability will not include factors such as the age and educational level of the accused, the Court has indicated that the accused's characteristics may be relevant if they render the particular accused incapable or unable to appreciate or avoid the prohibited risk. Justice McLachlin reasoned in *Creighton*[133] that "convicting and punishing a person who lacks the capacity to do what the law says he or she should

---

131 *Hibbert*, above note 70.

132 *Beatty*, above note 14 at para 40.

133 Above note 3 at 388.

have done serves no useful purpose." She contemplated, however, that such incapacity will "arise only exceptionally." The examples McLachlin J provided are not particularly helpful because they included an illiterate person mishandling a marked container (most containers have non-written warnings) and those already exempted from criminal liability because they are under twelve years of age or have a mental disorder defence. The Supreme Court has subsequently affirmed that "evidence of the accused's personal attributes (such as age, experience and education) is irrelevant unless it goes to the accused's incapacity to appreciate or to avoid the risk."[134] At the same time, the Court has yet to apply the incapacity exception in any case. Hence, the incapacity exception remains more theoretical than real.

The Quebec Court of Appeal has indicated that a mental disorder rendering the accused incapable of appreciating the physical consequences of actions or knowing that they were wrong would qualify as an incapacity to appreciate or control risk.[135] This seems correct, but incapacity may not be limited to such extreme circumstances and could include forms of mental disability or disorder that fall short of the strict requirements of the mental disorder defence under section 16 of the *Code*.[136] At the same time, courts have rejected factors such as the youth and inexperience of a driver[137] and a person's religious belief[138] as factors that produce incapacity to appreciate or control a risk that is relevant to the application of objective factors. The result seems to be that judges simply instruct triers of fact to consider whether there is a reasonable doubt that there is incapacity and inability to appreciate the risk,[139] with no defined jurisprudence having been developed. This raises the danger that objective standards of liability may be unfairly applied to those who are not really capable of living up to objective standards.

3) Degree of Negligence

A more important manner of adapting a negligence standard to the criminal context is to require not only unreasonable conduct or simple

---

134 *Roy*, above note 16 at para 38.

135 *Autorité des marchés financiers v Patry*, 2015 QCCA 1933 at para 95.

136 But see *R v CPF*, 2006 NLCA 70 at para 23, suggesting that fetal alcohol syndrome that did not result in a mental disorder defence did not amount to an incapacity to appreciate the risk for the purpose of objective components of an offence.

137 *R v Stuart*, 2017 MBQB 149.

138 *R v Canhoto*, 1999 CanLII 3819 at para 18 (Ont CA).

139 *R v Czornobaj*, 2017 QCCA 907 at paras 34–44.

negligence, but also conduct that amounts to a marked departure from that of the reasonable person. In *Hundal*,[140] the Court indicated that although dangerous driving was to be determined on an objective basis, "the trier of fact should be satisfied that the conduct amounted to a *marked departure* from the standard of care that a reasonable person would observe in the accused's situation." In *Beatty*, the Supreme Court suggested that a requirement of a *marked departure* from reasonable standards was necessary to distinguish criminal from civil negligence and to ensure restraint in the use of the criminal law.[141]

The Supreme Court has required a marked departure from the conduct of a reasonable person even when a criminal offence seems to require simple negligence. In *Finlay*[142] and *Gosset*,[143] the Supreme Court considered manslaughter charges based on the unlawful act of careless use of a firearm. The Court required that a person demonstrate a marked departure from the standard of care of a reasonably prudent person in the circumstances, even though the offence seemed only to require careless use of a firearm. A legislated careless or simple negligence standard was essentially read up to require a more severe form of negligence.[144] This is an important development that is now constitutionally required, given the Court's recognition in *Beatty* that a marked departure standard is required under section 7 of the *Charter*. A constitutional requirement would justify the court in disregarding Parliament's intent to criminalize simple carelessness in the use of a firearm and essentially to read the careless standard up to require a marked departure from reasonable conduct.

In *R v JF*,[145] the Supreme Court distinguished the *marked departure* standard that, following *Beatty* as well as *Finlay* and *Gosset*, applies as a minimal fault requirement to all forms of negligence used for purposes of criminal liability, from a slightly higher standard of *marked and substantial* departure that applies to criminal negligence. The Court cited a number of cases in which appellate courts had distinguished criminal negligence causing death or bodily harm from dangerous driving, on the basis that criminal negligence requires a marked

---

140 *Hundal*, above note 13 at 108 [emphasis added].

141 *Beatty*, above note 14. See also the discussion in Chapter 2.

142 *Finlay*, above note 36 at para 24.

143 *Gosset*, above note 36.

144 *Gosset, ibid* at 505, Lamer CJ; at 512, McLachlin J. See also *R v Gunning*, [2005] 1 SCR 627 at para 21, stating: "[T]he gravamen of the offence is conduct that constitutes a marked departure from the standard of care of a reasonably prudent person."

145 2008 SCC 60 [*JF*].

and substantial departure from reasonable conduct whereas dangerous driving required only a marked departure.[146] In the result, the Court held that the offence of failing to provide necessities of life required "a marked departure" from the standard of a reasonable caregiver whereas offences of criminal negligence causing death or bodily harm would require "*a marked and substantial departure* (as opposed to a *marked departure*) from the conduct of a reasonably prudent parent in the circumstances . . . ."[147] The Court justified its approach by noting that criminal negligence was subject to more serious maximum sentences than failing to provide the necessities of life. In addition, the definition of criminal negligence in section 219 of the *Code*[148] underlines the severity of the fault of criminal negligence by defining it as conduct that "shows wanton or reckless disregard for the lives or safety of other persons" and McIntyre J had previously defined criminal negligence as requiring a marked and substantial departure from reasonable conduct.[149]

The decision in *JF* recognizes subtle and fine distinctions in the degrees of objective fault between the general rule of proof of a marked departure from reasonable conduct, and the higher standard of marked and substantial departures from reasonable conduct that is required for criminal negligence. This complicates the law, but in a not altogether different way than distinctions between the various degrees of subjective fault. It also means that the fault required for manslaughter may differ depending on whether manslaughter by criminal negligence is charged (requiring marked and substantial departures) or manslaughter by the commission of an unlawful act (requiring a marked departure) is charged.[150]

---

146 See *R v L(J)* (2006), 204 CCC (3d) 324 (Ont CA); *R v Fortier* (1998), 127 CCC (3d) 217 at 223 (Que CA); *R v Palin* (1999), 135 CCC (3d) 119 (Que CA).

147 *JF*, above note 145 at para 9 [emphasis in original]. The Court did note, however, that the actual case which concluded that a conviction of criminal negligence causing death was inconsistent with an acquittal of failing to provide the necessities of life, did "not turn on the nature or extent of the difference between the two standards" (*ibid* at para 10).

148 Above note 2.

149 *R v Waite* (1999), 48 CCC (3d) 1 at 5 (SCC). In *Tutton*, above note 13 at 140, he formulated the criminal negligence standard slightly differently as a "marked and significant departure" from that expected of a reasonable person. His interchangeable use of "significant" and "substantial" in these two cases suggests that there is no real difference between the two terms.

150 See Chapter 10, Section A(6).

4) The Need to Consider All the Evidence Including the Accused's Subjective Perceptions

In a case dealing with the offence of dangerous driving causing death, Cory J maintained that objective fault must be determined in the context of all the evidence surrounding the incident. He stated:

> Although an objective test must be applied to the offence of dangerous driving, it will remain open to the accused to raise a reasonable doubt that a reasonable person would have been aware of the risks in the accused's conduct . . . .
>
> [I]n order to convict, the trier of fact must be satisfied that a reasonable person in similar circumstances ought to have been aware of the risk and danger involved in the conduct manifested by the accused.[151]

These comments suggest that the issue is whether the reasonable person in the same circumstances as the accused would have been aware of the risk of the prohibited act. The Court in *Beatty* cited with approval the reference by Cory J about the need to take a contextualized approach that considers, for example, whether the accused has suffered an unexpected heart attack, seizure, or detached retina.[152] At the same time and as discussed in Chapter 3, the majority of the Court in *Beatty* rejected the approach of the dissenters who would have applied the marked departure standard to the *actus reus* and would have held that a momentary lapse produced by falling asleep at the wheel without more did not satisfy either the *actus reus* or the *mens rea* of dangerous driving.[153]

The Court's decision in *Beatty* suggests that courts should not ignore factors subjective to the accused when determining whether the accused has the criminal fault level of negligence. The Court referred to situations where the presumption that a reasonable person in the accused's situation would have been aware of the risk "cannot be sustained because a reasonable person in the position of the accused would not have been aware of the risk or, alternatively, would not have been able to avoid creating the danger."[154] Consistent with basic criminal law principles including the presumption of innocence, the *mens rea* cannot be automatically deduced from the commission of the criminal act even if the act such as driving on the wrong side of the road

---

151 *Hundal*, above note 13 at 106–8.
152 *Beatty*, above note 14 at para 37.
153 *Ibid* at para 72, McLachlin CJ in dissent.
154 *Ibid.*

is itself dangerous or a marked departure from reasonable conduct.[155] Relevant factors to be considered in determining *mens rea* may include the accused's perception of the circumstances, including mistaken belief that the prohibited circumstances or consequences did not exist. The trier of fact should also consider other explanations offered by the accused and contextual factors such as the accused's sudden incapacity. Although this requirement runs some risk of confusing a jury (and students) about the distinction between subjective and objective fault, it makes sense given the need to consider all relevant evidence when assessing *mens rea*. For example, it would be overly harsh not to allow the accused to lead evidence that he subjectively but mistakenly believed the situation to be safe even though this mistake of fact may not absolve the accused of responsibility under objective fault standards based on marked departure from reasonable standards.

The purpose of examining factors subjective to the accused is not to determine whether the accused was subjectively at fault but only to determine whether there is a reasonable doubt about whether the accused's conduct in the circumstances constituted a marked departure from standards of reasonable care. The Court in *Beatty* warned that the same standard of reasonable conduct will be applied to all accused and that the accused will not be exonerated simply because he or she did not subjectively advert to the risk. *Beatty* makes clear that the mere fact that the accused has engaged in a dangerous act, such as driving on the wrong side of the road, is not determinative of the fault of a marked departure. Courts should consider all the evidence including the accused's actual state of mind and any explanation offered by the accused in determining whether the Crown has proven a marked departure from reasonable conduct beyond a reasonable doubt. The Court has, however, approved of a decision that characterized the accused's subjective perception as "the starting point, not the end of the analysis" of whether a driver had engaged in a marked departure from the standards of a reasonable driver that amounted to dangerous driving. It also stressed the need to examine the whole course of the driving and not just the driver's explanations.[156]

The Supreme Court subsequently affirmed its approach in *Beatty* of requiring a marked departure from a reasonable standard of care and not deducing such fault simply from the commission of an objectively

---

155 I disagree with Manning and Sankoff's assertion that "once it is determined that the accused's conduct was sufficiently dangerous to rise to the standard of criminal negligence, any other aspect of the analysis is simply going to be a formality." Manning & Sankoff, above note 63 at 4.148.

156 *R v Hecimovic*, 2015 SCC 54, aff'g 2014 BCCA 483 at para 70.

dangerous act. In *R v Roy*,[157] the Court unanimously acquitted a person of dangerous driving causing death after he drove into the path of an oncoming tractor-trailer when entering a highway at a difficult intersection in foggy and snowy weather. The Court stressed the seriousness of the criminal offence and the need to establish fault and not simply deduce it from the commission of an objectively dangerous act. Even at the *actus reus* stage, it emphasized that triers of fact should not reason backwards from the tragic consequences of traffic accidents, but rather should conduct a meaningful inquiry to determine whether the manner of driving was dangerous to the public given all the circumstances.[158] In addition, the trier of fact must find fault going beyond mere carelessness and amounting to a marked departure from the standard of care expected from a reasonable person. All the circumstances, including any evidence of the accused's state of mind or any explanation given for the commission of the *actus reus*,[159] should be considered in making this fault determination. At the same time, the ultimate issue is whether there was a marked departure from the standard of care that a reasonable person would take in the circumstances.

Consistent with *Creighton*,[160] the accused's age, experience, or education is not relevant unless it rendered the accused incapable of appreciating the risk.[161] The Court has stressed the importance of finding fault in addition to an *actus reus* and the need for a marked departure from reasonable conduct as a means of ensuring that any objective standard of fault is appropriate for determining criminal liability. *Roy* solidifies the majority decision in *Beatty* by indicating that only a marked departure from reasonable conduct and not mere carelessness will be sufficient to establish criminal liability, and that all the evidence must be examined and fault should not be automatically deduced even from a dangerous act. *Roy* also affirms that the accused's incapacity to appreciate or avoid the risk would prevent the imposition of objective standards of fault, but, as discussed above, the Court has yet to find or apply such incapacity.

---

157 Above note 16. The Court acquitted the accused on the basis that "[t]he record here discloses a single and momentary error in judgment with tragic consequences. It does not support a reasonable inference that the appellant displayed a marked departure from the standard of care expected of a reasonable person in the same circumstances so as to justify conviction for the serious criminal offence of dangerous driving causing death." *Ibid* at para 55.

158 *Ibid* at para 34.

159 *Ibid* at para 39.

160 Above note 3.

161 *Roy*, above note 16 at para 38.

D. MISTAKE OF FACT

Mistake of fact is a controversial defence that conceptually depends on the *mens rea* of the particular offence. If subjective awareness of prohibited circumstances is required, the Crown will not be able to establish the fault element if the accused honestly, but not necessarily reasonably, believes those circumstances do not exist. On the other hand, if the fault element of the offence requires only that a reasonable person would have recognized the prohibited circumstance or risk, then any defence based on mistake must be honest *and* reasonable. Finally, even a reasonable mistake of fact would not be a defence to an absolute liability offence. All that would matter would be whether the accused in fact committed the prohibited act.

Deducing the existence and nature of a mistake of fact defence from the fault element of the offence may, however, be too mechanical. It is possible that a mistake of fact may be based on a combination of subjective and objective factors. For example, section 273.2(b) of the *Criminal Code* provides that the accused's belief that the complainant consented to the sexual activity is not a defence if the accused did not take reasonable steps, in the circumstances known to him at the time, to ascertain that the complainant was consenting. As will be discussed below, this creatively combines objective and subjective fault elements.

1) Early Cases

Mistake of fact defences have frequently been influenced by policy concerns not derived from the fault element of the particular offence. Courts were initially reluctant to accept mistake of fact as a defence. In *R v Prince*,[162] an accused was convicted of unlawfully abducting an unmarried girl under sixteen years of age without her parents' permission, even though he had an honest *and* reasonable belief that the girl was eighteen. Bramwell B concluded: "The legislature has enacted that if anyone does this wrong act, he does it at the risk of her turning out to be under sixteen."[163] He did, however, concede that an accused would have no *mens rea* if he made a subjective mistake about other elements of the offence, such as whether he had received permission from the parents. Only one judge would have acquitted the accused on the basis that

---

162 (1875), LR 2 CCR 154.
163 *Ibid* at 175.

a mistake of facts, on reasonable grounds, to the extent that if the facts were as believed the acts of the prisoner would make him guilty of no criminal offence at all, is an excuse, and that such excuse is implied in every criminal charge and every criminal enactment in England.[164]

The above passage was adopted in the subsequent case of *Tolson*,[165] so that a mistake of fact was originally recognized as a defence on the basis that it must be both honest *and* reasonable.

2) Mistake Related to the Degree of Fault

With the rise of subjective *mens rea*, courts began to recognize the possibility that an accused could have an honest but not necessarily reasonable belief in a state of circumstances that would make his activity innocent. In *R v Rees*,[166] the accused was charged with knowingly contributing to the delinquency of a person under eighteen whom he believed to be older. Justice Cartwright concluded:

[T]he essential question is whether the belief entertained by the accused is an honest one and that the existence or non-existence of reasonable grounds for such a belief is merely relevant evidence to be weighed by the tribunal of fact in determining such essential question.

He conceded that the issue might be different if Parliament had not used the word "knowingly," or had specifically excluded a mistake about the girl's age as a possible defence. A year later, Cartwright J acquitted an accused found in possession of an illegal drug because the accused thought that the substance was harmless. He stressed that the offence required subjective *mens rea*, and that "in a criminal case there is in law no possession without knowledge of the character of the forbidden substance."[167] Two judges dissented, on the basis that Parliament had intended to enact an absolute prohibition of being in possession of the illegal drugs. An absolute liability offence would, of course, allow no defence of mistake of fact.[168] An offence based on negligence would afford a defence of mistake of fact "if the accused *reasonably* believed in

---

164 *Ibid* at 170.
165 *Tolson*, above note 1 at 181 and 189. In *DPP v Morgan* (1975), [1976] AC 182 (HL), the House of Lords reversed this decision and held in a 3:2 decision that the accused's mistaken belief in a woman's consent must be honest, but not necessarily reasonable, to be a defence to rape.
166 *Rees*, above note 18 at 11.
167 *Beaver*, above note 18.
168 *R v Pierce Fisheries Ltd*, [1970] 5 CCC 193 (SCC).

a mistaken set of facts which, if true, would render the act or omission innocent."[169]

In *R v ADH*, the Court divided on whether the offence of abandoning a child under section 218 required subjective or objective fault, but were agreed that the accused should be acquitted. The majority interpreted the offence as requiring subjective fault and affirmed the trial judge's acquittal on the basis that the accused made a subjective mistake that a baby she had unexpectedly delivered in a washroom was dead. Justice Moldaver held that the offence required only objective fault, but would have acquitted the accused on the basis that her mistake about whether her baby was alive was both honest and reasonable in the circumstances.[170] As will be seen in Chapter 6, a reasonable mistake of fact is also necessary when the accused is charged with a regulatory offence that requires strict liability, though the definition of a reasonable mistake of fact for the purpose of criminal liability should also take into account the requirement that negligence for the purpose of criminal liability must be a marked departure from reasonable standards.

3) Mistake of Fact and Drug Offences

As discussed above, an accused would have a defence of mistake of fact if he or she believed that a substance was a harmless substance and not illegal drugs.[171] Courts have, however, been unwilling to apply this strict logic when an accused makes a mistake as to the nature of an illegal drug. In *R v Burgess*,[172] an accused was convicted of possession of opium, even though he thought the drug was hashish. This reasoning was extended in *R v Kundeus*,[173] when an accused was convicted of trafficking in LSD that he thought was mescaline. Mescaline was a prohibited drug, but not one carrying as serious a penalty as LSD. Chief Justice of Canada Laskin dissented on the basis that it was unfair to convict an accused of a more serious offence when he had the *mens rea* only for the commission of the less serious offence. In his view, the accused did not have the *mens rea* required to be convicted of selling LSD because he never thought he was selling LSD.

---

169 *Sault Ste Marie*, above note 17 at 374 [emphasis added].
170 *ADH*, above note 20 at para 157.
171 *Beaver*, above note 18.
172 [1970] 3 CCC 268 (Ont CA).
173 (1975), 24 CCC (2d) 276 (SCC).

4) Mistake of Fact and Sexual Assault

Although the contours of a mistake of fact defence can be deduced at a conceptual level from the fault requirement of the specific offence, there may be a case for combining elements of subjective and objective fault for mistake of fact in some contexts. A purely subjective mistake of fact defence may not adequately protect victims of crime and social interests in giving people incentives to avoid unnecessary and harmful mistakes of fact, while a purely objective mistake of fact defence may punish those who, given their failure to correctly perceive circumstances, proceeded in a manner that did not indicate a flagrant disregard for the law.

In *R v Pappajohn*,[174] the Supreme Court held that an accused in a rape trial could have a defence of honest but not necessarily reasonable mistake that the complainant consented. Justice Dickson derived the defence of mistake of fact from the *mens rea* of the particular offence. He concluded that because the *mens rea* of rape was subjective intent or recklessness relating to all the elements of the offence, it was not necessary that an accused's mistaken belief about consent be reasonable. He stated:

> It is not clear how one can properly relate reasonableness (an element in offences of negligence) to rape (a "true crime" and not an offence of negligence). To do so, one must, I think, take the view that the *mens rea* only goes to the physical act of intercourse and not to non-consent, and acquittal comes only if the mistake is reasonable. This, upon the authorities, is not a correct view, the intent in rape being not merely to have intercourse, but to have it with a non-consenting woman. If the jury finds that mistake, whether reasonable or unreasonable, there should be no conviction. If, upon the entire record, there is evidence of mistake to cast a reasonable doubt upon the existence of a criminal mind, then the prosecution has failed to make its case.[175]

Justice Dickson added that although the accused's belief did not have to be reasonable, its reasonableness would be evidence considered by the jury to determine whether the accused actually had an honest belief in consent. The *Criminal Code* was subsequently amended to provide that the judge "shall instruct the jury, when reviewing all the evidence

---

174 *Pappajohn*, above note 20.
175 *Ibid* at 152.

relating to the determination of the honesty of the accused's belief, to consider the presence or absence of reasonable ground for that belief."[176]

Although the Supreme Court agreed on the conceptual nature of the defence of mistake of fact and its relation to the *mens rea* of the particular offence, it disagreed on its application in particular cases. In *R v Pappajohn*, Dickson J was in dissent in concluding that the jury should have been instructed to consider the defence of mistake of fact. Justice McIntyre for the majority held that the only realistic issue that could arise on the facts of the case was whether there was consent or no consent, not a third option of a mistaken belief in consent. In his view, there should be something more than the accused's assertion that he believed the complainant consented to justify instructing the jury on the mistaken belief defence.

The *Pappajohn* defence of an honest but not necessarily reasonable mistaken belief in consent remained controversial. This controversy was increased when the Supreme Court struck down so-called rape shield restrictions on the admission of the complainant's prior sexual conduct as a violation of the accused's *Charter* right to make full answer and defence, in part because the restrictions could deprive the accused of evidence to support the *Pappajohn* defence. Justice McLachlin stated that the *Pappajohn* defence

> rests on the concept that the accused may honestly but mistakenly (and not necessarily reasonably) have believed that the complainant was consenting to the sexual act. If the accused can raise a reasonable doubt as to his intention on the basis that he honestly held such a belief, he is not guilty under our law and is entitled to an acquittal. The basis of the accused's honest belief in the complainant's consent may be sexual acts performed by the complainant at some other time or place.[177]

In dissent, L'Heureux-Dubé J argued that the complainant's prior sexual activity with a person other than the accused would never provide an air of reality for the jury to consider a defence of mistake of fact, if they were "operating in an intellectual environment that is free of rape myth and stereotype about women."[178]

In response to *R v Seaboyer*, the law of sexual assault was amended in 1992 to restrict the availability of the mistake of fact defence. Section 273.2 states that the accused's belief that the complainant consented is

176 *Code*, above note 2, s 265(4). This was held to be consistent with ss 7, 11(d), and 11(f) of the *Charter* in *R v Osolin* (1994), 86 CCC (3d) 481 (SCC).
177 (1992), 66 CCC (3d) 321 at 393 (SCC).
178 *Ibid* at 363.

not a defence if it arose from the accused's "self-induced intoxication," his "recklessness or wilful blindness," or if "the accused did not take reasonable steps, in the circumstances known to the accused at the time, to ascertain that the complainant was consenting." This provision will be discussed in greater detail in Chapter 10, which examines sexual assault among other offences, but it is also relevant to the various levels of fault.

The reference to recklessness contemplates that an accused who adverted to the risk that the complainant did not consent has always had the *mens rea* required for sexual assault. The reference to wilful blindness would seem to codify *Sansregret* and preclude the defence when an accused is subjectively aware of the need to inquire into consent, but deliberately declines to inquire because he does not wish to know the truth. It will be recalled that in *Sansregret*,[179] the trial judge acquitted the accused on the basis of *Pappajohn*, even though she found that anyone in his right mind, but not the accused, would have been aware of the risk that the complainant was not consenting to the sexual activity. The Supreme Court reversed and entered a conviction on the basis that even if the accused was not subjectively aware that there was no consent, he was wilfully blind to that prohibited risk. The culpability in wilful blindness was the accused's refusal to inquire whether the complainant was consenting, when he was "aware of the need for some inquiry . . . [but declined] to make the inquiry because he . . . [does] not wish to know the truth."[180] *Sansregret* narrowed the *Pappajohn* defence by holding that the accused was presumed to have guilty knowledge of the absence of consent when, knowing the need for inquiry as to consent, he remained deliberately ignorant.

The denial in section 273.2(b) of the mistake of fact unless the accused takes reasonable steps in the circumstances known to him at the time to ascertain whether the complainant was consenting to the activity in question combines subjective and objective fault elements in a novel and creative manner. As such, it breaks away from the idea in *Pappajohn* that the contours of the mistake of fact defence can be deduced from the fault element of the offence and it represents a fault level that blends subjective and objective fault. On the one hand, section 273.2(b) bases the accused's obligation to take reasonable steps to ascertain consent on the basis of what the accused subjectively knows of the circumstances. The accused's obligation to take reasonable steps is only based

---

179 *Sansregret*, above note 21 (cited to CCC).

180 *Ibid* at 235. The accused had broken into his ex-girlfriend's apartment and threatened her with a knife. Less than a month earlier, the complainant had reported a rape after a similar incident with the accused.

on what he subjectively knows at the time. On the other hand, section 273.2(b) requires the accused to act as a reasonable person would in the circumstances by taking reasonable steps to ascertain whether the complainant was consenting. Further issues relating to the interpretation and constitutionality of section 273.2 will be discussed in Chapter 10 when the offence of sexual assault is examined in more detail.

E. MIXED SUBJECTIVE AND OBJECTIVE FAULT ELEMENTS

The classification of fault elements as subjective or objective adds analytical clarity and precision, but it would be a mistake to conclude that a particular offence must necessarily be completely subjective or objective. Some offences contain multiple elements and there is little reason why some of these elements may not require proof of subjective fault while others require proof only of objective fault. Justice L'Heureux-Dubé has stated "that the *mens rea* of a particular offence is composed of the totality of its component fault elements. The mere fact that most criminal offences require some subjective component does not mean that every element of the offence requires such a state of mind."[181]

A mixed approach allows the fault requirement to be tailored to the particular element of the offence, but it also requires judges and juries to understand clearly that for some elements of an offence they must consider all the evidence that is relevant to determining the accused's subjective state of mind, whereas for other elements of the same offence, all they need to consider is how the accused's conduct measures up to the reasonable person standard.[182] Justice Dickson in *Pappajohn*[183] argued that it was "unfair to the jury, and to the accused, to speak in terms of two beliefs, one entertained by the accused, the other by the reasonable man." Mixed fault elements require such an approach. Despite the added complexity,[184] both the Supreme Court and Parliament have been attracted in recent years to mixed forms of liability so that some elements of the offence require proof of subjective fault while others require proof of objective fault.

---

181 *R v Hinchey* (1996), 111 CCC (3d) 353 at 385 (SCC).
182 Assuming that the accused is not incapable of perceiving the prohibited risk or circumstances. See *Creighton*, discussed above note 3.
183 *Pappajohn*, above note 20.
184 The complexity can be overstated given the practical reality that even in determining a subjective *mens rea*, the jury must rely in part on inferences about what is reasonable.

In *R v Lohnes*,[185] the Supreme Court interpreted the offence of disturbing the peace as requiring proof of subjective fault as to the underlying act such as fighting or yelling, but objective fault in relation to the actual disturbance of the peace. Similarly, the offence of conspiracy to unduly lessen competition requires a subjective intention among the parties to agree on a course of action and the objective fault that it is reasonably foreseeable that the course of action would unduly lessen competition.[186] In both of these cases, the objective fault elements dominate and the subjective fault seems only to preclude a conviction if the accused unintentionally and almost accidentally engages in an act that disturbs that peace or lessens competition.

A more integrated blending of subjective and objective fault elements is found in section 273.2(b), which provides that the accused's subjective belief that the complainant consented is not a defence to a sexual assault charge if "the accused did not take reasonable steps, in the circumstances known to the accused at the time, to ascertain that the complainant was consenting." The accused's defence of mistake of fact is in part based on the accused's own subjective perception of the circumstances, provided they are not based on self-induced intoxication, recklessness, or wilful blindness.[187] At the same time, the accused's obligation to take reasonable steps is an objective fault element that requires the accused to act as a reasonable person would in situations where consent is not clear. This is a mixed standard of subjective and objective fault and one that may strike the appropriate balance in the circumstances. Those engaged in sexual activity are being required to take reasonable steps to ascertain consent, but they are only required to do what is reasonable given their own subjective perception or knowledge of the circumstances. Another integrated blending of subjective and objective fault elements is found in the new section 22.2(c) of the *Code*, which provides for organizational fault on the basis that a senior officer of a corporation subjectively knows that a representative of the organization is or is about to be a party to a subjective intent offence but fails to take all reasonable measures to stop the representative from being a party to the offence.[188]

---

185 (1992), 69 CCC (3d) 289 (SCC).
186 *R v Nova Scotia Pharmaceutical Society* (1992), 74 CCC (3d) 289 (SCC).
187 *Code*, above note 2, s 273.2(a).
188 This provision will be examined in Chapter 6, Section D(2)(e).

CONCLUSION

Many of the uncertainties surrounding the fault element for crimes could be addressed by legislative reform that provides generic definitions of the various levels of fault, that explains their relation to the *actus reus*, and that specifies what level of fault is required should Parliament not specifically address the issue in the drafting of a particular offence. The general rule should be that *mens rea* will relate to all aspects of the *actus reus* and that the lowest form of subjective *mens rea*, namely recklessness, should be the minimum form of fault for offences in the *Criminal Code*.[189] These standards are based on well-established common law presumptions. They are not constitutional standards under section 7 of the *Charter*, and Parliament can clearly depart from them when drafting particular offences.

Although not all levels of fault are the same, the number of fault elements could be reduced. Given the Court's determination to distinguish intent from motive or purpose[190] and its requirement that knowledge of the prohibited act is the constitutionally required fault element for murder,[191] it could be argued that knowledge, as opposed to intent, purpose, or wilfulness, should be the highest level of subjective *mens rea*.

At the same time, an intent or purpose *mens rea* would still be justified with respect to crimes of peripheral involvement, including parties, attempts, and conspiracies, and broadly defined statutory inchoate crimes relating to preparation and participation in organized crime or terrorism. It could also be justified with respect to other crimes, such as wilful promotion of hatred, in which caution should be exercised before employing the criminal sanction.

Knowledge should be defined as the accused's belief that the prohibited consequences or circumstances probably exist. Recklessness, the lowest form of subjective *mens rea*, should be defined as an awareness of the risk that the prohibited circumstances or consequences possibly exist. The idea that knowledge relates to subjective advertence of probabilities while recklessness only requires subjective advertence to the possibility that the prohibited circumstances exist or the prohibited consequences will occur allow for a principled distinction between these two forms of subjective fault.

If wilful blindness is included, it should be a form of subjective fault based on deliberate ignorance and knowledge of the probability, not the

---

189   *Sault Ste Marie*, above note 17 at 362; *ADH*, above note 20.
190   *Hibbert*, above note 70.
191   *Martineau*, above note 7.

mere possibility, that the prohibited act exists. Such an approach would allow wilful blindness to be equated with knowledge as a higher form of subjective fault.

Negligence is a constitutionally sufficient fault element for most criminal offences. The Court has indicated that it should be interpreted to require as a minimum a marked departure from the standard of care that a reasonable person would have taken in the circumstances. The Court in *Beatty* stressed that it was constitutionally necessary to clearly distinguish criminal negligence from civil negligence or the negligence that is presumed when a person or corporation charged with a regulatory offence fails to establish a defence of due diligence. It also stressed that courts should consider all the evidence including the accused's subjective state of mind and explanations offered by the accused to see if they raise a reasonable doubt about whether the accused engaged in a marked departure from standards of reasonable care. In other words, courts should not automatically deduce the *mens rea* of negligence from the commission of a negligent or dangerous *actus reus*. The courts have drawn some fine distinctions between degrees of negligence that are sufficient for purposes of criminal liability, distinguishing the requirement of a marked departure that is necessary for all criminal uses of objective fault from an additional requirement of a marked and substantial departure that is required for criminal negligence.

In some cases, subjective and objective standards can be blended. An example would be section 273.2(b), which requires the accused to take reasonable steps to ascertain the complainant's consent to sexual activity (that is, act as a reasonable person would have), but only based on the circumstances subjectively known to the accused at the time. Section 22.2(c) similarly requires that a senior officer know that a representative of an organization is committing an offence, but then requires the senior officer to take all reasonable steps to stop the offence from being committed. Blended fault levels may make sense in a particular context, but they may present a challenge to juries and judges who must administer them.

A final issue is whether the reasonable person standard used to determine criminal negligence can be made to account for the frailties and capacities of the particular accused without collapsing the distinction between individual and subjective fault elements. As will be seen in Chapter 9, the courts now consider the experience and characteristics of the accused when determining whether he or she acted reasonably for the purposes of most defences. In contrast, the Court in *Creighton* and in *Beatty* held that the characteristics of the accused are not relevant in determining whether there is a marked departure from the standard of care that a reasonable person would have taken in the circumstances except in the rare event that those characteristics render the accused incapable of appreciating or controlling the prohibited risk. This qualification is designed to ensure that objective forms of fault are not applied in situations where the accused is incapable of conforming with the law. It has, however, not been applied and so far has been an illusory restraint on objective forms of liability.

The real restraints on the use of objective forms of liability include the rebuttable common law presumption that criminal offences generally require proof of subjective fault. If Parliament displaces this presumption of subjective fault, the courts have insisted that the prosecution must prove at a minimum a marked departure from reasonable conduct in order to distinguish criminal from civil negligence or negligence in regulatory offences. Finally, the Court has warned triers of facts that they should not deduce objective fault from the commission of the *actus reus* and should consider all the evidence in the case, including evidence about the accused's subjective perceptions, when determining whether objective fault in the form of a marked departure from reasonable standards has been established beyond a reasonable doubt.[192]

FURTHER READINGS

ARVAY, J, & LATIMER, A. "The Constitutional Infirmity of Laws Prohibiting Constitutional Negligence" (2016) 63 *Criminal Law Quarterly* 325.

BRUDNER, A. "Guilt under the *Charter*: The Lure of Parliamentary Supremacy" (1998) 40 *Criminal Law Quarterly* 287.

CAIRNS-WAY, R. "The *Charter*, the Supreme Court and the Invisible Politics of Fault" (1992) 12 *Windsor Yearbook of Access to Justice* 128.

COLVIN, E, & S ANAND. *Principles of Criminal Law*, 3d ed (Toronto: Thomson Carswell, 2007) ch 5.

EDWARDS, JLJ. "The Criminal Degrees of Knowledge" (1954) 17 *Modern Law Review* 295.

MANNING, M, & P SANKOFF. *Criminal Law*, 5th ed (Markham, ON: LexisNexis, 2015) ch 4.

---

192 *Beatty*, above note 14. *Roy*, above note 16.

PACIOCCO, D. "Subjective and Objective Standards of Fault for Offences and Defences" (1995) 59 *Saskatchewan Law Review* 271.

PICKARD, T. "Culpable Mistakes and Rape" (1980) 30 *University of Toronto Law Journal* 75.

ROACH, K. "Mind the Gap: Canada's Different Criminal and Constitutional Standards of Fault" (2011) 61 *University of Toronto Law Journal* 545.

STEWART, H. *Fundamental Justice: Section 7 of the* Charter (Toronto: Irwin Law, 2011) ch 4.

STRIBOPOLOUS, J. "The Constitutionalization of 'Fault' in Canada: A Normative Critique" (1999) 41 *Criminal Law Quarterly* 227.

STUART, D. *Canadian Criminal Law: A Treatise*, 7th ed (Toronto: Thomson Carswell, 2014) ch 3 & 4.

REGULATORY OFFENCES AND CORPORATE CRIME

Regulatory offences are enacted by the federal, provincial, and municipal governments. They far outnumber offences under the *Criminal Code*. Regulatory or public welfare offences emphasize the protection of the public from the risk of harm and the regulatory interests of the modern state, as opposed to the punishment of inherently wrongful and harmful conduct. A person or a corporation is convicted for performing a regulated activity without a licence or for failing to take specified safety precautions, not because such non-compliance must be denounced and punished, but because it frustrates the regulatory ambitions of the modern state and creates a danger of harm. Courts have fashioned distinct rules to make it easier for the state to investigate and prosecute regulatory offences.

Traditionally, Canadian courts were faced with the stark choice of interpreting a regulatory offence to require either absolute liability, in which a conviction followed from the commission of the prohibited act, or proof beyond a reasonable doubt of a subjective fault element. The former standard could impose liability without fault, while the latter might frustrate the objectives of the regulatory scheme by requiring the Crown to prove that someone in a large organization had guilty knowledge. A third option, strict liability, has now emerged to dominate the field. Absolute liability offences are now vulnerable under section 7 of the *Charter*, at least when they deprive individuals of life, liberty, or security of the person by imposing terms of imprisonment.

Strict liability offences require fault based on negligence, and for this reason they satisfy the requirement under section 7 of the *Charter* that the morally innocent who act without fault not be punished. They do, however, violate the presumption of innocence under section 11(d) of the *Charter*. After the Crown proves the prohibited act of a strict liability offence beyond a reasonable doubt, negligence is presumed, and the accused must establish that it was not negligent. The accused makes its case by establishing on a balance of probabilities a defence of due diligence or reasonable mistake of fact. This approach violates the presumption of innocence by allowing a conviction even if there is a reasonable doubt about whether the accused was negligent. Nevertheless, it has been held to be justified because of the danger of acquitting an accused who has entered a regulated field and committed an *actus reus* when there is only a reasonable doubt about negligence. An accused who enters a regulated field can be expected to bear the burden of establishing that it was not negligent in allowing a harmful or dangerous act to occur.

Regulatory offences frequently apply to corporations that have engaged in harmful conduct such as pollution, misleading advertising, or violations of health, safety, or licensing requirements. The difficulty of establishing fault in a large organization is one of the reasons why it is the accused who must establish a lack of negligence when charged with a strict liability offence. Negligence for regulatory offences also does not have to be the marked departure from reasonable standards required when negligence is required for a criminal offence. When a corporation is charged with a criminal offence, however, it is necessary to find someone within the corporation who has the required fault. That individual must have enough responsibility within the corporation so that his or her fault can be attributed to the corporation and the Crown must prove fault beyond a reasonable doubt. This makes it considerably more difficult to convict a corporation of a criminal offence than a regulatory offence.

Traditionally, only the fault of a "directing mind" of the corporation could be attributed to the corporation for the purpose of establishing its criminal liability. At the end of 2003, Parliament introduced extensive reforms designed to make it easier to convict and punish corporations and other organizations for criminal offences. The common law concept of a "directing mind," which had previously been restricted to those who had enough power to establish corporate policy, was replaced by a new statutory concept of a corporate "senior officer." This position includes not only those who play an important role in establishing a corporation's policies, including its board of directors, chief executive officer, and chief financial officer, but also those who are "responsible for managing an important aspect of the organization's activities."[1] Parliament also specified the fault required by the senior officer in order to convict the corporation of a negligence-based criminal offence[2] and a subjective intent criminal offence.[3] The criminal liability of corporations and other organizations is still based on the attribution of the fault of individuals to the organizations, but Parliament has replaced the common law definition of a corporation's directing mind with a broader concept that allows the fault of its senior officers to be attributed to the organization.

A. ABSOLUTE LIABILITY OFFENCES

An absolute liability offence requires the Crown to prove the commission of the prohibited act beyond a reasonable doubt, but does not require proof of any additional fault element such as guilty knowledge or negligence. For offences of absolute liability, "it is not open to the accused to exculpate himself by showing that he was free of fault."[4] This form of liability has been controversial. Supporters of absolute liability argue that its imposition can persuade a person or an organization to take additional measures to prevent the prohibited act. Opponents stress that the imposition of absolute liability can punish the morally innocent, and that one who has not acted with subjective fault or negligence cannot be expected to do anything more to prevent the prohibited act.[5]

Courts have recognized offences as requiring absolute liability when they have been convinced that the legislature did not intend the Crown to prove fault or that such a requirement would frustrate the purpose of the statute. In *R v Pierce Fisheries Ltd*,[6] the Supreme Court

---

1   *Criminal Code*, RSC 1985, c C-46, [*Code*], s 2 (as amended by SC 2003, c 21).
2   *Ibid*, s 22.1.
3   *Ibid*, s 22.2.
4   *R v Sault Ste Marie (City)* (1978), 40 CCC (2d) 353 at 374 (SCC) [*Sault Ste Marie*].
5   In *R v Hess* (1990), 59 CCC (3d) 161 (SCC) [*Hess*], Wilson J argued for the majority that an absolute liability offence for statutory rape served no useful purpose and was unfair to the accused who believed that the girl was over fourteen years of age. In dissent, McLachlin J would have upheld the offence under s 1 of the *Canadian Charter of Rights and Freedoms*, Part I of the *Constitution Act, 1982*, being Schedule B to the *Canada Act 1982* (UK), 1982, c 11, on the basis that it would discourage men from having sex with girls who might be under fourteen years of age.
6   [1970] 5 CCC 193 (SCC) [*Pierce Fisheries*].

held that the possession of undersized lobsters contrary to regulations under the *Fisheries Act* was an absolute liability offence. Justice Ritchie refused to apply the Court's previous decision in *R v Beaver*[7] that a person could not be held to possess drugs without subjective knowledge. He reasoned:

> I do not think that a new crime was added to our criminal law by making regulations which prohibit persons from having undersized lobsters in their possession, nor do I think that the stigma of having been convicted of a criminal offence would attach to a person found to have been in breach of these regulations.[8]

This approach recognized that regulatory offences did not carry with them the same stigma as criminal offences and that it would be difficult to achieve the objectives of regulatory offences if proof of subjective fault was required. Justice Cartwright dissented and, following *Beaver*, would have required proof that the accused knew about the undersized lobsters.

There are problems with both the decisions in *Pierce Fisheries*. Under the minority's approach of requiring subjective *mens rea*, it would be difficult, if not impossible, to establish that individuals who were directing minds of the corporation[9] knew that they were catching undersized lobsters. Under the majority's absolute liability approach, however, the corporation could have been convicted even if it had taken reasonable precautions to ensure that undersized lobsters were not caught by, for example, training its employees properly and using proper equipment. The majority imposed absolute liability that could punish without fault while the minority insisted on proof of subjective fault that would often be very difficult for the state to establish beyond a reasonable doubt in the regulatory context.

1) The Common Law Presumption Against Absolute Liability

In *Sault Ste Marie*,[10] the Supreme Court indicated that it would not interpret public welfare or regulatory offences as absolute liability offences unless "the Legislature has made it clear that guilt would follow

---

7   (1957), 118 CCC 129 (SCC).

8   *Pierce Fisheries*, above note 6 at 201.

9   Only the subjective *mens rea* of a person classified as one of the corporation's directing minds could be attributed to the corporation. See Chapter 6, Section D(1). Now the fault of senior officers, including important managers, could be attributed to the corporation.

10 *Sault Ste Marie*, above note 4 at 374.

proof merely of the proscribed act." The Court, in effect, created a common law or judge-made presumption that regulatory offences would be interpreted as requiring strict liability unless the legislature clearly indicated that the offence was an absolute liability offence that would punish the accused who had acted reasonably and with due diligence.

In the actual case, the Court held that the offence of causing or permitting the discharge of pollution was a strict liability as opposed to an absolute liability or subjective *mens rea* offence. This meant that the accused had an opportunity to establish that it had acted reasonably or with due diligence to avoid the commission of the *actus reus*. The accused could also establish that it had made a reasonable mistake of fact. The Crown, however, did not have to prove subjective fault or even the fault of negligence beyond a reasonable doubt. The Supreme Court applied its new common law presumption against absolute liability in another case to hold that a prohibition on hunting within a quarter mile of a baited area was a strict liability offence.[11] The accused would again have an opportunity to demonstrate that it had exercised due diligence to avoid the prohibited act or made a reasonable mistake of fact. Negligence would be inferred as the fault element in these regulatory offences, even though it was not specifically mentioned in these offences. Under the *Charter*, the courts have generally been reluctant to interpret a statute as imposing absolute liability, unless the legislature has clearly indicated that this is its intent.[12] As will be seen, an absolute liability offence when combined with imprisonment may violate the *Charter*.

Offences will, however, be recognized as absolute liability offences if the legislature clearly indicates an intent that they not be interpreted as offences of strict liability. In making this determination courts examine multiple factors, including the subject matter and regulatory pattern of the legislation, the language used to define the offence, and the penalties. In the *BC Motor Vehicle Reference*, the legislature clearly indicated such an intent by stating that the offence of driving with a suspended driver's licence was "an absolute liability offence in which guilt is established by proof of driving, whether or not the defendant knew of the prohibition or suspension."[13] As will be discussed later, the Court ruled that absolute liability offences, when combined with imprisonment, violated

---

11   *R v Chapin* (1979), 45 CCC (2d) 333 (SCC).

12   *R v ILWU, Local 500*, [1994] 1 SCR 150; *R v Rube* (1992), 75 CCC (3d) 575 (SCC); *R v Nickel City Transport (Sudbury) Ltd* (1993), 82 CCC (3d) 541 (Ont CA) [*Nickel City Transport*]. But see *R v Polewsky* (2005), 202 CCC (3d) 257 (Ont CA), holding speeding offences to be absolute liability in part because the risk of imprisonment was remote.

13   *Motor Vehicle Act*, RSBC 1979, c 288, s 94(2).

section 7 of the *Charter* and could not be justified under section 1 especially as compared with the alternative of a strict liability offence.

Even after the British Columbia legislature deleted the specific reference to the offence of driving with a suspended driver's licence being an
offence of absolute liability, the Supreme Court held in a 5:4 decision that
the offence remained one of absolute liability.[14] The majority stressed
that the offence applied when the accused had his or her licence "automatically and without notice" suspended after conviction of a number of
offences. Given that any mistake that the accused made about whether
his or her licence was suspended would be classified as a mistake of law
and hence prohibited as a defence,[15] the majority concluded that the offence was one of absolute liability. The minority in this case, however,
would have interpreted the offence as one of strict liability. Thus, the
minority would allow a defence of due diligence in ascertaining whether
the accused had been convicted of a driving offence and a defence of reasonable mistake of fact about the existence of such a conviction. It also
warned that the majority was making an incursion into the principle
that ignorance of the law was not an excuse by holding that the legislation effectively deprived the accused of a due diligence defence. *Pontes*[16]
suggests that it is possible for an offence that does not clearly state it is
one of absolute liability still to be classified as one.

In *Lévis (City) v Tétreault*,[17] the Supreme Court indicated that it
would "be better to return to the clear analytical framework and classification approach adopted in *Sault Ste Marie*," which requires "clear
proof of legislative intent" for an absolute liability offence and does
not ask the additional question of whether the legislature intended a
due diligence defence to be available. Therefore, there is a presumption that all regulatory offences are strict liability offences that allow
a defence of due diligence. This presumption has subsequently been
applied to hold that relatively minor motor vehicle offences that have
been phrased as simple prohibitions are not absolute liability and allow
a defence of due diligence.[18] It has also been applied to a provincial

---

14   R v Pontes (1995), 100 CCC (3d) 353 (SCC) [*Pontes*]. As will be examined below,
     the absolute liability offence was not struck down, but the Court indicated that
     no one could be imprisoned for its violation.

15   See Chapter 3, Section A(4) on the principle that ignorance or mistake of law
     does not constitute an excuse.

16   *Pontes*, above note 14.

17   [2006] 1 SCR 420 at paras 19 and 17 respectively [*Lévis*].

18   *R v Kanda*, 2008 ONCA 22 (highway traffic offence of not having children wear
     seat belts interpreted as strict liability offence); *R v Raham*, 2010 ONCA 206
     [*Raham*] (highway traffic offence of street racing 50 km over speed limit inter-
     preted as strict liability offence).

statute that prohibited anyone assisting others to breach offences that applied to insurance companies. The Court rejected arguments that subjective *mens rea* requirements applicable under the *Criminal Code* to aiders and abettors were relevant. It stressed the regulatory context in holding that the offence was a separate strict liability offence where the accused was guilty once the Crown established the *actus reus* and unless the accused established a reasonable mistake of fact or due diligence.[19] As will be seen, interpreting a regulatory offence as an absolute liability offence raises constitutional problems that will not occur if the offence is interpreted as a strict liability offence.

2) The *Charter* and Absolute Liability

As discussed in Chapter 2, the Supreme Court of Canada held in the *BC Motor Vehicle Reference*[20] that absolute liability offences offend the principles of fundamental justice by allowing the conviction of the morally innocent. Justice Lamer observed that "it is because absolute liability offends the principles of fundamental justice that this Court [in *Sault Ste Marie*] created presumptions against Legislatures having intended to enact offences of a regulatory nature falling within that category." Yet the Court also held that an absolute liability offence would violate section 7 of the *Charter* "only if and to the extent that it has the potential of depriving of life, liberty, and security of the person."

Justice Lamer suggested that a person's liberty would be broadly construed to include not only the mandatory imprisonment that was at issue in the case, but also probation orders.[21] The Ontario Court of Appeal has, however, held that that a simple probation order not to commit a similar offence and appear before the court does not affect the right to liberty under section 7 triggering the rule against liability.[22] Courts are divided over whether a fine threatens a person's liberty thus engaging the section 7 *Charter* rule against absolute liability. Some hold that any possibility of imprisonment for not paying a fine triggers the

---

19 *La Souveraine, Compagnie d'assurance générale v Autorité des marchés financiers*, 2013 SCC 63 at paras 31–50 [*La Souveraine*].

20 *Re BC Motor Vehicle Reference S 94(2)* (1985), 23 CCC (3d) 289 at 311 (SCC) [*BC Motor Vehicle Reference*].

21 Justice Lamer stated: "Obviously, imprisonment (including probation orders) deprives persons of their liberty. An offence has that potential as of the moment it is open to the judge to impose imprisonment. There is no need that imprisonment, as in s. 94(2), be made mandatory." *Ibid.*

22 *R v Schmidt*, 2014 ONCA 188 at para 43 [*Schmidt*].

constitutional rule against absolute liability[23] while others have indicated that section 7 does not apply if the possibility of imprisonment is remote.[24] The Ontario Court of Appeal has held that the possibility of imprisonment for an offence of driving 50 km over the speed limit gave the normal common law presumption against absolute liability a constitutional dimension. It thus interpreted the offence as a strict liability offence that allowed a defence of due diligence and avoided running afoul of the section 7 *Charter* rule against combining absolute liability with imprisonment.[25]

The Supreme Court has refused to strike down an absolute liability offence in *Pontes* on the basis of a general provision in British Columbia's legislation that provided that no one could be imprisoned for violation of an absolute liability offence. Justice Cory indicated that "generally speaking, an offence of absolute liability is not likely to offend the *Charter* unless a prison sanction is provided." He refused to strike down an absolute liability offence on the basis that an individual convicted of driving without a licence "faces no risk of imprisonment and there is, accordingly, no violation of the right to life, liberty and security of the person under s. 7 of the *Charter*."[26]

The Ontario Court of Appeal subsequently refused to strike down an absolute liability offence that provided for the operator of a commercial motor vehicle to be fined at least $2,000 and not more than $50,000 when a wheel becomes detached from a vehicle on a highway. Although an absolute liability offence violates the principles of fundamental justice, there was no section 7 violation because the rights of life, liberty, and security of the person were not affected since the offence provided that no one could be imprisoned or placed on probation for violation of the offence. The Court of Appeal concluded that the offence did not involve state-imposed serious psychological stress on the accused that would trigger section 7 of the *Charter*. "The right to security of the person does not protect the individual operating in the highly regulated context of commercial trucking for profit from the ordinary stresses and anxieties that a reasonable person would suffer as a result of government regulation of that industry."[27] In the commercial context at least, significant and mandatory fines, as well as the stigma that may accompany

---

23 *R v Burt* (1987) 38 CCC (3d) 299 (Sask CA) [*Burt*]; *Nickel City Transport*, above note 12 at 572.

24 *London (City) v Polewsky*, 2005 CanLII 38742 at para 4 (Ont CA); *Schmidt*, above note 22 at para 44.

25 *Raham*, above note 18 at paras 37–38.

26 *Pontes*, above note 14.

27 *R v 1260448 Ontario Inc* (2003), 68 OR (3d) 51 (CA).

conviction for regulatory offences associated with deaths, appear not to engage the rights to life, liberty, and security of the person under section 7 of the *Charter*.

In the *BC Motor Vehicle Reference*, Lamer J suggested that an absolute liability offence would rarely, if ever, be justified under section 1 of the *Charter*, because only in exceptional cases "such as natural disasters, the outbreak of war, epidemics and the like" should the liberty or security of a person "be sacrificed to administrative expediency."[28] In *Hess*,[29] the Supreme Court held that a statutory rape offence of having sexual intercourse with a girl under fourteen years of age constituted an absolute liability offence because Parliament had specifically provided for the accused's guilt upon proof of the *actus reus* "whether or not he believes that she is fourteen years of age or more." The offence was one of absolute liability because the Crown was not required to establish subjective fault such as knowledge or objective fault such as negligence concerning an essential element of the statutory rape offence. The majority of the Court held that the offence was an unjustified violation of section 7 of the *Charter* when compared to a less restrictive alternative that would allow the accused a limited defence that he took all reasonable steps to ascertain the age of the complainant[30] and would thus require objective fault or negligence. In *R v Wholesale Travel Group Inc*,[31] the Court concluded that provisions that required the prompt correction of misleading advertising, even in cases where it was not reasonable for the accused to know that the advertising was misleading, amounted to absolute liability that could not be justified under section 1.

3) Corporations and the *Charter*

In the *BC Motor Vehicle Reference*, Lamer J recognized that there might be a case for the use of absolute liability offences against corporations "in certain sensitive areas such as the preservation of our vital environment and our natural resources." He hinted, however, that such concerns "might well be dispelled were it to be decided, given the proper case, that s. 7 affords protection to human persons only and does not extend to corporations."[32] Subsequently, the Court held that corporations were not protected under section 7 of the *Charter*, on the basis that only human beings can enjoy life, liberty, and security of the per-

---

28   *BC Motor Vehicle Reference*, above note 20 at 311.
29   *Hess*, above note 5.
30   *Code*, above note 1, s 150.1(4).
31   [1991] 3 SCR 154, 67 CCC (3d) 193 at 214–15 [*Wholesale Travel Group*].
32   *BC Motor Vehicle Reference*, above note 20 at 314.

son and that it would be "nonsensical to speak of a corporation being put in jail."[33] Despite this conclusion, a corporate accused can, when charged with an offence, bring a *Charter* challenge on the basis that the offence violates the section 7 rights of individuals who might be charged.[34] Legislatures can insulate absolute liability offences from invalidation under section 7 of the *Charter* by enacting offences that apply only to corporations. So far, legislatures have not made extensive use of this option to insulate absolute liability offences from *Charter* review. As will be seen, however, new provisions for organizational liability under the *Criminal Code* may be immune from section 7 review because they do not apply to natural persons who enjoy rights to life, liberty, and security of the person under section 7 of the *Charter*.

4) Corporate Liability for Absolute Liability Offences

Corporations have "automatic primary responsibility"[35] for absolute liability offences. A corporation may be guilty whenever one of its employees or someone under its control commits the prohibited act.[36] In a sense, this is a form of vicarious liability, because it attributes the acts of the employee to the corporation. Courts have not seen this as a problem, however, because it is only the acts of the employees that are attributed to the corporation and not some fault element. Corporations can also be guilty if they had an ability to control the commission of the *actus reus* by an independent contractor. In *Sault Ste Marie*,[37] Dickson J indicated that although a homeowner who hires a company to collect garbage is probably not responsible for polluting if the company dumps the garbage in a river, a corporation or a municipality may well be.

5) Defences to Absolute Liability Offences

A defence of honest or even reasonable mistake of fact will not be a defence to an absolute liability offence. Thus, an accused's subjective reliance on a faulty speedometer would not be a valid defence even if the reliance was reasonable.[38] The defences of automatism, mental

---

33 *Irwin Toy Ltd v Quebec (AG)*, [1989] 1 SCR 927 at 1003 [*Irwin*].

34 *Wholesale Travel Group*, above note 31.

35 *Canadian Dredge & Dock Co v R* (1985), 19 CCC (3d) 1 at 8 (SCC) [*Canadian Dredge & Dock*].

36 A corporation will not be guilty if an independent operator on its premises commits a crime. *R v FW Woolworth Co* (1974), 18 CCC (2d) 23 (Ont CA).

37 *Sault Ste Marie*, above note 4.

38 *R v Hickey* (1976), 30 CCC (2d) 416 (Ont CA).

disorder, extreme intoxication, or accident as related to involuntary conduct might possibly apply to an absolute liability offence, because they would indicate that the accused acted in an involuntary manner that is inconsistent with proof of the *actus reus*.[39] There is also some authority that the defence of necessity might apply to a person who committed an absolute liability offence such as speeding because of an urgent need to save a life.[40]

B. STRICT LIABILITY OFFENCES

A strict liability[41] offence requires the Crown to prove the prohibited act beyond a reasonable doubt, but then gives the accused an opportunity to prove due diligence or absence of negligence on a balance of probabilities. Strict liability offences are a halfway house between absolute liability offences and full *mens rea* offences. They "seek a middle position, fulfilling the goals of public welfare offences while still not punishing the entirely blameless."[42] In 1978, the Supreme Court indicated that all regulatory offences would be presumed to be strict liability offences, unless there was a clear indication from the legislature that either absolute liability or subjective *mens rea* was intended.

1) Simple Negligence

The blameworthiness of a strict liability offence is negligence. The Crown does not have to prove this fault element; rather, the accused is given an opportunity to establish on a balance of probabilities that it was not negligent.[43] In *Sault Ste Marie*, Dickson J contemplated that an accused who took all reasonable care, but still committed the prohibited act, would not be convicted of a strict liability offence. Given that regu-

---

39 In *R v Daviault* (1994), 93 CCC (3d) 21 at 25 (SCC), Lamer CJC stated that he preferred to characterize the mental element involved in voluntary and conscious activity "as relating more to the *actus reus* than the *mens rea*, so that the defence will clearly be available in strict liability offences." The same logic should apply to absolute liability offences.

40 *R v Kennedy* (1972), 7 CCC (2d) 42 (NS Co Ct); *R v Walker* (1979), 48 CCC (2d) 126 (Ont Co Ct).

41 Note that this terminology is distinctly Canadian, so that what other jurisdictions call strict liability would in Canada be classified as absolute liability. Similarly, strict liability in tort law is analogous to absolute liability in Canadian criminal law.

42 *Sault Ste Marie*, above note 4 at 374.

43 *R v Timminco Ltd* (2001), 42 CR (5th) 279 (Ont CA).

latory offences are designed to encourage people and corporations to take appropriate safeguards to avoid harmful results, such as pollution or workplace accidents, courts should not require negligence to amount to a marked departure from the conduct of a reasonable person, as they do when applying negligence in criminal offences.[44] The reasonableness of the accused's conduct also should be determined on the basis of the circumstances that a reasonable person would have seen, not the circumstances that the accused actually perceived. Thus, any mistake of fact would have to be both honest and reasonable.

To avoid a conviction for a regulatory offence, the corporation would have to demonstrate that it took reasonable steps to avoid the prohibited act or that it made an honest and reasonable mistake of fact.[45] It is important that the accused be given the opportunity to demonstrate that it was not negligent in order to avoid a strict liability offence becoming an absolute liability offence in which guilt is established simply by the prosecution proving the prohibited act beyond a reasonable doubt.

2) Negligence and the *Charter*

In *Wholesale Travel Group*,[46] the Supreme Court unanimously upheld negligence as a sufficient fault element for an offence of false or misleading advertising. The accused had argued that subjective *mens rea* was required because of the stigma that would accompany a conviction, and it relied upon *dicta* in *Vaillancourt*, which had suggested that proof of subjective *mens rea* might be required because of the stigma attached to theft. Chief Justice Lamer stated that a conviction for misleading advertising will not "brand the accused as being dishonest," but, in many cases, would indicate that the accused had been careless. Negligence was sufficient, even if the accused faced imprisonment. Adoption of a higher fault element was a matter of public policy for the legislature. Justice Cory similarly concluded that "the demands of s. 7 will be met in the regulatory context where liability is imposed for conduct which breaches the standard of reasonable care required of those operating in the regulated field."[47] Simple negligence will be a constitutionally sufficient fault element for all regulatory offences.

---

44   See Chapter 5, Section C.

45   *R v MacMillan Bloedel Ltd*, 2002 BCCA 510 [*MacMillan Bloedel Ltd*].

46   *Wholesale Travel Group*, above note 31.

47   *Ibid* at 252. See also *R v Eurosport Auto Co* (2002), 11 CR (6th) 327 (BCCA).

3) The Defence of Due Diligence

Although the fault element for a strict liability offence is negligence, the Crown need not prove negligence beyond a reasonable doubt. Rather, the accused must prove a defence of due diligence or lack of negligence on a balance of probabilities. Once the Crown has proved the wrongful act beyond a reasonable doubt, the fault element of negligence is presumed, unless the accused can demonstrate that it took reasonable care or acted under a reasonable mistake of fact. In *Sault Ste Marie*,[48] Dickson J stressed that the burden of establishing due diligence should fall upon the accused, because it "will generally have the means of proof." This is especially true when, as in the case, it was alleged that "a large and complex corporation" caused pollution. He concluded that the burden was not unfair, "as the alternative is absolute liability which denies an accused any defence whatsoever," and the accused need only prove the defence on a balance of probabilities. The burden on the accused is an important component of the halfway house approach of strict liability offences, because it means that the Crown is not required to prove negligence beyond a reasonable doubt and that the accused is not acquitted because there is a reasonable doubt as to negligence.

The due diligence defence requires more than passivity from the accused. In *Lévis (City) v Tétreault*,[49] the Supreme Court rejected the idea that an accused who thought that the date on his licence was a renewal notice as opposed to an expiry date had a defence of due diligence. The Court stated that the courts below, which had acquitted the accused on the basis of due diligence, had

> confused passivity with diligence . . . . He proved no action or attempt to obtain information. The concept of diligence is based on the acceptance of a citizen's civic duty to take action to find out what his or her obligations are. Passive ignorance is not a valid defence . . . .[50]

Due diligence requires an active and reasonable attempt to prevent the commission of the prohibited act. A defence of "human error" or honest but not necessarily reasonable mistake will not suffice.[51]

The due diligence defence does not apply to mistakes or ignorance of the law. In a 2013 case involving an insurance company, the Court upheld the conviction of an insurance company that had written to a regulator explaining why it thought its conduct was legal, but received

---

48 *Sault Ste Marie*, above note 4 at 373.
49 Above note 17 at paras 17 and 19.
50 *Ibid* at para 30.
51 *R v Pourlotfali*, 2016 ONCA 490 [*Pourlotfali*].

no reply until the regulator charged it with fifty-six regulatory offences six months later. The majority of the Court upheld the convictions on the basis that the corporation had committed the *actus reus* and failed to establish a defence of due diligence. It stressed that the due diligence defence "will not be available if the defendant relies solely on a mistake of law to explain the commission of the offence."[52] The Court recognized that the behaviour of the regulator was problematic and the difficulty of understanding the vast amount of regulatory laws. Nevertheless, it refused to recognize a new defence of reasonable mistake of law or apply mistakes of law to the due diligence defence in large part because of concerns that such developments could undermine the deterrent value of regulatory offences. Justice Abella in dissent would have extended the defence of officially induced error to situations where regulators were passive and would have stayed proceedings on that basis. Reliance on private legal advice will not support a due diligence defence because it is a mistake of law and not covered by the limited exception of officially induced error.[53]

One variant of a due diligence defence is that the accused made a reasonable mistake of fact, for example, in failing to detect a hazard that required remedial action. Even if the accused is aware of the hazard, it may have a due diligence defence if it establishes it took reasonable measures to prevent the commission of the prohibited act.[54]

The courts look to a large range of factors in determining whether the accused has established a defence of due diligence to a regulatory offence. Relevant factors include: the likelihood and gravity of the risk, including whether it was foreseeable and the effect that it could have on vulnerable people and neighbourhoods. Other factors look to the ability of the accused to control or manage the risk of the prohibited act from occurring. Factors such as alternative solutions, regulatory compliance, industry standards and preventive systems, efforts made to address the problem, and the promptness of the accused's response are significant. Other matters such as factors beyond the control of the accused, technological limitations, skill level expected of the accused, complexities involved, and economic considerations can be relevant in determining whether the accused has taken all reasonable steps to prevent the risk.[55] Courts will consider the perspective of the reasonable

---

52   *La Souveraine*, above note 19 at para 57.

53   *R v Stucky*, 2009 ONCA 151 at para 109.

54   *MacMillan Bloedel Ltd*, above note 45 at para 47.

55   These factors are taken from *R v Commander Business Furniture* (1992), 9 CELR (NS) 185 (Ont Prov Div). They are discussed at greater length in T Archibald, K Jull, & K Roach, *Regulatory and Corporate Liability: From Due Diligence to Risk Management*

person when applying the due diligence defence. They will examine the training and supervision that was or was not given to employees.[56] The focus in due diligence is on whether the accused has taken reasonable steps to prevent the commission of the offence.

a) Due Diligence in Relation to Other Defences and Legislative Requirements

The due diligence defence is flexible. It may include aspects of other defences, including self-defence, necessity, and mental disorder, provided that a healthy allowance is made for the basic requirement in strict liability that the accused must establish reasonable conduct or due diligence. Courts of appeal have accepted that the due diligence defence can be informed by elements of self-defence and necessity so as to include speeding to avoid a collision[57] and shooting a bear in self-defence, but in violation of a regulatory offence.[58] The Quebec Court of Appeal has held that the mental disorder defence (but not *Criminal Code* provisions governing the accused's disposition) can apply to regulatory offences under Quebec law.[59] Some commentators urge that such defences should be recognized directly rather than "strange due diligence variants."[60] In my view, including them seems to fulfill the purpose of the due diligence defence in preventing the conviction of those who have done nothing wrong even though they have committed the prohibited act of a regulatory offence.[61]

Legislatures can fill in the content of a due diligence defence by requiring specific content such as checking certain prescribed forms of identification to prevent prohibited under-age purchase.[62] At the same time, courts should be careful to allow for a more general due diligence or reasonable mistake defence that may not be captured by the specific statutory requirements.[63]

(Aurora, ON: Canada Law Book, 2004) (loose-leaf), ch 4, where it is suggested that the due diligence defence may require reasonable risk management.

56   *Ontario (Ministry of the Environment and Climate Change) v Sunrise Propane Energy Group Ltd*, 2017 ONSC 6954.

57   *Raham* above note 18 at para 49.

58   *R v Turnbull*, 2016 NLCA 25; *R v Klem*, 2014 BCCA 272 at para 31.

59   *Autorité des marchés financiers v Patry*, 2015 QCCA 1933 [*Patry*].

60   M Manning & P Sankoff, *Criminal Law* 5th ed (Markham, ON: LexisNexis, 2015) at 5.76.

61   One of the reasons given by the Quebec Court of Appeal for finding that the mental disorder defence would apply to regulatory offences is that it would also negate the commission of the *actus reus*. *Patry*, above note 59 at paras 73–81.

62   *R v Seaway Gas & Fuel Ltd*, 2000 CanLII 2981 (Ont CA).

63   *Pourlotfali*, above note 51.

The accused must be given an opportunity to establish due diligence or reasonable mistake of fact in order to ensure that a strict liability offence does not become an absolute liability offence in which a conviction follows automatically from the fact that the risk sought to be managed has been realized and the prohibited act occurred. It is an error of law to acquit the accused simply because there is a reasonable doubt about the due diligence defence: the defence must be proven on a balance of probabilities.

4) The Defence of Due Diligence and the *Charter*

In *Wholesale Travel Group*, the Supreme Court in a 5:4 decision upheld a statutory defence that required those who committed the wrongful act of false or misleading advertising to prove on a balance of probabilities that they exercised due diligence to prevent the occurrence of such error. Seven judges agreed that placing such a burden on the accused violated the presumption of innocence as protected under section 11(d) of the *Charter* because it allowed an accused to be convicted, even though there was a reasonable doubt as to whether it acted in a negligent fashion. Chief Justice Lamer, with three other judges in dissent, found that this restriction on section 11(d) could not be justified under section 1, because the legislature could achieve its objective by means of an evidential as opposed to a persuasive burden. He contemplated a mandatory presumption of negligence following proof of the *actus reus*, but one that could be rebutted by evidence that could raise a reasonable doubt as to whether the accused was negligent. Such a mandatory presumption would violate section 11(d) of the *Charter* but would constitute a less drastic means of advancing the legislature's objectives.[64]

However, a majority of the Court concluded that imposing the burden on the accused to establish due diligence on a balance of probabilities could be justified. Justice Iacobucci stated that an evidential burden "would shift to the accused the burden of simply raising a reasonable doubt as to due diligence and would not thereby allow the effective pursuit of the regulatory objective."[65] He argued that the accused, as participants in regulated activities, "are in the best position to prove due diligence, since they possess in most cases the required information" to prove that they were not negligent. Justice Cory also stressed that the accused would be in the best position to prove whether

---

64 *R v Downey* (1992), 72 CCC (3d) 1 (SCC); *R v Laba* (1994), 94 CCC (3d) 385 (SCC), discussed in Chapter 2, Section B(3)(g).

65 *Wholesale Travel Group*, above note 31 at 267 (CCC).

it exercised reasonable care, and concluded, "in the regulatory context, there is nothing unfair about imposing that onus; indeed, it is essential for the protection of our vulnerable society."[66] He feared that with only an evidential burden, the accused would always be able to point to some evidence of measures it had taken to prevent the prohibited act, and the Crown would then have the difficult task of proving beyond a reasonable doubt that the accused was negligent.

The majority's judgment in *Wholesale Travel Group* endorses the functional justifications given in *Sault Ste Marie* for requiring the accused to prove the defence of due diligence or lack of negligence. Although it is technically necessary to justify each reverse burden under section 1, the Court has applied the section 1 analysis used in *Wholesale Travel Group* to other regulatory offences in different contexts.[67]

5) Corporate Liability for Strict Liability Offences

The same considerations apply when holding corporations accountable for strict liability offences as apply for absolute liability offences. In *Canadian Dredge & Dock*,[68] Estey J stated:

> As in the case of an absolute liability offence, it matters not whether the accused is corporate or unincorporated, because the liability is primary . . . . It is not dependent upon the attribution to the accused of the misconduct of others . . . . [T]he corporation and the natural defendant are in the same position. In both cases liability is not vicarious but primary.

As with absolute liability offences, this approach suggests that the corporation will have committed the *actus reus* when one of its employees or another person subject to its control has committed the prohibited act. In *Sault Ste Marie*, the accused could be liable, even though it had contracted out the pollution-causing activity to another company.

The primary liability of a corporation for a strict liability offence suggests the corollary that the corporation must establish a defence of due diligence for the organization. In *Sault Ste Marie*,[69] however, Dickson J suggested that "the availability of a defence to a corporation will depend on whether such due diligence was taken by those who are the directing mind and will of the corporation, whose acts are therefore in

---

66   *Ibid* at 256–57.
67   *R v Ellis-Don Ltd* (1992), 71 CCC (3d) 63 (SCC); *R v Martin* (1992), 71 CCC (3d) 572 (SCC).
68   *Canadian Dredge & Dock*, above note 35 at 9.
69   *Sault Ste Marie*, above note 4 at 377–78.

law the acts of the corporation itself." As will be seen, this standard is no longer used for attributing subjective fault to a corporation and has been replaced by a broader concept of a senior officer who exercises policy-making or important managerial functions within the organization. There may be cases in large organizations where the directing mind or even the senior officers act with due diligence, but the corporation as a complex organization does not. An example of this would occur when no one informed a directing mind or senior officer about certain problems or warning signs that the *actus reus* was likely to occur. In that case, it is possible that the directing mind or senior officer will be found not to be negligent (unless he or she should have made inquiries) even though the corporation as an organization might be negligent. It would be more consistent with the logic of strict liability offences to require the corporation as an organization to prove a due diligence defence.

6) Requirements of Fault Beyond Negligence in Regulatory Offences

The Court in *Sault Ste Marie*[70] contemplated that while regulatory offences would be presumed to be offences of strict liability, they could also require proof of fault if the legislature specifically provided for fault elements such as knowledge, wilfulness, or recklessness. It held that the use of the words "cause" and "permit" in environmental legislation were not sufficient to move the regulatory offence into the full *mens rea* category.[71] In *Strasser v Roberge*,[72] the Supreme Court disagreed about whether there was an intent requirement with respect to the offence under Quebec labour legislation of participating in an illegal strike. The Court in *Strasser* divided 4:3 on the classification of the offence, with Beetz J holding for the majority that the offence was one of strict liability that required the accused to bear the burden of establishing the lack of intent and Dickson J in dissent holding that the offence was a *mens rea* offence that required the Crown to prove intent. In 2013, the Court rejected an argument that an offence that applied to those who assisted others to breach insurance regulations should require subjective fault similar to that which applies to parties under the *Criminal Code*. The Court stressed the regulatory context and the distinct nature of the offence. It concluded that it should not be

---

70   *Ibid.*
71   *Ibid.*
72   [1979] 2 SCR 953 [*Strasser*].

"surprising in the regulatory context to find strict liability offences that encompass forms of secondary penal liability for the ultimate purpose of vigilantly ensuring compliance with a regulatory framework established to protect the general public."[73]

If a regulatory offence requires proof of subjective fault, this raises the issue of burden of proof. If it is accepted that the offence remains one of strict liability even though the legislature has required fault above negligence, then *Wholesale Travel Group* should justify the reversal of proof that requires the accused to establish lack of intent. On the other hand, the dissenting position of Dickson J in *Strasser* that regulatory offences can still be classified as *mens rea* offences if they require proof of fault beyond negligence is attractive. In other words, there can be a small subset of regulatory offences that specifically require subjective fault as *mens rea* offences where the Crown has to establish both the prohibited act and the fault requirement beyond a reasonable doubt.

C. VICARIOUS LIABILITY

Vicarious liability occurs when the acts and fault of another person are attributed to the accused for the purpose of determining liability. It is used in tort law as a means of ensuring that employers are not allowed to profit from civil wrongs committed by their employees. Even before the *Charter*, courts resisted this doctrine on the basis that "criminal law regards a person as responsible for his own crimes only."[74] A judge-made or common law presumption against holding a person responsible for the acts and faults of another could, however, be displaced by clear legislative intent.[75] As will be seen in relation to corporate liability for *mens rea* offences, Canadian courts struggled to avoid holding corporations vicariously liable for crimes committed by their employees.

1) Vicarious Liability and the *Charter*

In *Bhatnager v Canada (Minister of Employment & Immigration)*,[76] the Supreme Court suggested that it might violate section 7 to hold ministers of the government vicariously liable for acts of criminal contempt

---

73   *La Souveraine*, above note 19 at para 49.
74   *Tesco Supermarkets Ltd v Nattrass* (1971), [1972] AC 153 at 199 (HL); *R v Stevanovich* (1983), 7 CCC (3d) 307 at 311 (Ont CA).
75   *R v Budget Car Rentals (Toronto) Ltd* (1981), 57 CCC (2d) 201 (Ont CA).
76   [1990] 2 SCR 217.

committed by their officials without their knowledge. Several *Charter* cases have considered statutes that make the owners of automobiles vicariously liable for violations committed by any person driving their cars. In *Burt*,[77] the Saskatchewan Court of Appeal concluded:

> The principles of fundamental justice simply do not recognize the ascribing to one person of another's state of mind. Accordingly, where a statute purports to make one person vicariously liable for another's *mens rea* offence the statute may be said to offend . . . the principles of fundamental justice.

An offence that bases the accused's liability on the acts and faults of another may be found to be an absolute liability offence that punishes the accused without fault. At a minimum, a person could not be imprisoned for such an offence.[78] Many motor vehicle offences that impose vicarious liability on the owner of a vehicle for offences committed with the vehicle contain a limited defence allowing the owner to establish that the vehicle was taken without his or her consent. Courts of appeal are divided on whether this limited defence makes a vicarious liability offence one of absolute or strict liability.[79] The statutory defence does allow the owner a limited opportunity to show that he or she was not at fault. At the same time, however, it does not exhaust the range of due diligence defences that an accused would ordinarily have to a strict liability offence. Thus, the better view is that even with this limited defence, the offence remains one of absolute liability because it can convict an accused who was not at fault. The accused may still be convicted but not imprisoned for the violation of a vicarious liability offence that imposes absolute liability.

---

77 *Burt*, above note 23 at 311. See also *R v Pellerin* (1989), 47 CCC (3d) 35 (Ont CA).
78 *R v Gray* (1988), 44 CCC (3d) 222 (Man CA); *R v Smith* (1989), 14 MVR (2d) 166 (YCA); *R v Free* (1990), 110 AR 241 (QB).
79 The British Columbia Court of Appeal has held that such a vicarious liability offence remains one of absolute liability while the Nova Scotia Court of Appeal has held that it makes the offence one of strict liability. *R v Geraghty* (1990), 55 CCC (3d) 460 (BCCA); *R v Sutherland* (1990), 55 CCC (3d) 265 (NSCA).

D. CORPORATIONS AND *MENS REA* OFFENCES

1) The Common Law Directing Mind Approach

Canadian courts resisted holding corporations vicariously liable for the *mens rea* offences of their employees. Instead, they identified the corporation with a senior official who acts as the corporation's directing mind and attributed the fault or mental element of that person to the corporation for the purpose of determining the corporation's liability for a criminal offence. In doing so, they followed English authorities that suggest that a corporation is liable only for what is done by "the directing mind and will of the corporation, the very ego and centre of the personality of the corporation."[80] Under this identification or alter ego theory, the wrongful action of the directing mind is attributed to the corporation so that the corporation has primary, not vicarious, liability for the acts and mind of an official who is a directing mind of the corporation.

A corporation could not insulate itself from the crimes committed by a directing mind by claiming ignorance or issuing instructions that the crime not be committed. Thus, the Supreme Court has stated: "Acts of the ego of a corporation taken within the assigned managerial area may give rise to the corporate criminal responsibility, whether or not there be formal delegation; whether or not there be awareness of the activity in the board of directors or the officers of the company, and . . . whether or not there be express prohibition."[81] One relatively narrow exception was that a corporation would not be held liable if the directing mind acted wholly in fraud and against the interest of the corporation. In that case, the corporation would be the victim of the crime, not responsible for it. The Court has restricted this principle so that the corporation remains liable if the directing mind's activities were "by design or result partly for the benefit of the company."[82] Thus, a corporation may be guilty of fraud if it receives kickbacks, even though the directing mind fraudulently keeps some of the kickbacks from the corporation.

Canadian courts defined the directing mind of the corporation somewhat more broadly than English courts, in part because of the decentralized nature of much corporate activity in Canada. In the leading

---

80 *Lennard's Carrying Co Ltd v Asiatic Petroleum Co Ltd*, [1915] AC 705 at 713 (HL). Note that s 2 of the *Code*, above note 1, defines "everyone" to include corporations and fines are generally available to punish corporations.

81 *Canadian Dredge & Dock*, above note 35 at 17.

82 *Ibid* at 38.

case of *Canadian Dredge & Dock*, the Supreme Court made clear that there could be more than one directing mind of a corporation. Directing minds could include "the board of directors, the managing director, the superintendent, the manager or anyone else delegated . . . the governing executive authority of the corporation." In *R v Waterloo Mercury Sales Ltd*,[83] the manager of a used car lot was held to be the corporation's directing mind for the purpose of determining whether it had committed fraud by rolling back odometers, even though the president of the corporation had no knowledge of the acts and had circulated written instructions not to roll back odometers. The manager was acting as the corporation's directing mind within the field of operation assigned to him. An employee with lesser responsibility, such as a salesperson or a mechanic, would not be a directing mind.

In the 1990s, Canadian courts placed limits on who might be classified as a corporation's directing mind. A directing mind must be an officer or manager of a corporation, acting in the scope of his or her responsibility. A directing mind must also have "an express or implied delegation of executive authority to design and supervise the implementation of corporate policy rather than simply to carry out such policy."[84] Under this test, both a tug captain who exercised considerable discretion[85] and a truck driver who was a corporation's sole representative in an area[86] were held not to be directing minds of their corporations. The courts reasoned that these employees did not have the power to design or supervise the implementation of corporate policy and that their fault could not be attributed to the corporation. This trend made it difficult to hold corporations criminally accountable for crimes committed in Canada. Not infrequently, those with the degree of responsibility required of a directing mind would be sheltered within the corporate hierarchy and not have the required fault, while those with the required fault would not have enough policy-making power within the corporation to be classified as the corporation's directing mind. The designers and even the supervisors of corporate policies in a large and economically dependent country such as Canada often were so far away from any criminal acts that took place that they did not have the *mens rea* required for the particular crime. Those closer to the ground who would have the required fault were not classified as directing minds because they did not design or supervise the implementation of

---

83 (1974), 18 CCC (2d) 248 (Alta Dist Ct).
84 *"Rhone" (The) v "Peter AB Widener" (The)*, [1993] 1 SCR 497 at 521 [*Rhone*].
85 *Ibid.*
86 *R v Safety Kleen Canada Inc* (1997), 114 CCC (3d) 214 (Ont CA) [*Safety Kleen*].

corporate policy, even though they exercised an important managerial role in the corporation.

2) 2003 Statutory Provisions for Corporate Criminal Liability

There were many calls to abandon the identification, alter ego, or directing mind approach in favour of less restrictive approaches. One option would be to hold corporations vicariously responsible for the actions of all their employees and agents, as is done in some American jurisdictions. This would run against the criminal law's reluctance to impose vicarious liability based on the fault of another. Such vicarious liability likely offends the principles of fundamental justice, but it may not violate section 7 of the *Charter* because corporations have no rights to life, liberty, and security of the person. In any event, vicarious liability would still only attribute the fault of individuals to corporations. Another option would have been to impose liability on corporations based on their organizational fault or "corporate culture," as is done in some Australian jurisdictions.[87] The focus under such proposals would not be on the fault of individuals within the corporation, but on the fault of the corporation as a whole.

In late 2003, Parliament enacted Bill C-45 that amended the *Criminal Code* to provide a new regime to determine when corporations and other organizations were guilty of criminal offences, and its provisions took effect at the end of March 2004. The Bill also provided a new punishment regime to allow courts not simply to fine corporations, but also to place them on probation in an attempt to ensure that the offences were not repeated. This new regime is a fundamental change to corporate criminal liability in response to corporate misconduct that led to the death of twenty-six miners in the Westray Mine disaster, as well as events such as the Enron scandal.

The new regime replaces the common law concept of a directing mind with a new and broader statutory concept of a senior officer, which now includes those who are responsible for managing an important aspect of the corporation's activities. At the same time, the new regime retains the idea that a senior officer of the corporation must be at fault before that person's fault can be attributed to the corporation for either a negligence or subjective fault offence under the *Criminal Code*.

---

87   D Stuart, "A Case for a General Part" in D Stuart, RJ Delisle, & A Manson, eds. *Towards a Clear and Just Criminal Law: A Criminal Reports Forum* (Toronto: Carswell, 1999) at 135–38.

The new provisions do, however, allow an organization to be found criminally liable for crimes of negligence because of the aggregate actions of more than one of its representatives and the aggregate or collective fault of more than one of its senior officers. It does not go as far as vicarious liability for the fault of all employees or fault that inheres in the corporation as an organization including "corporate culture" as opposed to the senior officers of the corporation.

The new regime also lends some structure to the *Criminal Code* by providing a separate provision for determining organizational liability for criminal offences of negligence and for criminal offences of subjective fault. It also builds on the parties provisions of the *Criminal Code* by tying organizational liability to individuals in the organization being a party to the specific offence. This underlines the reality that in many cases both individuals within the organization and the organization itself may face criminal charges. Nevertheless, it does make the new sections complex and can in some circumstances result in the corporation being found guilty for a subjective intent offence because its senior officers ought to have known that the offence would be committed or did not take reasonable steps to prevent an offence that they knew was being committed by representatives of the corporation.

a) Organizational Liability

The new provisions apply not only to corporations, but also to any "public body, body corporate, society, company, firm, partnership, trade union or municipality."[88] This makes sense because municipalities have long been held liable for regulatory offences and there is no reason in principle why other public bodies and alternatives to formal corporations should not be held responsible under the *Criminal Code*. All of these entities are united in not being natural persons who enjoy a right to life, liberty, and security of the person under section 7 of the *Charter*.[89]

The new provisions also apply to a less formal association that is "created for a common purpose, has an operational structure and holds itself out to the public as an association of persons."[90] This suggests that the formal legal status of the organization will not be determinative with respect to the applicability of the new principles. It also raises the novel possibility that prosecutors could charge associations like criminal gangs with a criminal offence as a means of fining the organization

---

88   *Code*, above note 1, s 2.
89   *Irwin*, above note 33.
90   *Code*, above note 1, s 2.

or placing the organization itself on probation as opposed to relying solely on prosecutions of individuals within the informal association.

b) Representatives of an Organization

The prohibited act or *actus reus* must be committed by one or more of the organization's "representatives." Representatives are defined broadly in section 2 of the *Criminal Code* as including not only the directors, partners, employees, and members of the organization, but also its agents and contractors. A public body or a corporation that contracts out work to non-employees can still be held liable for prohibited acts performed by the contractor or agent.

c) Senior Officers of an Organization

In general, the required fault element or *mens rea* for the offence must be found in a senior officer of the organization. The definition of a senior officer in section 2 of the *Criminal Code* is perhaps the most crucial feature of the new regime because the new statutory concept of a senior officer replaces the old common law concept of the corporation's directing mind. "Senior officer" is defined as a

> [r]epresentative who plays an important role in the establishment of the organization's policies or is responsible for managing an important aspect of the organization's activities and, in the case of a body corporate, includes a director, its chief executive officer and its chief financial officer.[91]

This definition follows the common law concept of directing mind to the extent that it provides that (1) directors, chief executive and chief financial officers, and (2) those who play an important role in the establishment of policies are senior enough in the organization that their fault can fairly be attributed to the corporation. The most important difference between the old directing mind concept and the new senior officer concept is that the latter also covers those responsible for managing an important part of the organization's activities. This last aspect of the definition of a senior officer overrules previous cases that suggested that those who exercised important managerial functions in an organization were not high enough in the corporate hierarchy to represent the corporation for the purpose of determining fault. Thus, it is likely the tugboat captain in *Rhone*[92] and the truck driver who

---

91   *Ibid.*
92   *Rhone*, above note 84.

represented a waste disposal corporation in *Safety Kleen*[93] would now be found to be senior officers whose fault could be attributed to the corporation. Even though such persons were held not to be directing minds because they did not play an important role in establishing corporate policy, they did manage an important aspect of the corporation's activities and on that basis would satisfy the expanded definition of senior officer in section 2 of the *Criminal Code*.

A regional manager who oversaw 200 service stations and six territory managers[94] as well as a contractor who was a site supervisor[95] have been held to be senior officers under section 2 of the *Code*. This underlines that Parliament has departed from the restrictive common law directing mind test. In its 2003 reforms, Parliament extended a corporation's criminal responsibility beyond the board room so that "a corporation should not be permitted to distance itself from culpability due to the corporate individual's rank on the corporate ladder or level of management responsibility."[96] In *Metron Construction Corp*, a company pled guilty to four counts of criminal negligence causing death and breaching a duty under section 217.1 of the *Code* to take reasonable steps to prevent employees from being harmed on the basis of the fault of a senior officer who was a contractor and a site supervisor. This senior officer was also one of four fatalities when proper safety equipment was not used on a construction site. The corporation was fined $750,000.[97] At the same time, the new concept of a senior officer is limited to managers and not mere employees and the manager, such as the site supervisor in *Metron Construction Corp*, must be responsible for managing an important aspect of the organization's activities.

d) Section 22.1 of the *Criminal Code* and Organizational Fault for Negligence Offences

As mentioned above, the new regime differentiates between organizational fault for criminal offences based on negligence and subjective intent. This helpfully differentiates between the two main varieties of criminal fault. As will be seen, the new legislation also incorporates the idea that negligence in the criminal context requires more than unreasonable conduct or simple negligence. Following cases such as *Creighton*, *Beatty*, and *Roy*, discussed in Chapter 5, the new regime requires

---

93   *Safety Kleen*, above note 86.
94   *R v Petroles Global Inc*, 2013 QCCS 4262 at para 202.
95   *R v Metron Construction Corp*, 2013 ONCA 541 at para 16.
96   *Ibid* at para 90.
97   *Ibid* at para 120.

a marked departure from a standard of reasonable care. Section 22.1 provides:

> In respect of an offence that requires the prosecution to prove negligence, an organization is a party to the offence if:
> a)   acting within the scope of their authority
>   i)   one of its representatives is a party to the offence, or
>   ii)   two or more of its representatives engage in conduct, whether by act or omission, such that, if it had been the conduct of only one representative, that representative would have been a party to the offence; and
> b)   the senior officer who is responsible for the aspect of the organization's activities that is relevant to the offence departs — or the senior officers, collectively, depart — markedly from the standard of care that, in the circumstances, could reasonably be expected to prevent a representative of the organization from being a party to the offence.

Section 22.1(a) defines how the representative(s) of the organization can commit the prohibited act, or *actus reus*, of the offence whereas section 22.1(b) defines how the senior officer(s) of the organization will have the required fault element for a negligence-based criminal offence. Such offences could include causing death or causing bodily harm by criminal negligence.[98]

i)   *The Commission of the Prohibited Act by the Organization's*
     Representative(s)

Section 22.1(a) requires that the representative(s) of the organization commit the prohibited act. The first requirement is that the representative(s) be acting in the scope of their authority. A corporation thus will not be liable for something done by employees, agents, or contractors outside the scope of their authority. For example, a corporation would not be guilty of criminal negligence causing death should an employee be involved in a fatal accident after he or she had stolen the company's truck.

In many cases, one representative of an organization acting within the scope of his or her authority will commit the prohibited act. Section 22.1(a)(ii), however, provides that multiple representatives of the

---

98   *Code*, above note 1, ss 220 & 221. Criminal negligence under s 219(b) can also be found on the basis of omissions. Section 217.1 of the *Code* now provides that "every one who undertakes, or has the authority, to direct how another person does work or performs a task is under a legal duty to take reasonable steps to prevent bodily harm to that person, or any other person, arising from that work or task."

organization may cumulatively be held responsible for commission of the prohibited act. This provision recognizes that corporate misconduct can often be the aggregate of the behaviour of separate individuals, each of whom taken by themselves may not have committed the prohibited act. A mining disaster, for example, may be caused by the combination of two or more individuals failing to take safety precautions. The failure of each may not have caused death, but the combined actions of the individuals may be sufficient to cause death.

ii) *Marked Departure from Reasonable Standards by the Organization's Senior Officer(s)*

Section 22.1(b) requires that senior officer(s) of the organization have the fault of departing markedly from the standard of care that could reasonably be expected to prevent a representative from being a party to the offence. The fault element does not require that a senior officer necessarily know that a representative of the organization was committing the offence. Nevertheless, it does require more than simple negligence or a lack of due diligence by the senior officer. The fault element that is required is criminal negligence in the sense that the departure from reasonable conduct must be a marked departure. This follows from the Supreme Court's repeated statements that negligence in the criminal context must be "marked."[99]

The relevant standard is the standard of care that in the circumstances could reasonably be expected to prevent a representative of the organization from being a party to the offence. This suggests that all organizations should establish systems designed to prevent their representatives from committing offences based on negligence, such as causing death or bodily injury by criminal negligence. The exact contours of this standard of care will depend on the particular circumstances and may be informed by some of the factors discussed above in relation to the due diligence defence.

In general, the requisite degree of negligence will be found in the conduct of the senior officer "who is responsible for the aspect of the organization's activities that is relevant to the offence." For example, the senior officer responsible for mine safety would generally be the relevant person in determining whether the mining company had acted with criminal negligence in the causing of death or bodily harm. It will be recalled that this senior officer need not establish corporate policy;

---

99   See *R v Creighton* (1993), 83 CCC (3d) 346 at 382–83 (SCC); *R v Hundal*, [1993] 1 SCR 867; *R v Finlay*, [1993] 3 SCR 103; *R v Beatty*, 2008 SCC 5; *R v Roy*, 2012 SCC 26, discussed in Chapter 5, Section C(2).

it is sufficient under the definition of senior officer in section 2 of the *Criminal Code* that he or she be responsible for managing an important part of the organization's activities. This could include a mine manager in Canada even though corporate policy is established in head office in some other country.

Section 22.1(b) also provides for an innovative form of aggregate fault by multiple senior officers. In a sense this mirrors the concept of the aggregate commission of the prohibited act by multiple representatives of the organization in section 22.1(a). Section 22.1(b) contemplates a conviction of an organization if "the senior officers, collectively, depart markedly from the standard of care that, in the circumstances, could reasonably be expected to prevent a representative of the organization from being a party to the offence." Even if the required criminal negligence cannot be located in one senior officer, it may be found in the collective fault of the senior officers, including the board of directors, the chief executive, and those who play an important role in establishing corporate policies or managing an important aspect of the organization's activities. Thus, in a case where no one at a mine is responsible for safety, the required level of criminal negligence might be found in the collective conduct of the senior officers of the mining company.

Corporate liability for criminal offences of negligence may in practice blur with corporate liability for strict liability regulatory offences as discussed above. Both are offences based on negligence in allowing a prohibited act to occur. The differences, however, are that criminal offences under section 22.1 of the *Criminal Code* must be based on (1) a marked departure from the standard of care and (2) the Crown must prove beyond a reasonable doubt that senior officer(s) had this fault whereas it is the accused corporation that must demonstrate that it took all reasonable steps to prevent the prohibited act from occurring when the offence is a regulatory offence of strict liability or simple negligence.

e) Section 22.2 of the *Criminal Code* and Organizational Fault for Subjective Intent Offences

Section 22.2 applies to organizational liability for all criminal offences other than those based on negligence. In other words, it applies when the organization is charged with a subjective intent offence such as fraud, obscenity, or facilitating terrorism. Section 22.2 provides:

> In respect of an offence that requires the prosecution to prove fault
> — other than negligence — an organization is a party to the offence
> if, with the intent at least in part to benefit the organization, one of
> its senior officers

a) acting within the scope of their authority, is a party to the offence;
b) having the mental state required to be a party to the offence and acting within the scope of their authority, directs the work of other representatives of the organization so that they do the act or make the omission specified in the offence; or
c) knowing that a representative of the organization is or is about to be a party to the offence, does not take all reasonable measures to stop them from being a party to the offence.

Section 22.2 contemplates subjective intent offences being committed by (1) senior officers acting on their own within the scope of their authority; (2) senior officers directing representatives so that they commit the offence; or (3) senior officers knowing that representatives are committing or will commit offences but failing to take all reasonable measures to stop them from doing so. Unlike section 22.1, it does not contemplate fault based on the collective or aggregate fault of multiple senior officers. In other words, one responsible senior officer must have the fault under section 22.2, which is then attributed to the organization.

i)   Senior Officers Being a Party to the Offence

The simplest form of organizational liability for a subjective intent offence is when the senior officer commits the offence. The only restrictions under section 22.2(a) are that the senior officer must (1) be acting within the scope of his or her authority and (2) have the intent at least in part to benefit the organization. The latter requirement codifies the holding in *Canadian Dredge & Dock*[100] that a corporation will not be held responsible if the senior officer acts totally in fraud of the corporation. Nevertheless, corporations can be held criminally responsible when they receive some benefits from the senior officer's activities, even though the senior officer is also defrauding the corporation.

Under section 22.2(a) the senior officer does not necessarily have to be the person who actually commits the offence. All that is required is that the senior officer be a party to the offence, which as discussed in Chapter 4 includes aiding and abetting under section 21(1)(b) and (c), common unlawful intent under section 21(2), and counselling the commission of an offence under section 22. Thus, the corporation could be liable for a subjective intent offence under section 22.2(a) on the basis that its senior officer intentionally assisted or counselled a representative of the corporation to commit the offence. Indeed, sections 21(2) and 22(2) suggest that in some circumstances a senior officer may be a party to a subjective intent offence on the basis that he or she

---

100 *Canadian Dredge & Dock*, above note 35.

ought to have known that the offence would be committed as a result of the carrying out of an unlawful purpose or as a result of intentionally counselling the commission of another offence.

ii) Senior Officers Directing Representatives to Commit the Offence

Section 22.2(b) is a complex provision that makes the corporation liable when a senior officer directs other representatives of the corporation so that they commit an offence. As under section 22.2(a), the senior officer must be acting within the scope of his or her authority. The senior officer must also be "directing the work of other representatives of the organization so that they do the act or make the omission specified in the offence." This requires not only that the senior officer directs the work of representatives, but also directs them in such a manner that they commit the prohibited act or omission. The wording of this provision, as well as the requirement that the senior officer must also have "the mental state required to be party to an offence," suggests that the reference to directing the work of representatives so that they commit the *actus reus* of the offence is a broader concept than counselling the commission of the offence. Indeed, a senior officer who intentionally and successfully counselled the commission of the offence under section 22 would be a party to the offence counselled and would already be covered by section 22.2(a), discussed above.

In addition to the direction requirement, the senior officer must "have the mental state required to be a party to the offence." As with section 22.2(a) discussed above, this incorporates the party provisions of sections 21 and 22 of the *Criminal Code* into the new corporate criminal liability provisions. Section 21(1)(b) and (c) make a senior officer liable if he or she intentionally and knowingly assists in the commission of a crime. The fact that the senior officer may have been motivated by a desire to save his or her job will not negate this fault element. Section 21(2) extends liability to offences that the senior officer either knew or ought to have known would be a probable consequence of carrying out a common unlawful purpose that was intentionally formed with at least one other person. Thus, if a senior officer intentionally forms an unlawful purpose to commit a fraud with another person, the corporation will also be liable for other offences that the senior officer either knew or ought to have known would be committed in carrying out that unlawful purpose. A senior officer would have the mental state required under section 22(1) if he or she counselled another person to commit an offence that is then in fact committed. Section 22(2) extends liability to include every offence that the senior officer would have known or ought to have known would have been carried out as a likely consequence of the counselling.

Both sections 21(2) and 22(2) could be applied to make an organization liable for a subjective intent criminal offence even though its senior officer only had objective fault in relation to that particular offence. In other words, the corporation could be liable if its senior officer, having formed a common unlawful purpose or having counselled the commission of an offence, ought to have known that some further offence would be committed. Any illogic or unfairness in this state of affairs is the fault of the party provisions incorporated as an important part of the new organizational liability provision of section 22.2 and have only been partially mitigated by cases such as *Logan*[101] that hold that the objective arm of section 21(2) should not be applied for offences such as murder and attempted murder that constitutionally require subjective fault.

iii) Senior Officers Failing to Prevent Representatives from Committing the Offence

The organization's liability for subjective intent offence is further extended by section 22.2(c), which applies when a senior officer knows that a representative of the organization is or is about to be a party to the offence but fails "to take all reasonable measures" to stop the representative[102] from being a party to the offence. This section requires subjective fault in the form of guilty knowledge by the senior officer about the commission of an offence. As discussed in Chapter 5, knowledge is a fairly high form of subjective knowledge and does not encompass recklessness or wilful blindness.

Section 22.2(c) also requires objective fault by the senior officer in the form of a failure to take all reasonable steps to stop the commission of the offence. The requirement of liability for a failure to take all reasonable steps is one usually associated with regulatory offences as opposed to criminal offences of subjective fault.[103] Indeed, this requirement is quite close to the due diligence requirement for strict liability offences and courts may well look to the multiple factors that are

---

101 *R v Logan* (1990), 58 CCC (3d) 391 (SCC). See Chapter 4, Section F.

102 The section at first refers to "a representative" but later uses the plural "them" in reference to the representative. This is confusing but fails to clearly introduce the novel concept of aggregate liability found in s 22.1, which applies to criminal offences of negligence.

103 But see s 150.1(4), requiring an accused to have taken "all reasonable steps" to ascertain the age of a complainant under the age of fourteen for the purpose of various sexual offences.

relevant in determining due diligence in order to determine whether a senior officer took all reasonable steps to prevent a representative from committing or continuing to commit the offence.

There are still some differences between section 22.2(c) as it applies to organizations charged with a criminal offence of subjective intent and the due diligence available to corporations charged with a regulatory offence. One difference is that an organization will not be liable under section 22.2(c) unless its senior officer also had guilty knowledge that a representative of the organization was committing or was about to commit the offence. A second difference is that the failure of the senior officer to take all reasonable steps must be proven beyond a reasonable doubt. Organizations are made liable under this section through a combination of subjective and objective fault elements,[104] both of which must be proven beyond a reasonable doubt.

CONCLUSION

Although the Supreme Court has disapproved of absolute liability offences since its decision in *Sault Ste Marie*[105] and declared them contrary to the principles of fundamental justice in the *BC Motor Vehicle Reference*,[106] it appears that such offences are constitutionally permissible so long as no imprisonment is imposed.[107] Absolute liability offences would also be permissible if only applied to corporations, which do not enjoy the rights to life, liberty, and security of the person protected under section 7 of the *Charter*. The Supreme Court has recently affirmed the common law presumption that regulatory offences should be assumed not to be absolute liability but rather to be strict liability offences that allow a defence of due diligence. The defence of due diligence requires an active attempt to prevent the commission of the prohibited act and not mere passivity.[108]

Strict liability offences have survived *Charter* challenge. The courts have not disapproved of the fault element of simple negligence, but they

---

104 See the discussion of s 273.2(b) in Chapter 5, Section D(4), for a somewhat similar combination of subjective and objective fault that requires a person arguing mistaken belief in consent to take "reasonable steps, in the circumstances known to the accused at the time, to ascertain that the complainant was consenting."

105 *Sault Ste Marie*, above note 4.

106 *BC Motor Vehicle Reference*, above note 20.

107 *Pontes*, above note 14.

108 *Lévis*, above note 17.

have noted that the mandatory presumption that the accused is negligent unless it establishes a defence of due diligence on a balance of probabilities does violate the presumption of innocence under section 11(d) of the *Charter*. The Court in *Wholesale Travel Group* did not accept that the less drastic alternative of an evidential as opposed to a persuasive burden would adequately advance the objectives of regulatory offences. It expressed concerns that regulatory objectives could be frustrated if accused were acquitted simply because there was a reasonable doubt whether they were negligent in allowing an *actus reus* to occur.

When a corporation is charged with a criminal offence, the required fault must now under new statutory provisions designed to facilitate the prosecution of corporations be attributed to senior officer(s) who either play an important role in establishing policy or who are responsible for managing an important aspect of its activities. If the criminal offence is based on negligence, the prohibited act under section 22.1 of the *Criminal Code* must be committed by representative(s) of the corporation (not only employees but also agents and contractors) acting within their scope of authority. No one individual need be responsible for the prohibited act, which can be committed in aggregate by multiple representatives. Either the responsible senior officer or the senior officers collectively must be at fault in the sense of a marked departure from the standard of care that could reasonably be expected to prevent the commission of the offence.

If the criminal offence requires subjective fault, a senior officer acting within the scope of his or her authority must be (1) a party to the offence; or (2) direct the work of the organization's representatives so that they commit the offence; or (3) fail to take all reasonable steps to stop the commission of the offence when he or she knows that representatives of the organization are committing an offence. Sections 22.1 and 22.2 of the *Criminal Code* are complex and largely untested provisions designed to facilitate the process of holding organizations responsible for criminal offences in a manner consistent with the requirements of objective and subjective fault found in the criminal law.

FURTHER READINGS

ARCHIBALD, T, K JULL, & K ROACH. "The Changed Face of Corporate Criminal Liability" (2004) 48 *Criminal Law Quarterly* 367.

———. *Corporate and Regulatory Liability: From Due Diligence to Risk Management* (Aurora, ON: Canada Law Book, 2004) (loose-leaf).

————. "Corporate Criminal Liability: Myriad Complexity in the Scope of Senior Officer" (2013) 60 *Criminal Law Quarterly* 386.

BRAITHWAITE, J. *Responsive Regulation and Restorative Justice* (Oxford: Oxford University Press, 2002).

COLVIN, E, & S ANAND. *Principles of Criminal Law*, 3d ed (Toronto: Thomson Carswell, 2007) ch 3 and 6.

EDWARDS, J, LLJ. Mens Rea *in Statutory Offences* (London: Stevens, 1955).

FISSE, B. "Corporate Criminal Responsibility" (1991) 15 *Criminal Law Journal* 166.

HANNA, D. "Corporate Criminal Liability" (1989) 31 *Criminal Law Quarterly* 452.

HARVARD LAW REVIEW ASSOCIATION. "Corporate Crime: Regulating Corporate Behavior through Criminal Sanctions" (1979) 92 *Harvard Law Review* 1227.

MACPHERSON, DL. "Extending Corporate Criminal Liability" (2004) 30 *Manitoba Law Journal* 253.

MANNING, M, & P SANKOFF. *Criminal Law*, 5th ed (Markham, ON: LexisNexis, 2015) ch 5 and 6.

ONTARIO LAW REFORM COMMISSION. *Report on Provincial Offences* (Toronto: Queen's Printer, 1992).

RUBY, C, & K JULL. "The *Charter* and Regulatory Offences: A Whole-Sale Revision" (1992) 14 *Criminal Reports* (4th) 226.

STUART, D. *Canadian Criminal Law: A Treatise*, 7th ed (Scarborough, ON: Thomson Carswell, 2014) ch 4 and 11.

STUESSER, L. "Convicting the Innocent Owner: Vicarious Liability under Highway Traffic Legislation" (1989) 67 *Criminal Reports* (3d) 316.

WELLS, C. *Corporations and Criminal Responsibility*, 2d ed (Oxford: Oxford University Press, 2001).

CHAPTER 7

INTOXICATION

Intoxication from alcohol or drugs may be a condition that prevents the Crown from proving that the accused had the fault element required for a particular offence (see Chapter 5). Some extreme forms of intoxication may even result in involuntary conduct that, as discussed in Chapter 3, is increasingly seen as inconsistent with proof of the prohibited act. Nevertheless, the intoxication defence has been influenced by policy considerations beyond those that relate to the fault element or the prohibited act of the particular offence. For these reasons, it will be examined here in a separate chapter.

Intoxication was historically considered an aggravating factor to a crime because it "was occasioned by [the accused's] own act and folly, and he might have avoided it."[1] In the nineteenth century, as greater emphasis was placed on subjective *mens rea*, courts became more concerned about the relevance of intoxication as a possible defence. The object was not to determine whether the accused was intoxicated, but whether intoxication, combined with any other factors, prevented the formation of the fault element required for the particular offence. At the same time, however, courts never completely abandoned the older idea that an intoxicated offender was not morally innocent, and they placed restrictions on the availability of the intoxication defence. Intoxication was admissible and could raise a reasonable doubt to the mental element for specific intent offences, which required a more

---

1   *Reniger v Fogossa* (1548), 75 ER 1 (Ex).

complex form of subjective fault, often an ulterior objective beyond the immediate act. It was not, however, admissible when the accused was charged with general intent offences, which required proof only of an intent to perform the immediate act or objective fault. In practice, this meant that intoxication could be a defence to more serious crimes such as murder and robbery, but not to less serious offences such as manslaughter and assault.

The distinction between general and specific intent offences has frequently been criticized. As examined in Chapter 5, there are different levels of *mens rea*, but fault elements are not usually classified as either general or specific intent. At best, the general/specific intent dichotomy serves as a rough and ready distinction between the various degrees of subjective *mens rea* and how they may be affected by the accused's intoxication.

The classification of a particular fault element as general or specific intent may be uncertain and has "proved formidable to those who have been schooled in criminal law, and daunting to those who have not."[2] In making this classification, courts should examine the complexity of the fault level for the particular offence. In cases of uncertainty, "logic, intuition, and policy" play a role. For example, the Court indicated that assaulting with intent to resist arrest is a specific intent offence that requires a complex *mens rea*. But in cases where evidence of intoxication creates a reasonable doubt about that particular fault element, the accused will often be convicted of the lesser included offence of assault, which has consistently been classified as a general intent offence. The same is true for the specific intent offence of murder and the general intent offence of manslaughter. The classification of intent as either general or specific remains a relevant and often decisive factor in the administration of the intoxication defence. Its continued relevance reveals concerns about whether voluntary intoxication by the accused should lead to a complete acquittal. As will be seen in this and the next two chapters, defences are often influenced by concerns about the ultimate disposition of the accused.

It would also be wrong to suggest that intoxication can never be a defence to a general intent offence in Canadian criminal law. The Supreme Court in the 1994 case of *R v Daviault*[3] controversially recognized a separate extreme intoxication defence that the accused must establish on a balance of probabilities and with expert evidence. Such an extreme intoxication defence would not simply raise a reasonable

---

2   *R v Tatton*, 2015 SCC 33 at para 31 [*Tatton*].
3   [1994] 3 SCR 63.

doubt about the accused's actual intent, as is the case with the ordinary intoxication defence that is available for offences classified as specific intent offences. Rather, the extreme intoxication defence would be inconsistent with the accused's capacity to have the minimal intent for offences classified as general intent offences and the accused's capacity to act in a voluntary manner, which has been recognized as a requirement for the commission of the prohibited act or *actus reus*. The Court held that the substitution of becoming voluntarily intoxicated for the fault and voluntariness of the general intent crime violated sections 7 and 11(d) of the *Charter* and could not be justified as a reasonable limit on the accused's rights. The extreme intoxication defence was controversial because it was recognized in a case where an accused was charged with the general intent crime of sexual assault. Although the Supreme Court accurately predicted that the extreme intoxication defence would be rare, it could result in an extremely intoxicated accused being acquitted of all criminal offences, even violent ones.

Within a year of the *Daviault* decision and even though intoxication has historically been a common law defence, Parliament enacted section 33.1–3 of the *Code* to deny an extreme intoxication defence whenever the accused is charged with an offence "that includes as an element an assault or any other interference or threat of interference by a person with the bodily integrity of another person."[4] This new provision follows the pre-*Daviault* caselaw deeming the fault of becoming voluntarily intoxicated as a sufficient and substituted form of fault even if the accused at the time of the commission of the prohibited act "lacked the basic intent or the voluntariness required" to commit the general intent violent offence such as manslaughter, sexual assault, or assault.

The constitutionality of section 33.1–3 still has not been definitely decided by the Supreme Court. It would seem that the substitution of the fault of voluntarily becoming extremely intoxicated for the fault and voluntariness of a general intent offence would still violate the accused's rights under sections 7 and 11(d) of the *Charter* unless the Court overrules *Daviault*. The fate of section 33.1–3 would then depend on whether it can be justified as a reasonable limit on the accused's rights. The restriction is designed to affirm responsibility for intoxicated violence and affirm the rights of those victimized by such violence. It denies the accused the benefit of the *Daviault* defence of extreme intoxication, but only with respect to general intent offences that involve an assault or interference or threatened interference with bodily

---

4   *Criminal Code,* RSC 1985, c C-46, s 33.1(3) [*Code*].

integrity. It does not apply to general intent property offences such as arson or mischief to property.

As a result of both judicial and Parliamentary decisions, there are a number of different intoxication defences making this area of the law especially complex. If an offence is classified as specific intent, intoxication can operate as a defence if it raises a reasonable doubt about the accused's intent. If, however, the offence is classified as general intent, only an extreme intoxication defence established by the accused on a balance of probabilities and with expert evidence is possible. Section 33.1–3 will, subject to a successful *Charter* challenge, deny the accused the benefit of the extreme intoxication defence but only when the charges involve an assault or other threat or invasion of bodily integrity. Finally, separate considerations apply in cases where the accused's intoxication is involuntary.

A. BEARD'S CASE

The genesis of the modern defence of intoxication is found in the House of Lords' 1920 decision in *DPP v Beard*.[5] In that case, the Court articulated the following propositions:

1) "[T]hat intoxication could be a ground for an insanity defence if it produced a disease of the mind."

2) "That evidence of drunkenness which renders the accused incapable of forming the specific intent essential to constitute the crime should be taken into consideration with the other facts proved in order to determine whether or not he had this intent."

3) "That evidence of drunkenness falling short of a proved incapacity in the accused to form the intent necessary to constitute the crime, and merely establishing that his mind was affected by drink so that he more readily gave way to some violent passion, does not rebut the presumption that a man intends the natural consequences of his acts."[6]

In the actual case, Beard had been drinking when he killed a woman in the course of a rape. Shortly after the killing, he was accepted into a trade union after answering "not unintelligently certain questions which were put to him." The House of Lords confirmed his conviction for constructive murder in the course of a rape by stating: "[D]runken-

---

5   [1920] AC 479 (HL) [*Beard*].
6   *Ibid* at 500–2.

ness in this case could be no defence unless it could be established that Beard at the time of committing the rape was so drunk that he was incapable of forming the intent to commit it, which was not in fact, and manifestly, having regard to the evidence, could not be contended."[7]

The first *Beard* proposition contemplates that in some cases intoxication could provide a basis for the mental disorder defence, but only if it produced a "disease of the mind" or what today is called a mental disorder.[8] The courts have been reluctant to classify voluntary intoxication as a mental disorder because of the temporary and voluntary nature of intoxication. The Supreme Court has held that a toxic psychosis produced by the consumption of the drug ecstasy was not a mental disorder even if it resulted in involuntary conduct. The Court refused to apply the mental disorder defence. It convicted the accused of the general intent offence of aggravated assault and applied the 1995 restrictions on the extreme intoxication defence but without deciding whether they violated sections 7 and 11(d) of the *Charter* or could be justified as reasonable limits on the accused's rights.[9] The accused had not brought a *Charter* challenge, but rather sought in vain to take advantage of the mental disorder defence.

B. THE DISTINCTION BETWEEN GENERAL AND SPECIFIC INTENT OFFENCES

Courts in England and Canada have taken the reference in *Beard* to "forming the specific intent essential to commit the crime" as drawing a distinction between crimes of specific intent and those of general intent. It is arguable, however, that the word "specific" was used in *Beard* only to refer to the particular crime, and not to a distinct category

---

7 *Ibid* at 504–5. Constructive or felony murder bases liability for murder on the commission of a serious underlying offence such as rape, whether or not the accused intended to kill the victim or knew that death was likely. If Beard's case arose today in Canada, he could not be charged with constructive murder. See *R v Vaillancourt* (1987), 39 CCC (3d) 118 (SCC), and *R v Martineau* (1990), 58 CCC (3d) 35 3 (SCC), discussed in Chapters 2 and 5. Evidence of intoxication would be relevant in determining not whether Beard would have the intent for sexual assault, but for murder. The focus today would be on intent, not capacity for intent. In other words, the question would be whether given the evidence of intoxication and any other factors, the prosecutor had established that Beard knew that his victim was likely to die.

8 *Code*, above note 4, s 2.

9 *R v Bouchard-Lebrun*, [2011] 3 SCR 575 [*Bouchard-Lebrun*], also discussed in Chapter 8, Section C(4).

of offences. No reference is made in *Beard* to "general intent" offences as a category of offences distinct from "specific intent" offences. Moreover, the relevance of intoxication to rape was considered even though that offence has subsequently been classified as a general intent offence. Nevertheless, *Beard* has been interpreted in England and Canada as establishing a distinction between crimes of specific and general intent, with intoxication traditionally being a defence only with respect to the former.

In *R v George*, the Supreme Court held that robbery was a specific intent offence to which drunkenness was relevant, but assault was a general intent offence to which evidence of intoxication was rarely, if ever, relevant. Justice Fauteux explained: "In considering the question of *mens rea*, a distinction is to be made between (i) intention as applied to acts considered in relation to their purposes and (ii) intention as applied to acts apart from their purposes."[10] Robbery fell into the first category because it required the application of force in order to facilitate the taking of property, while assault fell into the second category because it required only the minimal intent required for the application of force without consent. Justice Ritchie similarly distinguished

> between "intention" as applied to acts done to achieve an immediate end on the one hand and acts done with the specific and ulterior motive and intention of furthering or achieving an illegal object on the other hand. Illegal acts of the former kind are done "intentionally" in the sense that they are not done by accident or through honest mistake, but acts of the latter kind are the product of preconception and deliberate steps taken towards an illegal goal.[11]

In the result, the intoxicated accused was acquitted of robbery, but convicted of the included offence of assault.

The distinction between general and specific intent has been criticized as illogical and difficult to apply. The Supreme Court has recognized that the distinction is largely driven by policy concerns. In *R v Daviault*,[12] Sopinka J noted that specific intent offences were generally more serious offences requiring some ulterior intent, and that "failure to prove the added element will often result in conviction of a lesser offence for which the added element is not required. One example is the offence of assault to resist or prevent arrest which is a specific intent offence. Absent the intent to resist arrest, the accused would be con-

---

10   *R v George* (1960), 128 CCC 289 at 301 (SCC).
11   *Ibid* at 306.
12   (1994), 93 CCC (3d) 21 (SCC) [*Daviault*].

victed of assault *simpliciter*, a general intent offence."[13] The distinction between specific and general intent offences has often served the practical purpose of ensuring that even if the accused's voluntary intoxication prevents conviction for the specific intent offence, the accused will normally still be convicted of a less serious general intent offence. A classic example is when evidence of intoxication raises a reasonable doubt about the intent for murder, but the accused is then convicted of the general intent offence of manslaughter.

The Court revisited the specific/general intent distinction in *R v Tatton*.[14] Justice Moldaver explained that general intent crimes "do not require actual knowledge of certain circumstances or consequences, to the extent that such knowledge is the product of complex thought and reasoning processes. In each instance, the mental element is straightforward and requires little mental acuity."[15] He also explained that while specific intent offences may involve an intent to achieve an ulterior purpose, they may also involve other forms of complex thought and reasoning processes. For example, in murder, the accused must know that the victim will die, and in possession of stolen property, the accused must know that the property was stolen. Specific intent offences involve a "heightened mental element" in the form of an ulterior purpose or knowledge of certain consequences or circumstances where that knowledge is a product of "more complex thought and reasoning processes."[16]

Policy considerations will help resolve cases of uncertainty in classifying an offence as general or specific intent. The dominant policy consideration is whether intoxication is habitually associated with the crime as is the case with many violent and property offences. This factor pushes towards a classification of an offence as general intent. Other factors including whether there is a lesser included general intent offence and whether there is a heavy mandatory minimum sentence for the offence in question may also play a role and push the classification towards specific intent.[17]

The Court concluded that even without resort to policy considerations, arson under section 434 of the *Criminal Code* was a general intent offence because "damage by fire is typically obvious" and "no complex thought or reasoning process is required."[18] In the result, the Court

---

13   *Ibid* at 41 (in dissent, but not on this issue).
14   Above note 2.
15   *Ibid* at para 35.
16   *Ibid* at para 39.
17   *Ibid* at paras 40–45.
18   *Ibid* at paras 48–49. The case did not address other forms of arson. Arson for a fraudulent purpose under s 435 may be a specific intent offence because of its

ordered a new trial for a person who had been acquitted of arson on the basis of intoxication. The accused was an alcoholic who had been drinking heavily and had left bacon cooking on a stove while he drove to Tim Hortons to get a coffee. In the absence of an extreme intoxication defence, the accused would be convicted of the general and subjective intent offence of arson primarily on the basis of committing the criminal act while voluntarily intoxicated.

Murder, theft, robbery, breach of trust,[19] aiding and abetting a crime, counselling a crime,[20] and attempted crimes have all been held to be specific intent offences, on the basis that they require proof of an ulterior objective beyond the immediate act or a more complex thought process to identify the prohibited circumstances or consequences. Thus, intoxication is admissible and can raise a reasonable doubt about the mental element for these offences.

Manslaughter, assault, sexual assault, assault causing bodily harm, mischief, and arson, however, have all been classified as general intent offences on the basis that they require proof only of intent in relation to the prohibited act. In addition, crimes based on an objective fault element would also preclude considering the accused's intoxication as a defence. Recent developments, however, suggest that extreme intoxication may be a defence to general intent offences. To the extent that extreme intoxication negates the voluntariness of the accused's actions, it may also be a defence to crimes that require objective fault and even absolute liability offences.

C. THE INTOXICATION DEFENCE FOR SPECIFIC INTENT OFFENCES

Since *Beard*,[21] it has been possible for an accused to be acquitted of a specific intent offence where evidence of intoxication alone or in combination with other factors produced a reasonable doubt as to whether he or she had the intent required for the offence. The role of the intoxication defence in relation to specific intent offences has not been

---

more complex and ulterior intent. This indicates some of the complexity and uncertainty of dividing offences into specific and general intent offences.

19   *R v Upjohn*, 2018 ONSC 947.

20   But see *R v Vinet*, 2018 QCCA 334 at paras 66–67 where the Quebec Court of Appeal did not decide the issue while noting general statements in *Tatton* that violent and disorderly defences may tend to be classified as general intent crimes. The focus, however, should be on the particular intent and not the general nature of the crime.

21   *Beard*, above note 5.

as controversial as the possibility that extreme intoxication might be a defence to a general intent offence. The practical reason is that an accused acquitted of a specific intent offence because of intoxication will almost always be convicted of a lesser general intent offence. For example, evidence of intoxication could raise a reasonable doubt to the specific intent of murder, but would normally not be considered in determining whether the accused was guilty of the general intent offence of manslaughter. In *George*, the accused was acquitted of the specific intent offence of robbery because of intoxication, but was convicted of assault because his intoxication was not so extreme as to prevent the Crown from proving the minimal intent required for that general intent offence.

1) Intent Not Capacity to Commit the Offence

In *Beard*, the House of Lords referred to evidence of intoxication that would render the accused incapable of forming a specific intent. This seems to require the trier of fact to have a reasonable doubt about whether the accused was capable of forming an intent, whereas general *mens rea* principles would suggest that the actual intent, not the capacity for intent, should be the issue. Nevertheless, in a long line of cases, Canadian courts followed *Beard* and held that the issue was whether evidence of drunkenness raised a reasonable doubt as to the accused's capacity to form a specific intent.[22]

In *R v Robinson*,[23] the Supreme Court held that the *Beard* rules violated sections 7 and 11(d) of the *Charter* because they required the jury to convict even if it had a reasonable doubt about the accused's actual intent. In other words, the Court was concerned that an accused who was not so intoxicated as to lack the capacity to form the intent may nevertheless have not exercised that capacity and formed the specific intent. A conclusion that evidence of intoxication did not raise a reasonable doubt as to the accused's capacity to form the specific intent did not lead inexorably to the conclusion that the Crown had proven beyond a reasonable doubt that the accused had actually exercised that capacity and had the required intent. The *Beard* rule concerning capacity could not be justified under section 1 because social protection could be achieved without casting the net of liability so far as to convict all those who had the capacity to form the requisite intent, but who may nevertheless not have had the intent required for a murder conviction. The Court was

22   *R v MacAskill* (1931), 55 CCC 81 at 84 (SCC); *R v Leary* (1977), 33 CCC (2d) 473 at 482–84 (SCC) [*Leary*]; *R v Bernard* (1988), 45 CCC (3d) 1 at 26 [*Bernard*].
23   (1996), 105 CCC (3d) 97 (SCC) [*Robinson*].

less deferential to judge-made common law rules that infringed *Charter* rights than to legislation enacted by Parliament. The Court also noted that the capacity rule was not necessary because the intent rule only reduced the accused's culpability from murder to manslaughter.

After *Robinson*, judges could still instruct the jury to consider the accused's capacity to form the intent if evidence, such as expert evidence, was directed to the issue of capacity. Nevertheless, a judge who instructs on capacity has an onerous obligation to make sure that at the end of the day the jury understands that the ultimate issue is whether evidence of intoxication raised a reasonable doubt as to the accused's actual intent and not his or her capacity to form the intent. A new trial will be ordered if the jury is misled into thinking that the accused's capacity to form that intent was the ultimate issue because this could result in convicting an accused even though there might still be a reasonable doubt as to his or her actual intent.[24] In 2007, however, a majority of the Court in *R v Daley* indicated that henceforth judges should instruct the jury to consider only whether intoxication raises a reasonable doubt with respect to actual intent and that they should not make reference to capacity so as not to confuse the jury.[25] This approach has simplified charges to the jury and is consistent with basic *mens rea* principles in focusing on the issue of intent.

2) Threshold Air of Reality Tests

In cases involving either general or specific intent offences, the accused must establish that there is an air of reality that justifies instructing the trier of fact about the intoxication defence. Threshold air of reality tests are designed to ensure that the jury is not instructed about irrelevant defences. They have not generally been seen as presenting presumption of innocence problems. Nevertheless, they can keep the jury from considering defences such as mistake of fact, intoxication, and necessity and they may play an important role in the criminal trial.

With respect to murder, the threshold test is whether "the evidence of drunkenness was sufficient to permit a reasonable inference that the accused may not in fact have foreseen that his act of firing the gun at the deceased would cause her death."[26] This threshold was not satisfied

---

24 See, for example, *R v McMaster* (1996), 105 CCC (3d) 193 (SCC).

25 *R v Daley*, [2007] 3 SCR 523 at para 102 [*Daley*]. Four judges dissented on the facts of the case and held that the trial judge should have done more to instruct the jury about the evidence of intoxication and the *mens rea* requirements.

26 *R v Lemky* (1996), 105 CCC (3d) 137 at 144 (SCC). In *Robinson*, above note 23 at 116, the Court articulated the threshold standard in a seemingly less restric-

in the murder case of *Lemky*, where an accused with a blood alcohol level slightly above the legal limit for driving was capable before and after the shooting of being aware of the consequences of his actions. With respect to specific intent offences the evidential threshold is focused on actual intent and not capacity.

With respect to the *Daviault* test of extreme intoxication to a general intent offence, the threshold air of reality issue should be the capacity to have the minimal intent associated with general intent offences as opposed to the actual intent. A judge at the stage of applying the air of reality test should focus on whether a properly instructed jury could reasonably acquit on the evidence. The judge should not determine the credibility of the evidence or keep the defence from the jury on the basis that the accused may not be able to establish the defence on a balance of probabilities.[27]

D. LIABILITY FOR THE INTOXICATED COMMISSION OF GENERAL INTENT OFFENCES

In *R v Leary*,[28] the Supreme Court followed *R v Majewski*[29] and decided that intoxication could not be a defence to a general intent offence. In *Majewski*, Lord Elywn-Jones relied on the controversial proposition that the accused, by becoming voluntarily intoxicated, had committed the *mens rea* for a general intent offence such as assault causing bodily harm. He stated:

> If a man of his own volition takes a substance which causes him to cast off the restraints of reason and conscience, no wrong is done to him by holding him answerable criminally for any injury he may do while in that condition. His course of conduct in reducing himself by drugs and drink to that condition in my view supplies the evidence of *mens rea*, of guilty mind certainly sufficient for crimes of basic

---

tive manner by stating that the trial judge must instruct the jury concerning intoxication if "the effect of the intoxication was such that its effect *might* have impaired the accused's foresight of consequences sufficient to raise a reasonable doubt" [emphasis in original].

27 See *R v Fontaine*, 2004 SCC 27.
28 *Leary*, above note 22.
29 (1976), 62 Cr App Rep 262 (HL).

intent. It is a reckless course of conduct and recklessness is enough to constitute the necessary *mens rea* in assault cases.[30]

Under this approach, the recklessness of becoming drunk is deemed to be sufficient to supply the fault element for the commission of the particular general intent offence. This creates an exception to the general proposition, examined in Chapter 3, that the fault element should occur at the same time as the *actus reus*. The fault element would be formed not when the assault took place, but before that time while the accused was becoming intoxicated. At the time the assault was committed, the accused would have no fault element. It also creates an exception to the general proposition, examined in Chapter 5, that the fault element should be directed towards the *actus reus*. When applied to a case such as *Tatton*,[31] it would suggest that the accused could be convicted of a general intent offence of arson on the basis of the fault of becoming voluntarily intoxicated even if there was otherwise a reasonable doubt about the subjective intent of arson.

In a strong dissent in *Leary*,[32] Dickson J argued that the recklessness in becoming intoxicated was not legally sufficient because "recklessness in a legal sense imports foresight. Recklessness cannot exist in the air; it must have reference to the consequences of a particular act," namely, the crime charged. He argued that the dichotomy between general and specific intent was irrational and that evidence of drunkenness should be left to the jury regardless of the offence charged. "In the case of an intoxicated or drugged accused, the jury may have little difficulty in drawing an inference of intent or recklessness in the relevant sense, but that remains an issue of fact for the jury to determine in each particular case."[33] New Zealand and Australia follow this approach and allow evidence of intoxication to be considered by the trier of fact in all cases and without regard to the classification of offences as general or specific intent.[34]

---

30   *Ibid* at 270.
31   Above note 2.
32   *Leary*, above note 22 at 494.
33   *Ibid* at 495.
34   *R v Kamipeli*, [1975] 2 NZLR 610 (CA); *R v O'Connor* (1980), 54 ALJR 349 (HC).

E. EXTREME INTOXICATION AND GENERAL INTENT OFFENCES

1) The Development of the *Daviault* Defence

The rule in *Leary* that holds that becoming intoxicated could supply the *mens rea* for general intent offences was vulnerable under the *Charter* because (1) it departed from the requirement that the *mens rea* occur at the same time as the *actus reus*; (2) it transferred the general or at-large fault of becoming intoxicated for the fault of the particular general intent offence; and (3) it would allow the conviction of a person who was so severely intoxicated that he or she acted involuntarily or without the intent required for the particular general intent offence.

The Supreme Court first considered the constitutionality of the *Leary* rule in *Bernard*.[35] The Court was deeply divided. Two judges would have upheld the *Leary* rule in its full vigour so that even if the accused "was so intoxicated as to raise doubts as to the voluntary nature of his conduct," the Crown could demonstrate the necessary *mens rea* from the fact of voluntary self-intoxication. Justice McIntyre argued for the traditional position that proof of the accused's "voluntary drunkenness can be proof of his guilty mind"[36] even though this fault would not necessarily be present when the prohibited act was committed or have been directed at the prohibited act.

At the other end of the spectrum, Dickson CJ, with the concurrence of Lamer and La Forest JJ, not only adhered to his strong dissent in *Leary*, but argued that the *Leary* rule violated sections 7 and 11(d) of the *Charter* by substituting the intent of becoming intoxicated for the intent of the particular general intent offence. He concluded:

> The effect of the majority holding in *Leary* is to impose a form of absolute liability on intoxicated offenders, which is entirely inconsistent with the basic requirement for a blameworthy state of mind as a prerequisite to the imposition of the penalty of imprisonment [under section 7 of the *Charter*] . . . .
>
> The majority holding in *Leary* also runs counter to the s. 11(d) right to be presumed innocent until proven guilty. With respect to crimes of general intent, guilty intent is in effect presumed upon proof of the fact of intoxication. Moreover, the presumption of guilt created by the *Leary* rule is irrebuttable.[37]

---

35   *Bernard*, above note 22.

36   *Ibid* at 36.

37   *Ibid* at 16–17.

The exclusion of evidence of intoxication converted general intent offences to absolute liability offences by not considering a potentially crucial factor in determining whether the accused had the required *mens rea*. In addition, the presumption of innocence was violated when the fault of becoming intoxicated was substituted for the fault of the particular general intent offence. Chief Justice Dickson also concluded that the *Leary* rule could not be justified under section 1 of the *Charter* because it would require people to be convicted for unintended or unforeseen crimes. He argued: "[I]t has not been demonstrated that risk of imprisonment of a few innocent persons is required to attain the goal of protecting the public from drunken offenders."[38] If public protection required special measures to deal with intoxicated offenders, that should be done by Parliament, not the courts. This could be done through the creation of an offence that punished the accused for being drunk and dangerous.

Justice Wilson fashioned a novel compromise position that was later to command support from a majority of the Court in *Daviault*. Unlike Dickson CJ, she retained the distinction between general and specific intent offences. In most cases, the minimal intent required for the commission of a general intent offence could be inferred from the commission of the act. In *Bernard*, for example, the accused was guilty of the general intent offence of sexual assault causing bodily harm because it was clear that he engaged in "intentional and voluntary, as opposed to accidental or involuntary, application of force."[39] Justice Wilson also disagreed with Dickson CJ that the *Leary* rule violated section 7 of the *Charter*. An accused who voluntarily became so intoxicated as not to have the minimal awareness required for a general intent offence was not a morally innocent person who should be protected from conviction under section 7 of the *Charter*.[40] However, the "real concern" for Wilson J arose under section 11(d), because the fault of becoming drunk would under the *Leary* rule be substituted for the fault of the particular offence charged. Justice Wilson elaborated:

---

38   *Ibid* at 18.

39   She concluded: "There is no evidence that we are dealing here with extreme intoxication, verging on insanity or automatism, and as such capable of negating the inference that the minimal intent to apply force was present . . . . The evidence of intoxication in this case was simply not capable of raising a reasonable doubt as to the existence of the minimal intent required." *Ibid* at 39–40.

40   Such persons would nevertheless have rights under ss 7 and 12 of the *Canadian Charter of Rights and Freedoms*, Part I of the *Constitution Act, 1982*, being Schedule B to the *Canada Act 1982* (UK), 1982, c 11 [*Charter*] "to be protected against punishment that is disproportionate to their crime and degree of culpability." *Bernard*, above note 22 at 43–44.

While this court has recognized that in some cases proof of an essential element of a criminal offence can be replaced by proof of a different element, it has placed stringent limitations on when this can happen . . . . In my tentative view, it is unlikely that in those cases in which it is necessary to resort to self-induced intoxication as the substituted element for the minimal intent, proof of the substituted element will "inexorably" lead to the conclusion that the essential element of the minimal intent existed at the time the criminal act was committed.[41]

Justice Wilson would apply the basic *Leary* rule in a more flexible fashion that would allow "evidence of extreme intoxication involving an absence of awareness akin to a state of insanity or automatism" to go to the trier of fact in "those rare cases in which the intoxication is extreme enough to raise doubts as to the existence of the minimal intent which characterizes conscious and volitional conduct."[42]

Six years later, Wilson J's approach, with some variations, commanded support from a majority of the Supreme Court. In *Daviault*,[43] the Supreme Court decided that extreme intoxication could in rare cases be a defence to general intent offences such as assault or sexual assault. In such cases, the minimal intent required for a general intent offence could not be inferred from the commission of the prohibited act because "the very voluntariness or consciousness of that act may be put in question by the extreme intoxication of the accused."[44] The focus in *Daviault* was on extreme intoxication that negated the accused's capacity for voluntary conduct and the minimal *mens rea* necessary for a general intent offence as opposed to evidence of intoxication that could raise a reasonable doubt about the more complex mental processes required in specific intent offences. Moreover, the application of the *Leary* and *Majewski* rules would violate both sections 7 and 11(d) of the *Charter* by substituting the intent of becoming intoxicated for the intent of the offence. Justice Cory concluded:

The consumption of alcohol simply cannot lead inexorably to the conclusion that the accused possessed the requisite mental element to commit a sexual assault, or any other crime. Rather, the substituted *mens rea* rule has the effect of eliminating the minimal mental element required for sexual assault. Furthermore, *mens rea* for a crime is so

41 *Ibid* at 44.
42 *Ibid* at 42–43.
43 *Daviault*, above note 12.
44 *Ibid* at 58.

well recognized that to eliminate that mental element, an integral part
of the crime, would be to deprive an accused of fundamental justice.[45]

Not considering evidence of intoxication in cases of extreme intoxication could lead to conviction without proof that the accused had the
mens rea required for the general intent offence. Whatever fault element
could be inferred from becoming intoxicated did not prove beyond a
reasonable doubt that the accused had the fault element for a general
intent offence, in this case, sexual assault.

In *Daviault*, the Supreme Court purported to adopt Wilson J's position in *Bernard*, but the Court's reasoning differed in two respects. First,
the Court held that the *Leary* rule violated not only section 11(d), but
also section 7 of the *Charter*. In contrast, Wilson J suggested in *Bernard*
that a person who voluntarily became so intoxicated that he or she did
not have the minimal intent necessary to commit a general intent offence was not a morally innocent person protected from punishment
under section 7 of the *Charter*.[46] This is not a doctrinal quibble given
that the courts have been much more willing to uphold violations of
section 11(d) under section 1 than violations of section 7 of the *Charter*.[47]

Second, the Court in *Daviault* required an accused to prove extreme
intoxication as a defence to a general intent crime on a balance of probabilities, whereas Wilson J would have allowed such evidence to rebut
the Crown's usual duty to prove the fault element beyond a reasonable
doubt. Justice Cory explained that the burden on the accused to prove
extreme intoxication violated the presumption of innocence in section
11(d), but was justified because "it is only the accused who can give
evidence as to the amount of alcohol consumed and its effect upon him.
Expert evidence would be required to confirm that the accused was
probably in a state akin to automatism or insanity as a result of his
drinking."[48] Because of concerns about social protection, the Supreme
Court violated the presumption of innocence in its own development
of the common law. As will be seen in Chapter 8, an accused wishing
to take advantage of the mental disorder or automatism defences must
also prove the defence on a balance of probabilities. At the same time,
the reversal of the burden can be criticized as unprincipled. In countries
such as Australia and New Zealand, which have abandoned the specific
and general intent distinction, the accused has no burden to establish

---

45   *Ibid* at 60.
46   Justice Wilson, however, contemplated that such a person would be protected
     from disproportionate punishment under both s 7 and s 12 of the *Charter*, above
     note 40.
47   See Chapter 2, Section B(3)(g).
48   *Daviault*, above note 12.

the defence of intoxication and will be acquitted whenever the evidence of intoxication raises a reasonable doubt about the intent of the offence charged. There is no compelling evidence that social protection has been sacrificed by maintaining the presumption of innocence.

The defence contemplated in *Daviault* applies only if the accused is extremely intoxicated. Justice Cory argued:

> those who are a "little" drunk can readily form the requisite mental element to commit the offence. The alcohol-induced relaxation of both inhibitions and socially acceptable behaviour has never been accepted as a factor or excuse in determining whether the accused possessed the requisite *mens rea*. Given the minimal nature of the mental element required for crimes of general intent, even those who are significantly drunk will usually be able to form the requisite *mens rea* and will be found to have acted voluntarily . . . .
>
> It is obvious that it will only be on rare occasions that evidence of such an extreme state of intoxication can be advanced and perhaps only on still rarer occasions is it likely to be successful.[49]

Despite evidence suggesting that Daviault, a chronic alcoholic, had a blood alcohol level that would kill most people, and the trial judge's acquittal, the Court sent the case back for a new trial to require the accused to establish the defence of extreme intoxication on a balance of probabilities.

Daviault dealt with the crime of sexual assault, which, at the time, required subjective *mens rea*.[50] Other general intent offences, notably unlawful act manslaughter, require only proof of an objective fault element. An extremely intoxicated accused could still have objective fault if his or her conduct demonstrated a marked and substantial departure

---

49 *Ibid* at 67–68.

50 Subsequent amendments to sexual assault have introduced objective components in relation to the defence of mistake of fact and have affirmed that self-induced intoxication should not be considered in relation to that defence. *Code*, above note 4, s 273.2(b). In his dissent, Sopinka J concluded

> sexual assault does not fall into the category of offences for which either the stigma or the available penalties demand as a constitutional requirement subjective intent to commit the *actus reus* . . . . I cannot see how the stigma and punishment associated with the offence of sexual assault are disproportionate to the moral blameworthiness of a person like the appellant who commits the offence after voluntarily becoming so intoxicated as to be incapable of knowing what he is doing. The fact that the *Leary* rules permit an individual to be convicted despite the absence of symmetry between the *actus reus* and the mental element of blameworthiness does not violate a principle of fundamental justice.

Daviault, above note 12 at 37–38.

from what a reasonable person would have done in the circumstances. If, however, the extreme intoxication negates the voluntariness required for the *actus reus*, the accused may have a defence because he or she did not consciously and voluntarily commit the criminal act. In *Daviault*, Cory J indicated that when extreme intoxication produced a state akin to automatism it would "render an accused incapable of either performing a willed act or of forming the minimal intent required for a general intent offence." In their concurrences, both Lamer CJ and La Forest J indicated that such extreme intoxication would also raise a reasonable doubt as to the commission of the *actus reus*.[51]

Daviault raises the possibility that extreme intoxication would be a defence not only to general intent offences but to absolute or strict liability offences. The extreme intoxication contemplated under *Daviault* may negate the voluntariness that is increasingly seen as part of the *actus reus*.[52] Justice Cory recognized that "the mental aspect involved in willed or voluntary conduct may overlap to some extent in both the concept of *mens rea* and *actus reus*."[53] In their concurrences, both Lamer CJ and La Forest J stated that they preferred to characterize the minimal mental element of general intent offences "as relating more to the *actus reus* than the *mens rea*, so that the defence [of extreme intoxication akin to automatism] clearly be available in strict liability offences."[54] In such cases, it would not matter that the accused could not prove a defence of due diligence because of his or her negligence in becoming drunk, since the *actus reus* necessary for conviction would not be present. The accused would still bear the burden of proving the defence of extreme intoxication on a balance of probabilities, even though extreme intoxication might prevent the Crown from proving the commission of the *actus reus* beyond a reasonable doubt.

Daviault did not abolish the much-criticized distinction between general and specific intent offences, and it introduced two distinct intoxication defences with different burdens of proof. When an accused is charged with a specific intent offence such as murder, the ordin-

---

51   In Australia, extreme intoxication can be a defence to manslaughter if it indicates that the accused's acts were not voluntary. *R v Martin* (1984), 51 ALR 540 (HC). Presumably, a similar defence would apply in Canada after *Daviault*, above note 12, albeit one that requires the accused to prove on a balance of probabilities that the unlawful act for the manslaughter was not voluntary because of extreme intoxication.

52   See Chapter 3, Section C.

53   *Daviault*, above note 12 at 49.

54   *Ibid* at 25. The Chief Justice's reasoning would also seem to apply to absolute liability offences to the extent that they survive *Charter* scrutiny.

ary intoxication defence will apply if it raises a reasonable doubt about whether the accused had the required intent. In many cases, however, the accused would still have to face a charge on a general intent offence such as manslaughter or assault. With respect to general intent offences, evidence of intoxication will be relevant only in rare cases supported by expert evidence. The accused must prove on a balance of probabilities that he or she was so extremely intoxicated as to be incapable of having the minimal intent required for a general intent offence. An accused with the extreme intoxication defence may, however, not be convicted of any offences, because there are generally no lesser included offences to convict a person acquitted of a general intent offence.[55] For example, while a person acquitted because of intoxication of the specific intent offence of murder will often be convicted of manslaughter, a person acquitted of manslaughter, assault, or sexual assault because of extreme intoxication will often not be guilty of any lesser crime.

2) The Legislative Response to *Daviault*: Section 33.1

Although the Supreme Court believed the *Daviault* defence would apply only in rare cases, it recognized that Parliament might wish to respond to the social danger of an acquittal of a severely intoxicated accused who committed a general intent offence. The Court indicated that "it is always open to Parliament to fashion a remedy which would make it a crime to commit a prohibited act while drunk."[56] There are many ways that such legislation could be formulated. Parliament could have provided a new offence of being "drunk and dangerous," committing harm while extremely intoxicated, or committing a specific wrongful act while extremely intoxicated. All these options would mean that an extremely intoxicated person who did not have the minimal intent to commit a general intent offence would be acquitted of that offence, but convicted of a new offence that contained intoxication as an essential element. Such offences have long been proposed as a means to ensure public safety should the courts abolish the common law distinction

---

55   One exception may be offences such as impaired driving, which have intoxi-
      cation as an essential element. See *R v Penno* (1990), 59 CCC (3d) 344 (SCC)
      [*Penno*], discussed below at note 57. On the other hand, it could be argued that
      an accused should still have a *Daviault* defence, because the extreme intoxica-
      tion prevents the voluntary commission of even the *actus reus* required for
      intoxication-based offences. This is also suggested by the Court's recognition
      that involuntary intoxication may be a defence to impaired driving. See *R v King*
      (1962), 133 CCC 1 (SCC) [*King*].
56   *Daviault*, above note 12 at 68.

between specific and general intent offences, and allow evidence of intoxication to go to the jury in all cases. An offence that included intoxication as an element would undoubtedly be held consistent with the *Charter*. In *R v Penno*,[57] the Supreme Court rejected the notion that intoxication could be a defence to a crime of intoxicated driving and it has in several subsequent cases indicated that the denial of a defence that would be at odds with the very mischief that the offence seeks to prohibit would not violate the *Charter*.[58]

Another alternative would be to treat those with a *Daviault* defence in the same manner as a mentally disordered offender. They would then be found not criminally responsible but be subject to further detention and treatment if they are a significant danger to the public. The House of Lords in *Beard* seemed to contemplate that drunkenness could produce a state of insanity, but Canadian courts have been reluctant to hold that self-induced intoxication and other transitory states should qualify for the insanity or mental disorder defence.[59] In his dissent in *Daviault*, Sopinka J explicitly rejected this mental disorder option and argued that those who voluntarily become extremely intoxicated "deserve to be punished for their crimes" because their condition was self-induced and avoidable.[60]

In any event, Parliament did not respond to *Daviault* through the creation of a new intoxication-based offence or by creating a treatment disposition. Rather, it amended the *Criminal Code* so that those with a *Daviault* defence will be convicted of the same violent general intent offences that they would have been convicted of before the Court's decision.[61] Section 33.1(1) and (2) of the *Criminal Code* now contemplates that it will not be a defence that the accused "by reason of self-induced intoxication, lacked the general intent or the voluntariness required to commit the offence," because

---

57   Above note 55. Only Lamer CJ found that the denial of the intoxication defence might violate ss 7 and 11(d) of the *Charter* because it could convict a person on the basis of an involuntary act, but he held that such violations were justified under s 1 of the *Charter*. The rest of the judges found no *Charter* violation.

58   *R v Finta*, [1994] 1 SCR 701 at 865 [*Finta*]; *R v Ruzic*, 2001 SCC 24 at para 23 [*Ruzic*]; *Canadian Foundation for Children, Youth and the Law v Canada (AG)*, 2004 SCC 4 [*Canadian Foundation for Children*].

59   *R v Cooper* (1979), 51 CCC (2d) 129 (SCC); *Bouchard-Lebrun*, above note 9. See Chapter 8, Section C.

60   *Daviault*, above note 12 at 45.

61   Section 33.1(3) of the *Code*, above note 4, applies only to offences that include "as an element an assault or any other interference or threat of interference by a person with the bodily integrity of another person." An accused could still raise a *Daviault* defence and be acquitted of a general intent property crime such as mischief.

a person departs markedly from the standard of reasonable care generally recognized in Canadian society and is thereby criminally at fault where the person, while in a state of self-induced intoxication that renders the person unaware of, or incapable of consciously controlling, their behaviour, voluntarily or involuntarily interferes or threatens to interfere with the bodily integrity of another person.[62]

This confusing provision seems to deem that a person who has become so drunk as to engage in involuntary violence has departed markedly from an at-large standard of reasonable care "generally recognized in Canadian society." This marked departure from the standard of reasonable care is then substituted for the intent required to commit the particular general intent offence charged, whether it be assault or sexual assault.

Section 33.1–33.3 is a legislative reaffirmation of the controversial proposition in *Majewski* and *Leary* that if an accused charged with a general intent offence does not have the necessary *mens rea* at the time that the offence was committed, his actions and mind in voluntarily becoming so intoxicated can be substituted for the *mens rea* or the voluntary *actus reus* required for the particular offence. The only extra step is that the *Criminal Code* now deems that becoming so intoxicated is a marked departure from "the standard of reasonable care generally recognized in Canadian society." In a sense, what Dickson J originally criticized in *Leary* as "recklessness at large" has been codified for general intent offences, which involve assaults or other interference or threat of interference with bodily integrity. The following chart demonstrates the similarities between the *Leary* rule and section 33.1.

Leary Rule	
Becoming intoxicated "recklessness in the air"	⟶ fault for any general intent offence
Section 33.1	
Becoming intoxicated	⟶ fault for any general intent offence that includes an assault or threat of interference with bodily integrity (section 33.1(3))
Deemed to constitute marked departure from standard of reasonable care generally recognized in Canadian society (section 33.1(2))	

---

62   *Code, ibid*, s 33.1(2).

It is important to stress, however, that section 33.1 does not apply to general intent offences that do not involve an assault or threat of interference with bodily integrity. One example of such an offence would be arson.[63] In a case in which it applied section 33.1 but was not asked to rule on its constitutional validity, the Supreme Court observed that "the principles set out in *Daviault* still represent the state of the law in Canada, subject, of course, to the significant restriction set out in section 33.1 *Cr. C. Daviault* would still apply today, for example, to enable an accused charged with a property offence to plead extreme intoxication."[64]

3) The Constitutionality of Section 33.1

The Supreme Court has not ruled on the constitutionality of Parliament's "in your face" reply that takes away the *Daviault* defence for violent general intent offences. The Court has, however, applied section 33.1 to convict a person of the general intent offence of aggravated assault even though the person was acting in an involuntary manner and without intent as a result of a toxic psychosis produced by his voluntary consumption of a drug. The Court stressed that section 33.1 applies even to extreme intoxication and "toxic psychosis" produced by drugs that would render the accused incapable of knowing that his or her acts were wrong. The Court explained that section 33.1

> applies where three conditions are met: (1) the accused was intoxicated at the material time; (2) the intoxication was self-induced; and (3) the accused departed from the standard of reasonable care generally recognized in Canadian society by interfering or threatening to interfere with the bodily integrity of another person. Where these three things are proved, it is not a defence that the accused lacked the general intent or the voluntariness required to commit the offence.[65]

There is still no definitive ruling of the constitutionality of section 33.1 more than twenty years after its enactment. This may be a product of the rarity of the defence. The trend in lower courts has been to uphold section 33.1, usually under section 1 of the *Charter*, while concluding that its substitution of the fault of becoming extremely intoxicated for the fault and voluntariness of the general intent crime of violence violates sections 7 and 11(d) of the *Charter*. The fault of becoming ex-

---

63   *Tatton*, above note 2. A possible exception would be arson committed in disregard of human life under s 433.

64   *Bouchard-Lebrun*, above note 9 at para 35.

65   *Ibid* at para 89.

tremely intoxicated does not lead inexorably to the intent required for a particular general intent offence. Thus, the provision violates section 11(d) of the *Charter* by substituting the fault of becoming intoxicated for the fault of the particular general intent offence. The fact that Parliament has deemed such intoxication as departing from the standard of care generally recognized in Canadian society does not alter the fact that such fault is not the fault that Parliament has required for assault and sexual assault or any other general intent offences of violence covered by section 33.1.

Unless the Court reverts to Wilson J's position in *Daviault* that a person who commits a general intent offence while in an involuntary state produced by self-induced intoxication is not morally innocent, it would also seem that section 33.1 violates section 7 of the *Charter*. Even if a person who becomes extremely intoxicated is not morally innocent, a person who commits a crime in either a physically or morally involuntary manner would also be protected under section 7 of the *Charter*.[66] Section 33.1 clearly allows a person to be convicted of a crime even though he or she "lacked the general intent or the voluntariness required to commit the offence" and was "incapable of consciously controlling" the behaviour. The Court in both *Daviault* and a number of other nonintoxication cases has confirmed that it would violate the fundamental principles of justice to convict a person for involuntary actions.[67]

If section 33.1 violates sections 7 and 11(d) of the *Charter*, its fate will be decided under section 1 of the *Charter*. When enacting section 33.1, Parliament included a lengthy preamble emphasizing the legislative objective of responding to intoxicated violence. It expressed a particular concern that such "violence has a particularly disadvantaging impact on the equal participation of women and children in society and on the rights of women and children to security of the person and to equal protection and benefit of the law as guaranteed by sections 7, 15, and 28 of the *Canadian Charter of Rights and Freedoms*."[68] Such considerations may be used to urge the Court to view a *Charter* challenge to section 33.1 through a framework of reconciling competing rights, as was done

---

66   *Ruzic*, above note 58.

67   *R v Stone*, [1999] 2 SCR 290 at paras 155–58; *Ruzic*, above note 58 at paras 42–43.

68   The preamble generally speaks more to the importance of the objective rather than to the crucial issue of the proportionality of the means used to advance the objective. It does, however, refer to Parliament sharing with Canadians "the moral view that people who, while in a state of self-induced intoxication, violate the physical integrity of others are blameworthy in relation to their harmful conduct and should be held criminally accountable for it." See *An Act to Amend the Criminal Code (Self-Induced Intoxication)*, SC 1995, c 32 [*Code Amendment*].

when the Court upheld a law restricting access to the therapeutic records of complainants in sexual assault cases,[69] even though the legislation, like section 33.1, seemed at odds with a previous *Charter* decision of the Court.[70] Such a reconciliation of rights approaches runs the risk of undermining the obligation placed on the state under section 1 of the *Charter* to justify restrictions on rights and of ignoring the extent to which legislation may infringe one of the competing rights including, in this case, the basic principle that a person should not be convicted for involuntary conduct.

One judge who has held that section 33.1 was an unjustified violation of sections 7 and 11(d) of the *Charter* has been quite critical of the preamble, concluding that "victim's rights are, undoubtedly, a component of society's interests but society's interests must also include a system of law, governed by the principles of fundamental justice . . . . The section cannot accurately be said to address victim's section 7 rights; nor does it address any special needs of women or of children; rather, it sets out to protect victims against intoxicated automatons who act violently."[71] Section 33.1 does indeed apply to forms of violence committed by the accused and is not as specifically tailored to the interests of women and children as the legislation restricting access to confidential records in sexual offence cases.

A better approach than attempting to reconcile the rights of the accused and the victim may be to determine whether the infringements of sections 7 and 11(d) of the *Charter* in section 33.1 can be justified under section 1 of the *Charter*. A threshold issue will be whether a violation of section 7 of the *Charter* can ever be saved under section 1 of the *Charter*. The Court has suggested that a violation of section 7 could be justified only in "exceptional circumstances, such as the outbreak of war or a national emergency."[72] Such an approach runs the danger of undermining the structure of the *Charter* in contemplating that legislatures can place and then justify limits on all *Charter* rights.

The first step in a section 1 analysis would be to determine the objective of section 33.1 and whether it is important enough to justify limitations on the relevant *Charter* rights. Responding to alcohol-induced violence that could result in the complete acquittal of the accused is obviously a compelling objective that could justify the infringement of *Charter* rights. The fundamental question under section 1 of the *Char-*

---

69   *R v Mills*, [1999] 3 SCR 668.

70   *R v O'Connor*, [1995] 4 SCR 1411.

71   *R v Dunn* (1999), 28 CR (5th) 295 at 303 (Ont SCJ) [*Dunn*].

72   *Ruzic*, above note 58 at para 92.

ter will be whether section 33.1 is a proportionate response to these important objectives.

The Crown will argue that Parliament has adopted a more tailored rule than the previous common law rule. Thus, section 33.1 does not transfer the fault of becoming extremely intoxicated for the *mens rea* or voluntariness of all general intent offences as contemplated under the *Leary* rule, but only for crimes involving violence. Moreover, it will be argued that Parliament's policy decision not to respond to *Daviault* by introducing a new intoxication-based crime or treatment disposition deserves more judicial deference than the Court's previous common law rule in *Leary*.[73] It may be assumed that Parliament examined other options such as introducing new intoxication-based crimes but found them wanting for a variety of reasons, including their possible effects on police discretion and plea bargaining and the perceived need to label and punish a drunken sexual assaulter or assaulter as a person who nevertheless committed a sexual assault or an assault.[74] Parliament also heard evidence suggesting that alcohol cannot produce involuntary behaviour. This evidence, however, does not relate to other drugs. One judge has dismissed such scientific concerns: "[T]he issue is not whether an accused can scientifically prove [automatism]; the issue is whether it is constitutionally permissible to deny an accused even the opportunity to try to prove it just because his or her intoxication was self-induced. In my opinion, it is not."[75]

The accused will argue that Parliament rejected a number of more proportionate responses when it introduced new legislation that effectively reversed *Daviault* for general intent offences of violence. Section 33.1 follows the minority in *Daviault* and the *Leary* rule by substituting the fault of voluntarily becoming drunk for the fault of the general intent offence. It labels the drunken automaton as guilty of the same crime as the person who consciously committed an assault or sexual assault with the required *mens rea* at the time the offence was committed. It may thus run afoul of the principles that those who cause harm intentionally be

---

73   In *R v Swain* (1991), 63 CCC (3d) 481 (SCC), the Supreme Court indicated that "where a common law, judge-made rule is challenged under the *Charter*, there is no room for judicial deference" that can apply when Parliament as an elected body places limits on *Charter* rights.

74   The preamble, for example, states that Parliament "shares with Canadians the moral view that people who, while in a state of self-induced intoxication, violate the physical integrity of others are blameworthy in relation to their harmful conduct and should be held criminally accountable for it." See *Code Amendment*, above note 68.

75   *R v Brenton* (1999), 28 CR (5th) 308 at 331 (NWTSC), rev'd on other grounds, 2001 NWTCA 1 [*Brenton*].

punished more severely than those who cause harm unintentionally and that punishment be morally proportionate to the gravity of the offence.[76] There were other ways that Parliament could have advanced its interest in social protection that were more respectful of the accused's rights under sections 7 and 11(d) of the *Charter*. For example, a new intoxication-based crime would recognize that an accused with a *Daviault* defence did not have the voluntariness or *mens rea* required for an assault or a sexual assault even though he committed an act that caused harm and required punishment. It will also be argued that the harm caused by convicting an accused who acted involuntarily and without *mens rea* outweighs the benefits of section 33.1, especially with regard to the dubious proposition of deterring severely intoxicated people from violence and the rarity that an accused will be so extremely intoxicated as to be able to establish a *Daviault* defence on a balance of probabilities.

The constitutionality of section 33.1 has been considered in a few cases. In *Vickberg*,[77] a trial judge found that section 33.1 violated sections 7 and 11(d) of the *Charter* because it substituted "proof of voluntary intoxication for proof of the intent to commit an offence of general intent, most commonly assault." Nevertheless, these violations were held to be justified under section 1 of the *Charter* as a proportionate means to ensure accountability for violence related with intoxication.[78] In the actual case and as discussed in the next section, however, the trial judge did not apply section 33.1 to convict the accused on the basis that the accused's intoxication in taking an overdose of pills to treat an addiction was not voluntary. Should section 33.1 be held to be constitutional, it will be important that courts, as in *Vickberg*, expand the defence of involuntary intoxication to apply to unanticipated effects of self-induced drugs.[79]

In two recent cases, trial judges have held that section 33.1 violated section 7 of the *Charter* but was a justified response because the alternatives of an intoxication-based offence were problematic both with respect to penalties and the accountability of the offender. In one case, the judge stressed that Parliament acted on evidence that the notion

---

76 *R v Creighton* (1993), 83 CCC (3d) 346 (SCC). See Chapter 5, Section A(4).

77 *R v Vickberg* (1998), 16 CR (5th) 164 at 193 (BCSC) [*Vickberg*].

78 See also *R v Decaire*, [1998] OJ No 6339 (Gen Div), holding that s 33.1 of the *Code*, above note 4, is justified under s 1 of the *Charter* to deal with the harms of voluntary intoxication.

79 In *Brenton*, above note 75, the court held that unanticipated effects of marijuana consumption did not result in involuntary intoxication. The court, however, found that s 33.1 was an unjustified violation of the *Charter* and acquitted the accused on the basis of the *Daviault* defence.

of extreme intoxication producing involuntary conduct (as opposed to simply an alcoholic blackout and failure to remember) was a "dodgy scientific proposition."[80] In another case, the trial judge stressed that section 33.1 was a proportionate limit on section 7 rights because it "only relates to a limited number of offences, namely crimes of general intent including, as an element, an assault or any other interference or threat of interference by a person with the bodily integrity of another person. This leaves the defence of voluntary extreme intoxication akin to automatism or insanity available for all other general intent offences."[81] Section 33.1 has been held to be constitutional in another case on the basis that "the act of becoming voluntarily intoxicated to the extent of being incapable of controlling one's behaviour, constitutes criminal culpability sufficient to found criminal liability for offences committed against the bodily integrity of others . . . . The public outcry and the Parliamentary response to the *Daviault* case . . . strongly indicate that such a provision is not only consistent with the objectives of the *Charter* but is justifiable and essential in a free and democratic society."[82] The judge in that case also stated that a judge could use sentencing discretion to distinguish between "offences that were deliberately committed and those that were committed involuntarily because of self-induced intoxication."[83]

In some other cases, trial judges have found section 33.1 to be unconstitutional. In *Dunn*,[84] the judge stressed the importance of focusing on the objective of limiting the sections 7 and 11(d) rights as articulated in *Daviault*. The judge doubted that the objective of removing the *Daviault* defence for violent general intent offences was important enough to limit the accused's rights, but in any event concluded that the good of convicting such accused did not outweigh the harms of convicting a person who acted in an involuntary manner. "When an accused can be convicted without proof that he intended his actions or without proof that his actions were voluntary, then absolute liability has become a component of Canadian criminal justice, the presumption

---

80 *R v SN*, 2012 NUCJ 2 at para 114.

81 *R v Dow*, 2010 QCSC 4276 at para 144.

82 *R v BJT*, [2001] 4 WWR 741 at para 35 (Sask QB).

83 *Ibid* at para 36.

84 *Dunn*, above note 71. See also *R v Cedono* (2005), 195 CCC (3d) 468 at paras 35–36 (Ont Ct J), finding that s 33.1 was unconstitutional but that the *Daviault* defence did not apply because the accused had not established it on a balance of probabilities with expert evidence. In the result, the accused was convicted of sexual assault even though the judge would otherwise have had a reasonable doubt that the intoxicated accused had the necessary intent.

of innocence is eroded and the principles of fundamental justice are seriously compromised."[85] In *Brenton*,[86] section 33.1 was also struck down with the judge stressing that it "in effect re-enacts as legislation the very same common law rule that was held unconstitutional" in *Daviault*. By eliminating the need to prove either intent or voluntariness at the time the offence was committed, Parliament had created an absolute liability provision and ignored the more proportionate response of enacting a new offence based on the accused's intoxication. This decision was subsequently reversed on appeal on the basis that the constitutionality of section 33.1 did not arise on the facts of the case because the accused who had consumed marijuana had not established the *Daviault* defence of extreme intoxication on a balance of probabilities.[87] In *R v Jensen*,[88] the trial judge concluded that section 33.1 was an unjustified violation of sections 7 and 11(d). The accused's murder conviction was subsequently upheld with the Ontario Court of Appeal stating that it "may have been preferable for the trial judge to have explicitly instructed the jury that the level of intoxication required to negate the specific intent to kill could be less than intoxication akin to automatism"[89] that would be required to establish the *Daviault* defence with respect to manslaughter.

The Supreme Court will ultimately decide the fate of section 33.1. Although it is rare that violations of section 7 of the *Charter* will be held to be justified under section 1 of the *Charter*, it is possible that courts will defer to this strong articulation of legislative will. Section 33.1 is more narrowly tailored than the common law *Leary* rule because it is restricted to general intent crimes of violence. Although there were less drastic alternatives to section 33.1,[90] it is not clear that the creation of new intoxication-based crimes would be as effective as section 33.1 in achieving Parliament's objectives. In addition, unexpected forms of intoxication may be exempted from section 33.1 should they continue to be classified

---

85   *Dunn*, above note 71 at 307.

86   *Brenton*, above note 75.

87   *Ibid* (NWTCA).

88   [2000] OJ No 4870 (SCJ).

89   *R v Jensen* (2005), 195 CCC (3d) 14 at para 22 (Ont CA).

90   For arguments that Parliament's refusal to adopt this alternative makes s 33.1 disproportionate, see Gerry Ferguson, "The Intoxication Defence: Constitutionally Impaired and In Need of Rehabilitation" (2012) 57 *Supreme Court Law Review* (2d) 111 and Michelle Lawrence, "Voluntary Intoxication and the *Charter*: Revisiting the Constitutionality of Section 33.1" (2017) 40:3 *Manitoba Law Journal* 391. For contrary arguments, see Kelly Smith, "Section 33.1: Denial of the *Daviault* Defence Should be Held Constitutional" (2000) 28 *Criminal Reports* (5th) 350.

as involuntary intoxication that is not truly self-induced and as such not affected by section 33.1. Finally, the new legislation deserves a greater margin of deference than the previous judge-made common law rule because it was enacted by Parliament.

The Court may also hold that section 33.1 engages conflicting rights, even though such an approach would overestimate what the section actually accomplishes in convicting the rare accused who will be able to establish intoxicated automatism. The reconciliation of rights approach will also diminish the heavy burden that the Crown should bear in justifying the violation of the accused's sections 7 and 11(d) rights where the result is to convict someone who has acted in an involuntary manner and to base the conviction on the prior and unfocused fault of becoming extremely intoxicated. It is likely that the state can justify section 33.1–3 as a reasonable limit on the accused's *Charter* rights even without reliance on the conflicting rights approach, but provided that the Supreme Court is willing to allow a violation of section 7 to be justified under section 1 of the *Charter*.

F. INVOLUNTARY INTOXICATION

Under section 33.1 as well as the traditional approach taken in *Leary*, an accused may be convicted of a general intent offence on the basis of the fault or recklessness of voluntarily becoming intoxicated. This raises the question of what should the courts do if the accused becomes involuntarily intoxicated through no fault of his or her own? If the accused is to be held at fault for a general intent offence for voluntarily becoming intoxicated, it is only fair that he or she not be convicted if the intoxication was not the accused's fault.[91]

1) Involuntary Intoxication as an Independent Defence

The Supreme Court has long recognized that involuntary intoxication raises special issues. In *R v King*,[92] the Court indicated that an accused who had been impaired by a drug given to him by his dentist should not be convicted of impaired driving if he "became impaired through no act of his own will and could not reasonably be expected to have known that his ability was impaired or might thereafter become impaired when he

---

91   Courts in England have, however, convicted an accused despite his involuntary consumption of drugs. *R v Kingston*, [1994] 3 WLR 519 (HL).

92   Above note 55.

undertook to drive and drove his motor vehicle." It is also significant that the 1962 case of *King* seems to acknowledge that there could be a degree of intoxication that is inconsistent with the formation of the *mens rea* of a general intent offence such as impaired driving.

King is consistent with *Daviault* in suggesting that extreme intoxication can be a defence that may negate either the *mens rea* or the *actus reus* of a general intent offence. Evidence of either voluntary or involuntary intoxication could also be considered in determining whether the accused had the *mens rea* of a specific intent offence. At the same time, *King* places a restriction on the involuntary intoxication defence by requiring not simply that the accused not know that the substance might impair, but also that the accused could not reasonably know that the substance would impair.

King has been applied in a case in which the accused went into an automatic state and assaulted another person after overdosing on prescription pills that contained no specific warnings[93] or was surreptitiously given vodka in his drink.[94] It has been distinguished in cases in which the accused were convicted of impaired driving caused by overdoses of cold medication,[95] and by a deliberate overdose of prescription pills in an attempt to commit suicide. In that case, there was a conclusion that the accused's "reckless indifference" in taking forty-five antidepressant pills and fifteen sleeping pills deprived him of an involuntary intoxication defence.[96]

2) Involuntary Intoxication and Section 33.1

As discussed above, section 33.1 limits the *Daviault* defence of extreme intoxication to a general intent offence of violence by deeming that the fault of "self-induced intoxication" constitutes a marked departure from standards of reasonable care that can supply the fault for such offences even if the accused does not have *mens rea* and acts involuntarily at the time that the crime is committed. This raises the issue of whether involuntary and perhaps unexpected intoxication constitutes "self-induced intoxication" under section 33.1 or whether section 33.1 can be read down not to apply to such forms of intoxication.

---

93   *Vickberg*, above note 77 at 184. Section 33.1 of the *Code* places restrictions on when "self-induced intoxication" will be a defence.

94   *R v Tramble* (1983), 33 CR (3d) 264 (Ont Co Ct).

95   *R v Rushton* (1963), [1964] 1 CCC 382 (NSCA).

96   *R v Honish* (1991), 68 CCC (3d) 329 (Alta CA) aff'd [1993] 1 SCR 458.

In *Vickberg*, a trial judge held that the reference to "self-induced intoxication" in section 33.1 required voluntary intoxication. The judge decided that section 33.1 did not apply in the case because the accused became involuntarily intoxicated since he did not know and could not reasonably be expected to know that a drug he was given to assist with heroin withdrawal would intoxicate him.[97] In *Brenton*, a similar argument was made by the accused on the basis that smoking marijuana had an unexpected effect on the accused, but it was rejected by the courts on the basis that the accused knew that marijuana was intoxicating and that smoking it constituted self-induced intoxication under section 33.1.[98]

The Nova Scotia Court of Appeal has concluded that consumption of drugs or alcohol will be excluded as self-induced intoxication under section 33.1 only if the accused did not know and could not reasonably be expected to know the risk of becoming intoxicated. The Court of Appeal stressed that since *King* "courts have consistently held that 'voluntary intoxication' means the consuming of a substance where the person knew or ought to have had reasonable grounds for believing such might cause him to be impaired."[99] There is support in *King* for the proposition that intoxication may be held to be voluntary when the accused ought to have known that the substance was intoxicating even though he or she did not subjectively have that knowledge. Such an approach errs on the side of social protection, but fails to ensure subjective fault for voluntary intoxication. A broader definition of voluntary or self-induced intoxication that is more generous to the accused in focusing on the accused's subjective knowledge about the effects of taking an intoxicating substance could also mitigate some of the harsher effects of section 33.1 and make it easier to justify under section 1 of the *Charter* as a reasonable limit on the accused's rights under sections 7 and 11(d) of the *Charter*.

In any event, intoxication is a particularly complex issue in Canadian criminal law with four distinct types of intoxication defences. They are summarized in the following chart.

---

97   *Vickberg*, above note 77 at paras 68–70.
98   *Brenton*, above note 75 at 320.
99   *R v Chaulk*, 2007 NSCA 84 at para 45.

Summary Chart of Intoxication Defences

Defence	Issues
Ordinary intoxication defence to specific intent offences (i.e., murder, robbery)	Is there a reasonable doubt about intent?
Extreme intoxication defence to non-violent general intent offences (i.e., mischief, arson)	Has the accused established on a balance of probabilities lack of capacity for minimal *mens rea* or involuntary conduct?
Extreme intoxication defence to violent general intent offences (i.e., assault, sexual assault)	Has the accused established on a balance of probabilities lack of capacity for minimal *mens rea* or involuntary conduct? Does the deeming of the fault of becoming extremely intoxicated as sufficient for the fault and voluntariness of the offence in section 33.1 of the *Criminal Code* violate sections 7 and 11(d) of the *Charter*? Can it be justified under section 1?
Involuntary intoxication defence to specific or general intent offences	Did the accused know or ought to have known the intoxicating effect of the substance(s)? If the intoxication is involuntary, is it "self-induced intoxication" under section 33.1?

CONCLUSION

The Canadian law concerning intoxication is not only intensely controversial, but complex. As represented in the chart, there are four different ways in which intoxication can operate as a "defence" or, more accurately, prevent proof of the required fault for various criminal offences. The first and simplest is that evidence of intoxication can raise a reasonable doubt as to whether the accused had the intent required for a specific intent offence such as murder or robbery. The issue is the accused's actual intent, not whether intoxication impaired the accused's capacity to form the required intent.[100] The only difficult issues may be whether a particular offence will be classified as a specific intent offence that requires a complex mental process such as an intent directed

---

100 *Robinson*, above note 23; *Daley*, above note 25.

at some purpose beyond the immediate action and whether there is an air of reality to justify instructing the jury about this defence.

The second intoxication defence is the *Daviault* defence of extreme intoxication to general intent offences that do not include an element of an assault or any other interference or threat of interference with the bodily integrity of another person.[101] The accused must establish the *Daviault* defence of extreme intoxication to a general intent crime on a balance of probabilities and with expert evidence. The issue seems to be whether the accused was capable of forming the minimal intent required for general intent offences and not whether the accused actually had that intent, as in the case with the first intoxication defence to specific intent offences. The *Daviault* defence exists unimpeded by legislation only when the accused is charged with a general intent offence such as arson or mischief to property that does not involve an assault or threat of violence.[102] If the accused establishes the *Daviault* defence to such a general intent crime on a balance of probabilities, he or she will be acquitted. The *Daviault* defence does not apply to crimes that require intoxication as an element of the offence because such a defence would be inconsistent with the mischief of the offence.[103]

The most difficult issue is the classification of the offence. The Court has recently stated that specific intent offences are the product of more complex thought processes that produce either an ulterior objective to achieve certain consequences or knowledge of certain circumstances. In cases of uncertainty, courts will examine policy considerations with concerns about intoxicated violence and property damage pushing towards classification of an offence as a general intent offence that only allows an extreme intoxication defence, while the existence of a lesser included general intent offence or a mandatory minimum sentence may push towards classification of the offence as a specific intent offence.[104]

The third and most controversial intoxication defence is when the accused raises a *Daviault* defence to a violent general intent offence such as manslaughter, assault, or sexual assault. The Supreme Court's decision in *Daviault* suggests that it would violate the accused's rights under sections 7 and 11(d) of the *Charter* to convict a person who was

---

101 *Code*, above note 4, s 33.1(3). The extreme intoxication defence could also apply to regulatory offences to the extent that it prevents the Crown from establishing the prohibited act or *actus reus* beyond a reasonable doubt.

102 *Ibid.*

103 *Penno*, above note 55; *Finta*, above note 58; *Ruzic*, above note 58; *Canadian Foundation for Children*, above note 58. But see *King*, above note 55, recognizing involuntary intoxication as a defence to impaired driving.

104 *Tatton*, above note 2.

so extremely intoxicated at the time of the criminal act that he or she acted involuntarily and without the minimal intent required for a general intent offence. Parliament's reply to *Daviault* in section 33.1 of the *Criminal Code*, however, adds legislative support to the traditional rule in *Leary*. Section 33.1 substitutes the fault of becoming extremely intoxicated for the fault of committing the general intent crime of violence, even though the accused may have acted involuntarily at the time the assault occurs. It remains to be seen whether the Supreme Court will find that section 33.1 can be upheld under the *Charter.*

On the one hand, the substitution of the fault of becoming intoxicated for the fault of committing the general intent offence offends principles that require fault to be related to the *actus reus* and to overlap in time with the *actus reus.* As suggested by Wilson J in *Bernard,* this is mainly a substitution problem under section 11(d). In *Daviault,* the Supreme Court also held that basing the fault of sexual assault on the fault of becoming extremely intoxicated also violated section 7 of the *Charter* by punishing an accused who had no *mens rea* at the time of the act and who acted involuntarily. By deeming voluntary intoxication a marked departure from reasonable standards of conduct, section 33.1 may substitute the objective fault in voluntarily becoming extremely intoxicated for a subjective intent crime in possible violation of section 7 of the *Charter.* Although courts frequently accept violations of the presumption of innocence under section 11(d) as reasonable limits, they have been reluctant to accept violations of section 7 under section 1 of the *Charter.* The section 1 defence will likely focus on the fact that substitution of the fault of becoming extremely intoxicated for the fault of the particular offence is restricted under section 33.1 to general intent crimes of violence and that an intoxication-based offence may be less effective than section 33.1 in responding to intoxicated violence.

The time may have passed for general reforms that would abolish the much criticized distinction between general and specific intent offences and allow intoxication as a defence to all offences that require subjective *mens rea.* Such reform proposals were usually accompanied by proposals for the introduction of separate intoxication-based offences. After *Daviault,* there was reluctance to introduce new intoxication-based offences, in part because of a concern that a person who commits assault or sexual assault while intoxicated should still be labelled as an assaulter or sexual assaulter, and in part because of concerns about the impact of broad intoxication-based offences on the discretion of police and prosecutors in laying and reducing charges. There is no easy solution to the many dilemmas produced by the various intoxication defences and the most important immediate issue is whether section 33.1, restricted as it is to general intent offences of violence, will survive a *Charter* challenge.

The fourth intoxication defence is the rare defence of involuntary intoxication. It could apply to prevent the conviction of a person charged with a general intent offence who involuntarily becomes intoxicated and commits a criminal act,[105] as well as to a specific intent offence. Those who are involuntarily intoxicated, for example, by a drug slipped into a drink, might also be exempted from section 33.1, which applies only to self-induced intoxication. The defence of involuntary intoxication is based on the logic that if the fault of becoming voluntarily intoxicated can supply or be substituted for the fault for the particular offence, then a person who becomes intoxicated through no fault of his or her own should not be held culpable. In other words, the substitution of the fault of becoming intoxicated for the fault of the particular offence should not occur if the accused was without fault in becoming intoxicated.

FURTHER READINGS

COLVIN, E, & S ANAND. *Principles of Criminal Law*, 3d ed (Toronto: Thomson Carswell, 2007) ch 8.

"Criminal Reports Forum on *Daviault*" (1995) 33 *Criminal Reports* (4th) 269.

FERGUSON, G. "The Intoxication Defence: Constitutionally Impaired and in Need of Rehabilitation" (2012) 57 *Supreme Court Law Review* (2d) 111.

GRANT, I. "Second Chances: Bill C-72 and the *Charter*" (1996) 33 *Osgoode Hall Law Journal* 379.

HEALY, P. "Intoxication and the Codification of Canadian Criminal Law" (1994) 73 *Canadian Bar Review* 515.

———. "*Beard* Still Not Cut Off" (1996) 46 *Criminal Reports* (4th) 65.

LAWRENCE, M. "Voluntary Intoxication and the *Charter*: Revisiting the Constitutionality of Section 33.1" (2017) 40:3 *Manitoba Law Journal* 391.

MANNING, M, & P SANKOFF. *Criminal Law*, 5th ed (Markham, ON: LexisNexis, 2015) ch 10.

---

105 *King*, above note 55; *Vickberg*, above note 77.

QUIGLEY, T. "Reform of the Intoxication Defence" (1987) 33 *McGill Law Journal* 1.

SHAFFER, M. "*R. v. Daviault*: A Principled Approach to Drunkenness or a Lapse of Common Sense?" (1996) 3 *Review of Constitutional Studies* 311.

SMITH, K. "Section 33.1: Denial of the *Daviault* Defence Should Be Held Constitutional" (2000) 28 *Criminal Reports* (5th) 350.

STUART, D. *Canadian Criminal Law: A Treatise*, 7th ed (Toronto: Thomson Carswell, 2014) ch 6.

WILKINSON, J. "The Possibility of Alcoholic Automatism: Some Empirical Evidence" (1997) 2 *Canadian Criminal Law Review* 217.

CHAPTER 8

MENTAL DISORDER AND AUTOMATISM

Like intoxication, the defences of mental disorder and automatism apply to accused who commit criminal acts, but who cannot be found criminally responsible because their mental processes were impaired. It has long been accepted that an offender who, because of a mental disorder, is incapable of appreciating the nature and quality of a criminal act, or of knowing that it is wrong, should not be convicted. The verdict is not a pure acquittal, but rather a verdict of not criminally responsible on account of mental disorder or what used to be called not guilty by reason of insanity. The accused does not automatically go free and can be subject to detention or release with conditions until he or she is determined no longer to be a significant danger to society. In Canada, the mental disorder defence is set out in section 16 of the *Criminal Code*, and has been revised by both the Supreme Court and Parliament to take into account various *Charter* concerns.

The defence of automatism is more novel and applies to an accused who has committed a criminal act while in a state of impaired consciousness that results in involuntary behaviour. If that state is caused by a mental disorder, the accused will be held not criminally responsible by reason of mental disorder. If the cause of the automatism is some other factor such as a blow to the head, the disposition is to acquit the accused. The defence of non-mental disorder automatism is a common law defence that is not codified. If the cause of automatism producing involuntary behaviour is self-induced intoxication by alcohol or drugs, then the provisions of the intoxication defence discussed in Chapter 7 will apply.

Section 16(3) of the *Criminal Code* requires that the mental disorder defence be established on a balance of probabilities and the Supreme Court has also required the accused to establish the defences of both intoxicated and non-mental disorder automatism on a balance of probabilities. This violates the presumption of innocence in section 11(d) of the *Charter* by allowing a person to be convicted even though there is a reasonable doubt about guilt. Nevertheless, it has been held to be justified as a reasonable limit on the presumption of innocence on the basis that accused persons will be in the best position to adduce evidence about the impairment of their mental processes.[1]

Both the mental disorder and automatism defences have firm constitutional foundations in section 7 of the *Charter*. This is important as both defences can be unpopular because of public fears about violent acts that people may commit while suffering from a mental disorder and because of the stigma and lack of understanding of mental illness. The conviction of a person who acts in a state of automatism would likely violate the principle of fundamental justice that prohibits conviction for physically involuntary conduct. In other words, it would be unfair to convict a person for actions that the person cannot physically control.[2] That said, there is a very clear trend in the law to assume even in the absence of a medical diagnosis that automatism is caused by mental disorder. This trend is motivated by concerns about public protection, including the potentially indeterminate detention of a person found not criminally responsible on account of mental disorder.

A person who qualifies for a mental disorder defence under section 16 of the *Charter* acts in a morally involuntary manner because he or she has no "moral control"[3] over his or her actions. Such a person is

> incapable of morally voluntary conduct. The person's actions are not actually the product of his or her free will. It is therefore consistent with the principles of fundamental justice for a person whose mental condition at the relevant time is covered by s. 16 *Cr. C.* not to be criminally responsible under Canadian law. Convicting a per-

---

1   *R v Chaulk*, [1990] 3 SCR 1303 [*Chaulk*] (mental disorder defence); *R v Daviault*, [1994] 3 SCR 63 [*Daviault*] (extreme intoxication defence); *R v Stone*, [1999] 2 SCR 290 [*Stone*].

2   *R v Ruzic*, [2001] 1 SCR 687 at paras 45–46. On such a basis, the mental disorder defence could apply to regulatory offences as relating to the voluntary commission of the prohibited act. *Autorité des marchés financiers v Patry*, 2015 QCCA 1933 at paras 63 and 81.

3   *R v Bouchard-Lebrun*, 2011 SCC 58 at para 47 [*Bouchard-Lebrun*].

son who acted involuntarily would undermine the foundations of the criminal law and the integrity of the judicial system.[4]

This statement suggests that Parliament could not repeal or restrict the mental disorder defence without violating section 7 of the *Charter*.

A. PROCEDURAL CONSIDERATIONS IN THE MENTAL DISORDER DEFENCE

1) Unfitness to Stand Trial

The mental disorder defence applies to an accused who, at the time that the criminal act was committed, suffered from a mental disorder that made him or her incapable of appreciating the nature or quality of the act or omission or of knowing that it was wrong. It is possible that a person who suffered from a mental disorder at the time of the crime will continue to suffer from that condition and be found unfit to stand trial. Conversely, a person who was sane when the crime was committed might subsequently suffer a severe mental disorder that would make it unfair to have a trial. Section 672.23(1) allows the court on its own motion, or on an application from the accused or the prosecutor, to determine whether an accused is fit to be tried. A person is unfit to stand trial if he or she is

unable on account of mental disorder to conduct a defence at any stage of the proceedings before a verdict is rendered or to instruct counsel to do so, and, in particular, unable on account of mental disorder to

(a) understand the nature or object of the proceedings,

(b) understand the possible consequences of the proceedings, or

(c) communicate with counsel.[5]

The accused is presumed to be fit to stand trial, and unfitness must be proven on a balance of probabilities.[6] It is not necessary that a person be able to act in his or her own best interests or to employ analytical

---

4   *Ibid* at para 51.

5   *Criminal Code*, RSC 1985, c C-46, s 2 [*Code*].

6   *Code, ibid*, ss 672.22 & 672.23. The burden placed on the accused when the accused argues unfitness to stand trial has been held to be justified under the *Charter*. *R v Morrissey* (2002), 8 CR (6th) 41 (Ont SCJ), aff'd on other grounds 2007 ONCA 770 [*Morrissey*]. As will be seen, similar burdens on the accused to establish the mental disorder and automatism defences have also been held to be justified under the *Charter*.

reasoning, but it is necessary that he or she have "limited cognitive capacity to understand the process and to communicate with counsel."[7] This standard is a legal one that focuses on the fairness of the trial process and the accused's ability to participate in the trial process and not whether the accused clinically requires psychiatric treatment. A person who satisfies the minimal standards of the cognitive capacity test may still be found at trial to have a mental disorder defence. Courts of appeal have found that accused who lack testimonial competence and could not remember the crime were nevertheless fit to stand trial. They have found that accused with the permanent brain injury caused by fetal alcohol spectrum disorder were also fit to stand trial as were accused who were delusional.[8] Some lower courts, however, have argued for higher standards that would require accused persons be able to make rational decisions, especially in relation to their defence and against a restrictive approach to determining fitness to stand trial.[9]

A person found unfit to stand trial is subject to the same disposition hearing as a person found not criminally responsible because of a mental disorder. The difference, however, is that where an accused is found unfit to stand trial, the Crown may not have proven beyond a reasonable doubt that the accused committed the criminal act. For this reason, judges have the power to postpone the determination of fitness until the Crown has made its case and the accused has been found not to be entitled to an acquittal or a discharge. If the accused is found unfit to stand trial, the Crown is required to establish a *prima facie* case against the accused every two years until the accused is either found fit to be tried or is acquitted because the Crown cannot establish a *prima facie* case.[10] These safeguards are designed to ensure that a factually innocent accused is not subject to detention in the same manner as an accused who committed the criminal act, but was found not guilty by reason of a mental disorder.

A person with Downs Syndrome accused of sexual assault who was found unfit to stand trial and released after two months challenged the

---

7   *R v Whittle* (1994), 92 CCC (3d) 11 at 25 (SCC), approving of *R v Taylor* (1992), 77 CCC (3d) 551 (Ont CA).

8   *Morrissey*, above note 6 (Ont CA); *R v Jobb*, 2008 SKCA 156; *R v Krivicic*, 2011 ONCA 703; *R v Eisnor*, 2015 NSCA 64.

9   *R v Steele* (1991), 63 CCC (3d) 149 (Que CA); *R v Adam* (2013), 294 CCC (3d) 464 (Ont SCJ); see also *Dusky v United States*, 362 US 402 (1960). See, generally, Hugh Harradence, "Re-applying the Standard of Fitness to Stand Trial" (2013) 59 *Criminal Law Quarterly* 511.

10   *Code*, above note 5, s 672.33. The unavailability of an absolute discharge for a permanently unfit accused who does not pose a significant threat to society violates s 7 of the *Charter*. *R v Demers*, 2004 SCC 46 [*Demers*].

constitutionality of the provisions. The Supreme Court found Parliament had jurisdiction under the division of powers to legislate with respect to those unfit to stand trial because of concerns about trying the accused and also about preventing crime by the mentally disordered accused. The Court also rejected the accused's argument that subjecting him to review board proceedings violated the presumption of innocence under section 11(d) of the *Charter* given that the aim of review proceedings was not to punish the accused. The Court did, however, find that the unfitness to stand trial scheme violated section 7 of the *Charter* because it did not provide for an absolute discharge for an accused who is permanently unfit to stand trial and who did not present a continuing danger to the public. The Court ruled that the scheme was overbroad to the objectives of social protection by effectively providing that such a person could only be released subject to indeterminate conditions.[11] Parliament responded to this ruling with a new provision that allows a trial court to enter a stay of proceedings in such circumstances where an accused is not likely to ever become fit to stand trial, but also does not pose a significant threat to the safety of the public.[12]

2) Who Can Raise the Mental Disorder Defence?

Canadian courts have been more willing than British or American courts to allow the prosecutor to raise the mental disorder defence. The rationale is that society has an interest in not convicting an accused who may not be responsible because of a mental disorder, but who has chosen not to advance the insanity defence. This latitude presents dangers that (1) the Crown could bolster a weak case by presenting evidence of the accused's mental disorder, and (2) an accused could be exposed to indeterminate detention as a person found not guilty on grounds of mental disorder when he or she wishes either to plead guilty or to contest his or her innocence.

---

11 *Demers, ibid.*

12 *Code,* above note 5, s 672.851. The court may make this determination on its own initiative or with representations from the review board. To enter a stay the court must conclude not only that the accused is not likely ever to be fit to stand trial and that he or she does not pose a significant threat to the safety of the public, but also that a stay is in the best interests of the proper administration of justice considering factors such as the seriousness of the offence and any harm of a stay to public confidence in the administration of justice.

In *R v Swain*,[13] the Supreme Court found that the common law practice of allowing the Crown to raise the insanity defence violated the accused's right under section 7 of the *Charter* to control his or her own defence. Chief Justice Lamer stated:

> The mere fact that the Crown is able to raise a defence which the accused does not wish to raise, and thereby to trigger a special verdict which the accused does not wish to trigger, means that the accused has lost a degree of control over the conduct of his or her defence.[14]

The Court concluded that the principles of fundamental justice generally would allow the Crown to raise the insanity defence only after the accused had otherwise been found guilty. A permissible exception is that the Crown can raise the insanity defence in rebuttal if the accused has placed his or her capacity for criminal intent in issue. For example, if the accused raised a defence of non-mental disorder automatism, the Crown could then raise the defence of mental disorder and introduce evidence to indicate that section 16 of the *Code* should apply and the verdict should be not criminally responsible on account of mental disorder. An accused who argued that he or she went into a state of automatism because of a severe emotional blow may find the Crown arguing that the cause of the automatism was a mental disorder and that the appropriate disposition is further detention and treatment, not a complete acquittal.[15] It is even possible that the court will determine that there is no air of reality to the non-mental disorder automatism defence and only the mental disorder defence will be left for the jury to consider.[16]

3) Burden of Proof

Sections 16(2) and 16(3) of the *Criminal Code* provide that every person is presumed not to suffer from a mental disorder so as to be exempt from criminal responsibility and that the party who raises this issue must prove it on the balance of probabilities. In *R v Chaulk*,[17] the Supreme Court found that the requirement that an accused prove the defence of insanity on a balance of probabilities violated the presumption

---

13   (1991), 63 CCC (3d) 481 (SCC) [*Swain*].

14   *Ibid* at 506.

15   See, for example, *R v K* (1970), 3 CCC (3d) 84 (Ont HCJ) [*K*]; *R v Rabey* (1977), 37 CCC (2d) 461 (Ont CA), aff'd (1980), 54 CCC (2d) 1 (SCC) [*Rabey*], discussed later in this chapter.

16   See, for example, *Stone*, above note 1, discussed later in this chapter.

17   *Chaulk*, above note 1.

of innocence under section 11(d) of the *Charter*, because it allowed the conviction of an accused in spite of a reasonable doubt as to a factor essential to guilt, namely, sanity. Chief Justice Lamer reasoned:

> Whether the claim of insanity is characterized as a denial of *mens rea*, an excusing defence or, more generally, as an exemption based on criminal incapacity, the fact remains that sanity is essential for guilt. [The section] allows a factor which is essential for guilt to be presumed, rather than proven by the Crown beyond a reasonable doubt. Moreover, it requires an accused to disprove sanity (or prove insanity) on a balance of probabilities; it therefore violates the presumption of innocence because it permits a conviction in spite of a reasonable doubt in the mind of the trier of fact as to the guilt of the accused.[18]

The Chief Justice went on, however, to find that the statutory requirement that an accused prove the insanity defence on a balance of probabilities was justified under section 1 of the *Charter* because of the difficulties that the Crown would have proving beyond a reasonable doubt that an accused was sane. Justice Wilson dissented and held that, as in some American jurisdictions, once the accused produced some evidence of insanity, the prosecutor should bear the burden of proving beyond a reasonable doubt that the insanity defence did not apply.

The Court did not consider the burden of proof if the prosecutor raises the mental disorder defence. Section 16(3) suggests that the prosecutor, like the accused, would have to prove the defence on a balance of probabilities. Normally, however, the prosecutor must prove its case against the accused beyond a reasonable doubt. Given this general principle and the fact that the prosecutor would only be required to establish a mental disorder defence against an accused who did not wish to rely on such a defence, it would be best if the prosecutor was required to establish a mental disorder defence by proof beyond a reasonable doubt. Some model jury instructions, however, suggest that the prosecutor need only establish the mental disorder defence on a balance of probabilities.[19]

There must also be an air of reality before the mental disorder defence is even put to the jury. This requires some evidence that, if believed by the jury, would allow a reasonable jury to accept all of the

---

18   *Ibid* at 213.

19   See, for example, Canadian Judicial Council National Committee on Jury Instructions, "Model Jury Instructions," online: National Judicial Institute www. nji-inm.ca/index.cfm/publications/model-jury-instructions/#FC25EB9D-01E3-4794-76622AC40E00FEE2.

essential requirements of the mental disorder defence, namely, the existence of a mental disorder that renders an accused incapable of appreciating the nature and quality of the act or incapable of knowing that the act is wrong.

4) Disposition of an Accused Acquitted by Reason of Mental Disorder

An accused acquitted on grounds of insanity used to be subject to automatic indeterminate detention at the pleasure of the Lieutenant Governor in Council. In practice, this meant detention until a review board determined that release was in the accused's interests and not contrary to the public interest. In *Swain*,[20] the Supreme Court held that such automatic detention without a hearing and with no criteria to authorize detention violated the accused's rights under sections 7 and 9 of the *Charter*. That case raised the issue because the accused, who did not wish to plead insanity as a defence, was found to have been insane at the time of the crime but had successfully been treated with antipsychotic drugs at the time of sentencing. Chief Justice Lamer noted, however, that some automatic detention and delay following an acquittal by reason of insanity is a "practical reality," because the evidence of insanity at trial relates to the mental condition of the accused at the time of the offence and not the accused's "present mental condition and dangerousness."[21]

Amendments to the *Criminal Code* in the wake of *Swain* instruct the court to hold, if possible, a disposition hearing for the accused when the accused is found unfit to stand trial or not criminally responsible on account of mental disorder.[22] In any event, a review board of a judge and two mental health professionals is required to hold such a hearing "as soon as is practicable but not later than forty-five days after the verdict was rendered."[23] Courts or review boards no longer are faced with the draconian disposition of automatic indeterminate detention.[24] The Supreme Court has stressed that there is no presumption that a person found not criminally responsible by reason of mental disorder is dangerous. There is no burden or onus of proof on either the accused or the Crown. The court or review board may consider and seek evidence from a broad range of sources.

---

20   *Swain*, above note 13.
21   *Ibid* at 539.
22   *Code*, above note 5, s 672.45.
23   *Ibid*, s 672.47(1).
24   *Penetanguishene Mental Health Centre v Ontario (AG)*, 2004 SCC 20.

At the disposition hearing, the court or review board is instructed to discharge the accused absolutely if "the accused is not a significant threat to the safety of the public."[25] If an absolute discharge is not warranted, the court or review board was instructed to make the disposition "that is the least onerous and least restrictive to the accused," considering "the need to protect the public from dangerous persons, the mental condition of the accused, the reintegration of the accused into society and the other needs of the accused."[26] The Supreme Court interpreted this provision to require an absolute discharge unless the court or review board finds that release would present a significant risk to the safety of the public by the commission of a crime that presents a real risk of physical or psychological harm that is not merely trivial or annoying. The scheme did not violate sections 7 and 15 of the *Charter* because it avoided stereotypical assumptions about those who suffer a mental disorder and requires individual assessment of each and every person found not criminally responsible by reason of mental disorder and unconditional release if they do not present a significant threat to the safety of the public.[27]

Since that decision upholding the scheme under the *Charter*, however, Parliament responded to some high profile cases by changing the provision to make the safety of the public "the paramount consideration" at disposition hearings and to remove the requirement that the least restrictive measure be adopted.[28] It has also created a new disposition regime for "high-risk accused" found not criminally responsible on account of mental disorder. High-risk accused may be subject to less frequent reviews, and courts as well as review boards must be satisfied that there is not a substantial likelihood that the accused will use violence that could endanger the life and safety of another person before release.[29] Both the changes to the disposition criteria for all accused found not criminally responsible and the new regime for high-risk accused are likely to be challenged under the *Charter*.

Continued detention or conditions placed on those found not criminally responsible by reason of mental disorder are generally subject to yearly reviews by the review board.[30] The review board can order

---

25 *Code*, above note 5, s 672.54(a).
26 This provision was amended by SC 2014, c 6, s 9.
27 *Winko v British Columbia (Forensic Psychiatric Institute)* (1999), 135 CCC (3d) 129 (SCC) [*Winko*].
28 *Code*, above note 5, s 672.54, as amended by SC 2014, c 6, s 9.
29 *Ibid*, ss 672.54 and 672.84. Note a significant threat to the public is defined broadly in s 672.5401.
30 *Ibid*, s 672.81(1).

provincial authorities to provide an independent evaluation of a person's diagnosis, safety risk, and treatment plan, and to make assertive efforts to enroll an Indigenous person in a culturally appropriate treatment plan as an incident to its powers to supervise and make available treatment. At the same time, the review board does not have the power to order treatment for the person, such powers being within provincial authority with respect to the hospital where the person is detained.[31]

There were provisions in the *Criminal Code* never proclaimed in force that would have capped the ultimate period of time a person could be detained, or could be subject to conditions, based on the seriousness of the offence charged,[32] while also allowing the Crown to apply to have a person declared a dangerous mentally disordered accused, subject to a disposition cap of life.[33] The Supreme Court has disapproved of a court of appeal decision that held that the failure to proclaim the capping provisions produced overbreadth and disproportionality in the criminal law that violated section 7 of the *Charter*.[34] As a result, an accused found not criminally responsible still remains subject to potentially indeterminate detention or indeterminate conditional restraints on liberty. At the same time, the accused should be released without conditions if they are not a significant threat to the safety of the public.[35] The potential for indeterminate detention or indeterminate conditions, as well as the generally restrictive nature of the defence, helps explain why the mental disorder defence is rarely invoked despite evidence that many in our prisons suffer from a mental disorder of some form.

B. THE *M'NAGHTEN* RULES AND THEIR CODIFICATION

The substantive rules governing the insanity or mental disorder defence are derived from the 1843 decision of the House of Lords in *M'Naghten's Case*.[36] In that case, the accused was found by a jury to be not guilty by reason of insanity of murdering the prime minister's secretary. He suf-

---

31   *Mazzei v British Columbia (Director of Adult Forensic Psychiatric Services)*, [2006] 1 SCR 326.

32   *Code*, above note 5, s 672.64, repealed SC 2005, c 22, s 24.

33   *Ibid*, s 672.65, repealed SC 2005, c 22, s 24.

34   *Winko*, above note 27 at para 70, disapproving of *R v Hoeppner* (1999), 25 CR (5th) 91 (Man CA).

35   *Code*, above note 5, s 672.54(a).

36   (1843), 8 ER 718 (HL).

fered from delusions of persecution from the government. Subsequent controversy led to a reference to the House of Lords, which affirmed the availability of the insanity defence if it was "clearly proved that, at the time of the committing of the act, the party accused was labouring under such a defect of reason, from disease of the mind, as not to know the nature and quality of the act he was doing, or, if did know it, that he did not know he was doing what was wrong."[37] The House of Lords added that an accused suffering from delusions should have his responsibility determined on the basis that the delusions were real. Thus, an accused who killed another, supposing himself under deadly attack, may not be responsible, but one imagining only an injury to his character would be guilty of murder.[38]

In 1892 the M'Naghten rules were embodied in the Criminal Code of Canada with some variations. A person was defined as legally insane if he or she laboured "in a state of natural imbecility or disease of the mind, to such an extent as to render him incapable of appreciating the nature and quality of an act or omission, and of knowing that such an act or omission was wrong." This introduced the idea that an accused would have an insanity defence if he or she did not "appreciate," as opposed to "know," the nature and quality of the act. The 1892 Code also required the accused to be incapable of both appreciating the nature and quality of the act and of knowing that it was wrong. This was corrected as a misreading of the disjunctive M'Naghten rules.[39] Thus, either a failure to appreciate the nature and quality of the criminal act or to know that it was wrong will suffice to ground the mental disorder defence.

In 1992 the insanity defence was renamed the mental disorder defence, and the verdict of not guilty by reason of insanity was renamed the verdict of not criminally responsible by reason of mental disorder. The mental disorder defence now provides:

> No person is criminally responsible for an act committed or an omission made while suffering from a mental disorder that rendered the person incapable of appreciating the nature and quality of the act or omission or of knowing that it was wrong.[40]

---

37   Ibid at 722.
38   This provision was codified in Canada until its repeal. SC 1991, c 43, s 2. Delusions would now be considered with reference to whether the accused was able to appreciate the nature and quality of the act or was able to know that it was wrong. See R v Landry (1991), 62 CCC (3d) 117 (SCC) [Landry]; R v Oommen (1994), 91 CCC (3d) 8 (SCC) [Oommen], discussed below for two cases considering mental disorder defences based on the accused's delusions.
39   R v Cracknell (1931), 56 CCC 190 (Ont CA).
40   Code, above note 5, s 16(1).

This provision indicates more clearly that the accused must have committed the act or omission charged, but other changes are more cosmetic. Section 2 of the *Criminal Code* defines mental disorder as a disease of the mind, preserving the old jurisprudence on that issue. Section 16(1) preserves the traditional two-prong test that allows the defence on the basis that (1) a mental disorder "rendered the person incapable of appreciating the nature and quality of the act or omission," or (2) a mental disorder "rendered the person incapable . . . of knowing that it was wrong." The most significant changes in the 1992 amendments related not to the substantive defence, but rather to the abolition of automatic indeterminate detention as discussed above. For example, the 1992 amendments did not embrace American reforms that attempt to broaden the insanity defence so that it applied to crimes that were a product of mental disorder or to offenders whose mental disorder made them unable to obey the law.

Although Parliament could reformulate the mental disorder defence as it did in 1992, it could not repeal it in response to some controversial finding that a person cannot be convicted because of the mental disorder defence. The Supreme Court had indicated that a person who is incapable because of a mental disorder of appreciating the nature and quality of their actions or of knowing that they are wrong acts in a morally involuntary manner. In other words, the acts are "not actually the product of his or her free will" and the Court's refusal to convict such persons is "therefore consistent with the principles of fundamental justice" under section 7 of the *Charter*.[41] That said, the scope of the mental disorder defence should not be overestimated. It is not enough to establish that the accused has a mental disorder or even that the mental disorder caused the crime. The mental disorder must be so severe that it prevented the accused from either appreciating the consequences of his or her actions or of knowing that they were wrong.

C. MENTAL DISORDER OR DISEASE OF THE MIND

In order for the defence to apply, an accused must suffer from a disease of the mind or a mental disorder. A person who is unable to appreciate the nature and quality of an act or is incapable of knowing that the act is wrong, but does not suffer from a mental disorder, will not qualify

---

41   *Bouchard-Lebrun*, above note 3 at para 51.

for the defence.[42] However, holding that a person suffers from a mental disorder is not sufficient. As mentioned, the condition must be severe enough to render the person incapable of appreciating the nature and quality of the act, or incapable of knowing that it was wrong.

1) Policy Considerations

The categories of disease of the mind have expanded since 1843 when the *M'Naghten* rules were first defined. Judicial interpretation of what constitutes a disease of the mind will be influenced by medical developments, but it remains a question of law for the courts to define and may involve policy considerations not known to the discipline of psychiatry. These policy factors relate to concerns about how wide the mental disorder defence should be and the need to protect the public "by the control and treatment of persons who have caused serious harms while in a mentally disordered or disturbed state."[43] The Supreme Court in *Stone* has stated that it is open to trial judges to find new policy considerations to influence their interpretation of what constitutes a disease of the mind. "Policy concerns assist trial judges in answering the fundamental question of mixed law and fact which is at the centre of the disease of the mind inquiry: whether society requires protection from the accused and, consequently, whether the accused should be subject to evaluation under the regime contained in Part XX.1 of the Code."[44] The Court in that case endorsed a "holistic" approach to determining disease of the mind that includes an open-ended list of policy factors, including whether the accused presents a continuing danger and whether his or her conduct can be explained by an internal as opposed to an external cause.

2) Continuing Danger and Internal Causes

A disease of the mind has often been defined in relation to whether there is a continuing danger to the public,[45] or whether the disturbance is related to an internal cause stemming from the psychological make-up of the accused as opposed to an external factor.[46] Justice La Forest has warned against exclusive reliance on either the continuing danger or

---

42   As will be discussed later, they may have the common law defence of non-mental disorder automatism.

43   *Rabey*, above note 15.

44   *Stone*, above note 1 at 441.

45   *Bratty v AG for Northern Ireland* (1961), [1963] AC 386 (HL).

46   *R v Quick*, [1973] 3 All ER 347 (CA) [*Quick*]; *Rabey*, above note 15.

the internal cause theories, but has noted that they are united in their common concern for recurrence. In his view, however, even "recurrence is but one of a number of factors to be considered in the policy phase of the disease of the mind inquiry," and "the absence of a danger of recurrence will not automatically exclude the possibility of a finding of insanity."[47] Nevertheless, the danger of recurrence does seem to be the most important policy factor in determining whether a particular condition constitutes a disease of the mind. It is related to concerns about both the need to protect public safety and to treat and rehabilitate the accused.

In *Stone*,[48] the Supreme Court confirmed that the existence of a continuing danger or an internal cause are legitimate and non-mutually exclusive factors indicating that the accused may suffer from a mental disorder. The psychiatric history of the accused and the likelihood of the recurrence of violence or the stimulus that triggered violence in the past are important considerations in determining whether the accused is a continuing danger. "The greater the anticipated frequency of the trigger in the accused's life, the greater the risk posed to the public and, consequently, the more likely it is that the condition alleged by the accused is a disease of the mind."[49] Thus, an accused who goes into an automatic state[50] and assaults or kills another because of ordinary teasing or nagging is more likely to be classified as having a disease of the mind than a person who goes into an automatic state after a rare stimulus such as seeing a loved one assaulted or killed. At the same time, the Court warned that the absence of a continuing danger does not preclude a finding of a mental disorder or a disease of the mind.

The existence of an internal cause will be most relevant in cases of psychological blow automatism discussed later in this chapter. An internal cause may reveal itself when the accused goes into an automatic state when faced with something less than "an extremely shocking trigger"[51] that would send "a normal person" in similar circumstances into an automatic state. Comparing how the accused reacted with how a

---

47 *R v Parks* (1992), 75 CCC (3d) 287 at 310 (SCC) [*Parks*]; *Stone*, above note 1 at 438. See also *R v Sullivan* (1983), [1984] AC 156 (HL) [*Sullivan*].

48 *Stone*, above note 1.

49 *Ibid* at 440.

50 It is assumed that such a state will by definition produce a situation in which the accused is incapable of appreciating the nature and quality of his or her actions or knowing that they are wrong. The crucial issue in determining whether the mental disorder defence applies or not will be determining whether the accused suffers from a mental disorder or disease of the mind.

51 *Stone*, above note 1 at 436.

normal person would have acted in similar circumstances is motivated by concerns about public safety when an accused responds atypically and violently to what may be the ordinary stresses and disappoint- ments of life. There may be cases where a focus on internal causes is not helpful and the accused will be found not to suffer from a mental disorder even though there might be an internal cause to his or her ac- tions. As will be discussed later in this chapter, sleepwalking may be an internal cause of automatic behaviour, but it may not be classified as a disease of the mind. Conversely, a person might be classified as having a disease of the mind even though there is no apparent internal cause.

The existence of either a continuing danger or an internal cause is simply a factor that suggests the accused may have a mental disorder. The absence of these factors does not mean that for other policy reasons, concerning the need to protect the public by potentially indeterminate detention or conditions placed on a person found not criminally respon- sible by reason of mental disorder, an accused will not be classified as having a disease of the mind. In a fundamental sense, the definition of whether a person has a mental disorder or disease of the mind is driven by policy and public safety concerns about the ultimate dispos- ition of the accused. This means that courts can channel people into the mental disorder defence even if most health professionals would maintain that the accused does not have a mental disorder or the need for treatment.

3) The *Cooper* Definition

In R v Cooper,[52] Dickson J defined "disease of the mind" as

> any illness, disorder or abnormal condition which impairs the human
> mind and its functioning, excluding however, self-induced states
> caused by alcohol or drugs, as well as transitory mental states such
> as hysteria or concussion.

This is a broad definition of disease of the mind that includes all medic- ally recognized disorders except those in which transitory disturbances are caused by external factors such as drugs. Psychopathic personal- ities[53] or personality disorders[54] have been recognized as diseases of the mind. Brain damage including fetal alcohol spectrum disorder and severe mental disability may also be considered diseases of the

---

52   (1979), 51 CCC (2d) 129 at 144 (SCC) [Cooper].
53   R v Simpson (1977), 35 CCC (2d) 337 (Ont CA) [Simpson].
54   Rabey, above note 15.

mind.[55] *Delirium tremens*, or deterioration of the brain cells produced by chronic alcoholism, have also been recognized as diseases of the mind.[56] Thus, alcohol or drug use will generally fall under the mental disorder defence only when it produces a permanent condition as opposed to temporary intoxication.

The Supreme Court has held that sleepwalking is not a disease of the mind, so that a person rendered unconscious by this condition was entitled to a complete acquittal, rather than possible detention as a person found not guilty by reason of insanity.[57] This suggests that even though a condition might fall within the broad contours of an illness or abnormal condition that impairs the human mind, it will not necessarily be classified as a disease of the mind.

4) Mental Disorder and Transitory States

The House of Lords in *Beard* suggested that "if actual insanity in fact supervenes, as the result of alcoholic excess, it furnishes as complete an answer to a criminal charge as insanity induced by any other cause."[58] Canadian courts have not been willing to apply the section 16 defence in cases involving self-induced intoxication. The *Cooper* definition excludes self-induced states caused by alcohol and other drugs as a disease of the mind. In *R v Bouchard-Lebrun*,[59] the Supreme Court held that an accused who brutally assaulted a person after taking the ecstasy drug was not suffering from a mental disorder even though he was in a state of "toxic psychosis" that both Crown and defence experts agreed rendered him unable to know that the assaults were wrong. The accused had made religious comments during the assault about the coming of the Apocalypse and the devil. The Court stopped short of holding that "toxic psychosis" produced by intoxication could never

---

55 *R v Revelle* (1979), 48 CCC (2d) 267 (Ont CA), aff'd [1981] 1 SCR 576; *R v R(MS)* (1996), 112 CCC (3d) 406 (Ont Ct Gen Div); *R v CPF*, 2006 NLCA 70. In the last case, the permanent brain damage caused by fetal alcohol spectrum disorder was found to be a mental disorder but not one that satisfied the other requirements of the mental disorder defence, namely, that the mental disorder rendered the accused incapable of appreciating the physical consequences of their actions or knowing that they were wrong.

56 *R v Malcolm* (1989), 50 CCC (3d) 172 (Man CA); *R v Mailloux* (1985), 25 CCC (3d) 171 (Ont CA), aff'd (1988), 45 CCC (3d) 193 (SCC).

57 *Parks*, above note 47. The Court based this decision on the evidence presented in the particular case and suggested that it could reconsider its decision on different evidence.

58 *DPP v Beard*, [1920] AC 479 at 500 (HL).

59 Above note 3.

be a mental disorder. Nevertheless, applying the holistic test in *Stone*, the Court concluded that the drugs acted as an external cause of the behaviour and there was no evidence of a danger of recurrence if the accused did not take similar drugs.[60] It indicated that the mental disorder defence and various intoxication defences are "mutually exclusive"[61] as a matter of law even though they may overlap in a clinical or medical sense. The Court's refusal to find a mental disorder meant that the accused was convicted of aggravated assault even though at the time he committed the assault he was acting in an involuntary, delusional, and psychotic state and did not know that his acts were wrong. This seems to base his fault not on what he did at the time, but on the act of becoming voluntarily intoxicated. It should also be noted that the accused appeared to rely on the mental disorder defence and did not challenge section 33.1 of the *Code* under the *Charter*, which, as discussed in the last chapter, substitutes the fault of becoming extremely intoxicated for the fault and voluntariness of violent general intent offences such as aggravated assault.

In subsequent cases, some of the harsh effects of *Bouchard-Lebrun* have been partially mitigated. The Quebec Court of Appeal in *R c Turcotte* distinguished *Bouchard-Lebrun* and would have allowed section 16 to go to the jury in a case where there was both evidence of mental disorder and extreme intoxication. It held, however, that the judge erred in not making clear that the jury should consider the mental disorder defence without relying on the evidence of the accused's intoxication. "The defence of mental disorder must not, however, turn into another form of self-induced intoxication. Consequently, the jury must understand that, if it finds that there was a mental disorder, it must continue its analysis and ensure that the source of the accused's incapacity was truly the mental disorder, in spite of the intoxication."[62]

The *Cooper* definition of disease of the mind also excludes "transitory mental states such as hysteria or concussion." Those subject to a one-time mental disturbance because of external factors such as a blow to the head or an extraordinary trauma should probably not be subject to potential indeterminate detention or conditions as a person found not criminally responsible on account of a mental disorder. However, this more intrusive disposition may be appropriate when the accused's inability to appreciate the nature and quality of the acts or to know that

---

60   In the specific case, the accused was guilty of aggravated assault by virtue of the restrictions on the extreme intoxication defence in s 33.1 of the *Code* as examined in Chapter 7.

61   *Bouchard-Lebrun*, above note 3 at para 37.

62   *R c Turcotte*, 2013 QCCA 1916 at para 118; *R v Mock*, 2016 ABCA 293 at para 15.

they are wrong is caused by a "malfunctioning of the mind arising from some cause that is primarily internal to the accused, having its source in his psychological or emotional make-up, or in some organic pathology, as opposed to a malfunctioning of the mind which is the transient effect produced by some external factor such as, for example, concussion."[63] In R v Rabey, a dissociative state produced by the accused's disappointment at being romantically rejected was found to have been derived from internal factors within the accused that could constitute a disease of the mind. However, if the accused had been subjected to "extraordinary external events" such as being involved in a serious accident, escaping a murderous attack, or seeing a loved one killed, then a dissociative state could perhaps be explained "without reference to the subjective make-up of the person exposed to such experience."[64] In such a case, the dissociation would not be likely to recur, because of the extraordinary nature of the external factor. As such, it would be unduly intrusive to subject the accused to possible detention and treatment as a person found not criminally responsible on account of mental disorder.

5) Mental Disorder and Organic Conditions

A focus on factors internal to the accused has led English courts to conclude that various conditions that are not commonly considered mental disorders are nevertheless diseases of the mind for the purpose of the insanity defence. For example, epilepsy has been found to constitute a disease of the mind,[65] as has arteriosclerosis.[66] The focus on internal factors has produced strange results where diabetics are concerned. If the accused takes insulin and does not eat, the resulting dissociative state has been held not to be a disease of the mind, because it was caused "by an external factor and not by a bodily disorder in the nature of a disease which disturbed the working of the mind."[67] If, however, a diabetic goes into a dissociative state because he or she has not taken insulin, then the resulting condition is a disease of the mind because it is caused by the internal factor of the accused's diabetes.[68] In such cases, it would be better not to focus on whether the cause of the state was internal or external, but whether it was likely to recur and to present a continuing danger.

---

63   Rabey, above note 15 at 477–78.

64   Ibid at 482–83.

65   R v O'Brien, [1966] 3 CCC 288 (NBCA) [O'Brien]; Sullivan, above note 47.

66   R v Kemp (1956), [1957] 1 QB 399.

67   Quick, above note 46.

68   R v Hennessy, [1989] 2 All ER 9 (CA) [Hennessy].

The Supreme Court's holistic approach to categorizing a disease of the mind suggests that a focus on whether the cause was internal can and should be dispensed with in those cases in which it will produce an absurd result not necessary for public safety. In *Parks*,[69] sleepwalking was not classified as a disease of the mind even though it could be seen as an organic or hereditary condition internal to the accused. Canadian courts should not classify organic conditions such as epilepsy or diabetes as diseases of the mind simply because they are internal causes that explain the accused's behaviour. The ultimate issue should be whether the public requires protection through potentially indeterminate conditions or detention imposed on those found not criminally responsible on account of mental disorder. In a case subsequent to *Parks*, however, the Ontario Court of Appeal held that sleepwalking should be considered a mental disorder under the holistic *Stone* test because it was a matter internal to the accused, it was not triggered by specific external stimuli, and there was a continuing danger to the public from a risk of recurrence.[70] This case certainly underlines the tension between the Court's decision in *Parks* that sleepwalking was not a mental disorder and its more open-ended and holistic approach to defining a mental disorder in *Stone*.

D. CAPACITY TO APPRECIATE THE NATURE AND QUALITY OF THE ACT

Even if the accused is held to suffer from a mental disorder or disease of the mind, he or she must qualify under one of the two arms of the mental disorder defence. Canadian courts have stressed that section 16 of the *Criminal Code* refers to an inability to *appreciate* the nature and quality of acts, as opposed to the *M'Naghten* rules, which refer to an inability to *know* the nature and quality of the act. The ability to appreciate the nature and quality of an act involves more than knowledge or cognition that the act is being committed. It includes the capacity to measure and foresee the consequences of the conduct. In *Cooper*, Dickson J stated:

> The requirement, unique to Canada, is that of perception, an ability to perceive the consequences, impact, and results of a physical act. An accused may be aware of the physical character of his action (i.e.,

---

69   Above note 47.

70   *R v Luedecke*, 2008 ONCA 716 [*Luedecke*].

in choking) without necessarily having the capacity to appreciate that, in nature and quality, the act will result in the death of a human being.[71]

An accused who is unable to appreciate the physical consequences of his or her actions because of a mental disorder will have a valid section 16 defence. In a murder case, this also mirrors the *mens rea* requirement that the accused subjectively know that his or her actions would cause death. Of course, a successful section 16 defence could result in a disposition far more intrusive than an acquittal in a murder case.

The courts have not expanded the defence to apply to those who, because of mental disorder, were unable emotionally to appreciate the effect of their actions on the victim. In *Simpson*,[72] Martin JA stated that the defence did not apply to an accused

> who has the necessary understanding of the nature, character and consequences of the act, but merely lacks appropriate feelings for the victim or lacks feelings of remorse or guilt for what he has done, even though such lack of feeling stems from "disease of the mind." Appreciation of the nature and quality of the act does not import a requirement that the act be accompanied by appropriate feeling about the effect of the act on other people . . . . No doubt the absence of such feelings is a common characteristic of many persons who engage in repeated and serious criminal conduct.

An inability to appreciate that a victim may die can result in a mental disorder defence. An inability to have appropriate emotions about the death of another person, however, does not result in a section 16 defence, even if it is an indication of a mental disorder such as a psychopathic personality.

The courts have also held that an inability to appreciate the penal consequences of an act does not render an accused incapable of appreciating the physical consequences of the act. In *R v Abbey*,[73] the accused believed that he was protected by an external force from punishment for importing narcotics. The Supreme Court held that the trial judge had erred in law "in holding that a person who by reason of disease of the mind does not 'appreciate' the penal consequences of his actions is insane."

---

71   Above note 52 at 147.
72   Above note 53 at 355.
73   (1982), 68 CCC (2d) 394 at 405–6 (SCC) [*Abbey*].

In *Landry*,[74] the Supreme Court rejected the Quebec Court of Appeal's conclusion that an accused who killed while under the delusion that he was God, and the victim, Satan, did not appreciate the nature and circumstances of the act. Chief Justice Lamer reasoned that the prior precedents had clearly established that an accused would have an insanity defence only if a mental disorder prevented him from appreciating the physical, as opposed to the moral, consequences of the act. He also added that the Court of Appeal had erred in holding that section 7 of the *Charter* required it "to modify the established interpretation of this statutory provision."[75] As will be seen later in this chapter, however, the majority of the Supreme Court affirmed the verdict of not guilty by reason of insanity on the alternative basis that the accused's severe psychosis and resulting delusion rendered him incapable of knowing that the killing was wrong. It is important to be sensitive to how the two alternative arms of the mental disorder defence interact.

E. CAPACITY TO KNOW THAT THE ACT IS WRONG

Section 16(1) of the *Criminal Code* provides two alternative arms or formulations of the mental disorder defence. The first, discussed above, applies when a mental disorder renders the accused incapable of appreciating the physical consequences of the act. The second is when the disease of the mind renders the accused incapable of knowing that the act was wrong.

In *R v Schwartz*,[76] the Supreme Court divided 5:4, with the majority holding that an accused must be unable to know that an act was legally wrong. Justice Martland for the majority concluded that the test "is not as to whether the accused, by reason of mental disease, could or could not calmly consider whether or not the crime which he committed was morally wrong. He is not to be considered as insane . . . if he knew what he was doing and also knew that he was committing a criminal act."[77] Justice Dickson in his dissent seemed more concerned with giving the insanity defence a generous reading. He noted that Parliament had chosen in section 16 to use the word "wrong," which could refer to either legal or moral wrong. In most cases, there would be no practical

---

74   Above note 38.
75   *Ibid* at 124.
76   (1977), 29 CCC (2d) 1 (SCC) [*Schwartz*].
77   *Ibid* at 12.

difference, but he was concerned about a case in which an accused was capable of knowing that his or her acts were illegal but was not capable of knowing they were morally wrong. He cited the example of an accused who knew that it was legally wrong to kill but did so believing that his killing followed a divine order and therefore was not morally wrong. Justice Dickson held that the reference to wrong in section 16 should be interpreted to mean morally wrong. In his view, this broader definition would not give the amoral offender a defence, because the incapacity to know that an act was morally wrong must stem from a disease of the mind and indicate a complete loss of the "ability to make moral distinctions."[78]

In *R v Chaulk*,[79] the Supreme Court reversed *Schwartz* and concluded that accused should have an insanity defence if, because of a disease of the mind, they were incapable of knowing that an act was morally wrong, even if they were capable of knowing that the act was legally wrong. Chief Justice Lamer argued for the majority that this broader reading of the insanity defence

> will not open the floodgates to amoral offenders or to offenders who relieve themselves of all moral considerations. First, the incapacity to make moral judgments must be causally linked to a disease of the mind . . . . Secondly, as was pointed out by Dickson J. in *Schwartz*, *supra*, "'moral wrong' is not to be judged by the personal standards of the offender but by his awareness that society regards the act as wrong . . . .'" The accused will not benefit from substituting his own moral code for that of society. Instead, he will be protected by s. 16(2) if he is incapable of understanding that the act is wrong according to the ordinary moral standards of reasonable members of society.[80]

This distinction between the accused's own moral code and his or her ability to know society's moral standards may be difficult to draw in some cases. In *Chaulk*, the accused were young boys suffering from a paranoid psychosis that made them believe that they had the power to rule the world and that killing was necessary. It was clear that they did not have a defence under *Schwartz*, because they knew that killing was illegal. Unfortunately, the Supreme Court did not rule on the crucial issue of whether their belief that the law was irrelevant to them constituted an inability to know that what they did was morally wrong in the eyes of society.[81]

---

78   *Ibid* at 22.
79   Above note 1.
80   *Ibid* at 232–33.
81   The insanity defence did succeed at their subsequent trial.

A subsequent case suggested that the insanity defence would not apply to a "psychopath or a person following a deviant moral code" if such a person "is capable of knowing that his or her acts are wrong in the eyes of society, and despite such knowledge, chooses to commit them."[82] The insanity defence will also not apply if the act was motivated by a delusion, but the accused was still capable of knowing "that the act in the particular circumstances would have been morally condemned by reasonable members of society."[83] In another case, the Supreme Court upheld the denial of the section 16 defence because there was some evidence that the accused knew killing was morally wrong even though he shot a woman while suffering from a delusion that by killing her and her unborn child, he would save the world.[84]

The section 16 defence will also not apply if the accused understands society's views about right and wrong but, because of a delusion or mental disorder, believes that what he is doing is justified.[85] The Ontario Court of Appeal has explained that "a subjective, but honest belief in the *justifiability* of the acts — however unreasonable that belief may be — is not sufficient" for the section 16 defence. Rather, "[t]he accused person's mental disorder must also render him or her *incapable* of knowing that the acts in question are morally wrong as measured against societal standards, and therefore incapable of making the choice necessary to act in accordance with those standards."[86] All of these cases indicated that the section 16 defence does not apply to many mentally disturbed offenders despite the Court's ruling in *Chaulk* that the defence should apply if the accused was because of a mental disorder incapable of knowing that an act was morally wrong.

The Supreme Court applied the new moral wrong standard in *Landry*,[87] when it concluded that the accused had an insanity defence because his disease of the mind produced a delusion that he was God killing Satan. This condition rendered him "incapable of knowing that the act was morally wrong in the circumstances." The Court was presumably satisfied that the mental disorder was so severe that the accused was not capable of knowing that society would consider the killing immoral. In *Oommen*,[88] the Supreme Court indicated that an accused, even though he was generally capable of knowing that killing

---

82   *Oommen*, above note 38 at 19.
83   *R v Ratti* (1991), 62 CCC (3d) 105 at 113 (SCC).
84   *R v Baker*, [2010] 1 SCR 329.
85   *R v W(JM)* (1998), 123 CCC (3d) 245 (BCCA); *R v Ross*, 2009 ONCA 149.
86   *R v Campione*, 2015 ONCA 67 at para 41.
87   *Landry*, above note 38 at 124.
88   Above note 38 at 18.

was wrong, could have an insanity defence if his paranoid delusion "at the time of the act deprived him of the capacity for rational perception and hence rational choice about the rightness or wrongness of the act." The focus is on the accused's capacity for rational choice about the particular criminal act at the time the act was committed, not his or her general intellectual ability to know right from wrong.

F. IRRESISTIBLE IMPULSE

Canadian courts have long refused to recognize irresistible impulse as a separate category of the insanity defence. At the same time, however, evidence of an irresistible impulse, like evidence of delusions, may be relevant in determining whether an accused otherwise qualifies for the mental disorder defence.[89] Categorical rejections of the relevance of irresistible impulsion to the mental disorder defence would be especially inadvisable given the Court's statements that convicting a person who did not act through a voluntary expression of free will would violate the principle of fundamental justice that a person should not be convicted for a morally involuntary action. The section 16 defence should protect those who act in a morally involuntary manner because of a mental disorder and a person who faces a genuine irresistible impulse because of a mental disorder may well qualify for the defence.[90]

Evidence of "irresistible impulse" may also be relevant to proof of non-mental disorder automatism or of the required *mens rea*. In a case of multiple killings where the accused testified that he "lost control," the trial judge was correct in telling the jury to consider such testimony in relation to the Crown's burden to prove intent in relation to each killing and in relation to the accused's claims to have acted in a dissociative state.[91]

G. EFFECT OF A MENTAL DISTURBANCE ON MENS REA

Evidence of a mental disorder may fall short of establishing a mental disorder defence but may raise a reasonable doubt as to whether the accused had a subjective mental element required for a particular offence.

---

89   *Abbey*, above note 73; *Chaulk*, above note 1.
90   *Bouchard-Lebrun*, above note 3 at para 51.
91   R v Ng (2006), 212 CCC (3d) 277 at paras 28–31 (Alta CA).

The mental disorder defence focuses on capacity and has to be proven on a balance of probabilities, whereas the mental element focuses on actual intent and is rebutted by any evidence that raises a reasonable doubt. Thus, it should not be surprising that evidence of mental disturbance, short of establishing a full section 16 defence, could still raise a reasonable doubt about some forms of *mens rea*.

In *R v Baltzer*,[92] Macdonald JA reasoned that in order to determine what was in the accused's mind, the jury must have evidence of the accused's "whole personality and background including evidence of any mental illness or disorder that he may have suffered from at the material time." It is an error of law for a judge to instruct the jury to disregard evidence of mental disorder if the defence of insanity fails.[93] All the evidence, including that of mental disorder, should be considered in determining whether the accused had the requisite intent. The higher the degree of *mens rea*, the more likely it is that mental disorder may raise a reasonable doubt about the particular intent. For example, evidence of mental disorder short of establishing the insanity defence may raise a reasonable doubt as to whether murder was planned and deliberate.[94]

Some judges have confused the relevance of evidence of mental disturbance to the determination of *mens rea* with the separate issue of Parliament's choice not to create a defence of diminished responsibility to reduce a killing from murder to manslaughter.[95] Although there is no defence of diminished responsibility in Canadian criminal law, the growing consensus is that evidence of mental disturbance or illness should be considered when determining whether the accused had the required *mens rea*. Such evidence may prevent the Crown from proving that the accused had the subjective foresight of death required for a murder conviction. In such a case, an accused could be acquitted of murder but could still be found to have the *mens rea* necessary for manslaughter. This would occur through ordinary *mens rea* principles and not through the recognition of a separate defence of diminished responsibility.

---

92   (1974), 27 CCC (2d) 118 at 141 (NSCA).

93   *R v Allard* (1990), 57 CCC (3d) 397 (Que CA.); *R. v Jacquard* (1997), 113 CCC (3d) 1 (SCC) [*Jacquard*].

94   *Jacquard*, *ibid* at 14; *R v McMartin* (1964), [1965] 1 CCC 142 (SCC); *More v R*, [1963] 3 CCC 289 (SCC).

95   This is a defence in England. *Homicide Act 1957* (UK), c 11, s 2.

H. AUTOMATISM

Automatism is a legal term that refers to unconscious or involuntary behaviour. The Supreme Court has defined automatism as "unconscious, involuntary behaviour, the state of a person who, though capable of action, is not conscious of what he is doing. It means an unconscious, involuntary act, where the mind does not go with what is being done."[96] More recently, the Court has noted that an accused acting as an automaton may not necessarily be actually unconscious, but that his or her consciousness must be so impaired that he or she "has no voluntary control over that action."[97] Those who act while sleepwalking or in a dazed condition from a concussion are examples of those who may be acting in an automatic state.

1) Relation to Mental Disorder and Consequences of an Automatism Defence

Automatism is related to the mental disorder defence because both involve conditions in which the accused cannot be held criminally responsible for his or her actions owing to a lack of mental capacity. If an accused leads evidence of automatism, the Crown can counter with evidence that the cause of the automatism was a mental disorder. Because an accused who acts in an automatic state will generally satisfy either arm of the mental disorder defence, the crucial issue in automatism cases is whether the cause of the automatism is a mental disorder or some other factor. If it is established that the cause of the automatism is a disease of the mind, the accused is held not criminally responsible by reason of a mental disorder and is subject to a disposition hearing and potential indeterminate detention or conditions as outlined above in relation to the mental disorder defence.

If the accused's automatism is not caused by a mental disorder, however, then the verdict is a simple acquittal. In *R v Bleta*,[98] the Supreme Court affirmed the acquittal of an accused who, while in a dazed condition following a severe blow to his head, killed another person. The Court concluded that "the question of whether or not an accused person was in a state of automatism so as not to be legally responsible at the time when he committed the acts with which he is charged, is a ques-

---

96   *Rabey*, above note 15 at 6.
97   *Stone*, above note 1 at 417.
98   (1964), [1965] 1 CCC 1 (SCC) [*Bleta*].

tion of fact"[99] for the jury. In *Parks*,[100] an accused successfully raised
a defence of automatism after he stabbed two people, killing one of
them. The cause of his automatism was sleepwalking, and the Supreme
Court found this condition, on the evidence presented to it, not to be a
disease of the mind. The accused was acquitted and was not subject to
a disposition hearing or any form of treatment. Chief Justice Lamer expressed concerns about setting the accused "free without any consideration of measures to protect the public, or indeed the accused himself,
from the possibility of a repetition of such unfortunate occurrences."[101]
The majority of the Court held, however, that in the absence of a verdict
of not criminally responsible on account of mental disorder, the courts
did not have jurisdiction to make preventive orders.

The Supreme Court has also speculated that "anger conceivably
could, in extreme circumstances, cause someone to enter a state of automatism in which that person does not know what he or she is doing,
thus negating the voluntary component of the *actus reus*."[102] In such a
circumstance, the Court noted that the appropriate disposition would
be an acquittal. The possibility that the accused's state of automatism
may negate either the voluntary commission of the prohibited act or
the required fault element makes it even more anomalous that, as will
be discussed below, the accused has the burden of establishing the defence of automatism on a balance of probabilities.[103]

Federal proposals to amend the *Criminal Code*, made in 1993 but
not implemented, would have made an accused acquitted on the basis
of non-insane automatism subject to the same disposition hearing and
possible conditions or detention as a person held not criminally responsible by reason of mental disorder. If enacted, it would have for all
practical purposes eliminated the present distinction between a defence of mental disorder or non-mental disorder automatism by eliminating the different dispositions for the two defences. As will be seen, the
Supreme Court subsequently in *Stone*[104] narrowed the distance between
the two defences by requiring the accused to establish the defence of
non-mental disorder automatism on a balance of probabilities and by
indicating that automatism will be presumed to be caused by mental

---

99 *Ibid* at 58.
100 *Parks*, above note 47.
101 *Ibid* at 299.
102 *R v Parent* (2001), 154 CCC (3d) 1 at para 10 (SCC).
103 *Stone*, above note 1. See, for example, *R v Fontaine*, 2017 SKCA 72 at para 35
     [2017 *Fontaine*], affirming an acquittal for involuntary and reflexive actions on
     the basis that the *actus reus* had not been committed.
104 *Ibid*.

disorder unless the accused establishes otherwise. Nevertheless, non-mental disorder automatism still results in an acquittal.

2) Air of Reality and Persuasive Burdens of Proof

As late as 1992, the Supreme Court held that an accused who raised a defence of non-insane automatism was entitled to an acquittal if the evidence presented at trial raised a reasonable doubt as to whether the accused acted in a voluntary or conscious manner.[105] This was because such evidence would raise a reasonable doubt as to whether the accused acted with the required fault element (including the capacity to live up to an objective fault element) or, alternatively, whether the accused consciously and voluntarily committed the *actus reus*.

In the 1999 case of *Stone*,[106] however, the Supreme Court held that an accused claiming a non-mental disorder defence of automatism must establish on a balance of probabilities that he or she acted in an involuntary manner. The majority of the Court was concerned that an automatism defence might easily be faked under the traditional law that allowed the defence to go to the jury so long as the accused pointed to some evidence that, if believed, would raise a reasonable doubt about the voluntariness of his or her actions. The Court was also concerned about consistency in allocating burdens of proof given that the accused had the onus to establish on a balance of probabilities the *Daviault* defence of extreme intoxication producing a state akin to automatism and the mental disorder defence under section 16(3) of the *Criminal Code*.

The Court in *Stone* also concluded that the new persuasive burden on the accused to establish the automatism defence on a balance of probabilities also influenced the threshold decision by trial judges about whether there was a sufficient air of reality to justify instructing the jury about the defence. On the facts in *Stone*, the Court held that a trial judge was justified in not instructing the jury on the defence of non-mental disorder automatism because there was no "evidence upon which a properly instructed jury could find that the accused acted involuntarily on a balance of probabilities."[107] The Court indicated that even to satisfy this threshold air of reality burden, the accused will not only have to assert involuntariness, but also produce collaborating psychiatric evidence. Even these two factors will not necessarily

---

105 *Parks*, above note 47. The accused would have had an air of reality burden to point to some evidence in the case that makes automatism a viable issue, but not a persuasive burden.

106 Above note 1.

107 *Ibid* at 426.

suffice. Other relevant factors that should be considered include the severity of the triggering stimulus, the corroborating evidence of by-standers, the corroborating evidence of the accused being in states of automatism at other times, whether there was a motive for the crime, and whether the alleged trigger of automatism was also the victim of the crime. Finally, if the crime could be explained without reference to automatism, this suggested that the automatism defence should not be put to the jury. The Court not only imposed a novel persuasive burden on the accused to establish non-mental disorder automatism, but also raised the threshold air of reality burden considerably.

In a strong dissent joined by three other members of the Court, Binnie J noted the virtues of the traditional law in giving the accused the benefit of a reasonable doubt about the voluntariness of his or her actions. He persuasively argued that the majority's decision on the threshold air of reality test would deprive the accused of having claims of non-insane automatism considered by the jury. *Stone* indeed suggested a stringent test that may significantly reduce the number of claims of non-mental disorder automatism that are considered by the jury especially in cases in which the accused argues that he or she went into an automatic state because of an emotional blow.

In *R v Fontaine*,[108] the Supreme Court qualified *Stone* as it relates to the threshold air of reality burden but not the persuasive burden on the accused to establish automatism. Justice Fish stated for a unanimous Court that "there is language in *Stone* that may be understood to invite an assessment by the trial judge as to the likely success of the defence. This in turn, may be seen to require the judge to weigh the evidence in order to determine whether it establishes, on a balance of probabilities, that the accused perpetrated the criminal act charged in a state of automatism." The Court, however, held that a trial judge who followed such an approach erred and that the factors set out in *Stone* were better used to guide the trier of fact in deciding whether the automatism defence had been established on a balance of probabilities. A trial judge should not weigh evidence or judge its credibility in deciding whether there is an air of reality that justifies leaving the defence to the jury. The question should rather be whether there is "in the record any evidence upon which a reasonable trier of fact, properly instructed in law and acting judicially, could conclude that the defence succeeds."[109] The Court stressed that judges should not lightly deny

---

108 2004 SCC 27 at para 63 [*Fontaine*].

109 *Ibid* at para 57. Note, however, that other parts of this judgment suggest that the fact that the accused has to establish automatism on a balance of probabilities may still influence the threshold air of reality decision. Justice Fish stated:

the accused an opportunity to have a jury consider the defence. In this case, the Court determined that the jury should have been instructed about the defence of mental disorder automatism. The accused gave detailed evidence that he acted in an involuntary manner and did not simply assert that the defence existed in law. A psychiatrist also testified that the accused was suffering from a psychotic episode induced by substance abuse and was "seeing things" when he shot the victim. *Fontaine* lowers the air of reality burden in *Stone* but leaves intact the assignment of a persuasive burden on the accused to establish the defence of non-mental disorder automatism on a balance of probabilities.

If the accused or the Crown raises a defence of mental disorder automatism, then, under section 16(3) of the *Criminal Code*, that party must prove on a balance of probabilities that the accused suffers from a mental disorder and that this condition rendered the accused incapable of appreciating the physical consequences of his or her actions or of knowing that they were morally wrong. The jury can be left with a choice between mental disorder and non-mental disorder automatism if, for example, the accused places his or her capacity for the mental element in issue by claiming non-insane automatism, and the Crown argues that the cause of any automatism is a mental disorder.[110] After the Court's decision in *Stone*, however, it will be more difficult for the accused to satisfy the threshold air of reality burden to have the jury instructed about non-mental disorder automatism. As in *Stone* and in *Fontaine*, the judge may frequently be justified in only leaving the defence of mental disorder automatism to the jury. In such cases, a jury that accepts the accused committed the crime will only be left with the options of a guilty verdict, or if it finds the crime was committed while the accused was in an automatic state, a verdict of not criminally responsible on account of mental disorder.

In the case of 'reverse onus' defences, such as mental disorder automatism, it is the accused who bears both the persuasive and the evidential burdens. Here the persuasive burden is discharged by evidence on the balance of probabilities, a lesser standard than proof beyond a reasonable doubt. Reverse onus defences will therefore go to the jury where there is any evidence upon which a properly instructed jury, acting judicially, could reasonably conclude *that the defence has been established in accordance with this lesser standard.*

Ibid at para 54 [emphasis added]. The rest of the judgment, however, stresses the need to apply a consistent air of reality test to all defences regardless of whether the accused has a persuasive burden to establish the defence on a balance of probabilities or whether the Crown has to prove beyond a reasonable doubt that the defence does not exist.

110 See, for example, *K*, above note 15.

3) Automatism and Sleepwalking

An early American case recognized that sleepwalking could produce a defence of non-insane automatism because the "law only punishes for overt acts done by responsible moral agents. If the prisoner was unconscious when he killed the deceased, he cannot be punished for that act." An unconscious accused could not be held guilty for killing a person who tried to rouse him from a deep sleep even if the accused had committed "a grave breach of social duty in going to sleep in the public room of a hotel with a deadly weapon on his person."[111]

In *Parks*,[112] the Supreme Court upheld the acquittal of a man who drove twenty-three kilometres to his in-laws' house and attacked them with a knife, fatally wounding one of them. The jury had obviously concluded that the accused was acting in an involuntary or unconscious manner at the time of the attacks. Chief Justice Lamer concluded that the trial judge had acted properly in not instructing the jury on the defence of insanity because there was uncontradicted evidence that "sleepwalking is not a neurological, psychiatric, or other illness," but rather a sleep disorder from which "there is no medical treatment as such, apart from good health practices, especially as regards sleep."[113] The Supreme Court's definition of a disease of the mind in *Parks* does not follow English law, which somewhat mechanically assesses sleepwalking, like epilepsy, as a disease of the mind because it is a cause that is internal to the accused.[114] The Supreme Court stressed medical issues in *Parks*, not policy issues concerning whether the accused's condition was prone to recur or presented a danger to the public. However, the Court left open the possibility that, on different evidence, sleepwalking could be held to be a disease of the mind.

The Court's decision in *Stone*, while not overruling *Parks*, encourages judges to use policy concerns about the need to protect the public as a factor in concluding that the accused suffers from a disease of the mind. In *R v Luedecke*,[115] the Ontario Court of Appeal held that a trial judge had erred when following *Parks*; he had classified sleepwalking as a basis for non-mental disorder automatism in a case where an accused sexually assaulted a woman at a party while asleep. As in *Parks*, there was uncontradicted medical evidence led by the accused that a person could perform complex actions while sleepwalking and that

---

111 *Fain v Commonwealth of Kentucky*, 78 Ky Rptr 183 at 189 and 193 (CA 1879).
112 *Parks*, above note 47.
113 *Ibid* at 297.
114 *R v Burgess*, [1991] 2 QB 92 (CA).
115 Above note 70.

sleepwalking was not a mental disorder.[116] The trial judge determined
that there was no continuing danger under *Stone*, in part because the
accused had accepted a plan of sleep hygiene, modest alcohol consumption, and medication that "would reduce the risk of recurrence."[117] The
trial judgment in this case is more consistent with the medicalized
approach taken by the Court in *Parks* to determine the existence of a
mental disorder than the focus on public safety in *Stone*.[118]

The Ontario Court of Appeal reversed and held that sleepwalking
should for policy reasons be characterized as a mental disorder. In doing
so, the Court of Appeal rejected the medicalized approach in *Parks* and
followed the public safety approach taken in *Stone*. It candidly recognized
that the accused was not mentally ill and "the criminal law uses the concept of mental disorder very differently than the medical profession."[119]
The Court of Appeal stressed that *Stone* required it to assume that automatism was caused by a mental disorder and to focus on the risk of
recurrence of not simply violence, but the factors that caused the sleepwalking. It concluded that "social defence concerns, inevitably present in
such cases, must to a large degree drive the analysis in automatism cases
after *Stone*."[120] The Court of Appeal stressed dangers of recurrence given
that the accused had a history of sexual activities in his sleep, albeit in
situations with former girlfriends that did not lead to criminal charges.
Finally, the Court of Appeal expressed confidence that reforms to the disposition process examined above would ensure that a sleepwalking accused found not criminally responsible because of mental disorder would
not be detained or subject to conditions or stereotyped as dangerous unless he was a significant threat to the public.[121] The accused consented
to a verdict of not criminally responsible on account of mental disorder
at a new trial and subsequently received an absolute discharge from the
Review Board. The result in this case is inconsistent with *Parks* and could
only be justified on the basis that *Stone* overrules *Parks*, a decision that
the Supreme Court has yet to make.

The Saskatchewan Court of Appeal held that *Stone* has not completely eliminated non-mental disorder automatism even while establishing a
presumption that automatism is caused by mental disorder.[122] It upheld
an acquittal for aggravated assault where the accused struck his partner

---

116 *R v Luedecke* (2005), 35 CR (6th) 205 (Ont Ct J).
117 *Ibid* at para 48.
118 Eric Colvin & Sanjeev Anand, *Principles of Criminal Law*, 3d ed (Toronto: Thomson Carswell, 2007) at 451–54.
119 *Luedecke*, above note 70 at para 7.
120 *Ibid* at para 93.
121 *Ibid* at para 101. See Section A(4), above in this chapter.
122 2017 *Fontaine*, above note 103; see also *R v Graveline*, 2006 SCC 16.

as a reflexive action after being assaulted by her while he was asleep and there was no evidence that the accused had become conscious before he assaulted his partner.[123]

4) Automatism and Emotional Blows

In *Rabey*,[124] the Supreme Court considered whether an accused who committed a criminal act while in an automatic state caused by an emotional or psychological blow should have a defence of insane or non-insane automatism. The majority, following Martin JA in the Ontario Court of Appeal, decided that an accused would only have a defence of non-insane automatism if he or she went into an automatic state because of an "extraordinary event" such as being in a serious accident or seeing a loved one killed. Such an event "might reasonably be presumed to affect the average normal person without reference to the subjective make-up of the person exposed to such experience." The accused, who assaulted a fellow student a day after learning that she was not romantically interested in him, was held not to have a defence of non-insane automatism. The Court determined that the accused was only being exposed to "the ordinary stresses and disappointments of life which are the common lot of mankind."[125] If he had gone into an automatic state, the defence would have to be insane automatism because his "disassociative state must be considered as having its source primarily in the respondent's psychological or emotional make-up."[126]

Justice Dickson dissented in *Rabey* on the basis that the medical evidence in the case suggested that the accused did not suffer from psychosis, neurosis, personality disorder, or an organic disease of the brain and that his violence "was an isolated event" and "the prospect of recurrence of disassociation is extremely remote."[127] In its reliance on medical evidence, this dissent bears some resemblance to the Supreme Court's decision in *Parks*. Justice Dickson also objected to placing an objective threshold on when an emotional blow should be allowed as a basis for a defence of non-insane automatism. He stressed that "the fact that other people would not have reacted as [Rabey] did should not obscure the reality that the external psychological blow did cause a loss of consciousness."[128] He noted that in the case of a physical as opposed

---

123 2017 *Fontaine*, above note 103 at para 36.
124 *Rabey*, above note 15 at 7.
125 *Ibid*.
126 *Ibid*.
127 *Ibid* at 27.
128 *Ibid* at 29.

to a psychological blow, the only issue would be whether the particular accused, not a reasonable person, went into a dissociative state.[129]

In *R v Stone*,[130] the Supreme Court followed *Rabey* in holding that a trial judge did not err by refusing to instruct the jury about the defence of non-mental disorder automatism in a case in which an accused, after being provoked by his wife's verbal insults, felt a "whoosh sensation" and stabbed her forty-seven times before disposing of her body and fleeing to a foreign country. The Court indicated that trial judges should start from the proposition that involuntary and automatic behaviour was caused by a disease of the mind. They should only instruct the jury about non-insane automatism if there was confirming psychiatric evidence that established an air of reality for the defence of non-mental disorder automatism.[131] The Court held that the requirement in *Rabey* that the trigger of the involuntary conduct be an extraordinary event that could send a "normal person" in similar circumstances into an automatic state did not violate sections 7 and 11(d) of the *Charter*. The majority reasoned that the objective standard only affected the classification of the defence as mental disorder or non-mental disorder automatism and not whether the Crown had proven that the accused had voluntarily committed the offence as a matter relating to proof of the *actus reus* or the *mens rea*. This distinction is a fine and somewhat artificial one given that (1) the presumption of innocence applies to defences as well as to elements of the offence; (2) the different dispositions for the two automatism defences; and (3) the Court's novel imposition of a persuasive burden on the accused to establish automatism on a balance of probabilities. In any event, *Stone* reaffirms that the definition of disease of the mind, and the characterization of automatism as insane or non-insane, is driven by policy concerns about the ultimate disposition of the accused. Even if, as in *Rabey* and *Stone*, a psychiatrist would not agree that the accused suffered from a mental disorder, courts are reluctant to hold that an accused who responds violently but perhaps involuntarily to non-extraordinary emotional blows should receive the complete acquittal that follows a verdict of non-mental disorder automatism.

Justice Binnie's dissent in *Stone* followed Dickson J's dissent in *Rabey* in stressing that there was no medical evidence before the Court that the accused was suffering from a mental disorder and arguing that the accused had a right to have his defence of non-mental disorder au-

---

129 See, for example, *Bleta*, above note 98.

130 Above note 1.

131 As discussed earlier, the air of reality burden on the accused was onerous and reflected a new persuasive burden that the accused must establish a defence of non-mental disorder automatism on a balance of probabilities.

tomatism considered by the jury. Both judges were confident that juries would reject frivolous and untruthful claims of non-insane automatism. Justice Binnie also strongly argued against the majority's decision to require the accused to prove the defence of non-mental disorder automatism on a balance of probabilities. He was concerned that the Court's decision would deprive the accused of the traditional right to be acquitted if there was a reasonable doubt as to whether he or she acted in a voluntary manner.

5) Automatism and Organic Conditions

As discussed above, accused suffering from conditions such as epilepsy, diabetes, or sleepwalking have been held by English courts to have a disease of the mind. Even if their condition caused them to act in an automatic state and there was little or no need for possible indeterminate detention, their defence has been limited to insanity.[132] These results have most often been justified with reference to a conclusion that the automatic state was the product of a cause internal to the accused. These English cases should not be followed under the holistic Canadian approach to defining a disease of the mind. In *Stone*,[133] the Supreme Court indicated that whether automatic conduct was caused by an internal cause is only one factor in a holistic test to determine whether there is a disease of the mind. A focus on internal causes can and should be discarded when it would not accord with the underlying policy concerns, most importantly the need to protect the public through potentially indeterminate detention or conditions that can be applied following a verdict of not criminally responsible by reason of mental disorder.

The Ontario Court of Appeal held that a trial judge erred in acquitting an accused on the basis of non-mental disorder automatism when he committed out-of-character violent acts in part as a result of brain damage caused by a series of strokes. It stressed that, following *Stone*, there was a presumption that automatism was caused by a mental disorder. Moreover, the trial judge had erred by giving undue weight to expert testimony over policy-based holistic reasoning and by focusing on the recurring future danger of violence as opposed to future stressors that may lead to violence.[134] This decision suggests that the defence of non-mental disorder automatism will be exceedingly rare and

---

132 *O'Brien*, above note 65; *Sullivan*, above note 47; *Hennessy*, above note 68.
133 *Stone*, above note 1 at 438.
134 *R v SH*, 2014 ONCA 303 at para 82 [*SH*].

that determination of the existence of mental disorder will be driven by concerns about even remote risks to social protection.

6) Automatism and Intoxication

Long before *Daviault*, the Supreme Court seemed prepared to consider that involuntary intoxication might produce a state of automatism that could be a defence to any criminal offence. In *R v King*,[135] an accused drove while still under the influence of a drug given to him by his dentist. In his concurring judgment, Taschereau J came close to recognizing a defence of non-insane automatism when he stated "there can be no *actus reus* unless it is the result of a willing mind at liberty to make a definite choice or decision, or in other words, there must be a willpower to do an act."[136] An accused who acted in an automatic state because of *involuntary* intoxication would still have a defence that could lead to an acquittal of a general intent offence such as impaired driving. Unlike in *King*, however, the accused under *Stone* would likely have to establish the automatism defence on a balance of probabilities. Even the stress in *Stone* on social protection should not result in involuntary conduct produced by involuntary intoxication being categorized for policy reasons as a product of a mental disorder. The scenario is more complex and less certain for an accused who acted in an automatic state because of *voluntary* intoxication.

As discussed in Chapter 7, *Daviault* opened the possibility that a voluntarily intoxicated accused could be acquitted of a general intent offence if he or she established, on a balance of probabilities, that the intoxication was severe enough to produce an unconscious condition similar to automatism or insanity. Parliament responded to *Daviault* with section 33.1, which takes away the *Daviault* defence in cases of general intent offences that involve violence. The Supreme Court in *Bouchard-Lebrun*[137] held that there was no mental disorder in a case where an accused who took drugs acted in a toxic psychosis and brutally assaulted persons in part because of religious delusions. The Court's restrictive reading of mental disorder in this case is at odds with its broad reading of mental disorder in *Stone*, which as discussed earlier has been applied to cover even cases of sleepwalking. Self-induced intoxication thus seems to be a special case to which Canadian courts are reluctant to apply the mental disorder defence. The only link seems

---

135 (1962), 133 CCC 1 (SCC).
136 *Ibid* at 3.
137 Above note 3.

to be a common emphasis on social protection, with the accused in *Bouchard-Lebrun* being convicted for involuntary behaviour under the section 33.1 restrictions on the *Daviault* defence, and other accused who act in an involuntary manner because of sleepwalking, emotional blows, or organic conditions being held not criminally responsible by reason of mental disorder to ensure that they may be detained if they are dangerous.

7) Automatism and Other Defences

In *R v Stone*, the majority of the Court cautioned against leaving both mental disorder and non-mental disorder automatism to the jury. As suggested earlier in the chapter, *Stone* may require that the court classify the cause of automatism as a mental disorder in many cases for reasons relating more to public safety than medical diagnosis or the need for continued treatment. Indeed, courts have used *Stone* as a reason for classifying sleepwalking and organic brain conditions as mental disorders that can only produce a finding of not criminally responsible by reason of mental disorder should the trier of fact accept that the accused acted in an involuntary automatic state at the time that the *actus reus* was committed.[138] In such cases, an accused with an automatism defence will be exposed to the potentially indeterminate detention for those held not responsible on account of mental disorder.

In *R v Graveline*,[139] the Supreme Court upheld the jury's acquittal of a severely battered woman after the judge had left the defence of non-mental disorder automatism and self-defence to the jury with respect to her actions in shooting her sleeping husband. It was accepted that the accused had no memory of her actions, but the Crown's expert testified that this amnesia occurred after the shooting. The Court held that the Crown was not entitled to a new trial simply because the judge had left both defences to the jury. Justice Fish in dissent concluded that a new trial was necessary in part because the defences were "fundamentally inconsistent"[140] and there was no air of reality with respect to self-defence. The majority of the Quebec Court of Appeal had upheld the acquittal, despite the fact that the trial judge had not reviewed policy factors relating to the feigning of the defence of automatism, the accused's motive, or the alleged trigger for the behaviour said to be involuntary and unconscious. The decision may have limited precedential value

---

138 *Canada v Campbell* (2000), 35 CR (5th) 314 (Ont SCJ); *Luedecke*, above note 70; *SH*, above note 134.

139 [2006] 1 SCR 609, rev'g (2005), 200 CCC (3d) 247 (Que CA).

140 *Ibid* at para 24 (SCR).

because the Crown had conceded that there was an air of reality to justify putting the non-mental disorder automatism defence to the jury.

CONCLUSION

The classification of diseases of the mind or mental disorder has been the most dynamic and uncertain feature of the law defining the defences of mental disorder and automatism. In *Parks*,[141] the Supreme Court held that sleepwalking was not a disease of the mind and indicated that the proper verdict, if the jury found that the accused had acted in a physically involuntary state, was an acquittal. Although *Parks* has not been officially overruled, today under *Stone* there would be a strong presumption that sleepwalking should be classified as a mental disorder or disease of the mind for reasons of public safety. Under *Stone*,[142] accused no longer benefit from a reasonable doubt about the voluntariness of their conduct but must establish the automatism defence on a balance of probabilities. Following *Rabey*[143] in all but the most extraordinary cases, an emotional blow producing an automatic state will result in a verdict of not criminally responsible by reason of mental disorder, even if the accused was not diagnosed by a psychiatrist with a mental disorder. In contrast to its earlier decision in *Parks*, the Court in *Stone* has significantly restricted the defence of non-insane automatism. In doing so, the Court has made it much less likely that the jury will ever get to consider such a defence even in cases such as *Parks*, where the accused commits a crime while sleepwalking. This is unfortunate because there was no evidence that the defence was being abused in the period between *Parks* and *Stone*. An exception to the willingness to expand the concept of mental disorder or disease of the mind is the continued reluctance to characterize temporary intoxication — even extreme intoxication producing a toxic psychosis — as a mental disorder. In such cases, however, accused will often be convicted given restrictions on the intoxication defence, including even extreme intoxication that produces involuntary conduct.[144]

The exact contours of the two alternative arms of the section 16 defence are relatively settled. The Court has limited the reference to a mental disorder producing an inability to appreciate the consequences

---

141 Above note 47.
142 Above note 1.
143 Above note 15.
144 *Bouchard-Lebrun*, above note 3.

of actions to physical consequences as opposed to emotional or penal consequences. The Court is understandably concerned that the mental disorder defence not be expanded so far as to apply to psychopaths who lack empathy for victims and foresight of penal consequences.

Less clear are the exact contours of the accused being incapable of knowing that his or her acts were morally wrong. In *Chaulk*,[145] the Court indicated that the accused could not benefit by substituting his or her own moral code for that of society. Except in extreme cases such as *Landry*,[146] it is not always easy to distinguish the accused's own moral code from his or her ability to know what society generally regards as wrong. The reference in *Oommen*[147] to the defence applying if the accused did not have a capacity for rational perception and choice about the rightness or wrongness of the act does not clarify matters or respond to the danger of expanding the defence so far as to apply to psychopaths who assert their own moral code over society's. If the psychopath is capable of discerning society's moral code but decides to follow his or her own deviant moral code, the mental disorder defence should not apply because punishment, not treatment, would be the appropriate disposition.

In 2014, Parliament enacted new legislation that will make the release of those found not criminally responsible on account of mental disorder more difficult. These restrictions catered to public fears about notorious and horrific acts of violence by mentally disordered persons. They are likely to be challenged under the *Charter* because they alter the post-*Swain*[148] balance between ensuring that the mentally disordered are treated fairly and public safety. Statements by the Court in *Bouchard-Lebrun*[149] suggest that there are limits to how far Parliament can go in curbing the sometimes unpopular automatism and mental disorder defences. Complete repeal of the automatism defence would violate the principle of fundamental justice that a person not be convicted for physically involuntary conduct. In addition, complete repeal of the mental disorder defence would violate the principle of fundamental justice that a person not be convicted for morally involuntary conduct.

---

145 Above note 1.
146 Above note 38.
147 Above note 38.
148 Above note 13.
149 Above note 3.

FURTHER READINGS

BARRETT, J, & R SHANDLER. *Mental Disorder in Canadian Criminal Law* (Toronto: Thomson Carswell, 2006).

BERGER, B. "Mental Disorder and the Instability of Blame in Criminal Law" in F Tanguay-Renaud & J Stribopoulos, eds. *Rethinking Criminal Law Theory* (Portland: Hart, 2012).

BLOOM, H, & R SCHNEIDER. *Mental Disorder and the Law*, 2d ed (Toronto: Irwin Law, 2017).

BRUDNER, A. "Insane Automatism: A Proposal for Reform" (2000) 45 *McGill Law Journal* 67.

COLVIN, E, & S ANAND. *Principles of Criminal Law*, 3d ed (Toronto: Thomson Carswell, 2007) ch 8.

GULAYETS, M. "Exploring Differences Between Successful and Non-Successful Mental Disorder Defences" (2016) 58 *Canadian Journal of Criminology and Criminal Justice* 161.

HARRADENCE, H. "Re-applying the Standard of Fitness to Stand Trial" (2013) 59 *Criminal Law Quarterly* 511.

HEALY, P. "Automatism Confined" (2000) 45 *McGill Law Journal* 87.

HOLLAND, W. "Automatism and Criminal Responsibility" (1982) 25 *Criminal Law Quarterly* 95.

MANNING, M, & P SANKOFF. *Criminal Law*, 5th ed (Markham, ON: LexisNexis, 2015) ch 12 & 13.

MARTIN, GA. "The Insanity Defence" (1989) 10 *Criminal Lawyers Association Newsletter* 19.

McSHERRY, B. "Criminal Responsibility, 'Fleeting' States of Mental Impairment and the Powers of Self-Control" (2004) 27 *International Journal of Law & Psychiatry* 445.

O'MARRA, AJC. "*Hadfield* to *Swain*: The *Criminal Code* Amendments Dealing with the Mentally Disordered Accused" (1994) 36 *Criminal Law Quarterly* 49.

PACIOCCO, D. "Death by Stone-ing: The Demise of the Defence of Simple Automatism" (1999) 26 *Criminal Reports* (5th) 273.

SCHNEIDER, R, & D NUSSBAUM. "Can the Bad Be Mad?" (2007) 53 *Criminal Law Quarterly* 206.

STUART, D. *Canadian Criminal Law: A Treatise*, 7th ed (Toronto: Thomson Carswell, 2014) ch 6.

SUTTON, R. "Canada's *Not Criminally Responsible Reform Act:* Mental Disorder and the Danger of Public Safety" (2014) 60 *Criminal Law Quarterly* 41.

SELF-DEFENCE,
NECESSITY,
AND DURESS

This chapter will outline three defences that may apply when the accused faces external threats or pressures. Unlike mistake of fact or intoxication, these defences are not derived from the fault element of the particular offence, and they can apply even though the accused committed the *actus reus* in a physically voluntary manner and had the *mens rea* required for the offence. For example, a person who intentionally kills another may nevertheless have a defence of self-defence. Those who intentionally break into a house to save themselves from freezing to death may have a defence of necessity and a person who intentionally assists in a robbery because of death threats may still have a defence of duress.

All the defences examined in this chapter operate as complete defences that result in the accused's acquittal. In each case, there must be a reasonable doubt about each requirement of the defence. Unlike in the cases of mental disorder, automatism, or extreme intoxication, the accused does not have to establish self-defence, necessity, or duress on a balance of probabilities.

All three defences require a person to have acted reasonably in response to external pressures. In self-defence, these external pressures are violence, or threats of force from the victim; in duress, threats of serious harm from third parties; and in necessity, dire circumstances of peril. The Supreme Court has observed that self-defence, necessity, and duress "all arise under circumstances where a person is subjected to an external danger, and commits an act that would otherwise be criminal as a way of avoiding the harm the danger presents."[1]

The common requirement that the accused respond to these pressures in a reasonable fashion raises the familiar issue of how objective standards should be applied to ensure fairness towards individual accused. This issue first arose in the context of self-defence claims by women who killed abusive partners. The Court's landmark decision in *R v Lavallee*[2] to consider particular experiences and circumstances that the accused faced in determining whether the accused reasonably perceived a threat and acted reasonably has had implications for all the defences examined in this chapter.

The Supreme Court has accepted a modified objective standard that invests the reasonable person with the relevant characteristics and experiences of the accused for all three defences examined in this chapter, as well as the defence of provocation, which will be examined in Chapter 10, because it provides a partial defence that reduces murder to manslaughter. This approach to endowing the reasonable person with similar characteristics and experiences as the accused stands in contrast to the Court's decision that a modified objective standard based on an individuated or contextual reasonable person is generally not appropriate in applying the objective fault standards discussed in Chapter 5.[3] The modified objective standard used to administer these defences responds to the danger of holding accused to unreasonable standards of restraint, but it also risks blurring the distinction between subjective and objective standards and undermining social interests in requiring people to satisfy general standards of reasonable conduct.

Some of the defences examined in this chapter — self-defence, defence of property, and duress (as applied to principal offenders) — are codified, whereas others such as necessity and duress (as applied to secondary parties) are common law defences that the courts have recognized and developed.[4] Overly restrictive statutory or common law defences may violate section 7 of the *Charter* by allowing those who have acted in a morally involuntary manner to be punished. Moreover, defences should not be subject to any special deference under the

---

1   *R v Hibbert* (1995), 99 CCC (3d) 193 (SCC) [*Hibbert*].

2   (1990), 55 CCC (3d) 97 (SCC) [*Lavallee*], discussed below in this chapter.

3   *R v Creighton* (1993), 83 CCC (3d) 346 (SCC) [*Creighton*], discussed in Chapter 5, Section C(1).

4   Section 8(3) of the *Criminal Code*, RSC 1985, c C-46 [*Code*] has been interpreted as allowing courts to develop and recognize new defences. Entrapment, which was examined in Chapter 2, Section B(2)(d), has been developed as a common law defence.

Charter.[5] The Supreme Court has struck out the requirement in the statutory defence of duress that the threat must be of immediate death or bodily harm and that the threat must be from a person who is present at the time that the accused commits the crime under duress on the basis that they could result in the conviction of a person who has no other reasonable choice but to commit a crime.[6]

The Court has read in common law concepts to what remains of the section 17 duress defence. Consistent with the common law defence of duress and necessity, an accused who claims the section 17 defence must now demonstrate a reasonable basis for his or her belief in a threat, a close temporal connection between the threats and the commission of the alleged crime, the existence of no safe avenue of escape, and proportionality between the threats faced and the crime committed.[7] This has brought the section 17 defence that applies to principal offenders and the common law defence that applies to parties much closer. The section 17 defence still, however, has a categorical list of offences that Parliament has deemed too serious to be excused that is not present in the common law defence. In other words, Parliament remains more inclined to impose categorical restrictions on defences than courts, which, consistent with the common law method, shape defences on a case-by-case basis.

A. CONCEPTUAL CONSIDERATIONS

1) Excuses and Justifications

Criminal law defences are sometimes classified as excuses or justifications. A defence that excuses a crime is one that acknowledges the wrongfulness of the action but holds that in the circumstances the accused should not be punished for the crime. The Supreme Court has stated that excuses rest

> on a realistic assessment of human weakness, recognizing that a liberal and humane criminal law cannot hold people to the strict obedience of laws in emergency situations where normal human instincts, whether of self-preservation or altruism, overwhelmingly impel disobedience . . . . Praise is indeed not bestowed, but pardon is, when one does a wrongful act under pressure which . . . "overstrains human

---

5   *R v Ruzic* (2001), 153 CCC (3d) 1 (SCC) [*Ruzic*].
6   *Ibid.*
7   *R v Ryan*, [2013] 1 SCR 14 [*Ryan*].

> nature and no one could withstand . . . . . At the heart of [necessity conceptualized as an excuse] is the perceived injustice of punishing violations of the law in circumstances in which the person has no other viable or reasonable choice available; the act was wrong but it is excused because it was unavoidable."[8]

In other words, "excuses absolve the accused of personal accountability by focussing, not on the wrongful act, but on the circumstances of the act and the accused's personal capacity to avoid it." Because the accused has no realistic choice but to commit the crime, "criminal attribution points not to the accused but to the exigent circumstances facing him."[9] Section 17 of the *Criminal Code* provides that a person who commits a crime under duress from threats is "excused" from the commission of crimes, and both it and the common law defences of duress and necessity have been conceptualized as excuses.

In contrast, a defence that acts as a justification "challenges the wrongfulness of an action which technically constitutes a crime." The accused is not punished because, in the circumstances, "the values of society, indeed of the criminal law itself, are better promoted by disobeying a given statute than by observing it."[10] A justification is not conceived as a concession to normal human weakness. Most would classify self-defence as a justification on the basis that people have rights to defend their persons and their property. The Supreme Court has distinguished self-defence from necessity and duress by explaining that in self-defence, "less emphasis is placed on the particular circumstances and concessions to human frailty and more importance is attached to the action itself and the reason why the accused was justified in meeting force with force."[11]

As will be seen in the case of necessity and duress, whether a defence is conceptualized as an excuse or a justification can have a practical effect on its availability. Excuses are inherently limited by what is thought necessary for a realistic concession to reasonable human weaknesses, whereas justifications are more wide-ranging in holding that certain values are so important that they justify disobeying the law. The excuses of necessity and duress are more restrictive than the justification of self-defence because necessity and duress excuse the commission of crimes against innocent third parties while the justification of self-defence generally operates to justify the use of force against an

---

8   *R v Perka*, [1984] 2 SCR 232, 14 CCC (3d) 385 at 398 [*Perka*].

9   *Ruzic*, above note 5 at paras 40 and 46.

10   *Perka*, above note 8 at 396–97 (cited to CCC).

11   *Ryan*, above note 7 at para 24.

aggressor.[12] The Supreme Court has refused to apply duress in a case where a battered woman tried to hire a police officer to kill her abusive husband. The Court explained that if any defence applied in such a situation, it would be self-defence, that was a "less restrictive" defence than duress and did not require (like duress) "that any course of action other than inflicting the injury was 'demonstrably impossible' or that there was 'no other legal way out.'"[13]

Excuses may be more restrictive than justifications, but they are also a constitutional baseline because it is fundamentally unfair to punish a person for committing a crime when a reasonable person in the same circumstances would commit the crime. The Supreme Court has accepted the idea that a conviction of a person who committed a crime in a morally involuntary manner because the circumstances were so exigent that there was no realistic choice but to commit the crime would offend section 7 of the *Charter*. This acceptance is largely based on the self-defining and self-limiting nature of the juristic category of an excuse.[14] Nevertheless, the classification of a defence as an excuse or a justification does not affect the disposition of the accused. Duress and necessity are commonly seen as excuses, yet they lead to a complete acquittal just as the justification of self-defence does.

Although often recognized, the distinction between excuses and justifications has at times become blurred in Canadian law. A proportional relation between the harm inflicted by the accused and the harm avoided is commonly thought to be one of the defining features of a justification that makes a crime taken in the circumstances rightful. As will be seen, however, Canadian courts and legislatures have imposed proportionality requirements as part of necessity and duress defences, even though they are commonly seen as excuses. Recent reforms to self-defence and defence of property have dropped the language of justification that previously appeared in the *Criminal Code*, perhaps in recognition that proportionality is only one element to determine whether

---

12   *Ryan, ibid* at para 20. This is not absolute because accused can make a reasonable mistake that the persons they defend against are aggressors and because self-defence under s 34(1) of the *Code* can apply to the commission of crimes against innocent parties (such as stealing a vehicle to escape from an aggressor).

13   The Court elaborated that "if infliction of harm on a person who threatened or attacked the accused is not justified by the law of self-defence, it would be curious if the accused's response would nonetheless be excused by the more restrictive law of duress. For the sake of the coherence of the criminal law, the defence of self-defence ought to be more readily available, not less readily available, than the defence of duress in situations in which the accused responds directly against the source of the threat." *Ryan, ibid* at para 27.

14   *Ruzic*, above note 5.

self-defence was reasonable. This may recognize that some forms of self-defence may have elements of excuses as realistic concessions to human weaknesses and not simply act as a justification that challenges the wrongfulness of the act. It does, however, produce the paradoxical result that proportionality between the harm threatened and the harm inflicted is now required in Canadian criminal law for the so-called excuses of duress and necessity, but it is not absolutely required for the so-called justification of self-defence or defence of property.

2) Relation to Fault Element

The defences examined in this chapter are not conceived as an absence of *mens rea* in the same way as the mistake of fact or intoxication defences examined in previous chapters. At the same time, however, evidence relating to these defences could conceivably be relevant to proof of the mental element of some crimes. Evidence of self-defence, necessity, or duress, perhaps when combined with other factors such as intoxication, could possibly lead the jury to have a reasonable doubt as to whether the accused had the fault element for a particular crime. This would usually be possible only for offences with a high subjective level of *mens rea* and in situations where the defences of duress, necessity, or self-defence would not apply because the objective requirements of those offences are not satisfied. This possibility may, however, be more theoretical than real. As discussed in Chapter 5, the Supreme Court has indicated that duress will not negate the formation of a common intent under section 21(2) or the intent required under section 21(1)(b) and (c) when a party performs an act or omission for the purpose of aiding another person to commit an offence.[15] This means that situations of duress (and presumably necessity and self-defence) cannot undermine the relatively high subjective *mens rea* required of parties to an offence.

3) Subjective and Objective Components

In order to qualify for self-defence, necessity, or common law duress, the accused must not only subjectively and honestly perceive the need to respond to the relevant external pressures or threats, but the accused must also reasonably perceive a threat and respond reasonably to the threat.[16] The Supreme Court has explained that it is "society's concern

---

15   *Hibbert*, above note 1.
16   Section 34(1)(c) requires that acts of self-defence be "reasonable in the circumstances." The duress and necessity defences both require that the accused have

that reasonable and non-violent behaviour be encouraged that prompts the law to endorse the objective standard."[17] This restriction makes sense when it is recognized that an accused who qualifies for these defences will nevertheless have committed a crime, frequently one involving violence, with the required fault element.

At the same time, the use of objective standards raises the challenge of ensuring that accused with particular characteristics and experiences can fairly be expected to live up to the objective standard required by the law. The dilemma is to make the objective standard fair, without collapsing it into a subjective standard. This task can be attempted in several ways. One approach is to endow the reasonable person with some of the characteristics of the particular accused, such as the accused's age or sex. As examined in Chapter 5, the Supreme Court has rejected such a modified objective approach for administering objective fault elements in offences. The Court was concerned that such an approach could undermine the purpose of objective fault requirements in requiring that all persons abide by the same standard of conduct. As will be seen in this chapter, the Court has been more willing to factor in characteristics of the accused such as age and gender when applying objective standards to defences. At the same time, however, the Court has warned that such an approach should not be taken so far as "to subvert the logic of the objective test" so that objective standards imposed on defences fail to accomplish their purpose in encouraging that all persons act whenever possible in a reasonable and non-violent manner.[18]

Objective standards must also be contextualized or modified to reflect the particular circumstances that the accused faced. For example, the Court has recognized that evidence of past battering and expert evidence concerning how battered women respond to cycles of violence is relevant in assessing the reasonableness of claims of self-defence.[19] Such evidence may also be relevant to determining "the reasonableness of a battered woman's actions or perceptions" when duress or necessity defences are claimed. It has been suggested that such evidence is a means of ensuring that "the perspectives of women, which have historically been ignored, . . . equally inform the 'objective' standard

---

no safe avenue of escape and proportionality between what is threatened and the crime committed, and both of these concepts have an objective component.

17   *R v Hill* (1986), 25 CCC (3d) 322 at 330 (SCC) (in relation to provocation but the same principle applies for the purpose of the reasonableness standard in self-defence, duress, and necessity).

18   *R v Tran*, [2010] 3 SCR 350 at paras 33–34 [*Tran*] in relation to the ordinary person standard used in the provocation defence examined in Chapter 10, Section A(4).

19   *Lavallee*, above note 2; *R v Malott* (1998), 121 CCC (3d) 456 (SCC) [*Malott*].

of the reasonable person in relation to self-defence."[20] This contextual approach also suggests that the accused's particular experiences may be relevant to placing the external pressure faced by the accused in its proper context.

The emphasis in the modified objective standards discussed in this chapter (and in relation to provocation discussed in Chapter 10) is on how the accused's experiences affect context, not the level of self-control that the law expects. The fact that the accused had previously been beaten would not speak to the level of self-control expected, but could be considered so that the jury could fully understand the implications of the threats that the accused faced. For example, the fact that a woman had been previously battered by a man she assaults or kills may be relevant in determining whether she had a reasonable basis for believing that she was being threatened by the man and that the violence she used was reasonable in the circumstances. Of course, considering the full context of the pressures that the accused faced may have the practical result of making it easier to excuse the accused's conduct. The distinction[21] between modifying the objective standard in order to place the events in context and individualizing it in a manner that lowers the standard of reasonable conduct expected is a critical but sometimes difficult distinction to maintain.

4) Burden of Proof

Although the extreme intoxication, mental disorder, and automatism defences examined in the last two chapters must be proven by the accused on a balance of probabilities, the defences examined in this chapter must be disproved by the Crown as part of its burden to prove guilt beyond a reasonable doubt. Thus, if the jury has a reasonable doubt that an accused acted in self-defence, or under duress or necessity, it must acquit. In *R v Pétel*,[22] Lamer CJ stated that in a case of self-defence, "it is the accused's state of mind that must be examined, and it is the accused (and not the victim) who must be given the benefit of a reasonable doubt." The same is true with respect to the partial defence of provocation examined in the next chapter. In order to acquit, there must be a reasonable doubt about each of the required elements of

---

20   *Malott, ibid* at 470–71, L'Heureux-Dubé J (McLachlin J concurring).

21   In *Tran*, above note 18 at para 35, the Court warned "there is an important distinction between contextualizing the objective standard, which is necessary and proper, and individualizing it, which only serves to defeat its purpose" in encouraging reasonable behaviour.

22   (1994), 87 CCC (3d) 97 at 104 (SCC) [*Pétel*].

self-defence, necessity, and duress. Conversely, the prosecutor can disprove any of these defences by establishing beyond a reasonable doubt
that one of the essential elements of the defence does not exist.

5) Air of Reality

The judge does not, however, have to instruct the jury about every defence in every case. The accused has to overcome a threshold air of
reality burden in every case. In *R v Cinous*,[23] the Supreme Court indicated that a standard air of reality test should apply to all defences.
The appropriate air of reality test was whether a properly instructed
jury acting reasonably could acquit on the basis of the evidence. This
requires evidence on each necessary element of the defence and that a
properly instructed jury acting reasonably could acquit on the basis of
the evidence. In administering the air of reality test, the judge should
assume that evidence is true and leave the determination of its credibility to the jury.

The air of reality test does not impose a persuasive burden on the
accused. Once a judge determined there is an air of reality to any of
the defences examined in this chapter, the jury should be instructed
to acquit if it has a reasonable doubt about the existence of the defence.
The majority of the Court in *Cinous*, however, held that there was no air
of reality to the accused's claim that he acted reasonably in self-defence
when he shot the victim in the back of the head,[24] even though there
was an air of reality to the accused's claim that he reasonably believed
he would be attacked. Without an air of reality to each of the essential
elements of self-defence, the jury should not have even been instructed
about self-defence.[25]

---

23   (2002), 162 CCC (3d) 129 (SCC) [*Cinous*].

24   This case was decided under the old s 34(2)(b) that required that accused
     believe on reasonable grounds that they could not otherwise preserve them-
     selves from such harms. The Court held that the defence need not have been left
     with the jury because "there is absolutely no evidence from which a jury could
     reasonably infer the reasonableness of a belief in the absence of alternatives."
     Ibid at para 123. Under the current s 34(1)(c) of the *Code*, above note 4, the issue
     would now simply be whether a jury could reasonably infer that the accused's
     actions were "reasonable in the circumstances" without reference to the lack of
     any alternatives.

25   It may seem confusing that there must be an air of reality for each of the mul-
     tiple essential elements of self-defence, necessity, and duress but if there is an
     air of reality and the defence is left to the jury, the prosecutor must only prove
     beyond a reasonable doubt that one of the multiple essential elements of the

B. SELF-DEFENCE

The statutory provisions in the *Criminal Code* governing self-defence were notoriously complex. In 1995, the Supreme Court criticized them as "highly technical," "excessively detailed," and "internally inconsistent" and stated that "legislative action is required to clarify the *Criminal Code*'s self-defence regime."[26] The old provisions attempted to define the various circumstances in which an accused might act in self-defence. They drew distinctions on the basis of whether the accused intended to cause death or grievous bodily harm, or had no such intent. They also drew distinctions on the basis of whether the accused had assaulted or provoked the person against whom he or she claimed self-defence. In some cases, they imposed specific duties of retreat on accused. They also required in some circumstances that the accused reasonably believed that they could not otherwise preserve themselves from death or grievous bodily harm. They also contained distinctions between self-defence and defence of third parties under the protection of the accused and between the protection of personal property and dwelling houses. Although not without some defenders, these attempts to classify the various situations in which a claim of self-defence might arise were often criticized as artificial and unnecessary.

Amendments to the *Criminal Code* in 2012 adopt a simpler approach based on one encompassing provision in a new section 34, governing defence of self and others, and a new section 35, governing defence of all forms of property. These new provisions, which only apply to events committed after their proclamation into force on March 11, 2013,[27] simplify self-defence and defence of property considerably though at some expense to the predictability of the defences. As will be seen, the new self-defence provisions are less demanding of the accused than the defences of necessity and duress, which explicitly require proportionality between the harm inflicted and the harm avoided and that there be no legal way out. The new provisions instead simply require that the acts of self-defence and defence of property be reasonable in the circumstances.

The new provisions retain the basic structure of the previous self-defence provisions because they require both that the accused act with the subjective purpose of defending self or others and that they

---

defence does not exist. The explanation is the defence only applies and prevents the conviction of the accused if all of its multiple essential elements are present.

26 *R v McIntosh*, [1995] 1 SCR 686 at para 18 [*McIntosh*].

27 The new provisions have not been applied to events before their enactment on the basis that they substantively change the law and as such should be applied prospectively. See *R v Evans*, 2015 BCCA 46 [*Evans*]; *R v Bengy*, 2015 ONCA 397.

must act reasonably both with respect to the perceptions of the threat and the response to the threat. A fully subjective approach to self-defence, though used in some jurisdictions,[28] could encourage hot-headed and unnecessary resort to violent self-help. The defences of necessity, duress, and provocation also similarly blend subjective and objective requirements.

At the same time, the need for reasonable grounds and conduct in self-defence raises the difficult issue of whether and how objective standards should be contextualized to reflect the accused's circumstances and characteristics. The new section 34(2) continues the trend in recent self-defence jurisprudence to allow objective standards to be contextualized to reflect the accused's characteristics and history. It requires judges and juries to consider a variety of factors including the imminence and nature of the threat, whether there were other means to respond, and the proportionality of the force used by the accused to the force threatened against the accused or others. At the end of the day, however, it simply requires that any act of self-defence be reasonable in all the circumstances. The new section 34 provides:

34. (1) A person is not guilty of an offence if

    (a) they believe on reasonable grounds that force is being used against them or another person or that a threat of force is being made against them or another person;

    (b) the act that constitutes the offence is committed for the purpose of defending or protecting themselves or the other person from that use or threat of force; and

    (c) the act committed is reasonable in the circumstances.

(2) In determining whether the act committed is reasonable in the circumstances, the court shall consider the relevant circumstances of the person, the other parties and the act, including, but not limited to, the following factors:

---

28 For a subjective approach to self-defence, see *Beckford v R* (1987), [1988] AC 130 (PC). In *People v Goetz*, 497 NE2d 41 at 50 (NY 1986), the New York Court of Appeals stated that to base self-defence solely on the accused's subjective beliefs "would allow citizens to set their own standards for the permissible use of force" and risk acquitting individuals who use violence "no matter how aberrational or bizarre his thought patterns." At the same time, however, there is some evidence that contrary to the instructions it received from the judge in that case, the jury applied a subjective test in acquitting Goetz, the so-called subway vigilante, for shooting four African-American youths who approached him in the New York subway and asked him for $5; George Fletcher, *A Crime of Self-Defence* (New York: Free Press, 1988) at 186–88.

    (a) the nature of the force or threat;

    (b) the extent to which the use of force was imminent and whether there were other means available to respond to the potential use of force;

    (c) the person's role in the incident;

    (d) whether any party to the incident used or threatened to use a weapon;

    (e) the size, age, gender and physical capabilities of the parties to the incident;

    (f) the nature, duration and history of any relationship between the parties to the incident, including any prior use or threat of force and the nature of that force or threat;

    (f.1) any history of interaction or communication between the parties to the incident;

    (g) the nature and proportionality of the person's response to the use or threat of force; and

    (h) whether the act committed was in response to a use or threat of force that the person knew was lawful.[29]

1) Self-Defence and Defence of Others in the New Section 34

Section 34(1) now contains one defence for self-defence and defence of others. It provides that accused are not guilty of an offence if (a) they believe on reasonable grounds that force is being used against them or another person or that a threat of force is being made against them or another person; (b) the act is committed for the purpose of defending or protecting themselves or the other person from the use or threat of force; and (c) the act committed is reasonable in the circumstances.[30] There must be an air of reality about all three elements for the defence to be left with the jury, but the defence will not apply if the prosecutor proves beyond a reasonable doubt that at least one of the three essential elements of the defence is not present.

---

29   *Code*, above note 4, s 34(3), addresses self-defence in the context of legally authorized actions and provides: "3) Subsection (1) does not apply if the force is used or threatened by another person for the purpose of doing something that they are required or authorized by law to do in the administration or enforcement of the law, unless the person who commits the act that constitutes the offence believes on reasonable grounds that the other person is acting unlawfully."

30   *Ibid*, s 34 as amended by SC 2012, c 9.

a) Self-Defence Applies to a Broad and Expanded Range of Offences

The new provision makes clear that self-defence can be claimed not only as a defence to charges of violent crimes such as assault or murder undertaken in self-defence, but also to any offence. Thus, self-defence could apply if an accused stole a vehicle in order to protect him- or herself or others. In such circumstances, the theft could be justified under the new section 34 provided that the accused reasonably believed he or she was threatened and the theft was reasonable in the circumstances. This expansion of self-defence makes sense given that the alternative offence would often be a more proportionate response to real or threatened violence than the use of actual violence. The existence of less drastic means to respond to the potential use of force and the proportionality of the response are specifically enumerated factors under section 34(2)(b) and (g) in determining the reasonableness of self-defence. In some cases, the commission of a property or other offences to facilitate escape could be a preferred means of responding to a threat of violence than violent self-defence. The approach taken in Florida and a number of other states of extending the so-called Castle doctrine of no retreat beyond the home can encourage unnecessary violent self-help.

There are no restrictions on the offences to which section 34 can apply and, as under the old law, self-defence can apply to the most serious crimes including murder. As will be seen, it is an open question whether necessity or duress would be available to murder because of the explicit requirement of proportionality between the force threatened and the force used. In this way, self-defence is less demanding on the accused than common law duress and necessity, perhaps because the victim in self-defence will usually be an aggressor.

The new section 34 departs from the old law in not making the accused's intent to cause death or grievous bodily harm specifically relevant to the self-defence claim. Such determinations are best left to the determination of whether the accused has the fault required for the offence. The accused's intent may be relevant in determining the reasonableness of the self-defence, but it is not enumerated in the non-exclusive list of factors in section 34(2). At most, the accused's intent will be one among a range of factors that is relevant in determining the reasonableness of the act of self-defence.

b) No Specific Reference to Self-Defence as a Justification

The previous law on both self-defence and defence of property specifically incorporated the language of justification. As previously discussed, the Canadian courts have recognized a distinction between excuses conceived of as realistic concessions to human weaknesses and justifications that are challenges to the wrongfulness of the act.[31] Self-defence has traditionally been seen as a justification and not an excuse on the basis that accused have rights to defend themselves and their property. Those who act in proportionate self-defence are seen as right in defending themselves and not as persons who must be excused for committing a crime under dire circumstances. At the same time, Canadian criminal law is not entirely consistent in this regard and requires that crimes committed under duress and necessity be proportionate to the harm threatened even though those defences are characterized as excuses and not justifications. In addition, the use of the modified objective standard to determine reasonableness has introduced some excuse-like elements into self-defence in order to ensure that the reasonableness of an accused's perceptions of threats or his or her response to them is judged fairly and in a manner that is sensitive to the accused's particular characteristics and experiences.[32]

The new defences in both sections 34 and 35 refer to a person not being guilty of an offence and do not make reference to their acts being justified, as did the previous self-defence provisions. What effect, if any, will this change have? In most cases, acts of proportionate self-defence can still be seen as a justification, but the new approach recognizes that the theoretical distinction between justification and excuse can become blurred in some contexts. For example, the Supreme Court disapproved in 1990 of a case in which appellate courts had held that a battered woman could not claim self-defence or defence of others when she shot her sleeping husband.[33] If self-defence was recognized in such a case, it would bear some resemblance to an excuse that accommodated human frailties as opposed to a justification that would apply to rightful conduct.

Although the Court has appealed to the concept of an excuse to limit necessity and to some extent duress, they have generally not appealed to the concept of a justification to limit self-defence.[34] In this respect, the omission of the concept of justification in the new section 34 is

---

31   *Ruzic*, above note 5; *Perka*, above note 8.

32   *Lavallee*, above note 2.

33   *R v Whynot*, (1983), 9 CCC (3d) 449 (NSCA) [*Whynot*], disapproved of in *Lavallee*, above note 2 at 116.

34   But see *R v Ryan*, 2011 NSCA 30 at para 71, rev'd on other grounds 2013 SCC 3, refusing to allow self-defence to go to a jury because a battered woman could not be justified in hiring a hit man to kill her abuser but allowing the excuse of duress to go to the jury. To the extent that this decision relies on the statutory concept of justification in the old self-defence provisions, it should no longer be viewed as valid given that the new s 34 does not employ the language of justification.

consistent with recent developments in self-defence, especially in the context of battered women. A number of courts of appeal have suggested that the new provisions are generally more generous to the accused than the old provisions.[35] This is consistent with the idea that the new section 34 may contain excuse-like elements. At the same time, the Quebec Court of Appeal has noted that the new section 34(2), unlike the old section 34(2), requires some consideration of proportionality and whether alternative, less drastic means were available to the accused.[36] This suggests that the new defence contains some justification-like elements.

c) First Requirement: Belief on Reasonable Grounds That Force or Threat of Force Is Being Used Under Section 34(1)(a)

An accused under section 34(1)(a) must believe on reasonable grounds that force or the threat of force is being used against them or another person. In *R v Reilly*,[37] Ritchie J explained that in applying a similarly dual objective and subjective standard in the old law of self-defence, the jury can be guided by the accused's subjective beliefs "so long as there exists an objectively verifiable basis for his perception." A mistake by the accused as to the existence of force or threat of force is not fatal to a self-defence claim, but the mistake must be reasonable.

The old law of self-defence generally referred to unlawful assault or assaults as the triggering factor whereas section 34(1)(a) now refers to force or the threat of force. This approach should simplify matters by avoiding having to resort to the definitions of assault and the classification of unlawful assaults. The concept of responding to the threat of force may expand self-defence somewhat, but the old law rejected the idea that the accused must wait until an assault was underway in order to respond with self-defence.[38]

The new concept of a threat of force could be applied in a case such as *R v Pétel* in which the Supreme Court held that an accused can qualify for a self-defence claim even though he or she was in fact not being unlawfully assaulted. The case arose when a woman who had been threatened by one of two men shot both of them after one of them had given her his gun. She claimed that she reasonably, but perhaps

---

35   *Evans*, above note 27; *R v Cormier*, 2017 NBCA 10 at para 46 [*Cormier*].

36   *Levers c R*, 2017 QCCA 1266 at para 85. The Ontario Court of Appeal has also interpreted the new s 34(2) as requiring proportionality and not being available in a case where the accused stabbed a person eight times. *R v Breton*, 2016 ONCA 425 at para 12.

37   *R v Reilly* (1984), 15 CCC (3d) 1 at 7 (SCC) [*Reilly*].

38   *Lavallee*, above note 2 at 116.

mistakenly, believed she was being unlawfully assaulted by both men. Chief Justice Lamer stated:

> An honest but reasonable mistake as to the existence of an assault is . . . permitted . . . . The existence of an assault must not be made a kind of prerequisite for the exercise of self-defence to be assessed without regard to the perception of the accused. This would amount in a sense to trying the victim before the accused.[39]

The question for the jury was not "'was the accused unlawfully assaulted?' but rather 'did the accused reasonably believe, in the circumstances, that she was being unlawfully assaulted?'"[40] In determining the reasonableness of the belief, the jury could consider prior threats and violence received by the accused from the victim[41] and expert evidence concerning battered woman syndrome.[42] Under the new section 34(1), the relevant question for the jury would now be whether the accused reasonably believed that she faced force or a threat of force. As before, reasonable mistakes will not defeat a self-defence claim and past acts might be relevant in determining whether the accused reasonably perceived that force or the threat of force was being used.

The new concept of a threat of force is also consistent with the Supreme Court's landmark decision in *R v Lavallee*.[43] In that case, the Court held that there was no legal requirement that the accused wait until she faced an imminent attack from the deceased. In doing so, the Court upheld the acquittal of a woman who had shot her abusive partner in the back of the head after he had threatened that she would be harmed after guests had left their house. Justice Wilson stated that expert testimony about the effects of battering on women can cast doubt on the view expressed in a previous case that it was "inherently unreasonable to apprehend death or grievous bodily harm unless and until the physical assault is actually in progress."[44] Expert evidence may suggest "it may in fact be possible for a battered spouse to accurately predict the onset of violence before the first blow is struck, even if an outsider to the relationship cannot." She stressed

---

39   *Pétel*, above note 22 at 104.
40   *Malott*, above note 19 at 464. See also *R v Currie* (2002), 166 CCC (3d) 190 (Ont CA).
41   *Pétel*, above note 22.
42   *Malott*, above note 19.
43   *Lavallee*, above note 2.
44   *Ibid* at 116, citing *Whynot*, above note 33.

> [t]he issue is not, however, what an outsider would have reasonably perceived but what the accused reasonably perceived, given her situation and her experience . . . .
>
> I do not think it is an unwarranted generalization to say that due to their size, strength, socialization and lack of training, women are typically no match for men in hand-to-hand combat. The requirement . . . that a battered woman wait until the physical assault is "underway" before her apprehensions can be validated in law would . . . be tantamount to sentencing her to "murder by installment."[45]

In the context of spousal battering, "the definition of what is reasonable must be adapted to circumstances which are, by and large, foreign to the world inhabited by the hypothetical 'reasonable man.'"[46]

In subsequent cases, the Supreme Court affirmed that evidence of prior threats and beatings would be relevant to the determination of whether the accused could perceive danger from an abuser.[47] The accused's knowledge of the complainant's propensity for violence is also relevant.[48] Although the history of the relationship between the parties to the incident is mentioned explicitly only in section 34(2)(f.1) as a factor to be considered in determining whether the act of self-defence was reasonable in the circumstances, it should also be relevant in determining whether the accused believed on reasonable grounds that he or she faced force or a threat of force.

Although the imminence of the force is likewise only mentioned in section 34(2)(b) as a factor in determining the reasonableness of the act and there is no legal requirement of an imminent attack, the presence or absence of an imminent threat is a factor that can be considered in determining whether the accused had a reasonable belief of force or threat of force.[49] The concept of a threat of force extends the law of self-defence but only so far. Drawing on concepts under the old law of self-defence that it concluded were not changed in the new section 34, the Nova Scotia Court of Appeal has stated that the "accused need not wait until he or she is actually assaulted before acting, and an accused is not by law required to retreat before acting in self-defence."[50] Under section 34(1)(a), the focus is not on the reasonableness of the actions taken by the accused, but whether there was a belief on reasonable grounds that

---

45   *Lavallee*, above note 2 at 120.

46   *Ibid* at 114.

47   *Pétel*, above note 22; *Malott*, above note 19.

48   *R v Pintar* (1996), 110 CCC (3d) 402 at 435 (Ont CA).

49   *Cinous*, above note 23.

50   *R v Levy*, 2016 NSCA 45 at paras 112 and 124–29 [*Levy*].

force or a threat of force would be used. Factors such as the relationship between the accused and the victim can be relevant.

The jury should not be instructed about self-defence if there is no air of reality to the accused's claim that he had a reasonable belief that he or she was subject to force or a threat of force. For example, cases under the old law decided that an adult son could not claim to have reasonably apprehended that his frail, asthmatic seventy-five-year-old father presented a realistic danger of inflicting death or grievous bodily harm.[51] The question under the new section 34(1) would be whether a jury could reasonably conclude that there was a reasonable basis for the accused's belief that he or she faced force or threat of force from the victim.

d) The Protection of Others

Self-defence has been expanded in section 34(1)(a) not only by reference to threats of force, but also by the inclusion of force or threats of force against "another person." The old provision for the defence of others was limited to the defence of persons under the accused's protection. This term was not defined, but was commonly thought to include family members and others to whom the accused owed a duty of care. Now, defence of others could be claimed with respect to unrelated third parties, for example, in circumstances where an accused came across a stranger being beaten or threatened by others and acted in defence of that person. In this way, section 34(1)(a) has broadened self-defence to include the defence of all other persons. As such it now also supplements the more narrow provisions in section 27 that provide a separate defence for using reasonable force to prevent a commission of offences subject to arrest without warrant and that are likely to cause immediate and serious injury to persons or property.

Good Samaritans will be able to act in defence of all others, but they must under section 34(1)(a) believe on reasonable grounds that the other person is faced with force or the threat of force. They must also under section 34(1)(b) act with the subjective purpose of defending the other person. Moreover, the force they use under section 34(1)(c) must be reasonable in the circumstances. These requirements should exclude violent persons who are "itching for a fight" and who may use real or imagined threats to third parties as an excuse for violence. That said, a mistaken belief that a third party is threatened by force or threat of force may still qualify under section 34(1) if it is a reasonable mistake in the circumstances.

---

51   R v Hebert (1996), 107 CCC (3d) 42 at 50 (SCC) [Hebert].

e) Second Requirement: Subjective Purpose of Defending Oneself or Others Under Section 34(1)(b)

Section 34(1)(b) requires that those claiming self-defence have the subjective purpose of defending themselves or others. In most cases, this subjective inquiry will be the least challenging requirement for the accused of the three requirements of self-defence. It will, however, exclude those accused who do not subjectively intend to defend themselves or others but rather desire to seek vengeance, punishment, or vindication of honour against someone who has used force against them or threatened to do so. The more difficult cases will be those where such improper subjective purposes are combined with the required subjective purposes of defending self or others. One judge in applying this requirement has concluded that a battered woman was acting in subjective self-defence even though she was also angry at the accused.[52] This suggests that subjective defence of self or others is satisfied even if the accused also has other purposes or emotions.

The separation out of the inquiry into the accused's subjective purpose under section 34(1)(b) will make it important that the jury is clearly instructed that the subjective purpose of self-defence is not sufficient and that the accused must in addition have both a reasonable belief that they are threatened and that they respond reasonably. A completely subjective approach to self-defence could allow people who act on unreasonable, inaccurate, and even racist perceptions of threats from others to be acquitted.

f) Third Requirement: Acts Done in Self-Defence Must Be Reasonable in the Circumstances Under Section 34(1)(c)

In most self-defence cases, the critical issue will be whether the act done by the accused was reasonable in the circumstances. Section 34(1)(c) provides a more general and open-ended standard than the old law of self-defence which in some contexts specifically required that the accused use no more force than was necessary or use self-defence that was necessary to preserve the accused from death or grievous bodily harm. The new section 34(1) essentially delegates to the judge and the jury the issue of determining whether self-defence is reasonable in the circumstances.

Section 34(2) provides that the "court shall consider the relevant circumstances of the person, the other parties and the act, including,

---

52 *R v Knott*, 2014 MBQB 72 at para 104 [*Knott*]. In this case, the judge also found that the accused's actions were reasonable because "a tolerant approach is to be employed when measuring the proportionality of the force." *Ibid* at para 147.

but not limited to" nine specified factors. As originally introduced in Parliament, section 34(2) simply provided that the court may consider such factors. The mandatory nature of the requirements now means that the jury should consider all the listed factors and any other relevant circumstances as they relate to the accused, other persons, and the act that is claimed to be self-defence.

Although all relevant factors including the nine listed factors must be considered, it would be quite onerous to require either an air of reality or a reasonable doubt about all nine listed factors. As suggested previously, the three elements of self-defence remain those three factors listed in section 34(1), namely, the requirements of (1) a belief on reasonable grounds of force or threat of force; (2) subjective purpose of defending self or others; and (3) that the act be reasonable in the circumstances. Section 34(2) merely provides guidance to courts in determining whether the third requirement exists and its list of factors is not exhaustive of the relevant factors. Judges should read the long list in section 34(2) to the jury and the jury should consider all the listed factors, but they can also consider other relevant factors relating to the accused, the parties, and the act. This open-ended approach allows courts and juries to consider new factors that may be relevant. At the same time, however, it also makes self-defence less predictable and less structured and demanding than the necessity and common law duress defences that require proportionality between the harm threatened and inflicted and that there be no legal alternative.

g) Modified Objective Standard and the History of the Relationship Between the Parties to the Incident

As under the old law of self-defence, a modified objective standard should be used in determining whether acts of self-defence are reasonable in the circumstances. This standard should account for the history of the relationship of the parties to the incident. *Lavallee* is the landmark case in this regard because it was the Supreme Court's first decision embracing a modified objective approach that considered the accused's situation and experience. *Lavallee* has, however, sometimes been misunderstood as making the accused's status as a battered woman (or not) determinative of the self-defence claim. This is unfortunate because Wilson J specifically warned:

> [T]he fact that the accused was a battered woman does not entitle her to an acquittal. Battered women may well kill their partners other than in self-defence. The focus is not on who the woman is, but on

what she did . . . . Ultimately, it is up to the jury to decide whether, in fact, the accused's perceptions and actions were reasonable.[53]

The converse of the above proposition should also be true. A woman may act in self-defence against a threatening partner even if she does not satisfy clinical definitions of being a battered woman.

The contextual objective standard articulated in *Lavallee* was not limited to issues of gender and past battering. In *Nelson*,[54] the Ontario Court of Appeal held that an accused's diminished intelligence should be considered in determining whether he had a self-defence claim. The Court of Appeal stated that an accused with an intellectual impairment relating to his or her ability to perceive and react to an assault "may be in a position similar to that of the accused in *Lavallee* in that his or her apprehension and belief could not be fairly measured against the perceptions of an 'ordinary man.'" It has subsequently affirmed that diminished intelligence can be factored into the modified objective standard, but not an accused's "psychological make-up," unless, like diminished intelligence, it is attributed to matters outside the accused's control.[55] The Nova Scotia Court of Appeal indicated that the jury should have been instructed about both past altercations between the accused and the victim and that the accused had Asperger's Syndrome, which may have impaired his social functioning and made him anxious, paranoid, and distrustful.[56] The Supreme Court has approved of a decision that factored in expert evidence about prison environment in determining whether an inmate faced a threat from other inmates.[57] In general, the jury should be instructed to consider a reasonable person with any of the characteristics and experiences that are relevant to the accused's ability to perceive harm and to respond to it. The accused's age, gender, physical capabilities, and past interaction and communication with the person who presents a threat may be relevant to both perceptions of harm under section 34(1)(a) and the reasonableness of the response under section 34(1)(c).[58]

The reference to the reasonableness of the accused's response in section 34(1)(c) should be read in light of the Court's use of the modified objective standard since *Lavallee*. In addition, there are some specific-

---

53   *Lavallee*, above note 2 at 126.
54   *R v Nelson* (1992), 71 CCC (3d) 449 at 467 (Ont CA).
55   *R v Berry*, 2017 ONCA 17 at paras 72–73.
56   *R v Kagan* (2004), 185 CCC (3d) 417 (NSCA).
57   *R v McConnell*, [1996] 1 SCR 1075 [*McConnell*].
58   There is no need for a modified objective standard under s 34(1)(b), which focuses on whether the accused acts with the subjective purpose of defending oneself or others.

ally enumerated factors in section 34(2) that must be considered and that support the use of the modified objective standard. These include the reference in section 34(2)(e) to the "size, age, gender and physical capabilities of the parties to the incident"; in section 34(2)(f) to "the nature, duration and history of any relationship between the parties to the incident, including any prior use or threat of force and the nature of that force or threat"; and in section 34(2)(f.1) to "any history of interaction or communication between the parties to the incident." It could be argued that the specific reference to size, age, physical capabilities, and gender is exhaustive of the modified objective standard, but this would be a mistake given both the specifically non-exhaustive nature of the section 34(2) factors and the development of the modified objective standard to incorporate other factors that the accused cannot control, such as mental disabilities. Indeed, limiting the modified objective standard to size, age, gender, and physical capabilities might even result in a successful equality rights challenge on that basis.

The reference in section 34(2)(f) and (f.1) to the relationship between the parties including the use of force and threats between the parties and the history of their interaction and communication reflects a series of cases involving claims of self-defence by battered women. In *Lavallee*, the Supreme Court held that evidence of battering and expert evidence on the effects of battering was relevant in determining the reasonableness of the response. Such evidence would be particularly relevant in explaining why a woman did not leave an abusive relationship sooner. Justice Wilson stressed that "the jury must ask itself . . . whether, given the history, circumstances and perceptions of the [accused], her belief that she could not preserve herself from being killed by [the deceased] that night except by killing him first was reasonable."[59] In *Pétel*, the Supreme Court affirmed that the prior assaults suffered by the accused and her daughter would be relevant to determining the reasonableness of her "belief that she could not extricate herself otherwise than by killing the attacker."[60] In *Malott*,[61] the Court again affirmed that evidence with respect to past battering may be relevant to determine the reasonableness of the accused's response. The modified objective standard thus includes not only the size, age, gender, and other non-controllable characteristics of the accused, but also the history of the accused's relationship with the victim including any prior force or threat of force.

---

59   *Lavallee*, above note 2 at 125.
60   *Pétel*, above note 22 at 104.
61   *Malott*, above note 19.

One characteristic of the particular accused that should not be considered is his or her intoxication. In *Reilly*,[62] the Supreme Court held that the accused's intoxication could not be considered in determining whether he reasonably apprehended harm. The Court concluded:

> The perspective of the reasonable man which the language of s. 34(2) places in issue here is the objective standard the law commonly adopts to measure a man's conduct. A reasonable man is a man in full possession of his faculties. In contrast, a drunken man is one whose ability to reason and to perceive are diminished by the alcohol he has consumed.

The Court left open the possibility that an intoxicated accused could have a valid self-defence claim provided that he or she still had reasonable grounds for his or her beliefs. Although the new section 34(2) allows a non-exhaustive use of factors to be considered, intoxication is simply not relevant to determining whether an act of self-defence is reasonable in the circumstances.

The reference to particular characteristics and past circumstances in sections 34(2)(e) and (f) are not limited to those of the accused but extend to those of all parties to the incident. This recognizes the fact that it is relevant in cases such as *Lavallee* that the victim is a larger male with a past history of beating and threatening the female accused. At the same time, sections 34(2)(d) and (e) suggest that the old age or small size of a victim and the use or absence of a weapon could also be relevant to whether the accused responded reasonably to force or a threat of force. At the end of the day, however, the focus should be on the accused and the accused should be given the benefit of the doubt about whether he or she acted in self-defence.

h) Retreat from Homes and Other Situations

The concept of whether the accused should retreat before using self-defence has been controversial. The Supreme Court in *Lavallee* affirmed that there is no requirement that the accused retreat from his or her home.[63] The origins of this concept are in the old common law notion that "a man's home is his castle."[64] Justice Wilson argued that a "man's home may be his castle but it is also the woman's home even if it seems

---

62   *Reilly*, above note 37 at 8.

63   A statutory duty to retreat was formerly imposed under the old s 35(c) on those accused who committed the initial assault or provoked it.

64   *Semayne's Case* (1604), 77 ER 194 (KB). See also *R v Antley*, [1964] 2 CCC 142 at 147 (Ont CA) [*Antley*]; *R v Deegan* (1979), 49 CCC (2d) 417 (Alta CA) [*Deegan*], affirming the concept in the context of intruders on the accused's property.

to her more like a prison in the circumstances."[65] Courts of appeal have held that the jury should be instructed that retreat is not a reasonable option for those attacked in their homes.[56] This doctrine is not specifically mentioned in the new section 34, but a number of courts of appeal has affirmed its continued relevance.[67]

Any no retreat doctrine should, however, be administered cautiously because it could encourage unnecessary and perhaps disproportionate violent self-help. The new section 34(2)(b) suggests that courts may consider "whether there were other means available to respond to the potential use of force." These other means in some situations could include retreat. The fact that the new defence applies to all offences also means that it could provide a defence in situations where an accused stole a car or trespassed on other property in order to avoid a violent situation.

i)   The Proportionality of the Act Done in Self-Defence

In determining the reasonableness of the act done in self-defence, the trier of fact shall consider a number of specifically enumerated factors, including in section 34(2)(a) "the nature of the force or threat" to be avoided; whether the force "was imminent and whether there were other means available to respond" to it (section 34(2)(b)); whether weapons were used or threatened (section 34(2)(d)) and "the nature and proportionality of the person's response to the use or threat of force" (section 34(3)(g)). These factors can all be grouped under the general heading of the proportionality or relative harm of the force resisted or threatened and the force used by the accused. At the same time, the only absolute requirement in section 34(1)(c) is that the act done must be reasonable in the circumstances. There is no requirement that the force or threat faced by the accused must be imminent or even that the accused's response must be proportionate, though these factors must be considered in determining the reasonableness of the act done. Similarly, there is no requirement that the accused must retreat in all cases. This is consistent with the historical tendency of Canadian courts not to demand that all self-defence be strictly proportional or that the accused take all possible routes of retreat.[68]

---

65   *Lavallee*, above note 2 at 124.

66   *R v Forde*, 2011 ONCA 592 at para 56; *R v Proulx* (1998), 127 CCC (3d) 511 at paras 45–46 (BCCA); *Antley*, above note 64 at 147; *Deegan*, above note 64.

67   *Levy*, above note 50 at para 155; *R v Cunha*, 2016 ONCA 491 at para 9; *Cormier*, above note 35 at paras 57–59.

68   *R v Kong*, 2006 SCC 40.

Section 34(1)(c) is more generous than the old section 34(2) of the *Code* because it does not require accused to believe on reasonable grounds that the act done in self-defence was the only way to protect themselves from death or grievous bodily harm. In *R v Cinous*,[69] the Supreme Court held that there was no air of reality to put self-defence to the jury in a case in which a man shot another man in the back of the head while they were stopped at a service station on route to steal computers together. The accused feared that the deceased and a companion were planning to kill him because they had put on latex gloves. The accused also testified that he believed he had no alternatives. He had tried to avoid the deceased and he did not think of calling the police to help because he had spent his whole life running from the police. Chief Justice McLachlin and Bastarache J for the majority of the Court held that while the jury may reasonably have reached a conclusion that the accused reasonably apprehended an assault and death or grievous bodily harm, it could not have reasonably concluded that the accused reasonably believed he had no alternative but killing the person. Unlike in *Lavallee*, there was no evidence supporting why the accused may have reasonably believed that there were no other alternatives. The fact that the accused may have reasonably believed that the police could not protect him was not enough. He could still have fled the scene: "Section 34(2) does not require that an accused rule out *a few* courses of action other than killing. The requirement is that the accused have believed on reasonable grounds that there was *no alternative course of action* open to him . . . . This defence is intended to cover situations of last resort."[70] Under the new section 34(1)(c), however, the relevant question would not be whether the accused believed on reasonable grounds that there was *no* other course of action, but only whether the accused's actions were reasonable in the circumstances. It may well be more difficult for a judge to hold that there is no air of reality to a self-defence claim under this new and less structured self-defence provision. If so, the issue would ultimately fall to the jury to decide whether the accused's actions were reasonable in all the circumstances.

j)   The Accused's Role in the Incident

The old defences drew complex distinctions between assaults that were unprovoked and assaults provoked by the accused. This required com-

---

69   *Cinous*, above note 23.

70   *Ibid* at paras 123–24 [emphasis in original]. See also *R v Pilon*, 2009 ONCA 248 at paras 73 and 75, rejecting the idea that a criminal subculture of kill or be killed should be considered and that self-defence is a defence of last resort as measured by the standards of the ordinary community as represented by the jury.

plex instructions to the jury on multiple defences. Section 34(2)(c) much more simply allows the jury to consider "the person's role in the incident" in determining whether the act done in self-defence is reasonable in the circumstances. The jury will then apply their own judgment about the relevance and importance of what the accused may have done to provoke force or threats of force. This approach is certainly easier to administer, but underlines how self-defence claims under the general reasonableness standard of section 34(1)(c) may be more difficult to predict than under the old law.

The Nova Scotia Court of Appeal has indicated that the proper answer to a jury's question about whether an aggressor can use self-defence "when he starts losing a fight and believes he is in danger" is a simple "yes," albeit subject to the overriding requirement that self-defence be reasonable in the circumstances as required under section 34(1)(c). The Court of Appeal added: "In this way, a protection is hopefully present to prevent self-defence from becoming too ready a refuge for people who instigate violent encounters, but then seek to escape criminal liability when the encounter does not go as they hoped and they resort to use of a weapon."[71]

k) Excessive Self-Defence

If excessive self-defence leads to a conclusion that the act was not reasonable in the circumstances, the accused will, as under the old law of self-defence,[72] be convicted, at least absent another defence or a reasonable doubt about *mens rea*. Canadian courts have not recognized a partial defence for accused who engage in excessive and unreasonable self-defence, which in some other jurisdictions reduces murder to manslaughter. Justice Dickson has concluded in the context of an unsuccessful self-defence claim under the old section 34(2):

> Where a killing has resulted from the excessive use of force in self-defence the accused loses the justification provided under s. 34. There is no partial justification open under the section. Once the jury reaches the conclusion that excessive force has been used, the defence of self-defence has failed.[73]

This decision is also supported by section 26 of the *Criminal Code*, which provides that everyone authorized by law to use force is criminally

---

71 *R v Borden*, 2017 NSCA 45 at para 101.
72 Stephen Coughlan, "Duress, Necessity, Self-Defence and Provocation: Implications of Radical Change?" (2002) 7 *Canadian Criminal Law Review* 147 at 199–200; Eric Colvin & Sanjeev Anand, *Principles of Criminal Law*, 3d ed (Toronto: Thomson Carswell, 2007) at 320–23.
73 *R v Faid* (1983), 2 CCC (3d) 513 at 518 (SCC).

responsible for any excess of force. The result can make self-defence, especially when the accused has the intent required for murder, an all or nothing proposition. The options are either to acquit on the basis of self-defence or to convict the accused of the most serious offence with its mandatory penalty of life imprisonment. Concern about the ultimate disposition of an accused in cases such as *Lavallee* and *Pétel* may have influenced the development of the law of self-defence. The rejection of the idea that excessive or non-reasonable self-defence should be a partial defence that reduces murder to manslaughter also places significant pressure on the accused to accept a plea bargain to manslaughter should one be offered.

l)   Section 34(3): Self-Defence Against Law Enforcement Actions
Can a person use self-defence in resisting arrest or other law enforcement actions? Section 34(3) prevents such self-defence claims unless the accused "believes on reasonable grounds" that those enforcing the law are "acting unlawfully." This means that in order to claim self-defence against law enforcement actions the accused must both subjectively and reasonably believe that the law enforcement actions are unlawful. The requirements for both subjective and objective components are consistent with the general tenor of the self-defence provisions. It also suggests that those who resist arrests will only have a defence if they both subjectively and reasonably believe that the officer is acting unlawfully.

In many cases, the critical issue under section 34(3) will be whether the accused's belief that the law enforcement actions were unlawful is reasonable. The requirement of reasonableness is not a standard of perfection. The accused may have a reasonable belief that the police are acting unlawfully even though the police may actually be acting lawfully. The reasonableness standard should be a modified one at least to the extent of considering the history of the parties. The accused should also be given the benefit of the doubt as is the case with all other elements of self-defence. Even if the accused's belief that the law enforcement actions are unlawful is accepted as reasonable, accused must still under section 34(1)(a) have reasonable grounds to believe that they face force or threats of force; they must under section 34(1)(b) act for the purpose of defending themselves or others and the acts that they do must be reasonable in the circumstances under section 34(1)(c).

m)   Summary
The new section 34 is less structured and predictable than the old self-defence provisions or, as will be seen, the necessity and duress

defences. Nevertheless, the new section 34 retains the basic elements of self-defence in that the accused must subjectively perceive a threat and respond for the purpose of defending themselves or others and there must be a reasonable basis both for the accused's perceptions of force and the accused's response in the circumstances. The trend towards a contextual application of objective standards also continues with specific reference to the characteristics and history of the parties to the incident.

In order for self-defence to be left to the jury there must be evidence upon which a jury acting reasonably could find (1) a belief on reasonable grounds that force or threat of force is being made against the accused or another; (2) that the act was done for the subjective purpose of defending the accused or the other person; and (3) that the act was reasonable in the circumstances. In order to justify an acquittal, there must be a reasonable doubt about each of those three requirements.

2) Defence of Property in the New Section 35

Section 35 now contains one defence for defence of property and makes no distinction between various forms of property and dwelling houses. The new section 35 provides:

> 35. (1) A person is not guilty of an offence if
>
> > (a) they either believe on reasonable grounds that they are in peaceable possession of property or are acting under the authority of, or lawfully assisting, a person whom they believe on reasonable grounds is in peaceable possession of property;
> >
> > (b) they believe on reasonable grounds that another person
> >
> > > (i)   is about to enter, is entering or has entered the property without being entitled by law to do so,
> > >
> > > (ii) is about to take the property, is doing so or has just done so, or
> > >
> > > (iii) is about to damage or destroy the property, or make it inoperative, or is doing so;
> >
> > (c) the act that constitutes the offence is committed for the purpose of
> >
> > > (i) preventing the other person from entering the property, or removing that person from the property, or
> > >
> > > (ii) preventing the other person from taking, damaging or destroying the property or from making it inoperative, or retaking the property from that person; and
> >
> > (d) the act committed is reasonable in the circumstances.

2)   Subsection (1) does not apply if the person who believes on rea-
     sonable grounds that they are, or who is believed on reasonable
     grounds to be, in peaceable possession of the property does not
     have a claim of right to it and the other person is entitled to its
     possession by law.[74]

There are four requirements to defence of property. They are:

1)   the accused must believe on reasonable grounds that they are in
     peaceable possession of property (or reasonably believe that they
     are acting under the authority of or lawfully assisting such a per-
     son): see section 35(1)(a);
2)   the accused must also believe on reasonable grounds that another
     person is entering, taking, damaging, or destroying the accused's
     property: see section 35(1)(b);
3)   the accused must also act for the subjective purpose of protecting
     the property: see section 35(1)(c);
4)   finally, the accused's acts must be "reasonable in the circum-
     stances": see section 35(1)(d).

The judge must be satisfied that there is an air of reality on all four
of the above elements to put the defence to the jury. In cases where the
defence is left to the jury, the jury must have a reasonable doubt on all
four elements to justify an acquittal, or in other words, the prosecution
need only prove beyond a reasonable doubt that one of the four elements did not exist.

a)   Defence of Property Applies to a Broad and Expanded Range of Offences

As with the new self-defence provision, the new defence of property
applies not only to assaults and other acts of force done to protect property, but any other offence. Unlike in self-defence, however, proportionality is not a specifically enumerated factor in defence of property.
This omission creates the potential that the section 35 defence might be
claimed to serious offences of violence done to protect property. In any
event, an act of defence of property must under section 35(1)(c) be done
for the subjective purpose of protecting property and must under section
35(1)(d) be reasonable in the circumstances. This latter requirement

---

74   Section 35(3) addresses the defence of property against law enforcement and
     provides that there is no defence, "unless the person who commits the act that
     constitutes the offence believes on reasonable grounds that the other person is
     acting unlawfully."

should disqualify attacks on people for reasons not related to and not reasonable to the defence of property.

b) No Specific Reference to Defence of Property as a Justification

As under the new section 34, there is no specific reference in section 35 to the concept that defence of property constitutes a justification of rightful conduct as opposed to an excuse that makes a realistic concession to human frailties. The omission of the concept of justification is more than a theoretical quibble with respect to defence of property because the new section 35 omits the concept of using no more force than necessary that was found in several of the old defence of property provisions relating to defence of dwellings. Section 35 does not specifically require the proportionality of the response be considered as one of the relevant factors in determining whether an act done to defend property is reasonable in the circumstances. One of the features of a justification is that the harm inflicted is less serious than the harm avoided and this makes the conduct rightful in the circumstances. As will be seen, it is possible that seriously injuring or even killing a person solely to defend property could be considered to be a valid defence of property under section 35. If such an extreme defence was recognized under section 35, it would operate more as an excuse for conduct that would still be wrongful given the value of human life and health and not as a justification of rightful conduct.

c) No Deeming of Assault but Continued Overlap Between Defence of Property and Self-Defence

The old defence of property provisions provided that a trespasser who resisted an attempt to protect personal or real property would be deemed to have committed an assault. These complex provisions are not present in the new section 35. Nevertheless, this does not preclude frequent overlap between defence of property and self-defence provisions. For example, a person who is protecting property may also be able to claim self-defence if they have a reasonable belief that force or a threat of force is being made against them. The New Brunswick Court of Appeal has noted this overlap in a case where it concluded that, while it would not have been reasonable for the accused to have killed a person to prevent his trespass into an apartment, the trial judge had erred by not relating the evidence to self-defence under section 34 once the person was in the accused's apartment.[75]

---

75 *Cormier*, above note 35.

d) The Modified Objective Standard

Under section 35, there must be a reasonable basis for the belief that the accused has possession of the property (section 35(1)(a)); that the property is being threatened (section 35(1)(b)); and that the accused's actions are reasonable in the circumstances (section 35(1)(d)). In principle, the modified objective standard used with respect to self-defence should also be applied to defence of property. The accused's history and circumstances may be relevant to their belief in the peaceable possession of property and their belief that their property is being threatened. The age, size, gender, physical capabilities, and perhaps other personal characteristics of the parties may also be relevant to determining whether a particular act done in defence of property was reasonable in the circumstances. As always, care must be taken to ensure that the objective standard of reasonable conduct is contextualized but does not become a subjective standard or one that demands lower standards of restraint from some accused.

e) First Requirement: Reasonable Belief in Peaceable Possession and Claim of Right Under Section 35(1)(a)

The first requirement for defence of property is a reasonable belief by the accused that they are in peaceable possession of property. The old defence of property provisions also used the concept of peaceable possession. It has been interpreted to include control of property that was peaceable because it was not seriously challenged by others. Indigenous protesters who have occupied land have previously been held not to be in peaceable possession of the land.[76] The new section 35(1)(a) does not, as did the prior section, actually require peaceable possession of the property. It only requires a reasonable belief in such peaceable possession. This seems to open the door for a court to hold that a person claiming the defence had a reasonable belief in peaceable possession even if mistaken. This may be of particular relevance in cases such as Indigenous occupations where the actual question of possession may be contested and difficult to determine. The concept of a reasonable belief in peaceable possession may also make relevant the history of the accused's claims to possession and even perhaps legal and other advice received about the possession.

Section 35(2), however, places an additional requirement by requiring that an accused who has a reasonable belief in peaceable possession will not have a defence if they do "not have a claim of right to it and

---

76   *R v George* (2000), 145 CCC (3d) 405 (Ont CA) [*George*]; *R v Born with A Tooth* (1992), 76 CCC (3d) 169 (Alta CA).

the other person is entitled to its possession by law." A claim of right can include an honest mistake about entitlement even though the mistake is based on both fact and law.[77] In this way, the concepts of both reasonable belief in peaceable possession and claim of right represent some relaxation of the strict principle that ignorance or mistakes of law is not an excuse. At the same time, it is possible to read section 35(2) as denying the defence of property in cases in which the accused is not entitled to possession of the property. In my view, however, it would be unduly harsh to preclude a defence of property defence if the accused made an honest and reasonable mistake about their entitlement to the property.

f) Second Requirement: Reasonable Belief That Property Is Being Threatened Under Section 35(1)(b)

The second requirement for defence of property is that accused have a reasonable belief that the property in question is being threatened. This section specifies a number of ways in which property can be threatened including when a person is about to enter or enters property without being entitled in law to do so. This provision on its face seems to exclude defence of property as a defence if the accused wrongly, but even reasonably, believes that the person entering the property is not entitled by law to enter the property when in fact the person is so entitled. It would, however, seem to be within the general tenor of the defence provisions to allow an accused to have the benefit of a reasonable mistake that a person was a trespasser even though section 35(1)(b)(i) seems to require that the person actually have no entitlement to enter the property. This section also does not apply in cases where another person may have just entered property, but is no longer on property.

Section 35(1)(b)(ii) applies in cases where an accused believes on reasonable grounds "that another person is about to take property, is doing so or has just done so." This provision expands defence of property to include acts done when the accused reasonably believes that a person has just taken property. It could apply to a security guard or shopkeeper who restrains a person outside the store on the basis of a reasonable belief that the person has just shoplifted.

Section 35(1)(b)(iii) applies in cases where an accused believes on reasonable grounds that "another person is about to damage or destroy property, or make it inoperative, or is doing so." This section clarifies that defence of property applies not only against trespass and theft of

---

77 R v Lei (1997), 120 CCC (3d) 441, leave to appeal to SCC refused (1998), 123 CCC (3d) vi.

property but also vandalism. Like section 35(1)(b)(i), however, this section seems not to apply in cases where the accused has a reasonable belief that a person has just finished damaging property. On the one hand, it could be argued that in such cases the damage has been done and the proper response is to call the police. On the other hand, it is anomalous that the defence applies against those who have just taken property but not to those who have just entered or damaged property but are no longer doing so.

g) Third Requirement: Subjective Purpose of Protecting Property Under Section 35(1)(c)

The third requirement for the defence of property is that the accused have the subjective purpose of protecting property. Depending on the circumstances, this will be a purpose in preventing a trespasser from entering property or removing a trespasser or retaking property or preventing its damage. In many cases, such subjective purposes will be obvious from the circumstances, but this provision would preclude a person who assaults a trespasser, thief, or vandal for the purpose of vengeance or punishment. As under self-defence, courts may find that the accused has the subjective purpose even if he or she has other purposes or emotions such as anger.[78]

The specific reference to accused removing trespassers or retaking property may raise issues about whether such potentially forceful actions by the accused are reasonable in the circumstances. As will be seen, the new section does not incorporate old statutory provisions that frequently required the accused to use no more force than necessary and had been interpreted by the Supreme Court in a number of cases to require a degree of proportionality between the harm inflicted by the accused in defence of property and the harm of the threat to property.[79]

h) Fourth Requirement: Act Must Be Reasonable in the Circumstances Under Section 35(1)(d)

As with the new self-defence provision, the most critical issue with respect to defence of property will often be whether the accused's actions were reasonable in the circumstances. Unlike in self-defence, section 35 of the *Code* provides no enumerated factors that must be considered by judges and juries in determining whether any particular act of defence of property is reasonable in the circumstances. In addition, section 35

---

78   *Knott*, above note 52 at para 104.
79   *R v Gunning*, [2005] 1 SCR 627 at para 25 [*Gunning*]; *R v Szczerbaniwicz*, [2010] 1 SCR 455 at para 20 [*Szczerbaniwicz*]. See also *George*, above note 76 at para 49; *R v McKay*, 2009 MBCA 53 at para 23.

does not follow the frequent references in the old defence of property provisions to the need to use no more force than necessary. This is unfortunate because these phrases have been subject to extensive interpretation by the courts who had read them as requiring some proportionality between the force used to protect property and the harm to property interests that were avoided by the use of self-help.

Nevertheless, the old jurisprudence on proportionality should still inform determinations of the reasonableness of defence of property under section 35(1)(d). In *R v Gee*,[80] Dickson J quoted with approval an authority that stated it "cannot be reasonable to kill another merely to prevent a crime which is directed only against property." The Supreme Court in *R v Gunning* held that the force used by a person in peaceable possession of a dwelling house to eject a trespasser "must have been reasonable in all the circumstances . . . . Where the defence arises on the facts, the onus is on the Crown to prove beyond a reasonable doubt that Mr. Gunning did *not* act in defence of property." The Court indicated that "the intentional killing of a trespasser could only be justified where the person in possession of the property is able to make out a case of self-defence." Thus, the Court has concluded that it will always be unreasonable to intentionally kill a person in order to remove that person as a trespasser.[81] In the subsequent case of *R v McKay*, however, the Court refused to extend such categorical rules when it explicitly stated that it did not endorse the view of the Manitoba Court of Appeal that "'defence of property alone will never justify the use of anything more than minor force being used against a trespasser or that, in all cases, 'the defence of property alone will not justify the intentional use of a weapon against a trespasser.'"[82] The Court in that case did hold that aggravated assault was not justified by defence of property.

In *R v Szczerbaniwicz*[83] the majority of the Supreme Court held that a man had used more force than was necessary when he pushed his estranged wife as she was damaging his diploma. Justice Abella quoted with approval statements by GA Martin J to the effect that self-defence and defence of property provisions reflected the

> great principle of the common law that the use of force in such circumstances is subject to the restriction that the force used is necessary; that is, that the harm sought to be prevented could not be

---

80 (1982), 68 CCC (2d) 516 at 523 (SCC). See also *R v Clark* (1983), 5 CCC (3d) 264 at 271 (Alta CA).
81 *Gunning*, above note 79 at paras 25–26.
82 *R v McKay*, [2007] 1 SCR 793 at para 2.
83 Above note 79.

prevented by less violent means and that the injury or harm done by, or which might reasonably be anticipated from the force used is not disproportion[ate] to the injury or harm it is intended to prevent.[84]

Justice Abella stressed that the "proportionality approach" requires both subjective and objective standards related to the harm caused to property and the harm inflicted in defence of property. Dissenting judges in *Szczerbaniwicz* also accepted that the accused "must have a subjective belief of the necessity, and the belief must be based on reasonable grounds," but stressed that in "'quick response' situations an accused is not expected to 'weigh to a nicety' the exact measure of a defensive action or to stop and reflect upon the precise risk of consequences from such action."[85] The Court was united on the need for proportionate defence of property though they disagreed on how strictly proportionality should be required.

It is unfortunate that Parliament was silent on the proportionality issue under section 35. In my view, courts should read in such a proportionality requirement in the absence of clear legislation displacing the extensive proportionality jurisprudence. Although proportionality is only one of the enumerated factors in section 34(2) relating to self-defence, it has an important role in restraining disproportionately violent defences of property. Although some mechanical approaches to statutory interpretation might find that Parliament's failure to include proportionality in section 35 when it is mentioned in section 34(2) would suggest that Parliament did not intend proportionality to be a factor in section 35, it would be anomalous to restrain defence of life and health with proportionality principles, but not to restrain defence of property. The New Brunswick Court of Appeal has reached a similar conclusion, stating that under the new section 35(1)(d) "it is difficult to conceive how the killing of an individual solely to defend one's property could ever be found to be a reasonable response in the circumstances."[86] It held that while it was reasonable for an accused to have a weapon when opening the door, there was no air of reality for the new defence of property when the accused stabbed a trespasser.[87] At the same time, however, the Court of Appeal held that what started

---

84   *R v Baxter* (1975), 27 CCC (2d) 96 at 113 (Ont CA), quoted with approval in *Szczerbaniwicz*, above note 79 at para 19.

85   *Ibid* at paras 33 and 35.

86   *Cormier*, above note 35 at para 50.

87   *Ibid* at para 67.

as defence of property quickly escalated to self-defence and that self-defence under the new section 34 should have been left to the jury.[88]

i)   Section 35(3): Defence of Property Against Law Enforcement Actions

Section 35(3) prevents a defence of property claim against law enforcement actions unless the "accused believes on reasonable grounds that the other person is acting unlawfully." This follows the same pattern as section 34(3), examined earlier in this chapter. Consistent with the general tenor of the defence of property provisions, it has both subjective and objective components that require that a person have both an honest and a reasonable belief that they are resisting unlawful law enforcement efforts. The requirement of reasonableness is not a standard of perfection and the accused may have a reasonable belief that the police are acting unlawfully even though the police may actually be acting lawfully. The reasonableness standard should be a modified one at least to the extent of considering the history of the parties. The accused should also be given the benefit of the doubt, as is the case with all elements of defence of property.

Even if the accused's belief that the law enforcement actions are unlawful is accepted as reasonable, accused must still under section 35(1)(a) have reasonable grounds to believe that they are in peaceable possession and have a legal right to the property; they must under section 35(1)(b) have a reasonable belief about a threat to property; they must under section 35(1)(c) have the subjective purpose of protecting property; and under section 35(1)(d) their acts done in defence of property must be reasonable in the circumstances. These should be adequate restraints against unreasonable attacks on law enforcement officials.

j)   Summary

The new section 35 is less structured and predictable than the old defence of property provisions, but it should be easier to apply. Section 35(1)(a) requires a reasonable belief in peaceable possession of the property defended. Section 35(2) may restrict the defence to at least require a claim of right and may even preclude the defence when the accused is not in fact entitled to the property. The accused must under section 35(1)(b) also believe on reasonable grounds that the property is threatened or that the accused has just taken the property. In addition, the accused must under section 35(1)(c) act for the subjective purpose of protecting the property and not for other purposes such as vengeance

---

88   *Ibid* at para 62.

and punishment. Finally and most importantly, the act under section 35(1)(d) must be reasonable in the circumstances and courts may well read established principles of proportionality developed in defence of property cases under the old provisions. There must first be an air of reality on all four elements to justify putting the defence to the jury and there must be a reasonable doubt on all four elements to justify an acquittal.

The new sections 34 and 35 of the *Code* are overdue and are in many respects an improvement over the previous self-defence and defence of property provisions that were needlessly complex. They will make the life of judges, jurors, lawyers, and students easier. That said, however, the increased simplicity of these defences will come at a price of less certainty. Self-defence and defence of property are now less structured defences than the defences of necessity and duress, which clearly require proportionality between the harm inflicted and the harm avoided and that there be no legal alternative to breaking the law. Juries will often have to decide what is reasonable without much guidance from the judge or the law.

Previous law reform proposals explicitly required that a person use no more force than necessary and/or that the force used be proportionate to the harm avoided; in some cases it was explicitly stated that defence of property could not justify intentional causing of death or serious harm.[89] The government has chosen not to follow these proposals, but to use the more flexible requirement that self-defence and defence of property must simply be reasonable in the circumstances. To be sure, this does not go as far as a wholly subjective approach or the explicit no-retreat rule used in Florida and other American states. Nevertheless, it may open up new avenues for self-defence and defence of property. For example, cases like *Cinous*, where self-defence was held not to have an air of reality because there was no evidence to support a reasonable belief in lack of alternatives, could potentially be decided differently under the new section 34. The question at the air of reality stage will be whether there is evidence that would allow a jury acting reasonably to conclude that the act was reasonable in the circumstances.

Courts are capable and may well be inclined to read requirements of proportionality and necessity back into self-defence and defence of property. Courts should do so especially with respect to defence of property because of the dangers of killing and maiming people sim-

---

89 These previous proposals were made by the Law Reform Commission of Canada, the Canadian Bar Association, and by the government in a 1993 white paper. See Don Stuart, *Canadian Criminal Law*, 5th ed (Toronto: Carswell, 2007) at 510–11 and 517.

ply to protect property interests and because of the lack of guidance provided by Parliament in respect of what constitutes reasonable force. With respect to self-defence, courts will continue to maintain the flexibility of the contextual objective standard embraced in *Lavallee* and clearly endorsed in the new section 34(2). This approach, as well as the omission of hard and fast proportionality and necessity requirements in the new section 34, also blurs the distinction between justifications and excuses. It opens up the possibility that self-defence may in some circumstances operate more as an excuse and concession to human weakness than a justification that always requires that the force used be proportionate and necessary.

3) Related Defences

There are a number of other provisions that allow justifications for the use of force in specific situations. Section 43 justifies the use of force by way of correction by schoolteachers and parents towards children under their care, provided the force does not exceed what is reasonable under the circumstances. The Supreme Court has narrowly interpreted this controversial defence because it restricts the protection of the law afforded to young people from unconsented invasions of their physical security and dignity. It has held that section 43 does not apply to the discipline of adults with mental disabilities and only applies when used with the intent and for the benefit of correction and education.[90]

In *Canadian Foundation for Children, Youth and the Law v Canada (Attorney General)*,[91] the Supreme Court upheld section 43 as not violating section 7, 12, or 15 of the *Charter*. Although section 43 adversely affects children's security of the person, it was consistent with the principles of fundamental justice. The requirement that the force be reasonable in the circumstances was not unduly vague under section 7 of the *Charter*. The Court indicated that the force must be used for corrective purposes and not include corporal punishment for those under two or over twelve years of age, corporal punishment using objects, such as rulers or belts, or slaps or blows to the head.[92] The result of the decision is to place new restrictions on the section 43 defence. These restrictions are expressed in clear and categorical terms in the Court's judgment but alas not in the text of the section 43 defence. The majority of the Court justified this approach as a proper interpretation of the defence in light of expert evidence and Canada's international obligations, while a minority

---

90   *R v Ogg-Moss* (1984), 14 CCC (3d) 116 (SCC).
91   *Canadian Foundation for Children, Youth and the Law v Canada (AG)*, 2004 SCC 4.
92   *Ibid* at paras 37 and 40.

argued that it was an impermissible reading down of a vague and over-broad defence that should have been struck down.

Section 45 justifies the performance of a surgical operation for a person's benefit if the operation was reasonable in the circumstances and performed with reasonable care. A doctor's actions in stopping res-piratory support of a patient, at the patient's request that nature be allowed to take its course, has been held to be justified under this pro-vision on the basis that the doctor's actions were reasonable.[93]

Sections 25 to 33 provide various justifications for the use of force to prevent criminal offences and to assist in enforcing the law. The Su-preme Court has explained:

> Section 25(1) essentially provides that a police officer is justified in using force to effect a lawful arrest, provided that he or she acted on reasonable and probable grounds and used only as much force as was necessary in the circumstances. That is not the end of the mat-ter. Section 25(3) also prohibits a police officer from using a greater degree of force, that is, that which is intended or likely to cause death or grievous bodily harm, unless he or she believes that it is necessary to protect him- or herself, or another person under his or her protec-tion, from death or grievous bodily harm. The officer's belief must be objectively reasonable. This means that the use of force under section 25(3) is to be judged on a subjective-objective basis. If force of that degree is used to prevent a suspect from fleeing to avoid a lawful ar-rest, then it is justified under section 25(4), subject to the limitations described above and to the requirement that the flight could not rea-sonably have been prevented in a less violent manner.[94]

Although these provisions impose objective standards of using no more force than necessary, the Court has also indicated that police have demanding and difficult work and the amount of force should not be measured with exactitude.[95] A previous provision that authorized the shooting of fleeing felons without regard to whether or not they were dangerous was held to be an unjustified violation of section 7 of the *Charter* by threatening people's lives and security of the person in a disproportionate manner.[96]

---

93   *B(N) v Hôtel-Dieu de Québec* (1992), 69 CCC (3d) 450 (Que SC).

94   *R v Nasogaluak*, [2010] 1 SCR 206 at para 34.

95   *Ibid* at para 35.

96   *R v Lines*, [1993] OJ No 3248 (Gen Div).

C. NECESSITY

Courts were historically reluctant to recognize necessity caused by dire circumstances of peril as either an excuse or a justification. In *R v Dudley*,[97] men who killed a boy and resorted to cannibalism when lost at sea were convicted of murder. Noting that it was "the weakest, the youngest, the most unresisting" who was chosen to die, the court declared that any defence of necessity "appeared to us to be at once dangerous, immoral, and opposed to all legal principle and analogy." The Court conceded that the accused were subject to great suffering, but concluded:

> We are often compelled to set up standards we cannot reach ourselves . . . . [A] man has no right to declare temptation to be an excuse, though he might himself have yielded to it, nor allow compassion for the criminal to change or weaken in any matter the legal definition of the crime.[98]

The accused did not have a defence of necessity and they were convicted of murder. They were sentenced to death, but their sentences were commuted to six months' imprisonment in an exercise of royal mercy by Queen Victoria.

In the 1970s, necessity was pleaded as a defence to the crime of performing an abortion without the approval of an abortion committee. Justice Dickson stated for the Supreme Court that the defence of necessity was "ill-defined and elusive," and concluded that if it did exist in Canadian law, "it can go no further than to justify non-compliance in urgent situations of clear and imminent peril when compliance with the law is demonstrably impossible." He added that "no system of positive law can recognize any principle which would entitle a person to violate the law because on his view the law conflicted with some higher social value."[99] Chief Justice Laskin dissented and would have left the defence with the jury, allowing it to decide whether there was an immediate danger to the woman's life or health and whether it was certain that a legal and committee-approved abortion could be obtained to prevent that danger.

---

97   (1884), 14 QBD 273 at 287 (CCR) [*Dudley*].
98   *Ibid* at 288.
99   *R v Morgentaler (No 5)* (1975), 20 CCC (2d) 449 at 497 (SCC).

1) The Recognition of Necessity an Excuse and Not a Justification

The Supreme Court finally recognized necessity as a common law de-fence in *R v Perka*,[100] which involved drug smugglers who were forced to come ashore in Canada because of dangerous seas. Chief Justice Dickson was careful to restrict necessity to "circumstances of immin-ent risk where the action was taken to avoid a direct and immediate peril"; where the act was "morally involuntary" as "measured on the basis of society's expectation of appropriate and normal resistance to pressure"; and where it was clear that there was no reasonable legal alternative to avoid the peril. The Court recognized necessity as an excuse for morally involuntary conduct but not as a justification that made conduct rightful.

The idea that necessity excuses morally involuntary conduct now gives the common law defence a constitutional foundation, despite the fact that necessity was not recognized as a common law defence until 1984. In *Ruzic*,[101] the Supreme Court held that it was a principle of fundamental justice under section 7 of the *Charter* that a person who acts in a morally involuntary manner not be punished. In other words, those who commit an offence when there is no other realistic choice but to do so should not be punished because their actions are mor-ally involuntary. This means that attempts by Parliament to abolish the common law defence, or perhaps even to restrict it by precluding its use for serious offences, would likely be found to violate the principle of fundamental justice that prevents the punishment of those who act in a morally involuntary manner.

Chief Justice Dickson stressed in *Perka* that necessity could operate as an excuse only in the face of immediate and urgent circumstances, and that it should not be based on "the comparative social utility of breaking the law against importing as compared to obeying the law."[102] In her concurring opinion, Wilson J would have left open the possibil-ity that necessity could operate as a justification. In such a scenario, an accused could have the defence, even though he or she did not act in a morally involuntary manner in the face of an emergency. Rather, the accused could deliberate and decide that the "fulfillment of the legal duty to save persons entrusted to one's care is preferred over the lesser

---

100 Above note 8, headnote at 233 (cited to SCR).
101 Above note 5.
102 Above note 8 at 402 (cited to CCC). Thus, a moral belief that abortion was or was not moral could not be the basis for a necessity defence. *R v Bridges* (1990), 62 CCC (3d) 455 (BCCA).

offences of trespass or petty theft."[103] The English Court of Appeal has recognized necessity as a justification to a deliberate and intentional killing in a case of the conjoined twins where it was certain that they would both eventually die if they were not separated.[104] Whether necessity could be a justification as well as an excuse could have had a practical effect in the abortion context, where those who did not comply with the law had often made a deliberate decision to violate the law.

In R v Morgentaler,[105] the Ontario Court of Appeal held that the defence of necessity should not have been left to the jury when doctors were charged with violating a Criminal Code provision that required the approval of a hospital committee before an abortion was performed. The court stated that the doctors' deliberate and planned decision to violate the law was inconsistent with the morally involuntary response to an immediate peril to life or health that was required for a necessity defence. The Supreme Court[106] did not deal with this issue because it decided that the law requiring approval of an abortion by a hospital committee was an unjustified violation of the rights of women under section 7 of the Charter.

Necessity and duress are recognized in Canada only as excuses. Excuses have a self-defining feature because they are based on what is required by a realistic concession to human weaknesses and do not normally involve a calculation of the respective harms that are avoided and harms that are inflicted.[107] Chief Justice Dickson elaborated that necessity conceptualized as an excuse "rests on a realistic assessment of human weakness, recognizing that a liberal and humane criminal law cannot hold people to the strict obedience of laws in emergency situations where normal human instincts, whether of self-preservation or of altruism, overwhelmingly impel disobedience."[108] The Court's rejection of necessity as a justification could cause injustice especially if the courts take a narrow and restrictive approach to the question of the imminence of peril. At the same time, it avoids the danger of justifying illegal conduct by state officials such as breaking fingers or arms if such conduct can avoid greater harms to the lives of hostages or innocent victims of a reasonably suspected terrorist bomb.

---

103 Perka, above note 8 at 420 (cited to CCC).
104 A (Children) (Conjoined Twins: Surgical Separation), [2000] 4 All ER 961 (CA).
105 (1985), 22 CCC (3d) 353 (Ont CA) [Morgentaler].
106 R v Morgentaler (No 2) (1988), 37 CCC (3d) 449 (SCC), discussed in Chapter 2, Section B(4)(b).
107 As will be seen, however, a proportionality requirement was imposed in Perka, above note 8, out of an abundance of caution.
108 Ibid at 398 (cited to CCC).

a) The Relevance of Clean Hands or Contributory Fault and Illegality

The conceptualization of necessity as an excuse may as in *Morgentaler* preclude premeditated and deliberate decisions to violate the law. At the same time, it should also preclude a "clean hands" argument that would deny the necessity defence to those who were engaged in illegal activity when they were faced with circumstances of urgent and compelling necessity. In *Perka*, the Court rejected the argument that an accused who is engaged in illegal conduct should be disentitled to the necessity defence. This decision meant that the jury could consider the defence, even though the accused had been engaged in drug smuggling when a storm forced them to land on Canadian territory. This followed from the Court's conceptualization of the defence as an excuse that in no way justifies the conduct and the Court's focus on whether the accused had any realistic choice but to commit the crime. It also follows from the traditional focus of whether accused are guilty at the time they commit the prohibited act. Courts should resist any temptation to judge or punish the person because of their prior bad acts.

Nevertheless, Dickson CJ indicated that the defence of necessity would not apply "if the necessitous situation was clearly foreseeable to the reasonable observer, if the actor contemplated or ought to have contemplated that his actions would likely give rise to an emergency requiring the breaking of the law."[109] Those who place themselves in a position where it is reasonably certain that they will have to engage in a crime may be denied the necessity defence.[110]

b) Air of Reality Required on Three Elements of the Necessity Defence and the Crown's Duty to Disprove at Least One Element

The Supreme Court in *R v Latimer*[111] articulated three essential elements of necessity: (1) the requirement of imminent peril or danger; (2) the requirement of no reasonable legal alternative; and (3) the requirement of proportionality between the harm inflicted and the harm avoided. As will be discussed below, the first two requirements are evaluated according to the "modified objective standard . . . that takes into account the situation of the particular accused person"[112] while the third proportionality standard is assessed on a purely objective standard.

Before the jury is instructed to consider the necessity defence, the judge must determine that there is an air of reality to each of the three

---

109 *Ibid* at 403 (cited to CCC).
110 *R v CWV*, 2004 ABCA 208; *R v Nelson*, 2007 BCCA 490; *R v Maxie*, 2014 SKCA 103.
111 *R v Latimer* (2001), 150 CCC (3d) 129 (SCC) [*Latimer*].
112 *Ibid* at para 32.

requirements so that a properly instructed jury acting reasonably could acquit the accused. In *Perka*, the Court indicated that there was an air of reality to the necessity defence in a case where the accused put into shore with thirty-three tons of marijuana because they faced imminent peril on the ocean. In *Latimer*,[113] however, the Court unanimously held that there was no air of reality with respect to any of the elements of necessity when a father killed his daughter in order to prevent her from suffering severe pain that would be caused by a medically required operation.

If there is an air of reality on all three elements of necessity, the defence should be left to the jury. The accused does not have to establish the defence, but will be denied the defence if the Crown can prove beyond a reasonable doubt that at least one of the required three elements of the necessity defence was not present.

2) First Requirement: Reasonable Belief in Imminent Peril and Danger

Chief Justice Dickson indicated in *Perka* that necessity as an excuse applied only when the accused had no realistic choice but to violate the law. He suggested that "at minimum, the situation must be so emergent and the peril must be so pressing that normal human instincts cry out for action and make a counsel of patience unreasonable."[114] The requirement in *Perka* of an imminent peril might be in tension to the recognition six years later in *Lavallee* that some accused, because of their experience and situation, should not be required to wait until harm was just about to occur. Similarly, what may be a reasonable legal alternative for some accused may not be for others.[115]

In addition, the requirement in *Perka* that the peril be imminent might violate section 7 of the *Charter* if the accused responded in a morally involuntary fashion to a serious and unavoidable threat of future harm. In *Ruzic*,[116] a statutory requirement that the duress defence be limited to threats of immediate death or bodily harm was held to violate section 7 of the *Charter* because it could punish those who acted in a morally involuntary fashion.

Following *Ruzic*, the requirement of imminence in the related defence of necessity should not be restricted to immediate threats. It is difficult to distinguish between an accused who breaks into a cabin

---

113 *Ibid.*

114 *Perka*, above note 8 at 399 (cited to CCC).

115 In *R v Lalonde* (1995), 37 CR (4th) 97 at 109 (Ont Ct Gen Div), *Lavallee*, above note 2, was applied to expand the common law defence of necessity.

116 *Ruzic*, above note 5.

for food before he or she has reached a level of starvation or exposure that is life-threatening and one who waits until the peril is immediate. Similarly, it would be difficult to distinguish between a person who leaves a secluded location by driving while impaired to escape a serious attack that has not yet commenced and one who waits until the attack is actually underway. Both accused in these scenarios would have no safe avenue of escape and no realistic choice but to violate the law. A restrictive approach to the imminence requirement is particularly undesirable given the Court's categorical rejection of necessity as a justification that could apply to deliberate and well-thought-out decisions to break the law.

In *R v Latimer*,[117] the Supreme Court affirmed the requirement that "disaster must be imminent, or harm unavoidable and near. It is not enough that the peril is foreseeable or likely; it must be on the verge of transpiring and virtually certain to occur." This restrictive formulation of the imminence requirement creates a risk that the peril may not be held to be imminent until the accused faces an immediate threat. As discussed above, a requirement of an immediate threat would be at odds with developments in self-defence and duress. The focus should be on whether the threat would have an immediate impact on the accused so as to produce morally involuntary conduct, not on whether it is a threat of immediate harm.[118]

The Court indicated in *Latimer* that "where the situation of peril clearly should have been foreseen and avoided, an accused person cannot reasonably claim any immediate peril."[119] On the facts of the case, the Court held there was no imminent peril because Tracy Latimer's "ongoing pain did not constitute an emergency in this case" but was rather "an obstinate and long-standing state of affairs" and that the proposed surgery "did not pose an imminent threat to her life, nor did her medical condition."[120]

The accused's subjective belief that there is an imminent peril is not determinative. There must be a reasonable basis for that belief. Reasonableness will be determined on a modified objective standard. In *Latimer*, the Court held that there was no reasonable basis for Latimer's belief in imminence in part because "there was no evidence of a legitimate psychological condition that rendered him unable to perceive that there was no imminent peril."[121] Here an analogy to evidence of the

---

117 *Latimer*, above note 111 at para 29.
118 *R v Nwanebu*, 2014 BCCA 387 at paras 61–62 [*Nwanebu*].
119 *Latimer*, above note 111.
120 *Ibid* at para 38.
121 *Ibid*.

ability of battered women to predict when another round of battering was imminent might be made. In the absence of such psychological evidence, however, the Court rejected Latimer's subjective belief in the imminence of the peril as unreasonable. The British Columbia Court of Appeal has held that the modified objective standard requires consideration that a person accused of possessing a false passport was fleeing Nigeria and that he had post-traumatic stress disorder from prior beatings in that country. A modified objective standard reflecting the accused's experiences and mental health difficulties should be used in determining whether he had a reasonable belief in imminent danger.[122]

3) Second Requirement: Reasonable Belief in No Legal Way out or Safe Avenue of Escape

In *Perka*,[123] the Court suggested that "if there is a reasonable legal alternative to disobeying the law, then the decision to disobey becomes a voluntary one, impelled by some consideration beyond the dictates of 'necessity' and human instincts." In that case, there was no legal way out because the accused faced disaster and drowning at sea if they did not put ashore with their large cargo of drugs. Courts should not deny the necessity defence simply because the accused was acting illegally at the time that necessity arose, though they have denied the defence on the basis that it was foreseeable when the accused acted that the need to break the law would arise.[124] The principled focus should be on whether the accused acted in a morally involuntary manner at the time that the offence was committed.

In two *Morgentaler* cases,[125] there were legal ways out because a legal abortion could have been approved by a therapeutic abortion committee as then required under the *Criminal Code*. In *Latimer*,[126] the Court affirmed that "if there was a reasonable legal alternative to breaking the law, there is no necessity." It indicated that legal alternatives must be pursued even though they may be "demanding," "sad," and "unappealing."[127] In this case, the Court indicated that allowing Tracy Latimer to go through the required operation and inserting a feeding tube to assist with pain management were reasonable legal alternatives that the accused should have pursued. The determination

---

122 *Nwanebu*, above note 118 at para 84.
123 Above note 8 at 400 (cited to CCC).
124 *Ibid*; *R v John Doe* (2007), 228 CCC (3d) 302 (BCCA).
125 *Morgentaler (No 5)*, above note 99; *Morgentaler*, above note 105.
126 *Latimer*, above note 111 at para 30.
127 *Ibid* at para 38.

of no reasonable legal alternative should be determined on a modified objective standard so that any past experiences that the accused had with the victim's pain, pain management, and surgeries should have been relevant in determining the reasonableness of legal alternatives.

There is some overlap in the determination of the imminence of the peril and the existence of reasonable legal alternatives. In both cases, courts should be careful before demanding that the accused wait until the peril is immediate. The defence of necessity has been denied in a case in which an accused engaged in impaired driving to flee a possible attack because there were other safe avenues of escape.[128] This makes sense because the accused had a reasonable legal way out. It would not, however, make sense to deny the defence to a person with no safe avenue of escape on the basis that she did not wait until the attack was underway to drive away while in an impaired state. It would also be inconsistent with *Lavallee* to deny the necessity defence until the attack was underway. In other cases, courts have found that impaired driving was the only way that the accused could escape attack.[129]

In *R v Kerr*, LeBel J (Arbour J concurring) would have found a valid defence of necessity to a weapons charge laid against a prisoner who carried a shank in a lawless prison and used the shank in self-defence. They concluded that the accused "had a reasonable belief that the circumstances afforded him no legal way out. And the harm he sought to avoid — in the words of the trial judge, 'a lethal attack' — outweighed" the harm of the weapons offence.[130] Justice Binnie stated in dissent that the "argument that violent self-help in breach of the peace can be justified as a 'necessity' has been rejected since medieval times as inimical to public order and should not be given new credence in 21st century Alberta."[131] This dissent discounts both the fact that necessity was considered a defence to the weapons charge and not the homicide charge and the fact that the authorities had lost control of a prison beset by warring gangs.[132] The modified objective approach to both the

---

128 *R v Berriman* (1987), 45 MVR 165 (Nfld CA); *R v Gardner*, 2015 NLCA 44 [*Gardner*].

129 See cases described in D Paciocco, "No-one Wants to Be Eaten: The Logic and Experience of the Law of Necessity and Duress" (2010) 56 *Criminal Law Quarterly* 249 at 258–59. But see *Gardner*, above note 128, finding that there were reasonable alternatives other than impaired driving and no proportionality between the harm of impaired driving and a threat of an assault that had already occurred and was not likely to occur again.

130 *R v Kerr*, [2004] 2 SCR 371 at para 96. The other members of the majority of the Court acquitted on the basis of lack of *mens rea*.

131 *Ibid* at para 68.

132 At the same time, self-defence, especially under the new s 34, might be a more viable and generous option for the accused than claiming necessity.

imminent peril and no legal way out requirements of necessity should make allowances for the exigencies of the prison environment.[133] For example, the prior experience and persecution of a person seeking refugee status may be relevant to determining the reasonableness of the accused's perception of harm and the existence of a safe avenue of escape under the modified objective standard.[134]

4) Third Requirement: Proportionality Between Harm Avoided and Harm Inflicted

Even though he conceptualized necessity as an excuse and not a justification, Dickson CJ required that, as is the case with self-defence, there be proportionality between the harm sought to be avoided and the harm committed by the accused. He stated:

> Even if the requirements for urgency and "no legal way out" are met, there is clearly a further consideration. There must be some way of assuring proportionality. No rational criminal justice system, no matter how humane or liberal, could excuse the infliction of a greater harm to allow the actor to avert a lesser evil.[135]

In *Latimer*,[136] the Court affirmed the importance of the proportionality requirement and held that killing a person was "completely disproportionate" to "non-life-threatening suffering" should Tracy Latimer have had the proposed operation. This suggests that the Court saw the case as one "where proportionality can quickly be dismissed" so that it might not even be necessary to examine whether the above two requirements of the necessity defence can be applied. On the other hand, the Court recognized that "most situations fall into a grey area that requires a difficult balancing of harms." The Court warned that it was not necessary that the harm avoided "clearly outweigh" the harm inflicted, but only that the two harms be "of a comparable gravity."[137] In this vein, the Court declined to create an absolute rule that murder would be categorically excluded from the necessity defence as a disproportionate response to all possible perils. At the same time, the case

---

133 See *McConnell*, above note 57.

134 *Nwanebu*, above note 118 at paras 82–85.

135 *Perka*, above note 8 at 400–1 (cited to CCC).

136 *Latimer*, above note 111 at para 41.

137 *Ibid* at para 31.

stands for the proposition that killing is disproportionate to relieving non-life-threatening suffering.[138]

5) Modified and Contextual Objective Standard for Imminence and No Legal Way out but Not Proportionality

As in the other defences in this chapter, the reasonable person will generally be tailored to reflect the past experiences and frailties of the particular accused. In *Hibbert*,[139] Lamer CJ observed that

> The defences of self-defence, duress and necessity are essentially similar, so much so that consistency demands that each defence's "reasonableness" requirement be assessed on the same basis . . . [namely an objective standard] that takes into account the particular circumstances and frailties of the accused . . . . [I]t is appropriate to employ an objective standard that takes into account the particular circumstances of the accused, including his or her ability to perceive the existence of alternative courses of actions.

In *R v Latimer*, the Court confirmed that a modified objective standard that takes into account the situation and characteristics of the accused should be used for determining (1) whether there was an imminent peril and (2) whether there was a reasonable legal alternative. It cautioned that the modified objective standard must be distinguished from the subjective standard. Thus, the fact that an accused like Robert Latimer subjectively believed that there was imminent peril and no reasonable legal alternative was not enough because his beliefs must also be "reasonable given his circumstances and attributes."[140] In the absence of psychological evidence about caregivers for children who

---

138 The Manitoba Court of Appeal, in upholding the exclusion of murder under s 17 of the *Code*, above note 4, has appealed to *Dudley*, above note 97, as support for the proposition that the common law was based on the moral idea that those threatened with death should not kill another. As will be suggested below, this approach tends to define necessity and duress as justifications. Moreover, *Dudley* is more narrowly framed as denying necessity as a response to suffering not imminent death. Even the Manitoba Court of Appeal recognizes that *Dudley* may no longer be good law, at least in Ontario. *R v Willis*, 2016 MBCA 113 at para 153 [*Willis*]. See also Morris Manning & Peter Sankoff, *Criminal Law*, 5th ed (Markham, ON: LexisNexis, 2015) at 13.79, who similarly argue that the categorical exclusion of killing as disproportionate tends to view necessity or duress "as a justification and thus intrinsically intertwined with morality . . . ."

139 *Hibbert*, above note 1 at 227.

140 *Latimer*, above note 111 at para 33.

lived in much pain, the use of the modified objective standard made little difference in *Latimer*.

The Court in *Latimer* concluded that a modified objective standard should not be used when determining whether there was proportionality between the harm inflicted and the harm avoided. Proportionality was to be determined on a purely objective standard that is not modified by the characteristics and experiences of the accused or the victim. The Court was concerned that a modified objective standard would give too little weight to harms suffered by the victim who was severely disabled. Proportionality is a matter of the moral standards of the community and these standards are "infused with constitutional considerations (such as, in this case, the section 15(1) equality rights of the disabled)."[141] As will be seen, the Court has taken the opposite approach with respect to duress by applying the modified or contextual objective approach to the determination of the proportionality between the harm threatened and the harm inflicted under the duress defence. It is difficult to justify this divergent approach given the common juristic elements of necessity and duress as excuses designed to exempt the accused for morally involuntary conduct.

D. DURESS

Like necessity, duress occurs when an accused commits a crime in response to external pressure. In the case of duress, the pressure is threats of harm by some other person. The classic case is the person who commits a crime or assists in the commission of a crime with a gun to his or her head.

The defence of duress in Canada is complex because of the existence of two separate defences. Section 17 of the *Criminal Code* contains a restrictive defence that only applies to principal offenders. A more generous common law defence applies to parties to an offence. The most restrictive features of the section 17 defence have been held to violate section 7 of the *Charter* by punishing morally involuntary conduct,[142] but the long list of excluded offences under that section remains, though they are vulnerable to *Charter* challenge. The common law defence that applies to parties is more generous than the section 17 defence because no offences are categorically excluded.

---

141 *Ibid* at para 34.
142 *Ruzic*, above note 5.

The Supreme Court in *R v Ryan*[143] has narrowed the differences between common law and section 17 defence by reading in common law concepts to the section 17 defence and applying some statutory concepts found in section 17 to the common law defence. The result is that judge-made common law requirements relating to no safe avenue of escape, close temporal connection between the threat and the crime, and proportionality between the threat and the crime apply to and restrict the section 17 defence even though they are not present on the face of the legislation. Conversely, concepts found in section 17 such as the exclusion of those who are placed under duress as a result of a pre-existing conspiracy or association are under *Ryan* applied in the common law defence.

Finally, it should be noted that duress could be relevant to proof of fault. This is somewhat theoretical because the Court has indicated that duress cannot negate the most common form of fault in situations where people act in response to threats: namely the subjective *mens rea* required when a person under duress acts as a party in assisting the commission of an offence under section 21.[144]

1) Section 17 as Applied to Principal Offenders and Common Law Duress as Applied to Parties to an Offence

The Supreme Court has recognized that "the plain meaning of section 17 is quite restrictive in scope. Indeed, the section seems tailor-made for the situation in which a person is compelled to commit an offence at gun point."[145] Section 17 provides:

> A person who commits an offence under compulsion by threats of immediate death or bodily harm from a person who is present when the offence is committed is excused for committing the offence if the person believes that the threats will be carried out and if the person is not a party to a conspiracy or association whereby the person is subject to compulsion, but this section does not apply where the offence that is committed is high treason or treason, murder, piracy, attempted murder, sexual assault, sexual assault with a weapon, threats to a third party or causing bodily harm, aggravated sexual assault, forcible abduction, hostage taking, robbery, assault with a weapon or causing bodily harm, aggravated assault, unlawfully

---

143 *Ryan*, above note 7.
144 *Hibbert*, above note 1.
145 *Ruzic*, above note 5 at para 50.

causing bodily harm, arson or an offence under sections 280 to 283 (abduction and detention of young persons).[146]

Even before the *Charter*, the Supreme Court minimized the harsh impact of this restrictive defence by concluding that "s. 17 is limited to cases in which the person seeking to rely upon it has himself committed an offence."[147] Section 17 was thus read down only to apply to principal offenders, and the common law defence of duress was held to apply to those who aided, abetted, or formed a common unlawful purpose to commit an offence.[148] It is not, however, always clear who was the principal offender and who only acted as a party or accomplice. Thus, juries sometimes have to be instructed about both the section 17 defence and the common law defence.[149] As a result of the Court's decision in *Ryan*, however, this option is now less confusing for juries (and students) because the Court interpreted the section 17 and common law defences in an identical fashion except for a recognition that section 17 categorically excludes offences ranging from murder to arson. As will be seen, the common law defence remains more generous because the courts have contemplated that it could apply to a person charged as a party to even murder[150] or attempted murder[151] offences.

The Supreme Court has performed some major surgery on section 17 by holding that its requirement that threats must be of immediate death or bodily harm and made by a person who is present when the crime was committed violated section 7 of the *Charter* by denying the defence to those who have no realistic choice but to commit the offence and thus act in a morally involuntary manner. The Supreme Court has yet to rule whether the surviving parts of section 17 violate section 7 of the *Charter* because they categorically exclude from the defence those who commit offences such as murder, attempted murder, robbery, unlawfully causing bodily harm, and arson. It may well be that the categorical exclusion of such a long list of crimes will eventually be held to violate section 7 of the *Charter*. It seems pretty clear that a person who commits the excluded offences of arson, robbery, or assault with a weapon to escape threats of death will be acting in a morally involuntary

---

146 *Code*, above note 4.

147 The section uses the specific words "a person who commits an offence." It does not use the words "a person who is a party to an offence." R v *Paquette* (1976), [1977] 2 SCR 189 at 193 [*Paquette*].

148 *Code*, above note 4, ss 21(1)(b), (c), and 21(2). See Chapter 4, Sections E & F for an explanation of these terms.

149 R v *Mena* (1987), 34 CCC (3d) 304 at 320 (Ont CA).

150 *Paquette*, above note 147.

151 *Hibbert*, above note 1.

manner and responding as a reasonable person in the same situation would. Thus, the excluded offences in section 17 seem destined to be struck down with only the possible but in my view not desirable exception of murder.[152] In such an eventuality, the same defence of duress would apply to parties to a crime and also to principal offenders. The result would make the law both less complex and fairer to the accused.

a) First Requirement: Threats of Death or Bodily Harm Against the Accused or a Third Party

Section 17 required that the threats be of immediate death or bodily harm from a person who was present when the crime was committed. The Supreme Court held in *Ruzic* that the requirements of immediacy and presence violated section 7 of the *Charter* because they could result in the punishment of a person who committed a crime in a morally involuntary manner. In that case, the accused was charged with importing heroin after a person had threatened to kill her mother who lived in a foreign country, if she did not import the drugs. The Supreme Court in *Ruzic* clarified that threats of death or bodily harm against third parties such as the accused's family may be considered under section 17 of the *Criminal Code*.[153] This seems appropriate as threats to one's family or loved ones may be just as compelling as threats to oneself, and Parliament has not clearly excluded threats to third parties from section 17. In addition, other caselaw suggests that the threats need not be expressly from words or gestures but can be reasonably implied from the circumstances. For example, there could be an implied threat when a person instructs his cousin to assist him after the accused killed two other people.[154]

The Supreme Court in *Ryan* held that it was no longer necessary under the common law defence of duress for the threats to be of "grievous" or "serious" bodily harm.[155] This brings the common law defence into line with the wording of section 17 (albeit minus the unconstitutional reference to "immediate" death or bodily harm). Although the law should not excuse a person who committed a serious crime in response to a non-serious threat of harm, such matters are best determined under the proportionality requirement common to both section 17 and common law defences.

---

152 See Section D(2), below in this chapter, for discussion.
153 Above note 5 at para 54.
154 *R v McRae* (2005), 77 OR (3d) 1 (CA).
155 *Ryan*, above note 7 at para 59.

b) Second Requirement: Reasonable Belief That Threats Will Be Carried Out

Although section 17 is worded so as to require that the accused have only a subjective belief that threats of death or bodily harm will be carried out, the Supreme Court in *Ryan* has interpreted section 17 to require that the accused's belief be reasonable. This brings the section 17 defence into line with the common law defence of duress. The Court in *Ruzic*[156] observed that the common law defence of duress "rejects a purely subjective . . . assessment" of the threats. The reasonableness requirement is "analyzed on a modified objective basis, that is, according to the test of the reasonable person similarly situated."[157]

c) Third Requirement: No Safe Avenue of Escape

In *Hibbert*,[158] the Supreme Court concluded that the common law defence of duress will not apply to parties who had a safe avenue of escape and could have safely extricated themselves from the situation of duress. Chief Justice Lamer reasoned that the common law defence of duress, like necessity, applied only if the accused had no realistic choice when deciding whether to commit the crime. The lack of alternatives is not determined solely on the basis of the accused's subjective perception of the available choices, but on the basis of what a reasonable person in the accused's circumstances would have perceived as a safe avenue of escape and a legal way out. He noted:

> The defences of self-defence, duress and necessity are essentially similar, so much so that consistency demands that each defence's "reasonableness" requirement be assessed on the same basis . . . while the question of whether a "safe avenue of escape" was open to an accused who pleads duress should be assessed on an objective basis, the appropriate objective standard to be employed is one that takes into account the particular circumstances and human frailties of the accused . . . . When considering the perceptions of a "reasonable person" . . . the personal circumstances of the accused are relevant and important, and should be taken into account.[159]

In another case, the common law defence of duress was kept from the jury even though the accused honestly believed he had no safe avenue of escape when he picked up drugs from an airport some four months after he was threatened. The Alberta Court of Appeal stated:

156 *Ruzic*, above note 5 at para 61.
157 *Ryan*, above note 7 at para 64.
158 *Hibbert*, above note 1.
159 *Ibid* at 227–28.

"[t]he question is whether a reasonable person, with similar history, personal circumstances, abilities, capacities, and human frailties as the accused, would, in the particular circumstances, reasonably believe there was no safe avenue of escape and that he had no choice but to yield to the coercion," after having taken reasonable steps such as contacting the police, to discover his full range of options.[160] The Court in *Ryan* concluded that the duress defence would not apply if a "reasonable person in the same situation as the accused and with the same personal characteristics and experience"[161] would conclude that there was a safe avenue of escape that provided a reasonable alternative to committing the crime.

d) Fourth Requirement: Close Temporal Connection Between Threat and Harm Threatened

The Court in *Ruzic* held that there was a "need for a close temporal connection between the threat and the harm threatened." This requirement serves a similar purpose as the requirement under the necessity defence that the peril be imminent. It is difficult to justify the difference between the imminence requirement for necessity and the close temporal connection requirement for duress given the similarities between the two defences. A common focus on whether the threats have an immediate effect on the accused in both defences would be preferable. Nevertheless, the facts of *Ruzic* suggest that the Court will interpret the close temporal connection requirement in a flexible manner, and there is no magic in any particular time between receiving the threat and committing the crime. Ruzic was threatened over two months before she committed the crime of importing narcotics. It took her four days from receiving the heroin and a false passport to travel from Belgrade to Toronto via Budapest and Athens. The people who threatened her did not accompany Ruzic, but they remained in Belgrade where threats to Ruzic's mother could have been carried out. As under section 17 of the *Code*, threats to third parties can be the basis for the common law defence of duress.

The Court in *Ryan* indicated that one purpose of the temporal connection requirement is to reinforce the no safe avenue of escape requirement. It concluded: "If the threat is too far removed from the accused's illegal acts, it will be difficult to conclude that a reasonable person similarly situated had no option but to commit the offence."[162]

---

160 *R v Keller*, 1998 ABCA 357 at para 24.

161 *Ryan*, above note 7 at para 65.

162 *Ibid* at para 68.

Another purpose of this requirement is to ensure that the accused was under sufficient pressure to ensure that he or she acted in a morally involuntary manner as required by the logic of excuses. Indeed, greater symmetry with the necessity defence would be achieved if the close temporal connection requirement was subsumed into the no safe avenue of escape requirement. A person who is threatened with a remote harm would often, if not always, have a safe avenue of escape.

e) Fifth Requirement: Proportionality Between Harm Avoided and Harm Inflicted

In *Ryan*, the Court stressed that proportionality was required under both common law and section 17 defences. Proportionality requires 1) "that the harm threatened was equal to or greater than the harm inflicted by the accused" and 2) "a more in-depth analysis of the acts of the accused and a determination as to whether they accord with what society expects from a reasonable person similarly situated in that particular circumstance."[163]

The Ontario Court of Appeal has subsequently stressed that this two-part approach to proportionality goes beyond an abstract comparison of the harm threatened and avoided to a more fact specific examination. It observed:

> Moral involuntariness by its very nature demands a fact-intensive inquiry. Neither prong of the proportionality requirement will always favour sacrificing one's own life over assisting in the murder of another. Choosing to aid in the murder of another will not always amount to choosing an evil greater than the evil threatened. For example, a person may be presented with a choice between taking the life of an innocent third party and the killing of her own child. The putative victims are equally innocent. Surely, the harms flowing from either choice are "of comparable gravity."[164]

This approach makes sense of the Court's decision in *Ryan* not to base proportionality exclusively on the basis of comparative harms, but also to undertake a more in-depth analysis of what society would expect from a reasonable person in the accused's circumstances.

It is difficult to see what role the second part of the *Ryan* inquiry into proportionality would have under the Manitoba Court of Appeal's more absolutist stance that murder can never be excused under section 17 of the *Code*. The second more fact-based inquiry into proportionality

---

163 *Ibid* at para 73.
164 *R v Aravena*, 2015 ONCA 250 at para 65 [*Aravena*].

is also consistent with the Court's holding that the principles of fundamental justice under section 7 of the *Charter* prohibit the conviction of a person who acts in a morally involuntary manner.[165] It could also accommodate the Manitoba Court of Appeal's concern that in some cases the harm of inflicting an immediate death on an innocent victim might be greater than the harm of the accused avoiding an uncertain death sometime in the future.[166]

As discussed above, the Supreme Court has stressed the similarities between necessity and duress. The third requirement of the necessity defence is that there be proportionality between the harm avoided and the harm caused by the accused. In *Latimer*, the Court also indicated that proportionality should be determined on a purely objective standard. In both *Ruzic* and *Ryan*, however, the Court indicated that proportionality for purposes of the duress defence should be applied on a less restrictive modified objective standard.[167] In *Ryan*, the Court attempted to justify these different approaches on the basis that duress has a less robust requirement of an imminent threat than necessity. This argument, however, would logically suggest that a stricter standard of proportionality should be applied to duress, which as in *Ruzic* can apply to threats of future and quite contingent harm. In any event, it is unfortunate and needlessly confusing that the Court has maintained such differences between necessity and duress while appropriately recognizing that the two defences are closely related and based on the same juristic principles of an excuse.

At the same time, the Court's curious affirmation in *Ryan* that proportionality should be judged for the purpose of duress (but not necessity) on the basis of a modified or contextual objective standard may help explain cases such as *Paquette*[168] and *Hibbert*[169] that hold that the common law defence of duress could be a defence to very serious crimes such as murder and attempted murder. The modified objective standard has the ability to factor in the relationship and past interactions between the accused and the person issuing threats, something that may be relevant to the accused's perception of how serious and certain that threat is when claiming duress. In most necessity cases, however, the threat will come from objective circumstances such as threats from nature that will usually be experienced in the same way by most people. Despite this, the Court has clearly stated that a modified objective approach will be

---

165   *Willis*, above note 138.
166   *Ibid* at paras 158 and 167.
167   *Latimer*, above note 111 at para 74.
168   Above note 147.
169   Above note 1.

applied to determining proportionality in duress while an unmodified objective approach will be applied for necessity.

Ryan makes clear that proportionality as a requirement for duress does not depend simply on whether the crime committed is less serious or similar in gravity to the threat, but also a more fact-specific inquiry about whether the accused in all the circumstances acted in a morally involuntary manner. This second fact-based inquiry into proportionality may overlap with other requirements, especially the no safe avenue of escape inquiry.

f) Sixth Requirement: No Defence if Accused Knew They Would Be Subject to Threats as a Result of a Criminal Activity, Conspiracy, or Association

Under section 17, an accused who is "a party to a conspiracy or association whereby the person is subject to compulsion" is not eligible for the duress defence. In *Ryan*, the Supreme Court interpreted this exclusion only to apply to accused who subjectively know that they will be subject to threats and compulsion as a result of their voluntary decision to become involved in crime. The Court reasoned "that the subjective standard is more in line with the principle of moral involuntariness. If the accused voluntarily puts him or herself in a position where he or she could be coerced, then we cannot conclude that there was no safe avenue of escape and that the ensuing actions were morally involuntary."[170] The Court also applied the same subjective approach to the common law defence of duress.

The restrictive and subjective approach to the exclusion of voluntary assumption of risk through criminal conspiracies and associations narrows the tension between duress and the Supreme Court's statement in *Perka* that the accused's involvement in illegal activities did not preclude the related defence of necessity in circumstances of true moral involuntariness. The Court's approach in *Perka* is justified by the logic of excuses and the section 7 right against punishing a person for morally involuntary behaviour because it appropriately focuses on whether the accused had any realistic choice but to commit the offence at the time it was committed and not on the accused's prior bad acts and associations. This is also consistent with the general principles that the accused's guilt should be determined at the time that the prohibited act occurs.[171]

---

170 Above note 7 at para 80.
171 See Chapter 3, Section D.

g) Summary

The Supreme Court's decision in *Ryan* has eliminated most of the differences between the statutory section 17 defence that applies to principal offenders and the common law defence that applies to parties to an offence. It has done so largely by grafting common law concepts onto the section 17 defence as stripped of the reference to "immediate" death or bodily harm by a person "present" in *Ruzic*. The common law concepts that an accused must reasonably believe that the threats will be realized, that the accused have no safe avenue of escape, that there must be a close temporal connection between the threats and the harm threatened, and that there must be proportionality between harm inflicted and harm avoided have all been read into section 17. All of these common law glosses on the section 17 defence will be applied, as they are in the common law defence, on the basis of a modified objective standard that takes into account the accused's past experiences and characteristics while avoiding applying a purely subjective standard.

The Court in *Ryan* interpreted the exclusion of threats as a result of the accused's prior voluntary assumption of risk by entering into criminal associations and conspiracies restrictively to require that the accused actually know of the risk of such threats. The Court then applied this restriction to the common law defence of duress as well as to section 17.

2) Excluded Offences: The Remaining Difference Between the Section 17 and Common Law Defences

On its face, section 17 is not available if the accused is charged with a long list of offences including murder, attempted murder, sexual assault, forcible abduction, assault with a weapon or causing bodily harm, aggravated assault, unlawfully causing bodily harm, robbery, arson, and abduction of a young person. In contrast, the common law defence of duress has been applied to parties charged with the most serious offences, including murder[172] and attempted murder.[173] The Supreme Court in *Ryan*[174] recognized this remaining difference between the section 17 and common law defences as both "incoherent" and "unsatisfactory" but left the "questions of the status of the statutory exclusions and what, if any, exclusions apply at common law" to another day.

---

172   *Paquette*, above note 147.
173   *Hibbert*, above note 1.
174   *Ibid* at paras 83–84.

The question that arises in light of the *Ruzic* decision and the recognition that the conviction of a person for morally involuntary conduct violates section 7 of the *Charter* is whether any categorical restrictions on the duress defence can be justified if the accused is truly placed in a position in which he or she has no realistic choice but to commit one of the excluded offences. The excluded offences in section 17 will have to be measured against the constitutional principle that it violates the principles of fundamental justice to convict a person who commits a crime in a morally involuntary manner. Although it can be argued that an accused should not be able to commit a crime such as murder that is clearly disproportionate to a threat of bodily harm, it is also doubtful that the exclusion of offences such as robbery or assault with a weapon[175] can be justified under section 7 of the *Charter* when the accused or a third party has been threatened with death.

The easiest exclusion for the state to justify in section 17 is for murder. It is the subjecting of conflicting Court of Appeal decisions that will eventually have to be resolved by the Supreme Court. The Ontario Court of Appeal has suggested that the exclusion of murder from the duress defence violated section 7 of the *Charter* because it violates a "bedrock principle" that "[c]riminal liability requires voluntary conduct. Voluntariness reflects individual choice and with choice comes responsibility for one's actions."[176] In contrast, the Manitoba Court of Appeal upheld the exclusion of murder under section 17 for principal offenders. It held that the purpose of the statutory exclusion was "to prevent one descending into the moral quicksand of trying to determine whose life is more important (or less important) in a given context, when they have an inherent bias as to who should live and who should die."[177] This decision relies on the moral absolutism of the traditional common law rule that duress (and necessity) could never be a defence for murder in order to protect the sanctity of life. This approach, however,

---

175 *R v Allen*, 2014 SKQB 402 at para 58 [*Allen*], concluding "[i]t is not realistic, in every instance, to expect a person to conform to the ideal of self-sacrifice when pushed to commit robbery or assault with a weapon under threat of death. Such an expectation is overly exacting, and does not accord with the human drive for self-preservation . . . . It is not realistic to expect an accused, faced with the prospect of physical harm or death, to prefer the property interests of others over his or her physical well-being."

176 *Aravena*, above note 164 at para 46. In the actual case, it held that a trial judge erred in ruling that murder was excluded from the common law defence of duress, because the constitutional principle of ensuring that those who act in a morally involuntary way should not be convicted "by its very nature demands a fact-intensive inquiry." *Ibid* at para 65.

177 *Willis*, above note 138 at para 106.

seems to treat duress more like a justification than an excuse. As the Ontario Court of Appeal has observed: "While a person told to 'kill or be killed' could perhaps never justify killing the innocent third party as the lesser of two evils, it is much more difficult to assert that the two harms are not of 'comparable gravity.'"[178] The Manitoba Court of Appeal's approach also reintroduces the distinction between principal offenders who would under section 17 be denied the defence and other parties to the offence who would have access to the offence.[179]

The Manitoba Court of Appeal makes much of the distinction between the moral or deontological justification case for excluded offences and utilitarian concerns about deterrence and social protection. Such distinctions have a long philosophical pedigree, but it is not clear that they will be helpful in applying the section 7 *Charter* principle against convicting people for morally involuntary behaviour that should be excused but not praised. A person who kills another to avoid his or her own death may be acting in a morally involuntary manner. To be sure, some may sacrifice themselves for others when faced with the threat of death, but such people are heroes who lack the human frailties that most of us have.[180]

The Manitoba Court of Appeal's approach is inconsistent with the excuse-based logic of excuses as concessions to common human frailties, and the logic of the *Charter* that protects the accused's rights under section 7 while requiring that the government justify competing social interests under section 1[181] whether they be the promotion of moral values about the sanctity of life or more prosaic concerns about social

---

178 *Aravena*, above note 164 at para 63. As the Ontario Court of Appeal elaborates the moral view rooted in the English common law "reflects a conception of duress as a justification . . . . Canadian criminal law does not, however, regard duress as a justification. As outlined above, duress is an excuse. The person excused from criminal liability is not said to have accomplished a greater good, but is rather said to have had no realistic choice but to act as she did." *Ibid* at paras 81–82.

179 In *Willis*, above note 138 at paras 173–79, Mainella JA concludes: "Only the actual killer(s) cannot raise the defence of duress; there is no statutory restriction on someone who provides no more than peripheral assistance" when even the common law that he relies upon has ended up rejecting such sometimes arbitrary distinctions. *R v Hasan*, [2005] UKHL 22.

180 As the Ontario Court of Appeal has observed: "Society may regret or even deplore the accused's failure to 'rise to the occasion,' but it cannot, in a criminal justice system predicated on individual autonomy, justly criminalize and punish conduct absent a realistic choice: see *Perka*, at pp 249–50. *Ryan*, at para 40, confirmed the status of moral involuntariness as a principle of fundamental justice protected by s. 7 of the *Charter*." *Aravena*, above note 164 at para 52.

181 *Carter v Canada (Attorney General)*, 2015 SCC 5.

protection. To be sure, the protection of life is an important social value that could justify a limit on the accused's *Charter* rights. Moreover, the categorical exclusion of murder from the duress defence is rationally connected with such objectives. The problem, however, is that the categorical exclusion of all murders is a blunt and disproportionate means of achieving these objectives. This is especially true when compared to the more proportionate approach of requiring true moral involuntariness as measured by the common law requirements of proportionality and no legal way out before a defence of duress is recognized for the commission of any crime. The exclusion of murder from duress categorically and automatically prefers the life or safety of third parties over those of the accused,[182] whereas the application of the defence allows a facts-based application of proportionality principles based on the facts of the particular case. As the Ontario Court of Appeal has stated: "The availability of the defence of duress cannot be settled by giving automatic priority to the right to life of the victim over that of an accused. Instead, the right to life of the victim must be factored into the proportionality assessment as part of the broader moral involuntariness inquiry."[183]

Even if a bright line exclusion of murder is necessary to promote the sanctity of life, the fourth step of the section 1 test will require the court to measure the harm of imposing life imprisonment on a person who kills in a morally involuntary manner against the uncertain and even symbolic benefits of declaring that people should not kill even if they or others are threatened with death.[184]

3) Duress and *Mens Rea*

As previously discussed in Chapters 4 and 5, duress will not negate the *mens rea* required to be a party to an offence. In *Hibbert*,[185] the Supreme Court overruled its earlier decision in *Paquette*[186] to the extent that it suggested that an accused who participated in a robbery under duress did not have the intent to carry out the unlawful purpose as required under section 21(2) of the *Criminal Code*. The Court suggested that the duress faced by Paquette explained his motives and desires in assisting in the robbery but could not negate or raise a reasonable doubt about his intent. It held that duress including threats with a gun could

---

182   *Aravena*, above note 164 at para 84.

183   *Ibid*. See also *Allen*, above note 175 at paras 79–80.

184   *R v KRJ*, 2016 SCC 31 at para 79.

185   Above note 1.

186   Above note 147 at 423.

not negate the accused's intent required to form an unlawful purpose under section 21(2) or the intent required for doing something for the purpose of aiding an offence under section 21(1)(b).[187] Given that duress will frequently arise in situations where the accused reluctantly assists in the commission of the crime, this decision suggests that duress will rarely be relevant to determining *mens rea*. *Hibbert* means that the fate of those who reluctantly assist in crimes will depend on the common law defence of duress. Duress will be relevant only to high levels of *mens rea* and even then it remains to be seen whether courts will allow duress to negate *mens rea*. It is quite plausible that they will conclude in many cases that duress speaks only to the motive as opposed to the intent with which the accused commits the crime.

The Supreme Court in *R v Carker (No 2)*[188] rejected the accused's argument that the threats deprived him of the *mens rea* of wilfully damaging public property. Justice Ritchie stated that while the evidence suggested "that the criminal act was committed to preserve . . . [the accused] from future harm . . . there is no suggestion . . . that the accused did not know that what he was doing would 'probably cause' damage." If the *mens rea* of wilfulness had not been defined in the *Criminal Code* to include the lower subjective mental elements of knowledge or recklessness, there may have been a reasonable doubt about whether Carker wilfully destroyed the public property.[189] It might be possible, however, that a court would have concluded that Carker's motive was to avoid the threats of his fellow inmates and he still wilfully damaged the property.[190]

In *Hebert*,[191] the Supreme Court held that an accused charged with perjury did not have a section 17 defence of duress because he was not threatened with immediate death or bodily harm. The Court nevertheless gave the accused a new trial so that the effects of the threats could be considered in determining whether he had the *mens rea* required for perjury. The Court stressed that the mental element of perjury requires "more than a deliberate false statement. The statement must also have been made with intent to mislead. While it is true that someone who lies generally does so with the intent of being believed, it is not impossible, though it may be exceptional, for a person to deliberately lie

---

187 See also *Dunbar v R* (1936), 67 CCC 20 (SCC) to a similar effect. See Chapter 5, Section B for further discussion of these cases.
188 [1967] 2 CCC 190 at 195 (SCC).
189 *Code*, above note 4, s 429(1). See Chapter 5, Section B for further discussion of this aspect of the case.
190 On the distinction between motive and intent, see Chapter 5, Section B(2).
191 Above note 51.

without intending to mislead."[192] In this case, for example, the accused testified that he attempted to tell a deliberate lie so that the judge might be alerted to the fact that he had been threatened. Duress may well be relevant to the particular *mens rea* of perjury and other offences relating to interference with the administration of justice.

4) Summary

As discussed above, duress will rarely be relevant to the proof of fault. In most cases, duress will either be considered as part of the section 17 defence of duress that applies to principal offenders or as part of the common law defence of duress that applies to parties.

The Court's decision in *Ryan* has narrowed the difference between the two duress defences considerably. The Court has interpreted section 17 to impose common law requirements that are not present on the face of section 17 even after the Court in *Ruzic* struck out references to threats having to be of "immediate" death or bodily harm from a person who is present. The common law requirements that have been added to section 17 include (1) the requirement that the accused have a reasonable basis for believing in the threat to life or bodily harm, (2) the requirement of no safe avenue of escape, (3) the requirement of a close temporal connection between the threat and the harm threatened, and (4) the requirement of proportionality between the harm threatened and the harm inflicted by the accused. All of these requirements will be applied on a modified or contextual objective standard that takes into account the accused's past experiences and characteristics without, however, imposing a purely subjective approach that disregards society's interests.

The Court in *Ryan* also interpreted the exclusion of those who were threatened as a result of prior criminal conspiracy and association as requiring that the accused subjectively be aware that they might be compelled, and extended this requirement to the common law defence. The only remaining differences between section 17 and the common law duress defence is the former's long list of categorically excluded offences.

An eventual finding that section 17 should be struck down in its entirety because the categorical exclusion of offences could punish those who act in a morally involuntary manner would simplify and improve the law. The same duress defence would apply to all offenders regardless of whether they actually committed the offence or were parties to

---

192 *Ibid* at 64.

the offence. There is no need for a categorical exclusion of any offence given the otherwise exacting requirements of the duress defence including the more fact-based inquiry into the proportionality between the harm inflicted and avoided outlined in *Ryan*. The ultimate requirement that the accused must act in a truly morally involuntary manner is the principled way to ensure that the duress defence is not abused. Categorical and *ex ante* exclusion of certain offences is not necessary.

The related common law defences of duress and necessity have for the most part developed in tandem. This is appropriate because both defences are grounded in the same juristic concept of an excuse that prevents an accused from being convicted for morally involuntary behaviour and that is now protected under section 7 of the *Charter*. The requirements of both defences are roughly equivalent except that the requirement that the threat to the accused be imminent in the defence of necessity is more flexibly interpreted in the duress defence to require only a close temporal connection between the threat and the harm threatened. In addition, the proportionality requirement between the harm threatened and the harm inflicted by the accused is determined on a purely objective standard for necessity but a modified objective standard for duress. Both divergences remain difficult to justify.

CONCLUSION

Unlike the defences of due diligence (Chapter 6), extreme intoxication (Chapter 7), mental disorder and automatism (Chapter 8), accused do not have to establish self-defence, defence of property, necessity, or duress on a balance of probabilities. Provided the judge finds that there is an air of reality to all the elements of the defence, the defence results in the acquittal of the accused whenever there is a reasonable doubt about all of the requirements of the particular defence. The defences examined in this chapter do not relate to the fault element of particular offences and they have both subjective and objective requirements. In general, they apply if the accused subjectively and reasonably responds to external pressures such as threats from other people (self-defence and duress) and circumstances of peril (necessity).

In administering the objective requirements of these defences, the Supreme Court has taken a modified objective approach that not only places the reasonable person in the same circumstances that the accused faced, but also invests the reasonable person with the same characteristics and experiences as the particular accused. This, of course, stands in contrast to the Court's unwillingness to consider such factors when applying objective standards of liability.[193] The landmark decision in contextualizing the reasonable person was *Lavallee*,[194] which recognized that a woman's past abuse could be relevant in determining whether she had a valid claim of self-defence against her abuser. This trend has been continued in the new section 34(2)(f) and (f.1) which requires consideration of the relationship and history of interaction including prior use or threat of force between the parties to the incident as well as section 34(2)(e) which requires consideration of the size, age, gender, and physical capabilities of the parties to the incident when determining whether an act of self-defence or defence of others was reasonable in the circumstances. The issue is not whether the accused can be classified as a battered woman, but whether in light of her experiences and characteristics, her actions and perceptions were reasonable.

New self-defence and defence of property provisions have replaced old provisions that the Supreme Court has candidly recognized as "unbelievably confusing."[195] The new provisions no longer attempt artificially to categorize and restrict self-defence. They are, however, based on the basic principles that an accused must (1) believe on reasonable grounds that either force or threat of force is being used against them or another person (section 34(1)(a)); (2) they must respond for the subjective purpose of defending themselves (section 34(1)(b)); and (3) they must respond in a manner that is reasonable in the circumstances (section 34(1)(c)). The new defence will be less predictable than the old defence or the common law defences of necessity and duress because factors relating to the necessity of the force used and the proportionality between the force used and the force threatened are only two of nine enumerated but non-exhaustive factors listed in section 34(2) that must be considered in determining whether self-defence is reasonable in the particular circumstances. Nevertheless, the use of general standards based on reasonableness in the circumstances seems inevitable in this context. A totally subjective approach to self-defence would excuse irrational, unnecessary resort to violent self-help. It could also condone racist stereotypes that Indigenous and racialized people are inherently dangerous, something that is contrary to *Charter* values. Most of the concerns about the possible unfairness of objective standards to the accused have been addressed by the Court's willingness to invest the reasonable person with the same characteristics and experiences as the accused. Still, care must be taken to ensure that the modified objective approach does not become a subjective or individualized approach.

---

193 *Creighton*, above note 3.
194 Above note 2.
195 *McIntosh*, above note 26 at para 16.

The new self-defence provisions are more generous to the accused than the common law defences of duress and necessity because they do not explicitly require that there be no legal way or that the force used be proportional to the force avoided. This difference can be explained only by the fact that the victim of self-defence will usually, but not always, be an aggressor or a trespasser whereas the victims of necessity and duress will generally be innocent third parties. This justification cannot, however, be pushed too far given that self-defence and defence of property may still apply if the accused acts under a reasonable mistake with respect to the use of force or invasion of property.

The new defence of property provisions discard unnecessary distinctions between personal and real property in the old provisions. They require (1) a reasonable belief in peaceable possession of property combined with a claim of right to the property (section 35(1)(a), section 35(2)); (2) a reasonable belief that a person is threatening property (section 35(1)(b)); (3) that the accused must act for the subjective purpose of protecting property (section 35(1)(c)); and (4) that the act done in defence of property must be reasonable in the circumstances (section 35(1)(d)). There must be an air of reality for all four requirements to justify putting the defence to the jury and there must be a reasonable doubt about all four requirements for the accused to be acquitted. The new section 35 does not specifically include the proportionality requirement that the Supreme Court has elaborated in a number of defence of property cases, but courts should and have started to read in such a requirement to the critical requirement that acts done in defence of property be reasonable in the circumstances. In some cases, what starts as a defence of property case can escalate to a self-defence case.

Duress and necessity are similar defences that are both more demanding of the accused than self-defence. Both defences insist on no safe avenue of escape and proportionality between the harm done and the harm avoided in a way that self-defence does not. The Court in *Ryan* recognized that necessity and duress are more restrictive defences than self-defence in part because self-defence authorizes the use of force against an aggressor whereas necessity and duress often excuse the commission of crimes that harm innocent third parties. In *Ryan*, the Court stated that a battered woman could not claim duress when she tried to hire an undercover police officer to kill her abusive husband. The appropriate defence would be self-defence. *Lavallee* makes clear that courts would not demand that a battered woman face imminent harm and they would apply a modified objective standard that takes into account the woman's past experience and characteristics.

The new section 34(1) also opens the possibility that the accused in *Ryan* (who tried to hire someone to kill her abusive husband) could have claimed self-defence because the new defence can apply to any crime and is not restricted to the use of force to resist an ongoing assault. She would, however, have to have the subjective desire to defend herself and to have responded reasonably to a reasonable perception of force or threat of force. Although self-defence is a less restrictive defence than necessity or duress, there is a danger that this insight will be taken too far to authorize privatized punishment in the form of self-help. It is important to remember that self-defence may be used against an innocent non-aggressor if the accused makes a reasonable mistake about the identity of the aggressor. Moreover, even self-defence against an aggressor cannot be justified as a type of privatized punishment: it must accord with societal concepts of reasonableness.

Although duress and necessity are both excuses that prevent conviction for morally involuntary acts where the accused has no reasonable alternatives, the Court has created some differences between the necessity and duress defences. These include imposing a requirement of reasonable belief in imminent harm for necessity while requiring a less demanding close temporal connection between the threat and the harm threatened for duress. It also includes the use of a modified objective standard to determine the proportionality between the harm threatened and avoided for duress, but a purely objective standard for determining proportionality between harm inflicted and harm avoided for the necessity defence. These modifications produce a duress defence that is slightly more generous to the accused than the necessity defence, but they add needless complexity to the law.

The Court has been more successful with *Ryan* in harmonizing the common law duress defence that applies to parties and the section 17 defence that applies to principal offenders. The same concepts of reasonable belief in threats, close connection between threats and harm, no safe avenue of escape, proportionality between harm threatened and inflicted, and exclusion of those who because of criminal conspiracies and associations subjectively know that they will be threatened apply to both defences. The only remaining difference is the contrast between the long list of offences excluded under section 17 and the applicability of the common law defences to even murder and attempted murder.

It is doubtful that the long list of excluded offences in section 17 can survive review under section 7 of the *Charter*, because they could result in the conviction of a person who acted in a morally involuntary manner. The Ontario Court of Appeal's approach that categorical exclusions of murder cannot be justified is more consistent with the

Supreme Court's understanding of duress as an excuse informed by the section 7 *Charter* principle that prevents convictions for morally involuntary acts than the Manitoba Court of Appeal's more morally absolute approach which seems to treat duress as a justification as opposed to an excuse. It will be even more difficult to justify the excluded offences under section 17 in light of the more fact specific alternative of applying the two-part test articulated in *Ryan* that requires proportionality between the harm avoided and the harm caused. Striking down the entire section 17 defence on the basis that it violates section 7 of the *Charter* by allowing the conviction of a person who had no realistic choice but to commit the offence would both simplify the law and help ensure that no one is convicted for morally involuntary conduct.

FURTHER READINGS

AKHAVAN, P. "Should Duress Apply to All Crimes? A Comparative Appraisal of Moral Involuntariness and the Twenty Crimes Exception Under Section 17 of the *Criminal Code*" (2009) 13 *Canadian Criminal Law Review* 271.

BERGER, B. "Emotions and the Veil of Voluntarism: The Loss of Judgment in Canadian Criminal Defences" (2006) 51 *McGill Law Journal* 99.

BRUDNER, A. "Constitutionalizing Self-Defence" (2011) 61 *University of Toronto Law Journal* 867.

COLVIN, E, & S ANAND. *Principles of Criminal Law*, 3d ed (Toronto: Thomson Carswell, 2007) ch 7.

COUGHLAN, S. "The Rise and Fall of Duress (or How Duress Changed Necessity before Being Excluded by Self-Defence)" (2013) 39 *Queen's Law Journal* 83.

"Forum on the *Latimer* Case" (2001) 39 *Criminal Reports* (5th) 29*ff*.

"Forum on the *Latimer* Case" (2001) 64 *Saskatchewan Law Review* 469*ff*.

GORMAN, W. "Provocation: The Jealous Husband Defence" (1999) 42 *Criminal Law Quarterly* 478.

GRANT, I, D CHUNN, & C BOYLE. *The Law of Homicide* (Toronto: Carswell, 1994) ch 6.

HEALY, P. "Innocence and Defences" (1994) 19 *Criminal Reports* (4th) 121.

HORDER, J. "Self-Defence, Necessity and Duress: Understanding the Relationship" (1998) 11 *Canadian Journal of Law & Jurisprudence* 143.

MACDONNELL, V. "The New Self-Defence Law: Progressive Development or New Status Quo?" (2014) 92 *Canadian Bar Review* 301.

MANNING, M. & P SANKOFF. *Criminal Law*, 5th ed (Markham: Lexis-Nexis, 2015) ch 13 & 14.

PACIOCCO, D. "Applying the Law of Self-Defence" (2007) 12 *Canadian Criminal Law Review* 25.

————. "No-One Wants to Be Eaten: The Logic and Experience of the Law of Necessity and Duress" (2010) 56 *Criminal Law Quarterly* 240.

SHAFFER, M. "The Battered Woman's Syndrome Revisited" (1997) 47 *University of Toronto Law Journal* 1.

————. "Scrutinizing Duress: The Constitutional Validity of S. 17 of the *Criminal Code*" (1998) 40 *Criminal Law Quarterly* 444.

SHEEHY, E. *Defending Battered Women on Trial* (Vancouver: University of British Columbia Press, 2014).

STUART, D. *Canadian Criminal Law: A Treatise*, 7th ed (Toronto: Thomson Carswell, 2014) ch 7.

TROTTER, G. "Necessity and Death: Lessons from *Latimer* and the Case of the Conjoined Twins" (2003) 40 *Alberta Law Review* 817.

YEO, S. "Challenging Moral Involuntariness as a Principle of Fundamental Justice" (2002) 28 *Queen's Law Journal* 335.

————. "Defining Duress" (2002) 46 *Criminal Law Quarterly* 293.

————. "Revisiting Necessity" (2010) 56 *Criminal Law Quarterly* 13.

THE SPECIAL PART: HOMICIDE, SEXUAL, PROPERTY, AND TERRORISM OFFENCES

This book has so far provided an overview of the general principles of criminal liability and defences. These principles are sometimes called the general part of the criminal law because they provide general principles, excuses, and justifications that apply to all offences. It is important to have a sense of the principles that apply to all criminal offences. Such general principles also inform how the courts interpret the principles of fundamental justice found in section 7 of the *Charter*.

That said, the criminal law, as well as *Charter* jurisprudence, has in recent years taken a more contextual approach. The increased emphasis on context makes it helpful to have a sense of how the courts interpret some specific offences. Those parts of the *Criminal Code* that set out specific offences are often referred to as the special part of the *Code*.

As discussed in previous chapters, it is important when examining specific offences to distinguish between matters relating to the prohibited act or *actus reus* and matters relating to the required fault element or *mens rea*. In addition, there is one defence — provocation — that belongs to the special part because it applies only when a person is charged with murder. Unlike the other defences examined in the previous chapters, a successful provocation defence does not produce an acquittal: it reduces murder to only manslaughter.

Any attempt to discuss the special part, especially in a book such as this that is designed to provide a concise introduction to criminal law, must be selective. To this end, this chapter will examine only homicide, some sexual, some property, and some terrorism offences. Each of these offences could merit a book in its own right and there are indeed books on each of these subjects. The offences examined in this chapter have been selected because they are some of the most important offences and they have been informed by contextual considerations that may not naturally be discussed in the general part with its focus on the general principles of criminal liability, excuses, and justifications. Because of their severity, homicide, sexual, and terrorism offences are subject to frequent litigation in the appellate courts and amendment by Parliament.

A. HOMICIDE OFFENCES

There are three homicide offences: murder, manslaughter, and infanticide. Section 234 of the *Criminal Code* provides that manslaughter is the residual offence so that culpable homicide that is not murder or infanticide is manslaughter. All murder convictions carry with them a mandatory penalty of life imprisonment, whereas manslaughter without the use of a firearm and infanticide have no mandatory minimum penalty. Murder is classified as either first or second degree with first-degree murder under section 231 of the *Code* requiring that the accused serve twenty-five years in prison before being eligible for parole. Section 232 provides a defence of provocation that reduces murder to manslaughter. Murder with its special stigma and mandatory penalty of life imprisonment is distinguished from manslaughter or infanticide mainly on the basis of its higher requirements of subjective fault involving as a minimum the accused's subjective knowledge that the victim would die.

1) The *Actus Reus* of Causing Death

The common *actus reus* for all homicide offences is the causing of the death of a human being. A human being is defined as a child who has completely proceeded from its mother in a living state whether or not the child has breathed, has an independent circulation, or has had its navel string severed.[1] A person can commit homicide if he or she causes injury to a child before or during its birth and the child dies as a result after becoming a human being as defined above.[2]

---

1   *Criminal Code*, RSC 1985, c C–46, s 223(1) [*Code*].
2   *Ibid*, s 223(2). Section 238 also provides a separate offence punishable by up to life imprisonment for causing death in the act of birth before the fetus becomes

a) Statutory Provisions in Homicide Cases

Section 222(1) of the *Code* provides that a person commits homicide when, directly or indirectly, by any means, he or she causes the death of a human being. This is a broad definition that has been satisfied in a case where an accused abducted a child who subsequently was left in a car and died of hypothermia.[3]

There are a variety of specific statutory rules relating to causation in homicide cases. Section 224 provides that a person is responsible for a death even though it might have been prevented by resorting to proper means. This section would apply where victims die as a result of a wound but could have been saved if they had accepted or received proper medical treatment.[4] A person who stabs another in a remote location will be held responsible for causing that person's death even though the very same wound may not have been life threatening if inflicted in a place with medical facilities.

Section 225 provides that a person who causes a dangerous injury is responsible for death, notwithstanding that the immediate cause of death is proper or improper treatment rendered in good faith. A person who stabs another will be responsible for causing death even though the immediate cause of death might be negligent treatment of the wound by a doctor. Indeed, section 225 might be less favourable to the accused than judge-made common law, which has held that very bad treatment that overtakes the initial wound can break the chain of causation, so that it is unfair to conclude that the accused caused the death.[5] Section 225 might be vulnerable to *Charter* challenge as overbroad or grossly disproportionate to the extent that it holds an accused who caused a dangerous but relatively minor bodily injury such as a stabbing accountable for a death that is really caused by grossly improper treatment, such as giving the victim drugs that caused a severe allergic reaction, though courts have in the past judged causation tests

---

a human being, as defined in s 223 with an exemption for acts done in good faith to preserve the life of the mother. This offence is distinct from infanticide.

3   *R v Younger* (2004), 186 CCC (3d) 454 (Man CA). In that case, the accused was also convicted of first-degree murder under the stricter requirement that his actions were the "substantial cause" of the child's death. This requirement will be examined later in this chapter.

4   In *R v Blaue*, [1975] 1 WLR 1411 (CA), a manslaughter conviction was upheld when the victim refused a blood transfusion because of her religious beliefs. In *R v Smith* (1959), 43 Cr App Rep 121 (CA), the accused was held to have caused death even though proper medical treatment would have probably saved the victim's life.

5   *R v Jordan* (1956), 40 Cr App Rep 152 (CCA).

not only on their own but in light of fault requirements that also have to be proven beyond a reasonable doubt to have a conviction.[6]

Under section 226, a person is deemed to have caused death even though the bodily injury that results in death accelerates a pre-existing disease. This provision suggests that an accused must assume responsibility if the victim's "thin skull" takes the form of a pre-existing disease. Section 222(5)(c) provides that a person commits homicide when he or she causes another person by threats, fear of violence, or deception to do anything that causes the person's death. The Supreme Court has observed that "these statutory provisions and others like them preempt any speculation as to whether the triggering of a chain of events was then interrupted by an intervening cause which serves to distance and exonerate the accused from any responsibility for the consequences."[7]

b) General Principles of Causation in Homicide Cases

The *Criminal Code* does not comprehensively codify all causation issues that may arise in a homicide case. As the Supreme Court has stated, "[w]here the factual situation does not fall within one of the statutory rules of causation in the *Code*, the common law general principles of criminal law apply to resolve any causation issues that may arise."[8]

In *R v Smithers*,[9] the Supreme Court upheld a manslaughter conviction on the basis that the accused's action of kicking the deceased in the stomach "was at least a contributing cause of death, outside the *de minimis* range," even though the death was in part caused by the victim's malfunctioning epiglottis, which caused him to choke to death on his own vomit. The Court affirmed that the "one who assaults another must take his victim as he finds him" and that the accused could be responsible for causing death even if "death may have been unexpected, and the physical reactions of the victim unforeseen."[10] This test has been applied in a case to hold that the accused caused a victim's death by a minor assault that was followed by a fatal heart attack even though the victim had a history of severe heart disease.[11] The accused had to accept that the victim had a "thin skull," in this case heart disease and anxiety that may have led to the heart attack.

---

6   *R v Cribbin* (1994), 89 CCC (3d) 67 (Ont CA).
7   *R v Nette*, [2001] 3 SCR 488 at para 48 [*Nette*]. See also *R v Maybin*, 2012 SCC 24 at para 52.
8   *Nette*, above note 7 at para 48.
9   (1977), 34 CCC (2d) 427 (SCC).
10   *Ibid* at 437.
11   *R v Shanks* (1996), 4 CR (5th) 79 (Ont CA).

Despite its breadth, the *Smithers* approach to causation in homicide cases has survived under the *Charter*. In *R v Cribbin*,[12] the Ontario Court of Appeal concluded that the *de minimis* causation test and thin skull principles approved in *Smithers* were consistent with section 7 principles of fundamental justice. Justice Arbour stressed that "[b]oth causation and the fault element must be proved beyond a reasonable doubt before the prosecution can succeed. Combined in that fashion, both requirements satisfy the principles of fundamental justice"[13] that prevent the conviction of the morally innocent. A manslaughter conviction was upheld in *Cribbin* because the accused's assault had contributed to the victim's death, even though the victim had been subject to more serious assaults by another person and had died because he drowned in his own blood.

In *R v Nette*,[14] the Supreme Court held that "the causation standard expressed in *Smithers* is still valid and applicable to all forms of homicide" (that is, murder, manslaughter, and infanticide) but that to make it easier to explain to the jury it should be described as a requirement that the accused's act be a "significant contributing cause" to death.[15] This remains the operative standard today.

Justice L'Heureux-Dubé with three other judges dissented and would have maintained the negative formulation of a not insignificant cause contemplated under *Smithers*. She argued that "[t]here is a meaningful difference between expressing the standard as 'a contributing cause that is not trivial or insignificant' and expressing it as a 'significant contributing cause.'"[16]

All the judges in *Nette* were agreed, however, that the accused had caused the death of a ninety-five-year-old widow he had left hog-tied and alone after robbing her home. The victim died of asphyxiation some twenty-four to forty-eight hours later. Medical evidence showed that a number of factors contributed to the death, including the hog-tied position, a moderately tight ligature that the accused had left around the victim's neck, as well as the victim's age, asthma, and congestive heart failure. Justice Arbour concluded that "the fact that the appellant's actions might not have caused death in a different person, or that death might have taken longer to occur in the case of a younger victim, does not transform this case into one involving multiple causes."[17]

---

12 (1994), 89 CCC (3d) 67 (Ont CA).
13 *Ibid* at 88.
14 Above note 7.
15 *Ibid* at para 71.
16 *Ibid* at para 6.
17 *Ibid* at para 81. See also *R v Knight*, [2003] 1 SCR 156.

Courts now articulate causation in the positive terms of whether the accused's actions were a significant contributing cause of death as opposed to the older formulation of a cause that is not trivial, *de minimis*, or insignificant.[18] The Supreme Court in *R v Maybin*[19] affirmed that the test is whether the accused's acts were a significant cause of death. It indicated that whether a possible intervening cause was reasonably foreseeable or independent of the accused's actions are simply analytical aids in determining whether the accused's actions were a significant cause of death. In that case, brothers who started a bar room fight were held to have significantly caused the accused's death even though a bouncer who intervened also hit a victim in the head who later died of bleeding in the brain. It was reasonably foreseeable that either a bouncer or some other patron might strike the victim once the accused initially assaulted the victim. It could not be said that the bouncer's actions were so independent of the brothers' initial assault that they rendered the accused's actions "so remote to suggest that they were morally innocent of the death."[20] In another case, the Court ordered a new murder trial to determine whether the accused's actions in shooting an accused were still a significant cause of death when the victim died of a blood clot a few days after being released from hospital.[21] A new trial would include the possible verdict of attempted murder because even though the pathologist would not rule out the possibility that the blood clot was related to the shooting, it could have been caused by the independent act of the victim ingesting cocaine shortly before his death.[22]

c) Substantial Cause Requirements for Some Forms of First-Degree Murder

Although the Supreme Court stressed in *Nette* that there is one causation test for all homicide cases, it also recognized that an additional and more stringent causation test applies to some forms of first-degree murder. Section 231(5) requires that the death "be caused by that person" while the accused is committing or attempting to commit a list of enumerated offences, including sexual assault, kidnapping, and hostage-taking. The same phrase "caused by that person" is now also found in sections 231(6), (6.01), (6.1), and (6.2) that apply when the accused causes the death of a person by committing other serious crimes,

---

18   *R v Pangowish* (2003), 171 CCC (3d) 506 (BCCA), leave to appeal to SCC refused (2003), 176 CCC (3d) vi (SCC).
19   2012 SCC 24.
20   *Ibid* at para 59.
21   *R v Sarrazin*, 2011 SCC 54.
22   *Ibid* at paras 6, 20, and 42.

such as criminal harassment, a terrorist activity, a crime for a criminal organization, or the intimidation of a justice system participant. In *Harbottle*, the Supreme Court interpreted "the death caused by that person" formulation as requiring an accused's actions "form an essential, substantial and integral part of the killing of the victim." Justice Cory elaborated that "The substantial causation test requires that the accused play a very active role — usually a physical role — in the killing."[23]

The substantial causation test was satisfied in *Harbottle* because the accused had held the victim's legs to stop her from struggling while his co-accused strangled her to death. The Court rejected an even stricter causation test that would have required the Crown to prove that the accused's acts were a physical cause of death, because it would lead to impractical and non-purposive distinctions. On the facts of the case, it was impossible "to distinguish between the blameworthiness of an accused who holds the victim's legs, thus allowing his co-accused to strangle her, and the accused who performs the act of strangulation."[24] At the same time, interpretation of the "caused by that person" requirement as requiring that the accused's act be a substantial cause will in most cases require the accused to play a physical role in the killing.

In *Nette*,[25] the Supreme Court rejected the idea that the substantial causation standard articulated in *Harbottle* should apply in all homicide cases. Rather, it was restricted to those sections that use the statutory phrase when death is "caused by that person." In such cases, the jury must be given two different causation tests. The first that applies to the causing of death is "that the acts of the accused have to have made a 'significant' contribution to the victim's death to trigger culpability for the homicide." The second causation test under sections 231(5), (6), (6.01), (6.1), and (6.2) is that "the accused's actions must have been an essential, substantial and integral part of the killing of the victim."[26] Multiple causation tests, especially those that hinge on the fine distinction between "significant" and "substantial" causation, may be difficult for the jury to understand.

To further complicate matters, the *Harbottle* substantial cause test does not apply to all forms of first-degree murder. There is no substantial cause requirement in section 231(2) that provides for planned and deliberate murders, section 231(3) that applies to contract murders, and section 231(4) that applies to murders of police officers and prison guards. The substantial cause requirement for some forms of

---

23   *R v Harbottle* (1993), 84 CCC (3d) 1 at 13–14 (SCC).
24   *Ibid* at 12.
25   Above note 7.
26   *Ibid* at paras 73 and 82.

first-degree murder can be defended as a restriction on the most serious offence in the *Criminal Code* that requires the accused to be a substantial cause and usually play a physical role in the death. The substantial causation requirement recognizes that the ordinary causation test of a significant cause of death is quite broad. At the same time, the substantial cause requirement complicates the law and requires the trial judge to instruct the jury on two different causation tests in many first-degree murder cases.

2) Murder

The main offence for murder is section 229. Any person charged with murder, even first-degree murder, must now be charged under section 229. It provides:

> Culpable homicide is murder
> a) where the person who causes the death of a human being
>   i) means to cause his death or
>   ii) means to cause him bodily harm that he knows is likely to cause his death and is reckless whether death ensues or not;
> b) where a person, meaning to cause death to a human being or meaning to cause him bodily harm that he knows is likely to cause his death, and being reckless whether death ensues or not, by accident or mistake causes death to another human being, notwithstanding that he desires to effect his object without causing death or bodily harm to any human being; or
> c) where a person, for an unlawful object, does anything that he knows or ought to know is likely to cause death, and thereby causes death to a human being, notwithstanding that he desires to effect his object without causing death or bodily harm to any human being.

a)   The Constitutionally Required Fault for Murder

As discussed in Chapter 2, the Supreme Court has interpreted section 7 of the *Charter* to require that a few offences, because of the special stigma and penalty, require a minimum form of *mens rea* or fault element. The constitutionally required minimum *mens rea* for murder is subjective knowledge of the likelihood or probability of death. In *R v Martineau*, the majority of the Court explained:

> A conviction for murder carries with it the most severe stigma and punishment of any crime in our society. The principles of fundamental justice require, because of the special nature of the stigma attached to

a conviction for murder, and the available penalties, a *mens rea* reflecting the particular nature of that crime . . . . The rationale underlying the principle that subjective foresight of death is required before a person is labelled and punished as a murderer is linked to the more general principle that criminal liability for a particular result is not justified except where the actor possesses a culpable mental state in respect of that result . . . . In my view, in a free and democratic society that values the autonomy and free will of the individual, the stigma and punishment attaching to the most serious of crimes, murder, should be reserved for those who choose to intentionally cause death or who choose to inflict bodily harm that they know is likely to cause death. The essential role of requiring subjective foresight of death in the context of murder is to maintain a proportionality between the stigma and punishment attached to a murder conviction and the moral blameworthiness of the offender. Murder has long been recognized as the "worst" and most heinous of peace time crimes. It is, therefore, essential that to satisfy the principles of fundamental justice, the stigma and punishment attaching to a murder conviction must be reserved for those who either intend to cause death or who intend to cause bodily harm that they know will likely cause death.[27]

In that case, the Court struck down section 230(a) of the *Criminal Code*. That section provided for a murder conviction where the accused caused death while committing or attempting to commit one of a long list of serious crimes if he or she meant to cause bodily harm for the purpose of facilitating the underlying offence or escape from it. The Court held that section 230(a) violated sections 7 and 11(d) of the *Charter* because it substituted the intent to commit the underlying offence and to cause bodily harm for the constitutionally required *mens rea* of subjective knowledge of the likelihood of death. Proof of the intent to cause bodily harm would not lead inexorably to proof of the constitutionally required fault element of knowledge of the likelihood of death.

The Supreme Court in *Martineau* held that the violation of sections 7 and 11(d) could not be justified under section 1 of the *Charter*. Even though the deterrence of violence during the commission of serious crimes was an important objective, it could be pursued in a more proportionate way such as stiff manslaughter sentences. Chief Justice Lamer explained: "To label and punish a person as a murderer who did not intend or foresee death unnecessarily stigmatizes and punishes those whose moral blameworthiness is not that of a murderer."[28]

---

27 *R v Martineau*, [1990] 2 SCR 633 at 645 [*Martineau*].
28 *Ibid* at 647.

One judge, L'Heureux-Dubé J, dissented in *Martineau* and would have maintained that the only constitutionally required fault for murder was objective foresight of death. She stressed the need to consider not only fault, but also the harm caused by the *actus reus* of death and the fact that other democracies including the United Kingdom and the United States used "felony murder" or constructive murder provisions that applied even though an accused who killed while committing a serious crime would not have known that the victim would die. Justice L'Heureux-Dubé held that the fault requirement of objective foresight of death would be satisfied by proof of a subjective intent to cause bodily harm while committing another serious offence, but Sopinka J disputed this conclusion even though he otherwise agreed that only the constitutionally required fault for murder should be objective foresight of death. This disagreement underlines the malleability of judgments about objective foresight. In any event, the majority of the Court clearly established that the constitutionally required fault for murder is subjective knowledge of the likelihood of death and the objective foresight of death standard would not have maintained an appropriate distinction between murder as the intentional infliction of death and manslaughter as a negligent killing.

In a previous case, *R v Vaillancourt*, the Supreme Court had struck down section 230(d), which had provided for a murder offence when death results from the use or possession of a firearm while committing one of a long list of serious offences, on the limited basis that it did not even guarantee that there would be objective foreseeability of death in a case, for example, where a firearm accidentally discharged during a robbery.[29] In a subsequent case, the Court also held that section 230(c) violated sections 7 and 11(d) of the *Charter* by substituting proof of wilfully stopping the breath of a human for the constitutionally required fault of subjective knowledge of the likelihood of death.[30] In most cases, a person who wilfully stopped another's breath would know that the victim was likely to die, but this might not be true in every case. Consistent with concerns about the presumption of innocence and any presumptions that could prevent the jury from having a reasonable doubt, the Court struck down this provision. In the result, section 230 has been rendered a dead letter that is no longer used even though Parliament has formally repealed only section 230(d). Hence, all people charged with murder have to be charged under section 229. Those charged with

---

29   *R v Vaillancourt*, [1987] 2 SCR 636 [*Vaillancourt*].
30   *R v Sit*, [1991] 3 SCR 124.

first-degree murder will be charged under section 229, but the Crown will also have to prove additional fault under section 231.

b)   Section 229(a)(i)

Section 229(a)(i) requires that the person who causes the death of a human being means to cause death. "This clearly requires that the accused have actual subjective foresight of the likelihood of causing death coupled with the intention to cause that death." This fault requirement has been described as "the most morally blameworthy state of mind in our system."[31] It could be argued that a person who plants a bomb to achieve some political objective does not mean to cause the death of those killed by the bomb but rather means to cause the advancement of the political objective. Courts would reject this argument based on the distinction between motive and intention discussed in Chapter 5 on fault.

c)   Section 229(a)(ii)

Section 229(a)(ii) requires that the person who causes the death means to cause the victim "bodily harm that he knows is likely to cause his death and is reckless whether death ensures or not." This offence requires proof of (1) subjective intent to cause bodily harm; and (2) subjective knowledge that the bodily harm is of such a nature that it is likely to result in death. The Supreme Court has explained that the reference to recklessness in section 229(a)(ii) is an "afterthought"[32] because a person who knows of the probability of death will of necessity have the lesser form of fault of being reckless in the sense of subjectively adverting to the possibility of death. The reference to recklessness in this section is not only superfluous but dangerous. New trials have been ordered in cases in which trial judges erroneously left the jury with the impression that recklessness was a sufficient form of fault for a murder conviction or that the accused need only be aware of a danger or risk as opposed to the likelihood of death.[33]

Section 229(a)(ii) requires proof of subjective knowledge that the victim is likely to die. As Martin JA explained,

> An intention to cause bodily harm that the offender ought to have known was likely to cause death is merely evidence from which, along with all the other circumstances, the jury may infer that the

---

31   *Vaillancourt*, above note 29 at para 10.

32   *R v Nygaard*, [1989] 2 SCR 1074 at 1088 [*Nygaard*].

33   *R v Czibulka* (2004), 189 CCC (3d) 199 (Ont CA); *R v Patterson* (2006), 205 CCC (3d) 171 (Ont CA).

accused actually had the requisite intention and knowledge . . . . It does not, however, constitute the requisite state of mind.[34]

As with all crimes, there must be some degree of correspondence between the commission of the *actus reus* of causing death and the *mens rea* required under section 229. That said, the Supreme Court in *R v Cooper*[35] indicated that so long as the accused knew at some point during two minutes of strangulation that the victim was likely to die, then there was a sufficient overlap between the *actus reus* and the *mens rea*. In other words, "if death results from a series of wrongful acts that are part of a single transaction then it must be established that the requisite intent coincided at some point with the wrongful acts." As long as the *mens rea* existed at some point in the transaction leading to death, it would not matter that the victim died some time later.[36]

d) Section 229(b) and Transferred Intent

Section 229(b) codifies the common law doctrine of transferred intent. The *mens rea* of intentionally or knowingly causing death to one person is transferred to the killing of the victim, even though the accused "does not mean to cause death or bodily harm" to the victim and does so "by accident or mistake." This provision was applied in *R v Droste (No. 2)*[37] to convict an accused who, in a deliberate attempt to kill his wife, set fire to a car, causing two children buckled in the back seat to die of asphyxiation. The Supreme Court concluded that because the attempted murder of the accused's wife was planned and deliberate, the intent of planning and deliberation, as well as the guilty knowledge that death would result, could be transferred to the children's deaths.

The Manitoba Court of Appeal has decided that section 229(b) should not be applied when the accused intends to kill himself but ends up killing another person. The Court of Appeal held that a person who intends to kill himself does not have the same moral blameworthiness as a person who intends to kill another person, but then kills yet another person by accident or mistake.[38] The Court of Appeal also stated that "section 229(b) is ambiguous in its interpretation as to whether it is intended to be limited to the killing of another or to include the

---

34   *R v Simpson* (1981), 58 CCC (2d) 122 (Ont CA).

35   (1993), 78 CCC (3d) 289 (SCC) [*Cooper*].

36   *R v Meli*, [1954] 1 WLR 228 (PC), cited with approval in *Cooper*, above note 35 at 297.

37   (1984), 10 CCC (3d) 404 (SCC) [*Droste (No 2)*].

38   *R v Fontaine* (2002), 168 CCC (3d) 263 at paras 40–45 (Man CA) [*Fontaine*], rejecting *R v Brown* (1983), 4 CCC (3d) 571 (Ont HCJ), holding that an intent to commit suicide could be transferred under s 229(b) of the *Code*, above note 1.

killing of oneself. Where ambiguity is present in a piece of penal legislation, the statutory interpretation rule of strict construction should be
applied because of the potential for serious interference with individual rights."[39] This conclusion invoked the principle of strict construction of the criminal law discussed in Chapter 3. The Ontario Court
of Appeal has even further restricted section 229(b) by holding that it
did not apply in a case where an innocent bystander was killed during
a gunfight on Toronto's Yonge Street on the basis that the accused did
nothing by accident or mistake that caused the bystander's death.[40] It
could, however, be argued that any intent to kill a rival gang member
could be transferred to killing the bystander by accident or mistake.

e)   Section 229(c)

Section 229(c) provides that a person is guilty of murder where he or she
does (1) for an unlawful object (2) anything that he or she knows (3) or
ought to know is likely to cause death and (4) causes death (5) notwithstanding that he or she desires to effect his or her object without causing death or bodily harm.

In *R v Vasil*,[41] the Supreme Court held that the unlawful object must
be the pursuit of a serious crime "clearly distinct from the immediate
object of the dangerous (unlawful) act." This requirement is necessary
to ensure that section 229(c) does not eclipse other murder provisions.
For example, if an assault that resulted in death was a sufficient unlawful object then there might not be much of a need for section 229(a).
Courts have continued to confirm that the unlawful object be distinct
and not merge with the dangerous act that caused the victim's death.[42]
The British Columbia Court of Appeal has confirmed that "[t]here must
be an unlawful object that is distinct from the dangerous act. The act
must be committed in furtherance of the object. The object must be
something other than the intention described in s. 229(a). Both object
and act must be clearly identified so that they are not conflated."[43]

In *R v Martineau*,[44] the Supreme Court ruled that the objective arm
of section 229(c) violated sections 7 and 11(d) of the *Charter* because
it substituted proof of objective foresight of death for subjective knowledge of the likelihood of death, which was constitutionally required

---

39   *Fontaine*, above note 38 at para 34.
40   *R v JSR*, 2008 ONCA 544 at para 38 [*JSR*].
41   [1981] 1 SCR 469 at 500.
42   *R v Roks*, 2011 ONCA 526 at paras 126–27 [*Roks*]; *R v Shand*, 2011 ONCA 5 at
     para 153 [*Shand*].
43   *R v Learn*, 2013 BCCA 254 at para 18.
44   *Martineau*, above note 27.

because of the stigma and penalty of murder.[45] The Court also indicated that it would be difficult to justify the objective arm of section 229(c) under section 1 given that there were other more proportionate means to deter the use of violence in pursuing an unlawful objective.

The courts have been using section 229(c) more often minus its objective arm that has unfortunately[46] still not been repealed by Parliament. In *R v Meiler*,[47] section 229(c) was applied to an accused who killed a person while pursuing the unlawful objective of attempting to kill another person. He was approaching his intended victim, but was tackled by another person and the accused's gun went off, killing the victim. The application of section 229(c) in these circumstances comes perilously close to the old section 230 under which killings during the course of certain crimes could result in murder convictions. The critical distinction, however, is that section 229(c) requires not only the pursuit of an unlawful object, but also subjective knowledge that death is likely to occur in the pursuit of the unlawful object. Knowledge that death is likely to occur requires that the accused know that death is probable, not simply that it is possible, a risk, a danger, foreseeable, or a chance.[48] The courts also applied section 229(c) in a case in which a bystander was killed in the course of a gun battle on a busy Toronto street, noting that the accused was doing a dangerous act in shooting in pursuit of the unlawful objective of killing a rival gang member when he knew that firing shots in the crowded street was likely to cause the death of someone other than his intended target.[49] The courts have, however, held that section 229(c) did not apply in a case where an arson planned for insurance fraud purposes unexpectedly led to the death of one of the arsonists. The Ontario Court of Appeal stressed the importance of

---

45 Justice Lamer explained: "In my view, subjective foresight of death must be proven beyond a reasonable doubt before a conviction for murder can be sustained, and as a result, it is obvious the part of s 212(c) of the *Code* allowing for a conviction upon proof that the accused ought to have known that death was likely to result violates ss 7 and 11(d) of the *Charter*." *Martineau*, *ibid* at 648.

46 New trials have had to be ordered in a number of cases in which trial judges left juries with copies of the *Criminal Code* section including the unconstitutional "ought" to know section. See Kent Roach, "The Problematic Revival of Murder under Section 229(c) of the *Criminal Code*" (2010) 47 *Alberta Law Review* 675 at 685–86. Unfortunately, s 229(c) has still not been amended by Parliament to remove the unconstitutional reference to "ought to know." Some courts have subsequently held that reading s 229 (c) as written by Parliament will not require a new trial provided that the jury was otherwise adequately instructed. *R v Foerster*, 2017 BCCA 105.

47 (1999) 136 CCC (3d) 11 (Ont CA).

48 *Roks*, above note 42 at paras 134 and 146.

49 *JSR*, above note 40.

proving that the accused must know at the time of the act that death was probable and the dangers of reasoning backwards from the fact that a death resulted.[50] In the result, the accused who had planned the fire was convicted of manslaughter, not murder.

In *R v Shand*[51] the Ontario Court of Appeal held that section 229(c) minus the objective arm was consistent with section 7 of the *Charter* but stressed the importance of the subjective foresight of death requirement. In other words "vague realization that death is possible will not be sufficient."[52] The accused must know that death was likely to occur and not simply a risk or a possibility. Section 229(c) applied in that case in which the accused pointed a gun that accidentally discharged during a robbery. The murder conviction was sustained because the trial judge made it clear to the jury that the accused must actually know that the unlawful act was likely to cause someone's death.[53]

The recent revival of section 229(c) carries many dangers. One danger that the Ontario Court of Appeal recognized was that the jury might engage in "the logical fallacy of assuming that, because the victim died, the appellant must have known that death was likely. This type of analysis essentially amounts to the constitutionally prohibited reasoning that the accused 'ought to have known' that his or her act was likely to cause death."[54] The critical distinction between subjective and objective fault can be blurred, especially in cases where knowledge of death is extended to a broad range of victims.

Another danger is that section 229(c) could expand to take over murders that should fall under section 229(a). The Ontario Court of Appeal in *Shand* appeared to suggest that the emphasis in pre-*Charter* cases like *Vasil* on an unlawful object being separate from the act that caused death may be less important now that the Court has invalidated the objective arm under the *Charter*.[55] Even so, however, as a matter of statutory construction courts should be careful not to allow section 229(c) to eclipse other forms of murder. Practically, section 229(c) seems most important in those cases where the accused is pursuing an unlawful object that is a serious *mens rea* offence and kills someone whose identity is not known. That said, it will be important and perhaps a challenge for judges and juries to understand that section 229(c) should only apply if the accused actually knew that someone would die.

50   *Roks*, above note 42 at paras 134–35.
51   *Shand*, above note 42, leave to appeal to SCC refused, [2011] SCCA No 270.
52   *Shand, ibid* at para 152.
53   *Ibid* at para 203.
54   *Ibid* at para 210.
55   *Ibid* at para 133.

Accidental deaths during the commission of unlawful acts are better punished as a form of manslaughter, not murder.

Another danger in section 229(c) is that accidental deaths will be punished as murder in large part because the accused was pursuing an unlawful object at the time of the accidental death. Long before the *Charter*, the Supreme Court took care not to allow section 229(c) to be applied to accidental deaths[56] and such a possibility violates the principle of fundamental justice that unintentional harm should not be punished as severely as intentional harm.[57] The British Columbia Court of Appeal has ruled that references to accidental deaths in explaining section 229(c) to the jury may be "misleading because it conflates two questions: (i) whether the accidental discharge of a weapon would result in death ("accident" in the sense of an unintended action) and (ii) whether the accused had subjective foresight that such a situation would likely result in death ("accident" in the sense of an unintended consequence)."[58] In the result, a conviction was overturned and a new murder trial ordered after a trial judge had instructed the jury that section 229(c) still applies even if the discharge of a gun during a robbery was "accidental." Accidental deaths whether as a result of unintended actions or unintended consequences should not be punished with the high stigma and penalty of murder. When using section 229(c), judges and juries should be careful to require knowledge of the probability of death and not reason backwards from the fact that a death occurred during the commission of an unlawful object.

f) Parties to Murder Offences

As discussed in Chapter 4, section 21(1) makes people guilty of an offence both if they actually commit it and if they aid and abet the commission of an offence. The *Thatcher* case underlines that it is not necessary for the Crown to specify whether a person is guilty as the principal offender or as an aider or abettor of the offence.[59] The *Pickton* serial murder case goes even further as it upheld a murder conviction in a case where the trial judge had initially and according to the Crown's theory of the case instructed the jury that Pickton personally shot his multiple victims, but later in response to a question from the jury on its sixth day of deliberation said that Pickton would be guilty if he was "otherwise an active participant" in the killings and indicated that it was not necessary that he be the actual shooter to be guilty of

---

56   *R v Hughes*, [1942] SCR 517 at 523.

57   *R v Creighton*, [1993] 3 SCR 3 at 49 [*Creighton*].

58   *R v Belcourt*, 2015 BCCA 126 at para 102.

59   *R v Thatcher* (1987), 32 CCC (3d) 481 (SCC).

murder. Relying on the *Thatcher* case, the Court stressed that section 21(1) was designed to put the aider or abettor on the same footing as the person who actually committed the crime.[60] A number of accused could be convicted of murder if they all knowingly assisted in the victim's death even though it was unclear which one of the accused actually killed the victim.[61]

If charged as an aider or abettor of murder, the Crown must prove that the accused performed an *actus reus* that rendered aid, assistance, or encouragement to the killing and something more than mere presence and passive acquiescence. In *Kirkness*,[62] the Supreme Court stated that an accused aiding or abetting a murder "must intend that death ensue or intend that he or the perpetrator cause bodily harm of a kind likely to result in death and be reckless whether death ensues or not." The above holding ensures that no one will be convicted of murder without proof of at least subjective foresight of death. In the actual case, the Supreme Court affirmed the acquittal of an accused who during a break-in had not participated in suffocating the victim and had told the accused to stop choking the victim.

In *R v Briscoe*,[63] the Supreme Court held that wilful blindness as a form of "deliberate ignorance" could be substituted for this knowledge requirement even with respect to murder. Thus, an accused will be guilty of aiding and abetting murder if the accused (1) purposively aids and abets, and (2) knows or is wilfully blind that the victim will die. An accomplice that satisfies the above requirements could be held guilty of murder through aiding and abetting even if the principal offender was not guilty of murder, for example, because he or she had a defence such as provocation or intoxication that reduced murder to manslaughter.

---

60   *R v Pickton*, [2010] 2 SCR 198 at para 33. Justice Charron for the majority indicated that it would have been preferable had the jury been instructed specifically about aiding and abetting but that the omission of such an instruction could have benefitted only the accused, *ibid* at para 12. The dissenters in the case agreed that the alternatives of aiding and abetting could be put to the jury, but stated that "the phrases 'active participation,' 'acting in concert,' or 'joint venture' do not in and of themselves adequately convey the law of party liability to a trier of fact." *Ibid* at para 38.

61   *Chow Bew v The Queen*, [1956] SCR 124; *R v Issac*, [1984] 1 SCR 74 at 80–81; *R v McMaster*, [1996] 1 SCR 740 at para 33; *R v McQuaid*, [1998] 1 SCR 244; *R v Biniaris*, [2000] 1 SCR 381; *R v Suzack* (2000), 141 CCC (3d) 449 (Ont CA); *R v H(LI)* (2003), 17 CR (6th) 338 at para 60 (Man CA); *R v Portillo* (2003), 17 CR (6th) 362 at para 71 (Ont CA) [*Portillo*]; *R v JFD* (2005), 196 CCC (3d) 316 at para 14 (BCCA); *R v Rojos* (2006), 208 CCC (3d) 13 (BCCA).

62   *R v Kirkness* (1990), 60 CCC (3d) 97 at 127 (SCC).

63   *R v Briscoe*, [2010] 1 SCR 411 at paras 22–25 [*Briscoe*].

The basic principle is that accused must intend to aid and abet and also have the requisite fault of knowledge or wilful blindness of death for murder. In cases where the aider or abettor intends to assist, but does not know and is not wilfully blind that death was likely to occur, a manslaughter conviction may be possible and that form of liability will be discussed later in this chapter.

Special caution must be employed with liability for murder under the common purpose doctrine of section 21(2). In *R v Logan*,[64] the Supreme Court declared the phrase "ought to have known" to be an unjustified violation of the *Charter* when the accused is charged with murder or attempted murder on the basis that stigma and punishment of those offences require no less than proof of subjective knowledge of the probability that death would result.

In cases of murder and attempted murder, the objective arm of section 21(2) should not be left to the jury and the jury should convict only if a party has actual foresight or knowledge that the principal offender would kill a person while carrying out their common unlawful purpose.[65]

3) First-Degree Murder

First-degree murder is technically a sentencing classification that has its origins in the now-abolished offence of capital murder. A person charged with first-degree murder will be charged with murder under section 229, but also with murder under section 231. Section 231 requires the proof of additional fault elements and additional prohibited acts than contemplated in section 229[66] and, thus, section 231 has been interpreted as if it were an offence. All murder convictions result in a mandatory sentence of life imprisonment, but a first-degree murder conviction results in ineligibility for parole for twenty-five years, though an accused previously could apply for eligibility for parole after fifteen years' imprisonment.[67]

a) Planned and Deliberate Murder Under Sections 231(2) and (3)

The purest form of first-degree murder is a planned and deliberate killing. The accused is subject to increased punishment because of the increased culpability of killing in a calculated and planned manner as opposed to a more impulsive murder. A planned and deliberate murder is more than

---

64   (1990), 58 CCC (3d) 391 (SCC).

65   *R v Rodney* (1990), 58 CCC (3d) 408 (SCC); *R v Laliberty* (1997), 117 CCC (3d) 97 at 108 (Ont CA); *Portillo*, above note 51 at paras 72–73.

66   *R v Luxton*, [1990] 2 SCR 711.

67   *Code*, above note 1, ss 745–746.1.

an intentional murder. It must be "considered, not impulsive"[68] and it requires planning and consideration beforehand.[69] A lesser degree of intoxication or mental disturbance may be sufficient to raise a reasonable doubt about planning and deliberation under section 231 than knowledge of the likelihood of death under section 229. There is no requirement that juries always be instructed to that effect, but the differences between the relevance of intoxication in raising a reasonable doubt about planning and deliberation and the less complex mental element of knowledge should be made clear to the jury.[70] Although a person with a mental disorder can still engage in a planned and deliberate murder,[71] evidence of mental disorder well short of establishing the mental disorder defence may still raise a reasonable doubt about planning and deliberation.

Murders under section 229(a)(ii)[72] and under section 229(b)[73] may be planned and deliberate. In the former case, the accused could have planned and deliberated to have given the victim a sustained beating in order to collect debts that he knew was likely to result in the accused's death. It should be clear that what is planned is not simply a beating, but a beating that the accused knew was likely to cause death.[74] In the latter case, the accused could have planned and deliberated to kill one person but then by accident or mistake have killed another person. It is also possible that a murder under section 229(c) might be planned and deliberate if the accused planned and deliberated the commission of an unlawful object that he knew would result in death.

Section 231(3) provides as a specific example of planned and deliberate killings a contract killing where money or anything of value is promised, passed, or is intended to be passed in exchange for causing, assisting in causing, or counselling another person to do any act causing or assisting in causing death.

b) Killing Police Officers and Other Officials in the Execution of Their Duties

Section 231(4) provides that murder is first-degree murder where the victim is a police officer acting in the course of his or her duties or

---

68   *R v More*, [1963] 3 CCC 289 at 291 (SCC).
69   *R v Ruptash* (1982), 68 CCC (2d) 182 (Alta CA).
70   *R v Wallen*, [1990] 1 SCR 827.
71   *R v Kirkby* (1985), 21 CCC (3d) 31 (Ont CA).
72   *Nygaard*, above note 32.
73   *Droste (No 2)*, above note 37.
74   *R v Banwait*, 2011 SCC 55, rev'g 2010 ONCA 869 at paras 178–89 and approving of MacPherson JA's judgment in dissent.

other law enforcement officials acting in the course of their duties, including those working in prisons. This provision was enacted in order to provide additional protection to such officials. It has been interpreted in a purposive manner to apply to a whole tour of duty, including breaks and other periods when police officers are not necessarily actively engaged in exercising their powers or duties[75] and courts have understandably been reluctant to conclude that on-duty police officers were not exercising their powers or duties because of allegations that the police had engaged in excessive force.[76]

As with many offences, section 231(4) is completely silent on the fault issue of whether the accused must know or be reckless with respect to the elements of the prohibited act, in this case the fact that the person killed was a police officer or other justice official acting in the course of his or her duties. The Ontario Court of Appeal has held that the normal common law presumption of fault should apply to section 231(4) even though the section is technically a sentencing classification and the accused must also be found guilty under section 229. Thus, under section 231(4), the Crown must prove that the accused either knew or was reckless by subjectively adverting to the possibility that the victim was a police officer.[77] The Court of Appeal reasoned that some degree of subjective fault with respect to the identity of the police officer was necessary to justify the enhanced culpability and punishment of first-degree murder as well as to satisfy the purpose of the section in deterring violence against the police officer. It is not necessary, however, that the accused know for certain that the victim is a police officer acting in the course of his or her duties. Some subjective advertence to the risk, for example, that a person is an undercover officer should be sufficient to satisfy the fault requirement of recklessness.

c) Killing While Committing Other Serious Crimes

Section 231(5) provides that killing is first-degree murder "when the death is caused by that person while committing or attempting to commit" a short list of serious offences including hijacking an aircraft, hostage-taking, kidnapping and forcible confinement, and sexual assault including aggravated forms of sexual assault. Although the Supreme Court struck down a similar formulation under section 230, the constructive or "felony" first-degree murder provisions in the *Code* have

---

75   *R v Prevost* (1988), 42 CCC (3d) 314 (Ont CA).

76   *R v Boucher*, 2006 QCCA 1079; *R v Jaw*, 2008 NUCA 2, aff'd on other grounds, [2009] 3 SCR 326.

77   *R v Munro* (1983), 8 CCC (3d) 260 (Ont CA); *R v Collins* (1989), 48 CCC (3d) 343 (Ont CA).

been upheld under section 7 of the *Charter* on the basis that any person convicted of first-degree murder under section 231(5) would also have been convicted of murder under section 229. The requirement for a conviction under section 229 would guarantee that the accused would have the constitutionally required fault of subjective knowledge that the victim would die. The Court also ruled that basing the harsher punishment provided for murders under section 231(5) on the commission of a serious crime was not arbitrary or cruel and unusual.[78] Parliament has in recent years effectively added to the list of serious crimes through the enactment of sections 231(6) to 231(6.2), which now apply to serious and well-publicized crimes such as criminal harassment, terrorism offences, intimidation of a justice system participant, and offences for a criminal organization.

The most controversial of the underlying offences in section 231(5) has been forcible confinement. The Alberta and Quebec Courts of Appeal have stressed that there must be some evidence of unlawful domination that goes beyond the violence inherent in a robbery, which in itself is not an offence listed under section 231(5).[79] The Supreme Court, however, rejected this restrictive approach and held that section 231(5) applies as long as there is some element of unlawful confinement distinct from the killing and that this unlawful confinement can arise in the course of a robbery that is part of a single transaction ending in the victim's death.[80] An act of the accused in stopping the victim's attempted escape has been held to be sufficiently "distinct and independent" from the subsequent killing to constitute forcible confinement triggering section 231(5).[81] Similarly the act of detaining a child in an abusive manner that goes beyond normal parenting is also sufficient to constitute forcible confinement.[82] Physical acts of violence are sufficient but not necessary and forcible confinement can also be caused by fear and intimidation.[83]

The Supreme Court has also taken a broad approach to section 231(5) in other cases. In *R v Paré*,[84] it indicated that the section would apply so long as the sexual assault was committed during a continuous trans-

---

78 *R v Arkell*, [1990] 2 SCR 695.

79 *R v Strong* (1990), 60 CCC (3d) 516 (Alta CA); *R v Kingsley* (1995), 105 CCC (3d) 85 (Que CA).

80 *R v Pritchard*, [2008] 3 SCR 195 at paras 27–28.

81 *R v Newman*, 2016 SCC 7 at para 1.

82 *R v Magoon*, 2018 SCC 14 at paras 68–69.

83 *R v Kematch*, 2010 MBCA 18 at para 89. A victim's actions of locking herself in a room in an attempt to save herself from the accused can be unlawful confinement. *R v Johnstone*, 2014 ONCA 504 at para 47.

84 [1987] 2 SCR 618.

action of illegal domination and that it need not occur at exactly the same time as the killing. Appeal courts have taken an even broader approach and held that the section applies even in cases where the accused commits sexual assault shortly after and in the same transaction as killing the victim.[85] In *R v Russell*,[86] the Court went further and held that the underlying offence could be committed against a person other than the murder victim so long as there was a temporal and causal connection between the commission of the underlying offence and the killing. The Court stressed that Parliament had not precluded the application of section 231(5) in cases where there are multiple victims as it has in section 231(6), which specifically states that the person murdered must also be the victim of the underlying offence of criminal harassment. It stressed that Parliament wanted to more severely punish killings while the accused also committed one of the listed serious crimes.

As discussed earlier in this chapter, in *R v Harbottle*,[87] the Supreme Court held that the phrase "caused by that person" in section 231(5) requires that the accused be a substantial cause of the victim's death. The Court in that case did not preclude the application of section 231(5) to co-accused and held that an accused who held the victim's legs while another accused strangled her to death still was a substantial and integral cause of the victim's death. As suggested above, the substantial cause requirement in section 231(5) applies to sections 231(6), (6.01), (6.1), and (6.2) pursuant to recent amendments that all refer to "death caused by that person" meaning the accused.

4) Provocation

a) Introduction to a Controversial and Recently Restricted Partial Defence

Unlike self-defence, necessity, and duress examined in the last chapter, a successful provocation defence does not result in the acquittal of the accused. Provocation only reduces murder to manslaughter. Nevertheless, this is an important distinction that avoids the mandatory life imprisonment that accompanies a murder conviction.

As a partial defence that reduces murder to manslaughter, provocation does not fit easily into the excuse/justification framework discussed in Chapter 9. The Supreme Court has stated that the "provocation . . . neither justifies nor excuses the act of homicide. But the law

---

85   *R v Muchikekwanape* (2002), 166 CCC (3d) 144 (Man CA); *R v Richer* (1993), 82 CCC (3d) 385, aff'd on other grounds, [1994] 2 SCR 486.

86   [2001] 2 SCR 804.

87   Above note 23.

accounts the act and the violent feelings which prompted it, less blamable because of the passion aroused by the provocation."[88] Provocation could be said to operate as a partial excuse out of compassion to human frailty when an accused kills another person while in a rage provoked by a sudden act or insult. Although the origins of the provocation defence lie in the distinction between capital and non-capital murder, today it flows from the distinction between mandatory life imprisonment for murder and more discretionary penalties for manslaughter.[89]

Provocation is a controversial defence. Its origins lay in traditions of mitigating violent responses to marital infidelities and other affronts to "honour" and it contains archaic phrases about excusing a person who acts in the heat of passion. Some argue that it should be abolished as a defence because it allows deadly rage and violence, often directed against women and sexual minorities, to be treated less seriously than other intentional killings. The Supreme Court has, however, indicated that the provocation defence should accord with contemporary norms and reject sexist and homophobic beliefs and "inappropriate conceptualizations of 'honour.'"[90] Others argue that the provocation defence reflects the special significance of murder and the fact that murder, unlike manslaughter, carries a fixed penalty. Still others argue that the defence of provocation should apply to all crimes, not only murder. And some question why provocation privileges emotions such as rage in response to acts or insults, but not other emotions such as compassion and despair that may also prompt killings that while intentional may not merit mandatory life imprisonment. In England, the provocation defence has been broadened to one based on loss of self-control, but in New Zealand it has been abolished.

As defined in section 232 of the *Criminal Code* up to 15 July 2015, provocation required (1) a wrongful act or insult that is not provoked by the accused or the result of a victim exercising a legal right;[91] (2) sudden provocation; (3) subjective provocation;[92] and (4) a wrongful act or insult "of such a nature as to be sufficient to deprive an ordinary person

---

88   *R v Manchuk*, [1938] SCR 18 at 19–20 [*Manchuk*].

89   *R v Tran*, 2010 SCC 58 at paras 21–22 [*Tran*].

90   *Ibid* at para 34.

91   *Code*, above note 1, s 232(3), provides in part that "no one shall be deemed to have given provocation to another by doing anything that he had a legal right to do, or by doing anything that the accused incited him to do in order to provide the accused with an excuse for causing death or bodily harm to any human being."

92   *Ibid*, s 232(1), uses the archaic phrase that the accused must act "in the heat of passion caused by sudden provocation."

of the power of self-control."[93] There is a tendency to categorize the first three factors as relating to the subjective arm of provocation and the last factor as relating to its objective component.

Just before Parliament was dissolved for the 2015 election and as part the *Zero Tolerance of Barbaric Cultural Practices Act*,[94] Parliament added an additional requirement, namely that the provoking act must also constitute an indictable offence punishable by five years' imprisonment or more. If not struck down under the *Charter*, this new restriction will essentially limit provoking acts to assaults or sexual assaults. Practically it may make the provocation defence illusory because in cases where the provoking acts amount to an assault or a sexual assault, the accused will likely rely on self-defence, which if accepted results in an acquittal, whereas a successful provocation defence is only a partial defence reducing murder to manslaughter.

Even before the 2015 amendments, provocation was quite a restrictive defence. The accused's subjective anger and rage may help satisfy the subjective requirements but would not suffice.[95] The requirement that the ordinary person would lose self-control is designed to encourage reasonable and non-violent behaviour that is in accord with contemporary norms and values including equality under the *Charter*.[96] The ordinary person standard has been modified so that the ordinary person has the same age and gender of the accused and the same relevant experiences.[97] This led to concerns that the individuated reasonable person may diminish the level of self-control and afford defences in particular to jealous or homophobic males. The Supreme Court responded to many of these concerns in *R v Tran*[98] by holding that the ordinary person should only be modified to place the act or insult in context but not "to shift the ordinary person standard to suit the individual accused" or to individualize the ordinary person so as to defeat its purpose in encouraging self-control and non-violent behaviour.

---

93 *Ibid*, s 232(2). The proper formulation is whether the ordinary person would, rather than could, have lost self-control. *R v Hill*, [1986] 1 SCR 313 at 330 [*Hill*]; *R v Hibbert*, [1995] 2 SCR 973 at para 24 [*Hibbert*]; *R v Lees* (2001), 156 CCC (3d) 421 at paras 15–16 (BCCA).

94 SC 2015, c 29, s 7.

95 *R v Parent*, [2001] 1 SCR 761 [*Parent*].

96 *Hill*, above note 93 at 324; *Tran*, above note 89 at para 34.

97 *R v Thibert* (1996), 104 CCC (3d) 1 (SCC) [*Thibert*].

98 *Tran*, above note 89 at para 35.

b) Air of Reality and Burden of Proof

Like the defences discussed in Chapter 9, the provocation defence will apply if there is a reasonable doubt about all of its elements. It should be left to the jury only when there is an "air of reality" to the defence. In other words, there must be some evidence that if believed by the jury would allow them acting judicially to have a reasonable doubt about each element of the defence. In order for the provocation defence to apply, the jury must have a reasonable doubt about each of its constituent elements.[99] This mean that the prosecutor can defeat the defence by proving beyond a reasonable that only one of its essential elements does not exist.

The Supreme Court has not hesitated to hold that there is no air of reality to provocation defences if there is a lack of evidence about whether an ordinary person would lose self-control[100] or whether the accused was subjectively provoked.[101] Now courts will also have to decide whether there is an air of reality that the provoking act is also an indictable offence punishable by five years' imprisonment or more.

At the same time, it is important to allow juries to make judgments, and determining that the defence has an air of reality does not mean that the trier of fact must accept that the defence applies.[102] Judges should not render the defence a dead letter by always holding that there is no air of reality to the defence.

c) First Requirement: A Wrongful Act or Insult and Now an Indictable Offence Punishable by Five Years' Imprisonment

The courts had traditionally interpreted the requirement of a wrongful act or insult broadly to include scornful and contemptuous remarks and a broad range of wrongful acts including assaults. For example, a wife's denial of an affair and slapping her husband was considered a wrongful act or insult,[103] as were a victim's actions in holding the accused's wife in front of him and saying "come on big fellow shoot me."[104] In one controversial case, the victim's statement that she would not marry the accused because he was black was not considered a wrongful

---

99 *Ibid* at para 41.
100 *R v Cairney*, 2013 SCC 55 [*Cairney*].
101 *R v Pappas*, 2013 SCC 56 [*Pappas*].
102 *R v Buzizi*, 2013 SCC 27 at para 16 [*Buzizi*].
103 *Taylor v The King*, [1947] SCR 462.
104 *Thibert*, above note 97. Two judges dissented on this issue and argued that the words and actions were not contemptuous or scornful but legitimate reactions to being confronted by the accused who was pointing a loaded rifle. *Ibid* at para 63.

act or insult but only on the basis that the accused testified at trial that he had not heard the remark.[105]

In *Tran*, the Court took a more restrictive approach to the threshold requirement of whether there was an act or insult. It found that there was no wrongful act or insult when the accused entered the apartment of his estranged wife to find her naked with another man. The behaviour of the two lovers "was not only lawful, it was discreet and private and entirely passive vis-à-vis" the accused. There was no wrongful act or insult defined as scornful abuse or offences to modesty or self-respect.[106] What in previous generations may have been considered to be the paradigmatic act of provocation — the discovery of evidence of adultery and a sudden violent response to that evidence — has now been held by the Court not even to constitute a wrongful act or insult capable of being an act of provocation. This part of *Tran* imposed a categorical restriction on the provocation defence even though the defence was also denied on the basis of other subjective and objective factors.[107] With respect to the objective standard, the Court also stressed in *Tran* the need for it to be informed by contemporary social norms and values and for it to reject sexist attitudes that saw adultery as "the highest invasion of propriety."[108]

In 2015, Parliament imposed another categorical restriction on the provocation defence by replacing the traditional reference to acts or insults with a requirement that the "[c]onduct of the victim that would constitute an indictable offence under this Act that is punishable by five or more years of imprisonment . . . ." It is, however, likely that courts will still assume that provoking acts should also be acts or insults. For example, the Ontario Court of Appeal has observed that under the new requirements "an insult that is not criminal is no longer capable of constituting a provocative act."[109]

The new statutory provision requires not only that provoking acts be criminal, but that they be indictable offences punishable by five years' imprisonment. This would include assaults and sexual assaults, but exclude many other crimes that might, in some circumstances, also satisfy the other requirements of the provocation defence. For example, some crimes that would be categorically excluded because they are punishable by a maximum penalty of less than five years' imprisonment

---

105 *Parnekar v The Queen*, [1974] SCR 449. Chief Justice Laskin in dissent would have left the provocation defence to the jury.

106 *Tran*, above note 89 at para 44.

107 *Ibid* at para 46.

108 *Ibid* at para 34, disapproving of *R v Mawgridge* (1707), 84 ER 1107 at 1115.

109 *R v Suarez-Noa*, 2017 ONCA 627 at n 1.

include forcible entry into a dwelling (section 73), carrying a gun at a public meeting (section 89), breaching a court order (section 127), an indecent act (section 173), disrupting a religious meeting (section 176), using hate speech (section 319), and delivering false or indecent information (section 372). If the accused was provoked by an assault or sexual assault as seemingly required by the new section 232(2), then the accused will often rely on self defence as his or her primary defence because, if successful, it would result in an acquittal whereas provocation is only a partial defence that reduces murder to manslaughter.

The new categorical restrictions placed in section 232(2) in 2015 was introduced to ensure that the provocation defence was not available to reduce "honour killings" to manslaughter (even though no court had recognized such a defence in such circumstances). Unfortunately, the new amendment goes much further and places restrictions on the provocation defence that are overbroad and perhaps even arbitrary to the legislative objectives of limiting the provocation to prevent honour killings or for general social protection. The new restrictions on the provocation defence may also violate section 7 of the *Charter* by being grossly disproportionate, especially given that categorical and unjustified denials of the provocation defence will result in a murder conviction subject to mandatory life imprisonment.

If this new restriction survives a *Charter* challenge, the only realistic scenario for a successful provocation defence is when the act or insult that deprives an ordinary person of self-control and causes the accused to be subjectively provoked also amounts to an assault or sexual assault. Assaults under sections 265(1)(b) or (c) can include threats and impeding a person with a weapon. In cases of assault, however, the accused may prefer to plead self-defence, which, if accepted, and unlike provocation, would lead to a full acquittal.

i) No Legal Right Restrictions

There are other restrictions on what may constitute a wrongful act or insult or now on indictable acts punishable by five years or more as being provoking acts. Section 232(3) states that there is no provocation when the accused has incited the victim to commit the act or insult claimed to be provocation. The Court has approved of the proposition that there will generally not be provocation where an accused initiates a confrontation and invites a predictable response. However, such self-induced provocation "is not a special category" but "simply a contextual factor in determining whether the subjective and objective elements of the defence are met."[110] Moreover, "there is no absolute rule that a person who instigates a confrontation cannot rely on the defence of provocation."[111] This could apply to stop an accused who provoked the deceased to assault him from claiming the provocation defence.

Section 232(3) also restricts the definition of provocation by providing that "no one shall be deemed to have given provocation to another by doing anything he has a legal right to do."[112] The legal right exception to provocation has been interpreted narrowly. In *Thibert*,[113] the Court stated: "In the context of the provocation defence, the phrase 'legal right' has been defined as something which is sanctioned by law as distinct from something which a person may do without incurring legal liability." This is unfortunate because a broader reading of the deceased's legal rights could respond to concerns about the provocation defence excusing violence in response to rather trivial acts or insults or when women tell men that they are leaving a relationship. This criticism of the legal right exception to provocation was considered but rejected by the Supreme Court in *Tran*,[114] which has upheld the idea that legal right applies only to conduct such as self-defence specifically authorized by law and not to freedoms that are not specifically prohibited by law. The Court noted that while a spouse has a legal right to leave his or her partner, it was still possible that he or she might suddenly insult the other during the course of leaving. The Court did note, however, that the fact that the victim had "the 'legal right,' in the broad sense of the term to leave the relationship is an important consideration" in determining whether the insult would have deprived an ordinary person of self-control.

The legal right exception could be relevant even under the 2015 restrictions on provocation. As discussed above, an assault by the deceased on the accused could qualify as a provoking act because assault is an indictable offence punishable by five years' imprisonment or more. If, however, the deceased was acting in self-defence when he or she assaulted the accused, then the legal right exemption in section 232(3) would apply and the Crown could disprove the provocation defence by proving beyond a reasonable doubt that there was no provoking act

---

110 *Cairney*, above note 100 at para 42.

111 *Ibid* at para 56.

112 *Code*, above note 1, s 232(4), provides that an arrest that exceeds an individual's or a police officer's legal powers is not necessarily provocation, "but the fact that the illegality of the arrest was known to the accused may be evidence of provocation."

113 *Thibert*, above note 97 at 14.

114 Above note 89 at para 29.

because the deceased was exercising a legal right in committing an assault and/or responding to something that the accused had incited the deceased to do.

The act that constitutes provocation must generally come from the victim. Provocation cannot be used when the accused knows that the victim was not involved in the act.[115] Provocation may, however, be available when the victim participated with a third person in the act, or where the accused makes a reasonable mistake that the victim was involved in the provocation.[116] Cases of transferred intent under section 229(b) of the *Criminal Code* in which the accused intends to kill one person but kills another by accident or mistake may be mitigated by the provocation defence even though the accused was provoked by the person he or she intended to kill and not the person actually killed.[117]

d) Second Requirement: Objective Requirement That a Modified Ordinary Person Would be Deprived of Self-Control

The most important limitation on what acts and insults can amount to provocation is the requirement in section 232(2) that they be "of such a nature as to deprive an ordinary person of self-control." Chief Justice Dickson has stated that it is:

> society's concern that reasonable and non-violent behaviour be encouraged that prompts the law to endorse the objective standard. The criminal law is concerned among other things with fixing standards for human behaviour. We seek to encourage conduct that complies with certain societal standards of reasonableness and responsibility. In doing so, the law quite logically employs the objective standard of the reasonable person.[118]

The same could be said about self-defence, necessity, and the common law defence of duress, which also employ objective standards. A peaceful society does not want to excuse violence solely on the basis of the accused's subjective and perhaps idiosyncratic perceptions and reactions to the ordinary stresses and strains of modern life. The challenge, as is the case with objective standards for *mens rea*, is to ensure that the particular accused can reasonably be required to live up to the objective standard of self-control and reasonable and non-violent behaviour.

---

115 *Manchuk*, above note 88.

116 *R v Hansford* (1987), 33 CCC (3d) 74 (Alta CA) [*Hansford*].

117 *R v Droste* (1981), 63 CCC (2d) 418 (Ont CA), aff'd on other grounds (*sub nom R v Droste (No 2)*), above note 37.

118 *Hill*, above note 93 at 324–25.

There is no meaningful distinction between the ordinary person standard used for provocation and the reasonable person standard used for self-defence, necessity, and duress, except to the extent the ordinary person standard used in provocation may be slightly less demanding of the accused in reflection of the fact that provocation is only a partial defence that reduces murder to manslaughter and not a full defence that results in the accused going free.[119] As with these others defences, provocation may be grounded on a mistake by the accused, but only if the mistake is reasonable or one that the ordinary person in the circumstances would make.[120]

Courts traditionally interpreted the ordinary person without any reference to the accused's circumstances or characteristics. In *R v Wright*,[121] the Supreme Court held that the fact that the accused was insulted by his father should not be considered when determining whether an ordinary person would have lost self-control. In *R v Parnerkar*,[122] the Saskatchewan Court of Appeal held that the accused's race was not relevant in determining whether an ordinary person would have lost self-control, even though the accused had been told by the victim that she was "not going to marry you because you are a black man." This approach was harsh because it did not allow the Court to consider the relevant context and circumstances behind the act or insult, and could, in the case of a young accused, require "old heads be placed upon young shoulders."[123]

In *Hill*,[124] the majority of the Supreme Court upheld a murder conviction of a sixteen-year-old boy who killed the victim after he claimed the male victim made sexual advances. The trial judge, following *Wright* and *Parnerkar*, had instructed the jury that, in determining whether the acts and words constituted provocation, "you are not to consider the particular mental make-up of the accused; rather the standard is that of the ordinary person."[125]

For the majority of the Court, Dickson CJ stated that it would be fair to consider the accused's youth as an "important contextual

---

119 *Tran*, above note 89 at para 30.
120 *Manchuk*, above note 88 at 19–20; *R v Droste*, above note 117 at 424 (Ont CA), aff'd on other grounds, *R v Droste (No 2)*, above note 37; *Hansford*, above note 116; *R v Boukhalfa*, 2017 ONCA 660 at para 64.
121 [1969] 3 CCC 258 (SCC).
122 (1972), 5 CCC (2d) 11 (Sask CA), aff'd (1973), 10 CCC (2d) 253 (SCC).
123 *Ibid*.
124 Above note 93.
125 *Ibid* at 327–28. They could consider the accused's emotional and physical conditions and his age when determining if he had acted suddenly, before his passion had cooled.

consideration." He warned, however, that the accused's personal characteristics will not always be relevant. For example, an accused's race
would not be relevant if he or she was faced with an insult about a
physical disability. The accused's sex would not be relevant if the insult
was directed at his or her race. Even with regard to the accused's youth,
Dickson CJ held that the charge to the jury was acceptable and it was
not necessary for the judge to instruct the jury to consider whether an
ordinary sixteen-year-old would have lost self-control. He explained:

> [T]he "collective good sense" of the jury will naturally lead it to as-
> cribe to the ordinary person any general characteristics relevant to
> the provocation in question. For example, if the provocation is a ra-
> cial slur, the jury will think of an ordinary person with the racial
> background that forms the substance of the insult. To this extent,
> particular characteristics will be ascribed to the ordinary person.[126]

Although he did not require the jury to be instructed to consider the
accused's youth, Dickson CJ did not seem to believe that considering
youth was inconsistent with the purposes of the objective standard in
encouraging reasonable and non-violent behaviour. Subsequent cases
have considered the accused's youth when determining whether an ordinary person would have lost self-control.[127] Indeed, it would now be
an error of law not to instruct the jury to consider the reactions of an
ordinary person of the accused's own age when considering whether
an ordinary person would have been deprived of the power of self-
control.[128]

In *Thibert*,[129] a three-judge plurality of the Court affirmed a modified or contextualized ordinary person standard when they stated that:
"the 'ordinary person' must be of the same age, and sex, and share
with the accused such other factors as would give the act or insult in
question a special significance and have experienced the same series
of acts or insults as those experienced by the accused." In that case,
this meant the ordinary person was a "married man, faced with the
breakup of his marriage"[130] who had previously convinced his wife
to return to the marriage. The majority concluded that this ordinary
man would have lost his powers of self-control when the deceased
(who was his wife's lover) taunted him to shoot him while holding the
accused's wife in front of him. A two-judge minority dissented on the

---

126   *Ibid* at 331.
127   *R v Jackson* (1991), 68 CCC (3d) 385 at 410 (Ont CA) [*Jackson*].
128   *Thibert*, above note 97.
129   *Ibid* at para 18.
130   *Ibid* at para 24.

basis that the breakup of a marriage due to an extramarital affair and the deceased's participation in the affair should not be considered as wrongful acts or insults capable of depriving an ordinary person of the power of self-control.

The Court's decision in *Thibert* to judge conduct by the standard of the married man was criticized as too easily offering a partial excuse for male violence towards women simply because of a breakup of a relationship. This concern has been partially addressed by the more recent unanimous decision in *Tran* that a man who entered his estranged wife's apartment to find her naked in bed with another man was not provoked. The Court recognized the need for a modified objective approach that places the provoking acts in their proper context. Justice Charron, however, warned that "in adopting this more flexible approach, care must be taken not to subvert the logic of the objective test. Indeed, if all of the accused's characteristics are taken into account, the ordinary person *becomes* the accused."[131] This would undermine the purpose of the ordinary person standard in imposing the same standards of self-control on all people in order to encourage reasonable and non-violent behaviour.[132]

Justice Charron elaborated on the contextual or modified objective standard that should be applied by noting that it should aim to place the provoking act in context, but without individualizing the level of self-control expected from all or building in particular feelings of animus that the accused might have towards the person who provokes him or her. She added:

> It follows that the ordinary person standard must be informed by contemporary norms of behaviour, including fundamental values such as the commitment to equality provided for in the *Canadian Charter of Rights and Freedoms*. For example, it would be appropriate to ascribe to the ordinary person relevant racial characteristics if the accused were the recipient of a racial slur, but it would not be appropriate to ascribe to the ordinary person the characteristic of being homophobic if the accused were the recipient of a homosexual advance. Similarly, there can be no place in this objective standard for antiquated beliefs such as "adultery is the highest invasion of property", nor indeed for any form of killing based on such inappropriate conceptualizations of "honour".[133]

---

131 *Tran*, above note 89 at para 33.
132 *Ibid* at paras 33–34.
133 *Ibid* at para 34 (citations omitted).

She stressed that "there is an important distinction between context-ualizing the objective standard, which is necessary and proper, and individualizing it, which only serves to defeat its purpose."[134]

Tran distinguishes between considering personal characteristics when necessary to place the provoking act in context and the common standard of behaviour promoted by the use of objective and ordinary person standards. One possible exception to this distinction may be age. As Wilson J stated in *Hill*, the fact that the accused was sixteen years of age was relevant because "the law does not attribute to indi-viduals in the developmental stage of their youth the same degree of re-sponsibility as is attributed to fully adult actors."[135] Consistent with the approach subsequently taken in *Tran*, however, Wilson J also cautioned against allowing other factors, including the accused's sex, to deter-mine the amount of self-control expected. In her view, "the underlying principles of equality and individual responsibility cannot be under-mined by importing the accused's subjective level of self-control into the 'ordinary person' test."[136] She believed, however, that the accused's sex was relevant as a factor "to put the wrongful act or insult into con-text for the purposes of assessing its gravity," so that the jury would determine the effect of the act or insult on "the ordinary person simi-larly situated and similarly insulted" as the accused.[137] Today, in light of *Tran*, however, this would be amended to ensure that the level of self-control and perhaps even the context of sexual assault as a provoking act was not influenced by discriminatory homophobia.

Courts of appeal have held that the cultural background of the accused is only relevant when it provides a provoking act "a special significance."[138] The fact that the accused has a particular psychological or physical make-up or even diminished intelligence has been held not to be relevant to placing the provoking act in context.[139] The Ontario Court of Appeal has upheld a first-degree murder conviction where the trial judge specifically instructed the jury that while it could consider the accused's age, gender, and other factors that would give an insult a special significance, it should not consider "any peculiar or idiosyn-cratic traits" arising from the accused's Muslim faith or culture. The

---

134 *Ibid* at para 35.
135 *Hill*, above note 93 at 352.
136 *Ibid*.
137 *Ibid*.
138 *R v Nahar*, 2004 BCCA 77 at para 34.
139 *R v Hill*, 2015 ONCA 616 at paras 80–87 [2015 *Hill*]. The Court of Appeal recog-nized that size could be relevant if the accused was much smaller than the per-son who provoked him or her. *R v Berry*, 2017 ONCA 17 at paras 81–84 [*Berry*].

accused had stabbed his wife nineteen times after apparently learning that she had sexual intercourse with a business associate, but there was also some evidence that he had planned to kill her. Justice of Appeal Doherty concluded:

> Provocation does not shield an accused who has not lost self-control, but has instead acted out of a sense of revenge or a culturally driven sense of the appropriate response to someone else's misconduct. An accused who acts out of a sense of retribution fuelled by a belief system that entitles a husband to punish his wife's perceived infidelity has not lost control, but has taken action that, according to his belief system, is a justified response to the situation.[140]

He also stated that the "beliefs which give the insult added gravity are premised on the notion that women are inferior to men and that violence against women is in some circumstances accepted, if not encouraged. These beliefs are antithetical to fundamental Canadian values, including gender equality."[141] Without reference to this statement, the Supreme Court in *Tran*[142] subsequently made similar statements that "the ordinary person standard must be informed by contemporary norms of behaviour, including fundamental values such as the commitment to equality provided for in the *Canadian Charter of Rights and Freedoms*." This approach suggests that the ordinary person standard should be applied in a manner that supports and incorporates *Charter* and other contemporary norms of behaviour. *Tran* explicitly states that homophobia should not influence the standard of control promoted by the ordinary person standard and implicitly suggests that sexist and cultural values that are out of sync with contemporary norms of behaviour, including the equality of men and women, should not dilute the standard of reasonable behaviour required by the ordinary person standard.

The Supreme Court recently dealt with a case that may have had a cultural dimension. It held that the fact that a woman had immigrated to Canada from Sri Lanka in the same year she killed her sister-in-law

---

140 *R v Humaid* (2006), 37 CR (6th) 347 at para 85 (Ont CA), leave to appeal to SCC refused, [2006] SCCA No 232.

141 *Ibid* at para 93.

142 Above note 89 at para 34. On the connections between the two cases, see *R v Singh*, 2016 ONSC 3739 at para 67 where Fairburn J concluded, "While the ordinary person must live in the accused's world, it must be a world that comports with a basic level of contemporary values, mores and fundamental *Charter* rights. To approach the matter otherwise would be to sacrifice the very foundation upon which the criminal law rests, a concern for setting minimum standards of human behaviour that are consistent with fundamental values."

was relevant because such an accused might have a heightened sensitivity to insults relating to her education and ability to integrate into a new country. At the same time, the Court unanimously concluded that there was no air of reality to the accused's argument that an ordinary person in those circumstances would have lost self-control when ridiculed about her lack of education. In other words, the accused's characteristics, "while relevant, do not transform her conduct [in stabbing the deceased forty-five times] into an act an ordinary person would have committed."[143] This case appropriately does not reject the relevance of the accused's particular circumstances as a recent immigrant even when applying the ordinary person standard. At the same time, it maintains the distinction in *Tran* about not allowing a contextual objective standard to be so individualized that it becomes a subjective one that fails to serve the purpose of the objective standard in promoting reasonable and non-violent behaviour.

In summary, the ordinary person should be defined in a contextual manner that ensures the ordinary person is endowed with those characteristics and past experiences that are necessary to place the act or insult in context. *Tran* now makes clear that *Charter* equality values should inform the ordinary person standard and that homophobia and sexism should not influence the standard of self-control expected of the ordinary person.

i)   Proportionality Not Required
The courts in England stress proportionality when they state the issue is "not merely whether such person would in like circumstances be provoked to lose his self-control but would also react to the provocation as the accused did."[144] Proportionality also figures in the Canadian law applying to self-defence, necessity, and common law duress discussed in Chapter 9. Nevertheless, under the provocation defence, Canadian courts have focused only on whether an ordinary person in the circumstances would have lost self-control, not whether he or she would have done what the accused did.[145] This approach seems to eliminate any requirement that the accused's acts be even roughly proportionate to the act or insult. It also follows the wording of section 232, which refers only to whether an ordinary person would have lost self-control.[146] In the recent case of *Mayuran*,[147] however, the Supreme Court seemed to

---

143 *R v Mayuran*, 2012 SCC 31 at paras 30–31 [*Mayuran*].

144 *DPP v Camplin*, [1978] 2 WLR 679 at 686 (HL).

145 *R v Carpenter* (1993), 83 CCC (3d) 193 at 197 (Ont CA); 2015 *Hill*, above note 139.

146 *Berry*, above note 139 at 88.

147 *Mayuran*, above note 143.

be influenced by the disproportionate nature of the accused's response to an act and insult even though provocation has traditionally been interpreted only to require that an ordinary person would have lost self-control and not have responded as the accused actually did.

e)   Third Requirement: Subjective and Sudden Provocation

Although they have sometimes been separated, the requirement that the accused have been subjectively provoked by sudden provocation and have acted in the heat of passion in section 232(1) and (2) can conveniently be grouped together. In *Tran*, the Court stated: "the subjective element can also be usefully described as two-fold: (1) the accused must have acted in response to the provocation; and (2) on the sudden [provocation] before there was time for his or her passion to cool."[148]

The Supreme Court has stated that "'suddenness' must characterize both the insult and the act of retaliation"[149] and it is an error of law for a judge not to require an air of reality of both a sudden insult and a sudden response.[150] On this basis, the Court has denied the defence to an accused who had prior knowledge of his wife's unfaithfulness and abortion but had killed her when she informed him of these previously known facts;[151] to an accused who commenced an argument with his wife and followed her into a room and called her a name;[152] and to an accused who kidnapped the victim, who later provoked the accused by hitting him with a hammer.[153] In *Tran*, the Court held there was no sudden provocation when an accused who previously knew that his estranged wife was seeing another man entered the wife's locked apartment to find her in bed with the other man and when the accused responded to seeing his wife with another man by retrieving butcher knives from the kitchen and stabbing the man seventeen times. Both the wrongful act or insult and the accused's response to it must be sudden and unexpected; it cannot be a manifestation of a grudge, the affirmation of suspected conduct, or a foreseeable response to something that the accused has initiated.

---

148   *Tran*, above note 89 at para 26.
149   *R v Tripodi* (1955), 112 CCC 66 at 68 (SCC) [*Tripodi*]; *Tran*, above note 89 at para 38.
150   *Cairney*, above note 100 at para 36.
151   *Tripodi*, above note 149 at 68.
152   *Salamon v R* (1959), 123 CCC 1 at 12 (SCC) [*Salamon*].
153   *R v Louison* (1975), 26 CCC (2d) 266 (Sask CA), aff'd (1978), 51 CCC (2d) 479 (SCC).

In *R v Cairney*,[154] the Court again found no sudden provocation because the victim responded to the accused's gunpoint lecture to stop abusing a third party by telling the accused that he did not have the guts to use the gun and that he would do whatever he wanted with the third party, who the accused viewed as his little sister. The Supreme Court held that there was no air of reality because the victim's verbal responses to being threatened "fell within a range of predictable responses. There is nothing on the record to support the element of sudden shock required to cause an ordinary person to lose self-control." A minority, however, disputed the conclusion that the victim's assertion that he would continue to engage in domestic abuse was predictable. It criticized the majority for stressing that the law should "not condone" gunpoint lectures by noting that provocation is only a partial excuse, reducing murder to manslaughter.[155] In *R v Pappas*,[156] the Court also held that the element of suddenness was absent when the victim refused to stop extorting the accused. The Court noted that the victim had uttered similar statements in the past and concluded that the accused's action in killing the victim "was not the result of a sudden insult striking an unprepared mind. It was simply the final stage of doing what he had come to do — killing [the victim] if that was necessary to stop the extortion and threats."

These recent decisions are part of a move to restrict the provocation defence started in *Tran*. They are difficult to reconcile with the Court's controversial decision in *Thibert*,[157] where provocation was established even though the accused had confronted the victim with a gun and had known for some time that the victim was having an affair with the accused's wife. The only possible distinction is that the accused in *Thibert* was exposed to sudden provocation because he did not expect the victim (his wife's lover) to be present when he tried to talk to his wife.[158]

In addition to sudden provocation, the accused must be subjectively provoked and act "before there was time for his passion to cool." This test "is called subjective because it involves an assessment of what actually occurred in the mind of the accused . . . . [The] task at this point is to ascertain whether the accused was in fact acting as a result of provocation."[159] The accused must not only be angry and excited,

---

154 Above note 100 at para 61.
155 *Ibid* at paras 82–83.
156 Above note 101 at para 41.
157 Above note 97.
158 *Cairney*, above note 100 at para 55.
159 *Hill*, above note 93 at 336.

but must have subjectively lost self-control.[160] In determining this sub-jective component of the provocation defence, all factors particular to the accused can be considered, including intoxication,[161] his or her "mental state and psychological temperament,"[162] and the history of the accused's relationship with the deceased.[163] The fact that the accused is acting from a range of emotions including fear and a desire for self-protection does not preclude the provocation defence.[164]

Although the objective test based on whether an ordinary person would lose self-control is often the highest hurdle, accused can be de-nied the provocation defence because they were not suddenly or sub-jectively provoked. In *R v Malott*,[165] the Ontario Court of Appeal held that a battered woman did not qualify for the provocation defence in part because she had deliberately obtained a gun to shoot her husband and her "behaviour following the shooting was characterized by a lack of passion."[166] The requirement that the accused be subjectively pro-voked complements the requirement that the provocation be sudden and can be conveniently grouped together as the subjective elements of the provocation defence.

f) Provocation and the *Charter*

There are a number of issues raised by the interaction of the provoca-tion defence with the *Charter*. The first is whether the objective stan-dard discussed above violates section 7 of the *Charter*. The second is whether abolition or tightening of the provocation defence including the 2015 restriction that requires a provoking act to constitute an indict-able offence punishable by five years' imprisonment violates section 7 of the *Charter*.

The requirement that an act or insult be sufficient to deprive an ordinary person of self-control has been challenged as inconsistent with section 7 of the *Charter* and, in particular, the constitutional re-quirement that there be subjective fault for a murder conviction. In *R v Cameron*,[167] Doherty JA rejected this argument on the basis that

---

160 *Tran*, above note 89 at para 46.

161 *Salamon*, above note 152.

162 *Hill*, above note 93.

163 *R v Sheridan* (1991), 65 CCC (3d) 319 (SCC), rev'g (1990), 55 CCC (3d) 313 at 321 (Alta CA); *Thibert*, above note 97 at 10–11.

164 *Buzizi*, above note 102 at para 13.

165 (1996), 110 CCC (3d) 499 (Ont CA), aff'd on other grounds (1998), 121 CCC (3d) 456 (SCC).

166 *Thibert*, above note 97.

167 (1992), 71 CCC (3d) 272 at 273–74 (Ont CA). A majority of the Supreme Court has relied on this case and its reasoning that objective standards in a defence

"the objective component of the statutory defence of provocation serves a valid societal purpose . . . and cannot be said to be contrary to the principles of fundamental justice" and because it does not relieve the Crown of the burden of proving that the accused subjectively knew that the victim was likely to die.

Serious thought has recently been given to abolishing the defence of provocation as has been done in New Zealand. This raises the issue of whether the absence of a provocation defence would violate section 7 of the *Charter*. A person who kills while provoked is not a morally innocent person and probably does not act in a morally involuntary manner in the sense of having no realistic choice but to kill. He or she will have the minimum *mens rea* of subjective foresight of death, which is constitutionally required for murder.[168] It thus appears as if the abolition of the provocation defence would not violate section 7 of the *Charter*, though it might raise a question about whether imposing mandatory life imprisonment on those who might have previously had a provocation defence was a grossly disproportionate punishment under section 12 of the *Charter*.[169]

In 2015 and as part of its *Zero Tolerance of Barbaric Cultural Practices Act*, Parliament amended section 232(2) of the *Code* to require that the provoking act also constitute an indictable offence subject to at least five years' imprisonment. As suggested above, this drastically limits the provocation defence to cases where the provoking act also constitutes a serious offence such as assault or sexual assault. There is a strong case that this new restriction violates the *Charter*.

The objective of the new restriction was to prevent honour killings, but as suggested above, the courts have uniformly resisted the application of the provocation defence in such a context. Thus, there is a strong argument that the new section 232(2) violates section 7 of the *Charter* as an arbitrary restriction on liberty that is not rationally connected to the objective of preventing or punishing as murder honour killings. Even if the legislative objective is defined more broadly as advancing social protection from killings, there are also strong arguments that the

---

did not affect the Crown's obligations to prove the voluntary commission of the *actus reus* with the required *mens rea*. R v Stone (1999), 134 CCC (3d) 353 at 437 (SCC) [*Stone*]. See Chapter 8, Section H.

168 The Ontario Court of Appeal has observed that "the defence of provocation, unlike duress, does not raise an issue of moral blameworthiness because, even if successful, it does not lead to an acquittal." R v Ruzic (1998), 128 CCC (3d) 97 at 122.

169 The *Charter* jurisprudence concerning what constitutes cruel and unusual punishment will be examined in Chapter 11.

requirement that the deceased have committed an indictable offence punishable by at least five years' imprisonment is overbroad to such objectives. In addition, there is a case that section 232(2) also results in gross disproportionality, given that it imposes mandatory life imprisonment without responding to a pressing social harm relating to honour killings or other killings.

The provocation defence as it existed before 2015 and especially its requirement that an ordinary person would lose self-control when faced with an act or insult represents a more proportionate means of providing social protection against killings. Parliament also has less drastic and arbitrary ways to restrict the defence, including more tailored definitions of conduct that should not constitute provocation or the expansion of the notion that an accused is not provoked if the victim is exercising a legal right. Another alternative would be to abolish mandatory life imprisonment that follows from a murder conviction. As will be seen in the next chapter on sentencing, violence in the domestic context and violence motivated by hatred are aggravating factors that can increase an accused's sentence even when a mandatory sentence does not apply.

g) Relation of Provocation to the Fault Element

As noted earlier, the defence of provocation applies even though the accused has killed with subjective foresight of the likelihood of death.[170] In such a case, the defence of provocation reduces murder to manslaughter. It is possible, however, that evidence of provocation could prevent the Crown from proving the mental element of murder or even other crimes. Justice of Appeal Martin recognized this possibility in *R v Campbell*,[171] when he stated there may "be cases where the conduct of the victim amounting to provocation produces in the accused a state of excitement, anger or disturbance as a result of which he might not contemplate the consequences of his acts and might not, in fact, intend to bring about those consequences . . . . Provocation in that aspect, however, does not operate as a 'defence' but rather as a relevant item of evidence on the issue of intent." Provocation is more likely to raise a reasonable doubt about the higher levels of *mens rea*. An accused who damages property in a rage at an act or insult, for example, may not act with the intent or purpose to damage property. The accused would, however, probably be aware of the risk that the property would be damaged and, as such, could be said to have recklessly caused the damage.

---

170 *R v Oickle* (1984), 11 CCC (3d) 180 (NSCA).

171 (1977), 38 CCC (2d) 6 at 16 (Ont CA). See also *R v Flores*, 2011 ONCA 155; *R v Bouchard*, 2013 ONCA 791 [*Bouchard*]; 2015 *Hill*, above note 139.

In *R v Parent*,[172] the Supreme Court held that a trial judge had erred when he left the jury with the impression that anger alone could reduce murder to manslaughter even when the defence of provocation did not apply. The Supreme Court unfortunately did not discuss Martin JA's statement in *Campbell* or other statements by the Ontario Court of Appeal suggesting that evidence relating to provocation, perhaps combined with other evidence such as relating to intoxication, could be relevant to reasonable doubt of *mens rea* for murder.[173]

Parent should be restricted to the idea that anger is not in itself "a stand-alone defence."[174] The Supreme Court has subsequently recognized that a trial judge who did not clearly differentiate between the requirements of the provocation defence and the subjective intent for murder erred.[175] It affirmed a decision of Doherty JA that recognized that especially when an accused was intoxicated

> potentially provocative conduct that fails the ordinary person test and, therefore, cannot qualify as provocation under s. 232, must still be considered by a jury in assessing whether an accused had the necessary *mens rea*. In the context of the *mens rea* inquiry, the accused's intoxication could potentially play a significant role in support of the claim that a deceased's conduct caused the accused to act without regard to the consequences and without the necessary *mens rea*.[176]

The result in this case was to overturn a murder conviction and order a new trial in a case where the male accused testified that he killed his male friend after being kissed by his friend. This case affirms that the combined effects of provocation and intoxication can be relevant to the question of intent to murder under section 229(a) and that conduct that falls short of causing an ordinary person to lose self-control may still raise a reasonable doubt about the existence of subjective intent. It also illustrates how the determination of subjective fault does not allow for the same judgment about unwarranted discriminatory bias such as homophobia that can be applied to the administration of objective standards such as those determined on the basis of an ordinary or reasonable person's reactions.

---

172 *Parent*, above note 95.
173 *R v Nealy* (1986), 30 CCC (3d) 460 (Ont CA) [*Nealy*].
174 *Parent*, above note 95 at para 10.
175 *Bouchard*, above note 171, aff'd 2014 SCC 64.
176 *Ibid* at para 62 (ONCA).

i)   Relation of Provocation to Other Defences

If provocation resulted in automatism that could be explained only with reference to the accused's internal emotional make-up or that required the public to be protected from a continuing danger, then the defence would be mental disorder automatism. If the provocation could be explained on the basis of extraordinary external factors such as seeing a loved one killed or harmed, the defence might be non-mental disorder automatism, leading to a complete acquittal.[177] Either variety of automatism must be established by the accused on a balance of probabilities as opposed to the provocation defence that applies if there is a reasonable doubt about all the elements of the provocation defence.

Evidence of intoxication and provocation combined might prevent the Crown from proving the intent of murder beyond a reasonable doubt, even though the evidence considered separately would not be capable of producing either an intoxication or a provocation defence.[178] This follows the logic of subjective *mens rea*, which is open to the effects that all evidence might have on whether the particular accused had the required mental element.

5) Infanticide

Infanticide is a separate homicide offence punishable by no more than five years' imprisonment that applies when a woman by wilful act or omission causes the death of her newly born child (defined as under one year of age[179]) when, by reason of not fully being recovered from childbirth or the effect of lactation consequent to birth, her mind is disturbed.[180] It was enacted in 1948 in response to refusals by juries to convict mothers who killed their newborn children of murder or manslaughter. It is one of a large number of potentially overlapping offences relating to infants and children as victims.[181]

---

177   *R v Rabey* (1980), 54 CCC (2d) 1 (SCC); *Stone*, above note 167. See Chapter 8, Section H.

178   *Nealy*, above note 173; *R v Friesen* (1995), 101 CCC (3d) 167 (Alta CA).

179   *Code*, above note 1, s 1.

180   *Code*, above note 1, s 233. The equally authoritative French version refers to the mother's "*son esprit est alors déséquilibré*" and has been held to be substantially the same as the English reference to a disturbed mind in referring to a broader concept than the mental disorder defence. *R v Borowiec*, 2016 SCC 11 at para 30 [*Borowiec*].

181   These offences range from causing death in the act of birth punishable by life imprisonment under s 238; neglect to obtain assistance in childbirth punishable by up to five years' imprisonment in s 242; concealing the dead body of a child punishable by up to two years' imprisonment under s 243; abandoning a

The Supreme Court has held that the central concept in infanticide of a mother's "disturbed" mind "is unique to infanticide and does not appear elsewhere in the *Criminal Code*."[182] The disturbed mind need not reach the level of the mental disorder or automatism defences discussed in Chapter 8. It does not even require a substantial psychological problem, but includes being "mentally agitated," "mentally unstable," or "mental discomposure," which the Court recognizes are neither mental nor legal terms of art. Although the mental disturbance must be present at the time of the killing and related to the childbirth, it need not be the cause of the "willful act or omission" that resulted in the killing of the newly born child.[183]

Infanticide functions both as a stand-alone and discrete homicide offence and a partial defence to murder that results in a conviction of infanticide that has no mandatory penalty and a maximum penalty of five years' imprisonment.[184]

As an offence and despite the reference to the commission of a "wilful act or omission," infanticide applies to "both the mother who intends to kill and the mother who unlawfully assaults her child in circumstances where bodily harm to the child is foreseeable."[185] In other words, infanticide applies both to mothers who have the intent to kill and those who do not have that intent but do have the objective fault for manslaughter. This approach has been justified not so much by the statutory reference in section 233 to a "willful act or omission," but on the basis of the "hierarchy of culpable homicide established in the Criminal Code" and Parliament's decision "to treat infanticide as a culpable homicide, but one that was significantly less culpable than murder and even manslaughter."[186] The Supreme Court has recently approved of this interpretation of infanticide as an offence and disclaimed its prior *dicta* characterizing infanticide solely as an intentional killing.[187] This approach is consistent with the reduced penalty and stigma of infanticide and its inclusion along with manslaughter as an included offence to murder.[188] It also seeks to avoid the anomalous

---

child under ten years of age under s 218; and failing to provide the necessities of life to a child under sixteen years of age in s 215.

182 *Borowiec*, above note 180 at para 23.

183 *Ibid* at para 35.

184 *Code*, above note 1, s 237.

185 *R v LB*, 2011 ONCA 153 at para 115 [*LB*], leave to appeal to SCC refused, [2011] SCCA No 208.

186 *Ibid* at paras 114 and 121.

187 *Borowiec*, above note 180 at para 16.

188 *Code*, above note 1, s 662(3). Note that the offence of concealing a body of a child under s 243 is also a lesser include offence to infanticide.

result of a woman who killed her child but with a reasonable doubt about her intent for murder being excluded from the infanticide provisions and being convicted of manslaughter, which is a more serious offence than infanticide.

Infanticide also operates as a partial defence to murder when the Crown charges manslaughter or murder. Once an air of reality has been established for the defence, the Crown must then disprove at least one element of the defence beyond a reasonable doubt, as is the case with provocation. In R v Effert,[189] the Alberta Court of Appeal substituted an infanticide conviction for a second-degree murder conviction in a case in which a nineteen-year-old mother, who had hidden her pregnancy, strangled her newborn. It stressed that "the issue is not . . . whether a properly instructed jury must have found a 'disturbed mind' on a balance of probabilities, but whether such a jury would not even have been left with a doubt on the issue." The Supreme Court has subsequently made clear that if the Crown fails to disprove one of the elements of infanticide beyond a reasonable doubt (i.e., that the accused's mind was disturbed as a result of childbirth when the child was killed), the jury should acquit the woman of murder and convict her of the less serious offence of infanticide. If the Crown does disprove infanticide, then the jury should next consider whether it has proven murder beyond a reasonable doubt. If it has not proven murder based on subjective foresight of the probability of the infant's death, then the jury should consider whether it has established manslaughter, the residual homicide offence.[190] The courts assume that the mother's disturbed mind as a result of childbirth is related to the killing and significantly diminishes the blameworthiness of the killing. Infanticide is thus an alternative to murder with its mandatory life imprisonment.[191] As with provocation, infanticide emerges as a long-standing partial excuse driven by concerns about the ultimate disposition of the accused and in particular the mandatory sentence of life imprisonment for murder.

6) Manslaughter

Manslaughter is the residual offence for culpable homicides that are not murders or infanticides. Manslaughter is a much broader offence than either murder or infanticide. It can include killings that are only a

---

189 R v Effert, 2011 ABCA 134 [Effert]. See also Borowiec, above note 180 at para 24.

190 Ibid at paras 15–17; LB, above note 185 at para 137; Effert, above note 189 at para 21.

191 Section 238 also provides a separate offence of killing an unborn child during birth that while subject to punishment of life imprisonment avoids the mandatory penalty of life imprisonment that follows a murder conviction.

reasonable doubt short of murder to killings that are only slightly more than accidents but that involve marked departures from standards of reasonable conduct.

a)   Unlawful Act Manslaughter Under Section 222(5)(a)

Section 222(5)(a) provides that a person commits culpable homicide when he or she causes the death of a human being by means of an unlawful act. The *actus reus* for this offence is causing death and, as discussed earlier, this requires that the Crown establish that the accused's act was a significant cause of the death.

The unlawful act can include any federal or provincial offence provided that it is not an absolute liability offence and it is objectively dangerous.[192] At the same time, the Court indicated in *R v Gosset*[193] that there was a requirement of a marked departure from a reasonable standard of care even when the unlawful act was one such as careless use of a firearm that seemed on its face to contemplate a lesser form of negligence. If they form the basis for an unlawful act in a manslaughter charge, strict liability offences would be read up to require the Crown to prove a marked departure from a standard of reasonable conduct, even though the accused would have to establish the defence of due diligence if only charged with the regulatory offence. This approach is reaffirmed in *R v Beatty*,[194] which suggests that a marked departure from standards of reasonable care is required whenever negligence is used as a form of criminal liability that could result in a deprivation of liberty.

In addition to the act and fault of the underlying act, the majority of the Supreme Court in *R v Creighton*[195] established that the Crown must establish the independent fault that there is a reasonable foreseeability of the risk of bodily harm that is not trivial or transitory. The majority rejected the minority's position that the fault element should relate to all aspects of the prohibited act, holding that such a requirement was not a principle of fundamental justice.[196] Justice McLachlin held that the lesser stigma of a manslaughter offence did not require a fault element in relation to the foresight of death. The idea that fault elements should relate

---

192   *R v DeSousa*, [1992] 2 SCR 944.
193   [1993] 3 SCR 76. See also *R v Finlay*, [1993] 3 SCR 103 and *R v Naglik*, [1993] 3 SCR 122.
194   2008 SCC 5 [*Beatty*].
195   *Creighton*, above note 57.
196   Justice McLachlin concluded: "It is important to distinguish between criminal law theory, which seeks the ideal of absolute symmetry between *actus reus* and *mens rea*, and the constitutional requirements of the *Charter* . . . the Constitution does not always guarantee the 'ideal.'" *Ibid* at para 98.

to all aspects of the *actus reus* was characterized as criminal law "theory." There were sufficient exceptions to this theory that it did not constitute a principle of fundamental justice under section 7 of the *Charter*.[197] The majority also sought to justify its approach in only requiring objective foresight of bodily harm as consistent with the thin skull principle that informs the Court's broad approach to causation in homicide cases.

In *Creighton*, the Court divided 5:4 on the proper approach to the reasonable person, with the majority holding that the reasonable person should not have the same characteristics as the accused. The majority stressed the need to encourage common standards of reasonable behaviour. It would only make an exception in cases where the accused's characteristics rendered the accused incapable of appreciating the relevant risk. Justice McLachlin reasoned that "even those who lack the advantages of age, experience and education" may properly be held to standards of reasonable conduct when they engage in dangerous activities. She added:

> Mental disabilities short of incapacity generally do not suffice to negative criminal liability for criminal negligence. The explanations for why a person fails to advert to the risk inherent in the activity he or she is undertaking are legion. They range from simple absent-mindedness to attributes related to age, education, and culture. To permit such a subjective assessment would be "co-extensive with the judgment of each individual, which would be as variable as the length of the foot of each individual" leaving "so vague a line as to afford no rule at all, the degree of judgment belonging to each individual being infinitely various": *Vaughan v. Menlove* (1837), 3 Bing. (N.C.) 468, 132 E.R. 490, at p. 475; see A.M. Linden, *Canadian Tort Law* (4th ed. 1988), at pp. 116–17. Provided the capacity to appreciate the risk is present, lack of education and psychological predispositions serve as no excuse for criminal conduct, although they may be important factors to consider in sentencing.

---

197 Justice McLachlin concluded:

> It would shock the public's conscience to think that a person could be convicted of manslaughter absent any moral fault based on foreseeability of harm. Conversely, it might well shock the public's conscience to convict a person who has killed another only of aggravated assault — the result of requiring foreseeability of death — on the sole basis that the risk of death was not reasonably foreseeable. The terrible consequence of death demands more. In short, the *mens rea* requirement which the common law has adopted— foreseeability of harm — is entirely appropriate to the stigma associated with the offence of manslaughter.

Ibid at para 85.

This is not to say that the question of guilt is determined in a factual vacuum. While the legal duty of the accused is not particularized by his or her personal characteristics short of incapacity, it is particularized in application by the nature of the activity and the circumstances surrounding the accused's failure to take the requisite care.[198]

The Supreme Court has subsequently affirmed this approach while also stating that attention should be paid to the accused's actual state of mind in order to determine whether it suggests that the accused was incapable of appreciating the risk or whether there is a reasonable doubt that the accused was negligent.[199] The purpose of this approach is not to contextualize the reasonable person in the manner that is done with respect to defences, but rather to accommodate sudden and unexpected events such as a heart attack or a detached retina and all other relevant circumstances that may have to be considered even when administering the objective standard.

b) Criminal Negligence Manslaughter Under Sections 222(5)(b) and 220

Section 222(5)(b) provides that culpable homicide is manslaughter when a person causes death by criminal negligence, and section 220 provides a separate but identical offence of causing death by criminal negligence. Criminal negligence is defined in section 219 of the *Code* as doing anything or omitting to do anything that "shows wanton or reckless disregard for the lives or safety of other persons."

In 1989, the Supreme Court split 3:3 whether criminal negligence was an objective or subjective form of fault, with three judges stressing the idea that the conduct has to show negligence and three judges stressing the presumption of subjective fault and the concept of wanton and reckless disregard.[200] With the decision in *Creighton*, however, it is now settled that criminal negligence is an objective form of fault that requires a marked and substantial departure from the standard of reasonable care expected of a reasonable person in the circumstances.

Following the majority judgment of McLachlin J, the reasonable person would not have the characteristics of the accused, such as age and education, unless the characteristics would render the accused incapable of appreciating the relevant risk.[201] In addition, objective fore-

---

198 *Ibid* at para 137.
199 *Beatty*, above note 194. See also *R v Roy*, 2012 SCC 26.
200 *R v Tutton*, [1989] 1 SCR 1392.
201 *R v Ubhi* (1994), 27 CR (4th) 332 (BCCA). The majority's decision in *Creighton* casts doubt on prior cases that would apply the standard of a reasonable sixteen-year-old. *R v Barron* (1985), 23 CCC (3d) 544 (Ont CA).

sight of death is not required. As discussed earlier, the majority of the Court in *Creighton*[202] rejected the idea that it is a principle of fundamental justice that the fault element must relate to all aspects of the *actus reus* or that the stigma of manslaughter was sufficient to require objective foresight of death. The conclusion that objective foresight of death is not required for manslaughter by criminal negligence is also supported by the definition of criminal negligence in section 219 of the *Code*, which refers to conduct that "shows wanton or reckless disregard for the lives *or* safety of other persons" (emphasis added).

The Supreme Court's decision in *R v JF*[203] indicates that the fault element for manslaughter by criminal negligence is proof of a *marked and substantial departure* from the conduct of a reasonable person. This appears to be a slightly higher fault requirement than that required for unlawful act manslaughter where the unlawful act is a negligence-based offence such as failing to provide the necessities of life or careless use of a firearm. As discussed above, the fault requirement for those forms of unlawful act manslaughter is only a *marked departure* from reasonable conduct. In *JF*, the Court reversed a conviction of manslaughter by criminal negligence on the basis that it was inconsistent with the jury's decision to acquit the caregiver of manslaughter by the unlawful act of failing to provide the necessities of life. In other words, it was inconsistent for a jury to acquit a person of the unlawful act of manslaughter offence that required a lower degree of fault (i.e., marked departure) but then convict that person of a criminal negligence manslaughter offence that required a slightly higher level of fault (i.e., marked and substantial departure). This approach is quite complex and will require that the different degrees of negligence be carefully explained to the jury.

The additional requirement of proof of a marked *and substantial* departure from reasonable conduct is the main distinction between criminal negligence manslaughter and unlawful act manslaughter, at least where the unlawful act is a crime of negligence that, as discussed above, requires only a *marked* departure from standards of reasonable conduct. In other respects the two manslaughter offences are similar. They both require reasonable foresight of harm but not necessarily death and they both apply a non-individuated reasonable person standard that does not consider the characteristics of the accused unless they render the accused incapable of appreciating the risk. The *actus reus* of both manslaughter offences are identical in requiring that the accused's actions be a significant cause of death.

---

202 Above note 57.
203 2008 SCC 60 at para 9.

c) Manslaughter Under Sections 222(5)(c) and (d)

Sections 222(5)(c) and (d) are archaic sections that refer to manslaughter by causing a person's death by threats or fear of violence or by deception or by wilfully frightening a child or sick person. These offences are at most articulation of broad causation rules that would apply to the two primary manslaughter offences articulated above.

d) Parties to a Manslaughter Offence

As discussed earlier in this chapter, an accused will be acquitted of aiding or abetting a murder if he or she does not have subjective foresight of death or wilful blindness as a form of deliberate ignorance that is the equivalent of knowledge. At the same time, however, an accused could be convicted of aiding or abetting manslaughter if "a reasonable person in all the circumstances would have appreciated that bodily harm was the foreseeable consequence of the dangerous act which was being undertaken."[204] This follows from the fault element of manslaughter, which is satisfied by objective foreseeability of bodily harm.[205] In order to be guilty of aiding and abetting manslaughter, however, "it would still be necessary to establish that the accused did or omitted to do something for the purpose of aiding the principal to commit the offence."[206] Thus, an accused who acted with the subjective purpose of aiding an assault would be found guilty of manslaughter if there was objective foreseeability that the victim would be harmed. Such a person could be found guilty of aiding and abetting manslaughter even though the principal offender was guilty of murder.

e) Defence of Accident

The "defence of accident" is sometimes used when an accused is charged with murder. As discussed in Chapter 3 on the act and Chapter 5 on fault, this so-called defence should be distinguished as a factor that prevents the Crown from proving beyond a reasonable doubt either the essential elements of *actus reus* and/or the *mens rea*.[207] A claim of accident can, depending on the circumstances, raise a reasonable doubt as to whether the accused acted in a voluntary manner. This could lead to the conclusion that the act that caused death was not a voluntary act of the accused and lead to an acquittal of both murder and manslaughter.

In the context of homicide, the claim of accident often relates not to involuntary acts and *actus reus*, but to unintended consequences and

---

204 *Jackson*, above note 127 at 391.
205 *Creighton*, above note 57.
206 *R v Helsdon* (2007), 216 CCC (3d) 1 at para 37 (Ont CA).
207 *R v Belcourt*, 2015 BCCA 126 at para 102.

mens rea. In such cases, it may raise a reasonable doubt as to whether the accused had the necessary intent for murder under section 229, which as discussed above generally requires proof of subjective knowledge that death is a likely or probable consequence of the accused's action. In such cases, however, the Crown may still be able to prove beyond a reasonable doubt that the accused has voluntarily committed the *actus reus* of causing death with the required fault for unlawful act or criminal negligent manslaughter or infanticide as discussed above.

7) Suicide and Assisted Suicide

Section 14 of the *Code* provides that no person can consent to death and that consent does not affect the criminal responsibility of those who assist a willing person to commit suicide. This means that a person who agrees to assist another person, including a loved one, to commit suicide could be liable to prosecution for murder, including in cases of planning and deliberation of first-degree murder. As with infanticide, issues of prosecutorial discretion and the proper disposition of the accused are often more important than the legal definition of the offence.

Section 241 provides a separate offence of counselling or aiding and abetting a person to commit suicide whether or not suicide itself ensues. The offences of suicide and attempted suicide have been abolished so that it is only those who assist or counsel others to commit suicide who remain liable to criminal prosecution and punishment. The section 241 offence is punishable by terms of imprisonment up to fourteen years but no mandatory minimum sentence. This offence was unsuccessfully challenged under the *Charter* by Sue Rodriguez who argued that it infringed her equality rights because as a result of her terminal disease she would be physically unable to take her own life.[208] The majority of the Supreme Court stressed the role of the offence in protecting the vulnerable and protecting life. In *Carter v Canada (Attorney General)*[209] however, the Supreme Court ruled that the offence violated section 7 of the *Charter* because it was overbroad to the extent that it applied to competent adults with an incurable condition that causes intolerable suffering. Parliament responded with new legislation that provided new exemptions to the assisted suicide offences now outlined in section 241(2) to (7) of the *Code.* Sections 241.1 to 241.4 govern eligibility for medical assistance in dying provided by doctors and nurse practitioners if multiple criteria outlined in section 241.2 of the

---

208 *Rodriguez v British Columbia (AG)*, [1993] 3 SCR 519.
209 2015 SCC 5.

Criminal Code are satisfied. A particularly controversial requirement is that the person's condition not only be incurable but that natural death has become reasonably foreseeable.[210]

B. SEXUAL OFFENCES

1) Sexual Assault Offences

Sexual offences have been the site of much controversy and change over the past three decades of Canadian criminal law.

In 1982, Parliament abolished the offence of rape and replaced it with three new offences of sexual assault. The offences — sexual assault under section 271; sexual assault with a weapon, threats to a third party, or causing bodily harm under section 272; and aggravated sexual assault under section 273 — were deliberately modelled after the corresponding assault offences in sections 266 to 268 of the *Code* in an attempt to emphasize that sexual assault is a crime of violence. The *actus reus* was broadened from rape to sexual assault and the new offences, unlike the old offence of rape, applied to both genders and to a man who sexually assaulted his wife. Parliament also amended the *Code*[211] to require that triers of fact consider the presence or absence of reasonable grounds when deciding whether the defence that the accused had a mistaken belief in consent applied.

In 1992, Parliament again reformed the offence of sexual assault in order to emphasize factors that were particular to the context of sexual encounters and violence. Parliament defined consent to mean the voluntary agreement to engage in the sexual activity in question. It provided a "no means no" law that states that there will be no consent if the complainant, having initially consented to engage in sexual activity, expresses by words or conduct, a lack of agreement. The law also provides that there will be no consent if the complainant is incapable of consenting, is induced to consent by an abuse of a position of trust, power, or authority, or if a third party purports to provide consent.[212] The law also addressed the *mens rea* for sexual assault by providing that it was not a defence that the accused believed that the complainant consented to the sexual activity in question if the accused's belief arose out of self-induced intoxication or recklessness or wilful blindness or if

---

210   *Code*, above note 1, s 241.2(2)(d).
211   *Ibid*, s 265(4).
212   *Ibid*, s 273.1.

the accused did not take reasonable steps in the circumstances known to him at the time to ascertain whether the complainant was consenting to the sexual activity in question.[213]

In 2018, Parliament responded to several high profile and controversial acquittals in sexual assault cases and to the "me too" campaign of increased awareness of sexual assault by proposing to add several provisions to the 1992 reforms.[214] Under Bill C-51, the definition of consent in section 273.1 of the *Code* would make clear both that consent must be present at the time of the sexual activity in question and would not apply if the complainant was unconscious or incapable of consenting for any reason and that various restrictions on consent in sections 265(3) and 273.1(2) and (3) are questions of law, thus triggering the section 19 principle that mistake or ignorance of the law is not an excuse.

A new section 273.2(a)(iii) relating to when the accused's belief in consent is not a defence would provide that the accused's belief in consent will not be a defence when it arose from any circumstances referred to in section 265(3) or section 273.1(2) and (2) where consent is not valid. These include where the complainant submits or does not resist because of threats, fraud, or abuse of trust, power, or authority, where the complainant expresses by words or conduct a lack of agreement to engage or continue to engage in the sexual activity or is incapable of consenting. This underlines that mistaken beliefs by the accused about these definitions of consent would be precluded as errors of law that are not an excuse.[215]

A new section 273.2(c) would provide that the accused would not have a mistaken belief in consent defence if "there is no evidence that the complainant's voluntary agreement to the activity was affirmatively expressed by words or actively expressed by conduct." This would add to the 1992 amendments that denied the mistaken belief in consent defence in cases where it arose from the accused's self-induced intoxication, recklessness, or wilful blindness or if the accused did not take

---

213 *Ibid*, s 273.2.

214 Bill C-51, *An Act to amend the Criminal Code and the Department of Justice Act and to make consequential amendments to another Act*, 1st Sess, 42nd Parl, 2017 (in committee, Senate). The bill would also expand the "rape shield" legislation in s 276 to provide that evidence of the complainant's prior sexual conduct including electronic messages to the accused are not used for the purpose of suggesting that complainants are more likely to consent or less worthy of belief and it also expanded restrictions on the production and use of private records held by the complainant or third parties to also include those possessed by the accused. These evidentiary provisions are important but beyond the scope of this work, which focuses on substantive criminal law.

215 *Code*, above note 1, s 19 as discussed in Chapter 3.

reasonable steps in the circumstances known to him at the time to ascertain that the complainant was consenting.

The government's *Charter* statement about Bill C-51 (which as of the 2018 summer recess had been passed by the House of Commons but not the Senate) explained that the provisions are designed to deprive accused of a defence that

> is based on a mistake of law (that is, ignorance or a misunderstanding of the law) or if their belief is based on the complainant's passivity . . . the proposed amendments advance the Government's objective of promoting greater awareness of and adherence to the provisions of sexual assault law that protect complainants, the majority of whom are female. These reforms promote the equality rights of complainants as protected by section 15(1) of the *Charter*, and their security of the person as protected by section 7 of the *Charter*.[216]

There are other sexual offences that relate specifically to sexual activity with children. In 1990, the Supreme Court struck down the offence of statutory rape of a girl under fourteen years of age regardless of the accused's belief about the girl's age or the girl's consent. The Court concluded that the offence was an absolute liability offence because it required no fault in relation to the age of the girl.[217] It also concluded that the legitimate objective of protecting children could be satisfied by new and broader offences of sexual interference that would protect both boys and girls and provide the accused a limited defence if he or she took all reasonable steps to ascertain the age of the child,[218] as well as a defence in cases where the accused was close in age to the child.[219] These new offences, like the 1982 sexual assault reforms, expand the *actus reus*. They apply to sexual interference, invitation to sexual touching, and sexual exploitation.[220] The age of consent, including for those offences, has recently been raised from fourteen to sixteen years of age.[221] There is also a special offence of sexual exploitation of a person with a disability,[222] which was subject to similar amendments as sexual assault in 2018, but the focus in this chapter will be on sexual assault offences.

---

216 *Charter* Statement on Bill C-51 (6 June 2017), online: www.justice.gc.ca/eng/csj-sjc/pl/charter-charte/c51.html.

217 *R v Hess*, [1990] 2 SCR 906.

218 *Code*, above note 1, s 150.1(4).

219 *Ibid*, s 150.1(1).

220 *Ibid*, ss 151, 152, & 153.

221 *Ibid*, s 150.1(2).

222 *Code*, above note 1, s 153.1 also to be amended by Bill C-51, above note 214.

2) The *Actus Reus* of Sexual Assault

The *actus reus* of sexual assault is extremely complex because it involves a generic definition of assault, a specific definition of what constitutes consent for the purpose of sexual assault offences, the Court's interpretation of consent as depending on the subjective views of the complainant, as well as common law restrictions that vitiate consent. An additional complicating factor are provisions that deem the question of consent including the restrictions on consent under section 265(3) and 273.1(2) and (3) to be questions of law.[223]

a) Assaults under Section 265

Section 265 provides a generic definition that defines all assaults to include the intentional application of force, directly or indirectly, to another person without that person's consent[224] or attempting or threatening by acts or gestures to apply force if it causes the other person to believe upon reasonable grounds that the accused has the ability to effect his or her purpose.[225] These two provisions define different ways of committing an assault.[226] The result is a broad definition of assault that can include any touching and threats to apply force without consent.

b) Sexual Assaults Distinguished from Other Assaults and Sexual Offences

The courts have distinguished sexual assaults from assaults on the basis of whether the circumstances viewed objectively are sexual. The intent or motive of the accused to obtain sexual gratification may be a factor, but it is not a requirement. Sexual assault differs from the sexual offences with respect to young persons in sections 151 through 153.1 of the *Code* because it does not require that the touching be for a sexual purpose.[227] The courts will examine all the circumstances including "the part of the body touched, the nature of the conduct, the words and gestures accompanying the act and all other circumstances surrounding the conduct"[228] in determining whether the assault is sexual. The Supreme Court has determined that a man grabbing a fifteen-year-old around her breasts and shoulders while saying "Come on, dear, don't

---

223 *Code*, above note 1, s 273.1(1.2) as amended by Bill C-51, above note 214.
224 *Ibid*, s 265(1).
225 *Ibid*, s 265(2).
226 *R v MacKay*, [2005] 3 SCR 725.
227 *R v Lutoslawski*, [2010] 3 SCR 60.
228 *R v Chase*, [1987] 2 SCR 293.

hit me, I know you want it" was an assault of a sexual nature.[229] More controversially, that Court has also held that a father's actions in grabbing his three-year-old son's genitals causing bruising and severe pain in an attempt to discipline the child who had been grabbing the private parts of others was a sexual assault because it invaded the child's sexual integrity. Justice Sopinka dissented on the basis that the father's actions constituted assault, not sexual assault.[230] The Court has continued to confirm that with respect to sexual assault "the Crown need not prove that the accused had any *mens rea* with respect to the sexual nature of his or her behaviour."[231]

c)   Consent under Section 273.1

In 1992, Parliament enacted section 273.1, which defines consent for the purposes of the sexual offences as "the voluntary agreement of the complainant to engage in the sexual activity in question." This definition of consent was designed "to overcome the historical tendency to treat the complainant's *silence, non-resistance or submission* as 'implied consent'" and to require consent to the particular sexual activity in question and to make clear that the complainant must agree to each particular sexual activity and can revoke or limit the scope of consent at any time.[232]

As will be discussed in greater detail later in this chapter, the 1992 reforms were called the "no means no" reforms because they also provide a concrete list of circumstances in which consent would not be obtained. The idea was to provide a legal definition of what did and did not constitute consent. A person who thought that no meant yes or that consent could be given by a third party or by a person who was not capable of giving consent would have a mistaken belief about the law, which, as discussed in Chapter 3, cannot be an excuse for criminal conduct.

d)   Consent in *Ewanchuk*

In a very important decision rendered in 1999, *R v Ewanchuk*,[233] the Supreme Court interpreted the *actus reus* of sexual assault as requiring proof of three elements "i) touching, ii) the sexual nature of the conduct, and iii) the absence of consent." The Court held that the touching and sexual nature were determined on an objective basis, but that the third factor of absence of consent "is subjective and determined by reference

---

229 *Ibid*.
230 *R v V(KB)*, [1993] 2 SCR 857.
231 *R v Ewanchuk*, [1999] 1 SCR 330 at para 25 [*Ewanchuk*].
232 *R v Barton*, 2017 ABCA 216 at paras 180 and 217 [*Barton*].
233 Above note 231 at para 25.

to the complainant's internal state of mind towards the touching at the time that it occurred."[234] If the complainant says that she did not consent, the only issue is whether she is a credible complainant. "The accused's perception of the complainant's state of mind is not relevant"[235] when determining whether there was consent for the purpose of determining whether the *actus reus* has been committed. The accused's belief that the complainant consented is only relevant to determine the *mens rea* of the offence.

The Supreme Court in *Ewanchuk* rejected the defence of implied consent to sexual assault.[236] In other words, it rejected the idea that although the complainant did not actually consent, her conduct satisfied an objective standard of implied consent. Thus, as a matter of determining the *actus reus* of consent "[t]he absence of consent . . . is subjective and determined by reference to the complainant's subjective internal state of mind toward the touching, at the time it occurred."[237] The trier of fact "may only come to one of two conclusions: the complainant either consented or not. There is no third option. If the trier of fact accepts the complainant's testimony that she did not consent, no matter how strongly her conduct may contradict that claim, the absence of consent is established."[238]

On the facts of *Ewanchuk*, the Court reversed an acquittal in a case where a man repeatedly made sexual advances to a seventeen-year-old woman who was applying for a job. The Court held that the judge's determination that the woman subjectively did not consent to the repeated sexual touching and that she subjectively feared force from the accused should have been determinative that there was no consent for the purpose of determining whether the *actus reus* of sexual assault had occurred.

The existence of consent for the purpose of defining the *actus reus* of sexual assault as a result of *Ewanchuk* depends on the subjective perceptions of the victim as opposed to external and objective standards of law. Similarly, consent will be negated by the complainant's fear of the application of force regardless of the reasonableness of the fear or whether it was communicated to the accused. A statement by the victim that she did not consent or did so because of fear will be determinative unless it is found not to be a credible statement of her state of mind at the time the offence occurred. The Court is understandably concerned

234 *Ibid* at para 26.
235 *Ibid* at para 30.
236 *Ibid*.
237 *Ibid* at para 26.
238 *Ibid* at para 31.

about maximizing the physical and sexual integrity of women and rejecting the rape myths that women implicitly consent to sexual activity unless they protest or resist or clearly expressly fear. The Court's vehicle for rejecting these myths is to make the issue of consent for the purpose of defining *actus reus* dependent on the subjective perceptions of the complainant even if they are uncommunicated and unreasonable.

e) Specific Instances Where Consent Is Not Valid

Various provisions of the *Criminal Code*, as well as the common law, deem that consent even if apparently given by the complainant will not be valid in certain circumstances. The Supreme Court has indicated that reference should only be made to these provisions if the court finds that the complainant either voluntarily agreed to the sexual activity in question or there is a reasonable doubt about such consent.[239]

Section 265(3) of the *Code* provides that

> no consent is obtained where the complainant submits or does not resist by reason of
> a) the application of force to the complainant or to a person other than the complainant;
> b) threats or fear of the application of force to the complainant or to a person other than the complainant;
> c) fraud; or
> d) the exercise of authority.

In *R v Ewanchuk*, the Supreme Court held that under section 265(3) (b) "the complainant's fear need not be reasonable, nor must it be communicated to the accused in order for consent to be vitiated. While the plausibility of the alleged fear, and any overt expressions of it, are obviously relevant to assessing the credibility of the complainant's claim that she consented out of fear, the approach is subjective."[240]

Traditionally, consent has been vitiated only by fraud that relates to the nature of the act itself or the identity of the person conducting the act. This would mean that a person who has sex with another without disclosing the existence of a sexually transmitted disease would not be found guilty of assault or sexual assault. In *R v Cuerrier*,[241] Cory J, with the concurrence of three other judges, held that fraud could negate consent in a case where a dishonest act in the form of falsehoods or a failure to disclose would have "the effect of exposing the person

---

239   *R v Hutchinson*, 2014 SCC 19 at para 4 [*Hutchinson*].
240   *Ewanchuk*, above note 231 at para 39.
241   [1998] 2 SCR 371.

consenting to a significant risk of serious bodily harm." The Crown must also prove that the complainant would have refused to engage in unprotected sex with the accused had she been informed that he was HIV-positive. This approach was affirmed in R v Mabior,[242] with the Court concluding that the significant risk of harm standard was appropriate for the criminal law. It could be avoided only if an HIV-positive person who did not disclose both used a condom and had a low viral load at the time of intercourse.

In R v Hutchinson,[243] a majority of the Court held that a complainant still consented to sexual intercourse even though the accused had poked holes in a condom without her knowledge or consent. A minority of the Court would have held that there was no consent because the activity in question that the complainant agreed to was sexual intercourse with an intact condom. The majority reached this conclusion in part by stressing the importance of certainty and restraint in applying "the heavy hand of the criminal law."[244] Nevertheless the majority still convicted the accused of sexual assault in Hutchinson but on the separate basis discussed above that the complainant's consent was vitiated by fraud under section 265(3) of the Code. In applying this exception, the Court concluded that consent was vitiated by fraud that required both deception and deprivation or harm that could be caused by an unwanted pregnancy.[245] Some commentators have suggested that the result in making a man liable for sexual assault because of deception about contraception but not a woman "seems both improper and out of touch with Canadian values."[246] In my view, however, the Court's approach simply reflects the physical realities of unwanted pregnancy. It also should not be surprising if responses to the gendered nature of sexual violence do not result in the identical treatment of men and women.

In addition to defining consent for the purpose of sexual offences as the voluntary agreement to engage in the sexual activity in question, Parliament in 1992 provided in section 273.1(2) that no consent is obtained where

a) the agreement is expressed by the words or conduct of a person other than the complainant;

b) the complainant is incapable of consenting to the activity;

---

242 [2012] 2 SCR 584.
243 Hutchinson, above note 239.
244 Ibid at para 46.
245 Ibid at para 72.
246 Morris Manning & Peter Sankoff, Criminal Law, 5th ed (Markham, ON: Lexis-Nexis, 2015) at 21.124.

c) the accused induces the complainant to engage in the activity by abusing a position of trust, power or authority;

d) the complainant expresses, by words or conduct, a lack of agreement to engage in the activity; or

e) the complainant, having consented to engage in sexual activity, expresses, by words or conduct, a lack of agreement to engage in the activity.[247]

This provision defines certain examples where the accused will be precluded from arguing that the prohibited act of sexual assault did not occur because the complainant consented. It establishes as an objective statement of law that there cannot be consent if (a) agreement is given by a third party; (b) the complainant is incapable of consenting; (c) the complainant is induced to participate by abuse of a position of trust, power, or authority; or (d, e) the complainant expresses a lack of agreement, by either words or comments, to engage or continue to engage in sexual activity. The above examples of deemed non-consent are not exhaustive. It should be noted that the accused can still argue that although there was no consent in these situations and the *actus reus* was committed, he or she still did not have the *mens rea* to commit sexual assault.

Finally, courts have applied the *Jobidon* principle that consent can be vitiated for policy reasons when the accused intends to and causes serious bodily harm to forms of sexual activity that are intended to and do cause such harms. In a case where a complainant sustained bruising from a beating with a belt and bleeding from her rectum for a number of days (and also claimed that she did not consent), the Ontario Court of Appeal held that Parliament had not exhaustively defined consent for the purpose of sexual assault. It held that

the consent of the complainant, assuming it was given, cannot detract from the inherently degrading and dehumanizing nature of the conduct. Although the law must recognize individual freedom and autonomy, when the activity in question involves pursuing sexual gratification by deliberately inflicting pain upon another that gives rise to bodily harm, then the personal interest of the individuals involved must yield to the more compelling societal interests which are challenged by such behaviour.[248]

---

247 *Code*, above note 1, s 273.1, introduced in *An Act to Amend the Criminal Code (Sexual Assault)*, SC 1992, c 38, s 1.

248 *R v Welch* (1995), 101 CCC (3d) 216 at 239 (Ont CA). See also *R v Robinson* (2001), 153 CCC (3d) 398 at para 62 (Ont CA), extending this to less serious harms that deliberately inflicted pain causing bodily harm.

Following the post-*Jobidon* jurisprudence from the Supreme Court, the Ontario Court of Appeal has held that consent to sexual activity will only be vitiated for policy reasons when bodily harm is both intended and caused,[249] but the Alberta Court of Appeal has left open the possibility for a more contextual approach including in cases where the sexual activity resulted in death.[250]

f) Consent Requires the Complainant Be Conscious and Capable of Consenting at the Time of the Particular Sexual Activity in Question

In *R v JA*,[251] a majority of the Supreme Court held that consent required the conscious agreement of the complainant to the sexual activity in question and that there was no consent in a case where a complainant consented in advance to choking and sexual experimentation while she was unconscious. The majority stressed that Parliament "defined consent in a way that requires the complainant to be conscious throughout the sexual activity in question."[252] The rejection of advance consent was justified in part by reference to sections 273.1(2)(d) and (e), which contemplate that the complainants can revoke consent at any time as well as vulnerability of an unconscious complainant. Chief Justice McLachlin explained: "When the complainant loses consciousness, she loses the ability to either oppose or consent to the sexual activity that occurs. Finding that such a person is consenting would effectively negate the right of the complainant to change her mind at any point in the sexual encounter."[253]

The Court stressed the need for vigilance about consent in the context of sexual assault that might not be applicable to other contexts, such as the consent that an unconscious person may give to surgery. It recognized, however, that this doctrine may seem "unrealistic" in trusting relationships where one partner would be unable legally to consent in advance to sexual activity including kissing while that person is asleep. Nevertheless, the Court held that Parliament's requirement for conscious consent to the sexual activity in question "produces just results in the vast majority of cases" and helps combat stereotypes that have "undermined the law's ability to address the crime of sexual assault."[254] The Court also declined to create a *de minimis* exception because "even

---

249 *R v Quashie*, 2005 CanLII 23208 at para 58; *R v Zhao*, 2013 ONCA 293 at para 108.
250 *Barton*, above note 232 at paras 304–9.
251 [2011] 2 SCR 440 [*JA*].
252 *Ibid* at para 33.
253 *Ibid* at para 53.
254 *Ibid* at para 65.

mild non-consensual touching of a sexual nature can have profound implications for the complainant."[255] Justice Fish, with two others, dissented and argued that the Court's rejection of advance consent unreasonably limited sexual autonomy and overshot Parliament's policy concerns that were to protect women "who said no"[256] and not the complainant who agreed in advance to the sexual activity in question.

There is also no consent if the complainant is not capable of consenting at the time of the sexual activity in question. In 2018, Parliament proposed to codify the *JA* principle by providing in a new section 273.1(1.1) that "consent must be present at the time of the sexual activity in question takes place" and providing in section 273.1(2.1)(a.1) that there is no consent if "the complainant is unconscious." Parliament also confirmed that the specific examples of non-consent are not exhaustive. This is consistent with the original intent of the 1992 "no means no" amendment, which simply provided common but non-exhaustive examples of lack of consent.

In addition, Parliament proposed to add section 273.1(1.2) that would provide that the question of whether no consent is obtained either under section 273.1(2) and (3) or with respect to submission under section 265(3) because of threats or fear and other matters are questions of law. This amendment would make clear both that judges should instruct juries about these matters, but also that mistakes made by the accused such as the belief that no means yes are mistakes of laws that will not be a defence under section 19 of the *Criminal Code*. This responds to concerns that "with respect to sexual offences, courts sometimes allowed mistakes of law to enter the courtroom masquerading as mistakes of fact,"[257] especially with regards to the accused's mistaken belief in the complainant's consent.

The Alberta Court of Appeal in *R v Barton* stressed that consent requires subjective and voluntarily agreement to each sexual activity. On the facts of the case, the Court of Appeal concluded that "when a sex trade worker gives her consent to 'Intercourse, sex' that sex trade worker is not consenting to bodily harm from that sexual activity. When sex trade workers contract to sell sex, they do not agree to sign away their lives."[258] The Court of Appeal held that vague references in jury instructions to the use of force were unhelpful as were references to consent to "similar" activities the night before. It proposed the following as a new model instruction on the meaning of consent:

---

255 *Ibid* at para 63.
256 *Ibid* at para 112.
257 *Barton*, above note 232 at para 245.
258 *Ibid* at para 196.

Consent means the voluntary agreement of the complainant to engage in the sexual activity in question: did she subjectively consent in her mind to that activity at the time it was occurring? The consent must be to each and every sexual act in question. The complainant is under no obligation to express her lack of consent. Silence does not equal consent. Nor does submission or lack of resistance. Agreement to one form of penetration is not agreement to any or all forms of penetration and agreement to sexual touching on one part of the body is not agreement to all sexual touching. To be valid, the complainant must be conscious and capable of consent throughout the sexual activity. Consent cannot be implied from the relationship between the accused and the complainant. A complainant may revoke consent or limit its scope at any time.[259]

In a controversial case involving a severely intoxicated complainant found unconscious with her pants down in a cab with the cab driver being charged with sexual assault, the Nova Scotia Court of Appeal has stated that:

> a complainant lacks the requisite capacity to consent if the Crown establishes beyond a reasonable doubt that, for whatever reason, the complainant did not have an operating mind capable of:
>
> 1. appreciating the nature and quality of the sexual activity; or
> 2. knowing the identity of the person or persons wishing to engage in the sexual activity; or
> 3. understanding she could agree or decline to engage in, or to continue, the sexual activity.[260]

The Court of Appeal held that trial judge who had acquitted the accused erred in equating incapacity with unconsciousness and in not considering whether the complainant did not have the capacity to consent.[261] At the same time, it held that the trial judge's controversial comments that a drunk complainant can still consent were correct and that complainants need not have "the cognitive ability necessary to weigh the risks and consequences of agreeing to engage in the sexual activity . . . "[262] to be able to consent.

---

259 *Ibid* at para 217.
260 *R v Al-Rawi*, 2018 NSCA 10 at para 66.
261 *Ibid* at paras 116 and 131.
262 *Ibid* at para 61.

3) The *Mens Rea* of Sexual Assault

The *mens rea* of sexual assault requires an intentional application of force without consent. There is no requirement to demonstrate that the accused had a motive of sexual gratification. Traditionally, the *mens rea* for sexual assault has in accordance with common law presumptions been interpreted as requiring proof of subjective fault in relation to all aspects of the prohibited act of applying force without consent. Recklessness,[263] as well as knowledge and wilful blindness,[264] have traditionally been held to be a sufficient form of fault. It is an error of law not to make clear to the jury that "any one of knowledge, recklessness or willful blindness is sufficient in law."[265]

a)   Mistaken Belief in Consent

Before the 1992 reforms, the Court applied the traditional common law presumption of subjective *mens rea* to hold that the Crown had to establish that the accused had subjective fault in relation to all aspects of the *actus reus* of the crime of sexual assault. In *R v Pappajohn*,[266] the Supreme Court held that an accused in a rape trial could have a defence of honest but not necessarily reasonable mistake that the complainant consented. Justice Dickson derived the defence of mistake of fact from the *mens rea* of the particular offence. He concluded that because the *mens rea* of rape was subjective intent or recklessness relating to all the elements of the offence, it was not necessary that an accused's mistaken belief about consent be reasonable. He stated:

> It is not clear how one can properly relate reasonableness (an element in offences of negligence) to rape (a "true crime" and not an offence of negligence). To do so, one must, I think, take the view that the *mens rea* only goes to the physical act of intercourse and not to non-consent, and acquittal comes only if the mistake is reasonable. This, upon the authorities, is not a correct view, the intent in rape being not merely to have intercourse, but to have it with a non-consenting woman. If the jury finds that mistake, whether reasonable or unreasonable, there should be no conviction. If, upon the entire record, there is evidence of mistake to cast a reasonable doubt upon the existence of a criminal mind, then the prosecution has failed to make its case.[267]

---

263   *R v Pappajohn* (1980), 52 CCC (2d) 481 (SCC) [*Pappajohn*].
264   *R v Sansregret*, [1985] 1 SCR 570 [*Sansregret*].
265   *Barton*, above note 232 at para 227.
266   *Pappajohn*, above note 263.
267   *Ibid* at 497.

Although the accused's belief did not have to be reasonable, its reasonableness would be evidence considered by the jury to determine whether the accused actually had an honest belief in consent. The *Criminal Code* was subsequently amended to provide that the judge "shall instruct the jury, when reviewing all the evidence relating to the determination of the honesty of the accused's belief, to consider the presence or absence of reasonable ground for that belief."[268] At the same time, juries also continued to be instructed that while the mistaken belief in consent had to be honest, it did not have to be reasonable.[269]

b) Establishing an Air of Reality for a Mistake of Fact Defence

Although the Supreme Court agreed on the conceptual nature of the defence of mistake of fact and its relation to the *mens rea* of the particular offence, it disagreed on its application in particular cases. In *Pappajohn*, Dickson J was in dissent in concluding that the jury should have been instructed to consider the defence of mistake of fact. Justice McIntyre for the majority held that the only realistic issue that could arise on the facts of the case was whether there was consent or no consent, not a third option of a mistaken belief in consent. In his view, there should be something more than the accused's assertion that he believed the complainant consented to justify instructing the jury on the mistaken belief defence. In a subsequent case, however, a majority of the Court indicated that there need not be evidence independent of the accused to support a mistake of fact. It was possible that the defence could arise when the accused alleged consent, and the complainant alleged no consent.[270] At the same time, there must be some plausible evidence to support a claim of mistake of fact, and a bare assertion by the accused of a mistaken belief is not sufficient.[271] In one case, a majority of the Court found there to be an air of reality to the defence of mistaken belief in consent when the accused testified to consent and the complainant testified to absence of memory. Both McLachlin J and L'Heureux-Dubé J dissented on the basis that there was no plausible evidence of ambiguous conduct that could create the basis for the defence of mistake about consent.[272]

The controversy about when the jury should be instructed about the defence of mistaken belief in the complainant's consent continues. As will be seen, however, this debate should be influenced by changes

---

268 *Code*, above note 1, s 265(4). This was held to be consistent with ss 7, 11(d), and 11(f) of the *Charter* in R v Osolin (1994), 86 CCC (3d) 481 (SCC) [*Osolin*].

269 *Barton*, above note 232 at para 244.

270 *Osolin*, above note 268.

271 *R v Park* (1995), 99 CCC (3d) 1 (SCC).

272 *R v Esau*, [1997] 2 SCR 777.

to the sexual assault offence made in 1992. There will now not be an air of reality with respect to the mistake of fact defence unless the complainant communicated an agreement to engage in the particular sexual activity with the accused.[273] For example, there would be no air of reality to a mistaken belief in consent defence in a case where an accused relies on consent given by an unconscious complainant in advance. The Court explained it would be impossible for the accused to take reasonable steps to ascertain consent at the moment that the *actus reus* occurs because the complainant would be unconscious. During that time, the accused could not believe that the complainant had said yes and communicated consent to engage in the sexual activity.[274] This demanding approach to mistaken belief in consent follows from the definition of consent in section 273.1(1) as the voluntary agreement of the complainant to engage in the sexual activity in question and the application of the mistake of the law principle. As the Alberta Court of Appeal has explained, a belief that a complainant "gave her consent because she was silent, did not resist or object is a mistake of law, not a mistake of fact." [275] Similarly it would be a mistake of law to conclude that consent was given on the basis of prior or similar sexual activity or on the basis of silence or passive or ambiguous conduct.[276]

In 2018, Parliament proposed to amend section 273.2 to provide that there is no defence where the accused's mistaken belief in consent arose from the circumstances vitiating consent in sections 265(3) and 273.1(2) and (3) of the *Code* and that the mistake of fact defence is also precluded where "there is no evidence that the complainant's voluntary agreement to the activity was affirmatively expressed by words or actively expressed by conduct."[277] This new requirement would also affect

---

273 *Ewanchuk*, above note 231.

274 Chief Justice McLachlin has explained: "In *Ewanchuk*, this Court held that it is not sufficient for the accused to have believed that the complainant was subjectively consenting in her mind: 'In order to cloak the accused's actions in moral innocence, the evidence must show that he believed that the complainant communicated consent to engage in the sexual activity in question.' It thus is not sufficient for the accused to have believed the complainant was consenting: he must also take reasonable steps to ascertain consent, and must believe that the complainant communicated her consent to engage in the sexual activity in question. This is impossible if the complainant is unconscious." *JA*, above note 251 at para 48. Justice Fish in dissent argued that he "read s 273.2 differently" so that it could apply to a belief in prior consent and ascertainment of prior consent. *Ibid* at para 107.

275 *Barton*, above note 232 at para 249, citing *Ewanchuk*, above note 231 at para 51.

276 *Barton*, above note 232 at paras 254–57.

277 Bill C-51, above note 214, proposed amendment of s 273.1 (2.1).

the air of reality and ultimate tests requiring either the complainant's verbal agreement to engage in the particular sexual activity or conduct that "actively expressed" agreement.

Even if there is the belief based in words affirmatively expressed by the complainant or conduct of the complainant that actively express-es agreement to the particular sexual activity, section 273.2(b) would still require the accused to take reasonable steps in the circumstances known to him or her at the time to ascertain whether the complainant was consenting. Hence, there will not be an air of reality unless the accused takes reasonable steps to ascertain that the complainant was consenting.[278] Taking no steps to ascertain consent does not amount to reasonable steps.[279] The reasonable steps requirement could influence the determination of whether there was an air of reality to the mistake of fact, for example, in a case where there is no evidence that the ac-cused took any steps to ascertain whether the complainant consented.

c) Wilful Blindness in Relation to Consent

In *Sansregret*,[280] the Supreme Court entered a conviction for rape de-spite the fact that the trial judge had found that at the time that the accused had sex with his ex-girlfriend with whom he had lived that he honestly believed that she consented even though he had terror-ized her with a knife and blows after having broken into her house in the middle of the night. In an effort to calm down the accused after an hour of this behaviour, the complainant pretended that there was some hope of reconciliation and they had intercourse. A similar incident had occurred a month before and the complainant had reported the inci-dent to the police. The trial judge had found that "no one in his right mind could have believed that the complainant's dramatic about-face stemmed from anything other than fear. But the accused did. He saw what he wanted to see, heard what he wanted to hear and believed what he wanted to believe."

The Supreme Court reversed the acquittal and entered a conviction, holding that the accused should have been convicted on the basis that the accused was wilfully blind to the lack of consent. The Court ex-plained that in the circumstances, the accused had engaged in "self-deception to the point of willful blindness" and that "where the accused becomes deliberately blind to the existing facts, he is fixed by law with actual knowledge" on the basis that he is at fault "in deliberately failing

---

278 *R v Flaviano*, [2014] 1 SCR 270.
279 *Barton*, above note 232 at para 259.
280 *Sansregret*, above note 264.

to inquire when he knows there is a reason for inquiry."[281] In subsequent cases, the Court has affirmed that wilful blindness is a form of deliberate ignorance equivalent to knowledge and distinct from both recklessness and negligence and not satisfied by the accused's mere failure to inquire into whether prohibited circumstances or consequences exist.[282]

d) Restrictions on the Mistake of Fact Defence Under Section 273.2

The Supreme Court struck down so-called rape shield restrictions on the admission of the complainant's prior sexual conduct as a violation of the accused's *Charter* right to make full answer and defence, in part because the restrictions could deprive the accused of evidence to support the *Pappajohn* defence. Justice McLachlin stated that the *Pappajohn* defence

> rests on the concept that the accused may honestly but mistakenly (and not necessarily reasonably) have believed that the complainant was consenting to the sexual act. If the accused can raise a reasonable doubt as to his intention on the basis that he honestly held such a belief, he is not guilty under our law and is entitled to an acquittal. The basis of the accused's honest belief in the complainant's consent may be sexual acts performed by the complainant at some other time or place.[283]

In dissent, L'Heureux-Dubé J argued that the complainant's prior sexual activity with a person other than the accused would never provide an air of reality for the jury to consider a defence of mistake of fact, if it were "operating in an intellectual environment that is free of rape myth and stereotype about women."[284]

In response to *Seaboyer*, the law of sexual assault was amended in 1992 to restrict the availability of the mistake of fact defence. Section 273.2 provides:

> It is not a defence to a charge under section 271, 272 or 273 that the accused believed that the complainant consented to the activity that forms the subject-matter of the charge, where
>
> a) the accused's belief arises from the accused's
>
>   i)   self-induced intoxication or
>
>   ii) recklessness or willful blindness; or

---

281   *Ibid* at 584.

282   *Briscoe*, above note 63 at para 24.

283   *R v Seaboyer* (1991), 66 CCC (3d) 321 at 393 (SCC).

284   *Ibid* at 363.

b)   the accused did not take reasonable steps, in the circumstances known to him at the time, to ascertain whether the complainant was consenting.

The accused's belief that the complainant consented is not a defence if it arose from the accused's "self-induced intoxication," his "recklessness or willful blindness," or if "the accused did not take reasonable steps, in the circumstances known to the accused at the time, to ascertain that the complainant was consenting."

The reference to recklessness contemplates that an accused who adverted to the risk that the complainant did not consent has always had the *mens rea* required for sexual assault. The reference to self-induced intoxication not being relevant represents traditional but constitutionally suspect law that provides that intoxication may never be a defence to crimes classified as general intent.[285] This issue will be discussed in greater detail later in this chapter.

The reference to wilful blindness codifies *Sansregret* and precludes the defence when an accused is subjectively aware of the need to inquire into consent but deliberately declines to inquire because he does not wish to know the truth. The culpability in wilful blindness was the accused's refusal to inquire whether the complainant was consenting, when he was "aware of the need for some inquiry . . . [but declined] to make the inquiry because he . . . [does] not wish to know the truth."[286] *Sansregret* narrowed the *Pappajohn* defence by holding that the accused was presumed to have guilty knowledge of the absence of consent when, knowing the need for inquiry as to consent, he remained ignorant.

As discussed above, amendments proposed in 2018 that would add to section 273.2(a) that the accused's mistaken belief in consent is not a defence if it arose from the conditions of no resistance from application or fear of force, fraud, or the exercise of authority in section 265(3) or deemed no consent in section 273.1(2) or (3) because of incapacity to consent or lack of agreement or inducement through abuse of power,

---

285   *R v Leary* (1977), 33 CCC (2d) 473 (SCC). But for a recognition of a possible defence of extreme intoxication, see *R v Daviault*, below note 319. In addition, s 33.1 of the *Code*, above note 1, would deem the fault of self-induced intoxication sufficient to form the fault of sexual assault and other general intent offences involving an assault or interference or threat of interference with the bodily integrity of another person. See Chapter 7, Section E for further discussion.

286   *Sansregret*, above note 264 at para 22. The accused had broken into his ex-girlfriend's apartment and threatened her with a knife. Less than a month earlier, the complainant had reported a rape after a similar incident with the accused.

trust, or authority.[287] In addition, a proposed but not yet enacted section 273.2(c) would provide:

> c)   there is no evidence that the complainant's voluntary agreement to the activity was affirmatively expressed by words or actively expressed by conduct.[288]

e)   The Requirement of Reasonable Steps in Section 273.2(b)

The denial in section 273.2(b) of the mistake of fact unless the accused takes reasonable steps in the circumstances known to him or her at the time to ascertain whether the complainant was consenting to the activity in question combines subjective and objective fault elements in a novel and creative manner. As such, it breaks away from the idea in *Pappajohn* that the contours of the mistake of fact can be deduced from the fault element of the offence. On the one hand, section 273.2(b) bases the accused's obligation to take reasonable steps to ascertain consent on the basis of what the accused subjectively knows of the circumstances. The accused's obligation to take reasonable steps is based only on what he subjectively knows at the time. On the other hand, section 273.2(b) requires the accused to act as a reasonable person would in the circumstances by taking reasonable steps to ascertain whether the complainant was consenting. Much will depend on the courts' view of what reasonable steps are necessary to ascertain consent. Some judges may find that positive steps are required in most, if not all, situations regardless of the accused's subjective perception of the circumstances. Others may require such steps only if the complainant has indicated resistance or lack of consent in some way that is subjectively known to the accused.

In *Ewanchuk*,[289] the majority of the Court did not directly apply section 273.2 despite the fact pointed out by the dissenters that it applied to the sexual assault in question.[290] Justice Major for the majority followed the traditional *Pappajohn* view that mistake of fact was a denial of *mens rea* and was necessary to protect the morally innocent. In part drawing on the new definition of consent, however, he indicated:

---

287   Bill C-51, above note 214, proposed amendment of s 273.1 (2.1).

288   *Ibid*.

289   Above note 231.

290   Justice L'Heureux-Dubé argued that the mistake of fact defence would not arise unless the accused took reasonable steps to ascertain consent. She indicated that moving from a massage to sexual touching without inquiring about consent was not reasonable and that once that complainant had expressed non-consent "the accused has a corresponding escalating obligation to take additional steps to ascertain consent." *Ibid* at para 99.

In order to cloak the accused's actions in moral innocence, the evidence must show that he believed that the complainant *communicated consent to engage in the sexual activity in question*. A belief by the accused that the complainant, in her own mind, wanted him to touch her, but did not express that desire, is not a defence. The accused's speculation as to what was going on in the complainant's mind provides no defence.[291]

The above statement would seem to restrict the mistaken belief in consent defence to cases in which the complainant communicated in an ambiguous manner that she consented to sexual activity. The mistake of fact defence was thus influenced more by statutory definitions of consent in section 273.1 as the voluntary agreement to engage in sexual activity than the reasonable steps requirement in section 273.2. *Ewanchuk* suggests that the accused may have a mistaken belief defence only when he mistakenly believes that the victim said yes through her words or actions. The accused may not have a mistaken belief defence if he only claims not to have heard the victim say no. This would mean that the accused would have a defence in mistaken belief in consent only if (1) he believed the victim communicated consent to the sexual activity in question and (2) he had taken reasonable steps, given the circumstances known to him at the time, to discover whether the victim consented to the sexual activity in question.

In any event, the mistake of fact defence was denied in *Ewanchuk* because the complainant said no and "there is nothing on the record to support the accused's claim that he continued to believe her to be consenting, or that he re-established consent before resuming physical contact."[292] In another case, the Ontario Court of Appeal stressed that the complainant's prior rejection of the accused's advances, as well as her objections when the accused entered her apartment and tried to kiss her, required the accused to take reasonable steps before he engaged in sexual intercourse: "The legislative scheme replaces the assumptions traditionally — and inappropriately — associated with passivity."[293]

The Supreme Court has yet to interpret the new requirement in section 273.2(b) that the accused take reasonable steps in the circumstances known to him or her to ascertain consent, though it has held that it was an error not to instruct the jury about the reasonable step requirement in a case where he claimed the complainant consented to

---

291 *Ibid* at para 46 [emphasis in original].
292 *Ibid* at para 58.
293 *R v Cornejo* (2003), 68 OR (3d) 117 at para 21 (CA) [*Cornejo*].

sex with him after having sex with two others.[294] The Manitoba Court of Appeal has described it as "a quasi-objective" provision that requires the court to ascertain what circumstances the accused knew about and then to ask "if a reasonable man was aware of the same circumstances, would he take further steps before proceeding with the sexual activity?"[295] In her concurring judgment in *Ewanchuk*, L'Heureux-Dubé J interpreted section 273.2(b) to require that the accused take reasonable steps to ascertain consent in all cases when she stated that "until an accused first takes reasonable steps to assure that there is consent, the defence of honest but mistaken belief in consent does not arise."[296] She indicated that the fact that the complainant did not refuse a message from the accused was not a reasonable step because "the accused cannot rely on the complainant's silence or ambiguous conduct to initiate sexual contact."[297] This approach could require some sign of consent in all cases. In a case where a co-worker had made numerous sexual advances to a woman and been rejected, the Ontario Court of Appeal also indicated that there was a need for "steps *before* he engaged in sexual activity to ascertain whether she was consenting."[298] Although some might criticize a requirement to take positive steps in all cases as unrealistic, it is also supported by the idea expressed by the majority of the Court in *Ewanchuk* that an accused cannot take silence, passivity, or ambiguous conduct as consent and must believe that the complainant has affirmatively communicated consent through words or actions to the particular sexual activity. In any event, it is clear that the requirement to take reasonable steps will be tailored to the overall circumstances known to the accused.

It is also clear that section 273.2(b) contemplates what has been described as "a proportionate relationship"[299] between the circumstances known or believed by the accused and the reasonable steps that are required. Once a complainant has expressed an unwillingness to engage in sexual activity, the accused must make certain that the complainant has changed her mind. In such circumstances, the accused cannot rely on lapse of time, silence, or equivalent conduct.[300] As L'Heureux Dubé J indicated in *Ewanchuk*, "where a complainant expresses non-consent,

---

294 *R v Spicer*, 2016 SCC 3.

295 *R v Malcolm* (2000), 147 CCC (3d) 34 at para 24 (Man CA), leave to appeal to SCC refused (2000), 150 CCC (3d) vi.

296 *Ewanchuk*, above note 231 at para 99.

297 *Ibid.*

298 *Cornejo*, above note 293 at para 32 [emphasis in original].

299 *R v G(R)* (1994), 38 CR (4th) 123 at para 29 (BCCA).

300 *Ewanchuk*, above note 231.

the accused has a corresponding escalating obligation to take additional steps to ascertain consent."[301]

The Supreme Court has interpreted a somewhat similar provision that requires the accused to take "all reasonable steps" to ascertain the age of a complainant under sixteen years of age to suggest that "the more reasonable an accused's perception of the complainant's age, the fewer steps reasonably required of them." This suggests that what constitutes reasonable steps will be "highly contextual, fact-specific"[302] and require a proportionate relationship between the circumstances subjectively known or believed by the accused and the reasonable steps required. Given this, the Court was reluctant to articulate general requirements. For example, it indicated that there was not always a rule that the accused ask the complainant's age in every case. Conversely, if the question was asked, it would not always be reasonable for the accused to rely on the answer provided by the complainant. In the result, the Court affirmed the trial judge's acquittal on the basis that the Crown had failed to prove beyond a reasonable doubt that a thirty-five-year-old woman who had sex with a fourteen-and-a-half-year-old boy whom she believed to be sixteen years of age had not taken all reasonable steps to ascertain the boy's age. The Supreme Court concluded the trial judge had made no legal errors in acquitting the accused and that the Court of Appeal that reversed the acquittal had erred by translating its disagreement with the trial judge's factual inferences and the weight given to specific pieces of evidence into legal errors. The reasonable steps requirements in section 273.2(b) may also be similarly fact specific though it would be helpful for the Supreme Court to set out the basic legal principles that should govern its administration.

f) Mistake of Fact Precluded if Based on a Mistake of Law
The 1992 amendments not only altered the mistake of fact defence by introducing a requirement in section 273.2(b) that the accused take reasonable steps in the circumstances known to him at the time to ascertain consent, but it also eliminated some claims of mistaken belief in consent as errors of law through the definition of consent and specific instances of non-consent.

This would be made even clearer by 2018 proposals to add a new section 273.1(1.2), stating that "the question of whether no consent is obtained under subsection 265(3) or [section 273.1] subsection (2) or (3) is a question of law." These sections provide a number of examples

---

301 *Ibid* at para 99.
302 *R v George*, 2017 SCC 38 at para 9 [*George*].

where consent is deemed not valid, such as consent on the basis of threats, fraud, or exercise of authority (section 265(3)) or consent expressed by a third person or when a position of trust, power, or authority is abused or when a complainant is incapable of consenting (section 273.1(2)). The idea behind these provisions is in some tension to the fact-specific approach to interpreting reasonable steps. In other words, the mistake of law approach sets out bright lines based on legal statements of what conduct is deemed to be unacceptable regardless of the factual nuances of the particular case.

The Supreme Court in *R v Ewanchuk* has indicated that the accused's "belief that silence, passivity or ambiguous conduct constitutes consent is a mistake of law and provides no defence."[303] This means that an accused who argued that he mistakenly believed the complainant consented because he thought that no meant yes or that he thought that yes to one sexual activity meant yes to another would be precluded from arguing this as a mistake of fact because it now constitutes a mistake of law. Given the Supreme Court's ruling in *JA* that advance consent by a complainant who was unconscious at the time of the sexual activity was not legally valid, the accused's claim of mistaken belief in consent in such a situation may also now be precluded as a mistake of law.[304] In holding that there was no air of reality to put a mistake of fact to the jury, the British Columbia Court of Appeal has stated: "If an accused's personal beliefs do not accord with the legal definition of consent, then his mistaken belief is not grounded in a mistake of fact, but in a mistake of law, which affords no defence."[305] It elaborated that the accused's "purported belief that the complainant's expressed lack of agreement to sexual touching in fact constituted an invitation to more persistent or aggressive contact, and his testimony that he thought 'no means yes', provides him no defence as the appellant's belief amounts to a mistake in law."[306]

The Alberta Court of Appeal in *R v Barton* similarly made clear the danger "that with respect to sexual offences, courts sometimes allowed mistakes of law to enter the courtroom masquerading as mistakes of facts,"[307] particularly in support of claimed mistake of fact about the

---

303 *Ewanchuk*, above note 231 at para 51.
304 The majority of the Court in *JA*, above note 251, did not directly address this point, but Fish J in his dissent stated that the majority's position meant that the accused's belief in the validity of advance consent "would constitute a mistake of law, which cannot avail as a defence." *Ibid* at para 118.
305 *R v Gairdner*, 2017 BCCA 425 at para 18.
306 *Ibid* at para 25.
307 *Barton*, above note 232 at para 245.

existence of consent. It held that a number of mistakes of law had impermissibly been allowed to support arguments by an accused that he mistakenly believed that a sex worker had consented to sexual activity that resulted in her death. One mistake of law was the accused's belief that the sex worker consented to the particular sexual activity based on her consent to "similar" activity the night before. The Court of Appeal explained: "The mistake of law is that the accused does not understand that consent must be given to what happened the second night . . . . An accused's belief must be grounded in the complainant's *communication of consent* at the relevant time to the 'sexual activity in question'."[308] Another mistake of law was that the accused relied on his subjective perception that the complainant's silence or ambiguous conduct meant that she consented. The jury should have been instructed that the complainant's "silence, passivity or ambiguous conduct" were not consent and that "consent must be affirmatively communicated through express words or unambiguous affirmative conduct. To suggest otherwise is wrong in law."[309]

At the same time and as discussed in Chapter 3, the distinction between a mistake of fact, which can be a defence if it raises a reasonable doubt about the fault requirement of the particular offence, and a mistake of law is often not clear cut. The above cases including *Ewanchuk* demonstrate that courts have recognized that one of the intents of the 1992 reforms was to expand the range of myths and stereotypes about sex and sexual violence that would be impermissible mistakes of law that would not provide a basis for a defence. At the same time, the Supreme Court's 2017 decision in *George*[310] demonstrates that acquittals cannot be overturned simply because of disagreements over the trier of facts factual inferences or the weight given to particular evidence, especially when as in that case the accused was acquitted of a sexual offence. It also suggests that the Court is likely to interpret reasonable steps requirements to depend on the facts of a particular case, albeit hopefully in a manner that also accepts that Parliament has acted to preclude some undesirable basis for mistaken belief in consents as mistakes of laws that should never be accepted.

Although, the basis for impermissible mistakes of law in sexual offence have increased as a result of the 1992 and 2018 amendments to the *Code*, the process of fact-finding by judges and juries remains an important and perhaps less predictable area of the criminal trial

---

308 *Ibid* at para 254 [emphasis in original].
309 *Ibid* at paras 256–57.
310 Above note 302 at para 24.

process. This may help explain why, despite law reform designed to eradicate sexist myths that disadvantage women as complainants in sexual offences, both reporting and conviction rates for sexual offences remain lower than for other crimes.[311]

g)   The Constitutionality of Section 273.2(b)

The Ontario Court of Appeal upheld the constitutionality of section 273.2(b) in *R v Darrach*.[312] Although the provision introduced an "objective component into the mental element of the offence," it was "personalized according to the subjective awareness of the accused at the time" and did not require the accused to take all reasonable steps to ascertain whether the complainant consented. Morden ACJO concluded that the subjective *mens rea* requirement "remains largely intact" and that the new provision did not require a mistaken belief to be reasonable. He posited a situation in which an accused who made an unreasonable mistake about consent could be acquitted because he took reasonable steps to ascertain that the complainant was consenting. Although it is true that the provision combines subjective and objective fault elements, the likelihood that any mistake that remains after reasonable steps have been taken would still be unreasonable must be very small. The Supreme Court unfortunately did not deal with section 273.2(b) when it dismissed the accused's appeal in this case.[313]

Some have warned that section 273.2(b) is vulnerable under the *Charter* because it does not on its face require a marked departure from reasonable standards.[314] To the extent that section 273.2(b) bases liability on a failure to take reasonable steps to ascertain that the complainant is consenting, it can be argued that there is a need for the accused to engage in a marked departure from what would be reasonable in the circumstances as now required in *Beatty*[315] whenever negligence is used

---

311   Victimization studies suggest that eight in ten sexual assault incidents are not reported to the police. Shana Conroy & Adam Cotter, *Self-Reported Sexual Assaults in Canada, 2014* (Ottawa: Statistics Canada, 2017), online: www.statcan. gc.ca/pub/85-002-x/2017001/article/14842-eng.pdf. Of those sexual assaults reported to the police, only one in ten result in convictions compared to one in four assaults resulting in convictions. Cristine Rotenberg, *From Arrests to Conviction: Court Outcomes of Police-Reported Sexual Assaults 2009 to 2014* (Ottawa: Statistics Canada, 2017), online: www.statcan.gc.ca/pub/85-002-x/2017001/ article/54870-eng.pdf.

312   (1998), 122 CCC (3d) 225 at 252 (Ont CA).

313   *R v Darrach* (2000), 148 CCC (3d) 97 (SCC).

314   D Stuart, *Canadian Criminal Law*, 7th ed (Toronto: Thomson Carswell, 2014) at 336.

315   Above note 194.

as a form of criminal liability. On the other hand, section 273.2(b) can be interpreted as it was by the Ontario Court of Appeal in *Darrach* to stress subjective fault based on what circumstances are actually known to the accused. Such an interpretation might, however, add little to the already existing law that the accused's mistaken belief in consent is not a valid defence if it is based on wilful blindness.

Another restriction on the section 273.2(b) defence is that the accused will presumably not be allowed to rely on beliefs in consent that have been deemed to be mistakes of law under sections 265(3) and 273.1(2) or (3). This prevents the accused from claiming that after reasonable steps were taken he still believed that no meant yes or that yes meant yes when it was obtained by threats of force, fraud, or the complainant was incapable of consent or consent was communicated by a third party. As discussed in Chapter 3, the Supreme Court has not questioned the principle in section 19 of the *Criminal Code* that ignorance or mistakes about the law are not an excuse except in very limited instances such as colour of right or officially induced error defences that do not apply to sexual assault.

It has also been argued that section 273.2(b) may violate the principle of fundamental justice that intentional conduct should be punished more seriously than negligent conduct as articulated by the Court in *Creighton*.[316] This is a clearly established principle of fundamental justice that is invoked by those who argue that the appropriate way to have restricted the mistake of fact defence would have been to create a separate offence of negligent sexual assault.[317] This principle of fundamental justice would, however, only clearly apply if section 273.2(b) would convict the accused simply on the basis that he or she ought to have known that the victim was not consenting. As discussed above, section 273.2(b) is an innovative blended form of subjective and objective fault that has been interpreted in a manner that stresses its subjective components. As such, the principle of fundamental justice that requires the different culpability of intentional and negligent conduct is not clearly engaged. In addition, one practical reason for not introducing a new offence of negligent sexual assault would be concerns that in a criminal justice system where most cases do not receive a full trial many cases would be resolved by guilty pleas to this less serious offence.

---

316 Above note 57.
317 Stuart, above note 314 at 336.

h) Sexual Assault and Intoxication

Sexual assault has been held to be a crime of general intent where the intent does not go beyond the commission of the immediate act. This interpretation stresses the idea that sexual assault is a crime of violence that need not be committed for an ulterior purpose such as the achievement of sexual gratification.[318] As discussed in Chapter 7, the normal rule is that evidence of intoxication is not considered capable of raising a reasonable doubt about a general intent offence such as sexual assault.

The Court's decision in *R v Daviault*[319] raised the possibility that an accused charged with sexual assault could raise a defence of extreme intoxication. *Daviault* was a sexual assault case and the accused at the new trial ordered by the Court would have had an opportunity to establish on a balance of probabilties defence of extreme intoxication producing involuntary conduct. Such a defence would also have to be supported with expert evidence about the degree of intoxication. If successful, the defence would have produced a complete acquittal in contrast to the traditional intoxication defence that operates to raise a reasonable doubt about a specific intent offence, such as murder or robbery, but would not affect the ability to convict the accused of lesser included general intent offences such as manslaughter and assault.

As discussed in Chapter 7, concerns about possible acquittals in cases following *Daviault* led to the quick enactment of sections 33.1 to 33.3 of the *Code*. These provisions deny the *Daviault* defence in cases where an accused was charged with sexual assault or indeed any offence involving an assault or interference with bodily integrity. Parliament resisted the Court's suggestion that it enact a new intoxication-based offence to cover such cases in part because it was thought important to convict voluntarily intoxicated accused of sexual assault and not some other intoxication-based offence that would be regarded as a less serious offence. As discussed earlier in this chapter, similar concerns influenced the decision not to enact a new offence of negligent sexual assault as a means to restrict the mistaken belief in consent defence.

An accused charged with sexual assault would not have an intoxication defence absent a successful *Charter* challenge to sections 33.1 to 33.3 of the *Criminal Code* and the proof on a balance of probabilities of the *Daviault* defence of extreme intoxication. Even if, following the majority opinion in *Daviault*, the substitution of the fault of voluntarily becoming extremely intoxicated for the fault of sexual assault violated

---

318   *R v Bernard*, [1988] 2 SCR 833.
319   [1994] 3 SCR 63.

sections 7 and 11(d) of the *Charter*, there is a strong case that could justify the restrictions on these rights as a reasonable and proportionate limit on the accused's rights designed, as stressed in the 1995 law's preamble, to respond to intoxicated violence that "has a particular disadvantaging impact on the equal participation of women and children in society and on the rights of woman and children to the equal protection and benefit of the law as guaranteed by sections 7, 15 and 28"[320] of the *Charter*.

C. PROPERTY OFFENCES

A broad array of property crimes is found in the *Criminal Code* and it is possible to examine only a few of the crimes here. As with all criminal offences, it is important to distinguish the prohibited act and the prohibited fault elements. As will be seen, both theft and fraud follow trends to broadly defined act requirements. At the same time, theft has a particularly high *mens rea* requirement. Fraud has a slightly lower fault requirement that includes some forms of recklessness and does not require subjective appreciation that one is acting dishonestly.

1) Theft

The *actus reus* of theft under section 322 of the *Criminal Code* requires the taking or conversion of anything.[321] Anything must be a type of property that can be converted in a manner that deprives the victim. It does not include confidential information that has not been reduced to a list or other tangible thing.[322] Conversion can be affected by delivery of goods or the conversion of property to the accused's own use with the intent to deprive the other person of the property.[323] Section 322(2) broadens the *actus reus* by providing that a person commits theft when, with the intent to steal, he or she begins to cause anything to move or to become movable. Section 322(4) provides that it is not material whether the person in possession of the property is in lawful possession

---

320 *An Act to amend the Criminal Code*, SC 1995, c 32 (preamble). For further discussion, see Chapter 6, Section E(3).

321 *Code*, above note 1, s 322.

322 *R v Stewart*, [1988] 1 SCR 963. Note, however, that there are many other separate theft-based offences, including the offence of unauthorized use of a computer and theft of telecommunications signals. *Code*, above note 1, ss 342.1 and 326.

323 *R v Milne*, [1992] 1 SCR 697 [*Milne*].

of the property.[324] It could be argued that a person who knowingly receives double payment for his or her services or who buys something from a store does not commit the *actus reus* of the theft because there is no taking of property. Such approaches, however, ignore the breadth of the *actus reus* of theft, which includes not only taking but also conversion of property for one's own use.[325] Any concern about overreaching in defining the *actus reus* of theft should be addressed by the high *mens rea* requirement of the offence.

The *mens rea* of theft requires that a person take or convert something "fraudulently and without colour of right." The requirement of a fraudulent intent requires deceit, or an intention to deceive, and dishonesty.[326] A colour of right is, as discussed in Chapter 3, a form of *mens rea* that provides something of an exception to the general principle that ignorance or mistake of law is not an excuse. A person who has an honestly asserted proprietary or possessory claim to a thing may have a colour of right even if the claim is not founded in the law.[327]

In addition, the prosecution must establish that the accused intended to deprive the owner of the property either temporarily or permanently. This includes actions such as pledging the property in security or altering or dealing with it in a manner so that it cannot be restored to its original condition.

2) Fraud

The *actus reus* of fraud under section 380 of the *Criminal Code* is (1) a prohibited act of deceit, falsehood, or some other fraudulent means that (2) has the prohibited consequence of causing a deprivation either in the form of an actual loss or placing the victim's pecuniary interests at risk. What constitutes other fraudulent means will be determined objectively on the basis of what a reasonable person would consider to be dishonest even if these acts do not involve deceit or falsehood.[328] They can include the use of corporate funds for personal purposes, the unauthorized diversion of funds, and non-disclosure of material facts. In one case, other fraudulent means were defined to include the gambling

---

324 See also *Code*, above note 1, s 328.
325 *Milne*, above note 323; *R v Dawond* (1975), 27 CCC (2d) 300 (Alta CA).
326 *R v Howson*, [1966] 2 OR 63 (CA).
327 *R v DeMarco* (1973), 13 CCC (2d) 369 (Ont CA); *R v Lilly*, [1983] 1 SCR 794.
328 *R v Olan*, [1978] 2 SCR 1175.

practices of the accused with respect to money that was necessary to pay the accused's creditors.[329]

The *actus reus* has been defined in a broad but purposive manner that is driven by the focus on dishonesty. In addition to dishonesty, however, there has to be a deprivation that produces either an actual loss or the placing of the victim's interest at risk. In the case of a risk to financial interests, "proof of actual loss is irrelevant. Proof of risk to the economic interest of the victim is sufficient."[330] The dishonest act must play a significant role in the deprivation, but consistent with causation principles examined in Chapter 3, it need not be the exclusive or only cause. Thus, the fact that the victim may have been deprived in part because of his or her own actions or truthful representations by the accused does not necessarily mean that an accused will not have committed the *actus reus* of fraud if the accused's dishonest act was a significant cause of the deprivation. As with other offences, an accused could be charged with an attempt in a case where the *actus reus* of the completed offence, in this case dishonest conduct that causes a deprivation, is not present.

The *mens rea* of fraud was interpreted in *Théroux*[331] to require only subjective knowledge of the prohibited act combined with subjective knowledge that the act could result in a deprivation including the placing of the victim's pecuniary interest at risk. Justice McLachlin stated:

> The prohibited act is deceit, falsehood, or some other dishonest act. The prohibited consequence is depriving another of what is or should be his, which may, as we have seen, consist in merely placing another's property at risk. The *mens rea* would then consist in the subjective awareness that one was undertaking a prohibited act (the deceit, falsehood or other dishonest act) which could cause deprivation in the sense of depriving another of property or putting that property at risk. If this is shown, the crime is complete. The fact that the accused may have hoped the deprivation would not take place, or may have felt there was nothing wrong with what he or she was doing, provides no defence. To put it another way, following the traditional criminal law principle that the mental state necessary to the offence must be determined by reference to the external acts which constitute the *actus* of the offence (see Williams, *supra*, c. 3), the proper focus in determining the *mens rea* of fraud is to ask whether the accused intentionally committed the prohibited acts (deceit, falsehood,

---

329 *R v Zlatic*, [1993] 2 SCR 29 [*Zlatic*].
330 *R v Drabinsky*, 2011 ONCA 582 at para 82.
331 *R v Théroux*, [1993] 2 SCR 579 [*Théroux*].

or other dishonest act) knowing or desiring the consequences proscribed by the offence (deprivation, including the risk of deprivation).
The personal feeling of the accused about the morality or honesty of
the act or its consequences is no more relevant to the analysis than
is the accused's awareness that the particular acts undertaken constitute a criminal offence.[332]

Justice McLachlin added that "[r]ecklessness presupposes knowledge
of the likelihood of the prohibited consequences. It is established when
it is shown that the accused, with such knowledge, commits acts which
may bring about these prohibited consequences, while being reckless
as to whether or not they ensue."[333]

The Supreme Court justified the above articulation of the fault element for fraud, which does not require that the accused subjectively
know that his or her conduct was dishonest as relating to the breadth
of the *actus reus*. The Court built on a number of earlier decisions that
had made clear the fact that the accused's belief that he had done nothing wrong because he would return the property[334] or that the fraud
had been encouraged by others[335] did not prevent the formation of the
criminal fault. It concluded that the *mens rea* would not catch negligent
misstatements or sharp business practices: "to establish the *mens rea* of
fraud the Crown must prove that the accused knowingly undertook the
acts which constitute the falsehood, deceit or other fraudulent means,
and that the accused was aware that deprivation could result from such
conduct."[336] The Court's approach accords with a trend towards thinner
versions of intentional *mens rea* that is seen in the Court's decision that
the intent to assist a party in a crime or to commit an unlawful purpose
is not negated by the fact that the accused has been threatened and
commits intentional acts in the hope of avoiding the threat.[337]

The Court upheld a conviction for fraud in *Théroux* on the basis
that the accused had lied about insurance protection for deposits paid
towards the construction of new homes. The deprivation of not receiving the insurance protection was a sufficient *actus reus*, as was the risk
that the victims could lose the deposit money. The *mens rea* was also
present because the accused knew that he did not have insurance protection for the deposits and that he would be depriving the depositors

332 *Ibid* at para 24.
333 *Ibid* at para 26.
334 *Lafrance v The Queen*, [1975] 2 SCR 201.
335 *R v Lemire*, [1965] SCR 174.
336 *Théroux*, above note 331 at para 39.
337 See *Hibbert*, above note 93, discussed in Chapter 5.

of that protection even though he honestly believed that the houses would be built and the risk to the deposit money would not material- ize.[338] Justice Sopinka agreed with this result but warned that there may not be *mens rea* in a case where a deprivation would occur only in the event of some future event and the accused honestly believed that such an event would not occur.

This difference of opinion with respect to the fault element was soon revealed in a companion case. In *Zlatic*,[339] the majority of the Su- preme Court held that the accused had the necessary *mens rea* because he subjectively knew that when he gambled with money that was re- quired by creditors he was placing their financial interests at risk even though he also believed that he would win at the casinos and be able to repay his creditors. Chief Justice Lamer and Sopinka J dissented on the basis that there was no finding that the accused was reckless or knew that his gambling would place the creditors' interest at risk. Indeed, the trial judge had made findings that the accused honestly believed that he would be able to pay off his creditors after the gambling. The major- ity, however, rejected the relevance of these findings on the basis of its thinner understanding of criminal fault as relating only to the commis- sion of the *actus reus* and not including the accused's belief that the risk to the creditors' money would not be realized.

D. TERRORISM OFFENCES

The terrorism offences quickly enacted after 9/11 are of interest in their own right; but for the purpose of a book on the fundamental principles of criminal law, they are of special interest in the way that they create new offences for conduct that would otherwise be prosecuted as incho- ate offences, such as conspiracy, attempts, and counselling a crime[340] that is not committed, or as forms of participation, such as aiding or

---

338 The Ontario Court of Appeal has applied this reasoning to conclude that an ac- cused's "assertion that he believed that no one would be hurt by his conduct is no defence, because a subjective intent to mislead is not an essential element of the offence of fraud. Instead, all that is required is subjective knowledge of the prohibited act, and that the act could have as a consequence the deprivation of another." *R v Eizenga*, 2011 ONCA 113 at para 81.

339 *Zlatic*, above note 329.

340 A man was acquitted of counselling murder and other offences in 2017, with the trial judge stressing the high *mens rea* for counselling and concluding, given the accused's political intent as a Palestinian activist, that there was a reasonable doubt whether he deliberately encouraged or actively induced others to commit murder. *R v Hamdan*, 2017 BCSC 1770 at para 153.

abetting or committing crimes as a result of common unlawful purposes. Whatever the arguments at the time that existing offences would be adequate should terrorist plots be discovered, it is now clear that such conduct, as well as additional conduct, can be prosecuted as completed crimes of terrorism under Part II.1 of the *Criminal Code*. These terrorism offences, as well as organized crime offences on which they were modelled, demonstrate a reluctance to rely on the traditional inchoate offences and principles of party liability and a willingness to create broadly defined new crimes.

The new terrorism offences are also of interest to the extent that they built on previous and problematic extensions of criminal liability under sections 467.11 to 467.13 with respect to participation in a criminal organization or gang, instructing the commission of an offence, recruiting members of a criminal organization, and committing an offence for the benefit of, at the direction of, or in association with a criminal organization. These offences have been criticized for criminalizing conduct that may only remotely be connected with organized crime but have so far been upheld by the courts as neither vague nor overbroad, according to the Supreme Court's rather deferential approach to reviewing criminal offences on these bases.[341] In addition, the Supreme Court has stressed when interpreting one of these offences the need for an accused to have subjective knowledge about and not simply associations with the targeted group.[342]

1) The Offence of Participation in a Terrorist Group

With respect to both organized crime and terrorist groups, a decision was taken not to criminalize mere membership in those groups. In this way, Parliament decided not to create pure status-based crimes but instead to create offences that provided a broadly worded prohibited act but also required intent. Section 83.18(1) provides:

> Every one who knowingly participates in or contributes to, directly or indirectly, any activity of a terrorist group for the purpose of enhancing the ability of any terrorist group to facilitate or carry out a

---

341 *R v Terezakis* (2007), 223 CCC (3d) 344 (BCCA); *R v Lindsay* (2004), 182 CCC (3d) 301 (Ont SCJ). For criticism, see Stuart, above note 314 at 765*ff*. See also D Freedman, "The New Law of Criminal Organizations in Canada" (2006) 85 *Canadian Bar Review* 171.

342 "The Crown must also demonstrate that an accused *knowingly* dealt with a criminal organization. The stigma associated with the offence requires that the accused have a subjective *mens rea* with respect to his or her association with the organization." *R v Venneri*, 2012 SCC 33 at para 57.

terrorist activity is guilty of an indictable offence and liable to imprisonment for a term not exceeding ten years.

The *mens rea* of this offence requires that a person both knowingly participate or contribute to the activities of a terrorist group and have the purpose of enhancing its ability to facilitate or carry out a terrorist activity. The dual requirements of knowledge and purpose are high subjective fault standards that would be sufficient even if the courts determined that terrorism crimes because of their stigma and penalty should, like murder, attempted murder, and war crimes, require proof of subjective fault in relation to all elements of the prohibited act.[343]

The broader aspects of this offence are found in its definition of an *actus reus*. The *actus reus* involves participation or contribution to any activity of a terrorist group and includes a long but non-exclusive list of examples of participating in section 83.18(3). As with the *actus reus* of attempted crime, the *actus reus* here may involve otherwise legal activity that is not a crime or a social mischief. In addition, the offence incorporates the broad definitions of a terrorist group and terrorist activities in section 83.01 of the *Criminal Code*. The reference to facilitating the carrying out of a terrorist activity in section 83.18 has been interpreted to include the broad definition of facilitation in section 83.19(2), which does not require the accused to know any particulars about a planned terrorist activity.[344]

The Supreme Court in *R v Khawaja* upheld the participation offence from challenge under section 7 of the *Charter*, rejecting arguments that the offence was vague or overbroad. It reached this conclusion by interpreting both the *actus reus* and *mens rea* of the offence to exclude (1) innocent activity not undertaken with the purpose to facilitate the ability of a terrorist group to carry out terrorist activities or (2) conduct that a reasonable person would not view as materially enhancing the ability of a terrorist group to act. The Court concluded that a lawyer who acted

---

343 See Chapter 2, Section B(4)(d) for a discussion of constitutionally required fault elements.

344 In the course of finding an abuse of process, a judge has found that undercover officers who provided terrorist suspects with money and inert bomb material had knowingly facilitated a terrorist activity under s 83.19, noting that it did not have the purpose requirement of s 83.18 and concluding: "The offence described in s. 83.19 is committed when the offender knows that his or her actions are making it easier or helping to bring about a terrorist activity. It is therefore not essential to prove that the police intended that the defendants carry out a terrorist activity, provided the RCMP knew that this was generally the intention of the defendants." *R v Nuttall*, 2016 BCSC 1404 at para 802. The judge also concluded that the RCMP, by supplying with property, had committed the offence under s 83.03. *Ibid* at para 806.

for a terrorist would have the necessary *mens rea* only if "his intent was specifically to enable the client to pursue further terrorist activities, as opposed to simply affording his client a full defence at law."[345] Leaving aside whether this interpretation blurs the admittedly fuzzy distinction between intent and motive, it depends on Parliament's decision to require not only knowledge, but the slightly higher fault requirement of a terrorist purpose. Assuming that terrorism offences are stigma offences under section 7 of the *Charter* (something the Court has yet to decide), Parliament has in section 83.18 gone beyond the constitutional minimum of subjective knowledge of *actus reus* and required a terrorist purpose, something that could not be proven in relation to most service providers. The Court dismissed another hypothetical — those who march to lend credibility to a terrorist organization — on the basis that the *actus reus* of section 83.18 "does not capture conduct that discloses, at most, a negligible risk of enhancing the abilities of a terrorist group to facilitate or carry out a terrorist activity."[346] This approach interprets the *actus reus* in a restrained manner to avoid a challenge on the basis of overbreadth.

Subsequent to *Khawaja*, the Ontario Court of Appeal affirmed the conviction of a person who attended part of a training camp and provided his computer skills to assist the leader of a terrorist group with computer problems. The Court of Appeal interpreted the Supreme Court's reading down of the *actus reus* quite narrowly and stressed that the prohibited act of section 83.18 "does not require proof that what the appellant did *actually* enhanced the ability of the terrorist group to carry out or facilitate a terrorist activity, only that the conduct creates a risk of harm beyond *de minimis*."[347] The Court of Appeal also stressed that the jury that convicted the accused had rejected his primary defence that he did not act for the purpose of enhancing the ability of a terrorist group to facilitate or carry out terrorist activities.

2) Definition of a Terrorist Group

What constitutes a terrorist group? A "terrorist group" is defined under section 83.01 as either a group that has been listed by the Cabinet as a terrorist group under section 83.05 or "an entity that has as one of its purposes or activities facilitating or carrying out any terrorist activity." The listed entity part of this definition effectively substitutes a

---

345 R v *Khawaja*, [2012] 3 SCR 555 at para 47 [*Khawaja*].
346 *Ibid* at para 50.
347 R v *Ansari*, 2015 ONCA 575 at para 186.

judgment made by the Cabinet as part of the executive without trial or adversarial challenge and on the basis of secret intelligence for proof beyond a reasonable doubt in a criminal trial that the group is a terrorist group. The second part of this definition is very broad because it incorporates the definition of terrorist activities in section 83.01 as well as the definition of facilitation under section 83.19, which has a highly qualified fault element in relation to knowledge of the nature of the terrorist activity.

3) Definition of Terrorist Activities

Terrorist activities are defined in section 83.01(a) as a number of extraterritorial offences to the extent that they implement various listed international conventions against terrorism that Canada has signed. This means that the full ambit of the criminal sanction cannot be interpreted without consulting both domestic and international law.

An alternative definition of "terrorist activity" is found in section 83.01(b), which provides:

> an act or omission, in or outside Canada,
> (i) that is committed
>   (A) in whole or in part for a political, religious or ideological purpose, objective or cause, and
>   (B) in whole or in part with the intention of intimidating the public, or a segment of the public, with regard to its security, including its economic security, or compelling a person, a government or a domestic or an international organization to do or to refrain from doing any act, whether the public or the person, government or organization is inside or outside Canada, and
> (ii) that intentionally
>   (A) causes death or serious bodily harm to a person by the use of violence,
>   (B) endangers a person's life,
>   (C) causes a serious risk to the health or safety of the public or any segment of the public,
>   (D) causes substantial property damage, whether to public or private property, if causing such damage is likely to result in the conduct or harm referred to in any of clauses (A) to (C), or
>   (E) causes serious interference with or serious disruption of an essential service, facility or system, whether public or private, other than as a result of advocacy, protest, dissent or stoppage

of work that is not intended to result in the conduct or harm
referred to in any of clauses (A) to (C),

> and includes a conspiracy, attempt or threat to commit any such act or
> omission, or being an accessory after the fact or counselling in rela-
> tion to any such act or omission, but, for greater certainty, does not
> include an act or omission that is committed during an armed conflict
> and that, at the time and in the place of its commission, is in accor-
> dance with customary international law or conventional international
> law applicable to the conflict, or the activities undertaken by military
> forces of a state in the exercise of their official duties, to the extent
> that those activities are governed by other rules of international law.

The Supreme Court in R v Khawaja held that sections 83.01(b)(ii) A–D
all involved violence or threats of violence and as such did not prohibit activity protected under freedom of expression. The reference to
counselling, conspiracy, and being an accessory after the fact in the
above definition also constituted violence or threats of violence not
protected under section 2 of the Charter. The Court distinguished its
interpretative reluctance to combine inchoate forms of liability such
as its unwillingness to recognize an offence of attempted conspiracy[348]
from Parliament's ability to create complete crimes designed to prevent
terrorism. The Court recognized that section 83.01(b)(ii) E was more
problematic and might in future cases include expressive activity, in
which case the Court would have to consider whether the government
could justify its limitation under section 1. Nevertheless, the Court
indicated that, given the exemption for protests and strikes and the requirement that the disruption of essential services endanger life, even
subsection E when read as a whole and purposively "is confined to the
realm of acts of violence and threats of violence."[349]

4) The Requirement of Political or Religious Motive

In Khawaja, the Supreme Court reversed a trial judge who held that
the political or religious motive requirement in section 83.01(b)(i)(A)
was an unjustified violation of fundamental freedoms and should be
severed from the other parts of the definition of terrorist activities.
The Court held that any chill of expression was caused not by the motive clause, but "the post '9/11' climate of suspicion" or discriminatory

---

348 R v Déry, 2006 SCC 53, discussed in Chapter 4, Section B.
349 Khawaja, above note 345 at para 73.

enforcement.[350] The Court also indicated that any chill was based on an incomplete understanding of the definition of terrorist activity that did not include the exemption for the expression of political or religious beliefs under section 83.01(1.1) of the *Code*.[351]

CONCLUSION

This chapter has provided an overview of a few selected offences in order to illustrate how the general principles of criminal liability play out in some different contexts. With respect to homicide, the general principle of fault in relation to all elements of the *actus reus* is satisfied with respect to murder but not manslaughter. The Supreme Court has held as a principle of fundamental justice under section 7 of the *Charter* that murder requires proof of at least knowledge of the probability that the victim will die. This fault element is designed to reflect the stigma and mandatory life imprisonment that follows from a murder conviction. At the same time, the Court has held that objective foresight of bodily harm is a sufficient fault element for manslaughter and has rejected the idea that it is a principle of fundamental justice protected under section 7 of the *Charter* that the fault element must correspond with the prohibited act of causing death. In addition, the Court has held that the idea that the accused must take the risk that a victim may unexpectedly die as a matter of determining whether the accused caused death should also be reflected in the fault element of manslaughter. In recent years, however, the Court has articulated the causation requirement as requiring the accused's acts to be a significant cause of death. It is also now necessary for the Crown to demonstrate that the accused has engaged in a marked departure from standards of reasonable care with regard to negligence-based unlawful acts. It is necessary to demonstrate a marked and substantial departure for manslaughter by criminal negligence.

Although it is technically a sentencing classification, first-degree murder under section 231 of the *Criminal Code* has been influenced by principles of criminal liability. The courts have recognized that planning and deliberation under section 231(2) may be negated by lesser forms of intoxication or other mental disturbance than the *mens rea*

---

350 *Ibid* at paras 81 and 83.

351 *Ibid* at para 82. Note this exemption does not apply to a new offence in section 83.221 of knowingly advocating or promoting terrorism offences in general, added by SC 2015, c 20, s 16.

requirements of section 229. The courts have followed the traditional presumption of subjective fault by reading in a requirement that the accused must either know or be reckless that the victim was a police officer or other justice official under section 231(4) of the *Code*. The Supreme Court has interpreted section 231(5) to require stricter causation than in other homicide cases so that the Crown must establish that the accused was a substantial, and not only the significant, cause of the victim's death. Even here, though, it is not necessary to prove that the accused was the only cause of the victim's death.

The defence of provocation in section 232 is unique because it applies only when an accused is charged with murder. If there is a reasonable doubt that the accused was provoked, murder is reduced to manslaughter. As with self-defence, there are both subjective and objective arms of the provocation defence. The objective arm has, as in self-defence, been held to a modified objective standard based on a reasonable person of the same age, gender, and relevant experience as the accused. Courts have held that the accused's characteristics must be relevant to placing the provoking act in context but should not be individuated so as to undermine the purpose of the objective standard in promoting non-violent behaviour. Objective standards should also be informed by *Charter* values. In 2015, Parliament restricted the provocation defence by providing that the provoking act must also be an indictable offence such as an assault or sexual assault that is punishable by five years' imprisonment or more.

Sexual offences have been the subject of much legislative and judicial reform. The trend towards broad definition of the prohibited act can be seen in the replacement of rape with broader crimes of sexual assault and by the replacement of statutory rape with broader offences of sexual interference with children. In 1992, Parliament also provided objective definitions of consent and specific examples of situations that would not constitute valid consent to sexual activity. The Supreme Court has subsequently interpreted consent as a matter of *actus reus* to be based on the subjective views of the complainant regardless of whether they were communicated or reasonable. Parliament proposed in 2018 to codify Supreme Court rulings that an unconscious complainant cannot give prior consent; that the mistaken belief of consent be supported by evidence that the complainant's voluntary agreement "was affirmatively expressed by words or actively expressed by conduct";[352] and by making clear that the accused's belief in consent

---

352 Bill C-51, above note 214, proposed amendment of s 273.1(2.1).

cannot be based on factors that have been deemed in law not to constitute consent.

By applying basic principles of subjective fault, the courts historically reached the conclusion that the accused's honest belief that the complainant consented would raise a reasonable doubt about fault even if the belief was unreasonable in the circumstances. The courts were, however, hesitant about some of the logical implications of this conclusion and held in a number of cases that there was no air of reality that required the jury to be instructed about the mistake of fact defence. They also held that a mistaken belief in consent could not be based on either wilful blindness or self-induced intoxication. In 1992, Parliament modified the defence of honest but not necessarily reasonable mistaken belief in consent by providing that the accused must take reasonable steps in the circumstances known to him or her at the time to ascertain whether the complainant consented to the sexual activity in question. This approach blends subjective and objective fault requirements and has been held to be consistent with the *Charter*. Both the Court and Parliament has recognized that the legislative restrictions on what constitutes consent also have restricted the controversial mistake of fact defence by converting what once might have been the accused's mistakes about factual matters into mistakes of law that are precluded as a defence under section 19 of the *Code*.

Property offences remain an important part of the criminal law. For an offence that is less serious than homicide and sexual offences, theft has surprisingly high fault requirements that the accused act both fraudulently and without colour of right. The latter concept constitutes a partial exception to the principle that ignorance or mistake of law does not constitute an excuse because it allows the accused's honest but mistaken belief in his or her legal entitlement to the property to be a defence to a theft charge. Although some aspects of the *actus reus* or prohibited act of theft follow general trends towards broad definitions of the prohibited act, the idea that information has to be reduced to a tangible item to be capable of being stolen is a curiously narrow and, some would suggest, archaic view of the *actus reus*.

Fraud has a broad *actus reus* that includes an open-ended range of dishonest conduct that results in deprivation or risks to the financial interests of others. The Supreme Court has required subjective fault in relation to the commission of the broadly defined *actus reus* but not to the point of requiring that the accused subjectively recognize the dishonesty of his or her actions. This is consistent with the Court's reluctance to incorporate matters that can be described as motive in fault or *mens rea* requirements.

The new terrorism offences created after 9/11 demonstrate how Parliament can enact new crimes for what may otherwise be inchoate crimes or forms of participation in crimes and how it can expand criminal liability beyond those established forms of inchoate and party liability. The Court has upheld one of these offences in part by relying on their requirement of high fault levels and in part by restricting the interpretation of its broadly defined *actus reus.*

FURTHER READINGS

CRAIG, E. *Putting Trials on Trial: Sexual Assault and the Failure of the Legal Profession* (Montreal: McGill-Queens University Press, 2018).

FORCESE, C, & K ROACH. *False Security: The Radicalization of Canadian Anti-terrorism* (Toronto: Irwin Law, 2015).

HOLLAND, W. *The Law of Theft and Related Offences* (Toronto: Carswell, 1998).

MANNING, M, & P SANKOFF. *Criminal Law*, 5th ed (Markham, ON: LexisNexus, 2015) pt 4.

NIGHTINGALE, B. *The Law of Fraud and Related Offences* (Toronto: Carswell, 1996) (loose-leaf).

QUIGLEY, T. "Battered Women and the Defence of Provocation" (1991) 55 *Saskatchewan Law Review* 223.

———. "Deciphering the Defence of Provocation" (1989) 38 *University of New Brunswick Law Journal* 11.

RENKE, W. "Calm Like a Bomb: An Assessment of the Partial Defence of Provocation" (2010) 47 *Alberta Law Review* 729.

ROACH, K. "Terrorism" in M Dubber & T Hornle, eds. *The Oxford Handbook of Criminal Law* (Oxford: Oxford University Press, 2014).

SHAFFER, M. "Sex, Lies, and HIV: *Mabior* and the Concept of Sexual Fraud" (2013) 63 *University of Toronto Law Journal* 466.

STEWART, H. *Sexual Offences in Canadian Law* (Aurora, ON: Canada Law Book, 2004) (loose-leaf).

TROTTER, G. "Provocation, Anger and Intent for Murder" (2002) 47 *McGill Law Journal* 669.

VANDERVORT, L. "Sexual Assault: Availability of the Defence of Belief in Consent" (2005) 84 *Canadian Bar Review* 89.

WILSON, L. "Too Many Manslaughters" (2007) 52 *Criminal Law Quarterly* 433.

SENTENCING

The Supreme Court has recognized that "sentencing is, in respect of most offenders, the only significant decision the criminal justice system is called upon to make."[1] Sentencing in Canada has traditionally been a matter of judicial discretion because Parliament frequently defines offences broadly to cover behaviour of varying degrees of culpability and has generally set only high and infrequently used maximum penalties to limit the judge's sentencing discretion. In contrast, many American jurisdictions rely more on statutory gradations of crimes and minimum sentences attached to each degree of any particular crime. Such attempts to limit sentencing discretion may transfer discretion from the sentencing judge to the prosecutor, when he or she accepts a guilty plea to a particular charge. There is a recent trend in Canada towards the use of more mandatory sentences, though the Supreme Court has been increasingly willing to strike down such mandatory sentences on the basis that they can be grossly disproportionate in some cases and thus violate the right against cruel and unusual punishment under section 12 of the *Charter*.

Sentencing is a discretionary process because a judge can emphasize multiple purposes or justifications for punishment, and appellate courts have stressed the wide latitude given to sentencing judges not only with respects to facts but the emphasis that is placed on specific sentencing purposes. The basic purposes and principles of sentencing

---

1   *R v Gardiner* (1982), 68 CCC (2d) 477 at 514 (SCC) [*Gardiner*].

were first outlined in the *Criminal Code* in 1996. The fundamental principle of sentencing, as defined in section 718.1 of the *Code*, is that the sentence "must be proportionate to the gravity of the offence and the degree of responsibility of the offender." This is an important first principle, owing to the wide variety of conduct that may be caught by some crimes. For example, a person who planned and executed a robbery should receive a more severe sentence than a person who reluctantly assisted the robbery in some manner. The fundamental principle of proportionality also counters the danger that a judge might punish an offender more than the crime deserves because of concerns about deterrence and future danger. It directs the judge to look backwards at the seriousness of the crime and the offender's role in it as well as the offender's moral blameworthiness or responsibility.

Nevertheless, the *Criminal Code* recognizes other concerns as legitimate purposes in sentencing. Section 718 provides:

> The fundamental purpose of sentencing is to contribute, along with crime prevention initiatives, to respect for the law and the maintenance of a just, peaceful and safe society by imposing just sanctions that have one or more of the following objectives:
>
> (a) to denounce unlawful conduct and the harm done to victims or to the community that is caused by unlawful conduct;
>
> (b) to deter the offender and other persons from committing offences;
>
> (c) to separate offenders from society, where necessary;
>
> (d) to assist in rehabilitating offenders;
>
> (e) to provide reparations for harm done to victims or to the community; and
>
> (f) to promote a sense of responsibility in offenders, and acknowledgement of the harm done to victims and the community.

This provision allows courts to sentence in order to deter the offender or others from committing crimes in the future; to remove an offender from society where necessary to prevent future crimes; and to tailor the punishment to further the rehabilitation of the offender in the future or the ability of the offender to provide reparations for the harm done to victims and the community. Concerns about rehabilitation and reparation may also suggest the use of alternatives to imprisonment, such as probation, restitution, or fines.

Different purposes suggest different sentences. For example, a sentence of imprisonment might be thought necessary to deter the accused and others from committing a crime, but it may well not assist in rehabilitating the offender or providing reparation to the victims of crime. Much will depend on what sentencing purposes a judge believes are most important in any particular case and the Supreme Court has observed that "[n]o one sentencing objective trumps the others and it falls to the sentencing judge to determine which objective or objectives merit the greatest weight, given the particulars of the case."[2]

In addition to these multiple purposes, Parliament has also codified some other sentencing principles. The principle of parity in section 718.2(b) of the *Criminal Code* requires that a sentence "should be similar to sentences imposed on similar offenders for similar offences committed in similar circumstances." This is a broad principle of parity because it focuses not only on the crime committed, but also on the offender and his or her circumstances.

Offenders are often found guilty of two or more offences at one time and section 718.2(c) codifies the totality principle by instructing judges that where consecutive sentences are imposed, "the combined sentence should not be unduly long or harsh." Absent specific statutory direction to the contrary,[3] Canadian judges have the discretion to allow offenders to serve separate sentences on a concurrent basis, a matter that has led to controversy in some circles. Section 718.21 sets out specific factors that are to be taken into consideration in the sentencing of corporations and other organizations.

Sections 718.2(d) and (e) codify the principle of restraint in punishment by instructing judges not to deprive the offender of liberty "if less restrictive sanctions may be appropriate in the circumstances" and to consider "all available sanctions other than imprisonment that are reasonable in the circumstances and consistent with the harm done to victims or to the community should be considered for all offenders, with particular attention to the circumstances of aboriginal offenders." Canada has one of the highest rates of imprisonment of industrialized countries as well as gross overrepresentation of Indigenous people in prison.[4] These principles, as well as a broad array of

---

2   *R v Nasogaluak*, 2010 SCC 6, [2010] 1 SCR 206 at para 43 [*Nasogaluak*].
3   *Criminal Code*, RSC 1985, c C-46, s 718.3 [*Code*]. Even when sentences have to be served consecutively, the overall sentence should not be excessive: *R v Khawaja*, [2012] 3 SCR 555 at para 126.
4   The Supreme Court has observed that "although the United States has by far the highest rate of incarceration among industrialized democracies, at over 600 inmates per 100,000 population, Canada's rate of approximately 130 per 100,000 population places it second or third highest." *R v Gladue* (1999), 133 CCC (3d) 385 at 406 (SCC) [*Gladue*]. It also noted that in 1997, Aboriginal people constituted 12 percent of federal inmates but only 3 percent of the total population and that they constituted the majority of prisoners in provincial institutions in Manitoba and Saskatchewan. In 2015–16, Indigenous people including First Nations, Inuit, and Metis people represent 28 percent of admissions

community sanctions that may not result in actual imprisonment, encourage judges to use alternatives to imprisonment whenever appropriate. The conditional sentence of imprisonment, a sanction that allows an offender to serve a shorter imprisonment term in the community often under conditions of partial house arrest, was added to the *Criminal Code* in the 1996 sentencing reforms. It has been used frequently, but Parliament has increasingly placed restrictions on its use.

A. PROCEDURAL CONSIDERATIONS

1) Prosecutorial Discretion

The exercise of prosecutorial discretion in the form of selection of charges, Crown elections whether to prosecute by indictment or summary conviction, and decisions whether to offer evidence of prior convictions or aggravating factors and to make joint submissions with the accused on sentencing all have significant influences on sentencing. Prosecutorial influence on sentencing is especially powerful in the context of mandatory sentences.

The Court has distinguished between prosecutorial discretion, which can be reviewed only if it results in an abuse of process, and the exercise of sentencing discretion. In *R v Anderson*,[5] the Court rejected the idea that the prosecutor had a section 7 *Charter* duty to consider the proportionality of a possible sentence in a case where the exercise of a prosecutorial discretion would have required a judge to impose a mandatory minimum sentence of 120 days' imprisonment on an Indigenous offender for a repeat drinking and driving offence. At the same time, the Court indicated that evidence of Crown decisions "motivated by prejudice against Aboriginal persons" would meet the standard of abuse of process.[6] In *R v Nur*,[7] the Court held that the exercise of prosecutorial discretion could not save a mandatory sentence that could in a reasonably foreseeable case have grossly disproportionate effects. It rejected a dissenting opinion that had assumed that prosecutors would ensure that the sentence would not be applied in a grossly

---

to federal custody and 26 percent of admissions to provincial custody, but are only 4 percent of the population. Julie Reitano, *Adult Correctional Services in Canada 2015/2016* (Ottawa: Statistics Canada, 2017), online: www.statcan.gc.ca/pub/85-002-x/2017001/article/14700-eng.pdf.

5   2014 SCC 4 [*Anderson*].

6   *Ibid* at para 50.

7   2015 SCC 15 [*Nur*].

disproportionate manner or that courts could provide remedies for any abuse of prosecutorial discretion. The courts distinguish between sentencing and prosecutorial discretion despite the fact that the latter can affect the former.

2) The Guilty Plea

In most cases, the accused pleads guilty to an offence. A guilty plea by the accused means that there will be no formal determination of whether the Crown can prove the accused's guilt beyond a reasonable doubt, and the trial process will move directly to the sentencing stage. An early guilty plea is an important mitigating factor in sentencing, on the grounds that it indicates remorse and saves the victim and the state the costs of a trial.[8] Courts have held that an accused who is sentenced after a full trial is not deprived of his or her *Charter* rights by not having the advantage of a guilty plea considered in mitigation of sentence.[9] Sometimes a guilty plea is accompanied by a joint submission by the Crown and the accused concerning sentencing. This submission does not, however, bind the trial judge from exercising his or her sentencing discretion.[10]

Canadian courts have not required trial judges to determine whether there is a factual basis for a guilty plea. In the disturbing case of *Brosseau v R*,[11] the Supreme Court did not allow a young Indigenous accused to withdraw his plea to non-capital murder, even though the accused claimed that he did not understand the consequences of entering the guilty plea and spoke Cree. Chief Justice Cartwright indicated that a trial judge should usually make inquiries if there is a doubt as to whether the accused understands what he is doing, but concluded: "[I]t cannot be said that where, as in the case at bar, an accused is represented by counsel and tenders a plea of guilty to non-capital murder, the trial Judge before accepting it is bound, as a matter of law, to interrogate the accused."[12] In that case, the accused's lawyer had indicated to the judge after sentencing that he did not pretend to have any understanding of his client's intent, a matter quite relevant to whether the accused was guilty of murder.

In a subsequent case, the Supreme Court affirmed the *laissez-faire* approach of *Brosseau* over a strong dissent by Laskin CJ, who argued that judges should be required by law to ensure that the guilty plea "be

---

8   *R v Johnston*, [1970] 4 CCC 64 (Ont CA).

9   *R v M(CB)* (1992), 99 Nfld & PEIR 280 (PEICA).

10   *R v Rubenstein* (1987), 41 CCC (3d) 91 (Ont CA).

11   [1969] 3 CCC 129 (SCC).

12   *Ibid* at 138–39.

made voluntarily and upon a full understanding of the nature of the charge and its consequences and that it be unequivocal."[13] Chief Justice Laskin would also have required that in cases of doubt, the trial judge should ensure that there was a factual basis for the guilty plea.

The Laskin approach is more appropriate under the *Charter*, because a person who pleads guilty is waiving his or her rights under the *Charter* to a fair trial. Section 36 of the *Youth Criminal Justice Act* provides a model for reform: it requires the court to be satisfied that the facts support the charge. At present, section 606(1.1) of the *Code* requires only that the plea be made voluntarily by an accused who admits to the essential elements of the offence and who understands the nature and consequences of the plea including that the court is not bound by any agreement made between the accused and the prosecutor. A failure of the court to inquire into even these conditions does not affect the validity of the plea. There have been cases where innocent accused have pled guilty in order to receive a more favourable sentencing and courts have subsequently allowed them to introduce fresh evidence relating to their innocence.[14] There are proposals before Parliament to add the requirement of a factual basis for a charge to the requirements for taking a guilty plea.

Guilty pleas are sometimes accompanied by joint submissions by the accused and the prosecutor about the appropriate sentence, one that often reflects a sentencing discount for an early acceptance by the accused of responsibility for the offence. In *R v Anthony-Cook*,[15] the Supreme Court held that while sentencing judges can depart from joint submissions, they should only do so if "the proposed sentence would bring the administration of justice into disrepute or is otherwise contrary to the public interest." The Court concluded that trial judges should not reject joint submissions on a less stringent test focused on the fitness of

---

13   *Adgey v R* (1975), 13 CCC (2d) 177 at 183 (SCC).

14   *R v Marshall*, 2005 QCCA 852; *R v Hannemaayer*, 2008 ONCA 580 at para 18 where Rosenberg JA recognized that "the court cannot ignore the terrible dilemma facing the appellant. He has spent eight months in jail awaiting trial and was facing the prospect of a further six years in the penitentiary if he was convicted . . . . The justice system held out to the appellant a powerful inducement that by pleading guilty he would not receive a penitentiary sentence." See also *R v Sheratt Robinson*, 2009 ONCA 886; *R v CF*, 2010 ONCA 691; *R v CM*, 2010 ONCA 690; *R v Kumar*, 2011 ONCA 120; *R v Brant*, 2011 ONCA 362 (parents pled guilty to reduced homicide in the child's death in the face of forensic pathology evidence later shown to be unreliable). See also *R v Catcheway*, 2018 MBCA 54 (guilty plea overturned because Indigenous accused was in jail at the time of the offence to which he pled guilty).

15   2016 SCC 43 at para 32.

the sentence in order to maximize the benefits for accused, the victim, and the system of early guilty pleas that avoid the expense, delay, and trauma associated with criminal trials. In upholding a joint submission that eighteen months' imprisonment would be appropriate for manslaughter, the Court also stressed that the prosecutor and the accused will be more knowledgeable than the trial judge in deciding whether to accept a guilty plea on the strengths and weaknesses of the case.

3) The Sentencing Hearing

The sentencing hearing is less formal than the trial because of the greater range of information that is relevant when sentencing an offender. The accused does, however, retain procedural rights, such as the right to call evidence, cross-examine witnesses, and address the court. Judges may accept as proved any information disclosed at trial or at the sentencing hearing or any facts agreed by the prosecutor and the offender. If there is a dispute, the party wishing to rely on the disputed fact must establish it on a balance of probabilities. The prosecutor, however, must establish an aggravating factor or a previous conviction beyond a reasonable doubt.[16]

Sentencing judges have a discretion to require the production of evidence and compel the attendance of witnesses at sentencing hearings[17] and they are required to provide reasons for their sentence.[18] Sentencing judges are "bound by the express and implied factual implications" of the verdict. For example, they cannot consider a person's death to be an aggravating factor when the accused was charged with dangerous driving causing death but convicted only of dangerous driving. They can in some cases consider that the accused has since conviction been charged with new offences, but only for purposes related to sentencing for the offence of which the accused has been convicted.[19]

Victim impact statements and reports by probation officers may be introduced as evidence in the sentencing hearing. Recent amendments require judges to inquire whether victims have been informed of the availability of victim impact statements and allow victims to give their impact statements orally and with photographs of the victim.[20] Offenders may also speak before their sentence is imposed.[21] Judges in some

---

16   Code, above note 3, s 724; Gardiner, above note 1.
17   Code, above note 3, s 723.
18   Ibid, s 726.2.
19   R v Brown (1991), 66 CCC (3d) 1 at 5 (SCC); R v Angelillo, [2006] 2 SCR 728.
20   Code, above note 3, s 722. There can also be community impact statements under s 722.2.
21   Ibid, s 726.

cases have used sentencing circles, in which offenders, victims, and community and family members are allowed to speak informally as a means to enhance community participation and improve the quality of information when sentencing Indigenous offenders.[22]

The Supreme Court decided in a 5:4 decision that a presumption that young offenders should receive an adult sentence when convicted of murder, attempted murder, manslaughter, or aggravated sexual assault violates section 7 of the *Charter*. Justice Abella for the majority indicated that the principles that young offenders are presumed less morally culpable than adult offenders and that the state has to establish aggravating factors at sentencing beyond a reasonable doubt qualified as principles of fundamental justice.[23]

The Court has recognized that time spent in pre-trial custody has traditionally been credited against the remaining sentence on a 2:1 basis, both because of harsher conditions of confinement in pre-trial detention and because time spent in pre-detention would not generally count when determining eligibility for parole or earned remission. These factors justified courts crediting such time on a 1.5:1 ratio as allowed as the maximum under a 2009 *Truth in Sentencing Act* that added section 719(3.1) to the *Criminal Code*.[24] In 2016, the Court struck down that part of the provision which denied the 1.5:1 ratio credit for pre-trial custody to those denied bail because of their post convictions. The Court concluded that this restriction was overbroad to any legitimate interest in public safety.[25]

4) Sentencing Appeals

Unless the sentence has been fixed by law, both the accused and the Crown can appeal a sentence. The Court of Appeal has a broad jurisdiction to consider the fitness of the sentence and vary the sentence within the limits prescribed by law.[26] The Supreme Court has, however, consistently counselled deference to the decisions of sentencing judges and held that absent (1) an error in principle, (2) failure to consider a relevant factor, or (3) an overemphasis of the appropriate factor, a court of appeal should not normally intervene.[27]

---

22 *R v Moses* (1992), 71 CCC (3d) 347 (Y Terr Ct).

23 *R v DB*, 2008 SCC 25.

24 *R v Summers*, 2014 SCC 26.

25 *R v Safarzadeh-Markhali*, 2016 SCC 14 [*Safarzadeh-Markhali*].

26 *Code*, above note 3, s 687.

27 *R v M(CA)* (1996), 105 CCC (3d) 327 (SCC) [*M(CA)*]; *R v LM*, 2008 SCC 31 at para 14 [*LM*].

In *R v Lacasse*,[28] the Supreme Court again stressed deference to the sentencing judge and suggested that even an error in principle by the sentencing judge might not justify appellate intervention if the error did not render the sentence demonstrably unfit. It recognized the trial judge's sentence of six years and six months' imprisonment for two counts of impaired driving causing death was severe, but upheld the sentence because the sentencing judge was entitled to take into account the dangers of impaired driving in the particular community. It also held that the trial judge's departure from ordinary sentencing ranges was not a ground for reversing the sentence. Sentencing in Canada remains an individualized process that defers to the trial judge, and this can shelter sentences perceived to be either lenient or harsh from appellate review.

A departure from a starting point or sentencing range or category established by the court of appeal by itself is not a sufficient reason to overturn the sentence.[29] Sentencing appeals allow courts of appeal to develop legal principles to govern sentencing, but considerable deference is accorded the decision of the sentencing judge. In recent years, the Supreme Court has also been much more active in sentencing when hearing appeals that raise questions of law of national importance. This, along with the new sentencing provisions in the *Criminal Code*, may bring a greater degree of national uniformity to sentencing. Nevertheless, much will still depend on the discretion of trial judges. However, courts of appeal will only intervene if the sentence is demonstrably unfit and a marked and substantial departure from the sentences imposed for similar offenders committing similar crimes.

B. THE PRINCIPLES AND PURPOSES OF SENTENCING

In 1953 the Ontario Court of Appeal referred to "three principles of criminal justice requiring earnest consideration in the determination of punishment, *viz.*, deterrence, reformation and retribution."[30] The first two factors, deterrence and reformation, look to the future, while retribution looks to the past and the severity of the crime committed. Although the terms have changed, these remain the primary purposes

---

28   2015 SCC 64 at para 44 [*Lacasse*].

29   *Ibid; R v Shropshire* (1995), 102 CCC (3d) 193 (SCC); *R v M(TE)* (1997), 114 CCC (3d) 436 (SCC); *Lacasse*, above note 28 at paras 51 and 105.

30   *R v Willaert* (1953), 105 CCC 172 at 175 (Ont CA).

of sentencing, with some new concerns being introduced about reparation. The Supreme Court has recently explained:

> Far from being an exact science or an inflexible predetermined pro-
> cedure, sentencing is primarily a matter for the trial judge's compe-
> tence and expertise. The trial judge enjoys considerable discretion
> because of the individualized nature of the process.[31] To arrive at an
> appropriate sentence in light of the complexity of the factors related
> to the nature of the offence and the personal characteristics of the
> offender, the judge must weigh the normative principles set out by
> Parliament in the *Criminal Code*:
>
> - the objectives of denunciation, deterrence, separation of offenders
>   from society, rehabilitation of offenders, and acknowledgement of
>   and reparations for the harm they have done (*Criminal Code*, sec-
>   tion 718);
> - the fundamental principle that a sentence must be proportionate
>   to the gravity of the offence and the degree of responsibility of the
>   offender (*Criminal Code*, section 718.1); and
> - the principles that a sentence should be increased or reduced to ac-
>   count for aggravating or mitigating circumstances, that a sentence
>   should be similar to other sentences imposed in similar circum-
>   stances, that the least restrictive sanctions should be identified,
>   and that available sanctions other than imprisonment should be
>   considered (*Criminal Code*, section 718.2).[32]

One difficulty with the multiple purposes of sentencing is that much
depends on what purpose is stressed. For example, in some cases imprisonment might be thought necessary to achieve retribution for a past
wrong and perhaps to deter others from committing a crime in the future. At the same time, such a sentence may not be necessary and may
even be counterproductive in achieving the purposes of rehabilitation
or deterring the particular offender or allowing the offender to provide
reparation to the victim.

1) The Fundamental Principle of Proportionality

Parliament has raised one principle above the others by designating the
principle of proportionality as the fundamental principle of sentencing.
Section 718.1 provides that "a sentence must be proportionate to the

---

31 *Code*, above note 3, s 713.3; *R v Johnson*, [2003] 2 SCR 357 at para 22; *R v Proulx*,
    [2000] 1 SCR 61 at para 82 [*Proulx*].
32 *LM*, above note 27 at para 17.

gravity of the offence and the degree of responsibility of the offender."
This principle contemplates not only that punishment be proportionate
to the crime committed, but also to the responsibility or blameworthiness of the offender. This directs judges to pay attention to the offender's actual conduct. The person who reluctantly acted as a lookout for
a robbery does not require the same punishment as the person who
planned and executed the robbery, even though both may be convicted
of the offence of robbery.

Before the enactment of section 718.1, the Supreme Court stated:

> It is a well-established tenet of our criminal law that the quantum of
> sentence imposed should be broadly commensurate with the grav-
> ity of the offence committed and the moral blameworthiness of the
> offender . . . the principle of proportionality in punishment is fun-
> damentally connected to the general principle of criminal liability
> which holds that the criminal sanction may only be imposed on
> those actors who possess a morally culpable state of mind.[33]

This approach should guide the way courts approach the new fundamental principle of proportionality. Punishment should never exceed
that which is required to recognize the blameworthiness of the offender's crime and his or her conduct. Proportionality restrains and limits
punishment based on the offender's moral culpability and the need to
punish "the offender no more than is necessary." At the same time,
it also authorizes punishment through a "just deserts" philosophy of
sentencing, which seeks to ensure that offenders are held responsible
for their actions and that the sentence properly reflects and condemns
their role in the offence and the harm they caused and imposes "a form
of judicial and social censure."[34] The Court has recognized the dual
nature of proportionality as the fundamental purpose of sentence. On
the one hand, it "reflects the gravity of the offence" and as such is related to denunciation, "justice for victims and public confidence in the
justice system." On the other hand, it "ensures that a sentence does not

---

33 *M(CA)*, above note 27 at 348. The Court also quoted with approval Wilson J's
    statement in the *Reference re Motor Vehicle Act (British Columbia) S 94(2)* (1985),
    23 CCC (3d) 289 at 325 (SCC): "It is basic to any theory of punishment that the
    sentence imposed bear some relationship to the offence; it must be a 'fit' sen-
    tence proportionate to the seriousness of the offence. Only if this is so can the
    public be satisfied that the offender 'deserved' the punishment he received and
    feel a confidence in the fairness and rationality of the system." In that case, she
    held that a mandatory term of seven days of imprisonment was disproportion-
    ate to the absolute liability offence of driving with a suspended licence.

34 *Nasogaluak*, above note 2 at para 42.

exceed what is appropriate, given the moral blameworthiness of the offender" and, in this sense, "serves a limiting or restraining function and ensures justice for the offender."[35]

The Court has recently affirmed in R v Lacasse that determining a proportionate sentence is a "delicate task" and that "the more serious the crime and its consequences, or the greater the offender's degree of responsibility, the heavier the sentence will be. In other words, the severity of a sentence depends not only on the seriousness of the crime's consequences, but also on the moral blameworthiness of the offender."[36] It also stressed that proportionality is "determined both on an individual basis, that is, in relation to the accused him or herself and to the offence committed by the accused, and by comparison with sentences imposed for similar offences committed in similar circumstances. Individualization and parity of sentences must be reconciled for a sentence to be proportionate."[37]

Proportionality is a retributive concept that focuses on the offender's moral blameworthiness and seriousness of the crime as opposed to utilitarian concerns about the future effects of the punishment on the offender or others through deterrence or rehabilitation. Retribution is a legitimate concern in sentencing, but it should not be confused with revenge or vengeance, which produces an unrestrained and "uncalibrated act of harm upon another, frequently motivated by emotion and anger." In contrast, retribution is "an objective, reasoned and measured determination of an appropriate punishment which properly reflects the *moral culpability* of the offender." It restrains punishment to ensure "the imposition of a just and appropriate punishment, and *nothing more*."[38] Proportionality should restrain punishment by ensuring that offenders do not receive undeserved punishment for their own good or other social objectives. The existence of other sentencing purposes, some of which are utilitarian and forward-looking, however, suggests that retribution or "just deserts" restrains but does not determine punishment. The Supreme Court has indicated that the award of a maximum sentence under the law should be rare, but that it is not necessarily reserved for "the worst offender." Rather, it should be justified after consideration of all the multiple purposes of sentencing.[39]

Section 718.1 requiring that a sentence be proportionate to the offence and the offender's responsibility for the offence is a fundamental

---

35   R v Ipeelee, 2012 SCC 13 at para 37.

36   Lacasse, above note 28 at para 12.

37   Ibid at 53.

38   M(CA), above note 27 at 368–69 [emphasis in original].

39   R v Cheddesingh, [2004] 1 SCR 433 at 433; LM, above note 27.

and foundational principle of sentencing, but it does not have constitutional status as a principle of fundamental justice under section 7 of the *Charter*. Hence, section 718.1 could be changed or even repealed by Parliament subject to the constitutional requirement under section 12 of the *Charter* that no sentence should be grossly disproportionate.[40] As will be seen, a grossly disproportionate sentence will be unconstitutional and struck down as cruel and unusual punishment prohibited by section 12 of the *Charter*.

2) The Fundamental Purpose of Sentencing

Section 718 states that the "fundamental purpose of sentencing is to protect society and to contribute, along with crime prevention initiatives, to respect for the law and the maintenance of a just, peaceful and safe society by imposing just sanctions."[41] Courts often pass over this vague and inspirational purpose to focus on the enumerated objectives. Nevertheless, it should be given some meaning. It combines concerns about proportionality by its reference to just sanctions with concerns about the future through its concern for promoting a peaceful and safe society and protecting society. It also recognizes sentencing discretion through its recognition that appropriate and just sanctions may have one or more of the enumerated objectives. The Supreme Court has indicated that retribution alone does not determine punishment, and other legitimate purposes such as deterrence, rehabilitation, and the protection of society should be considered. The relative importance of these multiple factors will vary with the crime, the circumstances of the offender, and the needs of the community.[42]

3) Denouncing Unlawful Conduct

Like proportionality, denunciation is a retributive concept that focuses on the past. Unlike proportionality, however, the emphasis is on expressing society's disapproval of the crime committed as opposed to judging the culpability of the particular offender. The Supreme Court has stated:

---

40   *Safarzadeh-Markhali*, above note 25 at paras 71–73; *R v Lloyd*, 2016 SCC 13 at para 47 [*Lloyd*].

41   The reference to protecting society was added by *Victims Bill of Rights Act*, SC 2015, c 13, s 23.

42   *M(CA)*, above note 27 at 368–69.

The objective of denunciation mandates that a sentence should also communicate society's condemnation of that particular offender's conduct. In short, a sentence with a denunciatory element represents a symbolic, collective statement that the offender's conduct should be punished for encroaching on our society's basic code of values as enshrined within our substantive criminal law.[43]

A concern about denunciation, as well as deterrence, has motivated some courts to indicate that a custodial sentence should normally be imposed for domestic violence.[44] The Supreme Court has recently indicated that both denunciation and deterrence "are particularly relevant to offences [such as impaired driving] that might be committed by ordinarily law-abiding people."[45]

Another way of achieving the aim of denunciation is to enact a mandatory minimum sentence for a crime. For example, the mandatory sentence for murder is life imprisonment. Problems may arise, however, because such mandatory sentences apply to the most sympathetic and least blameworthy person that nevertheless has committed the crime with the required act and fault and without a valid defence. As discussed in Chapter 3, crimes are often defined quite broadly and capture both the actual perpetrator and those who may have assisted the perpetrator. As discussed in Chapter 5, a good motive is also no defence to a crime but may be relevant in determining punishment.

4) Deterring and Incapacitating Offenders

Section 718 draws a distinction between general deterrence, which is concerned with the effect of punishment in deterring others from committing similar offences, and specific deterrence, which is concerned with the effect of punishment in deterring the particular offender from committing subsequent crimes. The latter concern may also embrace concerns about the incapacitation or rehabilitation of the offender, if that is the only way to prevent him or her from committing future

---

43   *Ibid* at 369.

44   *R v Brown* (1992), 73 CCC (3d) 242 (Alta CA); *R v Inwood* (1989), 48 CCC (3d) 173 (Ont CA).

45   *Lacassse*, above note 28 at para 73. Note that Parliament has also provided that with respect to offences against children, justice system participants, and animals, courts should give primary consideration to the sentencing objectives of denunciation and deterrence. *Code*, above note 3, ss 718.01–718.03. In a different context, the Court has noted "it is permissible for Parliament to guide the courts to emphasize certain sentencing principles in certain circumstances without curtailing their discretion." *R v Boutilier*, 2017 SCC 64 at para 69 [*Boutilier*].

crimes. The effectiveness of any strategy designed to deter future conduct is commonly thought to depend on a combination of the certainty, speed, and severity of punishment. Courts at the sentencing stage focus on the severity of punishment, because they have little control over the certainty and speed of punishment.

a) General Deterrence

Courts have accepted that the deterrence of others is a legitimate objective of sentencing. In *R v Sweeney*,[46] Wood JA stated:

> The theory behind the general deterrence goal of sentencing is that the legal sanction imposed on actual offenders will discourage potential offenders. While there is little empirical evidence to support such a theory, common sense tells us that, to some extent, that must be so. Indeed, there can be little doubt that the very existence of a criminal justice system acts as a deterrent which prevents many people from engaging in criminal conduct.

Courts often consider general deterrence as a factor in crimes such as drunk driving, sexual assault, and domestic violence, where there is widespread concern about the prevalence of such crimes and a desire to change human behaviour. Section 718(b) recognizes the desire to deter both the offender and other persons from committing offences as a legitimate objective of the sentencing process. In addition, section 718.2 also indicates a concern with general deterrence by stating that hate crimes, spousal and child abuse, and crimes based on the abuse of a position of trust or authority should be punished more severely.

b) Specific Deterrence

"Specific deterrence" refers to the goal of preventing the offender from committing another criminal offence. This requires courts to consider the offender's history and other information that may help predict future dangerousness. One court has stated that if the concern is general deterrence, then judges should focus on "the gravity of the offence, the incidence of the crime in the community, the harm caused by it either to the individual or the community and the public attitude toward it," whereas if specific deterrence is the goal, "greater consideration must be given to the individual, his record and attitude, his motivation and his reformation and rehabilitation."[47] Concerns about specific deterrence can blur into concerns about rehabilitation when the best way to

---

46   (1992), 71 CCC (3d) 82 at 98 (BCCA).
47   *R v Morrissette* (1970), 1 CCC (2d) 307 at 310 (Sask CA).

ensure that an offender does not reoffend is to help get that person's life back on track. A more punitive approach to specific deterrence would advocate harsher punishments as a means to prevent future crimes. If it was relatively certain that an offender was bound to reoffend, incapacitation of the offender by imprisonment might be considered the only way to prevent the commission of an offence during that time. Section 718(c) recognizes this concern by naming the separation of offenders from society "where necessary" as a legitimate objective of sentencing. Separation or incapacitation may be necessary in the case of the most dangerous offenders, but it is an expensive strategy and one that does not necessarily protect fellow prisoners or guards from violence in prison.

Provisions in the *Criminal Code* providing for indeterminate detention of repeat dangerous offenders are largely concerned with the incapacitation of repeat violent offenders.[48] They have been upheld under the *Charter*, with the Supreme Court stressing that concerns about preventing future crimes "play a role in a very significant number of sentences . . . . Indeed, when society incarcerates a robber for, say, ten years, it is clear that its goal is both to punish the person and prevent the recurrence of such conduct during that period."[49] Justice La Forest also stated that it did not offend the principles of fundamental justice to punish people for preventive purposes, "which are not entirely reactive or based on a 'just deserts' rationale."[50] In subsequent years the dangerous offender provisions were toughened to remove a judicial discretion to impose a determinate sentence on a person found to be a dangerous offender[51] unless the judge is satisfied that there is a reasonable expectation that a lesser measure will adequately protect the public. The first parole hearing to determine if a dangerous offender should be released is also from three to seven years with subsequent hearings every two years after.[52] This new regime is significantly harsher than that upheld in *Lyons* or the regime for the detention of those found not criminally responsible by reason of mental disorder[53] but has been upheld under the *Charter*.[54] The new amendments also allowed

---

48 Part XXIV of the *Code*, above note 3.
49 *R v Lyons* (1987), 37 CCC (3d) 1 at 22 (SCC) [*Lyons*].
50 *Ibid.*
51 *Code*, above note 3, s 753.
52 *Ibid*, s 761.
53 See Chapter 8.
54 *Boutilier*, above note 45, holding no violation of ss 7 or 12 of the *Charter* in part because the amendments preserved some sentencing discretion and ability to consider all the purposes of sentencing.

long-term sexual offenders who present a substantial risk to reoffend to be sentenced to a minimum of two years and then supervised in the community for up to ten years after their release.[55]

5) Rehabilitating Offenders

Section 718(d) of the *Criminal Code* provides that one of the objectives of sentencing is "to assist in rehabilitating offenders." Sections 718.2(d) and (e) encourage courts not to deprive offenders of their liberty or to imprison them when less restrictive sanctions are appropriate and reasonable in the circumstances.

Although less popular than in the past, rehabilitation remains a valid consideration in sentencing, especially in cases where there is a prospect of not imprisoning the offender. In *R v Preston*,[56] the British Columbia Court of Appeal upheld a suspended sentence, with probation orders, for the possession of heroin on the basis that "the principle of deterrence should yield to any reasonable chance of rehabilitation which may show itself to the court imposing sentence." Justice of Appeal Wood stated:

> The notion that rehabilitation is a legitimate goal of the sentencing process is neither new nor experimental. Every Royal Commission, official report and extensive study done on sentencing in this country . . . has stressed the obvious, namely, that the ultimate protection of the public lies in the successful rehabilitation of those who transgress society's laws. Those same authorities have also unanimously concluded that rehabilitation is unlikely to occur while the offender is incarcerated.[57]

Given the fundamental principle of proportionality, a concern for rehabilitation should not be used to deprive the accused of greater liberty than is necessary to punish the offender. The traditional justification for restraint in punishment has been a concern about preserving as much of the offender's liberty as possible. In recent years, concerns about the costs of imprisonment and the disproportionate imprisonment of Indigenous people have also been raised.

---

55   *Code*, above note 3, s 753.1.
56   *R v Preston* (1990), 79 CR (3d) 61 (BCCA).
57   *Ibid* at 78.

6) Providing Reparations and Promoting a Sense of Responsibility

Section 718(e) provides that one of the purposes of sentencing is to provide reparations for harm done to victims or to the community. The idea that an offender should provide reparation for crime is quite ancient and was prevalent in both Indigenous societies and England before the monarchy asserted its power. Nevertheless, it is a relatively new concept in modern criminal law and, as will be discussed later in this chapter, there are limited means by which judges can require offenders to make reparation to victims. Judges may stress the idea of reparation to the community more than reparation to the victim, and this may be used to support retributive and denunciatory sanctions.

Section 718(f) provides that another purpose of sentencing is "to promote a sense of responsibility in offenders, and acknowledgement of the harm done to victims and to the community." This provision could also be used to support punitive measures, but it can be better advanced by sentences designed to achieve restorative justice among offenders, victims, and the community. The Supreme Court in R v Gladue noted that sections 718(e) and (f) introduce new concerns to sentencing that, along with rehabilitation and the need to examine alternatives to incarceration, promote restorative justice. "Restorative sentencing goals do not usually correlate with the use of prison as a sanction," but generally involve "some form of restitution and re-integration into the community."[58] Justices Cory and Iacobucci have explained:

> In general terms, restorative justice may be described as an approach
> to remedying crime in which it is understood that all things are inter-
> related and that crime disrupts the harmony which existed prior to
> its occurrence, or at least which it is felt should exist. The appropri-
> ateness of a particular sanction is largely determined by the needs of
> the victims, and the community, as well as the offender.[59]

In the subsequent case of R v Proulx, the Supreme Court affirmed that the 1996 sentencing reforms including sections 718(e) and (f) were designed to reduce reliance on incarceration and advance the restorative principles of sentencing. Chief Justice Lamer explained:

> Restorative justice is concerned with the restoration of the parties that
> are affected by the commission of an offence. Crime generally affects
> at least three parties: the victim, the community, and the offender.

---

58   *Gladue*, above note 4 at 403.
59   *Ibid* at 414.

> A restorative approach seeks to remedy the adverse effects of crime in a manner that addresses the needs of all parties involved. This is accomplished, in part, through the rehabilitation of the offender, reparations to the victim and to the community, and promotion of a sense of responsibility in the offender and acknowledgment of the harm done to victims and the community.[60]

The Supreme Court has indicated that restorative sentencing purposes should be considered for all offenders, but especially for Indigenous offenders because of their overincarceration and the primary emphasis upon the ideals of restorative justice in Indigenous traditions.

7) Sentencing Indigenous Offenders

Section 718.2(e) instructs judges to consider "all available sanctions other than imprisonment that are reasonable in the circumstances and consistent with the harm done to victims or to the community" for all offenders but "with particular attention to the circumstances of Aboriginal offenders." The Supreme Court has held that this provision is designed to remedy the overincarceration of Indigenous people and requires judges to pay attention to the unique circumstances of Indigenous offenders, including systemic discrimination that may explain why the offender has been brought to court. It also requires courts to consider the availability of restorative and other approaches that may be appropriate because of the offender's Indigenous heritage or connection. The Court stated that "the more violent and serious the offence,"[61] the more likely it will be that Indigenous offenders will receive the same sentence as non-Indigenous offenders. In the actual case, the Court did not allow the accused's appeal from a three-year sentence of imprisonment for manslaughter in part because the accused had been granted day parole after six months on conditions that she reside with her father, comply with electronic monitoring, and take alcohol and substance abuse counselling. In a subsequent case, the Court upheld a sentence of imprisonment of an Indigenous offender convicted of sexual assault.[62]

In *R v Ipeelee*,[63] the Supreme Court expressed concerns about the growing percentage of Indigenous offenders in jail in the course of holding that trial judges had erred by sentencing two long-term violent

---

60 *Proulx*, above note 31 at para 18.
61 *Gladue*, above note 4 at 417.
62 *R v Wells* (2000), 141 CCC (3d) 368 (SCC).
63 2012 SCC 13.

offenders to three-year imprisonments for breaching non-intoxicant provisions in their long-term offender designation. The Supreme Court reaffirmed that courts must take judicial notice of systemic and background factors affecting Indigenous people to explain why the Indigenous offender is before the court and what sentencing objectives and procedures should be used. The Court stressed that section 718.2(e) imposes mandatory duties on all trial judges and that it continues to apply in cases that are serious and violent. In the result, the Court held that one-year sentences of imprisonment would be appropriate and not the three years ordered by the trial judges.

As discussed earlier, the sentence imposed on an offender may be influenced by the exercise of prosecutorial discretion, including the choice of charge and whether the prosecutor tenders evidence of prior convictions. In *R v Anderson*, the prosecutor served notice that an Indigenous offender convicted of drinking and driving offences had prior offences, and this would trigger a mandatory sentence of imprisonment if the offender was convicted. The Supreme Court held that neither section 718.2(e) of the *Criminal Code* nor the principles of fundamental justice under section 7 of the *Charter* required that the prosecutor consider the background circumstances and sentencing options available to an Indigenous accused. This was a duty reserved to the trial judge.[64]

C. AGGRAVATING AND MITIGATING FACTORS IN SENTENCING

Courts consider a wide range of aggravating and mitigating factors in connection with the particular crime and the offender. They often consider the offender's degree of participation in a crime. This consideration is important because criminal offences are often defined to catch a broad range of conduct and people can be convicted of a crime as parties even though they did not actually commit the crime. Courts also consider planning and deliberation, breach of trust, use of violence and weapons, and harm to victims as aggravating factors. Section 718.2 directs the court to consider aggravating factors such as whether the crime "was motivated by bias, prejudice or hate" on group characteristics, involved spousal or child abuse, or involved an abuse of a position of trust or authority. The *Criminal Code* leans towards identifying aggravating as opposed to mitigating factors at sentencing though trial judges are

---

64 *Anderson*, above note 5 at para 25.

free to recognize mitigating factors and also to assign the weight they determine is appropriate to both aggravating and mitigating factors.[65]

Prior convictions are usually considered an aggravating factor, while the accused's good character, youth, old age, ill health, remorse, and early guilty plea will generally be considered mitigating factors. Even though it also operates as a partial defence that reduces murder to manslaughter, provocation can be considered a mitigating factor in sentencing for manslaughter[66] and presumably other crimes. The use of alcohol and drugs can either be a mitigating factor or an aggravating factor, depending on the circumstances and the purposes of punishment that are stressed. The same can be said of the accused's social status, which may be related to either prospects for rehabilitation and future danger or to the goals of general deterrence and denunciation. Courts also consider time served in custody, and the combined effect of consecutive sentences.

Charter breaches and other abuses of state power may be mitigating factors at sentencing subject to other sentencing rules and statutory minimums and "provided that the impugned conduct relates to the individual offender and the circumstances of his or her offence." The Supreme Court has justified this approach in part through reference to section 718, which provides that "the fundamental purpose of sentencing is to contribute . . . to respect for the law and the maintenance of a just, peaceful and safe society." It upheld the entry of a conditional discharge to guilty pleas to impaired driving and flight from the police, in part because of excessive force by the police in the arrest that broke the accused's ribs and punctured his lung.[67]

Judges also have discretion to consider a wide range of factors in sentencing, including collateral consequences "arising from the commission of an offence, the conviction of an offence, or the sentence imposed for an offence, that impacts the offence."[68]

The Court concluded in *R v Pham*:

> The general rule continues to be that a sentence must be fit having regard to the particular crime and the particular offender. In other words, a sentencing judge may exercise his or her discretion to take collateral immigration consequences into account, provided that the

---

65   *Lacasse,* above note 28 at para 78.
66   *R v Stone* (1999), 134 CCC (3d) 353 (SCC).
67   *Nasogaluak,* above note 2 at para 49.
68   *R v Suter,* 2018 SCC 34 at para 47.

sentence that is ultimately imposed is proportionate to the gravity of the offence and the degree of responsibility of the offender.[69]

This approach recognizes the importance of individualizing sentences while respecting the fundamental principle of proportionality.

D. CONSTITUTIONAL CONSIDERATIONS

Punishment is restricted by section 12 of the *Charter*, which prohibits cruel and unusual treatment or punishment.[70] In *R v Smith*,[71] the Supreme Court held that a mandatory minimum sentence of seven years for importing narcotics violated section 12 and could not be justified under section 1 of the *Charter* because it could in some cases result in punishment that was grossly disproportionate to both the offence and the offender. Justice Lamer noted that the offence covered a wide variety of behaviour, so that it could hypothetically catch a person importing one joint of marijuana. He also noted that it could be applied to a range of offenders, including a young person with no prior convictions. He stated that, in determining whether a sentence was "grossly disproportionate,"

> the court must first consider the gravity of the offence, the personal characteristics of the offender and the particular circumstances of the case in order to determine what range of sentences would have been appropriate to punish, rehabilitate or deter this particular offender or to protect the public from this particular offender.[72]

Punishment that is disproportionate for the particular offender, but which may be necessary to deter others, must be justified under section 1 of the *Charter*. The Court has subsequently indicated that sentences can only be invalidated under section 12 of the *Charter* on the basis that they are grossly disproportionate and it has distinguished this exclusive constitutional standard from the statutory principle of proportionality found in section 718.1 of the *Charter*.[73]

The Supreme Court has upheld a minimum sentence of seven days' imprisonment for driving with a suspended licence on the basis that the Court should only consider how a sentence would affect reasonable and not remote or extreme examples of hypothetical offenders

---

69   *R v Pham*, [2013] 1 SCR 739 at para 14.
70   See Chapter 2, Section B(5).
71   (1987), 34 CCC (3d) 97 (SCC) [*Smith*].
72   *Ibid* at 139.
73   *Safarzadeh-Markhali*, above note 25 at para 71.

who could be affected by the sentence.[74] As discussed in Chapter 5, the Court has held that if any defence by the accused would be precluded as a mistake of law, then the offence of driving with a suspended licence would be classified as an absolute liability, thus triggering the separate rule under section 7 of the *Charter* that prohibits punishing an absolute liability offence with imprisonment.[75]

The Supreme Court has held that life imprisonment for first-degree murder, without eligibility of parole for twenty-five years, does not violate section 12 of the *Charter* because of the seriousness of the crime committed and the possibility that after fifteen years a jury will allow the accused to be considered for early parole, royal mercy, and absences from custody for humanitarian and rehabilitative purposes.[76] Since that time, the availability of controversial faint hope hearings has been eliminated. The Supreme Court in *R v Latimer* also upheld the mandatory sentence of life imprisonment with ten years' ineligibility for parole for the offence of second-degree murder. It stressed the seriousness of the crime and the constitutional requirements of subjective *mens rea*. The Court rejected arguments that the accused's altruistic motives in killing his daughter to prevent her suffering from a needed operation was relevant to the proportionality of the punishment.[77] The problem with mandatory sentences is that by definition they will apply to the most sympathetic and least blameworthy person who nevertheless committed the criminal act with the required fault.

The Supreme Court has considered a range of mandatory sentences attached to various firearms offences. In *R v Morrisey*, it upheld a mandatory minimum sentence of four years' imprisonment for the crime of criminal negligence causing death when a firearm is used. The Court deferred to Parliament's attempts to deter the use of firearms during the commission of crimes.[78] The Court subsequently held that the four-year mandatory minimum sentence for manslaughter with a firearm was not cruel and unusual when applied to a police officer who shot a person in his custody. The Court also ruled that constitutional exemptions were not an appropriate remedy with respect to mandatory sentences because they would be inconsistent with Parliament's attempt to limit a judge's sentencing discretion and send a clear deterrent message

---

74 *R v Goltz* (1991), 67 CCC (3d) 481 (SCC). See also *R v Brown* (1994), 93 CCC (3d) 97 (SCC), upholding a then-minimum one-year sentence for using a gun in a robbery.

75 *R v Pontes*, [1995] 3 SCR 44, discussed in Chapter 5.

76 *R v Luxton* (1990), 58 CCC (3d) 449 (SCC).

77 *R v Latimer* (2001), 150 CCC (3d) 129 (SCC).

78 *R v Morrisey* (2000), 148 CCC (3d) 1 (SCC).

to offenders. The Court was also concerned that case-by-case constitutional exemptions would undermine the certainty, clarity, and predictability of the law by creating a gap between the mandatory sentence on the books and the actual sentences below that minimum that were ordered as a constitutional exemption.[79]

The Supreme Court of Canada has held that mandatory firearm prohibitions upon the conviction of offences do not constitute grossly disproportionate cruel and unusual treatment in light of a statutory provision that allows exemptions for employment and sustenance reasons.[80] In light of the Court's decision that judges cannot order constitutional exemptions from mandatory sentences, the presence or absence of such statutory exemptions will often be determinative. If a judge determines that a mandatory sentence will be grossly disproportionate and cruel and unusual either in a particular case or on the basis of a reasonable hypothetical case, the judge now has no alternative but to strike down the mandatory sentence as it applies to all offenders.

In 2015, the Court in *R v Nur* struck down mandatory minimum sentences for the first time since the *Smith* case in 1987. The majority held that both a mandatory minimum three-year sentence for a first offence and a mandatory minimum five-year sentence for a second offence of possession of a prohibited or restricted firearm with access to ammunition were cruel and unusual punishment. Although these minimum sentences would be appropriate for many offenders, including the accused in these cases, they would have cruel and unusual effects when applied to reasonably foreseeable offenders. In determining the latter, the Court indicated that personal characteristics of offenders and decided cases were relevant, but the ultimate issue was whether reasonably foreseeable applications of the sentence would be grossly disproportionate.[81] The Court's continued application of reasonable hypotheticals has the virtue of recognizing that mandatory sentences, even if not applied in the case at hand, can still affect plea resolutions. The Court in *Nur* distinguished *Morrisey* on the basis that the offences in *Nur* could apply in the absence of harm and without offenders knowing they were breaking the law.[82] It also rejected an argument accepted in dissent that the use of prosecutorial discretion could be relied upon to preclude grossly disproportionate applications of the mandatory

79   *R v Ferguson*, 2008 SCC 6.

80   *R v Wiles*, [2005] 3 SCR 895 at para 10. See s 113 of the *Code*, above note 3.

81   *Nur*, above note 7 at paras 73–76.

82   See *R v Macdonald*, [2014] 1 SCR 37, discussed in Chapter 3, Section A(4), holding that *mens rea* for the offence should not be interpreted to undermine the ignorance of the law is no excuse dictate in s 19 of the *Code*.

sentence, in part because the abuse of discretion standard to review a prosecutor's decision is "a notoriously high bar."[83] The Court held that the government had not justified the violation under section 1 on the basis that Parliament could have applied the mandatory sentences to a less sweepingly defined offence.

A year later, the Court held in *Lloyd*[84] that a mandatory minimum sentence of one year's imprisonment for a second drug trafficking offence violated section 12 because it could be applied to a reasonable hypothetical offender who for a second time shared (but did not sell) prohibited drugs with a friend even though the accused conceded that such a sentence would not be grossly disproportionate as applied to him. Three judges dissented, questioning whether such sharing would constitute trafficking and concluding in any event that the mandatory minimum penalty would not be grossly disproportionate for a second conviction. The Court held that the violation of section 12 could not be justified under section 1 and that Parliament could achieve its objectives of deterring drug trafficking more proportionately. More proportionate approaches that could protect mandatory sentences from invalidation under section 12 of the *Charter* would include allowing judges to justify departures from them in exceptional cases[85] or defining offences very narrowly so that they could not capture a wide variety of conduct.[86]

Legislation providing for the indeterminate detention of repeat violent offenders has been held not to violate the *Charter* because of its relation to society's legitimate interest in punishing, rehabilitating, deterring, and incapacitating repeat violent offenders.[87] At the same time, the Supreme Court stressed that regular reviews are necessary to ensure that continued detention was not disproportionate to the legitimate aims of punishment. The Court subsequently authorized, by the writ of *habeas corpus*, the release of an offender who served thirty-seven years for sexual offences and who, in its view, no longer presented a danger to society.[88] It subsequently upheld presumptive indeterminate

---

83   *Nur*, above note 7 at para 94.

84   Above note 40.

85   As recommended by the Truth and Reconciliation Commission, *Canadian Residential Schools: The Legacy*, vol 5 (Montreal: McGill-Queen's University Press, 2015) at 242.

86   For arguments that exemptions are necessary because reasonably hypothetical offenders will often be found to illustrate how mandatory sentences could have grossly disproportionate effects, see Kent Roach, "Reforming and Resisting the Criminal Law: Criminal Justice and the Tragically Hip" (2017) 40(3) *Manitoba Law Journal* 1.

87   *Lyons*, above note 49.

88   *Steele v Mountain Institution* (1990), 60 CCC (3d) 1 (SCC).

sentences for those designated as dangerous offenders, but only after stressing that judges can impose less drastic options and should consider all the purposes and principles of sentencing.[89]

E. SENTENCES OTHER THAN IMPRISONMENT

1) Alternative Measures

Alternative measures allow an accused who accepts responsibility for a crime to engage in supervised activities in the community, without a formal determination of guilt or innocence at trial. They are contemplated under section 10 of the *Youth Criminal Justice Act* and under section 717 of the *Criminal Code*. There must be sufficient evidence to proceed with the charge; the accused must accept responsibility for the offence charged and voluntarily agree to the alternative measures. There are a great variety of alternative measures. Some may focus on various forms of community service and/or education for the offender while others may be based on restorative justice.

2) Absolute and Conditional Discharges

When the accused is charged with an offence not subject to imprisonment for fourteen years or life and without a minimum sentence, the court can, instead of convicting the accused, order an absolute or conditional discharge if "it considers it to be in the best interest of the accused and not contrary to the public interest."[90] The best interests of the accused include the accused's good character and the harm that can follow from a conviction. The public interest includes society's interest in the general deterrence of the offence. Absolute or conditional discharges do not apply only to trivial or technical violations of the *Code*, but they should not routinely be applied to any particular offence.[91] If the conditions of a conditional discharge are breached, the offender may be sentenced for the original offence as well as for the crime of breaching the probation order.

---

89   *Boutilier*, above note 45 at paras 53–63.
90   *Code*, above note 3, s 730.
91   *R v Fallofield* (1973), 13 CCC (2d) 450 (BCCA).

3) Suspended Sentences and Probation

After convicting an accused, the court can suspend sentence and make a probation order, or make a probation order in addition to a fine or sentence of imprisonment of not more than two years. Probation orders can be made even though the accused's sentence would normally have been more than two years in the absence of consideration of time that the accused spent in pre-trial custody.[92] Probation orders may also be entered after absolute or conditional discharges.

Courts make probation orders "having regard to the age and character of the offender, the nature of the offence and the circumstances surrounding its commission."[93] Compulsory conditions of a probation order are that the offender keep the peace and be of good behaviour, appear before the court when required, and notify the court or probation officer of changes of address or employment. Optional conditions are regular reports to the probation officer, abstaining from the consumption of alcohol or other drugs, abstaining from possessing a gun, supporting dependants, performing up to 240 hours of community service, and complying with other reasonable conditions designed to protect society and facilitate the offender's successful reintegration into the community.[94] It is an offence not to comply with a probation order without a reasonable excuse.[95] Corporations and other organizations can now be placed on probation under section 732.1 of the *Code*.

4) Conditional Sentences of Imprisonment

If the court imposes a sentence of imprisonment of less than two years, it may, under section 742.1, order that the sentence be served in the community if the court is satisfied that this would not endanger the safety of the community and would be consistent with the fundamental purpose and principles of sentencing set out in sections 718 to 718.2. In *R v Proulx*,[96] the Supreme Court indicated that only offences with a mandatory minimum sentence of imprisonment are categorically excluded from conditional sentences, but section 742.1 of the *Code* now categorically excludes a long list of offences, often depending on whether the prosecutor selects to prosecute the offence by indictment.

---

92 *R v Mathieu*, 2008 SCC 21 [*Mathieu*].
93 *Code*, above note 3, s 731.
94 *Ibid*, s 732.1.
95 *Ibid*, s 733.1.
96 *Proulx*, above note 31.

The Supreme Court restricted the availability of conditional sentences in *R v Fice*[97] when it held that in determining whether a conditional sentence is excluded because the offender faces a penitentiary sentence of two years' imprisonment or more, the trial judge should include time spent in pre-trial custody. In other words, pre-trial detention should be considered part of the offender's punishment for determining whether the threshold for a conditional sentence is satisfied even though pre-trial detention may ordinarily be used to reduce the final sentence. This approach restricts the availability of conditional sentences in a manner that is not done with respect to probation orders. As discussed above, probation orders can be made even if the accused's sentence was only reduced below two years' imprisonment because of time the accused spent in pre-trial custody.[98]

A conditional sentence should be a more punitive sentence than a probation order and will generally include punitive conditions such as house arrest. In addition, a conditional sentence can be longer than an actual term of imprisonment. The judge must determine that the particular offender will not present a danger to the community, but the conditions imposed on the offender will be considered in determining the risk of reoffending and the gravity of the damage caused by reoffending.[99] A conditional sentence can fulfill both the restorative and punitive purposes of sentencing, but imprisonment may be required for offences where the objectives of denunciation and deterrence are particularly important. Breaches of the conditions only have to be proven on a balance of probabilities and can result in the offender serving the duration of the conditional sentence in prison or having the conditions changed.[100]

5) Fines

Fines are commonly used in addition to, or as an alternative to, imprisonment. There are no limits to the amount fined except in respect of indictable offences, which are limited for summary conviction offences to $5,000 for individuals[101] or $100,000 for organizations.[102] If fines are not paid, an offender may be imprisoned or exposed to collateral civil consequences such as non-issuance of a licence or civil enforcement. In the past, significant numbers of those serving short imprisonment

---

97 [2005] 1 SCR 742.
98 *Mathieu*, above note 92.
99 *R v Knoblauch* (2000), 149 CCC (3d) 1 (SCC).
100 *Code*, above note 3, s 742.6.
101 *Ibid*, s 787.
102 *Ibid*, s 735(1)(b).

terms were serving time because of a failure to pay their fines. Provinces may provide fine option programs to allow an offender who cannot pay a fine to work off the fine. Section 734(2) of the *Criminal Code* now provides that a court should order fines only when satisfied that an offender will be able to pay the fine or to work off the fine in a fine option program. In *R v Topp*,[103] the Supreme Court stressed that as a practical matter a party seeking a fine must satisfy the court on a balance of probabilities that the offender has the ability to pay and there must be an affirmative finding to this effect.

Imprisonment for failure to pay parking tickets has been held to be cruel and unusual punishment contrary to section 12 of the *Charter*.[104] As discussed in Chapter 6, a person convicted of an absolute liability offence cannot constitutionally be imprisoned.[105] A more drastic sentence, such as a conditional sentence, should not be used because the offender is unable to pay a fine.[106] Although a judge has no discretion to take the ability to pay principle into account when ordering a fine as an alternative to the forfeiture of the proceeds of crime, such a principle will be considered when determining the time that is required to pay the fine and whether imprisonment for failure to pay the fine is warranted.[107]

There are victim fine surcharges on fines, and these have been made mandatory. They constitute 30 percent of the fine or a minimum of $100 for a summary conviction offence and $200 for an indictable offence.[108] These mandatory provisions have been challenged as cruel and unusual punishment in a number of cases, and their constitutionality will soon be determined by the Supreme Court.

6) Restitution

Section 737.1 requires sentencing judges to consider making restitution orders. Section 738 of the *Criminal Code* allows judges to order restitution for property damage, pecuniary damage arising from offences involving bodily harm, and reasonable and readily ascertainable expenses when a spouse and children move from an offender's household in cases involving bodily harm or the threat of bodily harm to the spouse or child as well as readily expenses relating to identity theft or unlawful distribution of intimate images.

---

103 2011 SCC 43 at paras 20–22.
104 *R v Joe* (1993), 87 CCC (3d) 234 (Man CA).
105 See Chapter 6, Section A(2).
106 *R v Wu* (2003), 180 CCC (3d) 97 (SCC).
107 *R v Lavigne*, [2006] 1 SCR 392.
108 *Code*, above note 3, s 737.

The Supreme Court has cautioned that the restitution provisions should not be used as a substitute for the civil process.[109] Nevertheless, "in appropriate cases, compensation orders provide an extremely useful and effective tool in the sentencing procedure" that can help rehabilitate the accused, provide benefits for victims in a "speedy and inexpensive manner," and benefits for society by reducing the use of imprisonment. They can also provide "for the reintegration of the convicted person as a useful and responsible member of the community at the earliest possible date. The practical efficacy and immediacy of the order will help to preserve the confidence of the community in the legal system."[110]

Restitution orders are generally enforced as civil judgments. This can make them difficult to enforce. Restitution can be better ensured by requiring it as a condition of probation or a conditional sentence. Provinces, however, have the option under section 738(2) of enacting regulations to preclude judges from imposing restitution as a condition of probation or a conditional sentence. Although reparation to victims is now recognized as a purpose of sentencing, judges have limited instruments with which to pursue this purpose.

7) Forfeiture

There are various provisions that allow for the forfeiture of property that is the proceeds of crime or was offence-related property. In certain drug and criminal organization cases, forfeiture can be ordered of any property of the offender. The state is generally only required to establish on a balance of probabilities that the property is related to crime[111] and in some cases, the accused has to establish on a balance of probabilities that it was not so obtained.[112]

CONCLUSION

Sentencing is the most important and visible aspect of the criminal law. The 1996 amendments to the *Criminal Code* have created a statutory framework for the exercise of sentencing discretion, but much discretion remains. The fundamental principle is that the sentence must be proportionate to the gravity of the offence and the offender's degree

---

109 *R v Zelensky*, [1978] 2 SCR 940.
110 *R v Fitzgibbon*, [1990] 1 SCR 1005 at 1013.
111 *Code*, above note 3, ss 462.37(1) and 490.1.
112 *Ibid*, s 463.37 (2.03).

of responsibility. The offender's crime and responsibility, however, do not determine punishment, and judges are instructed to be concerned about a wide range of other factors including specific and general deterrence, rehabilitation, reparation, and promoting a sense of responsibility. The last three purposes, combined with other instructions to consider alternatives to imprisonment, suggest that restorative justice is a legitimate and important approach to sentencing, especially, but not exclusively, with respect to Indigenous offenders. There are a wide variety of alternatives to actual imprisonment including pre-trial diversion, probation, restitution, and conditional sentences that allow offenders to be punished and held accountable while remaining in the community.

Courts will strike down grossly disproportionate sentences as cruel and unusual punishment, but they have upheld mandatory minimum sentences that by definition apply to the most sympathetic offenders and least blameworthy crimes that are caught under often broad definitions of crime. Parliament has also moved in a more punitive direction by enacting more mandatory minimum sentences, restricting credit for "dead time" served in pre-trial custody, deeming deterrence and denunciation to be the paramount consideration in sentencing for some offences, and placing more restrictions on the use of conditional sentences of imprisonment.

FURTHER READINGS

ARCHIBALD, B, & J LLEWELLYN. "The Challenges of Institutionalizing Restorative Justice" (2006) 29 *Dalhousie Law Journal* 297.

BROCKMAN, J. "An Offer You Can't Refuse: Pleading Guilty When Innocent" (2010) 56 *Criminal Law Quarterly* 116.

CANADIAN SENTENCING COMMISSION. *Sentencing Reform: A Canadian Approach* (Ottawa: Queen's Printer, 1987).

CARLING, A. "A Way to Reduce Indigenous Over-representation: Reduce False Guilty Plea Wrongful Convictions" (2017) 64 *Criminal Law Quarterly* 415.

CAYLEY, D. *The Expanding Prison* (Toronto: Anansi, 1998).

COLE, D, & J ROBERTS. *Making Sense of Sentencing* (Toronto: University of Toronto Press, 1999).

FITZGERALD, O. *The Guilty Plea and Summary Justice* (Toronto: Carswell, 1990).

HEALY, P, & H DUMONT. *Dawn or Dusk in Sentencing* (Montreal: Thémis, 1998).

IRELAND, D. "Bargaining for Expedience: The Overuse of Joint Recommendations for Sentence" (2015) 38 *Manitoba Law Journal* 273.

KERR, L. "Sentencing Ashley Smith: How Prison Conditions Relate to the Aims of Punishment" (2017) 32 *Canadian Journal of Law and Society* 187.

MANSON, A. *The Law of Sentencing* (Toronto: Irwin Law, 2001).

ROACH, K. "Changing Punishment at the Turn of the Century: Restorative Justice on the Rise" (2000) 42 *Canadian Journal of Criminology and Criminal Justice* 249.

———. "Searching for *Smith*: The Constitutionality of Mandatory Minimum Sentences" (2001) 39 *Osgoode Hall Law Journal* 367.

ROBERTS, J, & A VON HIRSCH. "Sentencing Reform in Canada: Recent Developments" (1992) 23 *Revue générale de droit* 319.

———. "Statutory Sentencing Reform: The Purpose and Principles of Sentencing" (1995) 37 *Criminal Law Quarterly* 220.

ROBERTS, J, & R MELCHERS. "The Incarceration of Aboriginal Offenders: Trends from 1978 to 2001" (2003) 45 *Canadian Journal of Criminology and Criminal Justice* 211.

ROBERTS, J, & K ROACH. "Restorative Justice in Canada: From Sentencing Circles to Sentencing Principles" in A Von Hirsch et al, eds. *Restorative Justice and Criminal Justice* (Oxford: Hart, 2003).

RUBY, C, ET AL. *Sentencing*, 9th ed (Toronto: LexisNexis, 2017).

RUDIN, J, & K ROACH. "Broken Promises: A Response to Stenning and Roberts' 'Empty Promises'" (2002) 65 *Saskatchewan Law Review* 3.

STENNING, P, & J ROBERTS. "Empty Promises: Parliament, the Supreme Court and the Sentencing of Aboriginal Offenders" (2001) 64 *Saskatchewan Law Review* 137.

CONCLUSION

The criminal law in Canada has undergone significant changes. The most visible change has been the enactment of the *Canadian Charter of Rights and Freedoms*. As examined in Chapter 2, the *Charter* causes criminal courts to be concerned not only with the accused's factual guilt, but also with whether the police and prosecutors complied with the accused's legal rights in the investigative and trial process. Noncompliance with *Charter* rights can lead to the exclusion of relevant evidence. Entrapment that would bring the administration of justice into disrepute can result in a stay of proceedings even though the accused may have committed the crime with the required *mens rea*.

The *Charter* guarantees the presumption of innocence. It has been interpreted to be breached whenever the accused bears the burden of establishing an element of an offence, a defence, or a collateral factor. It can even be breached when the accused must satisfy an evidential burden to overcome a mandatory presumption. It is not breached, however, when a judge makes a preliminary decision about whether there is an air of reality to justify putting a defence to a jury. The *Charter* contains many procedural rights such as the right against unreasonable search and seizure that affect the investigation of crime and disclosure and speedy trial rights that affect the trial process.

In addition, the *Charter* has provided new substantive standards of fairness by which to measure criminal and regulatory offences and the availability of defences. Constructive murder has been struck down as inconsistent with the minimum *mens rea* for murder and absolute liability offences have been found to be unconstitutional when they result in imprisonment. The intoxication and duress defences have also been expanded in response to *Charter* concerns. The *Charter* has influenced both the procedure and the substance of the criminal process.

More recently, the Supreme Court has struck down offences relating to prostitution and assisted suicide on the basis that the principles of fundamental justice in section 7 of the *Charter* are breached by laws that are overbroad by infringing rights further than required to achieve their objective or laws that are grossly disproportionate. In both cases, Parliament responded with controversial new laws prohibiting the purchase of sex and limiting the right to assistance in dying. The dialogue between courts and Parliament that started under the common law continues under the *Charter*, albeit subject to the requirements of the reasonable limits provisions in section 1 of the *Charter* with Parliament's final option (not yet exercised) of enacting criminal laws notwithstanding *Charter* rights.

Although some of the effects of the *Charter* on the criminal law have been dramatic and unexpected, the overall effect can be overstated, particularly in relation to substantive criminal law, which has been the focus of this work.

Most cases in which the broad presumption of innocence has been violated have nevertheless been sustained under section 1 of the *Charter* as reasonable and proportionate limits on *Charter* rights. The Supreme Court has approved the pre-*Charter* compromise of strict liability for regulatory offences, including the requirement that the accused rebut a presumption of negligence by establishing a defence of due diligence. The courts have also found that no-fault absolute liability offences will not violate section 7 of the *Charter* if they do not result in imprisonment. With the exception of the limited defence of officially induced error, the Court has accepted the sometimes harsh consequences of the traditional principle that even reasonable ignorance or a mistake of the law is not an excuse. The Court has even violated the presumption of innocence itself by requiring the accused to establish the defences of extreme intoxication, non-mental disorder automatism, and officially induced error on a balance of probabilities. The Court itself has restricted the provocation defence that if successful reduces murder to manslaughter and, in 2015, Parliament also restricted this defence in a manner that is likely to attract *Charter* challenge, as have the restrictions that Parliament placed on the defence of extreme intoxication in 1995.

The *Charter* has in some respects protected fault principles less robustly than the common law. Before the *Charter*, the courts under the common law applied common law presumptions of subjective fault in relation to all the elements of the *actus reus*. Under section 7 of the *Charter*, the courts have required subjective fault only in relation to the prohibited result for murder, attempted murder, and war crimes. It has decided that the principle that fault be proven in relation to all aspects of the prohibited act or that there be symmetry between the *actus reus* and *mens rea* is a matter of criminal law "theory" but not a principle of fundamental justice under section 7 of the *Charter*. Fortunately, there are some signs that the courts are increasingly recognizing that common law presumptions of subjective fault and against absolute liability can still do important work in the *Charter* era.

Parliament could always rebut common law presumptions of subjective fault and the Court has accepted objective fault standards for many criminal offences under the *Charter*. Moreover, there is no constitutional requirement that the reasonable person used to administer objective fault standards has the same characteristics as the particular offender or that fault be proven for all aspects of the *actus reus*. That said, the Court has interpreted section 7 of the *Charter* to require that there be a marked departure whenever negligence is used as a form of criminal liability and that courts at least consider whether the subjective position of the accused raises a reasonable doubt about the accused's negligence.[1]

Even when the Supreme Court has ruled in favour of the *Charter* rights of the accused, Parliament has frequently responded with new legislation that reaffirms the public interest and the interests of victims and potential victims of crime. The most dramatic example is section 33.1 of the *Criminal Code*, which attempts to overrule the Court's decision in *Daviault*, so that an extremely intoxicated accused who acted in an involuntary or unconscious manner would still be convicted of crimes such as assault and sexual assault. In an attempt to ensure that "no means no," Parliament has in sections 273.1 and 273.2 of the *Code* defined consent for the purpose of sexual assault not to include specific conduct and has restricted the *Pappajohn* mistake of fact defence to require the accused to take reasonable steps, given the circumstances known to him, to ascertain whether a complainant consents to sexual activity. In its preambles to these new provisions, Parliament has asserted that the *Charter* rights of women and children as potential victims of sexual and domestic assault should be balanced with the *Charter* rights of the accused.

Charter decisions striking down warrantless searches have led Parliament to create new warrant provisions and to authorize some

---

1   *R v Beatty*, 2008 SCC 5 [*Beatty*]; *R v Roy*, 2012 SCC 26.

warrantless searches. Parliament revived tertiary grounds relating to public confidence in the administration of justice for the denial of bail after they were struck down by the Supreme Court and it has restricted credit for remand custody when an accused has been denied bail. The Court's decision that the unavailability of an absolute discharge for those found permanently unfit to stand trial because of a mental disorder but of no significant danger to the public has been cured by legislation, but the new legislation requires judges to consider any adverse effects on the administration of justice including any adverse effect on public confidence in the administration of justice.

The *Charter* has not prevented Parliament from responding to court decisions. Legislative replies may be challenged under the *Charter*, but Parliament frequently has had the last word in its dialogue with the courts over the values of the criminal law.

A. THE *CHARTER* AND THE CRIMINAL LAW

1) The *Charter* and the Due Process Model

In his landmark study of the criminal process, Herbert Packer outlined two contrasting models of the criminal process.[2] In the crime control model, the justice system resembled an assembly line, with the police and prosecutors being able to identify the factually guilty and to secure a guilty plea. In contrast, he saw an emerging due process model that resembled an obstacle course, because it required the state to comply with various legal rights in the investigative and trial process before it could secure a conviction. If the police or prosecutor violated the accused's legal rights, courts were prepared to exclude evidence or terminate the case regardless of whether the accused was factually guilty of the crime charged.

The *Charter*, as interpreted by the Supreme Court of Canada, has injected due process elements into the Canadian criminal process. As discussed in Chapter 2, suspects now have constitutional rights against unreasonable searches, arbitrary detentions, and the right to counsel. If the police do not comply with these rights, the evidence they obtain can be excluded under section 24(2) of the *Charter*. An accused also has rights in the criminal trial process not to be denied reasonable bail without just cause, to be tried within a reasonable time, to receive

---

2   HL Packer, *The Limits of the Criminal Sanction* (Stanford, CA: Stanford University Press, 1968) Part II.

disclosure of relevant evidence in the Crown's possession, and to be presumed innocent. The Court has interpreted the last right broadly, but governments have been able to justify many limitations on that right under section 1 of the *Charter* as reasonable and necessary means to facilitate the prosecution of various crimes.

The due process model describes some elements of the criminal justice system under the *Charter*. At the same time, the Supreme Court has refused to constitutionalize the liberal principle that the criminal sanction be used only to respond to proven harms. Although they have crafted some exemptions for medical use of marijuana, the courts have not invalidated drug laws.

Recent decisions, however, have overruled prior *Charter* precedents to strike down the assisted suicide and prostitution-related laws. Even here, however, the Court does not have the final word and its decisions provoked Parliament to make prostitution illegal by prohibiting the purchase of sex as well as the advertising of prostitution and to limit medical assistance in dying to those with incurable diseases. The dialogue between the Court and Parliament will, however, continue as these new offences are sure to be challenged under the *Charter*. The Court's recent rulings that some mandatory minimum sentences violated the *Charter*[3] stopped short of holding that all mandatory sentences violate the *Charter*. This means that Parliament could apply mandatory sentences to less broadly defined crimes or by providing sentencing judges with a discretion to justify departures below mandatory sentences.

As Packer observed, the due process model was nurtured by the appellate courts, most notably the Supreme Court, and was dependent on changes within that institution. In recent years, there has been a trend, albeit not invariable, to more deference to police actions. The Court has created police powers of investigative detention while at the same time holding them to *Charter* limits. It has also allowed the police to engage in prolonged interrogation of suspects who have invoked the right to silence. Counsel does not have to be present so long as a suspect has been given a reasonable opportunity to contact counsel and the statement obtained is involuntary. The Court's section 8 jurisprudence is complex and uneven, sometimes robustly protecting privacy but at other times not. Even when the Court protects privacy, the state can often invade it if they obtain a warrant and sometimes even without a warrant. These cases provide some support for the critical comments that "due process is for crime control" because they demonstrate how due process both enables and restrains law enforcement. The courts have also stopped short

---

3   *R v Nur*, 2015 SCC 15; *R v Lloyd*, 2016 SCC 13.

of requiring that police interrogations be recorded. Recent changes to the exclusion of unconstitutionally obtained evidence under section 24(2) underline that such evidence should never be automatically excluded.

Prison populations and Indigenous overrepresentation in prison have increased significantly since the enactment of the *Charter*. The accused is not the only actor in the criminal process that has claimed *Charter* rights, and a number of cases have been influenced by concerns about the rights of crime victims and groups such as women, children, and minorities who may be disproportionately subject to some crimes. Indeed, the criminal sanction has been enthusiastically used as a means to respond to risks of crime and as a means to respond to even slight risks of harm.

2) The *Charter* and the Crime Control Model

The enactment of the *Charter* has not eclipsed the utility of Packer's description of the crime control model. Most criminal cases continue to end with guilty pleas that are not well supervised by judges. An early entry of a guilty plea remains an important mitigating factor in sentencing, and there is little legislative or judicial regulation of plea bargaining even though it resolves most criminal cases and despite increasing evidence that even innocent people may be pressured into pleading guilty. A bill before Parliament, however, proposes to require judges to find a factual basis that the accused committed the crime before accepting a guilty plea, and if enacted this may provide some safeguard against guilty plea wrongful convictions that are increasingly recognized as happening.[4] One of the main responses to the Court's decision in *R v Askov*[5] to hold courts to speedy trial limits under section 11(b) was to encourage more plea bargaining. In this respect the due process decision of *Askov* was actually for crime control in the sense of increased plea bargaining. The same may be true for the more recent section 11(b) of *R v Jordan*,[6] though it appears not to have as dramatic effects as *Askov*, in part because the reasonable time standards it sets of eighteen months for cases in provincial court and thirty months for cases in superior courts are much longer than the *Askov* standards. The basic point is that even decisions that appear to vindicate the due pro-

---

4   *R v Hannemaayer*, 2008 ONCA 580. See Kent Roach "Prosecutors and Wrongful Convictions" in Benjamin Berger, Emma Cunliffe, & James Stribopoulos, eds, *To Ensure That Justice Is Done: Essays in Memory of Marc Rosenberg* (Toronto: Thomson Reuters, 2017).

5   [1990] 2 SCR 1199.

6   2016 SCC 27.

cess rights of the accused may have unintended effects in the criminal process and ones that affirm its function as a crime control assembly line.

Parliament remains the dominant player in the crime control model, and each year Parliament amends the *Criminal Code* multiple times and almost always in the direction of expanding and toughening the criminal sanction. Tough on crime remains politically popular. Since the enactment of the *Charter*, offences against sexual assault; proceeds obtained by crime; war crimes; impaired driving causing death or bodily harm; sexual interference with children; the possession of drug instruments, drug literature, and child pornography; and committing a crime for a criminal organization have all been passed. In the wake of September 11 and again in the wake of two terrorist attacks in October 2014, Parliament enacted new crimes of terrorism. It also expanded the provisions for holding corporations and other organizations criminally liable as a response to the Westray Mine disaster. The Supreme Court has rejected a *Charter* challenge to the criminal offence of possession of marijuana, though it will be decriminalized by Parliament in 2018. Sentencing provisions require crimes motivated by hate against identifiable groups, involving child or spousal abuse, or abuse of positions of trust or authority, or involving organized crime or terrorism, to be punished more severely. Sections 15 and 28 of the *Charter* have also been invoked by Parliament in support of claims that the criminal sanction is necessary to protect the rights of women, children, and other vulnerable groups.

Judicial interpretation of the *Charter* has not been oblivious to crime control values. The Court has accepted that random stops and roadside denials of counsel are reasonable limits necessary to deter drunk driving. Violations of the presumption of innocence protected under section 11(d) of the *Charter* have frequently been upheld to facilitate the prosecution of crimes such as drunk driving, living off the avails of prostitution, hate propaganda, and regulatory offences. The Supreme Court has required proof of subjective foresight of the likelihood of death for murder but has approved of manslaughter convictions when death was unforeseen by the accused and may have been unforeseeable by the reasonable person. The Court has based this latter ruling on the fact that the accused was acting unlawfully and should accept responsibility for the victim's "thin skull," and has continued to apply broad causation tests that result in manslaughter being a very broad crime that includes killings just short of murder and accidental deaths caused by illegal acts.[7]

The *Charter* has changed the way conflicting interests are described and balanced in the criminal justice system, but it has not done away with the need to balance these interests. Parliament still plays a leading role in defining the prohibited act, the fault element, and the punishment available for most criminal offences. Enthusiasm for the use of the criminal sanction has not diminished under the *Charter*. The criminal law is used as a practical and symbolic response to a wide range of social issues, including drunk driving, domestic violence, hate literature, hate crimes, degrading pornography, sex work, terrorism, sexual violence towards women and children, and corporate misconduct.

3) The *Charter* and the Punitive Model of Victims' Rights

In a few cases, the *Charter* has encouraged courts to consider the effects of laws in protecting victims of crime, and in particular women and minorities who may disproportionately be the victims of certain crimes. In *R v Keegstra*,[8] the Supreme Court upheld hate propaganda offences that violated freedom of expression and the presumption of innocence in large part because the law attempted to protect vulnerable minorities from being the targets of wilful promotion of hatred. In *R v Butler*,[9] the Court reinterpreted obscenity provisions so that they prohibited material that was found to be violent, or degrading, or dehumanizing, particularly in relation to its portrayal of women and children. In the *Prostitution Reference*,[10] the Court upheld a new crime of soliciting in a public place for the purpose of prostitution in part because of concerns for communities and women victimized by prostitution. A concern that people with disabilities might be coerced into suicide in part motivated the Court's decision in *Rodriguez v British Columbia (AG)*[11] not to strike down the offence of assisting suicide. The Court has, however, overruled the latter two cases in the face of new evidence in *Canada (Attorney General) v Bedford*[12] and *Carter v Canada (Attorney General)*[13] that

---

7 *R v Creighton* (1993), 83 CCC (3d) 346 (SCC) [*Creighton*]; *R v Maybin*, [2012] 2 SCR 30.

8 (1990), 61 CCC (3d) 1 (SCC).

9 (1992), 70 CCC (3d) 129 (SCC).

10 *Reference re ss 193 & 195.1(1)(c) of the Criminal Code (Canada)* (1990), 56 CCC (3d) 65 (SCC).

11 *Rodriguez v British Columbia (AG)* (1993), 85 CCC (3d) 15 (SCC).

12 [2013] 3 SCR 1101 [*Bedford*].

13 2015 SCC 5.

the crimes it previously upheld in part to protect sex workers and people with disabilities actually harmed them. These turnarounds underline the dangers about assuming that criminal laws always serve their intended purposes and do not have dangerous side effects. The Court's decisions, however, did not stop Parliament from responding with new offences prohibiting the purchase of sex and restricting the availability of medical assistance in dying despite concerns that these new laws enacted in part to protect victims could actually impose harms on groups such as sex workers and those living in irremediable pain.

Parliament and the provincial legislatures have been more active than the courts in protecting the interests of victims of crimes. They have enacted various laws designed to provide compensation for the victims of crime. The new sexual assault provisions enacted in response to *R v Seaboyer*,[14] and the legislative response to *R v Daviault*,[15] both include preambles that state that the laws were designed in part to promote the full protection of rights guaranteed under sections 7 and 15 of the *Charter* and to deal with the prevalence of sexual assault and other violence against women and children. Parliament has recently responded to the *Bedford* ruling with new legislation that criminalizes the purchase of sex but not its sale.[16] The government is confident that the legislation will not harm sex workers and will respond to their exploitation and the violence they often suffer, but that proposition is very much contested. In 2015, Parliament dramatically restricted the provocation defence as an attempt to prevent "honour killings" despite the absence of evidence that the provocation defence had condoned such killings. It also amended the sentencing provisions of the *Code* to allow victims and communities to read impact statements and present photos before sentencing and also provided that courts should give primary consideration to deterrence and denunciation in cases involving preferred victims — children, justice system participants, and animals.[17]

New offences against the purchase of sex and restricting medical assistance in dying have been defended by governments as necessary to

---

14   (1992), 66 CCC (3d) 321 (SCC). See *Criminal Code*, RSC 1985, c C-46, ss 273.1–273.2 and 276.1–276.5 [*Code*].

15   *R v Daviault* (1994), 93 CCC (3d) 21 (SCC) [*Daviault*]. See *Code*, above note 14, ss 33.1–33.3.

16   *Protection of Communities and Exploited Persons Act*, SC 2014, c 25, adding to the *Code*, above note 14, s 213(1.1) communication offences relating to places near schools and playgrounds, and ss 286.1–286.5 providing various offences for purchasing sexual services, receiving material benefits from their sale, procuring sexual services, and advertising sexual services.

17   *Code*, above note 14, ss 722, 722.1, 718.01–718.03 respectively.

protect the rights of the vulnerable, despite concerns that they may have the opposite effect. All political parties are concerned about crime victims and potential victims of crime. A Liberal government enacted restricted legislation in response to *Carter* because of its desire to protect vulnerable individuals and groups that might be pressured into agreeing to medical assistance in dying whereas a Conservative government restricted the provocation defence and made the purchase of sex illegal.

There are concerns about higher acquittal rates in sexual assault cases that may be influenced by sexist prejudice and aggressive cross-examination of complainants despite various legal reforms to sexual assault law.[18] There are also concerns, in light of the jury acquittal of Saskatchewan farmer Gerald Stanley in February 2018 of killing twenty-two-year-old Cree man Colten Boushie, about the fairness of jury selection and how prejudice against Indigenous victims, including the many missing Indigenous women and girls, may influence criminal investigations and trials. There are also concerns that terrorism offences have not been applied to political violence inspired by the far right but rather focused on terrorism inspired by al Qaeda and Daesh. There is a legitimate concern in the punitive victims' rights model that the benefits of criminal laws and prosecutions extend equally to all without discrimination. At the same time, it should not be assumed that even equal criminal prosecutions will respond to broader forms of discrimination.

There are real limits as to how far victim interests will be integrated into the present criminal justice system or the ability of criminal law to prevent victimization by crime. The *Charter* provides no explicit rights for crime victims and the interests of victims have to be squeezed into the interests protected under sections 7 and 15. In *Canadian Foundation for Children*,[19] the Supreme Court rejected arguments that section 43 of the *Code* violated procedural and equality rights of children by author-

---

18   Victimization studies suggests that eight in ten sexual assault incidents are not reported to the police. Shana Conroy & Adam Cottor, *Self-Reported Sexual Assaults in Canada, 2014* (Ottawa: Statistics Canada, 2017), online: www.statcan. gc.ca/pub/85-002-x/2017001/article/14842-eng.pdf. Of those sexual assaults reported to the police, only one in ten results in convictions compared to one in four assaults resulting in convictions. Cristine Rotenberg, *From Arrests to Conviction: Court Outcomes of Police Reported Sexual Assaults 2009 to 2014* (Ottawa: Statistics Canada, 2017), online: www.statcan.gc.ca/pub/85-002-x/2017001/ article/54870-eng.pdf. See also Elaine Craig, *Putting Trials on Trial: Sexual Assault and the Failure of the Legal Profession* (Montreal: McGill-Queens University Press, 2018).

19   *Canadian Foundation for Children, Youth and the Law v Canada (AG)*, 2004 SCC 4 [*Canadian Foundation for Children*].

izing the use of reasonable force by way of correction against them. Chief Justice McLachlin stated: "[T]hus far, the jurisprudence has not recognized procedural rights for the alleged victim of an offence" and that assuming that such rights existed, "the child's interests are represented at trial by the Crown . . . . There is no reason to suppose that, as in other offences involving children as victims or witnesses, the Crown will not discharge that duty properly. Nor is there any reason to conclude . . . that providing separate representation for the child is either necessary or useful."[20] This case sets real limits on the extent to which the rights of crime victims will be recognized within the existing criminal justice system. In addition, sexual violence against women and violence against Indigenous women continue despite the enactment of broad sexual assault laws and the disproportionate imprisonment of Indigenous people. Governments may promise that tougher criminal laws will make people safer, but reducing victimization requires more than reliance on the criminal law. Indeed, there is a danger that governments with punitive agendas will use victims as simply a way to legitimate crime control that increases the powers of legislators, police, and prosecutors.

4) The Non-punitive Model of Victims' Rights

A non-punitive model of victims' rights would devote more resources to multidisciplinary and multi-sectorial crime prevention and on restorative justice that attempts to build and repair social relations and has some potential to respond to the causes of offending.

A non-punitive approach to victimization would often take a public health approach to minimizing the harms of not only crime, but also other threats to human security. As the possession of marijuana is decriminalized by Parliament, it will be important that the government attempts to educate the populace about the health and safety hazards of the drug, as well as other drugs. It would also emphasize the importance of healthy infant and school experiences in decreasing crime. It would approach issues like terrorism with both a desire to counter radicalization that leads to terrorism and an appreciation of the full range of risks to human security, including harms caused by natural and man-made disasters.

The *R v Gladue*[21] decision has recognized the role of restorative justice in sentencing and its ability to respond to the needs of victims

---

20   *Ibid* at para 6.
21   (1999), 133 CCC (3d) 385 (SCC) [*Gladue*].

as well as offenders. *Gladue* represents a non-punitive model of victims' rights that places less emphasis on competing claims of rights and the imposition of punishment. Other examples of a non-punitive model would include the use of family conferences and victim offender mediation and a greater emphasis on crime prevention. In *R v Ipeelee*,[22] the Court stressed that judges must take judicial notice of distinct background factors, including the residential school experience that may help explain why Indigenous offenders commit offences and may provide background to determine what sentence is appropriate. A non-punitive model would take seriously the evidence that Indigenous people are both disproportionately victimized by crime and imprisoned and be open to solutions outside the criminal justice system to this crisis.

In *R v Proulx*,[23] Lamer CJ explained that restorative justice was a new objective of sentencing that applies to all offenders and was associated with the rehabilitation of the offender and reparation and acknowledgment of the harm done to the victims and the community. The Chief Justice explained:

> Restorative justice is concerned with the restoration of the parties that are affected by the commission of an offence. Crime generally affects at least three parties: the victim, the community, and the offender. A restorative approach seeks to remedy the adverse effects of crime in a manner that addresses the needs of all parties involved. This is accomplished, in part, through the rehabilitation of the offender, reparations to the victim and to the community, and promotion of a sense of responsibility in the offender and acknowledgment of the harm done to victims and the community.[24]

Restorative approaches that attempt to rehabilitate the offender depend on the willingness of prosecutors to divert cases out of the system and of Parliament not to restrict alternatives to imprisonment through mandatory minimum sentences and restrictions on conditional sentences. So far, Parliament has not followed the Truth and Reconciliation Commission's[25] thirty-second call for action that trial judges be able to justify departures from mandatory minimum sentences and mandatory restrictions on conditional sentences in any appropriate case. At the same time, restorative justice approaches may fail to rehabilitate and they can impose harms on victims.

---

22 2012 SCC 13.
23 (2000), 140 CCC (3d) 449 (SCC).
24 *Ibid* at para 18.
25 Truth and Reconciliation Commission, *Canadian Residential Schools: The Legacy*, vol 5 (Montreal: McGill-Queen's University Press, 2015) at 242.

The non-punitive model of victims is also open to the possibility that an offender's conduct may be related to his or her prior victimization even if such victimization does not excuse the conduct. The Supreme Court in the *Canada (AG) v PHS Community Services Society* case rejected the government's argument that the use of illegal drugs was simply a matter of choice. It held that the refusal of the Minister of Health to continue to grant a statutory exemption from drug laws to continue to allow a safe injection site to operate on Vancouver's Downtown Eastside violated section 7 of the *Charter* because it was arbitrary and grossly disproportionate given evidence that it helped save the lives of addicts who might be infected with HIV by dirty needles while not increasing crime in the community.[26]

B. TRENDS IN THE CRIMINAL LAW

1) Broad Definition of Crimes

The criminal law as enacted by Parliament sets a fairly wide net of criminal liability by defining criminal acts quite broadly. Courts will interpret prohibited acts in a purposive fashion, before resorting to the doctrine of strict construction of the criminal law that gives the accused the benefit of reasonable ambiguities. They are reluctant to hold laws to be void for vagueness or to apply a *de minimis* defence to criminal acts that are broadly defined by Parliament.

As examined in Chapter 4, people can be held guilty as parties to an offence for a wide range of conduct, including aiding, abetting, or counselling a crime, or forming a common unlawful purpose with either subjective or objective foresight that the crime charged will occur.[27] Separate offences of conspiracy, counselling a crime that is not committed, and being an accessory after the fact also exist. Courts have defined the prohibited act of attempted crimes broadly, so that anything beyond preparation will suffice, even if it is not otherwise illegal or harmful. The accused may be guilty of an attempted crime even though it was impossible to commit the complete crime and his or her actions

---

26　*Canada (AG) v PHS Community Services Society*, 2011 SCC 44; *Respect for Communities Act*, SC 2015, c 22, s 5.

27　If the crime is murder or attempted murder, there must be subjective foresight that death will result from the carrying out of the unlawful purpose with an accomplice. *R v Logan* (1990), 58 CCC (3d) 391 (SCC) [*Logan*].

were quite remote from the complete crime.[28] At the same time, courts have stressed that the Crown must prove that the accused acted with the intent to commit the crime.

Another alternative to inchoate crimes is to criminalize activities that are preparatory to the commission of crimes. Parliament has taken this approach with organized crime, terrorism, and online luring offences, and the courts have accepted that they can broadly design crimes that might not otherwise attract inchoate or party liability in an attempt to prevent serious harms.[29] Sometimes such statutory inchoate crimes are restrained by high fault requirements such as requiring that the accused act for purposes, but not always. The courts have not developed constitutional doctrines to restrain broad statutory inchoate crimes by high fault requirements as they arguably do when interpreting general inchoate crimes such as attempt or the broad parties provisions of the *Criminal Code*.

Various sexual offences have been defined by Parliament broadly in an attempt to protect the sexual integrity of women and children. Parliament has defined consent for the purpose of sexual assault not to include specific conduct[30] and the Supreme Court has held that consent as a matter of *actus reus* depends solely on the subjective intent of the complainant[31] and also cannot be given by an unconscious complainant.[32] In *R v Jobidon*,[33] the Supreme Court held that, for the purposes of assault, a person could not consent to the intentional infliction of serious hurt or non-trivial bodily harm. This has effectively expanded the law of assault to include consensual fights that result in injury. In the future it appears likely that Parliament will continue to define many crimes broadly, and the manner in which crimes are defined will be an important policy component of the criminal law.

The overall trend is towards legislative creation and judicial interpretation of broad crimes. One countervailing force is the recent willingness of the Court to strike laws down as constitutionally overbroad. In cases such as living off the avails of prostitution and assisted suicide, this forces Parliament to enact new and narrower offences.

---

28 *R v Deutsch* (1986), 27 CCC (3d) 385 (SCC); *United States of America v Dynar* (1997), 115 CCC (3d) 481 (SCC).

29 *R v Legare*, 2009 SCC 56; *R v Khawaja*, [2012] 3 SCR 555.

30 *Code*, above note 14, s 273.1.

31 *R v Ewanchuk* (1999), 131 CCC (3d) 481 (SCC).

32 *R v JA*, [2011] 2 SCR 440.

33 *R v Jobidon* (1991), 66 CCC (3d) 454 (SCC).

2) Subjective and Objective Fault Elements

It appears that proof of subjective *mens rea* in relation to the prohibited result of a crime will be a constitutional requirement for only a few offences, such as murder, attempted murder, and war crimes. The Supreme Court has stressed that the penalties and stigma that accompany these offences require proof beyond a reasonable doubt of subjective *mens rea* in relation to the prohibited result. It has struck down the constructive (or felony) murder provisions in section 230 of the *Criminal Code*, because they allowed accused who caused death while committing serious crimes to be convicted of murder even if they did not have subjective foresight that death would occur. Liability for murder based on objective, as opposed to subjective, foresight of death contemplated in sections 229(c) and 21(2) has also been struck down.[34] In a controversial decision, the Supreme Court held in *R v Finta* that section 7 of the *Charter* required proof of knowledge or at least wilful blindness in relation to the conditions that would make a war crime constitute a war crime. The Court has affirmed this approach but also indicated that recklessness may be a sufficient form of fault.[35] Constitutional requirements of fault do not seem to require the highest levels of fault that may be necessary to restrain inchoate and statutory inchoate forms of liability.

Constitutional requirements of fault are much more limited than common law presumptions of subjective fault. Recently, however, the Court has applied these common law presumptions, demonstrating that they still have an important role to play in the *Charter* era.[36] Common law presumptions of subjective fault, however, can be displaced by clear legislative language, and courts accept that objective fault could be used for most crimes, except those whose stigma requires subjective fault. For non-stigma offences, however, the *Charter* prohibits only imprisonment for absolute liability that follows from the commission of the prohibited act and without regard to either subjective or objective fault.

The Supreme Court has rejected, as a constitutional requirement, the principle that the fault element should relate to all aspects of the *actus reus*. Thus, the fault element of manslaughter relates not to the causing of death but the causing of non-trivial bodily harm. Many other crimes are based on the consequences of the accused's actions even though the accused may not have had subjective or objective fault in relation to those consequences.

---

34   *R v Martineau* (1990), 58 CCC (3d) 353 (SCC); *Logan*, above note 27.
35   *Mugesera v Canada (Minister of Citizenship and Immigration)*, [2005] 2 SCR 100.
36   *R v ADH*, [2013] 2 SCR 269.

The Court has upheld the constitutionality of objective standards of liability for serious crimes, including unlawful act manslaughter, unlawfully causing bodily harm, and dangerous driving. The courts have accepted the legitimacy of the use of objective fault standards in the criminal law while also holding that section 7 of the *Charter* requires more than simple negligence, but rather a marked departure from the standard of care expected from a reasonable person in the circumstances so that negligence as a form of criminal fault is adequately distinguished from mere civil negligence.[37] The new section 22.1 of the *Criminal Code*, for example, requires that senior officer(s) of a corporation demonstrate a marked departure from the standard of care necessary to prevent representatives of the corporation from committing a criminal offence based on negligence. The marked departure standard, as well as the onus on the Crown to prove fault beyond a reasonable doubt, is an important distinction between criminal and regulatory offences.

In *R v Creighton*,[38] a 5:4 majority of the Supreme Court rejected attempts to tailor objective standards to a particular accused by endowing the reasonable person with personal characteristics such as the accused's age and intelligence. The majority did keep open the possibility of considering the characteristics of individual accused but only if they meant that the accused lacked the capacity to appreciate the prohibited risk. This has not emerged as an important factor when applying objective standards. In most cases, however, the reasonable person used to administer objective standards will not have the same characteristics as the accused and the Court has expressed concerns about not blurring the distinction between subjective and objective standards of liability. More recent cases tailor objective fault for criminal purposes by requiring a marked departure from reasonable conduct to distinguish criminal negligence from lesser forms of negligence and consideration of whether the accused's own mental state raises a reasonable doubt about negligence.[39] In cases dealing with defences, however, the Court has indicated that courts should consider the particular accused's past experiences, characteristics, and frailties when determining whether perceptions and actions are reasonable.[40] This leads to more generous defences, but some blurring of the distinctions between subjective and objective standards.

---

37   *Beatty*, above note 1.
38   *Creighton*, above note 7.
39   *Beatty*, above note 1.
40   *R v Lavallee* (1990), 55 CCC (3d) 97 (SCC) [*Lavallee*]; *R v Pétel* (1994), 87 CCC (3d) 97 (SCC); *R v Hibbert* (1995), 99 CCC (3d) 193 (SCC); *R v Thibert* (1996), 104 CCC (3d) 1 (SCC) [*Thibert*], discussed in Chapter 9.

The different approaches to applying objective standards and defining the reasonable person introduce inconsistency in the law. A possible rationale for the divergent approach is that many accused will make a voluntary choice to undertake activities that are judged on a negligence-based standard, whereas the objective standard in defences must be modified to account for the characteristics and experiences of the particular accused in order to ensure that he or she is not found guilty for morally involuntary conduct. In other words, accuseds' characteristics and experiences may be relevant to determine whether the only realistic choice open to them in particular circumstances was to violate the law.

3) Regulatory Offences and Corporate Crime

Following *R v Sault Ste Marie (City)*,[41] most regulatory offences are interpreted as strict liability offences that require the Crown to prove the prohibited act, but then presume the existence of negligence unless the accused can establish a defence of due diligence on a balance of probabilities. This important presumption has been affirmed by the Court.[42] In *R v Wholesale Travel Group Inc*,[43] the Supreme Court held that the fault element of negligence was constitutionally sufficient for a regulatory offence of misleading advertising, and it approved the requirement that the accused demonstrate that it was not negligent by proving a defence of due diligence on a balance of probabilities. Absolute liability in which the Crown must prove only the prohibited act is unconstitutional when there is imprisonment. At the same time, there is a trend to using high fines for regulatory offences. In such cases, legislatures can generally constitutionally displace common law and constitutional presumptions against absolute liability offences that punish people and corporations simply on the basis that they have committed a prohibited act.

The Supreme Court's decision in *R v Pontes*[44] suggests that offences may be interpreted as absolute liability offences if the ignorance of the law is no excuse principle would deprive the accused of his or her only possible defence. This decision also suggests that absolute liability is constitutionally permissible so long as imprisonment is taken off the table.

---

41   (1978), 40 CCC (2d) 353 (SCC).
42   *Lévis (City) v Tétreault*, [2006] 1 SCR 420 [*Lévis*]; *La Souveraine, Compagnie d'assurance générale v Autorité des marchés financiers*, [2013] 3 SCR 756 [*La Souveraine*].
43   (1991), 67 CCC (3d) 193 (SCC).
44   (1995), 100 CCC (3d) 353 (SCC).

The Court has made a minimal intrusion into section 19 of the *Criminal Code* by recognizing a defence of officially induced error,[45] but while maintaining the distinction that even reasonable mistakes about or ignorance of the law will not excuse while mistakes about facts often will.[46]

Sections 22.1 and 22.2 of the *Criminal Code* now have replaced the old common law that only attributed the fault of a corporation's directing mind to the corporation for the purpose of determining criminal liability. Now the fault of senior officers can be attributed to the corporation. Unlike the old directing mind concept, a senior officer may include someone who manages an important aspect of the company's operations even when that person does not set corporate policy. Section 22.1 applies to criminal offences of negligence and requires that senior officer(s) depart markedly from the standard of care that would prevent representatives of the corporation from being a party to the offence. Section 22.2 applies to criminal offences of subjective fault and requires the senior officer to be a party to the offence or direct a representative so that he or she commits an offence or to fail to take all reasonable steps to prevent a representative from committing an offence when the senior officer knows that an offence is being committed. It remains to be seen whether these new provisions, as well as new sentencing provisions that allow a corporation to be placed on probation, will increase criminal charges and convictions against corporations and other organizations and whether this will effectively deter corporate misconduct.

4) Diminishing Defences

Although the *Charter* has expanded some defences such as extreme intoxication and duress under section 17, the trend line for both the Court and Parliament in recent years has been to restrict defences. This accords with rising punitive attitudes especially towards violence even in the face of evidence that crime has been declining.

a) Intoxication
In *Daviault*,[47] the Supreme Court recognized a defence of extreme intoxication akin to automatism. Such a rare state would deprive an accused of the voluntary and conscious behaviour necessary for general intent offences such as assault and sexual assault. Unlike evidence of intoxication, which can always raise a reasonable doubt about the

---

45   *Lévis*, above note 42.
46   *La Souveraine*, above note 42.
47   *Daviault*, above note 15.

mental element of specific intent offences such as murder or robbery, the defence of extreme intoxication to a general intent offence must be proved by the accused on a balance of probabilities and with expert evidence. Despite these Court imposed restrictions on the new extreme intoxication defence, Parliament responded with section 33.1 of the *Criminal Code*. It attempts to eliminate the *Daviault* defence with respect to violent offences by deeming that the marked departure from reasonable conduct involved in becoming extremely intoxicated can be substituted for the voluntary and conscious behaviour and fault required to convict a person of assault, sexual assault, or other violent general intent offences. The constitutionality of this provision has not yet been finally settled, but most courts have found that it violates the presumption of innocence by substituting the fault of becoming extremely intoxicated for the fault of committing the crime and that it violates the principles of fundamental justice by allowing the conviction of a person who commits a crime in an involuntary manner. The Supreme Court, however, had no trouble finding that the section 33.1 applied and denied a defence in a case where an accused committed an aggravated assault while subject to a "toxic psychosis" produced by drugs even though that condition produced delusions normally associated with mental illness.[48] The Court's decision also prevented the extension of the mental disorder defence to those who have voluntarily become extremely intoxicated even if their intoxication means that they were not capable of appreciating the physical consequences of their actions or knowing that they were wrong.

The Supreme Court has also held that the traditional intoxication defence for specific intent crimes violates the *Charter* by requiring a reasonable doubt about the accused's capacity to form the intent rather than the actual formation of the intent.[49] At the same time, it has also upheld the denial of this defence if an air of reality is not present and has expanded the range of general intent offences that only allows the rare extreme intoxication to include crimes such as arson. The Court has also indicated that in cases of ambiguity, courts should classify offences as general intent if they are associated with intoxication.[50] This means that people are routinely convicted and punished for actions done while intoxicated and that much crime in our courts is related to addictions.

---

48   *R v Bouchard-Lebrun*, 2011 SCC 58 at paras 89–91 [*Bouchard-Lebrun*].
49   *R v Robinson* (1996), 105 CCC (3d) 97 (SCC).
50   *R v Tatton*, 2015 SCC 33.

b) Mental Disorder and Automatism Defence

The mental disorder defence applies to a wide range of mental disorders that can expand with medical knowledge, but only when the mental disorder renders the accused incapable of appreciating the physical consequences of his or her actions or knowing that they are wrong. This essentially means that Canadian criminal law combines a modern understanding of mental disorder with a nineteenth-century under-standing rooted in *mens rea* principles about when it is unjust to con-vict a person who acts because of a mental disorder. In other words, the Court's understanding of moral blameworthiness including perceived needs for social protection rather than current medical sciences shapes the mental disorder defence.

In 1990, the Supreme Court expanded the mental disorder defence by holding that people should not be convicted if a mental disorder ren-dered them incapable of knowing that their acts were morally and not just legally wrong.[51] At the same time, the courts have not extended the defence to those incapable of appreciating the emotional or penal con-sequences of their actions, even if this lack of appreciation was caused by a mental disorder. The courts also still do not apply the defence to psychopaths who, although aware that society would regard their actions as wrong, decide to substitute their own moral code for that of society. The accused still bears the burden of establishing the mental disorder defence on a balance of probabilities.

The Court has recently suggested that those who have a valid men-tal disorder defence act in a morally involuntarily manner and this would suggest that Parliament could not repeal or significantly restrict the defence without violating the section 7 principle of fundamental justice that people should not be convicted for morally involuntary be-haviour.[52] That said, Canada's mental disorder defence is very restrict-ive. It has not fundamentally changed since the nineteenth century. The means that people are routinely convicted and punished for actions that are done as a result of a mental illness, including mental illness that might be amenable to modern forms of treatment.

In its 1999 decision in *R v Stone*, the Supreme Court imposed new restrictions on the related defence of automatism by both requiring the accused to establish automatism on a balance of probabilities and as-suming, largely for reasons of social protection, that automatism would be caused by a mental disorder.[53] As a result, most cases where the ac-

---

51   *R v Chaulk* (1990), 62 CCC (3d) 193 (SCC).
52   *Bouchard-Lebrun*, above note 48 at para 74.
53   *R v Stone* (1999), 134 CCC (3d) 353 (SCC).

cused has acted in an involuntary and automatic state including cases where the accused commits a crime while sleeping will no longer result in an acquittal but in a finding of not criminally responsible by reason of mental disorder, which could result in continued detention even though conditions like sleepwalking are not medical disorders readily amenable to treatment.[54]

Although the Court has expanded the mental disorder defence to include most forms of automatism for reasons of social protection, it has resisted the application of the mental disorder defence in cases of self-induced intoxication producing toxic psychosis that would otherwise result in the restrictive mental disorder defence applying because it renders the accused incapable of appreciating the physical consequences of his or her actions or knowing that they are wrong.[55] In the result, the Court applied the restrictions on the extreme intoxication defence and convicted the accused of aggravated assault. The only common theme in these cases seems to be the perceived imperative of social protection, though applying the mental disorder defence to a self-induced toxic psychosis would also have the effect of subjecting the accused to the same potential of continued detention as would occur in the case of the accused who acts in a state of automatism that the Court presumes is the result of mental disorder.

One exception to the trend to both restrictive application of the mental disorder defence is that the Court has defined infanticide as a partial defence broadly to include all forms of mental agitation and instability caused by a mother's recent birth or lactation and not limited to mental disorders or even substantial psychological problems. The Court also does not require that the mother's broadly defined mental disturbance be the cause of the wilful act or omission that results in her newly born child's death.[56] One continuity with the mental disorder defence cases and mental disorder automatism cases is that the courts shape infanticide on the basis of their understandings of moral blameworthiness as opposed to current medical science.

c) Provocation

The starkest example of the trend to restrict defences is provocation. There were justified concerns that the provocation defence that reduces murder to manslaughter had expanded too much and could in cases like *R v Hill* and *R v Thibert*[57] partially excuse killings motivated by

---

54   *R v Luedecke*, 2008 ONCA 716; compare with *R v Parks*, [1992] 2 SCR 871.
55   *Bouchard-Lebrun*, above note 48.
56   *R v Borowiec*, 2016 SCC 11.
57   *R v Hill*, [1986] 1 SCR 313; *Thibert*, above note 40.

homophobia and male rage and jealousy. In *Thibert* the Court indicated that the ordinary person considered for the purpose of the provocation defence should be the same age and sex as the accused and have any other characteristic or experience that would give the act or insult special significance. The Court has clarified this approach in the subsequent provocation case of *R v Tran*[58] by stressing that the personal characteristics of the accused are only relevant in placing a provocative act in context but that they do not change the reasonable standard of restraint required from all individuals. In that case, the Court found there was no air of reality to the provocation defence when the accused found his estranged wife in bed with another man. In other cases, the Court was increasingly reluctant to hold that the provocation defence had an air of reality that would allow a reasonable jury to acquit the accused of murder with its mandatory sentence of life imprisonment but convict of manslaughter.[59] The Court in rejecting the provocation defence also seemed to flirt with imposing new requirements of proportionality between the act and the insult and the accused's response.[60]

But all these restrictions on the provocation defence were not enough. In 2015 and as part of the *Zero Tolerance for Barbaric Cultural Practices Act*,[61] Parliament severely and categorically restricted provocation by replacing the requirement of a provoking act or insult with the requirement that the deceased must have provoked the accused by committing an indictable offence subject to five years' imprisonment or more. This effectively means that the deceased will have to have assaulted or sexually assaulted the accused. This is in addition to the requirements of sudden and subjective provocation and that the acts would have caused an ordinary person to lose self-control. To be sure, there are strong arguments that the provocation defence should either be abolished (along with the mandatory sentence of life imprisonment for murder) or expanded to include other emotions and extenuating circumstances. Nevertheless, at present it is an arguably unconstitutional and somewhat illusory defence.

d) Duress and Necessity

Duress may appear to be an exception to the trend towards diminishing defences. In 2001, the Supreme Court held that the requirement in section 17 of the *Code* that an accused has a duress defence only if he or she faced immediate death or bodily harm from a person who is

---

58 [2010] 3 SCR 350.
59 *R v Pappas*, 2013 SCC 56; *R v Cairney*, 2013 SCC 55.
60 *R v Mayuran*, 2012 SCC 31.
61 SC 2015, c 29.

present when the crime is committed has been found to violate section 7 of the *Charter* because it could result in the punishment of a person who responded reasonably and in a morally involuntary fashion to threats from which there was no safe avenue of escape.[62] This responded to the most severe restrictions on the section 17 defence that had already been mitigated by the Court's pre-*Charter* decision to only apply the restrictive statutory defence to those who actually committed the crime while allowing parties who assisted in an offence to claim a less constrained common law defence of duress.[63]

The Court has subsequently interpreted section 17, which applies to those who commit offences, and the common law duress defence, which applies to those who are parties to an offence, in a similar way, inspired in part by the common juristic basis of necessity and defence. Hence, the accused's perceptions of the threat, lack of alternatives, and the proportionality of response must all be reasonable as judged by a modified objective standard.[64] This achieves harmony with the common law defence, but also imposes additional restrictions on the section 17 defence.

The only remaining difference between the common law and statutory duress defence is that the section 17 defence still contains a long and constitutionally suspect list of excluded offences. The Manitoba Court of Appeal has held that the categorical exclusion of murder under section 17 is justified[65] but its approach seems to conceive of duress as a justification as opposed to an excuse. It also underestimates the ability of a fact-based inquiry into the proportionality between the threat faced by the accused and the harm inflicted to serve social protection interests. It is, however, consistent with a growing unwillingness to accept that serious criminal acts should ever be excused.

Necessity has also emerged as a defence in the *Charter* era. It is, however, tightly constrained by requirements of a reasonable belief in imminent peril: reasonable belief in no safe avenue of escape or legal way out and a requirement of proportionality between the harm inflicted and avoided. It remains a rare defence and one that the courts will not hesitate to withhold from the jury if there is not an air of reality that would allow a reasonable jury to have a reasonable doubt about all of the essential elements of the defence. In *R v Latimer*,[66] the Court affirmed that a modified objective standard would be applied in determining whether

---

62 *R v Ruzic*, 2001 SCC 24.
63 *R v Paquette* (1976), [1977] 2 SCR 189.
64 *R v Ryan*, [2013] 1 SCR 14.
65 *R v Willis*, 2016 MBCA 113.
66 *R v Latimer*, 2001 SCC 1.

the accused faced an imminent harm and had no safe avenue of escape or legal way out. At the same time, however, the Court indicated that the requirement of proportionality between the harm avoided and the harm inflicted should be determined on a purely objective standard and one that did not devalue the life of a victim who was severely disabled.

e) Self-Defence

The most significant exception to the trend to diminishing defences is self-defence. In *R v Lavallee*[67] and *R v Pétel*,[68] the Court stressed that when determining whether self-defence was reasonable, the trier of fact should consider the accused's past experience, including the fact that she had been battered by the man she killed. In *Lavallee*, the Supreme Court rejected the idea that self-defence was justified only in response to an immediate threat of harm. The self-defence provisions subsequently enacted in 2012 codify parts of *Lavallee* by providing that triers of fact should examine the size, age, gender, and physical capabilities of the parties to the incident and any prior use or threat of force between them when determining whether an accused's actions were reasonable in the circumstances.[69]

At the same time, the Supreme Court has made clear that a woman will not necessarily have a self-defence claim just because she had previously been abused by the person she uses violence against.[70] In many cases, a battered woman charged with murder may face an agonizing choice if offered a plea to manslaughter because a murder conviction will result in life imprisonment if the self-defence claim is not accepted.[71] *R v Cinous*[72] suggests that in other contexts self-defence may not even be put to the jury in a case in which an accused has alternatives other than killing the person whom he believes threatens him.

Parliament's 2012 reforms of self-defence and defence of property demonstrate a salutary Parliament interest in simplifying the criminal law, but they may also make these defences somewhat less predictable. The new section 34 imposes only general requirements that accused believe on reasonable grounds that force or threat of force is being used and that they act reasonably in the circumstances. Similarly, the new section 35 requires only a reasonable belief of a threat to property held in

---

67   Above note 40.
68   Above note 40.
69   *Code*, above note 14, s 34(2).
70   *R v Malott*, [1998] 1 SCR 123.
71   Elizabeth A Sheehy, *Defending Battered Women on Trial* (Vancouver: University of British Columbia Press, 2014).
72   *R v Cinous* (2002), 162 CCC (3d) 129 (SCC).

peaceable possession and reasonable actions in the circumstances. Proportionality in particular is only a factor that should be considered under section 34(2) and one that is not even specifically mentioned in section 35 with respect to defence of property, though it is one that courts may be inclined to read into section 35.[73]

The Court has also restricted the use of reasonable force to correct pupils or children with several restrictions that are not apparent on the face of section 43 of the *Code*. These restrictions may be good social policy to discourage violence against children, but they are unfortunately not reflected in the text of section 43, which simply authorizes the use of reasonable corrective force against children.[74] With some exceptions, the trend seems to be for both Parliament and the Court to define defences quite narrowly.

CONCLUSION

Canadian criminal law is constantly evolving. Parliament adds more offences each year. It has recently simplified self-defence and defence of property and had restricted the defence of provocation. The courts continue to interpret offences and statutory and common law defences and the *Charter*. On occasion, courts recognize new common law defences such as entrapment and officially induced error. Parliament can respond to the extension of defences and has done so with respect to the Court's controversial recognition of a defence of extreme intoxication. Fault requirements are designed to ensure that the morally innocent, such as those who are unaware that they possess drugs, are not punished. Although objective standards of fault are constitutionally sufficient for most criminal offences other than murder, attempted murder, and war crimes, the Supreme Court has emphasized that objective fault must be based on a marked departure from the reasonableness standard to distinguish it from mere civil negligence.

FURTHER READINGS

BOYLE, C, ET AL. *A Feminist Approach to Criminal Law* (Ottawa: Status of Women Canada, 1986).

---

73   *R v Cormier*, 2017 NBCA 10.
74   *Canadian Foundation for Children*, above note 19.

CAIRNS-WAY, R. *Dimensions of Criminal Law*, 3d ed (Toronto: Emond Montgomery, 2002).

CAMERON, J. *The Charter's Impact on the Criminal Justice System* (Toronto: Carswell, 1996).

————, & J STRIBOPOULOS, EDS. *The Charter and Criminal Justice Twenty-Five Years Later* (Markham, ON: LexisNexis, 2008).

CRAIG, E. *Putting Trials on Trial: Sexual Assault and the Failure of the Legal Profession* (Montreal: McGill-Queens University Press, 2017).

ERICSON, R, & P BARANEK. *The Ordering of Justice: The Study of Accused Persons as Dependants in the Criminal Process* (Toronto: University of Toronto Press, 1982).

FRIEDLAND, ML. "Criminal Justice in Canada Revisited" (2004) 48 *Criminal Law Quarterly* 419.

MANDEL, M. *The Charter of Rights and the Legalization of Politics in Canada*, rev ed (Toronto: Wall & Thompson, 1994).

MANITOBA PUBLIC INQUIRY INTO THE ADMINISTRATION OF JUSTICE AND ABORIGINAL PEOPLE. *Report of the Aboriginal Justice Inquiry of Manitoba* (Winnipeg: The Inquiry, 1991).

MARTIN, D. "Retribution Reconsidered: A Reconsideration of Feminist Criminal Law Strategies" (1998) 36 *Osgoode Hall Law Journal* 151.

MORAN, M. *Rethinking the Reasonable Person* (Oxford: Oxford University Press, 2003).

PACIOCCO, D. *Getting Away with Murder* (Toronto: Irwin Law, 2000).

PACKER, H. *The Limits of the Criminal Sanction* (Stanford: Stanford University Press, 1968).

ROACH, K. *Due Process and Victims' Rights: The New Law and Politics of Criminal Justice* (Toronto: University of Toronto Press, 1999).

————. "A *Charter* Reality Check: How Relevant Is the *Charter* to the Justness of Our Criminal Justice System?" (2008) 40 *Supreme Court Law Review* (2d) 717.

————. *The Supreme Court on Trial: Judicial Action or Democratic Dialogue?* rev ed (Toronto: Irwin Law, 2016).

SHEEHY, E. *Defending Battered Women on Trial* (Vancouver: University of British Columbia Press, 2014).

SIMON, J. *Governing through Crime* (New York: Oxford University Press, 2007).

GLOSSARY

Absolute discharge: a disposition in which no conviction is recorded. It is available if there is no minimum penalty, the offence is not punishable by life or fourteen years' imprisonment, and the judge determines that it is in the accused's best interests and not contrary to the public interest.

Absolute liability: an offence for which the accused is guilty once it is proven that the prohibited act, or *actus reus*, was committed and regardless of the existence of any fault, including negligence.

Actus reus: the prohibited act in a criminal or regulatory offence. Proof of the *actus reus* may also include the requirement that the prohibited act be voluntarily and consciously committed by the accused.

Aiding or abetting: intentionally assisting or encouraging a crime and, by doing so, becoming a party to the crime.

Appellate court: a court that reviews the accused's conviction or acquittal at trial. In summary conviction matters, appeals are usually heard by superior courts, while in indictable matters, appeals are heard by the provincial courts of appeal. Courts, such as the Supreme Court of Canada, which hear subsequent appeals are also called appellate courts.

Arbitrariness: A principle of fundamental justice that is infringed by a law that does not advance or is inconsistent with its objective.

Attempt: an attempted crime occurs when the accused does something beyond mere preparation for the purpose of committing a crime. It is a separate crime of attempting the specific offence and is usually subject to less punishment than the completed crime.

Attorney General: the elected official ultimately accountable for prosecutions. For *Criminal Code* offences, this is normally the Attorney General of the province, but can also be the Attorney General of Canada.

Automatism: a state in which the accused acts in an involuntary manner. It is known as mental disorder automatism if it is caused by a mental disorder and non-mental disorder automatism if it is caused by some other factor such as a blow to the head.

Bail: also known as judicial interim release. It refers to the release of an accused person pending trial on the grounds that he or she is likely to appear for trial, not likely to commit offences in the meantime, and release will not undermine public confidence in the administration of justice.

Causation: an issue in determining whether the accused has committed the *actus reus*, or prohibited act, by causing the prohibited consequences, usually death.

Common law: judge-made law as opposed to legislation passed by the legislature.

Conditional discharge: a disposition in which no conviction is recorded so long as the accused successfully satisfies prescribed conditions. This disposition is available only if there is no minimum penalty and the offence is not subject to life or fourteen years' imprisonment.

Conditional sentence: a disposition in which the accused is found guilty and sentenced to imprisonment but serves the sentence in the community so long as he or she successfully fulfills conditions.

Counselling: procuring, soliciting, or inciting a person to commit a crime. A person who does this counselling can become guilty as a party to an offence that is committed by the person counselled or can be convicted of a separate crime of counselling if the offence is not committed.

Defence of property: A justification to a crime under section 35 of the *Criminal Code* generally available when persons reasonably apprehend threats to their property and respond in a reasonable manner.

Disease of the mind: a condition necessary for an accused to be found not criminally responsible on account of mental disorder. Diseases of the mind are now defined as mental disorders. They can include any mental disorder but not transitory or self-induced states.

Division of powers: the constitutional allocation of authority between the federal and provincial governments to enact legislation.

Due diligence: a defence available in strict liability offences that allows the accused to prove on a balance of probabilities that it was not negligent.

Duress: a defence available to those who commit crimes because they are threatened with serious harm. A codified defence of duress is found in section 17 of the *Criminal Code* and applies to principal offenders. The requirements of immediacy and presence in section 17 of the *Code* have been severed from the defence as unconstitutional. A common law defence of duress applies to parties to offences. In some rare circumstances, duress may also be relevant to the proof of the fault element.

Entrapment: objectionable police conduct such as offering a suspect an opportunity to commit a crime without a reasonable suspicion that he or she is involved with crime or when the police are not pursuing a *bona fide* inquiry in a high-crime area. It also includes disreputable police conduct that goes beyond providing a suspect an opportunity to commit a crime and actually induces the commission of the crime. The remedy for entrapment is a stay of proceedings.

Exclusion of evidence: the situation when evidence that would otherwise be relevant to determining the accused's guilt or innocence is kept out of a criminal trial because it was obtained in a manner that violated the *Charter* and its admission would bring the administration of justice into disrepute. Unconstitutionally obtained evidence is excluded if its admission would affect the fairness of the trial or if the seriousness of the *Charter* violation outweighs the harmful effects of excluding the evidence.

Fault element: the culpable state of mind that must be proven by the state. Fault elements can require proof of a subjective state of mind of the accused, such as wilfulness, knowledge, or recklessness, or can be based on objective fault such as negligence.

General intent: an offence in which the fault element relates only to the performance of the act in question, with no further ulterior intent or purpose. Intoxication has traditionally not been a defence to general as opposed to specific intent offences. Subject to section 33.1 of the *Criminal Code*, extreme intoxication producing involuntary behaviour may be a defence to a general intent offence.

Gross disproportionality: Grounds for invalidating sentences as cruel and unusual punishment under section 12 of the *Charter*.

Indictable offences: the most serious category of criminal offences. In most cases, the accused has the option to be tried before a provincial court without a preliminary inquiry or a jury, or tried in a superior court with a preliminary inquiry and/or a jury.

Intoxication: evidence of intoxication by alcohol or drugs that prevents the Crown from proving beyond a reasonable doubt that the accused had the *mens rea*, or fault element, required for the particular crime.

Judicial interim release: *see* bail.

Mens rea: the prohibited mental or fault element for the commission of a criminal offence. It may include intent, purpose, wilfulness, knowledge, recklessness, wilful blindness, criminal negligence, or negligence depending on the offence.

Mental disorder: *see* disease of the mind.

Mental disorder or insanity defence: a defence put forth when a person commits a crime while suffering from a mental disorder that renders him or her incapable of appreciating the nature and quality of the act or knowing that it is wrong. An accused found not criminally responsible by reason of mental disorder will be released unless a court or review board concludes that he or she is a significant threat to the public.

Mental element: *see mens rea;* fault element.

Moral innocence: The quality of a person who commits a prohibited act with no fault such as negligence or subjective *mens rea*. A morally innocent person cannot be imprisoned under section 7 of the *Charter*.

Moral involuntariness: The quality of a person who commits a crime but who because of emergency circumstances has no realistic choice but to commit the crime. A person who commits a crime in a morally involuntary manner cannot be convicted under section 7 of the *Charter*.

Necessity: a common law defence available as an excuse when an accused acts in response to an urgent and immediate peril that cannot be avoided by obeying the law.

Omission: the *actus reus* when a person is found guilty for failing to perform a specific legal duty, such as providing the necessities of life to a child.

Overbreadth: A principle of fundamental justice that is violated when a law infringes rights to life, liberty, or security of the person more than is necessary to achieve its objective.

Parole: discretionary release of an accused serving a term of imprisonment granted by a parole board.

Preliminary inquiry: a hearing to determine whether the prosecution has introduced enough evidence that, if believed at trial, would support a conviction.

Presumption of innocence: requirement in section 11(d) of the *Charter* that the Crown prove the accused's guilt beyond a reasonable doubt. The Crown must prove not only the elements of the offence but all matters essential for conviction, including the non-availability of relevant defences.

Principles of fundamental justice: basic tenets of the legal system that can be identified with precision and for which there is sufficient consensus that they are basic norms.

Probation: a court order that allows an accused to be supervised in the community. The breach of a probation order is a crime.

Prohibited act: The act or omission that is prohibited in the offence. *See also actus reus.*

Provincial courts: the court where most criminal cases are resolved. The judges are appointed by the provincial government and cannot sit with a jury.

Provocation: a partial defence that reduces murder to manslaughter. It is available when deceased commits an indictable offence punishable by five years' imprisonment or more (such as assault or sexual assault) in circumstances would make an ordinary person lose self-control, and which caused the accused suddenly and subjectively to have been provoked and killed before his or her passions had cooled.

Public welfare offences: *see* regulatory offences.

Regulatory offences: offences enacted by federal, provincial, or municipal governments that are used primarily to regulate risky behaviour that may cause harm. They are presumed to require strict liability.

Search and seizure: any state activity that invades a reasonable expectation of privacy.

Self-defence: a justification to a crime under section 34 of the *Criminal Code* generally available when a person reasonably apprehends a threat and responds in a reasonable manner.

Specific intent: an offence that requires the Crown to prove not only a fault or mental element that relates to the performance of the act in question, but also some ulterior intent or purpose. Evidence of intoxication is always relevant when the accused is charged with a specific intent offence and operates as a defence if it raises a reasonable doubt about the existence of the mental element.

Stay of proceedings: a disposition where the court does not allow a prosecution to proceed because of objectionable police or prosecutorial conduct and/or a violation of the accused's rights. This remedy is not the moral equivalent of an acquittal because it does not reach the merits but has the same practical effects.

Strict liability: an offence for which the Crown must prove the commission of the prohibited act beyond a reasonable doubt. The existence of negligence is then presumed unless the accused establishes a defence of due diligence on a balance of probabilities.

Summary conviction offences: the least serious offences in the *Criminal Code*. They are generally subject to a maximum penalty of six months and/or a fine of not more than $5,000, but can be subject to a higher maximum period of imprisonment such as eighteen months.

Superior courts: the highest level of trial court in a criminal case that hears all jury trials and the first level of appeal in summary conviction offences.

Suspended sentence: a disposition after conviction where the judge suspends passing sentence, while imposing conditions on the accused's release by means of probation orders. If the conditions are breached, the court may sentence the accused for the original offence.

Unfit to stand trial: a determination that an accused, on account of a mental disorder, cannot be tried because he or she cannot understand the nature or possible consequences of the proceedings or communicate with counsel.

Vagueness: A principle of fundamental justice that is offended by a law that does not provide a framework for legal debate that provides fair notice to citizens and limits law enforcement discretion. Vagueness can also be relevant to determining whether an objective constitutes a just cause for the denial of bail and whether a limit on a *Charter* right is prescribed by law.

TABLE OF CASES

INDEX

ABOUT THE AUTHOR

Kent Roach, CM, FRSC, is a professor of law at the University of Toronto, where he holds the Prichard-Wilson Chair in Law and Public Policy. In 2002, he was elected a Fellow of the Royal Society of Canada by his fellow academics and in 2015 was appointed a member of the Order of Canada. In 2013, he was awarded a Trudeau Fellowship and in 2017 the Canada Council awarded him the Molson Prize for his contributions. He has taught criminal law since 1989 and been editor-in-chief of the *Criminal Law Quarterly* since 1998. He is the co-editor of *Cases and Materials on Criminal Law and Procedure,* numerous collections of essays and thirteen books, including *Constitutional Remedies in Canada* (winner of the 1997 Walter Owen Book Prize); *Due Process and Victims' Rights: The New Law and Politics of Criminal Justice* (shortlisted for the 1999 Donner Prize); *The Supreme Court on Trial: Judicial Activism or Democratic Dialogue* (shortlisted for the 2001 Donner Prize); (with Robert J. Sharpe) *Brian Dickson: A Judge's Journey* (winner of the 2003 Defoe Prize); *The 9/11 Effect: Comparative Counter-Terrorism* (co-winner of the 2012 Mundell Medal); and (with Craig Forcese) *False Security: The Radicalization of Canadian Anti-Terrorism* (winner of the 2016 Canadian Law and Society book prize). Professor Roach has served as research director of the Commission of Inquiry into the Bombing of Air India and the Goudge Inquiry into Forensic Pathology and was volume lead on the Truth and Reconciliation's Commission volume of the legacy of Residential Schools for Indigenous children. Acting pro bono, he has represented civil liberties and Indigenous groups in interventions before the Supreme Court, including in *Golden* and *Ward* on strip searches; *Khawaja* on terrorism; *Latimer* on mandatory sentencing; *Gladue, Ipeelee,* and *Anderson* on sentencing Indigenous offenders; and *Sauve* on prisoner voting rights.